E.F. GUERITZ

1982.

THE SECOND WORLD WAR

Essays in Military and Political History

edited by

Walter Laqueur

SAGE Readers in 20th Century History 4

SAGE Publications
London & Beverly Hills

For information address
SAGE Publications Ltd
28 Banner Street, London EC1Y 8QE

SAGE Publications Inc
275 South Beverly Drive
Beverly Hills, California 90212

British Library Cataloguing in Publication Data

Laqueur, Walter
The Second World War: essays in military and political history.—(Sage readers in 20th century history; 4)
1. World War, 1939-1945
I. Title
940.53 D743 81-86067

ISBN 0-8039-9780-9
ISBN 0-8039-9781-7 Pbk

Contents

1 Introduction

Walter Laqueur

The second world war was the most important event of this century, the changes it caused were so enormous and so lasting that it continues to attract more interest and to provoke more controversy than any other topic. Its political and military history is heavily documented: at the last count there were 164,000 cubic feet of second world war material in the National Archives in Washington. But this was ten years ago and refers only to military records. There are other depositories in the United States, where the overall amount of material available is bound to be considerably larger. The same is true with regard to Britain and France, Germany and Italy, and presumably also the relevant archives of the Soviet Union and the other East European countries, most of them inaccessible so far to Western students. There have been many Soviet and East European publications on the war years, but the reception given in the 1960s to Nekrich's book on June 1941 clearly marked the outer limits of de-Stalinization.

Much important source material is not yet available in the West, and some presumably never will be. But even if it were, the debate would still continue. History is constantly being rewritten and the historiography of the second world war, not surprisingly, has been under attack from both 'right' and 'left' revisionist schools. The former was mainly preoccupied with the pre-history and the early phase of the war, the latter with the last phase and its aftermath. The former tried to prove that, broadly speaking, both Nazism and the Japanese were less to blame for the outbreak of the war than commonly supposed, that they had not really planned the war, that German and Japanese ambitions could have been contained but for the bellicose intentions of such Western statesmen as Lord Halifax and President Roosevelt, that Hitler's war against the Soviet Union was preventive in character.

'Left' revisionism, on the other hand, maintains that the Western governments mainly went to war to protect their imperial and economic interests which were threatened by the Axis powers. This school is less interested in the second world war per se, and sees it mainly as a prelude to the cold war. Responsibility for the break-up of the war-time alliance is put squarely on the shoulders of the Western leaders, whose main war aim was the suppression of the 'European revolution'.

The use of the terms 'left' and 'right' in this connection is, of course, quite misleading in some respects; 'right-wing' revisionists have drawn much of their inspiration from the writings of A.J.P. Taylor and Charles Beard who can hardly be classified as men of the right. Furthermore, beyond a certain point, the dividing line between 'left' and 'right' is altogether blurred, for even though they proceed from very different starting points, they reach conclusions which, in some ways, are strikingly similar. If it was mainly a war between rival imperialist powers, Hitler and Mussolini cannot possibly have been as evil as commonly thought, whereas Churchill and Roosevelt should not be regarded as fighters for freedom and democracy.

These writings are now largely a thing of the past; the impact of the revisionist schools on historians has been on the whole negligible, even though it had a certain success among the general public, in line with political sympathies and national sensibilities. Most of the articles published in this book first appeared in two special issues of the *Journal of Contemporary History* (January and July 1981); a few were first published in earlier issues of the same journal. They are fairly typical of the current preoccupations of historians, which are quite different from those of the 1950s and 1960s. For example, during the war and immediately after, great importance was attributed to the activities of the German Fifth Column in many European countries which allegedly made an important contribution to German successes. Research has shown, however, that while there was a great deal of appeasement and defeatism among Germany's neighbours, there were few Fifth Columnists in the specific sense; militarily they played no significant role at all. It also became clear after the war that the degree of German economic preparation and mobilization had been greatly exaggerated, certainly for the period up to Stalingrad.

Other controversies still continue albeit in a lower key; it is still debated whether any military benefit was drawn by Britain and France from the delay offered by the Munich treaty; whether Hitler really intended to invade Britain in 1940; whether the turning-point in the war came in late 1942 or well before. There is no full agreement on the importance of the air offensive against Germany and of the North African theatre within the general framework of the war. Mr Ralph Bennett criticizes in his contribution, rightly I believe, the newly fashionable tendency among some writers to 'depose the heroes of the past and to replace the story of five years uphill struggle with an insistence that the economic balance was so heavily weighted in favour of Britain, Russia and the United States that they were always bound to win, and with the assertion that the Allies should rather be blamed for the foolishness or timidity which prevented them from gaining a quicker victory than praised for the determination which enabled them to triumph in the end'.

In recent years, the impact of intelligence on the conduct of the war has been a bone of some contention. So far, only a small part of the German decrypts has been accessible — more apparently, of 'Magic', the intercepted Japanese messages. While the history of the war may not have to be completely rewritten, much of it will definitely have to be re-examined in the light of these revelations. Thus Mr Ralph Bennett discounts all talk about completely rewriting the history of the war in the light of Ultra whereas Mr Ronald Lewin elsewhere in the present volume takes a different stance: most of the significant volumes in the United Kingdom series of Official Histories of the Second World War are fundamentally misleading, inadequate and out of date: an exception, in this respect, being Professor Hinsley's history of British intelligence. But essential information was available during the war from other sources also; for example, I found to my surprise much interest in a postal censorship survey. These surveys will not be declassified for many years to come. In any case, the problem facing the historian is not just to establish that certain information existed at a given time, which is relatively easy, but whether it reached those who were taking decisions, whether it was correctly interpreted and what inferences were drawn from it — which, needless to say, is much more difficult. The time factor has always to be remembered: information may have been received, and even correctly interpreted, but it may have come too late for operational purposes; or the recipient may have been unable to use it for other reasons, such as overwhelming enemy superiority. In short, other things being equal, intelligence provides an advantage, sometimes a great advantage, but its limitations should always be remembered.

Poland was routed in 1939 despite the fact that it had broken the German code, and if Britain did not lose the war in 1940-41, this was due to a great many factors, of which superior intelligence was only one.

There is always the temptation facing the historian to assume that everything eventually happened as it did because it could not have happened in any other way. There is always the inclination to exaggerate necessity, to underrate the importance of historical accident. Lord Dacre (Professor Trevor Roper) rightly pointed out some time ago that if General Franco at Hendaye on 23 October 1940 had said 'yes' to Hitler rather than 'no', the assault on Gibraltar would have succeeded, the Mediterranean would have been closed to the Allies, the outcome of the war might have been reversed, and the shape of the post-war world would have been quite different. Some may argue that since the fate of the war was not decided in the Mediterranean, the importance of Franco's decision to prevaricate should not be exaggerated. Perhaps so, but then Hendaye was not the only historical accident during 1940-42. If there had been no determined leadership in Britain during the critical summer of 1940, if Hitler had given priority to the construction of nuclear weapons, there were a great many occasions during the first two to three years of the war on which the decision could have gone the other way. If the outcome of the war had been certain from the very beginning, interest in the subject would have abated long ago. But, of course, it was not, and this too is one of the basic reasons for our continuing preoccupation with it.

I

The Coming of the War

It is usually taken for granted that democracies enter a war totally unprepared and there is unfortunately more than a grain of truth in this popular assumption. As far as equipment and training are concerned, neither the British nor the American or French armed forces were a match for the Germans in the early phase of the war. This lack of preparation stemmed not so much from lack of information as from lethargy. There was no lack of information: the French Deuxième Bureau actually exaggerated the number of German units (and even more the number of German tanks) on the eve of the attack in May 1940. Yet nothing was done to face the danger. It may come therefore as a surprise that in some fields thought was actually given to future action well before the outbreak of the war. This refers to the question of Swedish iron ore, a problem of major importance for the German war economy, and also to the need for a Ministry of Information in Britain. The great miracle was not that the Ministry of Information entered the war (to quote Mr Taylor) hopelessly ill-prepared, inarticulate, though not altogether speechless as in 1914. It was in many ways surprising that any thought at all had been given to the necessity to engage in propaganda. Mr Lowenthal shows in his essay that given the isolationist mood prevailing in the United States between 1937 and 1939, there was little that President Roosevelt could have done over and above what he actually did. In 1939 and in 1940, he kept in mind better than his subordinates the political requirements of the allied war effort. In 1941, however, he wavered and showed lack of resolution. By that time, all the President's major advisers (with the possible exception of Secretary of State Hull) believed that war could no longer be avoided. Roosevelt, on the other hand, by keeping his options open failed to define clear policy goals, thus creating a vacuum 'which was never authoritatively filled for the United States during the course of the war'.

2 'If War Should Come':[1] Preparing the Fifth Arm for Total War 1935-1939

Philip M Taylor

When British representatives set off for Russia in September 1941 to attend the Moscow Conference, they went fully expecting the Soviets to enquire exactly how Britain proposed to win the war against Nazi Germany. The delegation had been instructed to reply:

> We shall undermine them by propaganda; depress them with the blockade; and, above all, bomb their homelands ceaselessly, ruthlessly, and with ever increasing weight of bombs.[2]

Two years earlier, one of the British Cabinet's earliest decisions following the outbreak of the Second World War had foreshadowed this statement. Within hours of the Anglo-French declaration of hostilities on 3 September 1939, authorization was given for the Royal Air Force to initiate the psychological offensive against the Third Reich.[3] That same night, Whitley bombers from RAF 4 Group showered six million leaflets over selective targets on German soil. This exercise, the technical success of which helped to pave the way for Bomber Command's crippling night-time bombing raids later in the war,[4] launched what was to become the most vociferous war of words yet waged by belligerent powers.

That such emphasis should have been placed upon the weapon of propaganda from the very outset of the conflict stands out in sharp contrast to the situation which had existed in August 1914 when the British government had entered the First World War almost completely unprepared for the conduct of psychological warfare. Although some prior consideration had been given to the related question of censorship,[5] as reflected by the immediate severance of the German transatlantic cables, the government was thereafter forced to improvise the machinery required for more positive forms of action in order to combat the widespread activities of an already fully-operational German propaganda machine. However, despite the establishment of Charles Masterman's War Propaganda Bureau at Wellington House in September 1914,[6] and despite the undervalued work of the various Whitehall departments in this direction,[7] it nonetheless took three and a half years for a full Ministry of Information to emerge and before a specific Enemy Propaganda Department was created at Crewe House.[8] The mistake, if such it was,[9] was not to be repeated in September 1939. On the outbreak of the Second World War, not only did a Ministry of Information spring immediately into action but preparations for the conduct of psychological warfare were also sufficiently well advanced to enable the British to launch their first offensive strike against the enemy with leaflets rather than with bombs.

That the government should have been prepared for propaganda in 1939 in a way that it had not been in 1914 was made all the more remarkable in light of the situation which had existed during the Munich crisis merely twelve months before. On 5 September 1938, Stephen King-Hall, the distinguished publicist and expert on international affairs, had been convinced that

> a moment might arrive when the whole situation might be saved by an immediate and nation-wide appeal to the German people. If we are involved in a war, a shower of pamphlets over Germany should precede a shower of bombs over the Ruhr (I hope we've got the bombers).[10]

Yet even if the bombers had been available, the Air Ministry had still to be consulted as to its willingness to release the necessary men and machines for what would obviously be a highly dangerous mission. Moreover, there did not at that time exist a pamphlet, even in draft form, let alone one translated, printed and ready for dissemination. There was thus a very real danger, as King-Hall warned, that 'if the crisis gets worse . . . we may be caught with our trousers down' in so far as propaganda was concerned.[11]

Despite some impressive improvisation in the weeks that followed, including the drafting of various leaflets[12] and some experimental leaflet-dropping raids carried out by the RAF in the north of England,[13] such an embarrassment was avoided only by Neville Chamberlain's third flight to Germany to bring Europe back from the brink of war by signing the Munich Agreement. In other words, Britain would almost certainly not have been prepared for psychological warfare in September 1938. Clearly, therefore, much progress was made during the final year of peace. Several recent publications, most notably Ian McLaine's *Ministry of Morale*[14] and Michael Balfour's *Propaganda in War*,[15] have thrown much new light on that progress but, overall, the authors tend to be somewhat critical of the pre-war planning process in view of the disastrous start made by British propagandists during the initial stages of the Second World War. Whereas many of those early mistakes can undoubtedly be attributed to the peacetime preparations, others cannot. The difference between the anticipated nature of a future war and the reality of experience is often very wide. When, for example, the long feared 'knock-out blow' from the air failed to materialize in 1939, British propagandists had to deal with the peculiar problems (such as boredom) raised during the period of the 'phoney war'.[16] Similarly, when the *Luftwaffe* did begin to appear over British cities, it was learned that aerial bombardment often served to consolidate rather than shatter civilian morale. Moreover, not only do Balfour and McLaine tend to examine the pre-war preparations from the retrospective standpoint of the 1940s, but they also examine the planning process in isolation from the considerable peacetime propaganda machinery which the British government had been developing throughout the 1930s and in isolation from developments elsewhere in Whitehall which were to affect considerably the wartime organization for propaganda. This article will therefore attempt to re-examine those preparations in light of these factors and in light of the lessons provided by the 1914-18 war and by the Munich crisis.

During the 1930s, there was a widely held conviction that, if war should come, it would be a long war of attrition in which a strong economy would serve as the fourth arm of defence.[17] Although Chamberlain's policy as Prime Minister was to suffer dearly from his own restraining influence while serving as Chancellor of the Exchequer,[18] he remained determined to ensure that Britain's preparations for war did not weaken the nation's capacity to actually wage war. The roots of this conviction lay in the experience of the First World War. The use of the economic weapon, whether in the form of the Allied blockade of the Central Powers or Germany's attempt to starve Britain into submission by the unrestricted U-boat campaign, had been designed to weaken the capacity of the other side to continue the struggle on the field of battle. From the British point of view, the successful application of the former, combined with her ability successfully to resist the stranglehold of the latter, was felt to have played a critical role in determining the final result. The cost of doing so, however, had been high. True, Britain had emerged victorious, seemingly at the height of her power, but in reality Britain also emerged from the war in a process of both relative and absolute decline. A repetition might signal her complete collapse as a great world power.

But the blockade had not simply been designed to deprive the enemy's armed forces of their basic equipment and supplies. It was also directed towards the mass of the enemy population. Indeed, the First World War substantially narrowed the distance which had previously existed between the military and civilian theatres of operation. Sections of the community which had hitherto remained generally uninvolved in the exigencies of national survival now found themselves directly affected by events at the front line. Nor could the military afford to ignore events on the home front. For the British, the introduction of conscription in 1916 was a major step on her road to total war in which the entire resources of the nation had to be mobilised against the entire resources of the enemy before victory could be secured.[19]

The impact of these developments, combined with the lessons to be drawn from the alarming frequency of mutinies within the mass conscript armies and the outbreak of revolutions in Russia, central Europe and elsewhere, led to a heightened appreciation within the British governing élite of the role which the masses would henceforth play in the survival of the state or, alternatively, in its destruction. This in turn led to an acceleration of the development of means to influence and control the opinions of people whose actions were becoming increasingly more significant with improving standards of literacy and education, growing politicization, and the broadening base of political power. Morale and opinion thus became military assets and propaganda began to emerge as the principal instrument of control over them. By 1918, it had become the fifth arm of defence.

In Germany, British war propaganda seemed more like an effective weapon of attack than of defence. Evidence of its profound impact was readily available in the form of testimonies by such prominent enemy personalities as Ludendorff and Hindenberg. In the 1920s, Adolf Hitler was to perpetuate further the British reputation for success by stating in *Mein Kampf* that the German army had not been defeated on the field of battle but had lost the war due to the disintegration of morale from within, a process which had been 'brilliantly' exploited by British propaganda. Admittedly, Hitler used this line of argument for propaganda reasons of his own — the 'stab-in-the-back' theory was but its logical conclusion — but the fact remains that British propaganda was believed by friend and former foe alike to have played such a decisive role in Allied victory that its revival in any future war seemed virtually guaranteed.

However, at the close of the 'war to end all wars', such a possibility seemed inconceivable. Accordingly, just as the British armed forces were gradually demobilized and reduced, so also was the wartime propaganda machinery dismantled in optimistic anticipation of a lasting peace in which neither would be necessary. Although a skeleton organization remained in the form of the Foreign Office News Department upon which to build in future should the need arise, the likelihood of it being so used seemed remote. Not that the British were particularly proud of their wartime reputation for being successful propagandists. Propaganda, as Baldwin said in 1918, was 'not a word that has a pleasant sound in English ears'.[20] It was regarded as a necessary evil of war, an 'un-English' activity associated with subversion and secrecy. Indeed, such was the overwhelming degree of prejudice against its continued use in peacetime that the British government was prepared to forfeit the considerable lead it had gained by 1918 and surrender the initiative to other governments which were less reluctant to put this new weapon to peacetime use. As a result, during the inter-war years, Soviet Russia, Fascist Italy and Nazi Germany utilized the lessons of the British wartime experience and combined them with new developments in communications technology in order to mould propaganda into a powerful weapon of peacetime nationalistic expansion.

As the lofty idealism of the post-war era came to be progressively eroded by the aggressive policies of Japan, Italy and Germany, the prospect of another war had to be considered as a distinct possibility. When, therefore, British defence planners were forced to consider the question of contingency plans for a future war in the wake of the abandonment of the Ten Year Rule, the painfully slow death of the World Disarmament Conference and the production of the Defence Requirements Committee's first major report, there was every reason to assume that propaganda would play an even greater role in the next war than it was believed to have done in the last. The advent of the first truly mass media in the form of radio and sound film, combined with the widespread peacetime exploitation of propaganda by the totalitarian regimes, merely served to reinforce this conviction. But there was one significant addition to the anticipated nature of total war: the bomber. During the 1930s, the fear of the bomber and of an aerial knock-out blow 'critically affected the making of British defence and foreign policy'.[21] It also affected the planning for propaganda in the next war.

Britain's insular position could no longer protect her people from direct involvement in a continental war as the bomber reduced still further the distance between soldier and civilian. British cities were vulnerable to attack in a way that they had not been before. If this threat was portrayed as something of a fantasy in Alexander Korda's 1936 science fiction film, *Things to Come*, the reality could only have been driven home by newsreels showing the bombing of Guernica and Madrid during the Spanish Civil War.[22] It was therefore not unnaturally assumed that, if war should come, civilian morale was likely to prove a critical factor, and indeed it might be assumed that film would have a key role to play in helping to sustain the populace through the dark hours of saturation bombing. But, in fact, the overriding assumption that the bomber would always get through led to the decision to close all cinemas in the event of war in an attempt to reduce the potential devastation and loss of life.[23] Clearly, only if Britain could survive the *Luftwaffe*'s anticipated initial knock-out blow from the air would the fourth and fifth arms of defence begin to play a decisive role. Even so, during that crucial initial phase, propaganda would still have an important role to play, both at home and abroad, and it was therefore felt that Britain would need to be sufficiently well-equipped for such work from the outset.

Significantly, the initiative came from the Air Ministry. The precise origins of the decision to begin planning for propaganda in the next war remain somewhat vague but it does appear that, during the summer of 1935, as the Committee of Imperial Defence (CID) was preparing for the impending clash with Italy in the

Mediterranean over the Abyssinian affair, one of its sub-committees was deliberating over the delicate question of censorship in time of war. It was recognised that propaganda and censorship were different sides of the same coin; some method of releasing news would be required to work in conjunction with the system for controlling it.[24] C. P. Robertson, press attaché at the Air Ministry, appears to have taken the initiative in proposing that plans for the establishment of a Ministry of Information should be set in motion so that 'we should not merely start off in the case of a future conflict where we ended in the last'.[25] In September 1935, Robertson produced a lengthy memorandum which argued that the wartime system had been deficient from an organizational point of view largely because of the multiplicity of bodies engaged in official propaganda. Crewe House had been responsible for enemy propaganda, with the exception of Turkey which had been the responsibility of the Ministry of Information, which in turn had been responsible for allied and neutral propaganda. The National War Aims Committee had been responsible for home propaganda, although the Press Bureau also had a strong interest. The War Office had been responsible for propaganda in military zones. In other words, Robertson's point was that in any future war propaganda must be conducted from under one roof. Centralization was, in his opinion, an essential precondition of success.

Robertson's memorandum was considered by the CID on 14 October 1935 when it was decided to establish a sub-committee to prepare plans for the establishment of a Ministry of Information on the outbreak of war.[26] The chairman and Minister of Information Designate was Sir John Colville, at that time Parliamentary Secretary to the Department of Overseas Trade but shortly to become Parliamentary Under-Secretary of State for Scotland. His sub-committee boasted an impressive membership: Sir Warren Fisher represented the Treasury and Sir Robert Vansittart the Foreign Office; Sir Russell Scott, the Permanent Under-Secretary at the Home Office and his counterpart at the Dominions Office, Sir Edward Harding; J. A. G. Troup and Major-General J. G. Dill, respectively the Directors of Naval and Military Intelligence; Sir Donald Banks and Sir John Reith, the Directors-General of the GPO and of the BBC; and Sir Maurice Hankey, Secretary to the Cabinet and to the CID, Rex Leeper, head of the Foreign Office News Department, and Stephen Gaselee, the Foreign Office Librarian, were also present in view of their considerable experience of propaganda in war and peace. The government was certainly taking the whole business very seriously. Warren Fisher informed the only member who was not a government official — Sir John Reith — that this was 'as strong a CID committee as had ever been called'.[27] This may well have been so, but it was also true that few of its members had any detailed knowledge or experience of propaganda. This was presumably the reason why meetings of the sub-committee proved to be infrequent; only five full meetings were convened between 1935 and 1939, three of which were held within the first nine months of its creation. Rather, the detailed planning was undertaken largely by subordinate officials.

Those officials were faced with a formidable task for an alarming eventuality. The defensive thinking which characterized all aspects of war preparations also permeated the planners of the Ministry of Information. For example, little time or thought appears to have been given to the question of enemy propaganda until 1938, and the decision to close all cinemas on the outbreak of war was perhaps one reason why film received relatively little attention until 1939. Because there was felt to be no effective form of defence against the bomber, the RAF devised the retaliatory strike against the Ruhr, a strategy which remained in force until after Munich when the emphasis was shifted more on to the air defence of Great Britain. Paradoxically, however, it was only then, when the RAF was concentrating upon the development of the fighter in conjunction with radar, that thoughts of a psychological offensive against the enemy began to determine an alternative use for the bomber.

A major problem for the planners was that although the march of technology ensured that the character of the next war would almost certainly be radically different from that of the last, they had only the precedent of the Great War on which to model their new structure — unless of course they chose to model their organization upon that of Goebbels. If that was effectively what happened, as Michael Balfour has argued, it created a ridiculous situation: 'in the war of words the British imagined that they were copying from the Germans something which the Germans imagined they had copied from the British!'[28] But, as Ian McLaine has pointed out, references to the German propaganda organization are extremely rare in the records of the shadow Ministry of Information, 'and no reference whatsoever to Goebbels by name'.[29] The British were, after all, planning for an entirely different set of criteria and a liberal democracy with its own peculiar historical idiosyncracies required different propaganda techniques than that of a dictatorship.

If the lessons of the past were to prove of any real value for the future, they had first to be discovered. During the 1930s, this proved easier said than done because the records of the various wartime propaganda organizations had largely been destroyed in 1920, or else 'lost' in the years that followed. Detailed information on the wartime experiment was simply not available. Instead, the planners were forced to consult the memoirs of former participants, such as E. T. Cook's *The Press in Wartime* (1920), Douglas Brownrigg's *Indiscretions of the Naval Censor* (1920) and Sir Campbell Stuart's *Secrets of Crewe House* (1920). This exercise meant that the planning proceeded from a highly misleading premise because these works tended to exaggerate the role which British propaganda was believed to have played either in bringing the United States into the war on the Allied side in 1917 or in bringing Germany to her knees the following year. As a result, Robertson's initial warning went unheeded. The second Ministry of Information would, it seemed, merely turn out to be a more streamlined version of the first after all.

The outcome might well have been different, however, if the Foreign Office had originally been allowed to have its way. At the first meeting of the CID sub-committee on 25 October 1935, Leeper challenged the basic assumption of Robertson's memorandum that the ministry should be an entirely separate entity. Alternatively, he argued, the Foreign Office News Department should constitute the nucleus of any future wartime organization. Although he failed to mention it, he did have the support of a CID decision made in October 1923 which inserted into the War Book a clause which stated that, in the event of another war or emergency, the Foreign Office should be responsible for propaganda 'or for recommending if and when a separate body for dealing with such work should be constituted'.[30] Leeper considered that in the News Department, with its reservoir of resident experts and its links with the fast growing peacetime propaganda organizations such as the British Council,[31] there already existed an ideal basic structure capable of expansion and conversion to wartime requirements.[32] Under his scheme, it would merely be necessary to appoint a large advisory committee to maintain close contacts with the Foreign Office, the BBC and with other government departments. In effect, Leeper's proposal amounted to the reintroduction of the system which had existed in

1917 prior to the establishment of the Ministry of Information and Crewe House, a system which had enabled the Foreign Office to control the policy and direction of Britain's overseas propaganda before losing that control on Lloyd George's instructions to Beaverbrook and Northcliffe.[33]

The scheme divided the sub-committee. Hankey, Gaselee and, if to a lesser extent, Colville, considered the peacetime apparatus capable and worthy of expansion and conversion if war should come. But theirs was a minority view. Warren Fisher considered Leeper's proposal 'too parochial and narrow' and dismissed it as beyond the sub-committee's terms of reference, which clearly called for the creation of a separate ministry. He also pointed out that the experience of the Foreign Office was limited to overseas propaganda in peacetime; there was no guarantee that its News Department could undertake home propaganda and censorship in time of war. Fisher's objections gained the support of the rest of the sub-committee and it was decided that smoother running and greater efficiency would ensue if the ministry was created as a unit apart from the existing machinery and free from the interference of Whitehall. The implication was that a return to the 1918 system was infinitely preferable to a return to the arrangements which had existed before the Ministry of Information had taken charge of propaganda from the Foreign Office.

That the planners were subsequently prepared to accept the 1918 model as a blueprint for their work was entirely understandable, particularly as their sources of information gave them little reason for starting afresh and in view of the fact that the planning was undertaken on a part-time basis by civil servants who were already overworked in their normal peacetime duties. Small wonder, therefore, that progress was slow. Moreover, their hands were tied to a considerable extent by the somewhat rigid conception of the ministry laid down in a report of 27 July 1936 and accepted by the CID as the basis for planning some months later.[34] They were also restricted by decisions made before they had even been appointed. For example, in September 1935, another CID sub-committee had recommended that, in the event of war, a Ministry of Information should assume control over broadcasting and over the BBC.[35] This proposal was embodied in a report[36] and approved by the full CID on 14 October 1935 — nearly a fortnight before the first meeting of the sub-committee to establish a Ministry of Information. This decision meant that a disproportionate amount of time was devoted by the planners to working out the wartime structure of the BBC and its position in relation to the ministry. Whereas broadcasting would undoubtedly prove an invaluable medium of wartime propaganda, there were other important instruments which demanded equal attention but which were denied their due consideration at first because of the determination of the BBC to be effectively exploited while, at the same time, preserving its autonomy and reputation.

The intolerable situation which resulted from these hindrances was shortly reflected in the plea of one official who wrote after being forced to consult an article on propaganda in the *Encylopaedia Britannica*, 'there must be experts somewhere'.[37] In fact, there were. In the first place, there was an abundant supply of experience and expertise within the existing peacetime propaganda machinery. For example, Lord William Tyrrell, the first chairman of the British Council, had not only served in the wartime propaganda organization but had also been head of the News and Political Intelligence Department of the Foreign Office for a brief period after the war. He was also currently serving as President of the British Board of Film Censors. John Buchan (Lord Tweedsmuir) had been in charge of the Department of Information in 1917. Lord Beaverbrook was still alive, as indeed was Sir Campbell Stuart, Northcliffe's right-hand man at Crewe House. Arthur Willert, head of the Foreign Office News Department from 1925 to 1934, had served in Britain's American propaganda organization while working as Washington correspondent of *The Times*.[38] There were also many journalists working in Fleet Street who, at one time or another, had been connected with the wartime organization, men such as Henry Wickham Steed, the former editor of *The Times*, and Sir Roderick Jones, the Managing Director of Reuters. H. Noble Hall, the Travel Association's Paris representative, had worked in Wellington House. So had Arnold Toynbee and various other Chatham House experts. Rex Leeper, Willert's successor as head of the News Department, was perhaps the leading Foreign Office exponent of increased peacetime propaganda, being personally responsible for the foundation of the British Council to conduct cultural propaganda in 1934 and for persuading the BBC to inaugurate broadcasts in foreign languages in 1938. Leeper had, in fact, been appointed Assistant Director-General Designate of the proposed News Division of the Ministry but was forced to withdraw his services in 1938 in order to concentrate upon his normal peacetime duties. Even Miles Lampson (Lord Killearn), Britain's ambassador in Egypt, had been involved in film propaganda work in 1916.[39] Sir William Jury, head of the Cinema Department of Beaverbrook's Ministry of Information, was still alive. Sir Joseph Ball, who in 1939 was placed in charge of the ministry's film work, was currently serving as deputy director of the National Publicity Bureau. In the private sector, there existed a growing body of industrial publicity experts such as Sidney Rogerson, the public relations officer at Imperial Chemical Industries, whose influential book, *Propaganda in the Next War*, was published in 1938.[40] The list is endless. But the only man, apart from Leeper, with any real idea of the problems involved who was directly involved in the planning before 1938 was Sir Stephen Tallents, who was appointed Director-General Designate in late 1936. Tallents had been Secretary of the pioneering Empire Marketing Board, 1926-32, and it had been under his aegis that John Grierson had been able to launch the British documentary film movement.[41] Following the Board's closure, he had been appointed public relations officer at the GPO, a post he held for three years before he became the BBC's public relations officer. But Tallents took up his appointment in the shadow Ministry of Information after the complete acceptance by the CID of the July 1936 report.

Essentially, the principal reason why Tallents was unable to consult the considerable body of expertise available derived from the intense secrecy which surrounded the planning for propaganda in the next war. It was felt that, should the preparations become public knowledge, it might create a political outcry at home. Despite the enormous progress which had been made in so far as the peacetime machinery was concerned, there was still a great deal of suspicion of official propaganda in Britain.[42] The first Ministry of Information had been disliked because it was directly responsible to Lloyd George and was financially independent of Treasury control.[43] During the only major wartime debate on the subject, the attitude of Parliament had been hostile, to say the least.[44] It was not beyond the imagination of many people to suspect that an unscrupulous government might utilize such a body as a means of sustaining political power. Moreover, a Ministry of Information essentially meant war, and the government could not allow the impression to form that it had resigned itself to such a probability. Knowledge of the planning might also provoke Hitler. However, the effect of this policy of secrecy was to impose a severe brake upon the progress of the preparations.

By February 1938, a critical stage of the planning was reached. Tallents urged that, although 'considerable progress' had been made, the time had now come for the preparatory process to be extended 'beyond the limits of government departments and the BBC, so as to enlist representatives of such interests as the press and the film industry in the discussion of the machinery appropriate to the changed conditions of 1938'.[45] He then warned that the planning was not sufficiently well advanced to enable the ministry to spring into existence in the event of a sudden emergency. He wrote:

> Even in a war in which the actual operations were geographically restricted, public opinion might come to be engaged on a world-wide front, and might materially affect its issue. Our preparations for the conduct of war on land, by sea and in the air, are the concern of powerful existing departments, and their planning the subject of continuous study by specialised staffs. Our preparations for the conduct of wartime operations of great possible variety and extent in the field of public opinion have no comparable peacetime basis, and their planning is dependent on a handful of men, all, with one exception, very fully employed on other work.[46]

Both his sub-committee and the full CID agreed. With Hitler's annexation of Austria, the time had clearly arrived for a greater sense of urgency to be injected into the planning process.

When, however, a crisis did erupt over the question of the Sudetenland, the preparations were found to be hopelessly inadequate. The shadow Ministry of Information was partially mobilized on 26 September 1938 amidst chaos and confusion. Important decisions concerning appointments, accommodation and demarcation of duties had still to be resolved, while its relationship with the peacetime propaganda machinery had still to be clarified. The planners had still not consulted the media and there did not exist any draft leaflets or pamphlets. Tallents admitted to Leeper that the important foreign section of the proposed Publicity Division was 'not yet organised'.[47] Arrangements were made for the Foreign Office to transfer certain of its staff and facilities to the ministry, and on the 27 September the Foreign Office made arrangements with the Air Ministry and Stationery Office to print ten million leaflets in German which would be dropped by the RAF immediately war was declared, but not before.[48] The theme to be adopted was to be that employed in 1918 — the destruction of the German governing regime rather than of the German people.

These improvisations did, however, raise a serious problem. At precisely what point was the ministry to assume responsibility for propaganda from the Foreign Office? Before the outbreak of war? Or immediately after? If the ministry sprang into existence prior to a formal declaration of hostilities, it might provoke opposition at home, particularly if war was averted at the last minute. Such action would also provide the enemy with advanced warning of what to expect in so far as psychological warfare was concerned, thereby providing him with an opportunity to prepare, say, for a leaflet raid, which in turn would merely serve to increase the considerable risks involved in such a mission. If, on the other hand, the Foreign Office was left in charge right up to the last minute, serious confusion might result from the wartime organization suddenly taking over from established Whitehall departments without any advanced preparation.

But there was a further complication. The Ministry of Information was not the only organization being prepared for the conduct of propaganda. In the wake of the Anschluss, two organizations came into being which were designed to conduct subversive activities against the enemy, including covert or 'black' propaganda (i.e. that emanating from an unattributable official source). The first of these, established under the auspices of MI6 and known as Section D, was set up 'to investigate every possibility of attacking potential enemies by means other than the preparation of military forces'.[49] Major Lawrence Grand was placed in charge of Section D's preparations in the fields of espionage, subversive propaganda designed to cause disaffection amongst the enemy, and what was described as 'moral sabotage'; it 'handled the unavowable'.[50] Together with another outfit known as GS(R), Section D was eventually to evolve into SOE.[51] The other organization which appears to have come into existence at about the same time was known as Department EH, after the initials of its headquarters at the Imperial Communications Committee at Electra House on the Victoria Embankment. Established initially under the auspices of the Foreign Office, Department EH was eventually to evolve into the Political Warfare Executive.[52] During the penultimate week of September 1938 (the exact date remains vague, but on or about the

24th),[53] Campbell Stuart was called in to take charge of Electra House and he began his work in complete secrecy, albeit too late to prove effective when the possible need of psychological warfare arose at the height of the Munich crisis.

Whether Tallents knew of the existence of these two organizations is not certain. It was subsequently discovered, however, that on 26 September Major Grand had been instructed (by whom is not known) to secure the dissemination of leaflets in German 'through all channels outside this country' — presumably this meant the Secret Intelligence Service — 'and had apparently got a few of them into Germany'.[54] Confirmation of this event is not available. Nor is it known what Electra House was doing during those critical days, although it does appear that Campbell Stuart had hardly begun to gather his staff together when the Prime Minister 'felt that in the Munich meeting he had achieved world peace, and I was instructed to suspend my operations'.[55]

From the point of view of the shadow Ministry of Information, the lessons of Munich were only too clear but, as Tallents wrote shortly afterwards, 'the sharpest and most urgent of them was the need of properly co-ordinated arrangements for the conveyance of information into enemy countries'.[56] On 5 October, he accordingly established contact with Section D, seemingly for the first time, in order to establish clear lines of demarcation and thus avoid the danger of overlapping. Grand informed the planners that there was no real problem for his concern was largely with black propaganda.[57] For example, in November 1938, he invited Hilda Matheson, a former Director of Talks and News at the BBC, to set up what came to be known as the Joint Broadcasting Committee and examine the possibility of broadcasting black propaganda 'from stations outside Great Britain, primarily to Germany but also to any other countries which proved available'.[58] Matheson began her work in February 1939 for a six month experimental period. Following a fact-finding tour of European radio stations, she discontinued an unprofitable arrangement recently made with Radio Luxembourg and instead advised the creation 'of a "goodwill" committee to sponsor broadcasts arranged through the broadcasting authorities of friendly countries, while the possibilities of getting programmes into Germany were explored.'[59] The Joint Broadcasting Committee of Section D was the result. Little more is known about this particular development, except that

Matheson chose as her liaison officer with the Ministry of Information one Guy Burgess, but the peacetime work of this unit remains a tantalizing mystery.

Tallents meanwhile continued to establish contacts with other interested concerns, such as the Air Ministry, SIS and the War Office. On 6 October 1938, he met with Majors E. K. Page and W. T. Stephenson (later known as 'Intrepid') to establish a liaison with military intelligence.[60] But of the various Whitehall departments consulted, the Foreign Office proved the most reluctant to accept his demarcation lines and, in the aftermath of Munich, there developed a major inter-departmental struggle for control over propaganda. Although the 1936 report had specified that the Ministry of Information was to be responsible for all propaganda at home and abroad in time of war, the events of September 1938 had merely served to cloud the issue. Now there existed a separate body for black propaganda and one for enemy propaganda. The ministry, it seemed, was now to be in control only of overt or 'white' propaganda (i.e. that conducted from an attributable government agency). Moreover, on 27 September, the Treasury had authorized the recreation of the Foreign Office Political Intelligence Department to supervise the collection and analysis of information of value to the propagandists and to the government as a whole.[61] In 1918, struggle for control over this temporary wartime department had frequently led Beaverbrook and Northcliffe to despair.[62]

Leeper did not believe in the idea of a Ministry of Information in peacetime. He was keen to maintain the Foreign Office News Department as the nerve-centre of Britain's peacetime propaganda overseas, particularly as the government was devoting renewed attention to the subject, as reflected in the appointment of the Vansittart Co-ordinating Committee for British Publicity Abroad earlier in 1938.[63] He had lost the 1935 battle to ensure a central role for the Foreign Office in the planning for propaganda in war, but when Tallents submitted a proposal in November 1938 to revise the ministry's terms of reference so that it could come into being immediately prior to the outbreak of hostilities, he was determined not to lose this one. Essentially, Tallents proposed a six-stage mobilization process, the first three phases of which would take place in peacetime. Of the first stage, which he termed 'Undisturbed Peacetime Conditions', Tallents wrote:

> Nothing has struck me more forcibly in my recent exploration of this field than the emphasis spontaneously and separately laid by representatives of all three Service Departments on the need in present continental conditions, in which the boundaries between peace and war are so largely obliterated, of an efficient peacetime centre for the close study of 'enemy' public opinion, and the conveyance through channels appropriate in peace of truth about events and British policy to both 'enemy' and other foreign countries. They have recognised that the country needs specialised armament in the world of opinion not less than in that of munitions of war, and have bluntly remarked that such equipment might well make the difference between future war and peace.[64]

The second stage, which Tallents described as 'Peacetime Conditions Disturbed by Factors which might lead to War', provided for the establishment of machinery to conduct propaganda immediately prior to a possible explosion in a last-ditch attempt to save the peace while other forms of evasive action were being explored. Stage three would provide for complete mobilization 'immediately preceding a decision for peace or war'.[65] Tallents further sought authorisation for the advanced preparation of propaganda material such as leaflets so that they would be ready for use at short notice.[66]

Leeper found these proposals completely unacceptable. He reminded the planners that not only was the Foreign Office the proper authority for the conduct of all official propaganda overseas in time of peace but was also responsible for the study of foreign opinion. The News Department had already examined means of disseminating the British case into Germany in consultation with the Berlin Embassy, the British Council and with SIS and was about to submit its own proposals to the Cabinet. Besides, he added, propaganda material prepared well in advance might become obsolete by the time war did come.[67] He therefore requested that his objections to Tallents's proposals be formally recorded at the full meeting of the CID sub-committee scheduled to take place on 14 December.

On that same day, the Cabinet considered a memorandum signed by the Foreign Secretary, Lord Halifax (but almost certainly written by Leeper), in which the Foreign Office sought permission to increase its peacetime propaganda in Germany. The Nazi government, it was felt, feared counter-propaganda to such a degree that any British activity in this direction 'should be unobtrusive and unprovocative, as the German government will do their best to counteract it or even stop it, but it also means that our propaganda, if wisely done, may produce a big effect'.[68] Various specific proposals were made including the extension of the BBC's German news bulletins (which had begun on 27 September), increased personal contacts among businessmen, the expansion of the British Council's long-term cultural and educational activities such as student exchanges, lecture tours and so on. 'Money so spent', it was argued, 'may rightly be regarded as an important item in our general defence programme.'[69]

It has been suggested that these proposals were 'a pitiful package of barrel-scrapings' and that the Foreign Office merely put them forward as the latest exchange in an inter-departmental battle.[70] But that the Foreign Office wished to retain control over a system which it had championed since the end of the First World War in the face of continuous opposition was entirely reasonable. If war should come, it would surprise neither Leeper, who had been warning of the German danger since at least 1935, nor those few officials who supported his innovative ideas in the field of peacetime propaganda. Yet Leeper's success had very much been determined by the degree of acceptance which others, particularly in the Treasury, were prepared to allow in light of financial stringency and, at times, of overwhelming prejudice. In the aftermath of Munich, there was a real chance that his ideas would begin to gain much wider support.

Nevertheless, when the Cabinet discussed the Foreign Office proposals, strong doubts were expressed concerning the suitability of the News Department serving as the nucleus for any programme of increased peacetime propaganda because its press office 'had not always been in complete harmony with Government policy' — a reference to Leeper's recent behaviour during the Munich crisis when he had been responsible for issuing the unfortunate communiqué of September 26.[71] Moreover, the financial implications of the proposals were severe, and the Cabinet decided to defer any decision pending further investigation by the Exchequer.[72]

Later that day, 14 December 1938, the CID sub-committee on the Ministry of Information convened to discuss Tallents's proposals. Grave concern was expressed at the lack of preparedness during the Munich crisis, and Tallents attracted most of the criticism. Warren Fisher poured cold water over the six-stage mobilization plan and warned that a shadow ministry must not be allowed to 'usurp in peacetime the functions of existing agencies or Departments, which should remain responsible for working out their own plans'.[73] In this inter-departmental struggle for control over propaganda in peacetime, Leeper's objections had won through while Tallents was chosen as the sacrificial lamb for the débâcle of Munich as, shortly afterwards, he was dismissed as Director-General Designate and replaced by Sir Ernest Fass, the Public Trustee. This was an astonishing decision. The only full-time planner with any real idea of the problems raised by Munich was replaced by a man with no prior experience of propaganda. Although the precise reasons for his dismissal remain unknown, it would appear that Tallents had upset too many influential people to warrant his replacement by a man who was less willing to rock the Whitehall boat. Conversely, the Foreign Office proposals for increased peacetime activity were approved by the Cabinet a week later.[74]

Not surprisingly, Fass did not prove to be a success, although he was certainly more willing than Tallents had been to accommodate the wishes of the established government departments. Sir Samuel Hoare, the Home Secretary, reluctantly assumed overall responsibility for the planning, although his level of commitment to the cause of propaganda in the next war was, as he himself admitted later, half-hearted to say the least.[75] In other words, both men were entirely unsuited to the enormous task of rectifying the serious deficiencies which had been exposed in the planning by the Munich dress-rehearsal.

Apart from the decision to increase the number of full-time planners working on the preparations from one to three, the only other satisfying outcome of the sub-committee's meeting of 14 December was a decision to appoint a new sub-committee under the chairmanship of Sir Campbell Stuart to re-examine the entire question of enemy propaganda in time of war. The first and only formal meeting of this body took place at Electra House on 26 January 1939. Discussion largely centred around a lengthy memorandum written by Leeper which revealed the considerable amount of propaganda currently being conducted by, or under the auspices of, the Foreign Office.[76] The Foreign Office was then confirmed as the proper authority in time of peace for the conduct of propaganda abroad and for the official study of foreign opinion.[77] Different arrangements would come into force on the outbreak of war when Campbell Stuart would assume responsibility for the conduct of enemy propaganda. Meanwhile, Leeper was to ascertain the views of the British Council concerning the possible role of cultural propaganda in wartime, while negotiations with the BBC and with the Air Ministry concerning the role of broadcasting and leaflets in enemy propaganda were to be accelerated.[78]

Campbell Stuart continued his own preparations in complete secrecy. Arrangements were made to move his organization from Electra House to Woburn Abbey on the outbreak of war.[79] He also began to recruit a small nucleus staff and to establish contact with the service departments, the Foreign Office, BBC and shadow Ministry of Information, from which he was to be completely separate[80] (as in 1918). Alternative methods of distributing propaganda into enemy countries were also investigated but were not disclosed 'in the public interest'.[81]

Despite these improvements in the planning for enemy propaganda, the preparations for the Ministry of Information were still being conducted at a relatively leisurely pace. The German invasion of Prague in March 1939 was to provide the necessary injection of urgency and realism which had not always been evident before, even after Munich. In May 1939, the Prime Minister authorized the appointment of a special ministerial committee composed of the Home and Foreign Secretaries and the Minister for the Co-ordination of Defence to consider 'what steps should be taken during peace to counteract anti-British propaganda and to institute a more active policy of British publicity overseas'.[82] Although there appears to be no available record of any formal proceedings, the committee did submit a report to the Cabinet containing two major recommendations to expand the existing propaganda programme and to facilitate the planning for propaganda in war. Hoare proposed the removal of two of the principal obstacles which had hitherto tied the hands of the wartime planners, namely the obligation of strict secrecy and the lack of funds made available to the shadow organization (which had up to now been carried on the Secret Service Vote). Moreover, because the Ministry of Information intended to assume responsibility for propaganda abroad from the Foreign Office in time of war, it had now become important to ensure 'continuity between the peacetime activities of the Foreign Office in relation to publicity abroad and the work that will in war fall upon the Ministry of Information.'[83]

This recognition was certainly long overdue, and Hoare's report produced two important results. The first was the re-organization of the Foreign Office News Department. The purely propaganda side of the department's work was separated from the press work and placed under the auspices of a new body called the Foreign Publicity Department of the Foreign Office.[84] The head of this new department was to be Lord Perth, the recently retired Ambassador to Rome. Perth was also made Director-General Designate of the shadow Ministry of Information, replacing Fass. Hoare felt that this dual role would greatly ease the transition from peace to wartime arrangements, and the Cabinet agreed,[85] although not without causing a major scandal in the process.[86] Perth was certainly an unusual choice. Despite his enormously distinguished diplomatic career, like Fass he had little or no personal experience of propaganda matters, and many believed that Leeper should have got the job.[87] When announcing the decision in Parliament on 15 June, thereby revealing the existence of plans for a Ministry of Information for the first time publicly, Chamberlain was subjected to a series of difficult questions which failed to dispel the suspicion that Perth's appointment was 'a ramp of Sam Hoare's'.[88]

The other major outcome of Hoare's report was the establishment by the Treasury of the Overseas and Emergency Publicity Expenditure Committee, known as OEPEC. This body was set up in late June 1939 under the chairmanship of Sir Alan Barlow, a senior Treasury official, assisted by Mr J. Cairncross as his secretary.[89] It was designed to cut across the normal time-consuming process of sanctioning expenditure for requests which required immediate action. For example, when the Foreign Office submitted to the Treasury a proposal to authorize its missions at Bucharest, Belgrade, Sofia, Athens and Budapest 'to spend up to £100 each, if necessary, to induce newspaper editors to print articles . . . calculated to put across the British point of view', Cairncross minuted: 'as we have already agreed to the "Operational Expense" (i.e. palm-greasing) . . . I do not think we need boggle at this further analogous charge'.[90] But OEPEC was also designed to provide speedy decisions to requests from the planners of the shadow Ministry of Information and other wartime propaganda bodies. As the drift towards war increased during the summer of 1939, it naturally concerned itself more with propaganda in the coming war than with the conduct of propaganda during the final months of peace.

There can be no doubt that the Ministry of Information entered the Second World War hopelessly ill-prepared for the tasks which lay before it. Despite the considerable progress made during the final year of peace, there still remained much more preparatory work to be done, particularly in the areas of propaganda techniques and content. Small wonder that it should become something of a public joke, the subject of Evelyn Waugh's satire,[91] at least until Brendan Bracken took over in 1941. The same could not be said of the enemy propaganda department which had sufficiently prepared the ground to enable the RAF to conduct a leaflet raid on the opening night of the war. So why was it that, despite five years of pre-war planning, Britain entered the war of words in September 1939 not speechless, as she had effectively been in August 1914, but certainly inarticulate? It was not due simply to the fact that new machinery tends to need running-in before it can begin to operate smoothly and effectively, because Goebbels' Ministry of Propaganda, which after all had had six years of practice, also entered the war in chaos and confusion.[92] Nor would it be entirely accurate to attribute the planning deficiencies solely to inter-departmental rivalry and squabbling, although that undoubtedly played its part. Perhaps the answer lies in the fact that before Hitler's seizure of Prague in March 1939 few people in British governmental circles were prepared to accept the idea that a Ministry of Information would be necessary. A Ministry of Information did, after all, mean war.

NOTES

1. *If War Should Come* is the title of a film, alternatively known as *Do it Now* and *If War Comes*, made by the GPO for the Ministry of Information in September 1939.

2. L. Woodward, *British Foreign Policy in the Second World War* (London 1971), II, 38.

3. CAB 65/1, 1 (39) 2, 3 September 1939.

4. C. Webster and N. Frankland, *The Strategic Air Offensive Against Germany, 1939-45* (London 1961), I, 201-204.

5. P. Towle, 'The debate on wartime censorship in Britain, 1902-1914' in B. Bond and I. Roy (eds.), *War and Society: A Yearbook of Military History* (London 1975).

6. M. L. Sanders, 'Wellington House and British Propaganda during the First World War', *Historical Journal*, XVIII, I (1975), 119-146.

7. P. M. Taylor, 'The Foreign Office and British Propaganda during the First World War', *Historical Journal*, XXIII, IV (1980).

8. The best accounts of the work at Crewe House remain C. Stuart, *Secrets of Crewe House: The Story of a Famous Campaign* (London 1920) and G. C. Bruntz, *Allied Propaganda and the Collapse of the German Empire in 1918* (Stanford 1938). There is still no satisfactory account of the work of the Ministry of Information.

9. See the forthcoming reappraisal of the wartime experiment by M. L. Sanders and P. M. Taylor, *British Propaganda during the First World War*, to be published by Macmillan in 1982.

10. King-Hall to S. G. Tallents, 5 September 1938. FO 898/2.

11. Ibid.

12. They can be found in FO 898/1.

13. Memorandum by Tallents, 'Information in Enemy Countries', 7 November 1938. CAB 16/127, MIC 15.

14. London 1979.

15. London 1979.

16. McLaine, *Ministry of Morale*, ch. 2.

17. D. N. Dilks, 'The Unnecessary War? Military Advice and Foreign Policy in Great Britain, 1931-39' in A. Preston (ed.), *General Staffs and Diplomacy before the Second World War* (London 1978).

18. D. J. Wrench, 'The Influence of Neville Chamberlain on Foreign and Defence Policy, 1932-35', *RUSI*, 125, 1, March 1980, 49-57.

19. M. Howard, 'Total War in the Twentieth Century: Participation and Consensus in the Second World War' in B. Bond and I. Roy, op. cit.

20. *Hansard*, 5th series, Vol. 109, 5 August 1918, col. 999.

21. U. Bialer, 'The Danger of Bombardment from the Air and the Making of British Air Disarmament Policy, 1932-34' in B. Bond and I. Roy, op. cit.

22. A. Aldgate, *Cinema and History: British Newsreels and the Spanish Civil War* (London 1979).

23. F. Thorpe and N. Pronay, *British Official Films in the Second World War: A Descriptive Catalogue* (Oxford 1980), 17.

24. Balfour, *Propaganda in War*, 53.

25. Memorandum by C. P. Robertson, 12 September 1935. CAB 16/127, MIC 2.

26. CAB 16/127, MIC 1.

27. C. Stuart (ed.), *The Reith Diaries* (London 1975), 122.

28. Balfour, op. cit., 54.

29. McLaine, op. cit., 12-13.

30. Extract from the minutes of the CID's 177th meeting, 12 October 1923. FO 371/9405, W 8762/293/50.

31. P. M. Taylor, 'Cultural diplomacy and the British Council, 1934-39', *Brit. J. International Studies*, 4 (1978), 244-65.

32. First meeting of the CID sub-committee to prepare plans for the establishment of a Ministry of Information in time of war, 25 October 1935. CAB 16/127.

33. P. M. Taylor, 'The Foreign Office and British Propaganda during the First World War', *H.J.*, XXIII, IV (1980).

34. The report is paper number 12538, PREM 1/388. Its acceptance is recorded in CAB 16/129, MIC (CC) 1.

35. CID sub-committee on the general policy of broadcasting in time of war, 25 September 1935. CAB 16/120.

36. CAB 16/120, BW 14.
37. H. V. Rhodes to Tallents, 12 July 1938. INF 4/1A.
38. A. Willert, *Washington and Other Memories* (Boston 1972).
39. Lampson to H. Montgomery, 28 July 1916. FO 371/2835, 184995.
40. London, Bles, 1938.
41. P. Swann, *The British Documentary Film Movement, 1926-46.* Unpublished Ph.D. thesis, University of Leeds, 1979.
42. P. M. Taylor, 'British Official Attitudes Towards Propaganda Abroad, 1919-39' to be published in a collection of essays edited by N. Pronay and D. Spring entitled *Film, Politics and Propaganda* (London 1981).
43. K. Middlemas and J. Barnes, *Baldwin* (London 1969), 68.
44. *Hansard*, 5th series, Vol. 109, 5 August 1918, cols. 947-1035.
45. Progress report by Tallents, 23 February 1938. CAB 16/127, MIC 10.
46. Ibid.
47. Note of a discussion between Leeper and Tallents held on 27 September 1938. INF 1/442.
48. Minute by H. Knatchbull-Hugessen, 27 September 1938. FO 898/1.
49. M. R. D. Foot, *SOE in France* (London 1966), 2.
50. Ibid.
51. Ibid; see also B. Sweet-Escott, *Baker Street Irregular* (London 1965).
52. R. Bruce Lockhart, *Comes the Reckoning* (London 1947).
53. See Tallents's account in his memorandum of 7 November 1938. CAB 16/127, MIC 15.
54. Ryan to Tallents, 5 October 1938. FO 898/1.
55. C. Stuart, *Opportunity Knocks Once* (London 1952), 185.
56. Tallents to Sir Donald Banks, 4 October 1938. FO 898/1.
57. Ryan to Tallents, 5 October 1938. FO 898/1.
58. Memorandum on the Joint Broadcasting Committee, 24 August 1939. Appendix to OEPEC paper 82. T 162/858, E 39140/4.
59. Ibid.
60. Record of a meeting held at the BBC, 6 October 1938. FO 898/1.
61. Memorandum by Warner, 6 October 1938. FO 395/624, P 2853/2853/150.
62. See Lord Beaverbrook, *Men and Power, 1917-18* (London 1956), 290; R. Pound and G. Harmsworth, *Northcliffe* (London 1959), 652-653.
63. See the chapter on this committee in the forthcoming book by P. M. Taylor, *The Projection of Britain; British Overseas Publicity and Propaganda, 1919-1939* to be published by Cambridge University Press in 1981.
64. Memorandum by Tallents, 7 November 1938. CAB 16/127, MIC 18.
65. Ibid.
66. Ibid.
67. Leeper to Ryan, 7 December 1938. CAB 16/127, MIC 18.
68. Memorandum by Halifax, 'British propaganda in Germany', 8 December 1938. CAB 24/281, CP 284 (38).
69. Ibid.
70. C. Cruickshank, *The Fourth Arm: Psychological Warfare, 1938-45* (London 1977), 14.
71. K. Middlemas, *The Diplomacy of Illusion* (London 1972), 388; I. Colvin, *Vansittart in Office* (London 1965), 266-267.
72. CAB 23/96, 59 (38) 5.

73. Fifth meeting of the CID sub-committee to prepare plans for the establishment of a Ministry of Information in time of war, 14 December 1938. CAB 16/127.

74. CAB 23/96, 60 (38) 3, 21 December 1938.

75. Viscount Templewood, *Nine Troubled Years* (London 1954), 420-421.

76. Memorandum by Leeper, 'British Publicity Abroad', 20 January 1939. CAB 16/130, MIC (P) 2.

77. Undated draft report by Campbell Stuart. CAB 16/130, MIC (P) 5.

78. CID sub-committee on Propaganda in Foreign Countries in time of war, first meeting, 26 January 1939. CAB 16/130, MIC (P).

79. Balfour, *Propaganda in War*, 88-89.

80. Memorandum by Campbell Stuart, 8 February 1939. CAB 16/130, MIC (P) 3.

81. Undated draft report by Campbell Stuart. CAB 16/130, MIC (P) 5.

82. Memorandum by Hoare, 2 June 1939. CAB 24/287, CP 127 (39).

83. Ibid.

84. FO 366/1071.

85. CAB 23/99, 31 (39) 12, 7 June 1939; CAB 23/99, 32 (39) 9, 14 June 1939.

86. J. Harvey (ed.), *The Diplomatic Diaries of Oliver Harvey, 1937-40* (London 1970), 292.

87. Ibid., 294.

88. Ibid., 292.

89. T 162/858, E 39140/2.

90. Minute by Cairncross, 31 August 1939. T 162/858, E 39140/2.

91. *Put Out More Flags* (London 1942).

92. R. E. Herzstein, *The War that Hitler Won* (London 1979).

3 British Plans for Economic Warfare against Germany 1937-1939: The Problem of Swedish Iron Ore

Patrick Salmon

Swedish iron ore occupies a special place in both the history of the first months of the Second World War, and the scholarly debate on the character of the German war economy. Schemes for diplomatic, naval or military action in Scandinavia — all more or less ineffectual — dominated the strategy of Britain and France in the winter of 1939-40. Though given impetus and a pretext by the outbreak of the Soviet-Finnish Winter War in November 1939, these plans were principally aimed at the complete or partial denial of supplies of Swedish iron ore to Germany. German strategy too was concerned with Scandinavia — partly in response to the ill-concealed Allied interest in the area, but also in pursuit of broader strategic objectives. According to Hitler's directive of 1 March 1940, the German invasion of Denmark and Norway, carried out on 9 April, 'would anticipate English action against Scandinavia and the Baltic, would secure our supplies of ore from Sweden, and would provide the Navy and Air Force with expanded bases for operations against England.'[1]

The British preoccupation with Swedish ore was not merely due to the fact that the German steel industry was more dependent on supplies from Sweden than from any other source: this was a matter of common knowledge. It also derived from the much more questionable belief, expressed most authoritatively in a memorandum by the Ministry of Economic Warfare (MEW) of 18 December

1939, that a total stoppage of these supplies would bring production to a standstill in a matter of months — perhaps by the spring of 1940 — with 'a profound effect on the duration of the war'.[2]

The revival of this claim by the Swedish historian Karlbom in 1965 provoked considerable controversy in the pages of the *Scandinavian Economic History Review* and elsewhere.[3] It was initially discredited on statistical grounds, and by pointing out that the German war economy was designed to cope with just such a short-term interruption as the Allies were trying to bring about.[4] More recently emphasis has been placed on the technical aspects of German steel production, in which the supply of Swedish ore was only one of many variables, and on the wider context of Swedish-German trade relations.[5] The complex picture that has emerged demonstrates that Allied expectations of rapid results were wholly unfounded, without diminishing Germany's dependence on Swedish ore in the long term.

Yet these studies have shed little light on the reasons why such mistaken assumptions were held in the first place; nor has it been their intention to do so. The present study is intended to fill the gap: to reconstruct the process by which a particular view of the importance of Swedish iron ore became fixed in British minds in the years immediately preceding the Second World War. It will also examine the methods evolved for dealing with the problem by Britain's planners, and finally the effect — if any — of these pre-war assessments and proposals on wartime policy. It therefore explores in detail one aspect of a phenomenon peculiar to Britain in the interwar period: the prominent role assigned to 'economic warfare' in strategic theory and practice. In the words of its official historian, ' "Blockade" was a familiar enough thing in European warfare; but, adorned and transmogrified with a new name and an ill-defined promise, it had become in 1939 Britain's secret weapon.'[6]

The attraction of economic warfare derived in the first instance from Britain's traditional advantages as a maritime power with access to overseas sources of supply, and the capacity to deny a large proportion of these supplies to a continental power such as Germany. The experience of the First World War had inculcated an exaggerated belief in the effectiveness of the blockade in bringing about Germany's defeat, together with a revulsion from the material and human cost represented by the Western Front. To these were added Britain's new commitment to the League of Nations, with the latter's emphasis on economic as opposed to military sanctions against aggression; and the doctrine of the strategic bombing offensive against selected economic targets.

The potential effectiveness of such methods against Germany was greatly increased by the territorial provisions of the Treaty of Versailles — above all the loss of the Lorraine ore fields, which meant that Germany's 60 per cent self-sufficiency in iron ore before the First World War was immediately transformed into a 75-80 per cent dependence on foreign sources. Efforts were naturally made to reduce this economic vulnerability, including the establishment of closer trade relations with neighbouring neutrals in northern and south-eastern Europe, and the development of substitute raw materials or the intensified exploitation of domestic sources, as exemplified by the 'Four Year Plan' of 1936.

These activities were the object of continuous scrutiny and assessment in Britain. The machinery of economic intelligence and planning established by the Committee of Imperial Defence (CID) from 1923 onwards has been described in several official histories and one recent article.[7] The point at which planning was directed primarily against Germany, and as part of a military strategy, not merely in support of League sanctions, is marked by the formation in July 1937 of the committee on Economic Pressure on Germany (EPG), in succession to the Economic Pressure (EP) committee of May 1933. By the middle of 1938 the EPG's preparatory work had been substantially completed, and the nucleus of the future MEW had been formed. It was then the responsibility of the Coordination Section of the Foreign Office to make arrangements for the new ministry to come into existence immediately on the outbreak of war. The information on which these preparations depended was supplied principally by the Industrial Intelligence Centre (IIC), established in 1931 with the task of reporting on 'the state of industrial and economic preparedness of foreign countries to make war.'

The IIC, which was to become in 1939 the Intelligence Division of MEW, enjoyed an unusual degree of influence. This was due not only to its expertise, but also to the personality of its head, the forceful and persuasive Major Desmond Morton. In numerous memoranda the IIC examined both Germany's war potential and that of other countries, whether prospective enemies, allies or neutrals. To a large extent its authoritative views and striking modes of expression defined the terms in which economic warfare (the term itself was an IIC coinage) was debated in government circles both before and during the war. Having identified a potential weakness in the economy of a country such as Germany, the IIC went on to suggest ways in which it might be exploited: it thus became much more than an intelligence-gathering body, and an integral part of the policy-making process.[8]

Any attempt to examine the relationship between economic intelligence and the formulation of policy is confronted with the problem of documentary evidence. Official secretiveness and dispersal or accidental destruction prevent direct access to the records of most of the bodies concerned. It is therefore necessary to search laboriously and often at random through the files of government departments whose activities overlapped with theirs. The field is potentially vast, but has been narrowed by efficient 'weeding'. Apart from the Foreign Office and MEW, only the Air Ministry and Ministry of Supply have proved particularly fruitful. Since it is impossible to estimate the nature and extent of the material that is unavailable, the present account is necessarily tentative.

The official historians have drawn attention to the deficiencies of Britain's economic warfare preparations, and their criticisms are of particular relevance to the iron ore question. On the administrative side, Hinsley points out that the CID's economic intelligence system was understaffed and hampered by a lack of advice from civil departments such as the Treasury: it therefore 'remained somewhat isolated from the main stream of economic thought and discussion in Whitehall'; while at the highest level — among ministers and senior officials — 'interest in economic intelligence was at best moderate.'[9] A more serious criticism concerns the nature of the information available to the IIC. In its important series of memoranda prepared for the EPG from July 1937 onwards, the IIC was unable to make adequate assessments of Germany's financial and manpower situations: 'Thus the appreciations were concerned mainly with the position in food, raw materials and fuel, and were largely based on published figures inadequately supported by reliable high-grade intelligence.'[10] This in turn contributed to a fundamental conceptual error: a failure to understand the nature of the German 'Blitzkrieg economy', which led to the belief that by 1939 the economy was fully mobilized for war, and hence highly vulnerable to action against its raw material supplies.[11]

In this last respect, too, the British approach to economic warfare displayed a characteristic weakness. Although the EPG's 'Plan for Economic Warfare against Germany' of July 1938 acknowledged that 'it is only by creating a sufficient scarcity of a large number of commodities that important results can be obtained', there was always a tendency, as Medlicott puts it, to 'search for Achilles' heel — some specific shortage which would bring the whole industrial machine to a standstill'.[12] It was clear from the outset that only two commodities qualified in this category — iron ore and oil — and the IIC had no doubt where the priority lay: 'It is not at all unlikely that Germany's greatest difficulty and the point at which successful economic pressure would hit her first and hardest would be in regard to iron ore.'[13]

The close connection between Swedish iron ore and German steel dated from the late nineteenth century, when the adoption of the Thomas process on a large scale made possible for the first time the exploitation of phosphoric ores — both those of France and Germany, and the much richer ores of Swedish Lapland, with an average iron content of over 60 per cent.[14] Transported by rail from the main mining centres of Kiruna and Gällivare either to Luleå on the Gulf of Bothnia (ice-bound for at least five months of the year) or to the Norwegian port of Narvik (ice-free throughout the winter), the ore reached the Ruhr principally via Rotterdam and the Rhine, or Emden and the Dortmund-Ems Canal. A smaller quantity was exported from central Sweden, where the ore was generally lower in iron and phosphorus content, through the southern Swedish port of Oxelösund (normally ice-free). This was utilized in the production of high-grade steel (for, e.g., armaments) by the Martin process, while Thomas steel was of a lower quality and mainly used in building, road and railway construction.

Successive Swedish governments were fully aware of the economic and political significance of the iron ore industry. 95 per cent of production and 90 per cent of the total export was controlled by the Grängesberg Company, either in its own right or in partnership with the state (which had a 50 per cent holding in the Lapland mines). Until 1937, exports were limited by the so-called 'Grängesberg Law' of 1927 to 9 million tons annually from the northern fields, and 1.5 million from central Sweden.[15] Germany was by far the largest purchaser of Swedish ore, taking in most years about 75 per cent of the total export (Britain, the second largest, rarely took more than 12 per cent) — amounting in the years 1936-

38 to an annual average of nearly 9 million tons. In terms of iron content, this represented almost 60 per cent of Germany's iron ore imports, and about 45 per cent of her total requirements.

The rapid revival in German consumption of Swedish ore after 1933, from the extremely low levels of the Depression period, revived the British strategic interest that had been largely dormant since the First World War.[16] As early as December 1933 the IIC devoted a report to Germany's 'Imports from Scandinavian Countries in Case of War'; and a year later iron ore figured prominently among the 'points where Swedish assistance would be of great value to Germany in war-time' in an IIC survey of Sweden's war potential.[17] It was not, however, until towards the end of 1936 that such interest became more than intermittent. In that year, Germany's aggressive intentions appeared no longer open to doubt, while the consequences of rearmament-based recovery were revealed in a foreign exchange and raw materials crisis which led to Göring's ascendancy as 'economic dictator', and the establishment of the Four Year Plan under his direction.

Germany's inability to pay for adequate imports of iron ore and other raw materials led the EP committee to make a less than usually gloomy estimate of the effects of economic pressure (short of war) in their report of October 1936, where they noted that 'a successful prevention of imports of iron ore and, of course, pig iron, steel and scrap as alternatives, would produce a rapid and serious effect upon German industry and national life.'[18] At this stage the IIC was not so sure, and blamed Germany's shortage of iron and steel on a fall in imports of manganese from the USSR, possibly for political reasons.[19] Iron ore was, however, the most serious problem, not least because of growing British competition for Swedish ore. New works such as Corby were capable of utilizing phosphoric ore, and demand was already rising when the outbreak of the Spanish civil war threatened supplies from Britain's largest source (30 per cent) of imported ore. The British Iron and Steel Federation (BISF) took an active part in securing ore from Sweden — paying higher prices than the Germans and, unlike the latter, in cash.[20]

In spite of German suspicion, the British were not buying for strategic reasons (although there was some concern for *British* supplies in wartime),[21] but simply to satisfy the boom conditions of 1936-37. German efforts to obtain increased supplies of ore, in which Göring played a leading role, were equally conspicuous; and the 'scramble for Swedish iron ore' aroused much attention in the

Scandinavian press and elsewhere.[22] It was clear that if production were to be increased, the Grängesberg Law would have to be revised; and after delicate negotiations it was raised with effect from 1938, primarily for Britain's benefit, by 2.2 million tons a year.[23] As it happened, Britain was hit by recession in 1938, and the extra ore was taken by Germany instead.

German anxiety in the winter of 1936-37, reflected in a visit to northern Norway and Sweden by Blomberg, the Defence Minister, and 'certain prominent German steel magnates' was noted by the IIC and in January 1937 provided the occasion for a memorandum dealing exclusively with Swedish iron ore.[24] It was a straightforward survey, and Morton's main purpose was to draw attention to Germany's urgent interest in the problem, and the likelihood that the export quota for 1936 had been virtually exhausted. No particular response appears to have been aroused in the Foreign Office, where interest was focused on Spanish ore, and the reactions of other departments are unknown.[25]

But the IIC continued to devote much attention to Germany's raw materials situation, and in June 1937 produced a major study of German supplies of iron ore in war, intended by Morton to be an 'invitation to controversy' among the departments to which it was circulated.[26] After discussing Germany's heavy dependence on imported ore, and taking into account variations in iron content, the memorandum concluded that Germany would have to import at least 9 million tons of Swedish iron ore 'in the first year of a war against Great Britain, France and Belgium in 1939' — even if the Four Year Plan was fully successful and Germany could obtain the entire output of the Luxemburg and Austrian mines. There appears to have been little criticism of the IIC's analysis (though the Air Ministry disputed its proposed methods: see note 44 below); and its conclusions were utilized in an important memorandum prepared by the IIC for the first meeting of the EPG committee.[27]

The IIC's assertion that 'were Sweden alone to refuse to supply Germany with iron ore, German Industry would come to a stop in a very short time, possibly measurable in weeks', appears to have made a deep impression on the committee, since their discussion returned repeatedly to Swedish ore. The chairman, Walter Elliot (Secretary of State for Scotland), suggested that 'it would be worth while facing a lot of trouble with neutrals in order to interfere with the trade to Germany in that particular commodity.'

It is worth stopping at this point to consider the IIC's memoranda in the light of the general criticisms noted earlier; for it is scarcely an exaggeration to suggest that between the middle of 1937 and the beginning of 1940, no significant advance was made in terms of either information or analysis. It seems that the IIC had to rely more on published sources for iron ore than for non-ferrous metals such as nickel, for which they were able to rely on the International Nickel Company, and more for Swedish iron ore than for Spanish, where the Rio Tinto Company was a regular informant.[28] Diplomatic and consular representatives in Scandinavia were of some value, but the Grängesberg Company was extremely secretive about certain matters, such as statistics of ore shipments from Narvik.[29] Contacts with the company's management were friendly but not very productive, although after the outbreak of war its London representative, Frisell, provided MEW with information (not always reliable) on several occasions.[30] But there was a general problem with the information the IIC obtained by informal means: Morton complained that although City contacts were entirely sincere and willing to help, 'when one has to pin them down to facts and, above all, figures, their statements tend to vanish like the Cheshire Cat, leaving little but the grin.'[31]

Although the IIC's analysis of Germany's ore requirements was realistic as far as it went, it was highly generalized and took no account of the varying phosphorus content of the ore, or of the different steel-making processes employed. This omission has been criticized, and it is certainly the case that it was not until January 1940, when MEW was searching for arguments in favour of immediate action against the Narvik traffic, that Morton drew attention to the ore's high phosphorus content.[32] The enhanced importance of low-phosphorus ore in wartime, when German armament production was increasing, was not anticipated at all; though here the IIC and MEW may be forgiven since the Germans themselves attached little importance to this ore before 1939.

There are, however, indications that the character and requirements of the German steel industry were better understood in Britain than the IIC's memoranda suggest. The fact that they were not alluded to was perhaps due to a desire to avoid overloading the argument with technicalities. But the danger of such oversimplification was that a selective picture could be mistaken for reality, contributing to the belief in the indispensability of a few key commodities which was, as we have seen, fully established by 1937.

If little was added to the picture after the completion of the basic economic warfare preparations in 1938, the IIC did not, as we shall see, relax its vigilance where *methods* of depriving Germany of iron ore were concerned. And in at least one area continued scrutiny was imperative: the extent to which the increased exploitation of Germany's low-grade domestic ores might reduce dependence on foreign supplies. The IIC's initial scepticism about the benefits, at least in the short term, of the Hermann Göring works at Salzgitter (founded in July 1937 on the model of Corby) was reinforced by information from the American expert H. A. Brassert, who had advised on the construction of both plants.[33] Morton's belief in the importance of Swedish ore remained unshaken, and was shared by Brassert himself, who let it be known in October 1939 that he felt that 'this supply is the thing to prevent as far as ever possible.'[34]

The British concept of economic warfare observed a distinction between 'Direct action against the German economy and industry' (including detention and capture of cargoes, prohibition of trading with the enemy, air attack and sabotage), and 'Indirect action by agreement with neutrals or pressure upon them.'[35] Where Swedish iron ore is concerned, the second category should be widened to include the possibility of increasing British purchases in order to deny supplies to Germany. This was feasible because maximum production was fixed by law, although there had to be some confidence that the Swedes would not succumb to German pressure to set the legal limit aside. Pre-emptive purchase of the entire ore export was occasionally suggested, but was quite impracticable: the British steel industry was incapable of absorbing such a huge quantity, the possibility of Swedish cooperation was remote and, as Elliot put it in 1937, 'the Germans would not allow themselves to be prevented from obtaining iron ore almost within sight of their shores merely because Sweden said that it had been sold to someone else.'[36]

A more modest increase was both practicable and welcome to the Swedes, since it was in accordance with Sweden's neutrality policy for ore exports to be divided as equally as possible between the two potential belligerents. As we have seen, the BISF negotiations of 1937 were not directed against Germany, and had inadvertently permitted German imports to be increased. The Swedes warned in July 1938 that the shortfall in British purchases could not 'fail to affect the exports of Swedish iron ore as a whole', and returned to the question in March 1939 when hints from Robert Hudson, the Secretary for Overseas Trade, who was shortly to visit Stockholm for trade talks, indicated that the British attitude might now be more receptive.[37] Prytz, the Swedish Minister in London, suggested that Britain should consider a long-term policy of buying up to 50 per cent of the total export. Although little could be done to implement such a policy at this late stage, the Swedes argued that it was still imperative for Britain's purchases to be increased at least to the level demanded by the BISF in 1937. If they were not, the Germans might offer to buy up to the revised legal limit, and the Swedes would scarcely be in a position to refuse. After much delay, a decision by the CID in July 1939 to create a war reserve of 500,000 tons of Swedish ore, together with an estimate of 2 million tons for the BISF's requirements, offered the hope that Britain would be able to take the 2.5 million tons necessary to ensure that there would be no surplus for the Germans.[38]

But it was too late for any significant results, and by the outbreak of war it seemed that, at best, the Swedes would 'cut down supplies of iron ore to Germany as far as they dare — which will probably not be very far.'[39] In pursuit of this objective, MEW devoted much effort in the autumn of 1939 to the negotiation of a war trade agreement with Sweden. The details are well known, and it is sufficient to mention that a combination of skilful Swedish negotiating tactics and British inexperience led to an agreement by which Germany would still receive at least 8 million tons of ore annually.[40] The Swedes were in turn forced by the Germans to accept a figure of 10 million, while contracts had in fact been exchanged for a total of 11 million tons in 1940.[41]

Even before the war it was realized that although such indirect methods might prevent an *increase* in Germany's ore supply, they could do little to bring about a substantial *reduction*. Hence the appeal of direct action. The measures discussed between 1937 and 1939 may be broadly classified in three categories: those aimed at the *destination* of the iron ore; those aimed at *interception* between source and destination; and those aimed at or near the *source*. Each corresponds to a particular form of action: the first, aerial bombardment; the second, naval action; and the third, sabotage. It is significant that while only the first two were discussed in 1937, by 1939 the emphasis had shifted to the third. The growing belief in the value of 'stoppage at source' was clearly connected with the retreat from their League obligations into strict neutrality on the part of Sweden and other small states, in response to the deteriorating international situation.

The IIC's memorandum on Germany's iron ore supplies of June 1937 placed much emphasis on the routes by which the ore was transported from Scandinavia to the continental ports, and from the ports to the Ruhr. It considered that the Narvik route would remain essential in wartime owing to the closure of Luleå in winter, and assumed that imports via Rotterdam would be prevented by naval interception in the North Sea. There appears to have been no suggestion in pre-war discussions that interception should be carried out in either Dutch or Norwegian territorial waters, although both — especially the latter — were considered after the outbreak of war.[42] Nor was serious consideration given to the possibility of Soviet action against the Baltic route in summer, until the Anglo-French-Soviet staff talks of August 1939.[43]

The closure of Rotterdam, together with the inadequate capacity of the German Baltic ports, would oblige most of the ore to be transported via Emden and the Dortmund-Ems Canal. It was on this potential bottleneck that the IIC based its chief recommendation for action, phrased in characteristically dramatic terms: 'Were it found possible to block the Dortmund-Ems Canal the effect on the steel output of the Ruhr would almost certainly be catastrophic.' Although the Air Ministry's Intelligence Division doubted the effectiveness of such an operation (not on technical grounds, but because they believed that the Germans would be able to transfer much of the ore from the canals to the railways), the idea of disrupting the transportation of ore within Germany continued to be favoured by the IIC and MEW, and coincided with the initial priorities of the strategic air offensive.[44]

Apart from the existence of an IIC memorandum of June 1938 entitled 'Routing of Swedish Iron Ore Imports', there is no evidence of any extensive discussion of the problem in 1938, and no indication that special measures were taken at the time of the Munich crisis.[45] But in February 1939 — only a week before the Swedish purchasing initiative — the IIC returned to the subject with a new and more drastic approach. Reminding the Foreign Office that iron ore was 'the most important commodity of all to stop reaching our enemy', Morton suggested that strike action at the mines — which, he had been informed by an unnamed source, was a possibility 'by no means remote' — might have this effect:

> Hitherto I at least have assumed that in practice it would be impossible to prevent the Germans continuing to receive most of the iron ore they require from Sweden — at any rate in the early stages of war. On the other hand, it seems undeniable that a rapid and decisive effect would be achieved were it found possible abruptly and completely to cut off the Swedish supply.[46]

The idea of a strike was not new to the Germans and had already been discounted by them; and it does not appear to have been pursued much further by the British.[47] But Morton went on to make a more far-reaching proposal. The prospect that Germany 'might threaten the Swedish Government with a military landing unless they put a stop to the strike by force' raised the possibility of British military support for Sweden; and this, Morton thought, deserved further discussion: first at an interdepartmental level, and ultimately by the CID.

Two alternatives had now been raised: that Britain should buy more ore, and that some form of military guarantee should be offered to Sweden as an inducement to resist German pressure. The extent to which either would produce significant results was clearly open to doubt, and led to consideration of various forms of direct action against the ore supply at source. It is at this point, for obvious reasons, that official reticence most effectively obscures our view of the discussion. We are forced to rely mainly on oblique references in Foreign Office minutes, though stray indications exist in the Swedish records and in the post-war reminiscences of one important witness: Morton himself.

Morton's idea was already under consideration by the Foreign Office Coordination Section (in an untraced file) when Prytz's proposal was made, and the latter was judged in its light.[48] The response was generally sympathetic: both Collier, head of the Northern Department, and Nicholls of the Coordination Section thought that it would be 'more advantageous than reliance on the alternative dealt with in our E. W. file P/3'. But Lascelles, Collier's deputy, was more sceptical and thought it conceivable that the kind of German pressure feared by the Swedes 'might actually benefit us by bringing on a rupture between Sweden and Germany and thus enabling us to take direct action against the mines'.

It was agreed that consideration should be given to the Swedish proposal at the interdepartmental meeting scheduled for Morton's; and when this took place, on 27 March, only the former was in fact (favourably) discussed.[49] The latter was deferred to a second meeting some time in April, but there is no indication whether it ever took place. Some aspects of the Foreign Office discussion during April can be traced, but there are no further references to direct action until shortly before the outbreak of war.

On 13 April Nicholls revived the idea of approaching the CID with the question of offering Sweden military assistance.[50] Lascelles, again dubious about the value of such an approach, took the opportunity to develop his own preference further by suggesting that an enquiry should be added 'as to the feasibility of direct action (through Narvik) on the Swedish mines', as an alternative to direct military assistance:

> My own feeling is that the Swedes are probably too weak-kneed to be worth trying to support — (and how, in any case, could we afford them military assistance, with the Baltic closed to us, except through Norway?) — and that direct action at Kiruna is the only thing for it. If such action could be disguised as 'military assistance for Sweden', so much the better: but the disguise would be a bit thin!

Collier suggested that an approach to the CID should be delayed until he had sounded out Prytz on the likelihood of Swedish resistance to German pressure. The response was fairly reassuring, and it may have been for this reason that no approach was made.[51]

The timing of these discussions is important for their bearing on Hudson's visit to Stockholm at the beginning of April. The Swedes were expected to raise the question of buying more ore, and the Department of Overseas Trade had hoped that the proposed interdepartmental meeting would provide Hudson with guidance.[52] The first meeting had not taken place by the time he left England in mid-March, and there is no sign that its conclusions were communicated to him. But he was accompanied by Ashton-Gwatkin, head of the Foreign Office Economic Relations Section, who was aware of the tenor of his colleagues' thinking on the subject.

Both men appear to have been remarkably indiscreet, giving the Swedes a startling insight into the importance now attached to iron ore by the British, and its dangerous implications for Sweden. Hudson threatened that the only solution might be 'to treat Sweden as a hostile power, because then at least we should be able to try and take steps by military or naval means to hinder, if not completely prevent, the supply of ore', while Ashton-Gwatkin, in a phrase taken much to heart by the Swedes, declared, 'I am afraid we have to destroy your mines.'[53] Such candour, while perhaps calculated, was not well judged. Swedish officials made no secret of their annoyance to the Germans, and a wholly accurate report of Hudson's threat reached the German legation in Oslo through a Swedish informant within a few days.[54]

It appears from Lascelles' and Ashton-Gwatkin's remarks that a military attack on the ore fields through Narvik was the principal form of action under consideration in the spring of 1939. Quite apart from its incalculable moral and political consequences, such an operation would have been of extremely limited practical value. The vast, open-cast mine-workings could not be 'destroyed' in any meaningful sense — a conclusion reached in 1937 by the British military attaché to the Scandinavian countries and a colleague from the War Office after a journey on the Narvik-Luleå railway.[55] There is no sign of any further discussion of this option after April 1939, but at least one other, more feasible, operation was investigated.

This was action against the port of Narvik and/or the railway — which, as the military attaché had noted in 1937, 'could be easily damaged by either blowing it up or causing part of the mountains from above falling on it.' On 1 September 1939 Lascelles referred, in connection with proposals for a military guarantee to Norway, to the possibility that the Norwegians might 'connive at the destruction by sabotage of the Narvik-Luleå railway, ostensibly by "internal" saboteurs whom the Norwegian Government would "strive without success" to control.'[56] He added, 'There are, it will be remembered, "other papers" about this aspect of the problem; but they are rather inconclusive.'

Morton's recollections in a letter of 1960 are more definite:

> With the joint planners, we put up a paper *before* the outbreak of war, showing the effects on Germany of the destruction of the very vulnerable railway joining the iron mines of Sweden with the West Norwegian ports. When war broke out, we referred to this, but adding reasons why it must be carried out in September or October 1939 *or not at all*.[57]

He refers elsewhere to the operation as 'an extended raid to destroy the Norwegian iron port for Swedish ore *and* the railway leading to the Swedish frontier.'[58] No such plan appears among the papers of the Joint Planning Committee; nor does it resemble the well-known but much more modest plan for naval action against the Narvik traffic actually proposed by Churchill to the War Cabinet on 19

September. But Lascelles' remark does lend credibility to Morton's account, in its essentials if not in detail.

A further operation — the sabotage of the ore-loading facilities at Swedish ports, especially Oxelösund — was proposed in the autumn of 1939 and actually attempted in 1940.[59] There is no direct evidence that it was of pre-war origin, but the confession to the Swedish authorities of one would-be saboteur — Alfred Rickman, author of *Swedish Iron Ore*, published in September 1939 — shows that Rickman was researching his book in Sweden late in 1938; and it has been suggested that he may already have been a British agent at this time.[60]

It is now possible to draw some conclusions as to the effect of these pre-war ideas on British policy after the outbreak of war. It is worth noting first that although iron ore was of paramount interest to MEW, as it had been to the IIC, it had to compete at Cabinet level with Germany's other major deficiency commodity: oil. By September 1939 arrangements were already in hand for the pre-emptive purchase of Rumanian oil and the destruction of the oil wells; and in October a special Cabinet committee was set up to investigate the question of Germany's oil supplies — a status never attained by iron ore.[61] This priority did not change significantly until Scandinavia came to dominate the War Cabinet's interest from December 1939 onwards.

As for the methods known to have been discussed before the war, none was actually put into effect — unless the Oxelösund sabotage scheme belongs to this category. Strategic bombing was not begun until May 1940, and although two isolated attacks on the Dortmund-Ems Canal were carried out with some success in June and August, 'the improbability of hitting such a target at night with the means available became more evident and inland waterways tended to recede into the background.'[62] Sabotage of the Narvik railway was ruled out by the Chiefs of Staff in December 1939 on the grounds that it was politically undesirable and difficult to carry out and, if successful, would deprive Britain as well as Germany of iron ore.[63]

Little reference has so far been made to the approach championed so persistently by Churchill: naval action against the Narvik traffic in Norwegian territorial waters. I have suggested in a previous article that this idea was discussed before the war, but only at the Admiralty, in isolation from the main stream of economic warfare planning.[64] Nor has any mention been made of the dominant idea pursued by the leaderships of Britain and France between December 1939 and March 1940 — that of a military expedition to occupy the ore fields of northern Sweden — since this was entirely a product of the special circumstances of the Winter War. There is no sign that large-scale land operations in the Scandinavian peninsula were ever seriously considered before the outbreak of war.

But in a more general sense the IIC approach to the iron ore question (and to a lesser extent that of other strategic raw materials) did have a decisive effect on wartime policy. The IIC was the product of a vastly over-optimistic view of economic warfare — a view which its own activities did much to reinforce. There *was* good reason to believe that Germany would have greater difficulty than Britain in coping with the economic effects of a long war; and to this extent economic pressure was worthwhile. But there was much less justification for making it, as it had become by 1939, the cornerstone of British strategy.[65] And there was also a fatal tendency to look to it for quick solutions: to regard economic warfare not only as the key to victory in the long term, but also as offering the possibility of a single knock-out blow that would render a long war unnecessary. Cabinet ministers needed no excuse for wishful thinking, but Morton's pronouncements pointed them in this direction. He does not appear to have believed before February 1939 that an immediately decisive blow could be made against Germany's ore supply, but he was always convinced that if some means could be found, it would have almost instantaneous results. To the Chamberlain Cabinet, worried about public morale and fearful of the consequences of provoking active hostilities on land or in the air, such views had an irresistible appeal.

NOTES

I am grateful to the Institut für Europäische Geschichte, Mainz, and the Stiftung Volkswagenwerk for financial support in connection with the research project, 'Die Interdependenz politischer und wirtschaftlicher Entwicklung in der Innen- und Aussenpolitik des Versailler Staatenssystems 1919-1939'.

All documents cited are in the Public Record Office, London, except where indicated by UD (Utrikesdepartmentets arkiv, Stockholm) or PA (Politisches Archiv des Auswärtigen Amts, Bonn).

1. H. R. Trevor-Roper (ed.), *Hitler's War Directives 1939-1945* (London 1964), 22-24.
2. CAB 67/3, WP(G) (39)153.
3. Rolf Karlbom, 'Sweden's Iron Ore Exports to Germany 1933-1944', *Scandinavian Economic History Review*, XIII (1965), 65-93. The debate is summarized in Martin Fritz, 'Swedish Iron Ore and German Steel 1939-1940', ibid., XXI (1973), 133-144, and in Alan S. Milward, *War, Economy and Society 1939-1945* (London 1977), 308-313.
4. Alan S. Milward, 'Could Sweden have stopped the Second World War?', *Scandinavian Economic History Review*, XV (1967), 127-138; Jörg-Johannes Jäger, 'Sweden's Iron Ore Exports to Germany 1933-1944', ibid., 139-147.
5. Martin Fritz, *German Steel and Swedish Iron Ore 1939-1945* (Gothenburg 1974); Klaus Wittmann, *Schwedens Wirtschaftsbeziehungen zum Dritten Reich 1933-1945* (Munich and Vienna 1978), 113-128.
6. W. N. Medlicott, *The Economic Blockade*, I (London 1952), xi.
7. Medlicott, op. cit., 12-24; Sir Charles Webster and Noble Frankland, *The Strategic Air Offensive against Germany 1939-1945*, I (London 1961), 92-93, 260-261; F. H. Hinsley, with E. E. Thomas, C. F. G. Ransom and R. C. Knight, *British Intelligence in the Second World War*, I (London 1979), 30-34, 59-73; Robert J. Young, 'Spokesmen for Economic Warfare: The Industrial Intelligence Centre in the 1930s', *European Studies Review*, 6 (1976), 473-489.
8. Not without opposition from the Air Ministry: Webster and Frankland, op. cit., 93.
9. Hinsley, op. cit., 32-34.
10. Ibid., 63-64.
11. Ibid., 66-73. See also the criticisms in Milward, op. cit., 294-328.
12. CAB 47/14, ATB 181, 22 July 1938; Medlicott, op. cit., 47.
13. CAB 47/13, ATB (EPG) 2, 5 July 1937.
14. A. F. Rickman, *Swedish Iron Ore* (London 1939); D. L. Burn, *The Economic History of Steelmaking 1867-1939* (Cambridge 1940), 154-160; Fritz, op. cit.
15. These amounts could be raised by 10 per cent in any one year, so long as the total export in three consecutive years did not exceed 27 million and 4.5 million tons respectively.
16. M. W. W. P. Consett, *The Triumph of Unarmed Forces (1914-1918)* (London 1923), 79; A. C. Bell, *A History of the Blockade of Germany* (London 1937), 656. But see SUPP 3/71, PSO(BT)53, of January 1929, for correspondence on the relationship between the Grängesberg Company and the German steel industry, and its implications for Britain's steel supply in war.
17. The title of the first is given in Young, op. cit., Appendix II, 484-485; The second, dated 13 December 1934, is in FO 419/29, N1525/18/42.
18. CAB 4/25, No. 1272-B, 29 October 1936.
19. ICF/66, 12 November 1936, FO 371/19937, C8595/99/18.
20. J. C. Carr and W. Taplin, *History of the British Steel Industry* (Oxford 1962), 566-567; Prof. Dr. E. Haarmann to Göring, 13 July 1936, PA, HaPol VI Schweden: Rohstoffe und Waren, Eisenerz, I; Meynen (Stockholm) to Auswärtiges Amt (AA), 6 October 1936, ibid.

21. CAB 4/26, No. 1337-B, 8 July 1937.

22. Joachim Joesten, 'The Scramble for Swedish Iron Ore', *Political Quarterly* (1938), I, 58-67; Wittmann, op. cit., 124-125; Gunnar Hägglöf, *Svensk krigshandelspolitik under andra världskriget* (Stockholm 1958), 20-22.

23. Hägglöf, op. cit., 22-24; FO 371/21082, file N230/63; FO 371/21110, file N1509/42; UD, H 40 Ba VII, H 40 Ct XIII.

24. ICF/86, 14 January 1937, FO 371/20713, C470/13/18; Morton to Baxter (FO), 14 January 1937, ibid.

25. Charles E. Harvey, 'Politics and Pyrites during the Spanish Civil War', *Economic History Review* XXXI (1978), 89-104.

26. ICF/66, 25 June 1937, FO 371/20715, C5426/13/18 (also CAB 47/13, ATB(EPG)6); Morton to Group Captain K. C. Buss (Deputy Director of Intelligence, Air Ministry), 3 September 1937, AIR 5/1154.

27. Morton to Buss: 'The Treasury, Foreign Office, Admiralty and War Office have at present not found themselves able to undermine the arguments'; CAB 47/13, ATB(EPG)2 (note 13 above); CAB 47/12, ATB(EPG) 1st Meeting, 29 July 1937.

28. E.g. ICF/231, 16 January 1937, FO 371/20713, C451/13/18; ICF/261, 13 January 1937, and Morton to Garran, 15 January 1937, ibid., C472/13/18.

29. Paus (Commercial Attaché, Oslo) to Department of Overseas Trade (DOT) (for IIC), 19 February 1937, FO 371/21080, N1742/143/63.

30. E.g. marginal note by Nicholls (Coordination Section, FO) on Blaker (IIC) to Nicholls, 11 November 1938, FO 837/796; and the inconclusive exchanges between Morton and Axel Johnson (a director of the Company) in July-August 1939, FO 371/23656, N3435/64/63, FO 371/23657, N4018/64/63. Ingram (MEW) to FO, 9 September 1939, FO 371/23652, N4292/31/63; Sporborg (MEW) to Collier (FO), 2 April 1940, FO 371/24821, N4063/19/63.

31. Morton to Fennelly (Board of Trade), 10 February 1937, SUPP 3/55, SO 305.

32. Fritz, op. cit., 103; CAB 66/4, WP(40)11, 9 January 1940.

33. Morton to Baxter, 8 September 1937, FO 371/20715, C6342/13/18; Carr and Taplin, op. cit., 532-534; Matthias Riedel, *Eisen und Kohle für das Dritte Reich* (Göttingen 1973).

34. Col. M. G. Christie to Vansittart, 13 November 1939 (citing letter from Brassert of 30 October), FO 371/23049, C18652/454/18; Morton to Roberts (FO), 20 November 1939, ibid.

35. CAB 47/14, ATB 181.

36. Minutes by Ashton-Gwatkin, 29 July 1937, and Collier, 30 July, FO 371/20715, C5426/13/18; British strategical memorandum for Anglo-French staff talks, 14 March 1939, CAB 16/209, AFC(39)1; ATB(EPG) 1st Meeting, CAB 47/12 (note 27 above).

37. Sandler (Swedish Foreign Minister) to Stanley (President of the Board of Trade), 14 July 1938, UD, H 40 Ba VIII; Prytz to UD, 21 February 1939, ibid.; Hudson to Halifax, 1 March 1939, FO 371/23706, N1189/1189/42.

38. FO 371/23652, N3298/31/63; Carr and Taplin, op. cit., 590-591.

39. Lascelles minute, 31 August 1939, FO 371/23657, N4050/64/63.

40. Medlicott, op. cit., 141-152, 180-192; Hägglöf, op. cit., 52-76, 90-92; Erik Boheman, *På vakt*, II (Stockholm 1964), 78-90.

41. Hägglöf, op. cit., 77-89, 92-98; Wittmann, op. cit., 160-169.

42. For Dutch waters, see proposal by Naval Attaché, The Hague, 21 September 1939, and Admiralty comments, ADM 199/892. For Norwegian, see note 64 below.

43. Strang minute, 28 July 1937, FO 371/20715, C5426/13/18; CAB 16/183B, DP(P)71, 31 July 1939, and DP(P)70, 15 August 1939.

44. Comments by Buss, sent to IIC 27 August 1937, AIR 5/1154; CAB 47/14, ATB 181; MEW memoranda I/610, 22 September 1939, FO 371/23049, C14886/454/18, and I 81/1, 27 October 193-, ibid., C17724/454/18; Webster and Frankland, op. cit., 28-29, 97-98.

45. The title appears in CAB 4/27, No. 1442-B, 6 July 1938, Appendix II, and in Young, op. cit., Appendix II, 484-485. For Munich, see Erik Lönnroth, *Den svenska utrikespolitikens historia 1919-1939* (Stockholm 1959), 171; Blaker (IIC) to Nicholls, 11 November 1938, and Walker (Stockholm) to Nicholls, 8 December 1938, FO 837/796.

46. Morton to Nicholls, 22 February 1939, ibid.

47. Below (Stockholm) to AA, 12 May 1938, PA, HaPol VI Schweden: Rohstoffe und Waren, Eisenerz, I; Oberkommando der Wehrmacht to AA, 23 November 1938, ibid., II; AA conference, 17 January 1939. *Documents on German Foreign Policy*, Series D, V, 610-613.

48. FO minutes, 7-14 March 1939, FO 371/23706, N1189/1189/42.

49. Collier minute, 27 March 1939, ibid., N1556/1189/42.

50. FO minutes, 6-25 April 1939, FO 371/23652, N1824/31/63.

51. Collier-Prytz conversation, 27 April 1939, ibid., N2168/31/63.

52. Mullins (DOT) to Palmer (BOT), 22 March 1939 (as note 49 above).

53. Hudson minute, recording conversation with Marcus Wallenberg, Junior, 2 April 1939, FO 371/23652, N1910/31/63; memoranda by Hägglöf and Kumlin, 15 April 1939, UD, H 40 Ct XV; Hägglöf, op. cit., 24-27.

54. Wied (Stockholm) to AA, 4 April 1939, PA, Abt Pol VI Po 2 Schweden; Sahm (Oslo) to AA, 13 April 1939, ibid.

55. 'Notes on a journey Boden-Narvik', 20 August 1937, FO 371/21084, N4639/4639/63; Collier minute, 18 September 1937, FO 371/21080, N4585/143/63.

56. FO 371/23657, N4041/64/63.

57. Morton to R. W. Thompson, 16 August 1960, printed in R. W. Thompson, *Churchill and Morton* (London 1976), 72-73.

58. Letter of 8 September 1961, ibid., 180.

59. References to this operation have appeared in several works of varying reliability, e.g. H. Montgomery Hyde, *The Quiet Canadian* (London 1962), 20-23; William Stevenson, *A Man Called Intrepid* (London 1976), 53-58; Bickham Sweet-Escott, *Baker Street Irregular* (London 1965), 26-27. The most authoritative account is in Tomas Munch-Petersen, 'Britain and Sweden, 1939-40: Foreign Policy Issues in Northern Europe' (unpublished Ph.D. thesis, University of London 1979), 30-31, 77-78, 112-113, 225-226.

60. Munch-Petersen, op. cit., 30-31.

61. Medlicott, op. cit., 250-257; Webster and Frankland, op. cit., 265, 284-292.

62. Webster and Frankland, op. cit., 296, 305.

63. CAB 66/4, WP(39)169.

64. 'Churchill, the Admiralty and the Narvik Traffic, September-November 1939', *Scandinavian Journal of History*, 4 (1979), 305-326.

65. COS memorandum of February 1939, quoted in Michael Howard, *The Continental Commitment* (London 1972), 133.

4 Roosevelt and the Coming of the War: The Search for United States Policy 1937-42

Mark M Lowenthal

The controversy over the pre-war foreign policy leadership of Franklin D. Roosevelt continues forty years after the fact, an interesting reflection of doubts over the course of more recent foreign policy decisions. Was Roosevelt the plotter painted by revisionists such as Tansill and Beard, who willingly forced events to bring the US into the war? Or was he the sagacious national leader who saw valid US interests at stake in the conflict and moved along a recognized path as quickly as domestic opinion would allow? These have been the two main poles around which arguments and interpretations have centred.

A third interpretation is possible, one which denies many of the basic arguments of both schools. President Roosevelt's policy, for all of the linearity later imposed on it, was actually a series of fits and starts whose interconnection the President himself denied at the time. These policy decisions can be grouped into three broad consecutive periods. Each of these periods was dominated by a thematic unifying search for a type of policy, or a very broad and general outcome which, while not always apparent at the time, particularly to subordinates, shaped most of Roosevelt's preferences and decisions. In each period Roosevelt knew, at least vaguely and usually within broad general outlines, what he wanted and what he hoped to avoid. Unfortunately, he regularly failed to define this for those subordinates responsible for executing this policy, leaving them to arrive at their own conclusions upon which to base and carry out their plans. Each of these three searches for policy was ill-defined at the outset, and was abandoned through the pressure of events, requiring the beginning of yet another search.

United States pre-war policy was the result of a dynamic tension between these two areas of responsibility, between a President who was disinclined to define his purposes or fundamental policy goals or the limits to decisions he had made, and his subordinates, who saw themselves forced to move tentatively beyond the President in response to events while frequently attempting to elicit greater policy guidance from him as they drafted US grand strategy.[1]

The Search for Influence, October 1937-May 1940

The Search for Influence was actually marked by two sequential policy goals: first, finding some means of using what international authority and power the United States had to prevent the outbreak of war; second, when war did begin, an effort to influence a favourable outcome within a hopefully limited conflict. Both goals were in part undercut by a sine qua non of this policy period, the avoidance of US commitments.

The origin of this policy phase was probably more coincidental in its relationship with international events than it was a case of immediate reaction to those events. Throughout his first years in office, domestic needs had been the necessary preoccupation of Franklin Roosevelt, but 1937 proved to be something of a disappointment. In the early part of the year there were numerous labour strikes. The contentious Supreme Court packing-plan failed that summer, and in October the economy slipped into recession, raising doubts about the efficacy of the New Deal. As both administrator and policy-maker Roosevelt did not have a long attention-span. Given these setbacks and his working methods, it was understandable that he then turned more to international affairs, especially when this sector began to show some dangerous trends.

The initial moves were vague at best, a vagueness which typified this entire policy period, a desire to do 'something' without a clear sense of exactly what to do. Thus, there was an initial flourish in the famous 'Quarantine Speech' of 5 October 1937, which did not so much herald some new departure by means of a 'trial balloon', as has often been argued, but rather sought to prod others to help formulate a programme.[2]

More significant was the idea of an international conference vaguely aimed at achieving a new international order. This idea had first surfaced in mid-1937, although it soon died under opposition from Secretary of State Cordell Hull and Secretary of the Treasury Henry Morgenthau, as well as from the press of domestic events.[3] However, in October 1937 it was revived under the prodding of Under-Secretary of State Sumner Welles. Welles was both a close friend of the President's and a rival of his nominal superior, an arrangement which Roosevelt allowed if not encouraged, as it suited his preference for rival subordinates. But once again Hull objected, fearing the effect of the US moving without Britain and France, and being uneasy about the general vagueness of the proposal.[4] Again the idea was put off, although tentative feelers between Germany and Britain between November 1937 and January 1938 seemingly offered the US the role of an 'honest broker', as Welles now suggested.[5] But now Roosevelt, vacillating as he often did, sided with Hull on the need for British support. Further, his own initiatives in a related area undermined the entire concept.

The President had been discussing the need for closer collaboration with Britain as early as January 1937. These early feelers, including the possibility of exchanges of military information,[6] came to nothing until Japan inadvertently provided a catalyst through its continued aggression in China. Although the United States rejected British feelers in November 1937, the sinking of the USS *Panay* on 12 December 1937 evidently moved Roosevelt to change his mind. In a conversation with Ambassador Sir Ronald Lindsay on 16 December 1937 the President, amid a rush of ideas, agreed to talks.[7]

These first naval contacts, conducted in London in January 1938 by Captain Royal E. Ingersoll, Director of US Navy War Plans, were arranged to discuss possible US and British actions should they be involved in a war against Japan.[8] This fitted in well with growing British concerns over their weak naval presence in the Far East owing to demands in Europe,[9] although not with their desire for an immediate demonstration against Japan as well. Ingersoll's instructions were vague in the extreme, and he informed his frustrated hosts at the Admiralty that he was more a liaison officer than a consultant.[10] The 'Record of Conversations' largely stated each side's planned naval moves, with a long section of inter-fleet communications.[11] Nonetheless, the fact that these talks were held at all was a significant step, although on the American side their purpose was shrouded in uncertainty. For the United States the talks were more a recognition of shared interests than a willingness to plan ahead, an understandable caution given current isolationist sentiment.

Towards the end of these talks Welles moved to revive the international conference. Now the President was willing to sound out the British, who were understandably confused by specific military talks and grandiose idealistic gestures.[12] Prime Minister Neville Chamberlain preferred his own more specific approaches to the fascist states. However, the Cabinet's Foreign Policy Committee, fearful of alienating the US, agreed to the concept with caveats, including no overt British support.[13] But now Roosevelt backed off, no doubt influenced by Hull's continued opposition and the recent narrow defeat in the House of Representatives of a requirement for a national referendum for declarations of war, and perhaps recognizing the limited nature of British backing.

What the President did not seem to appreciate was that his two initiatives ran counter to one another. In the Ingersoll mission he had given the British what they most wanted, some sign of naval co-operation in the Far East. The limited gains of this initiative undercut the vaguer goals of the conference proposal, and gave Britain less incentive to cooperate in this second scheme.

Interestingly, parallel to all of this activity was the beginning of a major change in US war planning, the revision of war plan Orange, a plan for war against Japan. Beginning in November 1937 the Joint Board, the army-navy body responsible for interservice cooperation, sponsored a revision of Orange, largely at the insistence of Army Chief of Staff General Malin Craig, who found the current plans 'unsound in general and specifically . . . wholly inapplicable to the present conditions'.[14] As had been the case in earlier revisions of Orange the two services had difficulty compromising between the army's desire largely to abandon the Philippines, and the navy's desire for a forward position in the Pacific.

But the arrival of Ingersoll's report in February 1938 led Chief of Naval Operations Admiral William D. Leahy to advise his commanders that it would be necessary to take into account cooperation with Britain in the Far East, and the possibility that conditions in Europe might curtail British efforts elsewhere.[15] In short, the Ingersoll talks helped the navy see beyond its parochial interests. A compromise over Orange was achieved that month, in which both services withdrew from their extreme positions, agreeing to an initial priority for defending the Pacific Triangle of Alaska, Hawaii and the Panama Canal, allowing time for the situation in both oceans to be evaluated first.[16]

Two points are significant in the Orange revision. First, the military planners were proceeding on their own, making strategic choices in response to events and without reference to or guidance from President Roosevelt. Second, the Ingersoll mission had helped foster a recognition of wider security problems, buttressing General Craig's initial criticism of Orange. There was a subtle interaction at work, the President's initiative affecting the military's planning, but it was more accidental than planned.

Through most of the spring and summer of 1938, Roosevelt's major concerns were again domestic, especially the so-called 'purge' of Democratic ranks in order to safeguard 'the continuing struggle for liberalism' after the expiration of his second term. The growing German-Czech crisis forced renewed focus on foreign affairs. The President's attitude vacillated wildly during the early stages of the crisis. After the first Hitler-Chamberlain meeting on 15 September 1938, Roosevelt characterized the Prime Minister as being for peace at any price, and discussed the best means of prosecuting a war against Germany. But in conversations with Ambassador Lindsay four days later he was more pessimistic, and reverted to his international conference concept as one way of avoiding war.[17] This became Roosevelt's basic role through the rest of the crisis, urging all parties to keep negotiations open in the hope that this would lead to a peaceful solution. In part Roosevelt was reflecting on the experience of Woodrow Wilson in 1914, whom he felt had not exerted any influence when he could have.[18]

Beyond these limited efforts, Roosevelt played no major role in Munich, although Sumner Welles went to great efforts to determine whether certain cables from the President to Mussolini had influenced the Duce to intervene in the course of negotiations.[19] The President's options had been extremely limited, and he had played them out as best he could, in favour of a somewhat disagreeable settlement rather than a dreaded and perhaps lost war for the Allies.

More significant than this outcome, however, was the effect of Munich on Roosevelt's perceptions. Still torn between his instinctive caution and fear of isolationist sentiment, and his desire to act as a leader of the democracies, the President evidently recognized the temporary nature of the Munich settlement and the need to increase visible means of US power.[20] This latter desire translated itself into a desire to build up the air force.

At a meeting with top civil and military advisers on 14 November 1938, the President stated his desire to have an air force in being of

10,000 planes, backed by an annual productive capacity for 10,000 more which could be doubled, to serve as a striking force in support of foreign policy. Roosevelt's plans were general at best, citing round, almost off-the-cuff figures of types of aircraft, ignoring military concerns about the need for a balanced and effective force. Roosevelt was not interested in a balanced fighting force, but rather a visible deterrent to safeguard the Western Hemisphere.[21]

Here was a significant change in Roosevelt's approach, a recognition of the need for military support for his foreign policy. Interviews from the post-Munich period confirmed this shift in the President's thinking. He now spoke more harshly of Chamberlain, emphasizing what he saw as the Prime Minister's pessimism.[22] Not a natural pessimist himself, Roosevelt resented it in others, especially when he felt he had found a means of solving the problem. Visible air power was such a means.

Once again there was a significant parallel development within the Joint Board, also in November 1938. There was now a growing perception of the threat from Europe, and a presumption that Germany, Italy and Japan had reached some sort of agreement. A new plan would be needed to respond to such a threat to United States interests across two wide and disparate fronts.[23] But once again the military was proceeding on its own, and in this case in advance of the President's thinking, which was still firmly focused on Europe. Acting on presumptions about the President's thinking, the Joint Board, and its subsidiary Joint Planning Committee, began to define perceived and presumed threats to the United States.

This willingness of the military to take politico-military initiatives was evident as the new plan emerged. By April 1939 the Joint Planners saw Germany as the main threat, especially against Latin America. The specific target seemed to be north-eastern Brazil, and from there the Panama Canal. This necessarily made Japan a less important threat.[24] The Joint Board accepted these premises in most generous terms, and ordered war plans based upon them in variations, including basic defence of the Western Hemisphere, control of the Western Pacific, and the extension of military power into the Eastern Atlantic.[25]

By June 1939 the Joint Planners had drafted the familiar Rainbow plans, five cases for possible strategic scenarios.[26] Once again the military was venturing out on its own in terms of strategic and political premises. While this was necessary as part of their responsibility for national defence, it also represented a continuing lack of coordination between their needs and the more limited policy goals envisioned by the President. Not only had the Joint Planners and the Joint Board outdistanced Roosevelt's policy, they had also gone beyond US capabilities to fulfil even the most basic contingency, Hemispheric Defense (Rainbow 1), the only plan which the President actually approved at that time.[27]

During this period of renewed military planning, Roosevelt was again permitting other military initiatives as well, in this case the visit of Commander T.C. Hampton, RN, to Washington as a follow-up to the Ingersoll talks. Meeting with Admiral Leahy in June 1939 Hampton reiterated the uncertainty of British deployments to the Far East, but Leahy avoided making any commitments or even speculations over US policy if Britain were involved in a war.[28] The mission was largely a disappointment to the British, although it once again indicated Roosevelt's multi-track approach to these issues.

Despite his efforts to do so, Roosevelt did not play a large role in the final pre-war crisis in 1939. Instead, he made one last effort at influencing the European situation during the lull of the Phoney War. On 9 February 1940 it was announced that Under-Secretary of State Welles would go to Europe on an advisory mission for the President.

Undoubtedly strongly abetted by the ambitious Welles, Roosevelt evidently hoped to help bring about a peaceful settlement before large-scale operations ensued.[29] That Roosevelt was casting about for influence was evident by the emphasis which the mission put on Mussolini, who was seen as a lever with which to restrain Germany and thus prevent an escalation of the war. Here was an even greater insight into the mission's main purpose, an effort to insure continuation of the apparent military stalemate so that a peace-making effort would be necessary for a comprehensive settlement, a return to the 1937 conference proposal.[30] Roosevelt's policy had come full circle.

However, these goals were very long-range, and either not totally realized or unarticulated. This left the mission with few specific goals and no real guidelines for success. In short, it was an open-ended gamble.

It is unnecessary to go into the detail of Welles' talks in the four European capitals. In Rome, Welles seriously misjudged his hosts, overestimating the Duce's influence within Europe and especially within the Axis. In Berlin, he heard little to indicate any basis for negotiations, an impression reinforced in Paris and London. With the British, Welles naïvely clung to efforts to find some basis for talks, ignoring the very fundamental differences which he had heard first-hand. Returning to Paris he urged the need for disarmament, and in Rome once again he argued, without much basis, that the Allies were willing to talk once their security was assured.[31]

All told, there was an increasing aura of desperation about the mission, both for the personal goals of Welles himself, and for those wider goals which he shared with President Roosevelt. The two men were still eager to act as the mediators on the international scene, although to a certain extent Welles was now acting on his own as well, though the President was kept informed at each stage. Welles returned to Washington on 29 March 1940, and in his report to the President he stressed the central role of Mussolini, and held that disarmament was the key to future peace. Only a United States-led initiative could bring peace, he concluded.[32]

Although his object had been to prolong the lull, the information Welles brought back could only confirm the depths of the war's causes. Eleven days after Welles' return, Germany invaded Norway. A month later the *blitzkrieg* erupted across Belgium and France. The Search for Influence ended because the United States had no influence without military power per se, which it would have been unwilling to use had it existed, without political commitments which its leaders felt unable to make, and because the United States could not possibly cast itself as a disinterested neutral, certainly not in the eyes of Adolf Hitler.

The Search for Alternatives, May 1940-December 1941

Events between 10 May and 22 June 1940 transformed the international strategic picture. France had been defeated and forced from the war, Britain had been routed from the Continent and stood alone, and Hitler was now the arbiter of virtually all Europe. The interests of the United States in the struggle were clear. Indeed, they had already been defined in the early Rainbow planning in April 1939. The key and primary question which now faced the US was: could the outcome of the war be influenced in Britain's favour without requiring US entry? The search for means to apply this influence short of war became the hallmark of policy deliberations. All other issues were subordinate to that, including the question of

Japan, whose continued deterrence was seen, in part, as an effort to defuse distractions or diversions from the central issue, the struggle in Europe.

As early as 22 May 1940, the military began to seek policy guidance from the President, in the form of a 'National Strategic Decisions' memorandum prepared by Army War Plans and revised by Chief of Staff General George C. Marshall. Noting the sudden wealth of potential threats, the army argued for an immediate concentration on Hemispheric Defense, the only strategy within current capabilities. Above all, the memorandum noted the need for early policy decisions as to US action upon which planning could be based. Roosevelt agreed with the substance of the paper, but no decisions followed.[33]

At the end of May 1940 Rainbow 4 (US acting alone, projecting forces into the Eastern Atlantic) was moved to the top planning priority.[34] While moved up largely to give some basis for more detailed plans and preparations, the priority of Rainbow 4 also indicated the pessimistic although not unrealistic views of the military planners, namely that the US would have to stand alone in the near future. Roosevelt evidently did not agree, presenting the military with a strategic hypothesis of his own on 13 June 1940, which presumed for the end of 1940 the survival of Britain and its empire, France still fighting from its empire, and US naval and air units co-operating with the Allies on the periphery of occupied Europe.[35]

Here was a reassertion of the President's own confidence, although one built largely on false hopes, as France left the war four days later. Nonetheless, the strategic hypothesis of 13 June offered some insight into what Roosevelt wanted or was willing to see six months hence. Significantly, he accepted an active role for the United States, but one which eschewed ground forces.

But Roosevelt's optimism was not the sort of direction the military needed. Instead, on 17 June 1940, General Marshall and his navy counterpart, Admiral Harold R. Stark, Leahy's successor as CNO, considered three alternative strategies: concentrating on the Pacific, seen to be of little sense; aid to the Allies to insure a victory, not just to prevent their defeat, a course beyond current capabilities; or a continued concentration on Hemispheric Defense, the preferred course.[36] These choices, after policy discussions with the State Department, were embodied in a new memorandum, 'Basis for Immediate Decisions Concerning the National Defense', which Marshall and Stark presented to the President on 24 June 1940. The military chiefs now urged a major fleet transfer to the Atlantic should the French fleet go over to Germany, a curtailment of aid to Britain, increased war production, and the institution of a military draft. Roosevelt, while agreeing with the premises of the threats to the US, pointedly refused to take any of these steps.[37] Although he saw the urgency of the situation, he preferred to stand by the primary basis of his 13 June hypothesis, the continued resistance of Britain. Indeed, as long as Britain was an active belligerent, Roosevelt could avoid the more radical steps now being proposed. Thus ended the first round of policy debate and the definition of the basic question.

It is not clear when President Roosevelt first made the connection between the continuation of British survival and his own desires to limit the role that the US might be required to play. Some of this was evident in the 13 June hypothesis, although in this document Roosevelt accepted the probability of US sea and air action. At least two factors were at work here, the President's natural optimism, and his continuing desire to avoid war. But sometime between 13 June and the meeting of 24 June, the President evidently drew back from his assumption of US entry. However, his revisions of the 'Basis for Immediate Decisions' memorandum only reflected the differences in perception between the President and the Chiefs, without offering any firm policy directions.

One probable source of this change in the President's thinking was Britain itself. From his first message to Roosevelt after becoming Prime Minister, one of Winston Churchill's major goals had been to convince the President that Britain was worth supporting, both for the sake of common interests and as a way of keeping the United States out of the war.[38] This message was repeated with increased urgency in the latter half of June 1940 as the British government sought to convince Roosevelt to transfer needed first-world-war destroyers to Britain.

The British argument was two-fold: if the destroyers were sent they could be crucial to keeping Britain in the war; if not, Britain could well be defeated, raising the spectre of German control of the British fleet.[39] Indeed, the fate of the British fleet became the major bargaining point for Britain. A limited US naval investment would help maintain a much larger force-in-being. But the British request also represented an important decision for Roosevelt, over and above the transfer of the ships. If accepted, it implied a fundamental policy decision to support the British war effort, a decision which would either be open-minded or necessarily abandoned at some later date.

This was brought home clearly to the President by Philip Kerr, the Marquis of Lothian, who had become the British Ambassador in August 1939. On the evening of 17 June 1940, Lothian asked the President if it was not time to be frank with Congress and the public about the British naval situation and the implications of a British defeat.[40]

Roosevelt was naturally reluctant to transfer the ships, initially citing doubts about the efficacy of such a step. However, by 18 June 1940, Secretary of the Treasury Morgenthau had amassed and presented statistics answering these qualms.[41] Pressure on Roosevelt, both from within his Cabinet and from Britain, continued unabated. In essence the President was being forced to re-examine the very premises of his assumptions about British survival. This could be achieved, but the United States would have to act now, not at the end of the year. At the same time, here was a way of aiding Britain indirectly, although a highly risky way in terms of US domestic politics.

The President evidently reached his decision in the last two weeks of July 1940, as advisers presented legal justifications for the transfer, and as the separate thread of acquiring bases in British possessions interwove with the request for destroyers.[42] In effect, Roosevelt was stating that the survival of Britain as an active belligerent was in the national security interests of the United States. But Roosevelt, as he was often to do, either did not recognize or chose to ignore the broader implications of this decision.

This was evident in the renewed frustration expressed by General Marshall at a meeting of the Standing Liaison Committee, the war-navy-state coordinating group, on 23 September 1940. The military had now received first-hand reports on the military situation in Britain from Generals Delos C. Emmons and George V. Strong, who stressed the high quality of British morale and Britain's ability to withstand invasion. Significantly, the military observers concluded: 'sooner or later the United States will be drawn into this war'. At the Standing Liaison Committee, Marshall urged that US political and military preparedness to meet these conditions be re-examined.[43]

But the fall of 1940, with President Roosevelt in the midst of his controversial bid for a third term, was not the best time to elicit a more positive policy direction. Yet just as Marshall and Stark sought to put pressure on the President, they too were subject to similar pressure from below for policy definition. This was especially true of Stark, who had two major commands under him, the US Fleet at Hawaii, and the Asiatic Fleet at Manila, which were virtually front-line units. In order to sort out his own thinking, Stark began drafting a paper on the strategic situation, which he then circulated to his own staff.

This study, which eventually became known as the Stark Memorandum, was a classic of policy and strategic planning. In it the Chief of Naval Operations forthrightly addressed the most fundamental question. Given the possibility of US involvement in the war 'We should see the answer to the question: "Where should we fight the war, and for what objective?" ' With this resolved, Stark argued, plans could be drawn, preparations made, and diplomatic activity coordinated with available military means.[44]

Stark, of course, had his own views on the subject, feeling that US goals were its own territorial, economic and ideological integrity and that of the Western Hemisphere, protection of its Far East interests, and 'the prevention of the disruption of the British Empire, with all that such a consummation implies'. This was not new, as it had been the basis of the Destroyer-Base deal, but Stark took it one step further, arguing that Britain could only win by defeating Germany in Europe, and to do this would require US aid in manpower and material. To pursue these goals Stark offered four strategies, favouring Plan D, an offensive in the Atlantic allied with Britain, coupled with a defensive stance in the Pacific.[45]

By 12 November 1940, when the final memorandum was presented, Stark had admitted that he had wider purposes, informing Admiral J.O. Richardson, Commander US Fleet, that he hoped that Roosevelt would 'give some definite pronouncement on it in order that I may send you something more authoritative than I otherwise could do'.[46] But once again Roosevelt did not choose, although he did make comments on the memorandum which were not recorded. Still lacking guidance from above, the Joint Planners began work on Rainbow 3 (US acting alone, defending the Western Hemisphere and projecting forces into the Western Pacific), as the most likely immediate need.[47]

To a certain extent, the significance of the Stark Memorandum was diluted by the time it took to be processed in the US planning apparatus, as well as by Roosevelt's own hesitancy in acting upon its premises. The memorandum had clearly gone beyond the President's conception of policy by drawing out US support for Britain to its logical conclusion, the probable necessity for active US participation in the war.

Less than a month after Stark presented his memorandum, Roosevelt also got firm indications from Britain that the current level of US assistance was no longer sufficient. Churchill, in his famous letter of 8 December 1940, informed the President that 'the moment approaches when we shall no longer be able to pay cash for shipping and other supplies'. Roosevelt, exactly one month earlier, had been considering loaning equipment to Britain rather than selling it. Now, motivated by Churchill, the President moved with uncharacteristic speed to prepare the public for such a change in policy, noting that the proposed Lend-Lease did not increase the risk of war as it did not involve US ships or crews.[48]

From the President's point of view this was an ideal move, as it allowed the policy of aid to Britain to continue without unduly alarming those who feared US entry into the war. However, Roosevelt was not facing an important part of the problem which was already worrying his more interventionist advisers, the growing difficulty of getting the material to Britain. For the time being this part of the issue simply was not addressed.

Roosevelt ended 1940 with a fireside chat in which he explained his foreign policy to the nation. The speech was an accurate summary of his motives and hopes. He pointed out the irreconcilability of the US and the Axis, and the importance of Britain to US security. The President dismissed the notion that these struggles were of no importance to the US. The core of the address stressed the commonality of US and British interests, and the concept that the best way for the US to avoid war was fully to support Britain. Roosevelt admitted that such a policy ran risks, but he still felt that it was less risky than the alternatives.[49] Thus, Roosevelt agreed with the basic premises of his advisers and subordinates, but he did not see the same probable or necessary conclusion to this policy, or if he did, he refused to say so.

1941 opened with US and British preparations for a full military staff conference to be held in Washington. In terms of the evolution of US policy or any shift in Roosevelt's position the fact that the conference was being held was of greater significance than its outcome. The talks had been proposed by Britain in November

1940, and Roosevelt had given his permission at the end of the month.[50] Although these talks were to be wider in scope than the earlier ones, there is little to suggest that this indicated any major change in the President's view. Instead, he probably viewed these conversations as continuations of the earlier missions, and of the ongoing naval talks then being conducted by Rear-Admiral Robert Ghormley in London. The ABC talks, as this new round became known, was only another in a sequence of prudent precautions.

Roosevelt actually had little to do with US preparations for the conference, beyond a meeting with Secretaries of War and the Navy Henry Stimson and Frank Knox, General Marshall and Admiral Stark on 16 January 1941. The President laid his emphasis on the continuation of US aid to Britain, stating that this was one of Hitler's greatest concerns and that the US should avoid involvement in either Europe or the Pacific which would curtail this aid. Roosevelt also discussed convoying, but saw this as a remote rather than an imminent possibility. In reviewing the United States' opening statement for the conference Roosevelt made a point of altering the phrase 'decide to resort to war' to 'be compelled to resort to war'.[51]

What the President had not provided was a policy basis for US military plans, and this proved to be a negative factor during the talks. The British delegation arrived with a well-integrated, coordinated strategy. The US delegation was forced to negotiate internally several times during the course of the two month conference. In addition to these methodological differences, ABC revealed significant strategic differences. Britain assumed a war against the European Axis and Japan; US planners presumed, for the time being, that Japan would remain neutral. Thus, Far Eastern policy became the sticking point, with Britain favouring a strong US presence as far west in the Pacific as possible, while the United States was willing to accept territorial losses in that theatre.[52]

After a major rupture over these differences and British efforts to seek a compromise through US channels beyond the conference, agreement was reached. The final report of 27 March 1941 left open the question of Japan's role, but agreed on the need to defeat Germany first. How this would be accomplished also remained vague, although greater emphasis was placed on British concepts of indirect means for the present.[53] ABC-1, as the report was called, was an important step forward, a means of fleshing out grand strategic agreement. It was also a dangerous precedent, in that serious areas of disagreement were either vaguely compromised or largely omitted, resulting in either unresolved differences, or differing views as to what the resolution actually was.

While Roosevelt was familiar with ABC-1, and approved of the methods called for, even allowing letters sent out by Stark to his commanders based on the joint war plan, the President pointedly avoided giving formal approval to the report. At the same time he did not disapprove it, and so Marshall and Stark took this to mean acquiescence and therefore used ABC-1 as the basis for further planning. This took the form of developing Rainbow 5, which was completed on 14 May 1941 and signed in early June by Stimson and Knox. This, too, Roosevelt did not formally approve.[54] Thus, the United States had entered a realm of grand strategic planning by acquiescence, in which the President refused to be drawn out further as to his goals or intentions, and allowed his military staffs to proceed on their own. As he was familiar with the direction of their thinking he was, in effect, acquiescing. Yet at the same time he offered little policy guidance of his own upon which they could base their plans.

This continued vagueness led to the most identifiable policy crisis that President Roosevelt faced during the pre-war period. The catalyst for this was Lend-Lease, which became law on 11 March 1941. Not everyone in the government agreed as to the significance of the act, although Assistant Secretary of State Adolf Berle was probably closest to the truth when he envisaged 'a steady drift into a deep grey stage in which the precise difference between war and peace is impossible to discern'. It was this grey area which bothered Secretary of War Stimson, who now saw a logical extension of Lend-Lease: the provision of supplies was meaningless unless their safe arrival was also guaranteed.[55]

British shipping losses reached new levels in February and March 1941. Churchill saw two alternatives: US protected convoys in the Western Atlantic, or at least an increased naval presence in the Atlantic.[56] However, either solution would require a decrease in the fleet at Hawaii, whose strength Roosevelt was committed to maintain as a means of deterring Japan. An increased presence in the Atlantic would also increase the risk of war with Germany. Underlying this conundrum was evidence that past US efforts at keeping the problems of Europe and the Far East separate were beginning to fail.

Nevertheless, Stimson and Knox began putting pressure on the

President in early April to commence convoys. He refused, citing the state of public opinion. Stark vaguely sided with the service secretaries, warning his Pacific and Atlantic commanders to be ready for a transfer of units. Roosevelt did take the step, on 10 April 1941, of extending the proclaimed US security zone to include Greenland and everything west of 25° west longitude. This allowed the President to take another limited step and yet to remain under the guise of Hemispheric Defense. But in real terms this did little immediately to aid Britain, especially as Roosevelt implemented the change without publicizing it beyond informing Churchill.[57]

Rumours now abounded about imminent German moves into Spain or the various eastern Atlantic island groups, increasing the anxiety of the interventionists, as did continued British shipping losses. Stimson and Secretary of the Interior Harold Ickes became convinced that some decision was necessary if Roosevelt was not to lose public support. Roosevelt finally announced the new patrol zone on 23 April 1941, but he carefully distinguished between this step, a supposed reconnaissance, and convoying or armed escort. His critics did not see the difference and accused him of sham. Operational instructions for the patrol gave credence to this view.[58]

A long debate now ensued over the need to transfer ships to the Atlantic. Stimson led the proponents, supported by Marshall, presidential confidant Harry Hopkins, and a more reluctant Stark. Interestingly, the British, who were aware of this debate, were also divided, desiring US support in the Atlantic but fearful of a lessened restraint on Japan. Following the line advocated by Churchill, they eventually agreed with the transfer.[59]

During the first part of May 1941 the transfer of ships had several false starts. Roosevelt now admitted that if a war came it would have to be at German provocation. The policy debate shifted somewhat, focusing on a planned major policy address by the President, which passed through several drafts as the interventionists and the more cautionary advisers, such as Hull, read it. The final draft, delivered on 27 May 1941, was a typical Rooseveltian compromise, vividly describing the ever nearer Nazi threat, the importance of the Battle of the Atlantic, and the fundamental issues at stake. But the only response, in terms of policy, was a declaration of unlimited National Emergency.[60]

The National Emergency speech suited Roosevelt's own needs by effectively rallying public opinion, giving him something further to build on, and also buying him more time. But it did little to resolve the policy dilemma. Indeed, at his press conference the following day, President Roosevelt eschewed any further steps and even undercut the declaration, frustrating the interventionists.[61] His advisers did not necessarily appreciate the difference that Roosevelt felt as the person ultimately responsible for policy decisions and their consequences, just as Roosevelt had not when he had served as Assistant Secretary of the Navy under Wilson.

In mid-June 1941 there was an important change in British military thinking. The Joint Planning Staff now concluded 'that the active belligerency of the United States has become essential for a successful prosecution and conclusion of the war'. However, this perception was not revealed by the British when the senior military leaders of both nations met at the Atlantic Conference in August 1941, and in preparing for this meeting the US military continued to limit their discussions to aid to Britain short of war. Once again Roosevelt failed to give his military subordinates any policy guidelines, which in a way was even more restrictive as they then had to err on the side of caution.[62] This being the case, the military discussions at Argentia resulted in another coherent presentation of British strategy and limited American responses. Where the two staffs openly disagreed, as on the relative importance of the Middle East, the US representatives tended to be more adamant, reflecting, in part, their inability to take major new strategic directions in the absence of policy guidance. Thus, the US military clung stubbornly to ABC-1, rather than tamper with this one source of seemingly agreed policy and strategy.[63]

In July 1941, Roosevelt instructed Stimson and Knox to examine 'the overall production requirements required to defeat our potential enemies'. The President was still viewing the US as a supplier, not a belligerent, and his request made no mention of possible US entry into the war. In making this request Roosevelt left 'appropriate assumptions as to the probable friends and enemies and to conceivable theaters of operation' to the drafters.[64] This vagueness notwithstanding, the President was asking for a global assessment, one which necessarily would have to assume eventual US belligerency. The President apparently believed he still had alternatives, ones which may even have grown given the recent invasion of the Soviet Union.

The inherent vagueness of the request frustrated the responsible army planners. Each officer in the chain of responsibility from the drafter, Major Albert C. Wedemeyer, to General Leonard Gerow,

Acting Assistant Chief of Staff, War Plans, asked his superior what the assumptions were to be on national policy. Gerow, after complaining to Marshall that policy was still 'nebulous', told Wedemeyer to draft his own assumptions.[65] Once again the military was responsible, owing to abdication, for defining fundamental policy. The final presentation was made on 25 September 1941. Called the Victory Program, it included an estimate signed by the Joint Board. In it the military defined national policy along lines largely similar to those of the Stark Memorandum, but went on to call for US entry in order to defeat Germany and Japan.[66]

In the Victory Program, Roosevelt undoubtedly received much more than he wanted. He was now being told that his alternatives had run out, that war was the best course for the pursuit of national interests. Yet the President still did not want to agree, nor did he seize the seeming opportunities offered by the growing naval incidents with Germany in the Atlantic, opportunities he had once suggested he wanted. By November 1941, not one of the President's major advisers, with the possible exception of Hull, felt that war could be avoided. Roosevelt, however, no longer felt that these incidents at sea were sufficient provocation.[67]

When the war came, it arrived in that secondary theatre, the Pacific. Even after the Japanese attack Roosevelt refused to act against the European Axis. He had resolved to wait for their declarations.[68] Hitler, in one of his most irrational policy decisions, obliged on 11 December 1941. One wonders what might have been the effect on US strategy and the war itself had he not.

Thus, the Search for Alternatives, like the Search for Influence, was overthrown by events, not by any realization that policy had actually reached a failed conclusion. Once again, President Roosevelt had clung to his preferred policy until he was forced to abandon it, producing the need for yet another search.

The Search for Strategy, December 1941-January 1943

The advent of the war had solved one set of problems, while giving rise to others. Beyond a general agreement on broad grand strategic concepts, specifically the defeat of Germany first, there was no agreed Allied strategy for the successful prosecution of the war. Arriving at such a strategy took up most of the next year.

The Search for Strategy was complicated by a number of factors.

One was purely national goals. To whatever degree was possible the British had put these aside before the United States entered the war. Now that both nations were in the war these issues, such as the importance of the Middle East, took on added prominence. Another was the changed role of Franklin Roosevelt. He no longer saw himself as an embattled national leader, hampered by a strong isolationist bloc. Instead, he seems to have arrived at a conception of himself as the leader of a great coalition, and as such he had to give added attention to the needs of other coalition members. These needs might not always be in accordance with the preferences of the newly-formed Joint Chiefs of Staff, who were not thinking in these terms. Interestingly, while pre-war domestic political factors had led Roosevelt to want to do less, wartime international political factors led him to want to do more.

Roosevelt was initially willing to follow the advice of his military planners when they advocated a build up in Britain (Bolero) and an invasion of Western Europe in April 1943 (Roundup). It is not clear that the Present understood that such a concept largely precluded action in 1942,[69] a fact which General Marshall possibly obscured in order to maintain Roosevelt's support.

Four months of negotiations, from April to July 1942, failed to bring Allied agreement on these plans. Roosevelt, uncharacteristically, informed his military advisers on 6 May 1942 that is was essential 'that active operations be conducted in 1942 . . . The necessities of the case call for action in 1942 — not 1943.' In other words, he would not wait for Roundup in 1943, about which the British had expressed grave and reasonable doubts.[70]

A number of concerns were now motivating the President, including the need to placate, rally and focus public opinion; competing demands from the Pacific; and the need to do something against Germany in order to ease the pressure on the Soviet Union. Indeed, in a meeting with Soviet Foreign Minister Vyacheslav Molotov in May 1942 the President had basically promised the creation of a second front that year.[71]

But when agreement could not be reached on an emergency landing in Western Europe for 1942 to aid Russia, code-named Sledgehammer, the Joint Chiefs staged a brief rebellion. Feeling that the British had continually reneged on agreed strategic decisions, Marshall and the new Chief of Naval Operations, Admiral Ernest J. King, proposed that the United States turn its main attention to the Pacific. The President rejected this in a memorandum he signed 'Roosevelt, Commander-in-Chief'. Instead, he intervened for the second time, sending Hopkins, Marshall and King to London to reach agreement on either Sledgehammer or an alternative, which would most likely be Gymnast, an invasion of North Africa, which had first been proposed at the Arcadia conference in December 1941. However, they were also instructed that the chosen strategy was not to preclude Roundup in 1943.[72]

Even though this presidential order resulted in agreement for Gymnast, soon to be renamed Torch, there was wide disagreement as to what this meant. The US military insisted that Torch would preclude Roundup; the British disagreed.[73] Roosevelt chose to play an intriguing role in this long and often tedious strategic debate. He seemed to rise above parochialism to try and moderate between the Joint Chiefs and the British Chiefs of Staff, rather than support the Joint Chiefs. In so doing he showed no conviction that either side was correct, only that they must both eventually agree. Thus, the Joint Chiefs felt rather isolated after the Torch decision, and this was redoubled when the Casablanca Conference proved their fears to be correct and Sicily, not Roundup, became the goal for 1943.

Much of the confusion in 1942 can actually be attributed to Roosevelt's reluctance to face the realities of 1941. By refusing to accept the likelihood of war he never took the time to ponder US goals should war come. In the absence of political guidance, which the President was still working out in 1942, the US military chose the only agreed course, quick victory. While this was desirable, it was also a narrow conception, one often divorced from political necessities or realities. Roosevelt knew he wanted something more than just victory; it had to be victory of a certain sort, with a certain significance. Unable, and perhaps unwilling to enunciate these ideas fully in 1942, he helped contribute to yet one more policy search. It is interesting to note, however, that twice in 1942 Roosevelt intervened directly in military planning to state minimum desiderata which would have to be taken into account. Just as his concept of his role changed, so did some of Roosevelt's tactics in carrying it out.

A political leader can be judged by the clarity with which he enunciates his goals, the methods he chooses to carry them out, and the availability of the options he faces at crucial junctures. Franklin Roosevelt's record for the years 1937-42 remains uneven at best.

During the first policy phase, the Search for Influence, Roosevelt's goals were unclear. Indeed, that was the basic issue at stake, an uncertain effort to influence events from a safe distance. During the second phase, the Search for Alternatives, Roosevelt knew that he did not want Britain to lose the war. However, he did not come to translate this into a higher necessity, helping Britain to win the war, until much later than virtually all of his advisers. His own abhorrence of war blinded him to the implications of many of his major policy steps. Indeed, unlike the members of the Joint Board, Roosevelt seemed to have given little or no thought whatsoever to a possible successful conclusion to the British-German struggle. Maintaining Britain as a belligerent, which also meant keeping the US out, was the primary focus, even though each further policy decision increased both the potential and the necessity for US entry if previous policy was not to be abandoned. Finally, during the Search for Strategy, Roosevelt personally transformed his role, and adopted a set of higher goals which, once again, he did not fully articulate.

Given the vagueness of goals, the methods chosen for pursuing them also had to be either vague or inconsistent. During the Search for Influence the very limitation of means of effecting the situation, either real or self-imposed, was built into policy deliberations. There was a certain casting about for means, accompanied by vacillations in the President's own outlook. During the Search for Alternatives, more means became available, but they would only be used with reluctance by Roosevelt. While the evolution of policy was more direct and linear than it had been before, it still moved by fits and starts, with little sense of cohesion. Rather, each major policy decision, such as the Destroyer-Base deal of Lend-Lease, while largely predicated on the necessity of maintaining the previous policy goals, was looked at in isolation by the President, who preferred not to face the broader implications of his decisions. Roosevelt's methodology changed once again during the last policy phase, although it was again for reasons which he largely did not explain.

This method of approach fostered a great deal of divergence between fundamental policy and grand strategy. While Roosevelt seemingly kept his options open, he was also failing to define policy goals, leaving this to subordinates who were then forced to make plans based on the realities of the situation as they saw them. However, erring on the side of caution as military staffs often do, they then reached necessary conclusions which had not been accepted by the President, and which he would not yet endorse. This then reduced planning to educated assumptions rather than definitive statements, which hampered US preparations and helped create the final policy search in 1942.

While Roosevelt's shortcomings in the enunciation of goals and in their execution were largely self-imposed, one must look finally at the options he faced. Certainly, given isolationist sentiment, either real or perceived, and the limitation of means, there was little Roosevelt could do during the years 1937-39. It is conceivable that Roosevelt could have identified US interest more closely with those of the Allies, but this would have run grave domestic risks and have had little effect on Hitler, whose own distorted view of the United States would probably have discounted this, especially given current US military strength. During the Search for Strategy, Roosevelt was probably responding to his options better than he had in the other phases. He pointedly refused to take a narrow nationalist path when strategic agreement could not be reached, and kept in mind better than his subordinates the political requirements of an allied war effort.

Roosevelt's great failure came during the Search for Alternatives. Not only did his unwillingness to face the implications of his decisions disrupt coherence between policy and planning, it also denied Roosevelt an opportunity to make clear, beyond vague generalities, what was at stake for the United States in the war and what the nation might hope to accomplish by entry. This created a fundamental policy vacuum which was never authoritatively filled for the United States during the course of the war.

NOTES

1. For a fuller discussion of the concepts of fundamental policy and grand strategy and their inter-relationship see B.H. Liddell-Hart, *Strategy*, second revised edition (New York 1967), 333-51.

2. See Dorothy Borg, 'Notes on Roosevelt's "Quarantine Speech" ', *Political Science Quarterly*, LXXII (September 1957), passim 405-24.

3. Arnold A. Offner, 'Appeasement Revisited: The United States, Great Britain and Germany, 1933-1940', *The Journal of American History*, LXIV (September

1977), 378; William E. Kinsella, *Leadership in Isolation* (Cambridge, Mass. 1968), 82-83; Borg, op. cit., 409; Robert Dallek, *Franklin D. Roosevelt and American Foreign Policy, 1932-1945* (New York 1979), 147.

4. Various sources refer to the Welles-Hull rivalry. See, for example, Sumner Welles, *Seven Decisions that Shaped History* (New York 1950), 8-12, 61; Henry L. Stimson, *Henry Lewis Stimson Diaries* (New Haven, Yale University Library, microfilm edition), 4 and 7 January 1941, 19 August 1941, 2 June 1942; Adolf A. Berle, *Navigating the Rapids, 1918-1971: From the Papers of Adolf A. Berle*, Beatrice Bishop Berle and Travis Beal Jacobs (eds.) (New York 1973), 205, 214, 286.

5. See Welles' comment to Berle in Berle, op. cit., 149-50 (2 December 1937); Memorandum, Welles to Roosevelt, 10 January 1938, *Foreign Relations of the United States* [hereafter *FRUS*], 1938, I, 115-17.

6. Record of Conversation with President Roosevelt and Mr. Hull by Walter Runciman, 8 February 1937, Paper A 1095/93/45, FO 371/20656, Public Record Office [hereafter PRO], London; Letter No. 247, Sir Ronald Lindsay to Eden, 22 March 1937, Paper A 2378/38/45, FO 414/274, Part XLVII, PRO.

7. Telegrams Nos. 481, 482, 483, Lindsay to Foreign Office [hereafter FO], 17 December 1937, FO 371/20961, PRO.

8. See Ingersoll's testimony in US Congress. *Pearl Harbor Attack*, 79th Congress, 2d session (Washington 1946), IX, 4273-76.

9. Telegram No. 464, Lindsay to FO, 13 December 1937, and Telegram No. 594, FO to Lindsay, 14 December 1937, Paper F 10976/10816/10, FO 371/21021, PRO. Cabinet Meeting 47 (37), 15 December 1937, CAB 23/90A, PRO.

10. Ingersoll commented on his instructions in a letter to the author, 16 May 1973. Also see Ingersoll's report, Memorandum for Chief of Naval Operations, nd, Navy War Plans Division records, Naval History Division [hereafter NHD], Washington. British records of the talks are in Papers F 95, F 96 and F 337/84/10, FO 371/22106, PRO. For a good summary of the talks see Lawrence Pratt, 'The Anglo-American Naval Conversations on the Far East of January 1938', *International Affairs*, XLVII (October 1971), 745-63.

11. Record of Conversations, appended to Ingersoll Memorandum cited in n. 10.

12. David Dilks (ed.), *The Diaries of Sir Alexander Cadogan, 1938-1945* (New York 1972), 36 (12-13 January 1938); Cabinet Meeting (1) 38, 24 January 1938, CAB 23/92, PRO.

13. Message, Chamberlain to Roosevelt, 14 January 1938, *FRUS*, 1938, I, 117-20; Dilks, op. cit., 40 (21 January 1938); Cabinet Meeting (1) 38, 24 January 1938, CAB 23/92, PRO.

14. JB No. 325 (Serials 617 and 618), War Plan Orange, 1938: Memorandum, Craig to Joint Planning Committee, 10 November 1937, Record Group 225 [hereafter RG], National Archives [hereafter NA], Washington.

15. Letter Op-12-MG/2-2-38/Serial 218: Chief of Naval Operations to Commanders-in-Chief, US Fleet and Asiatic Fleet, 2 February 1938, Navy War Plans Division Files: Correspondence Re British-US Conversations in London, NHD.

16. See War Plan Orange (1938), cited in n. 14. See also Louis Morton, 'War Plan ORANGE: Evolution of a Strategy', *World Politics*, XI (January 1959), 221-50.

17. Harold L. Ickes, *The Secret Diary of Harold L. Ickes* (New York 1954), II, 468-69 (18 September 1938); Telegram No. 349, Lindsay to FO, 19 September 1938, Paper A 7504/64/45, FO 371/21527, PRO.

18. Ickes, op. cit., II, 481 (30 September 1938).

19. Telegram No. 181, Welles to Ambassador Hugh Wilson (Berlin), 18 October 1938, *FRUS*, 1938, I, 274.

20. Anne O'Hare McCormick, 'As He Sees Himself', *New York Times Magazine*, 16 October 1938, 1-6, 19; 'Notes of certain conversations between President Franklin D. Roosevelt and Colonel Hon. Arthur Murray . . . October 16th to 24th, 1938', PREM 1/367, PRO.

21. Memorandum of White House Conference, 14 November 1938, Miscellaneous Conferences, 1938-1942, RG 165/30, NA.

22. Ickes, op. cit., II, 571; Letter, Roosevelt to Prof. Roger B. Merriman, 15 February 1939, PSF, Box 35: Diplomatic Correspondence, Great Britain, 1939, Franklin D. Roosevelt [hereafter FDR] Library, Hyde Park, NY.

23. Joint Board Meeting, 9 November 1938, JB No. 301: Minutes, 1934-1940, RG 225, NA.

24. Joint Planning Committee Exploratory Study: Joint Action in Event of Violation of Monroe Doctrine by Fascist Powers, JB No. 325 (Serial 634), 21 April 1939, RG 225, NA. Roosevelt was also concerned about threats to north-eastern Brazil; see Standing Liaison Committee Meeting, 21 January 1939, Minutes of the Standing Liaison Committee, RG 353, NA.

25. Joint Board Meeting, 6 May 1939, JB No. 301, Minutes 1934-1940, RG 225, NA.

26. JB No. 325 (Serial 642): Rainbow Nos. 1, 2, 3, 4 and 5, RG 225, NA. The plans' premises were as follows:
Rainbow 1: US defending Western Hemisphere (north of 10° south latitude) alone.
Rainbow 2: war in concert with Britain and France. Allies responsible for Europe, US to defend Western Hemisphere and responsible for the Pacific, including the defeat of enemy forces there.
Rainbow 3: US acting alone, defending Western Hemisphere and projecting forces to control Western Pacific.
Rainbow 4: US acting alone, defending entire Western Hemisphere and projecting forces into Eastern Atlantic.
Rainbow 5: war in concert with Britain and France. Defense of Western Hemisphere, and projection of US forces to Eastern Atlantic and to Europe and/or Africa to defeat Germany and Italy.

27. Roosevelt gave verbal approval of this fundamental plan on 14 October 1939 through his naval aide, Captain Daniel J. Callaghan. See JB No. 325 (Serial 642-1), Rainbow No. 1, RG 225, NA.

28. The US and British versions of the Hampton-Leahy talks differ as to whether or not the scenario under discussion envisaged both the US and Japan as being neutral (the British version), or only the US (the US version). See Report by Commander T.C. Hampton, 27 June 1939, Paper F 7010/456/23, FO 371/23561, PRO; and Memorandum of an informal conversation at the residence of the Chief of Naval Operations, 12 June 1939, by Rear-Admiral Robert L. Ghormley, in Navy War Plans Division, file noted in n. 15, NHD.

29. Sumner Welles, *The Time for Decision* (New York 1944), 73-74; Stimson, op. cit., 8 May 1940; Berle, op. cit., 290 (12 February 1940).

30. Welles, *The Time for Decision*, 74; and Welles' testimony, *Pearl Harbor Attack*, II, 547.

31. Welles' report on his mission is in *FRUS*, 1940, I, 21-117. See also Ickes, op. cit., III, 464-65 for Welles' opinion of Mussolini. Foreign accounts of Welles' mission can be found in US Department of State, *Documents on German Foreign*

Policy, Series D, 1937-1945, VIII, 829-30; and in PREM 4-25/2, FO 371/24406 and FO 115/3421, PRO.

32. Welles Report, op. cit., 116-17.

33. WPD 4175-7: National Strategic Decisions, Memorandum by Army War Plans, 22 May 1940; WPD 4175-120: Memorandum by Major Ridgway, 23 May 1940, and Memorandum by Marshall, 23 May 1940, all in RG 165/281, NA.

34. JB No. 325 (Serial 642-4): Rainbow 4, 31 May 1940, RG 225, NA.

35. WPD 4199-1: Op-12-CTB: Memorandum, Captain Russell S. Crenshaw (Director, Navy War Plans) to Admiral Stark, 29 June 1940, RG 165/281, NA.

36. WPD 4250-3: Decisions as to National Action, Memorandum, Marshall to Colonel O. Ward (Secretary, General Staff), 17 June 1940, RG 165/281, NA.

37. WPD 4250-3: Basis for Immediate Decisions Concerning the National Defense, Memorandum, Stark and Marshall to Roosevelt, 22 June 1940, RG 165/281, NA. The final version, with Roosevelt's changes, is in the same file, dated 27 June 1940.

38. See Churchill's first message as Prime Minister to Roosevelt, 15 May 1940, in Francis L. Loewenheim et al. (eds.), *Roosevelt and Churchill: Their Secret Wartime Correspondence* (New York 1975), 94-95.

39. This message was repeated over and over again. See, for example, Telegram No. 1271, Churchill to Roosevelt, 29 May 1940, Map Room File, Box 1: FDR-Churchill Messages, FDR Library; and Telegram No. 1579, Churchill to Roosevelt, 10 June 1940, 740.0011 European War 1939/3487 5/10 Confidential File, RG 59, NA.

40. Telegram No. 1019, Lothian to FO, 17 June 1940, Annex 1 to Enclosure 5A, WO 193/311, PRO.

41. Memorandum, Morgenthau to Roosevelt, 18 June 1940, Map Room File, Box 1, cited in n. 39.

42. William L. Langer and S. Everett Gleason, *The Challenge to Isolation, 1937-1940* (New York 1952), 746-48.

43. WPD 4368: Observations in England, Memorandum, Emmons and Strong to Marshall, 25 September 1940, RG 165/281, NA; Standing Liaison Committee meeting, 23 September 1940, Minutes of the Standing Liaison Committee, 1938-1943, RG 353, NA.

44. Memorandum, Stark to Knox, 4 November 1940, PSF, Box 3, Departmental Correspondence, Navy Department, November-December 1940, FDR Library.

45. Ibid., Stark to Knox. The other alternative strategies were:
Plan A: Hemispheric Defense, keeping the US out of war but minimizing influence on the outcome.
Plan B: offensive against Japan, defensive in the Atlantic, leaving Britain to fight alone and possibly be defeated, forcing the US to reorient its strategy.
Plan C: equal efforts in the Atlantic and Pacific, running the risk of spreading US forces thin without effect in either theatre.

46. Letter, Stark to Richardson, 12 November 1940, and see also Letter, Stark to Ghormley, 16 November 1940, both in File: Ghormley — Official Correspondence concerning war plans, 1940-41, COMNAVEU, Series II, Item 65, NHD. See also Mark M. Lowenthal, 'The Stark Memorandum and the American National Security Policy Process', in Robert William Love, Jr. (ed.), *Changing Interpretations and New Sources in Naval History* (New York 1980), 352-59.

47. WPD 4175-15: Memorandum, Stark to Marshall, 22 November 1940, RG 165/281, NA.

48. Letter, Churchill to Roosevelt, 8 December 1940, *FRUS*, 1940, III, 18-26; William L. Langer and S. Everett Gleason, *The Undeclared War, 1940-1941* (New York 1952), 237ff. See also Roosevelt's press conference, 17 December 1940 in Samuel I. Rosenman (ed.), *The Public Papers and Addresses of Franklin D. Roosevelt* (New York 1941), IX, 604-12.

49. Fireside Chat, 29 December 1940, ibid., IX, 633-34.

50. Notes by Rear-Admiral Roger M. Bellairs, RN, for Historical Officer, US Naval Forces Europe, November 1946 in File: Anglo-American Standardization of Arms Committee Item 9 in COMNAVEU cited in n. 46. Ickes, op. cit., III, 388-89 (1 December 1940); and Telegram No. 2851, Lothian to FO, 29 November 1940, Annex I to COS (40) 1014, 5 December 1940, CAB 80/24, PRO.

51. WPD 4175-18: White House Conference of Thursday, 16 January 1941: Memorandum, Marshall to General L.T. Gerow (Assistant Chief of Staff, War Plans), 17 January 1941, RG 165/281, NA. The revised Opening Statement is in JB No. 325 (Serial 674), RG 225, NA.

52. The British and US minutes are identical, but the British collection is easier to use. See CAB 99/5, PRO. Most US internal documents can be found in OPD Exec No. 4, Item 11; WPD 4402, WPD 4175-18, WPD 4434, all in RG 165/281, NA.

53. ABC-1, 27 March 1941, ibid.

54. Tracy B. Kittredge, *US-British Naval Cooperation, 1940-1942* (MS), Vol. I, Sect. IV, Part A, 374-75; Letter, Ghormley to Admiral of the Fleet Sir Dudley Pound, 26 April 1941, CAB 205/9, PRO; Letter, Ghormley to British Chiefs of Staff, 12 June 1941, COS (41) 371, 12 June 1941, CAB 80/28, PRO; Maurice Matloff and Edwin M. Snell, *Strategic Planning for Coalition Warfare, 1941-1942* (Washington 1953), 46-47; JB No. 325 (Serial 642-5): Rainbow 5 (Revised), 19 November 1941, RG 225, NA.

55. Berle, op. cit., 362 (9 March 1941); Stimson, op. cit., 17 March 1941.

56. War Cabinet meeting WM 29 (41), 17 March 1941, CAB 65/18, PRO.

57. Stimson, op. cit., 24 March, 11 April 1941; Letter, Stark to Admirals Kimmel, Hart and King, 3 April 1941, *Pearl Harbor Attack*, XVII, 2463; Telegram No. 1230, Roosevelt to Churchill, 11 April 1941, *FRUS*, 1941, II, 836-37.

58. *FRUS*, 1941, II, 836-37; Ickes, op. cit., III, 485-87 (26 April 1941); Stimson, op. cit., 21-22 April 1941; Roosevelt Press Conference, 25 April 1941, in Rosenman, op. cit., X, 132-36; Ernest J. King and Walter Muir Whitehill, *Fleet Admiral King* (New York 1952), 339.

59. Stimson, op. cit., 23 and 24 April, 5 and 6 May 1941; Defence Committee meetings DO (41) 21st meeting, 30 April 1941 and 22nd meeting, 1 May 1941, CAB 69/2, PRO. For a good synopsis of the decision to transfer US naval units see Robert J. Quinlan, 'The United States Fleet: Diplomacy, Strategy and the Allocation of Ships (1940-1941)', in Harold Stein (ed.), *American Civil-Military Decisions* (Birmingham, Alabama 1963), 155-62, 177-85.

60. Samuel I. Rosenman, *Working with Roosevelt* (New York 1952), 280-81; Stimson, op. cit., 24-25 May 1941; Rosenman, *Roosevelt Papers*, X, 181-95.

61. Robert E. Sherwood, *Roosevelt and Hopkins* (New York 1948), 298-99; Ickes, op. cit., III, 526-27 (30 May 1941); Stimson, op. cit., 27 and 29 May 1941.

62. British Joint Planning Staff: Future Strategy, JP (41) 444, 14 June 1941, in COS (41) 213th Meeting, 16 June 1941, CAB 79/2, PRO; Interview with Admiral Stark by Joint Chiefs of Staff Historical Section, 14 May 1947, copy in author's possession; testimony by General Marshall, *Pearl Harbor Attack*, III, 1389.

63. COS (41) 504: RIVIERA, CAB 80/30, PRO; Telegram Boxes No. 86, British

Chiefs of Staff to Joint Staff Mission, Washington, 23 August 1941, CAB 105/37, PRO.

64. Letters, Roosevelt to Stimson and Knox, 9 July 1941, PSF, Boxes 66 (Knox) and 86 (Stimson), FDR Library.

65. Interview with General Albert C. Wedemeyer, 4 January 1974; Albert C. Wedemeyer, *Wedemeyer Reports!* (New York 1958), 64; Mark S. Watson, *Chief of Staff: Prewar Plans and Preparations* (Washington 1950), 341.

66. Army and Navy Estimate of United States Over-all Production Requirements, 11 September 1941, JB No. 325 (Serial 707), RG 225, NA.

67. Rosenman, *Roosevelt Papers*, X, 438-44, 462-64; James MacGregor Burns, *Roosevelt, The Soldier of Freedom, 1940-1945* (New York 1970), 148-49.

68. Stimson, op. cit., 7 December 1941; Ickes, op. cit., III, 664 (14 December 1941).

69. Basis for preparation of attached outline plan for Invasion of Western Europe, Memorandum, Marshall to Roosevelt, 2 April 1941, PSF, Box 3, Safe File: Marshall, FDR Library.

70. For a synopsis of this period see Matloff and Snell, op. cit., 174ff; see the various Memoranda from Roosevelt to Marshall, Hopkins, Stimson, King, and Arnold, 5 and 6 May 1942, all in PSF, Box 86, Departmental Correspondence, War Department: Marshall, FDR Library.

71. Rober Dallek, *Franklin D. Roosevelt and American Foreign Policy, 1932-1945* (New York 1979), 339; Richard W. Steele, *The First Offensive, 1942* (Bloomington, Indiana 1973), 86; *FRUS*, 1942, III, 575-77.

72. Joint Chiefs of Staff, 24th meeting, 10 July 1942, CCS 334 — Joint Chiefs of Staff (6-23-42), RG 218, NA; Memorandum, Marshall and King to Roosevelt, 10 July 1942, and Memorandum, Roosevelt to Marshall and King, 12 July 1942, both in OPD Exec No. 1, Item 10a, Tab 3, RG 165/422, NA; Instructions for London Conference, 1942, Roosevelt to Hopkins, Marshall and King, 16 July 1942; PSF, Box 3, Safe File: Marshall, FDR Library. See also Mark A. Stoler, 'The "Pacific-First" Alternative in American World War II Strategy', *The International History Review*, II (July 1980), 432-52.

73. Combined Chiefs of Staff, 32nd meeting, 24 July 1942, CAB 88/1, PRO.

II

Clausewitz and German War Doctrine

Clausewitz (like Hegel) has been claimed by the left as well as by the right, by Lenin and by Hitler. The Nazis invoked him as the precursor of absolute war, the Vernichtungskampf, *which, as Mr Baldwin points out, had been for Clausewitz no more than an abstract philosophical concept. In view of the ambiguities and contradictions in Clausewitz he was constantly reinterpreted in Nazi Germany and used for different purposes, both at times of victory and defeat. Ludendorff had suggested in 1935 that Clausewitz was outmoded. Hitler quoted him on the superiority of the political aim over the military when his generals proved to be too old-fashioned and temperate to follow Hitler's radical political demands.*

Clausewitz had cautioned in 1827 that if an early death should interrupt his work, it would be subject to endless misunderstandings. His fears came true.

5 Clausewitz in Nazi Germany

P M Baldwin

I

A study of Clausewitz's influence on the thoughts and minds of those who made Nazi Germany is an exercise in the futility of traditional intellectual history, at least in so far as it applies to the events of recent times. In an age of demagogy, mass propaganda and irrational ideology, the accepted, commonsense standards of intellectual influence and causation prove largely worthless. Books are read, if at all, not as a source of enlightenment but of justification for dogmas already held. Ideas and their formulators no longer represent public values to be appropriated by anyone able and willing to do so, but become the medium of barter, mere tokens in a war of words which any and all sides may dole out in return for power and support. It comes, therefore, as no great surprise to find this frankly admitted with respect to Clausewitz, as in the following passage from the officer's periodical of the German army in the penultimate year of the Second World War:[1]

> Never before, as in these war years, has all history so clearly recognized its duty: the mobilization of the past in the interests of the preservation of the present and the future . . . . In accordance with this fundamental conviction, Clausewitz is here treated in a manner which does not, of course, satisfy the historical thirst for knowledge and the requirement of completeness, but in one which may nevertheless demonstrate the continuing importance and relevance of this truly great German.

With this in mind, it is less difficult to make sense of the wild fluctuations of opinion which vie for the honour of explaining Clausewitz's role in Nazi Germany and the Second World War. For, employing the standard criteria of intellectual history, it is possible to dress Clausewitz up to fit any part desired: evil genius of Prussian militarism; sober philosopher, misunderstood and perverted by the National Socialists; spiritual forefather of the German resistance. All these positions can be argued for and have been supported with approximately equal force.

The simplest view of the matter, one advanced by allied and neutral observers during and immediately following the war, stated that Hitler, although perhaps the black sheep of the family, was nonetheless a direct descendant of Clausewitz, the father of Prussian militarism.[2] This was usually meant to refer to Hitler's war aims and conduct. But Wyndham Lewis, a man of piquant and often flippant style, now more fondly remembered for his literary efforts than for his political views, saw in the tactics with which the Nazis battled their competitors before being lifted legally to power, an embodiment of Clausewitz's teachings on the nature of war.[3]

Another, more sophisticated approach does not stop at an assertion of the continuity of the Prussian military tradition, but singles out various Clausewitzian doctrines for attack. Particular opprobrium is reserved for the idea that war, by definition, involves a maximum exertion of effort, force and therefore violence. This idea, so runs the argument, laid the foundation of the so-called *Vernichtungsgedanke*, which regards as the only legitimate goal of war the complete decimation of enemy forces, ideally in one, all-decisive battle, the *Vernichtungsschlacht*. No war effort can, according to the dictates of this theory, ever aim at lesser goals or employ limited means. That not all wars have been of this extreme sort can therefore be explained only by the interference of extra-martial factors which deflect the war effort from its original, ferocious intent. This is the gist of Liddell Hart's argument, presented in the early 1930s, in which he traced much of the horror of the First World War back to the influence of Clausewitz.[4] More recently, this position has been expanded and elaborated to include the Second World War.[5] At the same time, however, more subtle analyses have emphasized the pernicious contribution of Schlieffen to the formulation of the *Vernichtungsgedanke* and have credited the Clausewitzian doctrine of the primacy of the political viewpoint over the purely military conduct of war with a moderating if, perhaps, therefore largely neglected character.[6] The rehabilitation of Clausewitz reaches its pinnacle in those studies that attempt to portray him as an important spiritual force behind the internal German resistance to Hitler. As is so often the case with rehabilitations, however, this one too leans occasionally towards the other extreme, as for example when, with disconcerting naiveté, the reader of a popular edition of *Vom Kriege* is assured that, 'The First World War would have been different, the Second would probably never have taken place, would never have been allowed to take place, had those responsible studied Clausewitz carefully and drawn practical lessons from him.'[7]

Various and opposing factions made use of Clausewitz's theories for their own purposes. In the period under consideration, however, the importance of his ideas lies less in their purely philosophical impact than in their role as an intellectual shibboleth. For the Nazis, the name Clausewitz lent an aura of respectability to their theories, their use of him suggested an unbroken line of historical continuity from Brandenburg to Berchtesgaden. But in order to enlist his reputation, they had to do violence to his ideas. For the anti-Nazis, it was precisely this impermissible deviation from true Clausewitzian doctrine which demonstrated that the Nazis were an aberration. Those who disputed Clausewitz's spiritual legacy were thus at odds on a comparatively narrow range of topics; it was primarily the honour of standing in the mainstream of the Prussian military tradition which was at stake. Yet within this limited scope vehement disagreement was possible. This essay considers two closely related ideas in particular: first, the well-known Clausewitzian leitmotiv that war is but a continuation of politics with other means, *la Formule* as Raymond Aron calls it; second, the notion of 'absolute war'.

II

Clausewitz's theories are widely known. It is therefore not so much their content as the ambiguity that plagues their formulation which deserves emphasis. The unfinished state of his writings at his death in 1831 has made them a treasure of often contradicting, mutually compromising statements which may submit to synthesis and harmonization at the hands of the patient scholar, but which can also be taken by the more pragmatic-minded statesman or soldier as a source of widely varying opinion. Thus, for example, everyone knows that, according to Clausewitz, war is subordinated to politics. But does this, to test one common assumption, mean that war is somehow subdued or tamed by political control, that politics act in a moderating, restraining fashion on the tempest which martial zeal left to itself would unleash? 'Thus politics', writes Clausewitz, 'makes of the all-overwhelming element of war a mere instrument. Out of the dreadful broadsword which seeks to be grasped with both hands and swung with full force, thus to strike once and for all, it fashions a light, handy sword which can on occasion even be handled as a rapier to exchange thrusts, feints and parries.'[8] In the same chapter, however, he also argues that it is a misunderstanding to speak of the detrimental influence of politics on warfare. If a war is unsuccessful, then not the political influence, but rather the nature of the politics in question is to blame. 'If the politics are right, that is, if they hit their mark, then they can work only to the advantage of war . . . '. This would seem to place politics and war on equal footing and might even be construed as a reversal of the usual sense of the *Formule*.[9]

Similar problems arise concerning the idea of absolute war. For Clausewitz, absolute war is a strictly philosophical concept, an abstraction on the analogy of the Kantian *Ding an sich*. In its purely military essence, war is a struggle fought with all available means until one side is unable to offer any further resistance. Two rational creatures, locked in combat, both realize that the victory will go to whichever exerts the most effort. Thus a continual escalation of force follows until one is completely vanquished. True to his philosophical calling, when Clausewitz writes that, 'never can a principle of moderation be introduced into the philosophy of war itself without committing an absurdity', he is making a statement about the nature of war in a logical sense.[10] He is not, as he is often misunderstood to say, advocating utmost brutality as the way to conduct any actual war.[11] Absolute war is the peak of the escalation of violence in the struggle between two rational creatures. It is the ideal type of war, never found in reality, which all real wars approximate but never attain. Clausewitz thought that, in his own day, Napoleonic warfare represented a new type of people's war which came much closer to the absolute form of war than the cabinet wars of the previous era.

To explain why absolute war is never met in reality, Clausewitz borrows the image of friction from physics. Not all forces can, in actuality, be deployed simultaneously, nor will those in charge of making the appropriate decisions ever be of one mind. Due to such 'modifications of reality', actual wars do not escalate to the absolute stage as a purely theory-bound consideration would expect.

Nevertheless, although Clausewitz did at one time think that all wars, however limited in scope and objective they might on occasion be, aimed at the idea of absolute war and were prevented from achieving this goal only through the interference of the frictions of reality, the development of his thought led him to argue that limited wars with circumscribed aims and motivations might represent a special class of war, one no less 'ideal' than absolute war.[12] He distinguishes various types of war in accordance with the intensity and importance of their motivations. The stronger the motives, the more every aspect of the peoples concerned is involved, the more war approaches its abstract form, the more it aims solely at crushing the enemy and, consequently, the more completely the military and political objects overlap, 'the more purely military and less political the war seems to be.' The weaker the motives, the more the war takes on a political cast.[13]

Thus Clausewitz distinguishes the purely military aims of war, the aim of struggle as a theoretical concept (destruction of the enemy), from the political manoeuvres which make use of war for ends which may very well be far more modest than those dictated by military considerations. Yet he wrote in the eighth book of *Vom Kriege* (one he did not live to revise) that, given sufficiently urgent political motives, it is possible for political and military goals to coincide. 'If war belongs to politics, then it will assume its character. As politics become greater and mightier, so does war; this can continue to the point at which war attains its absolute form.'[14] Given the ultimate motives of a battle for sheer survival, war can *apparently* lose its political aspect and be characterized wholly by the military goal of a completely vanquished opponent. 'It would be conceivable that the political viewpoint should lose its influence at the outbreak of war only if war were fought out of pure hatred as a struggle for life or death . . . '[15] This is not to say that, prompted by even the strongest of motivations, war is not actually political, but rather that at this extreme the political and military intentions seek one and the same object.

The point, therefore, is not that Clausewitz did not regard war as subordinate to politics or that he thought of limited wars as mere aberrations of the ideal war of utmost violence, but that his thought is genuinely ambiguous and therefore easily used and abused. 'Should an early death interrupt my work', he cautioned in his preface of 1827, scant years before one did, 'then what is here will, of course, only deserve to be called a shapeless mass of thoughts, . . . subject to endless misunderstandings . . . '.

III

However else they may have made use of him, the National Socialists regarded Clausewitz as a good Prussian, a valiant German, a dedicated soldier and therefore, it was assumed, an example that every Nazi might be proud to emulate. The National Socialists thought of themselves as fighting for Germany and her survival much as Clausewitz and others had done during the wars of national liberation. 'Who liberated Germany? 1813', Hitler scribbled in his notes for a speech already in the twenties. 'Not the host of the meek, but the hardheads. Not the Simons — Wirts — Erzbergers — Rathenaus, etc., but the Blüchers, Scharnhorsts, Yorcks and Gneisenaus. The spirit that Clausewitz expressed in a pamphlet: Clausewitz's Bekenntnis.'[16] 'Thus Clausewitz stretches out his hand to us over the civilian nineteenth century', wrote a fledgling National Socialist scholar in his Heidelberg dissertation from 1934.[17] It was only natural then that *Vom Kriege* should have shared the honour of inclusion on the list of the first hundred books for Nazi bookstores, along with the works of such luminaries as Rosenberg, Darré, Nietzsche, Bismarck, Ranke, Wagner and Jünger.[18]

Just as the Nazi rise to power was accompanied by a train of references to Clausewitz, so during the decline the philosopher's name was invoked, although now in a less optimistic, more desperate sense. As the war drags on toward the end, allusions to the man and his works turn up with increasing frequency as a sort of spiritual talisman. His *Bekenntnis*, read by Heinrich George, precedes Hitler's midnight address over the radio on New Year's Eve 1944. Snippets of his writings appear in military periodicals *zur Beherzigung*, or as a source of 'the power of inspiration in difficult times'. And, finally, in his political testament to Dönitz shortly before his suicide, Hitler appeals to 'the ideals of the great Clausewitz', for which he exhorts Germany to continue fighting.[19]

But the National Socialists made use of Clausewitz in more than this primarily ceremonial fashion. A quick check of the indexes to Hitler's various writings reveals that, with the exception of Ludendorff and Wagner, no other figure who could properly be considered an intellectual influence is mentioned or referred to as often as Clausewitz. This lends support to the observation that Hitler used Clausewitz as a source and justification for his thoughts in a fundamentally different sense than he did any of his other purported spiritual predecessors.[20]

It is often suggested that Hitler and the Nazis turned Clausewitz's *Formule* on its head, treating politics as the continuation of war and thus blurring the distinction between peace and war. This gave the Nazis a measure of freedom from the constraints of traditional diplomacy and foreign policy, which they exploited to full measure by militarizing what would normally be regarded as peaceful international relations up to the actual outbreak of hostilities in 1939.[21] 'Anyone familiar with the thinking of Clausewitz and Schlieffen knows that military strategy can also be used in the political battle', Hitler told Richard Breiting in 1931.[22] A decade later as Germany reaped the fruits of this doctrine, a German lieutenant-general looked back and concluded:

> Already before the outbreak of this war, we were witnesses to how the Führer made use of war, that is, the determination to go to war, as the most effective means of his politics, in the occupation of the Rhineland, the *Anschluss* of Austria, in the liberation of the Sudetenland and in the annexation of the protectorates of Bohemia and Moravia. Doesn't this correspond exactly to Clausewitz's view when he writes: 'If one concedes the influence of the political goal on war, . . . then there is no longer any limit and one must put up with descending even to such wars that consist merely in threatening the enemy and in negotiations.'[23]

Some observers assert that by reversing the *Formule*, Hitler subordinated politics to war and that the insanity of the Second World War is best explained by the predominance of the military element and the exclusion of a restraining political conception — a sort of war for war's sake.[24] This view ignores the redefinition of the nature of politics and war which the Nazis undertook. It rests on evidence provided by Ludendorff who, drawing on his experience in the First World War and his belief in the *Dolchstosslegende*, suggested in 1935 that Clausewitz had been outmoded. In the future, the leadership of the entire war effort should go to the military. For the military, thought the general, would be more willing to pursue a hard line than the civilian leadership.[25] Hitler did not see it this way. Although he considered himself the great general and shouted, '*I* shall make war', at Rauschning, he thought of the fight itself as political, though political, to be sure, in a new sense of the word: as a fanatical, uncompromising battle, 'the execution of a nation's struggle for existence', inspired by Nazi ideology.[26] This sort of politics, unlike that Clausewitz had in mind, was more savage than anything the military, left to its own devices, could ever dream up; the new political conception raised the possibility of brutality to unprecedented levels. 'The lack of a great, creative, renewing idea means at all times a limitation of fighting force', Hitler had written in 1926. 'Firm belief in the right to apply even the most brutal weapons is always bound up with the existence of a fanatical faith in the necessity of the victory of a revolutionary new order on this earth.'[27] Hitler complained of his generals that they were a moderating influence, bound by moribund conceptions of war and its limits. Of the war against the Soviet Union, he said in 1941,

> It is a fight with the great opponent of our Weltanschauung, a struggle for life and death in which each soldier must feel like a political fighter and act accordingly. The German officer and soldier is far too deeply rooted in the conceptions of an antiquated era. It is impossible ever to overcome Bolshevism with these principles of a chivalrous, purely military conduct of war.[28]

In fact, Hitler quoted Clausewitz on the superiority of the political aim over the military — a stricture which the generals of the First World War had ignored as too restrictive of their freedom of action — against his generals when they proved to be too old-fashioned and temperate to follow the radical new political demands he made of them. The document 'Die Kriegführung als Problem der Organisation' was issued by the OKW, over which Hitler has assumed personal control in February, on 19 April 1938, that is, shortly after the Fritsch-Blomberg affair had cleared some of the conservative underbrush out of the General Staff so that Hitler could implement his war plans unhindered. In it Clausewitz is quoted in support of the assertion that the soldier has no higher duty than to obey the dictates of the political command. 'If the assertion is advanced that one cannot demand of a Commander in Chief of the army that he conquer in accordance with a "foreign concept", then it should be recalled that we soldiers are all bound by the duty to conquer according to the political concept of the head of state . . . . To lead the complete war effort is the affair of the Führer and Reichskanzler.'[29] Similarly, in later disputes over Russian strategy, Hitler invoked Clausewitz to subdue his recalcitrant generals.[30]

What Hitler and the National Socialists did do was to take the *Formule* and, in combination with their new definition of politics and war, vitiate the distinction between the two, turning belligerence and peace, war and politics into one continuous whole. '. . . Clausewitz says that "war is the continuation of politics, although with different means",' Hitler told the Industrie-Klub of Düsseldorf in 1932. 'Conversely, Clemenceau thinks that today peace is nothing but the continuation of war and the pursuit of the war aim, though again with other means. In short: politics is and can be nothing other than the safeguarding of a people's vital interests with every means.'[31] It was no longer the distinction between politics and war which was of interest, but rather that which separated the 'political (diplomatic) and military (strategic) duties of the conduct of war', as Konstantin Hierl, Nazi military expert and later authority on labour policy questions, wrote as early as 1929.[32] Consequently, a duality of leadership, military and civilian, could not be tolerated. One man, alone responsible for the *Gesamtpolitik* of the day would secure for Germany its continued existence and prosperity. Where if in 1934 it was still possible to express doubts as to whether the complexity of modern political and military functions would ever allow the emergence of a new Alexander, Frederick the Great or Napoleon, later this position was specifically attacked and rejected.[33] Also Clausewitz was brought into line. The academic specialists were now quick to present the argument that, despite the common misconception, nothing in Clausewitz's thought indicates that war is in any way moderated or restrained by politics; on the contrary, war can only be fully pursued when assured of the complete support of politics.[34] 'In the current German fight for freedom, the German people . . . turns to Clausewitz, the German philosopher of war; for it has, admiringly and gratefully, experienced the unity of political combat and ingenious generalship in its Führer Adolf Hitler to an historically unique extent', the readers of a Clausewitz anthology were told.[35]

The unity of politics and war was, of course, closely linked with the concept of total war, which in turn owes much to a misuse of Clausewitz.[36] Employing the new National Socialist conception of politics, the following passage demonstrates the ease with which the transition from Clausewitz to total war was effected:[37]

> The primacy of politics over war is the axis around which Clausewitz's thought concerning war revolved.
>
> Thus Clausewitz had attained the peak of his conception of the uninterrupted nature of war . . . War is *one* side, peace the *other* of *an indivisible* historical reality . . . . Thus the liberal idea that war is an unfortunate interruption of peaceful conditions . . . was overcome. Only this overcoming brought forth for the first time, as a possibility, the character of the concept 'total war' as we know it today.

The nature of total war ideology was most succinctly described in the appendix to the OKW memorandum of 19 April 1938, entitled 'Was ist der Krieg der Zunkuft?':[38]

> War in its absolute form is the violent conflict of two or more states using all means.
>
> Despite all attempts to proscribe war, it remains a law of nature which may be checked but never eliminated, and which serves the maintenance of the people and the state or the assurance of its historical future.
>
> This high moral aim gives war its total character and its ethical justification.
>
> It lifts it above being a purely military act or a military duel for the sake of some economic advantage.
>
> Stakes, winnings and losses rise to hitherto unsuspected heights. Not only damage, but the annihilation of state and people threatens the loser of any war.
>
> Thus the war of today becomes a national emergency and a fight for survival for each individual.
>
> Since each person has everything to win and everything to lose, each must contribute the utmost.

The use of Clausewitzian terminology at the beginning was no coincidence. The great philosopher of war was hailed also as the prophet of total war and as a star witness for the accuracy of the assertion that, 'only those nations can maintain themselves which can and are determined to throw themselves completely onto the scales of war'.[39] Total war was thought of as the practical realization of absolute war, the overcoming of the 'modifications of reality'. Prompted by the strongest of motives, military and political goals coincided and utmost effort was to be expended in the attempt to destroy utterly the enemy that would not hesitate to do likewise. 'Already Clausewitz', Hitler confided to Horthy and Antonescu in 1943, 'had quite rightly labelled this uncompromising war of allies against a merciless enemy as the natural form of war and had distinguished it from those wars which are conducted like a joint-stock company, in which, instead of capital, one contributes 30,000 or 40,000 men. We must stake everything; we have everything to win or everything to lose.'[40] Early in 1945, Hitler described the war he had begun in terms which all but duplicate Clausewitz's account of the logical form of war: 'In a ghastly conflict like this, in a war in which two so completely irreconcilable ideologies confront one another, the issue can inevitably only be settled by the total destruction of one side or the other. It is a fight which must be waged, by both sides, until they are utterly exhausted . . . '[41]

The motivations of war, which Clausewitz had linked with its nature, were presented time and time again as absolute: life or death, complete victory or utter defeat as the only alternatives. The possibility of limited wars was abruptly dismissed. 'The time of cabinet wars and wars with limited political goals is over. They were often more like armed robberies than a struggle of profound moral justification as is the total war for the survival of a people.'[42] That Hitler should have thought of the alternatives only as life and death is perhaps not surprising late in the war.[43] But already in 1936 as he was unveiling the Four Year Plan to prepare Germany militarily, he argued that, 'the victory of Bolshevism over Germany would not lead to a Versailles Treaty, but to a final destruction, yes, extermination of the German people.'[44] It is also clear that his antisemitism, stemming largely from his belief that the Jew, as 'the mightiest counterpart to the Aryan', represented a most potent threat to the very existence of Germany, was closely tied to his conception of war, especially that against Russia.[45] But the Russians and the Jews were not the only ones who could force the issues to such extremes. When, at Casablanca, Roosevelt declared the allied war aim to be the unconditional surrender of Germany, Goebbels responded on 18 February 1943 with his infamous speech proclaiming the total war. 'Everyone knows that this war will destroy us all if we lose it. And therefore the people along with their leaders are determined to seize the most radical means of self-help.'[46] 'Unconditional surrender', Ernst Jünger, who knew a lot about the subject, wrote in his diary at the end of the war, '*that* is the counterpart to total war.'[47]

IV

While Hitler and the National Socialists were plundering Clausewitz's writings for their own purposes, others were making use of him for quite different reasons. The Nazis themselves intimated that Clausewitz's thought contained potentially subversive traits. 'The Führer has referred repeatedly to Clausewitz', one retired lieutenant-general whose hobby it was to reinterpret Clausewitz in the spirit of the new age assured his readers. 'Thus it is clear, in the battle over Clausewitz's heritage, that a supporter of Scharnhorst's gifted apprentice could not also be against Adolf Hitler.'[48] At about the same time, as Hitler was presenting the General Staff with his war plans and eliminating those members too conservative to back him, a German expatriate in Paris, Albert Schreiner, was pointing out the presence of a conflict within ranking German military circles between the Clausewitzians who continued to believe in the primacy of politics and its restraining influence and those who thought Ludendorff's reversal of Clausewitz correct. This latter faction he identified with the National Socialists. Although at the moment, he warned, the Clausewitzians still held their ground, the future boded a swing in the opposite direction.[49]

Others, outside of Germany, commented on the use of Clausewitz as a justification for the unprecedentedly belligerent nature of German foreign policy before the war, or used his ideas as an argument against the theoretical validity of total war ideology.[50]

More interesting, however, is the use to which Clausewitz was put by members of the internal German opposition, especially by Colonel-General Ludwig Beck, Chief of Staff of the Army from 1935 to 1938, but also by Karl Goerdeler, sometime Lord Mayor of Leipzig.[51] Both were participants in the assassination attempt of 20 July 1944 and perished in its aftermath. Conservative in outlook and intention, these two looked back to the days of Bismarck and his relations to Moltke for the ideal, traditional relationship of politics to war, wherein politics guided and restrained the otherwise directionless fury of unleashed martial energy. 'Only the failure of the political leadership during the last fifty years has made possible the fateful error of speaking of total war in the sense that in war any means are permissible', Beck and Goerdeler argued in a collaborative memorandum early in 1941.[52] Commenting on the failure of German foreign policy during the First World War in 1944 they observed that, 'A situation in which ever greater risks were taken was allowed to develop. Thus, in the face of the clear understanding of Clausewitz and the experiences of 1866 and 1870, war became total and the military leadership predominated.'[53]

In strict Clausewitzian fashion, they pointed out that, since war as such has no aim other than the destruction of the enemy, it can be no more than a tool in the political workshop. 'Wars may not be waged for their own sake', Goerdeler wrote in a memorandum from 1940. 'Even Moltke emphasized this; Clausewitz and all great statesmen have acknowledged it; reason and a sense of responsibility dictate it. The goal is always and alone an honourable and equal peace.'[54] 'For it is precisely the aim of politics', the two continued in 1941, 'flexibly to find and determine the right thing for each step of the development. Politics therefore do not grant the soldier every form of warfare; for example, it must be evaluated whether the effect at which destruction aims brings one closer to the considered and possible goal of an advantageous peace and its desired form and whether it serves to preserve this.'[55] Like many later commentators, Beck saw Hitler's conduct of the war in terms of an unrestrained, hypertrophied militarism. In a draft of his 'Aufruf an die Wehrmacht' from the fall of 1943, he wrote, in allusion to Bismarck: 'that leadership which no longer regards politics as the art of the possible and strives to attain its goal with the most sparing use of effort, but which revels in fantastic plans of limitless conquest, which recognizes no moral obligations whatsoever towards either its own people or towards others, can never arrive at peace with foreign nations.'[56]

With respect to total war, Beck has left behind a remarkable testimony to the various uses to which Clausewitz was put. In 1938 he had remained content with the charge that no one, however much a genius he might fancy himself, could, as the dictates of total war required, be a modern Napoleon, commanding both the military and political aspects of a future war. Two years later he set forth the usual opinion that Clausewitzian absolute war dominated military thinking and had found its realization and expansion in total war.[57] In June 1942, however, he delivered a lecture before the Mittwochsgesellschaft, a distinguished intellectual gathering of which he was a member, in Berlin. Here he attacked the Ludendorffian concept of total war and argued for a return to the diversity and therefore limitation of war in the sense that Clausewitz had depicted.

Whereas Clausewitz thought of absolute war as being an

abstract, philosophical concept, Beck accurately noted, Ludendorff and the other prophets of total war mistook this conception for a new form that war takes on in reality, one which excludes all other types of conflict. He suggested that Ludendorff diverged from Clausewitz in that, failing to understand the theoretical nature of absolute war, he attempted to impose this purely logical concept directly on reality. Of total war and Ludendorff, he said:

> With the creation of this new, exclusive concept, he is forced — to use the Clausewitzian expression — to extremes by moving in the abstract realm of pure concepts. These extremes are nothing but a play of ideas and prevent the return from abstraction to reality. Only through this return do the probabilities of real life replace the most radical and absolute aspects of the concept and only thus is the strict law according to which force must always tend toward the utmost invalidated for the entire military act.[58]

A very concrete manifestation of Beck's rejection of total war ideology may be found in his approach to the question of its motives. In a memorandum from 2 January 1940, he noted that in his New Year's address Hitler had told the army that the coming struggle would be a matter of life or death. To this Beck replied that, although Germany's position could and should be much improved in many respects,

> Neither our own situation, nor the desire of the people, nor our enemies force the German people into a struggle over existence or non-existence. In these circumstances, intentions to force, or beliefs that one is obliged to force, the German people through a fight for existence or non-existence, over matters actually or supposedly essential to its survival . . . can no longer be described with the vocabulary appropriate for politics and strategy and place themselves beyond the pale of the laws which govern these areas.[59]

Another, perhaps the most remarkable document on Clausewitz from this period, was left by the historian Gerhard Ritter who was a member of an anti-Nazi circle of conservative academics and theologians in Freiburg. Entitled 'Die Lehre Carls von Clausewitz vom politischen Sinn des Krieges', it was published in the 1943 volume of *Historische Zeitschrift*, the most important German historical periodical. Although his article seems at first glance to be but one of many similar scholarly contributions to the topic in question,[60] if read in conjunction with the arguments of this essay, its between-the-lines meaning suddenly becomes clear and quite a bit more interesting than the ostensible subject. For what Ritter did was to bring forth the themes discussed here and refute the Nazi interpretation of Clausewitz point by point. In strong contrast to the historical attitude quoted at the beginning of this essay, he rejected the tendency of each age to interpret Clausewitz after its own whims and insisted on going back to what Clausewitz himself meant.

If one considered only his early writings, Ritter granted, one might be led to interpret Clausewitz's *Formule* in the sense that is prevalent today:

> That politics is nothing but a continuous fight for power, that war is only the intensification of this with an admixture of violent means, that political and military aims are essentially identical: the overwhelming of enemy forces. According to this, the role of the leadership of the state in war would be determined in a purely military fashion, as the preparation of all material and spiritual means for the *Vernichtungskampf*.

This interpretation, however, he insisted, would represent 'an inadmissable modernization of the true Clausewitz'. Like Beck, Ritter emphasized the equal status which Clausewitz accorded to wars with limited goals and motivations, carried out with limited means. Similarly, he went back to a traditional interpretation of the moderating influence of politics: Clausewitz clearly states that political and military goals are not necessarily identical, and rather than assign to politics 'an ancillary and auxiliary role in war, he determinedly maintains its primacy . . . . Thus politics in no way appears as the intensifying element, but as the moderating.'

Turning to the question of absolute war, Ritter argued that, as a purely theoretical construct, this can never embody an actual political goal. The aim of war does not, without exception, always require the greatest exertion of force. Moreover, he continued, what Clausewitz meant by absolute war cannot without further ado be equated with modern *Vernichtungskrieg*. Not every war need be the catastrophe of total war:

> What Clausewitz does not see, or what in any case he will not allow, is the possibility of war, once it has broken loose, developing its own logic, . . . raging forth like an avalanche over all original war aims, over all wishes and considerations of politicians, like the First World War,[61] until it has destroyed not only millions of human lives, but also the possibility of any lasting European peace for generations. Clausewitz knows absolutely nothing of a 'total' conduct of war.

V

At the risk of ending on a sour note, one final group of Clausewitz's interpreters must be mentioned. This consists primarily of young academics who made their fortunes in the wake of the National Socialists without ever becoming mere propagandists. Sophisticated sycophants, they clearly recognized what was being done to Clausewitz, but, instead of objecting like Ritter even in so covert a fashion, they glossed over the problem with overly subtle distinctions and protestations that what was said was not also meant.

Karl Linnebach, for example, an *Oberarchivrat*, in 1934 cited — preposterously — Clausewitz as evidence for the statement that a *Vernichtungskrieg* aims at the destruction of the enemy state and 'in certain cases even the extermination of the enemy people'.[62] He then, however, went on to draw an acute and accurate distinction, occasionally neglected even by recent observers. He separated the conception of total war as the development of military technology and its increasing power and destructiveness from that conception of total war which was also Hitler's, by which the capacity to carry out the military aim is not synonymous with the decision to do so, in which the *Vernichtungs*-aim is a political decision. But, Linnebach hastened to add, as the National Socialist state holds the national rights of other countries in high regard, a *Vernichtungskrieg* is, for it, an impossible political goal. Similar is the case of another disputation on the nature of total war from 1937. The author understood perfectly well that, as the discussion stood at the moment, what was meant by total war was really *Ausrottungskrieg*, wherein peace is not honourably concluded with an eye to re-establishing an equilibrium of relations, but, as he said with a phrase that could have been lifted from Hitler's *Table Talk*, 'which one concludes on the grave of the enemy people in order to enslave the survivors'.[63] But this, the author was certain, although on what basis remains unclear, is a misunderstanding, and future wars will not be of this nature.

Walther Malmsten Schering, who made something of a career studying Clausewitz and, by adding doses of Nietzsche and Schopenhauer, concocting a murky intellectual brew called *Wehrphilosophie* for which he was appointed to a professorship in Berlin, is perhaps the classic example of this unappetizing species. He was conscientious and serious enough in his studies to realize and indicate that absolute war is merely a theoretical construct, that it should not be confused with total war, and that by *Vernichtung* Clausewitz meant nothing more catastrophic than *wehrlos zu machen*. Nevertheless, he made his peace with the problem of reconciling his knowledge of what Clausewitz had said to what he was being made to say through specious distinctions with which he separated the innocuous from the unpleasant and dismissed the latter as outside his domain. 'As with most catchwords, the expression "total war" includes too much and in this lies the danger', he wrote. 'For by it is understood that which belongs in the concept "natural war", that is, actual destruction or even extermination of a people due to a one-sided predominance of emotion and passion. It can hardly be assumed that this is what the European peoples want.'[64]

VI

The usual attempts to determine the intellectual origins of National Socialism, in particular the *Sammelsurium* of prejudices, *Lebensphilosophie* and snippets of fact, bound together by the glue of pseudo-scientific pretension that passed for a coherent view of things in Hitler's mind, take place in a manner which can perhaps best be described as an intellectual police line-up. As a row of suspicious, unpleasant, perverse or merely asocial thinkers squint and sweat under the blinding glare of arclights, historians, armed with a knowledge of Hitler's intellectual deviations, search their faces for tell-tale similarities. Nietzsche, Houston Stewart Chamberlain, Gobineau, Wagner and so forth have all been picked out in much this fashion and damned accordingly. Conversely, when attempting to rehabilitate any such figure, it has usually been necessary to argue at great length and with much subtlety that in his work can be discerned a certain core of thought which, when divested of its nebula of contradictions and reversals, may not rightly be confused with the misinterpretations foisted on it by the likes of Hitler. Such is the way, for example, in which Walter Kaufmann has rehabilitated Nietzsche. This may be a valid approach in some abstract sense, but it rests on a — for the historian — fruitless attachment to questions of timeless verity in favour of the misunderstandings, questionable associations and unjustified appropriations that characterize the thinking of those who shape the not so lofty aspects of the world. The *true* Nietzsche, the *essential*

Wagner, or whatever, cleansed of his sins, sits purified in the academician's heaven while his mortal coil is dismissed as of only secondary importance and left to the scavengers to rip apart.

Clausewitz has borne the brunt of both these efforts: damnation and rehabilitation. Neither is convincing, though not because the Nazis did not, in fact, misuse his thought or because Beck and Ritter did not tend to go back to the heart of his thinking. Clausewitz's ambiguity facilitated misinterpretation; it did not cause it. The problem is more fundamental. Those who had power did not learn from Clausewitz, but sewed his name like a fashionable label into their pirated, imitative intellectual vestments which would not have differed substantially in cut or quality had he never existed. Those who may have learned from him were not men in a position to have much effect: hesitant conspirators, incapable of acting until threatened with catastrophe; scholars writing for each other and posterity. Clausewitz, in other words, is not as important or interesting in this context and time as those who used him, the ways in which they did so and the reasons why. The really intriguing question concerns the extent to which this may be said of all similar figures.

NOTES

I am indebted to Ernest R. May and Agnieszka Kolakowska for comments and suggestions, both substantive and stylistic.

1. Walter Hauschild, 'Clausewitz. Ein Vermächtnis', *Offiziere des Führers*, 3 (1944), 23.
2. Random examples include: G. Reimann, *Germany. World Empire or World Revolution* (London 1938), 24; G. E. F. Boldt-Christmas, *Fraan Clausewitz till Liddell Hart* (Stockholm 1939), 33; P. Birdsall, *Versailles Twenty Years After* (New York 1941), 3, 304; G. Sava, *School for War* (London 1942), 24; H. Orb, *Nationalsozialismus* (2nd ed.; Olten 1945), 46-48.
3. Wyndham Lewis, *The Hitler Cult* (London 1939), 6.
4. B. F. Liddell Hart, *The Ghost of Napoleon* (New Haven [1934?]).
5. Johs. Nielsen, *Demokratiet og krigen. En undersøgelse af samspillet mellem demokrati, nationalisme og krigsførelse* ([Copenhagen] 1971), chap. VIII; J. F. C.

Fuller, *The Conduct of War 1789-1961* (New Brunswick 1961), 60ff; E. F. Szczot, *Die deutsche Doktrin des totalen Krieges*, Diss. Freiburg i.d. Schweiz (Vienna 1946), 15; J. Engel 'Der Wandel in der Bedeutung des Krieges im 19. und 20. Jahrhundert', *Geschichte in Wissenschaft und Unterricht*, 19, 8 (August 1968).

6. J. L. Wallach, *Das Dogma der Vernichtungsschlacht. Die Lehren von Clausewitz und Schlieffen und ihre Wirkung in zwei Weltkriegen* (Frankfurt/M. 1967), 57-58; G. Förster, *Totaler Krieg und Blitzkrieg* (East Berlin 1967), 60 ff. Also Raymond Aron, *Penser la guerre, Clausewitz* (Paris 1976), II, 92. In general on the entire topic, an excellent survey is Werner Hahlweg 'Das Clausewitzbild einst und jetzt', *Vom Kriege*, ed. W. Hahlweg (18th ed.; Bonn 1972).

7. W. R. von Schramm 'Zum Verständnis des Werkes', in *Vom Kriege*, eds. W. Pickert and W. R. v. Schramm (n.p. 1963), 258.

8. *Vom Kriege*, VIII.vi.B.

9. This point is made in Nielsen, op. cit., 168-169.

10. *Vom Kriege*, I.i.3. See also, very intelligently, on the relationship of absolute to real war in general, W. B. Gallie, *Philosophers of Peace and War* (Cambridge 1978), chap. 3.

11. For example: 'Just a century earlier, Clausewitz . . . had indoctrinated the Prussian Officers' Corps with exactly the same principles . . . . [H]e warned his pupils against attempting to disarm an enemy without *the maximum* of "blood-shed", begged them to avoid a "benevolent" spirit towards a stricken foe, dismissed all humanitarian restrictions on the conduct of war as "hardly worth mentioning", and denounced "moderation" in an officer as "an absurdity".' J. H. Morgan, *Assize of Arms* (New York 1946), 148-149.

12. Concisely on this very important development is P. Paret, *Clausewitz and the State* (New York 1976), 356 ff.

13. *Vom Kriege*, I.i.25. Also see H. Rothfels 'Clausewitz', in *Makers of Modern Strategy*, ed. E. M. Earle (Princeton 1943), 106.

14. *Vom Kriege*, VIII.vi.B.

15. Ibid.

16. W. Maser, trans. A. Pomerans, *Hitler's Letters and Notes* (New York 1974), 317. Two decades later, another group of Germans would seek inspiration in Clausewitz's life, but for quite different reasons. These Germans, banded together on Russian soil as the anti-Hitler, pro-Soviet group Freies Deutschland recalled Clausewitz's tenure in the Russian Army during his fight against Germany's enemies in the wars of liberation. See the 'Manifest des Nationalkomitees "Freies Deutschland" an die Wehrmacht und an das deutsche Volk' (1943?) in E. von Frankenberg, *Meine Entscheidung* (East Berlin 1963), 326.

17. A. Brügmann, *Staat und Nation im Denken Carls von Clausewitz*, Diss. Heidelberg (Heidelberg 1934), 90.

18. Reichsstelle zur Forderung des deutschen Schrifttums, *Die ersten hundert Bücher für nationalsozialistische Büchereien* (7th ed.; Munich 1934).

19. W. von Oven, *Mit Goebbels bis zum Ende* (Buenos Aires 1950), II, 204; 'Bekenntnis von der Ehre des Soldaten', *Was uns bewegt* (1943); 'Ein Clausewitz-Wort zur Beherzigung', *Wissen und Wehr*, 24, 11/12 (1943), 359; 'Kraft des Glaubens in schwerer Zeit', *SS Leitheft*, 10, 1 (1944), 3; 'Clausewitz über Beharrlichkeit im Kriege', *Militärwissenschaftliche Rundschau*, 9, 1 (1944), 56; A. Hitler, ed. M. Domarus, *Reden und Proklamationen 1932-1945* (Neustadt a.d. Aisch 1962), 2237.

20. W. Maser, *Adolf Hitler* (5th ed.; Munich 1973), 243.

21. A. Bullock 'Hitler and the Origins of the Second World War', *Proceedings of the British Academy*, 53 (1967), 275; Aron, op. cit., II, 77. Clear formulations of such a reversal may be found in B. F. Liddell Hart, *The Other Side of the Hill* (2nd ed.; London 1973), 295; A. Günther 'Staatsführung und Kriegswesen', *Militär-Wochenblatt*, 119, 21 (4 December 1934), 810; Vice-Admiral Groos, 'Fundamental Problems of Military Policy and Military Strategy', *Jahrbuch für Wehrpolitik und Wehrwissenschaft 1939*, quoted in W. Necker, trans. E. Fitzgerald, *Nazi Germany Can't Win* (London 1939), 13-14.

22. Edouard Calic, trans. R. Barry, *Unmasked. Two Confidential Interviews with Hitler in 1931* (London 1971), 48.

23. Fritz Willich, 'Clausewitz und der jetzige Krieg', *Militär-Wochenblatt*, 125, 1 (5 July 1940), 7. The Clausewitz quotation is from *Vom Kriege*, VIII.6.A.

24. Wallach, op. cit., 449. Conversely and, I think, rightly, see Hahlweg, loc. cit., 108.

25. E. Ludendorff, *Der totale Krieg* (Munich 1935), 10.

26. *Hitler's Secret Book*, trans. S. Attanasio (New York 1961), 7; Hermann Rauschning, *Hitler Speaks* (London 1939), 20.

27. *Mein Kampf*, trans. R. Manheim (Boston 1943), 533.

28. B. von Lossberg, *Im Wehrmachtführungsstab* (Hamburg 1949), 118-119. Similarly, OKW, *Kampf gegen die Sowjets* (Berlin 1943), 12. Compare W. Ehmer 'Weshalb sind Kompromisse unmöglich?', *Was uns bewegt*, 6 (1943), 11 and W. Kayser, *Die nationalpolitische Bedeutung der Wehrmacht* (Hamburg 1937), 6-7.

29. Doc. 211-L, International Military Tribunal, *Trial of the Major War Criminals* (Nuremberg 1949), XXXVIII, 39-42.

30. Paul Hagen, *Will Germany Crack?* (New York 1942), 150 ff. See also Major-General Nehring's complaint about Hitler's misunderstanding of Clausewitz during the Russian compaign, quoted in *Hitlers Lagebesprechungen*, ed. H. Heiber (Stuttgart 1962), 831, n. 4.

31. Hitler, *Reden und Proklamationen*, 69-70. This was echoed exactly by Goebbels a decade later in his speech on 30 September 1941, 'Politik und Kriegführung', in *Die Zeit ohne Beispiel* (Munich 1941), 590.

32. Konstantin Hierl, 'Politik und Strategie', *Ausgewählte Schriften und Reden* (Munich 1941), I, 113. See also Paul Schmitthenner, *Politik und Kriegführung in der neueren Geschichte* (Hamburg 1937), 9.

33. H. Metz 'Wehrpolitik und Wehrverfassung', in *Die Wehrwissenschaften der Gegenwart*, ed. F.v. Cochenhausen (Berlin 1934), 27; G. Scherff 'Die Einheit von Staatsmann und Feldherr', *Militärwissenschaftliche Rundschau*, 6, 3 (1941), 194-195.

34. W. M. Schering 'Clausewitz' Lehre von Zweck und Mittel', *Wissen und Wehr*, 17, 9 (1936), 607; 'Einleitung', in Clausewitz, *Geist und Tat*, ed. W. M. Schering (Stuttgart 1941), xxv.

35. W. Falz, 'Zur Einführung', in Clausewitz, *Politisches Soldatentum*, ed. W. Falz (3rd ed.; Berlin 1944), 12.

36. See especially, Hans-Ulrich Wehler, ' "Absoluter" und "totaler" Krieg. Von Clausewitz zu Ludendorff', *Politische Vierteljahresschrift*, 10, 2/3 (September 1969); Berenice A. Carroll, *Design for Total War* (The Hague 1968), chap. 1.

37. Hauschild, loc. cit., 28.

38. IMT, XXXVIII, 48.

39. Horst von Metzsch, *Der einzige Schutz gegen die Niederlage. Eine Fühlungnahme mit Clausewitz* (Breslau 1937), 8-9; Metzsch, *Zeitgemässe Gedanken um Clausewitz* (Berlin 1937), 5.

40. Quoted as a *freundliche Mitteilung* from Paul Carell by Norbert Krüger 'Adolf Hitlers Clausewitzkenntnis', *Wehrwissenschaftliche Rundschau*, 18 (1968), 471.

41. *The Testament of Adolf Hitler*, ed. F. Genoud, trans. R. H. Stevens (London 1961), 103-104.

42. Ludendorff, op. cit., 6.

43. For example, Hitler's speech, after the final defeats at Stalingrad, read by Goebbels in the Sportspalast on 30 January 1943, where he says that this war will not leave behind it victors and the vanquished, but only survivors and the annihilated. *Reden und Proklamationen*, 1978-79.

44. 'Denkschrift Hitlers über die Aufgaben eines Vierjahresplan', *Vierteljahreshefte für Zeitgeschichte*, 3, 2 (April 1955), 205.

45. *Mein Kampf*, 300; Eberhard Jäckel, *Hitlers Weltanschauung* (Tübingen 1969), 79 ff.

46. *Goebbels-Reden*, ed. H. Heiber (Düsseldorf 1971-72), II, 186.

47. Ernst Jünger, *Jahre der Okkupation* (Stuttgart 1958), 111.

48. Horst von Metzsch, *Clausewitz Katechismus* (Berlin 1941, copyright 1937), 4.

49. Albert Schreiner, *Vom totalen Krieg zur totalen Niederlage Hitlers* (Paris 1939), 45 ff.

50. *Hitler treibt zum Krieg. Dokumentarische Enthüllungen über Hitlers Geheimrüstungen*, ed. Dorothy Woodman (Paris 1934), 41 ff; Joseph M. Goergen, *Mensch, Staat und Krieg* (New York 1940), 94.

51. This is the hobbyhorse of Wilhelm Ritter von Schramm, who has repeated his argument in several places: 'Von der militärischen zur politischen Verantwortung. Was Generaloberst Beck von Clausewitz gelernt hat', *Zeitschrift für Politik*, n.s. 5, 4 (1958); 'Wege und Unwege der deutschen Kriegstheorie', *Revue militaire générale* 8 and 10 (October and December 1960); 'Generaloberst Beck und der Durchbruch zu einer neuen deutschen Wehrtheorie', *Aus Politik und Zeitgeschichte. Beilage zur Wochenzeitung 'Das Parlament'*, 8 (21 February 1962).

52. 'Das Ziel', in *Beck und Goerdeler. Gemeinschaftsdokumente für den Frieden 1941-1944*, ed. W. R. v. Schramm (Munich 1965), 85.

53. 'Der Weg', ibid., 178-179.

54. 'Denkschrift zur Kriegs- und aussenpolitischen Lage', ibid. 265.

55. 'Das Ziel', ibid. 85.

56. 'Aufruf an die Wehrmacht', in Gerhard Ritter, *Carl Goerdeler und die deutsche Widerstandsbewegung* (Stuttgart 1954), 606.

57. 'Betrachtungen über den Krieg' and 'Deutschland in einem kommenden Kriege', in L. Beck, *Studien*, ed. H. Speidel (Stuttgart 1955), 61, 121.

58. 'Die Lehre vom totalen Kriege. Eine kritische Auseinandersetzung', ibid., 241. It is interesting to note the resemblance between Beck's criticism of Ludendorff and National Socialist conceptions of total war and Hannah Arendt's brilliant and still eminently useful insight into the nature of totalitarian ideology in general: 'An ideology is quite literally what its name indicates: it is the logic of an idea . . . . The ideology treats the course of events as though it followed the same "law" as the logical explanation of its "idea".' *The Origins of Totalitarianism* (New York 1973), 469.

59. 'Denkschrift', in Helmuth Groscurth, *Tagebücher eines Abwehroffiziers 1938-1940*, eds. H. Krausnick and H. C. Deutsch (Stuttgart 1970), 497.

60. It was in fact reprinted with only minor changes in chapter 3, volume I of his *Staatskunst und Kriegshandwerk* (Munich 1959), English translation, *The Sword and the Scepter* (Coral Gables 1969).

61. The later version, not surprisingly, adds the Second.

62. K. Linnebach, 'Zum Meinungsstreit über den Vernichtungsgedanken in der Kriegführrung', *Wissen und Wehr*, 15, 11 (1934), 743. Here a comparison with arguments possible before the Nazi accession to power is instructive — for example, Günther Gründel 'Die Krise des Vernichtungsgedankens in der neuzeitlichen Kriegführung', *Militär-Wochenblatt*, 117, 7 (18 August 1932), who argues that not *Vernichtung* but only ' "painless" disarmament' can be the goal of future wars.

63. Hans-Heinrich Ambrosius 'Zur Totalität des Zukunftkrieges', *Wissen und Wehr*, 18, 3 (1937), 187-188.

64. W. M. Schering, *Wehrphilosophie* (Leipzig 1939), 241; 'Clausewitz' Lehre von Zweck und Mittel', 613. Also, in general, his *Die Kriegsphilosophie von Clausewitz* (Hamburg 1935).

III

The Darkest Hour

The dismissal of Britain's army minister four months after the outbreak of the war has never been satisfactorily explained before. Major-General Trythall shows that it was not the result of incompetence, or opposition against certain reforms, certainly not violent strategic disagreements but, above all, a matter of personal grievances: the fear that the minister would replace senior officers of the British Expeditionary Force in France. The incident shows that there was little teamwork and less leadership in the conduct of the war at the time. The popular notion that there was in the US unanimous and overwhelming readiness to help Britain at the time of its greatest peril in summer 1940 is challenged in Mr Haglund's article. Many members of the Roosevelt administration were violently opposed to the policy of draining America of military hardware for supplying Britain and 'no top official was more convinced of the lack of wisdom in sending increased aid across the Atlantic than the Chief of Staff, George C. Marshall'.

Louis de Jong once pointed out that the real life in the countries of Occupied Europe was between the two extremes of collaboration and resistance. Dr Hirschfeld shows that while there was little collaboration (in the Quislingian sense) in the Netherlands, there was certainly co-operation and attentism in 1940-41 and the Dutch populace was prepared at the time to accept the political consequences of the defeat.

6 Collaboration and Attentism in The Netherlands 1940-41

Gerhard Hirschfeld

The publicity which surrounded the bizarre case of the Amsterdam businessman and art-collector Pieter Nicolaas Menten[1] shed some sidelight upon one of the darkest pages of recent Dutch history: the collaboration of certain groups of the Dutch population with the German occupying power and the follow-up during the *Zuiveringen* (purges) after the war, when judicial action was taken against thousands of collaborators.[2]

The verdict of the Czech historian Tomás Pasák, that every fascist has inevitably been a collaborator, but that not every collaborator has been a fascist,[3] is of course also valid with regard to the Nazi occupation of the Netherlands and the reaction of the Dutch populace towards it. But it is exactly here that the problem begins. As far as fascist ideological collaboration is concerned — mainly supported and carried out by the *National Socialistische Beweging* (National Socialist Movement) under its leader Anton A. Mussert — the case seems quite obvious. For collaboration with the occupying power was regarded as an *ultimate objective*, either as a long-term and unlimited co-operation with Germany or as a total absorption into a future Germanic empire which would be newly created under the auspices of Himmler's SS.[4] All the same, I consider it debatable whether a linguistic distinction should be made, as suggested by Werner Warmbrunn, Louis de Jong et al., between the 'collaborator' as the non-Nazi or non-fascist, and the 'traitor' as a member of a fascist organization,[5] since such a differentiation is almost exclusively orientated to an ethical system of values, which can only be a hindrance to a critical analysis of the unquestionably diverse motivations.

But how shall the phenomenon of collaboration be dealt with? It seems to me that one should attempt to indicate the specific motives behind the individual collaboration, as well as behind the cooperation between the populace and the occupying power, and the forms which it took. At the same time, one should try, as far as possible, to take into account the functionality of certain modes of behaviour, especially their impact on the social system of an occupied country.

The use of the rather neutral term 'co-operation' here as a synonym for the concept of 'collaboration' with its political, ideological and moral overtones, makes it clear that the term 'collaboration' will by no means only be restricted to extreme forms of individual and collective behaviour, but will apply equally to the necessary day-to-day arrangement, to what has been called the 'unwilling adjustment'.[6] Given this framework, collaboration should be understood as every form of rapprochement or arrangement in a system of domination (based on the actual or any possible military occupation) whereby different degrees of collaboration emerge from the various possible relationships between the occupiers and the occupied.[7]

The supposed special position of the Netherlands within the Nazi sphere of rule and power, in accordance with a racially determined political conception (which, however, in the long run tended rather to reduce considerably the political tolerance level) creates, in addition, the necessity of placing the collaboration in the continuous sphere of tension between the political and ideological claims of the occupying power and the actual occupation policy. An assessment of collaboration without dealing thoroughly with the concepts and forms of fascist rule would, inevitably, be incomplete. Thus the following emerges: a history of collaboration by the populace of a country is always simultaneously a history of the occupying power; a study of collaboration as such would be pointless. Nowhere, with the possible exception of the fascist parties, is this more obvious than in the founding and development of the *Nederlandse Unie* (Netherlands Union). In the summer and autumn of 1940, an attempt was made by a popular patriotic movement for solidarity and unity to introduce a new political orientation, by eliminating the still formally existing parliamentary system. This, however, was doomed to failure from the moment the occupation authorities realized that the leadership of the Union, although in line with National Socialist intentions on certain programmatic points, was far removed from adopting or submitting to National Socialism.

All previous attempts to establish a gradual modification in social behaviour during the occupation were determined by considerations — mostly ethically motivated — in which collaboration and resistance were seen as opposite poles. According to many authors, this choice outweighed all other considerations in the mind of the population. In his foreword to Werner Warmbrunns' study, Louis de Jong, without doubt the most distinguished scholar on the history of the Netherlands during the second world war, asserts: 'the real life of people of occupied Europe lay between the two extremes of collaboration and resistance'.[8] What should not be forgotten, however, is that at least during the first months of German occupation in the Netherlands this 'pair of opposites' did not present an adequate 'either — or'.

During the first phase of the occupation, the majority of the Dutch populace was prepared to accept the political consequences of the military events and, on the basis of the new power structure, to agree upon a modus vivendi with the victors, for the sake of maintaining peace and security. The willingness to co-operate with the Nazi occupation authorities was given expression primarily by representatives of the conservative bourgeoisie who would have liked to combine with it a revision of the traditional Dutch state and social system. This attitude, which was strongly marked in the emergence of the Netherlands Union could be characterized by a term which was created after the French capitulation in June 1940, that of 'Attentism'. Several French contemporaries have maintained that the openly confessed willingness to submit to German rule already constituted collaboration and have thus considered 'Attentism' and 'collaboration' as one and the same thing. Thus Albert Fabre-Luce writes in his *Journal de la France 1939-1944:* 'L'attentisme déclaré, c'était, virtuellement, l'acceptation de l'occupation intégrale. La collaboration, c'était le véritable attentisme.'[9]

In contrast to this, I see 'Attentism', as far as the Netherlands are concerned, as a condition thoroughly characteristic of the first phase of occupation, in which not only the essential elements of the subsequent collaboration were formulated, but also the determining factors for a later resistance were established. As regards administrative and economic collaboration, collaboration by social groups and organizations, including various parties, there is an abundance of evidence for this. However, attentist behavioural patterns in these fields are superseded at a very early stage by original motivations, inherent in the individual institutions and organizations. An example of this is the 'New Order' discussion amongst Dutch economists and civil servants (i.e., collective 'Reorientation' to the realities in Europe created by the Reich, dismantling of a hyper-national economic system, new spheres and methods of production, reorganization of the social system, restructuring of the administrative spheres after the removal of the political controlling authorities). This discussion was ultimately dominated by fear of economic and social chaos, and concern for the maintenance of industrial production and jobs, even though the original causes of political attentism continued to play their part.[10]

In the summer of 1940, a mere two and a half months after the German occupation of the Netherlands, there emerged a collective movement of a magnitude and kind never before experienced in Dutch history. Now this raises the question: why did it emerge at that particular time and what were the decisive conditions for its formation? It seems that there were four reasons for the emergence of this popular mass movement, the Netherlands Union, each of which individually only partially explains the formation of this collective movement, but which, taken together, provide the essential conditions for its appearance:

1. The external condition, incorporated in the concrete plans of the occupying power, for establishing a popular 'collaboration movement'.
2. The lasting political and social tensions in the Netherlands. Criticism of the parliamentary democracy and the fact that it no longer had any function.
3. The sudden presence of an alternative ideology. Longing for identity when faced by a widely-felt threat and at the same time overcoming the pre-war social segmentation.
4. An alternative to the actual defensive action. Defence against native fascism since fighting the German enemy was no longer possible.

Before officially taking office, the newly appointed *Reichskommissar* in the Netherlands, Artur Seyss-Inquart, had two audiences with Hitler (19 and 25 May), during which he was put in the picture regarding the Führer's ideas for a 'New Order' in the *Reichskommissariat Niederlande* and the basic principles of the policy to be pursued. Hitler's decision to appoint a *Reichskommissar* must be considered in conjunction with his appointment, a month earlier, of a *Reichskommissar* for Norway; it reflected a certain amount of improvisation and also Hitler's desire to have a free hand with regard to future developments.[11] In his First Report, which was presented to Hitler on 23 July 1940,[12] Seyss-Inquart formulated his instructions again, pointing out that they consisted of 'securing public order and public life for the protection of the Reich's interests'; then he specified the political mission bound up with these instructions 'of economically linking the Netherlands as closely as possible to the Reich, but at the same time preserving their formal independence in order to maintain control over the Dutch-Indian areas'. This could be achieved most readily 'if we succeed in formulating a series of political objectives which make an economic link with the Reich seem to be the will of the Dutch people'.[13]

The *Reichskommissar* was well aware of the difficulties and contradictions which were, of necessity, fundamental to such an undertaking. The interests of the occupation force demanded on the one hand 'the complete suppression of all possible forms of public activity'; on the other hand it was desirable, 'in order to awaken and manoeuvre the political objectives, to allow such freedoms as will make the end result a decision which the Dutch have made themselves'. By his own definition, the task would have to be considered as accomplished when the adhesion of the Netherlands to National Socialism and the German Reich was accepted as an autonomous and unforced act on the part of the populace. The cautious tactics of the occupation authorities in the first months were thus determined by the desire to create a broad basis as quickly as possible from which to assist the breakthrough of the concept of 'self-nazification'.[14]

Seyss-Inquart and his four *Generalkommissare* were agreed that this would be impossible either with the support of the small fascist *Nationaal-Socialistische Beweging* (NSB) or with the help of any of the other fascist splinter parties. The NSB, which had been constantly rejected under the 'Accusation of Treason' and was despised by the majority of the Dutch people, was admittedly to be further built up, but at this stage Seyss-Inquart expected nothing from re-shaping this party with the active (or rather passive) assistance of the German authorities.[15] The main objective was a Dutch concentration and revival movement which would win over a large section of the populace for 'political collaboration' on the basis of an induced free-will. The conditions for such an internal political development seemed not unfavourable to the head of German administration, since, as Seyss-Inquart wrote in his First Report to Hitler, he had the impression 'that the Dutch people had emerged from their political reticence' and that 'the general as well as the political interest in the Reich was increasing'.[16]

The military victories of the German Wehrmacht over Denmark, Norway, the Netherlands and Belgium, the retreat of the defeated British at Dunkirk (4 June) and the surrender of France (22 June 1940) had an enormously strong psychological impact on the people in the conquered and occupied countries of Western Europe. The atmosphere there was overwhelmingly characterized by hopelessness, confusion and a deep feeling of helplessness resulting from the conviction that the war was 'over', that the Germans had achieved a 'final and total victory' and — on a rather more individual level — that the thing to do now was to draw the necessary political conclusions by recognizing this fait accompli.[17]

This attitude, which the Dutch historian J. S. Bartstra has characterized by the term 'Pétainisme',[18] referring to the head of Vichy-France, was primarily supported in the Netherlands in the summer of 1940 by a representative of the protestant-conservative bourgeoisie, the five-times Prime Minister and leader of the orthodox Calvinist 'Anti-revolutionary' party, Dr Henrij Colijn. After two vain attempts to co-operate with the occupying power on the possible establishment of a 'provisional' government,[19] Colijn finally, at the end of June, committed to paper his ideas on future collaboration between the Netherlands and the German Reich, as a sort of provisional credo.

The former Prime Minister no longer had any doubts that the continent of Europe, 'since a defeat of the Germans is no longer possible, will in future be led by Germany'. 'Germany and Europe are an entity which in the foreseeable future will not be divided.' The consequence for the Netherlands is this: '. . . [In this Europe] we will have to accept a German instructor on political, economic and social questions, even if this means that we have to copy him'. As far as Colijn was concerned, the only way of maintaining relative independence for the Netherlands and the Royal House was for them to do without a foreign policy of their own and to co-operate closely with the German Reich on economic matters. Over and above that, it would be necessary to modify certain national establishments and institutions in accordance with the German model. From the political point of view, he considered that the only way to enter into the necessary direct negotiations with Germany was to create a concentrated national movement, a so-called 'National Front', whose representatives would be empowered to speak on behalf of the Dutch people ('*namens een overweldigende meerderheit van het nederlandse volk*').[20]

This leaflet, which gained wide-spread distribution in the Netherlands causing a 'great sensation',[21] was not the only statement during the summer months which was understood by large sections of the population as a signal that they should adjust their political attitude to the new conditions, or at least 'come to terms with the new situation'.[22] Looking at the various pamphlets and programmes which appeared in those weeks, something remarkable can be found. Besides the desire to maintain the highest possible degree of national sovereignty in a Europe dominated by Germany, the intention of re-structuring the Dutch state and social system now became the driving force in the question of an arrangement with the occupying power.

Criticism of the parliamentary democracy and its lack of function had already been expressed before 10 May 1940 and was not only characteristic of anti-democratic and fascist groups. The dissatisfaction amongst the middle classes, but also amongst the working class, resulted primarily from the unresolved crises of the thirties, the general lack of leadership and the unhealthy party-political and social segmentation of the country.[23] Particularly in the strongly Catholic south, small bourgeois discussion groups formed which had set themselves the task of overcoming the social and political segregation, the *hokjesgeest* of the Dutch people, replacing the 'out-dated' parliamentary system by a non-party, conservative-authoritarian form of state and society. One such group was formed in 1937 in Noord-Brabant, *Brabantia Nostra*, which aimed at a corporative state system, based on Catholic ideas of morality. Another was Groning-Community which was active in North Holland and pleaded its cause in an emphatically trans-confessional, socio-political fashion.[24]

In addition, there were a number of individual agitators such as the young catholic politician and university lecturer, C.P.M. Rommé, who was fighting for a parliament constructed according to corporations and a stronger position for the Queen which would enable her to act — if the need be — against the interests of the parliament. At the beginning of the thirties, the Middelbourg sociologist, P.J. Bouman, leaning distinctly on National Socialist ideas, had already called for 'new ideals, a new way, and renewed national consciousness' for the Netherlands. Referring to Max Weber's criticism of the work of the German Reichstag, he declared that in the Netherlands too 'the parliamentary system is disintegrating' and recommended, to prevent 'the petrification of the party system', the establishment of a corporative state, which would have to be run on the basis of 'general interest before group interest' and rigorous 'withdrawal from class warfare'.[25]

The powerlessness of the government when faced with defeat during the 'tragic days of May 1940', and the helplessness with which it agitated, initially from exile in London, were regarded in these circles as 'merely the final proof that the arteries of the political party system were hardening'.[26] The victory of National Socialist Germany over the democratic Netherlands was not only the result of a failed and wrongly implemented policy of neutrality. It was also — in the opinion of the critics of the parliamentary system — a result of this wrongly conceived democracy.

This basic questioning of the democratic parliamentary system and the pleading for a society constructed along authoritarian lines were very much in accordance with the ideological intentions of the Nazi occupying power, and increased the *Reichskommissar*'s hope of provoking those leading personalities, 'with whose help an inconspicuous nazification might be achieved'. However, Seyss-Inquart's attitude to the statements of Colijn, Brouwer et al., which were doubtless intended for the ears of the occupying power, was reticent. The significance for him of a Colijn, whom he considered to be 'ready for action' and a personality strikingly different from the 'uniformity' of the political party leaders, but also 'craving admiration', was 'potential rather than actual'.[27] For in the meantime, Seyss-Inquart's objective, a Dutch solidarity and revival movement, had taken on definite contours, without the help of the 'system parties' he despised.

The 'Netherlands Community' (*Nederlandse Gemeenschap*), which made its first public statement in June 1939, was also part of the extra-parliamentary, conservative protest movement of the late thirties. It too saw itself as an answer to the established parties, which were considered to have failed to deal with 'national issues' and also in their attempt to overcome the lamentable social segmentation in Dutch society. In the view of many of its members, the political parties could in any case be regarded as 'vieux jeu', as Mr H. J. Reinink, the then chairman of the *Nederlandse Gemeenschap*, tried to characterize it after 1945.[28]

It was predictable, therefore, that only a month after the Dutch capitulation, and without the knowledge of the parliamentary parties, its leading representatives should make overtures to the *Reichskommissar*, in the hope of developing from a small non-parliamentary organization into a large-scale unitary movement. This leading group, from which the leadership of the Netherlands Union, the so-called 'Triumvirat' (*Het Driemanschap*), was later to come, consisted of its chairman, Reinink, department chief in the Education, Culture and Science Ministry; the former Royal Commissioner in the province of Groningen, Mr Johannes Linthorst Homan; the Government Commissioner for employment organization and lecturer at the School of Economics in Tilburg, Professor Jan Eduard de Quay, and the Chief Commissioner of the Rotterdam police, Louis Einthoven.[29]

Meanwhile, attempts to reach agreement with the chairman and floor leaders of the six major parties in the pre-war parliament concerning a common national movement had failed because of the divergent intentions of those involved. The party leaders (including Colijn, who in the meantime had been reprimanded by his political friends) saw in a wide-spread unification movement the possibility of replacing the parliament (which in fact no longer existed) by a new representative authority which, they hoped, would be recognized by the majority of the Dutch people as their legitimate representative, and accepted by the occupation authorities as a political opposite number.[30] The representatives of the 'Netherlands Community', however, saw in what was now called a 'National Solidarity and Concentration Movement', an unexpected opportunity to convert their ideological objectives into reality, without having to consider parliamentarianism which they altogether rejected.

Armed with a manifesto previously approved by Schmidt, the German Commissioner for Special Affairs (*Generalkommissar zur besonderen Verwendung*), in which there was no mention of the retention of the monarchy (which the party leaders had declared to be essential), nor a word about the re-establishment of national sovereignty, the 'Triumvirat' turned to the Dutch public. Now — going by the tone of the statement — it was a question of 'recognizing the changed situation', and together with the national authorities and the occupying power 'of striving for a new Dutch feeling of solidarity' which would enable the nation to accomplish the tasks which lay ahead.[31] The 'Programme' of the new movement (which was announced at the end of July) also did nothing to make the objectives of the self-appointed 'Triumvirat' more explicit, nor did it provide a more precise definition of their relationship with the occupying power. The *Nederlandse Unie* which —

according to the preamble to the statement — 'was founded at a difficult hour in the history of our fatherland in order to gather all Netherlanders to work for the conscious reinforcement of the fatherland and the community of the people' (!), has set itself 'the task of securing and strengthening the unity of the people in the political, cultural and socio-economic spheres'. 'In full awareness of reality' (!) and in a 'loyal relationship' with the occupation authorities, the *Unie* wanted to go about its work — no mention of how this relationship must look in view of a situation which in reality many of the Netherlanders considered as highly oppressive.[32]

As far as its political objectives were concerned the 'Programme' spoke only of a 'strong Dutch nation, closely linked with the regions abroad' (i.e. the colonies in the Far East), which 'under the leadership of a powerful and decisive authority' should organize itself in 'organic construction'.

This 'organic construction' or corporativism, as propagated by the Union leadership, emerges, on closer examination, as a conglomeration of very diverse ideas and concepts. Its kinship with the significant standpoints of the Catholic social doctrines of the twenties and thirties is certainly unmistakable and there is more than one direct reference to the Encyclical of Pius XI (*Quadragesimo anno*) and to corresponding adherent publications of the Catholic Employers Organization and of the Roman Catholic Trade Union (*Rooms-Katholiek Werkliedenverbond*).[33] But even political ideas which seem at odds with this objective were simply incorporated and given a quasi new relevance by means of such attributes as 'Dutch' and 'Corporative'. Thus the authors of a later paper on theoretical premises declared that in its Dutch variety, socialism could only be realized and completed by 'the formation of a corporative order'.[34] The proponents of the 'Corporative Ideas' did not even recoil from using unmistakably National Socialist terminology, as proved by the uninhibited use of 'socialist folk community' (*Volksgemeenschap*). Critical objections from Union members were countered by pointing out that such ideas 'must necessarily find their own form in each country, because every country and every people has its own national character. . . . And of course a Netherlander is not a German. He is not less, nor more, but he is different, fundamentally different.'[35]

Despite the vague and ambivalent formulations and the fact that the Royal House was not mentioned, the challenge of the Union leadership met with wide approval amongst the public. Above all, by means of a propaganda and recruitment campaign carried out in August 1940, the membership of the new organization reached proportions previously unkown in the Netherlands. In the first two weeks 25,000 members had already joined, who, in accordance with the organization's statutes had to be eighteen years of age and prepared to pay a minimum subscription of 50 cents per year. By the middle of October, a mere two months after its founding, the Union already had half a million members and in February 1941 as many as 800,000 Dutch people had joined (out of a population of approximately eight million).[36]

The organizational framework of the new 'unity movement' was able to keep pace with this development only with the greatest difficulty, but thanks to the great commitment of numerous members, contact offices and co-ordination posts (*Secretariaaten*) could soon be found in almost all the cities in the country. At the same time numerous 'councils' were formed on a provincial and local level, on which Dutch people, whose previous party-political affiliations were most divergent, came together. Admittedly, the function of these 'councils' within the organization was purely as a means of communication, but as regards the self-sufficiency of the Union, and the internal process of opinion-forming they were, precisely because they comprised such diverse elements, of a significance which should not be underestimated. The weekly newspaper *De Unie*, published for the first time at the end of August 1940, became an important link between the Union leadership and the grass-roots. After three months its circulation was already 200,000 copies, of which five out of six were sold on the street by the so-called 'Union-colporteurs'.[37]

The reasons for the development of the membership of this most heterogeneously-structured mass organization are extremely varied. Undoubtedly large sections of the bourgeoisie were convinced that by supporting a non-party 'unification movement' they would overcome the much-lamented political and social fragmentation. The vast majority of its supporters, however, considered the Union as an opportunity to express their 'anti-German, but even more their anti-NSB sentiments' — as one local official put it.[38] The 'flood of members from all classes of the population, including members of those parties whose leaders had advised against joining the Netherlands Union, was also carefully registered by the German intelligence services.[39] What did it result from? Firstly, a widespread desire to express dissatisfaction with recent political events, which up to then had only been channelled publicly to a most inadequate degree. Secondly, the possibility of creating a platform on which to give massive representation to the longing for national identity, particularly in view of the increasing powerlessness of the former parliamentary parties. Thirdly, the fact that all this was tolerated by the occupation authorities; in other words, it could be done without endangering personal safety or existence.

Unaware of the negotiations that had preceded the founding of the Netherlands Union, many of its members initially shared the hopes (which were fostered by suitable statements from the leadership) that the continually demanded 'loyal co-operation' with the occupying power would guarantee far-reaching self-sufficiency and independence for the country and, in addition, prevent the feared seizure of power by the much hated Mussert-movement, the NSB.

The relationship of the Union and its members to the NSB requires closer consideration. In September 1940, Mussert had been received by Hitler. In the Netherlands, the Berlin visit by the leader of the NSB was seen as a sure sign that a national fascist government, with Mussert as Prime Minister (following the example of Vidkun Quisling in Norway) was soon to be 'called'. The decisive rejection by the Union of a possible NSB rule ('The NSB is un-Dutch'; 'the Dutch people will not accept the NSB'; 'we refuse to believe that the NSB will manage to come to power with the help of the German authorities, since these have declared that they do not want to question Dutch values [!]'), was regarded by the Dutch public as demonstrative proof that the new 'unity movement' had 'declared war' on the native National Socialist party.[40] Membership of the Union was at the same time — and the leadership were at pains to give this suitable emphasis — a passionate rejection of the NSB. The first physical confrontations between the colporteurs of the weekly newspaper *De Unie* and uniformed members of the fascist *Weer Afdelingen* (Defence Troops) also contributed to the fact that, according to the German security reports, '90% of the lower officials and the vast majority of the members of the Union considered that they were building a dam against Mussert's NSB'.[41]

However, there were also those within the officials' camp who considered partial co-operation with the NSB and with another extreme right-wing party (Arnold Meijer's clerical-fascist and extremely anti-semitic *Nationaal Front*) possible and even desirable. In the autumn of 1940 sporadic contact was made between the

Union and the NSB, but this was far more a result of the initiative of individual lower officials than part of an official rapprochement strategy by the Union leadership, especially as it was only Linthorst-Homan within the 'Triumvirat' who expressed a possible willingness to have discussions with the NSB.[42] Homan and some of his colleagues doubtless reflected that only some kind of link between the NSB or individual groups from its camp and the 'unity movement' could, in the long run, establish the claim of the Union leadership to be the strongest political force in the Netherlands. However, permanent rivalries between the two organizations would not only increasingly sap their strength, but also provide the occupation authorities with an opportunity — and there was enough evidence for this — of playing off one 'movement' against the other and thus of using them to further their own ends.

Interestingly enough, the ideas of the Homan faction coincided with corresponding plans made by the German *Generalkommissar* Schmidt. The representative of the NSDAP in the Netherlands was convinced that the development within the 'unity movement' (the 'wild growth' which, due to the expansive development in membership, could now scarcely be controlled) could only be channelled along ordered lines by incorporating the organization into a common front with the NSB and other fascist groups. Continuing pressure-tactics (raids, temporary arrests) would also make it clear that the occupation authorities were no longer prepared to tolerate even the most minimal acts of independence, unless it had been established that the purely instrumental character of the undertaking was in accordance with the German occupation policy.

The competition between the Netherlands Union and the NSB for the favours of the occupying power, which now in fact existed despite the failure of Schmidt's idea, forced the Union leadership into an increasingly blackmailable position. The fact that the Union was formally open to Jews and that some of its members had taken part in illegal activites became a long-term weapon which could, at any time, be used by the Germans against the movement. Obviously, the thing to do was to escape from this potential 'position of weakness', in order to be less impeded when dealing with the occupation authorities.

In January 1941 the leadership of the Union issued several statements warning members against joining underground activities; four months later Jews were excluded from full membership.[43] Other measures seemed comparatively less significant: right from the start of the Netherlands 'Winter Help', this organization enjoyed financial as well as moral support from Union officials, as did the (at the time still voluntary) Dutch Labour Service.[44] Despite all these efforts, the relationship between the Union and the German authorities was far from cordial.

The 'loyal co-operation' with the occupying power, so often propagated by the Union, had been shown to be an empty cliché right from the start and indeed there was not even agreement within the 'Triumvirat' about it. As far as the majority of the members were concerned, these requirements by the leadership were seen as only of tactical value, in so far as it secured for the Union a relative degree of protection against the German measures. For the occupation authorities, on the other hand, it opened the door to all possible sorts of political interference and manipulation. The discrepancies in objectives and in ideas about their own political role between the officials and the members inevitably became obvious and led to conflict when neither the expected approval from the German administration was forthcoming, nor was there any further agreement on the degree of compromise necessary to cope with the evident division regarding internal and external policies.

The strike in Amsterdam in February 1941 and the ruthless and brutal reaction of the German police,[45] signified not only a caesura in the history of the occupation, but had a catalytic effect on both camps. In front of NSDAP officials, the *Reichskommissar* finally bid farewell to all plans for national solidarity and called instead for a radical policy of 'for or against us'.[46] At the same time, even amongst the Union leadership, support was growing for the view that further concessions would be wrong and that the gauntlet should be thrown down.

Five days after the German invasion of Russia, on 27 June 1941, at a mass meeting in Amsterdam (organized jointly by officials from the *Reichskommissariat* and the NSB), Seyss-Inquart called upon the Dutch people ('Netherlands, look to the East') to take part in the fight against the Russian 'Monster state' in this 'common European task'. An end must be finally put, he said, to 'all establishments and political ideas which, being retrogressive, stand in the way of new developments'[47] — an undisguised reference to the Union. The Union leadership, however, was not prepared to join the 'Crusade' against Bolshevism just like that. On 3 July 1941, the 'Triumvirat' made a very carefully prepared statement, agreed upon in advance with other leading officials: 'Together with

Dr Seyss-Inquart, the Dutch people are convinced that Bolshevik rule in Europe would mean the end of European culture. However, the situation in which our people find themselves makes it quite impossible for us to take up a stance regarding a war between Germany and Russia. Such a decision can only be made in complete freedom and by our own government.'[48]

The 'own government' was the Dutch government-in-exile in London which was just in the process of joining the alliance with the Soviet Union, in accordance with the policy of its British protectors. The proclamation by the Union leadership (to which Linthorst-Homan had also agreed without reservation) was received with surprise and delight amongst the membership. Within this choir, however, worried voices could soon be heard who expected a ban on the Union any day. It was certainly to be several months before the *Reichskommissar* had the 'unity movement' dissolved, but serious constraints and drastic restrictions on its activities meant that officials and members no longer had any real basis on which to work. On 13 December 1941, the same day on which the fascist splinter parties were banned, the *Reichskommissar* also dissolved the Netherlands Union by way of decree. On the following day, Anton Mussert's NSB was declared the only party still recognized.

The *Nederlandse Unie* is a quite unique phenomenon in the history of the Netherlands and even during its existence opinions as to its political function varied considerably. The historical assessment and evaluation remains equally controversial even today. Recent interpretations have stressed in particular the 'catalytic effect' on the traditional party system and on political thinking at that time. Ger van Roon has tried to see the function of the Union as similar to that of the 'German Christians' in giving rise to the formation of the 'Confessional churches' (*Bekennende Kirchen*) in Nazi Germany.[49] Roon's comparison sounds impressive but it is only appropriate to a certain extent, since it proceeds from false premises. It should be borne in mind that the recognizable 'catalytic effect' was qualified by the heterogeneity of the movement and its adherents. For it was just the former true followers of the respected parties who now joined the Union en masse and turned out to be its most active members. On the other hand, the party leaders failed to offer any effective alternative. Their divergent assessments concerning Union policy and half-hearted rejection of Union ideology proved totally inadequate.[50]

In his fundamental history of *The Netherlands during the Second World War*, Louis de Jong points to the differences existing between the leadership and the mass of Union members, whose intentions were often, as he defined it, 'diametrically opposed'. According to de Jong, the 'Triumvirat' and other leading officials were convinced for a long time that 'loyal collaboration' with the occupation authorities would create favourable preconditions for an internal re-structuring of the Netherlands and was essential for the success of their own fight against the only other serious contender for power, the NSB. The people, however, the mass of the members and lower officials, soon found themselves in a 'common defence front' against the NSB and the occupying power.[51]

Certainly these opposing views are a fundamental component of the phenomenon of the Netherlands Union. On the other hand, such an antagonism — ethically motivated and exaggeratedly formulated — between the 'false' (*foute*) objectives of the leadership, even if they varied in intensity and personal commitment, and the 'correct' (*goede*) attitude of the grass-roots, who in fact turned the leadership's actual intentions into the exact opposite, raises further questions. In view of the far-reaching differences, why was there never any serious conflict within the 'movement', apart from a leadership crisis at the end of January 1941, which was resolved relatively quickly? Was it merely political naivety which caused Union supporters to accept without resistance the appeasing statements and concessions which higher Union officials directed towards the occupation authorities?

We have established that a decisive element in the attraction of the Union in the late summer and autumn of 1940 was, for many members, the prospect of filling the existing political vacuum which had become apparent with the (partly forced, partly self-inflicted) withdrawal of the established parties and trade unions. This had not only enabled them to give expression to the newly-awakened national consciousness, but also provided massive opposition to the ambitions of the NSB — which indeed for many of the members was one and the same thing. The leadership did not lose the opportunity of turning this line of attack to their own advantage and of pointing out the necessity for a strong national force to overcome the current difficulties. At the same time, however, virtually no opportunity presented itself for them to prove their reliability to the German occupation authorities and for presenting themselves as the only party in the Netherlands which should be taken seriously, and which also, moreover, had a considerable number of members at its disposal. This self-imposed dual role, in which the motivation should be taken quite seriously, makes both the initial success and the later failure of the Union quite understandable. In the same proportion as the 'Triumvirat' gained the trust of the members, it lost the interest of the *Reichskommissar*. While the mass of its supporters was even prepared to regard rather dubious statements and actions on the part of the leadership as necessary and unavoidable 'camouflage', as far as the *Reichskommissar* was concerned the 'unity movement' was a write-off from the moment it refused to agree to every single step the occupying power was going to take. Even the pressures which the German authorities put on the leadership, in the hope of still being able to divert the Union onto the desired course, no longer had the expected success and indeed often created (quite intentionally) waves of solidarity amongst those concerned.

In spite of this, however, the German measures did not release the leading officials of the Union from the self-inflicted vicious circle of increasing political corruption. The concessions and compromises before and even after the strike of February 1941 are clear evidence of this. However, the critical intensification of the domestic political situation due to the Amsterdam strikes and the increasing pressure caused by the military-political events in Europe accelerated the clarification process, which by now had become overdue, not only amongst the Union supporters, but in the relationship between the occupation authorities and the Union leadership.

Corresponding to this dualism in political behaviour, the basic ideological premises also show a characteristic ambivalence. The ideas of the Union on a new authoritarian, non-party order, on a corporate basis, as the conception for an independent state in the Netherlands after the occupation were to become elements in a later conservative resistance, just as, at the time, they seemed, to some extent, to be an opening for the nazification objectives of the German masters. The inability of the 'corporationists' to develop any real definition of or concrete meaning for their ideas, which would have made them clearly distinct from national socialist and fascist concepts, left them highly vulnerable to the prophets and agents of precisely those concepts. The fact that there was no final ideological rapprochement between the occupying power and the Union seems then to have been caused less by those elements opposed to radical fascism in corporate thinking than by simple lack of interest on the part of those already firmly in power towards a programme proclaimed by a 'movement' that had turned into an uncalculated risk, since it could possibly infringe upon their claims to unlimited rule.

NOTES

1. Besides the coverage of the Menten case by the daily press, see (despite some grave mistakes and wrong assessments) the summarizing article by Reuben Ainsztein, 'The Collector', *New Statesman* 13, 20 and 27 February 1981.

2. Still the best account of the purges is in Henry L. Mason, *The Purge of Dutch Quislings. Emergency Justice in the Netherlands* (The Hague 1952).

3. Tomáš Pasák, 'K problematice česke kollaborace a fašismu za druhé suětové války', in *Přispěvky k dějinám fašismu v Československu a Madarsku* (Bratislava 1969), 134; also quoted in Hans Lemberg, 'Kollaboration in Europa mit dem Dritten Reich um das Jahr 1941' in K. Bosl (ed.), *Das Jahr 1941 in der europäischen Politik* (Munich/Vienna 1972), 152.

4. For SS policies towards the Netherlands see the excellent edition compiled by N.K.C.A. In't Veld, *De SS in Nederland. Documenten uit SS-Archieven, 1935-1945*, 2 vols. (The Hague 1976).

5. Werner Warmbrunn, *The Dutch under German Occupation, 1940-1945* (Stanford, Calif./London 1963), 272-75; Louis de Jong, 'Zwischen Kollaboration und Résistance' in *Das Dritte Reich und Europa* (Munich 1957), 141, though it should be mentioned that de Jong does not maintain this differentiation in his momentous history of the Dutch under German occupation *Het Koninkrijk der Nederlanden in de Tweede Wereldoorlog*, 10 vols. (The Hague 1969-80).

6. De Jong in his Foreword to Warmbrunn, op. cit., v.

7. See my forthcoming book on *Die Kollaboration mit der deutschen Besatzungsmacht in den Niederlanden während des zweiten Weltkrieges*, esp. ch. 1.

8. Foreword to Warmbrunn, op. cit., v.

9. Albert Fabre-Luce, *Journal de la France 1939-1944* (Paris 1969), 511-12.

10. Cf. ch. V of my forthcoming book (n.7).

11. Cf. Konrad Kwiet, *Reichskommissariat Niederlande. Versuch und Scheitern nationalsozialistischer Neuordnung* (Stuttgart 1968), 46-61, 92-109.

12. Artur Seyss-Inquart, 'Erster Bericht über die Lage und Entwicklung in den besetzten niederländischen Gebieten, Berichtszeit 29. Mai bis 19. Juli 1940', *International Military Tribunal* (*IMT*), Vol. XXVI, Doc. 997-PS, 413-29.

13. Ibid., 413.

14. A.E. Cohen, 'Opmerkingen over de notitie van dr. De Pater over het doel van het Duitse civiele bestuur in Nederland' in A.H. Paape (ed.), *Studies over Nederland in Oorlogstijd*, Vol. I (The Hague 1972), 50-51; also Kwiet, op. cit., 93-94.

15. Seyss-Inquart, op. cit., 416.

16. Ibid., 424.

17. Thus Paul Struye (the post-war Belgian Minister of Justice) in *L'évolution du sentiment public en Belgique sous l'occupation allemande* (Brussels 1947), 17.

18. J.S. Bartstra, 'Vergelijkende Stemmingsgeschiedenis in de Bezette Gebieden van West-Europa 1940-1945', *Mededelingen der Koninklijke Nederlandse Akademie van Wetenschapen*, Afd. Letterkunde, Nieuwe Reeks, Deel 18, No. 6, (Amsterdam 1955), 9-14.

19. Cf. de Jong, *Het Koninkrijk*, Vol. IV, 1, 414-15.

20. H. Colijn (Minister van Staat), *Op de grens van twee Werelden* (Amsterdam 1940), 43-53.

21. Rijksinstituut voor Oorlogsdocumentatie (RvO), Amsterdam: Archiv Höherer SS- und Polizeiführer (HSSPF), SD-Meldung No. 3 (6 July 1940).

22. Seyss-Inquart, op. cit., 425.

23. The sociological term for this segmentation is *Verzuiling*; cf. J.P. Kruijt and W. Goddijn OFM, 'Verzuiling en Ontzuiling als Sociologisch Proces' in A.N.J. den Hollander et al., *Drift en Koers* (Assen 1962), 227-63; also H. Daalder, 'The Netherlands: Opposition in a Segmented Society' in R.A. Dahl (ed.), *Political Opposition in Western Democracies* (Yale 1968), 188-236.

24. Cf. A.A. de Jonge, *Crisis en Critiek der Democratie. Anti-democratische stromingen en daarin levende denkbeelden over de staat in Nederland tussen de wereldoorlogen* (Assen 1968); also F.J.H.M. van der Ven, *Economische en sociale opvattingen in Nederland* (Utrecht 1952); H.W. von der Dunk, 'Conservatisme in vooroorlogs Nederland', *Bijdragen en Mededelingen* 90 (1975), 13-37.

25. P.J. Bouman, *Het Socialisme aan de Tweesprong* (Zutphen 1933); id., *Structuurcrisis en National-Socialisme in Nederland* (Zutphen 1935).

26. J. Rogier, *Katholieke herleving. Geschiedenis van Katholiek Nederland sinds 1853* (The Hague 1956), 565.

27. Seyss-Inquart, op. cit., 415.

28. For the pre-war history of the Netherlands Union see the semi-official study by J.J.H.A. Bruna, 'De Nederlandse Unie', Ms. 1966 (RvO, Amsterdam).

29. The biographies of the 'Triumvirat' are covered by de Jong, *Het Koninkrijk*, Vol. IV, 2, 512-19; cf. the (rather uncritical) memoirs by L. Einthoven, *Tegen de strooming* (Apeldoorn 1974) and J. Linthorst-Homan, *Wat zijt ghij voor een vent* (Assen 1974); also P. Geyl, 'De Quay in 1940 en De Quay in 1959', *Nederlandse Figuren* 2 (Amsterdam/Antwerpen 1962), 105-18.

30. Cf. the article by the post-war Prime Minister and former floor leader of the Social Democratic Party, Willem Drees, 'Uit de Voorgeschiedenis van de "Nederlandse Unie" ' in *Onderdrukking en Verzet. Nederland in Oorlogstijd*, Vol. II (Amsterdam/Arnhem 1950), 76-91.

31. 'Manifest aan het Nederlandsche Volk' (24 July 1940) in de Jong, *Het Koninkrijk*, Vol. IV, 2 (Nr.52).

32. 'Het Programma van de Nederlandsche Unie' (27 July 1940), RvO, Amsterdam: CNU I (1048).

33. Circular 'Betreft: De Corporatieve Orde' (20 November 1941), RvO, Amsterdam: CNU I a (1114).

34. Circular 'Grondslagen van de Nederlandsche Unie' (17 September 1941), RvO, Amsterdam: CNU I a (998).

35. Ibid.

36. For the organizational structure, see Bruna, op. cit.; de Jong, *Het Koninkrijk*, Vol. IV, 2, 824-28.

37. Bruna, op. cit., 51-52.

38. J.G. Suurhoff, 'De Nederlandse Unie en haar betekenis voor de bevrijdingsstrijd' in *Onderdrukking en Verzet*, Vol. II, 98-99.

39. RvO, Amsterdam: 'Informationsbericht' No. 41 (3 September 1940) of the Dept. 'Sonderfragen' at the *Generalkommissar z.b.V., Referat 73 d*; SD-Meldung No. 16 (8 October 1940).

40. *De Unie*, 14 September 1940, 3.

41. RvO, Amsterdam: 'Stimmungsbericht' No. 3 (29 January 1941). Dept. 'Sonderfragen'.

42. Cf. de Jong, *Het Koninkrijk*, Vol. IV, 2, 833-37.

43. *De Unie*, 18 January 1941; circular letter to 'Union' secretariats (12 December 1940), circular letter to 'Union' secretariats (31 May 1941), RvO, Amsterdam: CNU Ib I (741).

44. *De Unie*, 23 November 1940; circular letter to 'Union' secretariats (24 January 1940), RvO, Amsterdam: CNU I (34).

45. Cf. B.A. Sijes, *De Februari staking, 25-26 Februari 1941* (The Hague 1954).

46. Seyss-Inquart's address to a meeting of the 'Arbeitsbereich der NSDAP in den Niederlanden' on 12 March 1941 in Artur Seyss-Inquart, *Vier Jahre in den Niederlanden. Gesammelte Reden (1940-1944)* (Berlin/Amsterdam 1944), 45-53.

47. Seyss-Inquart's speech at the Museumsplein (Ijsclubterrein) in Amsterdam on 27 June 1941, in ibid., 92-93.

48. *De Unie*, 3 July 1941, 1 ('Waar wij staan').

49. G. van Roon, *Protestants Nederland en Duitsland* (Utrecht 1973), 300.

50. Cf. for the reactions of the traditional parties during the Nazi occupation, J.J. Bolhuis, 'De Politieke Partijen' in *Onderdrukking en Verzet*, Vol. II, 7-23; W. Verkade, *Democratic Parties in the Low Countries and Germany* (Leiden 1965), 199-203; de Jong, *Het Koninkrijk*, Vol. IV, 2, 556-64.

51. de Jong, *Het Koninkrijk*, Vol. IV, 2, 553; Vol. V, 1, 220-21.

7 The Downfall of Leslie Hore-Belisha

Major-General A J Trythall

The dismissal of the army minister of one of the chief belligerents only four months after the outbreak of the second world war, and before its armed forces had been involved in any serious hostilities, has never been satisfactorily and fully explained. Such a divisive and popularly unexpected event must surely have been brought about, it would seem not unreasonable to suppose, by some great clash of strategic or political principles or some swelling upsurge of revolt against incompetence or bad judgement, particularly as the minister in question had successfully held office since 1931, had been in the Cabinet since 1936 and at the War Office since May 1937, and was extremely well-known to and popular with the press and the average man. The most widely-held contemporary journalistic view, particularly on the left, was that Hore-Belisha had been sacked as a consequence of a plot hatched against him by senior army officers who resented his measures of military reform and democratization. Hugh Cudlipp in the *Sunday Pictorial* went so far as to claim that because Hore-Belisha promoted Gort over the heads of sixty other men, a 'small clique of brass-hats and aristocrats to whom Chamberlain so weakly surrendered resolved to intrigue Belisha out of his job'. 'The public will not stand for this abject surrender by Chamberlain to the high-caste brass-hats. You haven't heard the last of Hore-Belisha or of his miserable mean dismissal', he most unprophetically concluded.[1] Only the *Daily Worker* believed that the whole affair was one of principle, claiming that Hore-Belisha was dismissed because he opposed the opening of a 'second front' in Finland against the Soviet Union.[2] Many other reasons, of great variety, were put forward by the press. It is a fact, however, that after his replacement by the conservative Oliver Stanley, son of Lord Derby, there were few changes of policy or organization at the War Office until the débâcle of May 1940, so perhaps neither principles, incompetence or judgement were at the heart of the matter. On the other hand, although some of his reforms related to terms and conditions of service in a regular rather than a conscript army, and so were not of so much interest in wartime, there was never any serious attempt, either during or after the war, to turn the clock back — indeed many of the reforms were welcomed in the officer corps as well as in the ranks — only, of course, a silent re-emergence in places of the more traditional military values based on the regimental system and the public school.

If, therefore, his dismissal was not primarily the result of a reaction against reform or incompetence, or of violent strategic or political disagreements in the War Office or the Cabinet, it is important to discover just why he was dismissed, particularly as the answers may deepen our understanding of such a complex institution as the British Army and of its relations with its political masters.

Many explanations have been put forward since those early ones in the newspapers of January 1940 but none of them fits all the known facts with any completeness or rings wholly true. Minney, in *The Private Papers of Hore-Belisha,* concludes that in addition to creating great opposition to change, Hore-Belisha also aroused the enmity of those officers he passed over, and of the military generally, because of his energetic interventions in military affairs, his search for publicity and his occasional inconsiderateness and impatience.[3] Alastair Buchan believed that a contributory factor in Hore-Belisha's fall was Chamberlain's preference for Cabinet solidarity over departmental vigour coupled with a series of chinks in the Hore-Belisha armour — among them his race, his bounciness, his deafness to the criticism his energetic methods aroused, his lack of reverence for 'high brass' and Churchill's jealousy once in office.[4] Michael Foot, on the other hand, believed that the forces which got him out were military snobbery, obscurantism and intrigue.[5] General Sir Ronald Adam, Deputy Chief of the Imperial General Staff under Hore-Belisha and subsequently a corps commander in the BEF and Adjutant General, puts it down to a clash with Gort and Ironside mainly on personality grounds but also to a reaction against his interference in tactics and strategy.[6] He does not believe that there was any formal conspiracy. Chamberlain himself denied this and stated that no general had ever taken the initiative in complaining to him or 'asking directly or indirectly that he should be moved. The friction is due entirely to personal incompatibility, and not policy or administration.'[7] Lord Woolton thought he had political ability but 'had little knowledge of how to encourage people in the work they were doing'.[8] Major-General J. C. Haydon, once his Military Assistant, believed that differences of character and attitude to life split Hore-Belisha and Gort, and that Hore-Belisha's readiness to consult outside experts such as Liddell Hart did not help.[9] Hore-Belisha obviously felt a need to prove himself at frequent intervals.[10] Colville was convinced that the Pill Box affair 'would have done no more than ripple the tea in the cup of a more popular S of S, but it became the occasion for unleashing the pent-up dislike which most senior soldiers, many civil servants and latterly a number of Ministers felt for Hore-Belisha'.[11]

Before his dismissal is examined further it will be helpful to consider the origins and background of the man himself, the broad outline of his life and career and some salient points about the military and political background against which he had to play his dramatic role as Secretary of State for War. A brief analysis of his personal virtues and failings and his achievements in office will then lead on to a closer examination of the Pill Box affair which actually led directly to his dismissal. It will then finally be possible to offer, tentatively, a fuller explanation of his downfall than has hitherto been attempted, although one which must remain essentially a hypothesis until much more research has been carried out than the author has yet been able to undertake and until Hore-Belisha's own papers become available.[12]

Isaac Leslie Hore-Belisha was born in London in 1893. His father's family were Sephardic Jews driven from Spain under the inquisition, who eventually founded a cotton import firm in Manchester. His father died when Hore-Belisha was a baby. His mother, a very dominating person and an important influence in his life, sent him to Clifton where he entered Polack's House in 1907. Polack's House was entirely Jewish — a creation of Rothschild, among others, in 1877. Polacks didn't go to Chapel of course — the Chapel outside which is the statue of Haig, himself an Old Cliftonian, like Birdwood and Montgomery-Massingberd. Other Old Cliftonians included Hugh Elles, the Master-General of Ordnance Hore-Belisha sacked, Inskip, his first Minister for the Coordination of Defence, Venning, his Quarter-Master-General,

Bonham-Carter, once Governor of Malta, Hobart, whom he allowed to be removed from the post of Director of Military Training, and Morgan the planner.

At school he became quite a useful house rugby player, a three-quarter who was difficult to bring down once he had got into his stride, a strong attacker, but weak at 'collaring'. He could not get into the school team because, being a Jew, he could not play on saturdays. *Polack's House Magazine* reported prophetically in its 1908 winter number that he could 'play with plenty of dash when he chooses and what he chiefly wants is a better knowledge of the game'.[13] He also sprinted well, played cricket and was a witty speaker. However, he 'spoke more than he listened'[14] and was on the stout side for a boy. He had a lot of quarrels and good manners were not his strong point.[15]

He left Clifton in 1912, went to Paris and Heidelberg and in 1913 went up to St John's to read law. He became a Major in the ASC but early in 1918 was invalided out after serving in France and Greece. Back at Oxford he became the first post-war President of the Union and then went into journalism as a social and political columnist. In 1923 he won Devonport as a Liberal; in 1931 he organized the Liberal Nationals and brought them over to the government, achieving minor office himself and in 1932 became Financial Secretary to Chamberlain at the Treasury. In 1934 he became Minister of Transport where his reforms, which he pushed through with flair and energy, included the institution of the famous beacons, driving tests, the highway code and silent zones. In 1937 Chamberlain gave him the War Office, but the wilderness followed in 1940 until his death in 1957. He married Cynthia Elliott in 1944, but had no children and she left him in 1956. He was made a baron in 1954; he left his fortune, such as it was, to his two secretaries.[16]

The military scene into which Hore-Belisha was thrust by Chamberlain as principal actor in May 1937 was one in which resistance to mechanization and modernization, against which Fuller had fought with only very modest success,[17] had at last broken down in many quarters but which still lingered in the minds and attitudes of many of those officers who regarded the army as one of the last bastions of a disappearing social system and way of life. The mechanization issue was linked with the continental commitment and conscription and it is probable that support for a substantial commitment and conscription was motivated in part by a desire to have a large unmechanized army. There were, of course, numbers of others who were dedicated to change and reform.[18]

The regimental system was of vital importance and great strength, and spread its ramifications far beyond the ranks of serving officers. Teeth Arm regiments and corps were of course very powerful. For instance, from 1904 to the present, all Army Councillors (or Board Members) have been Infantry, Cavalry, Tanks, Gunners or Sappers and of those 23.3 per cent have been Gunners, whereas all but seven of the twenty-one Sappers have been Masters-General of Ordnance or Quarter-Masters-General and of the mere four Tank Corps/Regt. men only one was Chief of the General Staff and one Adjutant-General. But even among the Teeth Arm regiments there has been a certain selectivity; for instance the only English infantry regiments, excluding Foot Guards and the Light Division, which produced a Chief of the General Staff, were the West Yorks (who produced the very officer Hore-Belisha sacked!) and the Royal Warwickshire regiment who produced Monty (who outdid Hore-Belisha with his democratizing) — unless you count Slim as a Warwick. No Welsh regiment has ever done so. The Light Division (of all sorts) have on the other hand had five Chiefs of the General Staff, three Adjutant-Generals, five Quarter-Masters-General and one Vice-Chief of the General Staff. Some Infantry regiments have never produced an Army Councillor.[19] Hore-Belisha therefore was taking on a pretty select and powerful group of men.

It is also important to realize that the close-knit regimental structures, within which officers began their military lives, provided excellent informal communications networks because officers left the regiment to fill staff and command appointments outside it or became politicians, but obviously kept in touch with their friends. In late 1939, for instance, the Grenadier Guards, which happened to contain some of the principal figures in the Hore-Belisha affair, had Gort in post as Commander-in-Chief British Expeditionary Force, the Earl of Munster, Hore-Belisha's Under Secretary of State from February to September 1939, by his side as one of his ADCs, Colonel Fraser as Military Attaché in Paris and Major-General Beaumont-Nesbitt, who had been Brigade Major in the brigade in which Gort commanded a battalion in 1918, as Director of Military Intelligence in the War Office. In addition to this the King's private secretary, Major Sir Alexander Hardinge, was a Grenadier.[20] On top of that, Major-General Pakenham-Walsh, Engineer-in-Chief in the BEF, had been the CIGS's Brigadier

General Staff when the latter was GOC Eastern Command.[21] At one time, on a visit to France in 1937, Hore-Belisha, never particularly discrete, actually chose Beaumont-Nesbitt to question about the Army Councillors he later sacked. Beaumont-Nesbitt naturally told Gort, the new Military Secretary, all about it when he next visited England.[22]

Another aspect of the military setting which ought to be borne in mind is that whereas in many government departments the minister quite properly, through and with the advice of his civil servants, directs and manages operations, things are different in a service ministry in which the minister normally takes military advice on purely military matters or simply does not become involved in them. It is not always easy, of course, to determine what is, and what is not, a purely military matter, but Hore-Belisha wanted to direct and manage everything on the principle that if something went wrong on the battlefield his head would roll. A more commonly accepted view would be that the Secretary of State cannot be held responsible for military failure if he acts with military advice. In neither the first nor second world war did the Army Council direct operations. This was generally the responsibility of commanders, the Chiefs of Staff, the War Cabinet and the Prime Minister. Grigg, for instance, when Secretary of State later in the war, dealt with administrative matters but left operations alone.[23]

In a short article there is only space to make one or two vital points about the political setting which has in any case been analyzed and described a hundred times. The first is that Chamberlain's inner cabinet contained no ex-officers and had no feel for or understanding of the military. Chamberlain himself seems not to have understood generals, his conservatism had its roots in Birmingham rather than broad acres. Perhaps this is why he saw no incongruity in appointing a clever, ambitious, publicity-seeking Jew to the War Office in the first place. Hore-Belisha had an open mind, drive, energy and ability. What more suitable man could there be to get things moving when rearmament was beginning? Indeed, at first Chamberlain was delighted and wrote to his sister: 'My new S of S is doing what I put him there for and has already stirred the old dry bones up till they fairly rattle'.[24] The second point is that Hore-Belisha's political strength stemmed from his management of the Liberal National move in 1931. In 1935 the number of Liberal Nationals returned to the Commons was only thirty-two and by 1940 they were politically irrelevant and Hore-

Belisha therefore had no power-base. The third point is that another rising star, Winston Churchill, may have been jealous of Hore-Belisha, his one substantial competitor for popular appeal; Hore-Belisha, in addition, had probably offended Churchill over his handling of the 'Sandys Storm' in which the young TA Second Lieutenant Duncan Sandys, Churchill's son-in-law, and an MP, was hounded for putting down a question in the Commons allegedly based on classified information. Hore-Belisha could have avoided so much public trouble by seeing Sandys before the question was asked, and it also seems that he may not have told the whole truth about being unable to avoid a Court of Enquiry.[25] In addition Liddell Hart found out that the classified information had been distributed to all twenty-four units in 1AA Division.[26] Even these three points are enough to indicate that Hore-Belisha's political position was unsound.

However, he certainly had strong points as a minister.[27] He was a brilliant speaker, a warm and engaging personality, a go-getter and a persistent driver, a master of the unconventional or indirect approach, a patriot and a man of moral and physical courage, not a great intellect but an original with a flair for imaginative gestures and for public relations. He also had personal weaknesses. He was extremely self-centred and had a fine conceit of himself. At times he was accused of sharp practice as, for instance, over his very late comment at the Army Council meeting of 24 November 1939, when Pakenham-Walsh was leaving the room, that his remarks about 'the shortage of pill boxes were of course in no way meant as criticism of the C-in-C. All he wanted was to give him all possible help in the strengthening of his defences.'[28] He was accused of having this comment added to the minutes, and this is what Gort believed, but in fact he had said earlier at the meeting that he wished 'to do everything possible to help the C-in-C', and Pakenham-Walsh later admitted that Lieutenant-General Collins, the Controller Engineer Services, who was also present, told him subsequently that as Pakenham-Walsh left the room Hore-Belisha had said that the message he was taking to Gort 'was not meant to cast aspersions on the C-in-C'.[29] This incident is one of the almost unbelievable convolutions of the Pill Box affair which will be outlined later. Sharp practitioner or not, Hore-Belisha's quickness of mind and tongue, and transparent ambition to be seen to succeed, made him vulnerable to smears. He certainly sought publicity and most of the senior officers regarded this as beneath contempt

— reporters should, many believed, actually be horse-whipped.[30] He affected a flamboyance of dress which was aesthetic to say the least and the decor of his house in Stafford Place was not in the robust English taste. It is difficult actually to imagine Viscount Gort having to watch 'Belli', as he called him, eating breakfast there.[31] Another of Hore-Belisha's failings was his over-assertiveness which led him to appear inconsiderate of the feelings and views of others. He thought, in particular, that he could deal with generals; as early as November 1937 he told Liddell Hart that 'soldiers seemed to revel in each other's misfortunes' because he had heard Knox, then Adjutant-General, chuckling over Elles's removal as Master-General of the Ordnance.[32] A fortnight later he told Liddell Hart that he would sack Knox a week later and added: 'These soldiers took such a delight in each other's downfall that it was not difficult to deal with them separately'.[33] Above all, though, he was unable to perceive accurately enough the boundaries of his legitimate area of activity and authority. He made the mistake of believing that being Minister of War was much the same as being Minister of Transport and, of course, it was not. The army was to some extent a state within a state, with a complex and fiercely reverenced and cherished system of sub-loyalties within it. Senior soldiers could not be ordered about with impunity, and particularly not on matters within the heartland of tactics, command and *la vie militaire*. Moreover the Army Council was not a board of directors or even a cabinet. Hore-Belisha never really understood and accepted his constitutional and social limitations — and because in his heart he felt he did not belong (in a sense Polacks were worse than grammar school boys) he had to prove himself anew every day — and this increased his unacceptable assertiveness. On the other hand, he made a good point for himself when he told Liddell Hart in March 1938 that he was 'painfully impressed at the way so many senior soldiers seemed to regard the army as a matter of their personal interests instead of thinking what services they could render'. He was 'ready to go to any office for which he was detailed'.[34] Of course, in the end he was not ready, but for a very different reason. In the end he chose the wilderness.

His achievements, often initiated in the first year of office at the persistent behest of Liddell Hart, were, up to the outbreak of war, mostly wholly admirable — at least when he steered clear of attempting to influence or formulate strategic policy which he did not often understand — but many of them upset numbers of influential people. He turned the Army Council, and its two subordinate committees which he created, into effective tools of management.[35] He retired very senior officers when he considered them ineffective or unsuitable (this involved him in sacking three Army Councillors at the end of 1937), made enormous improvements in other-rank terms and conditions of service, barracks and recruiting, reformed and doubled the size of the territorial army, merged the posts of Master-General of Ordnance and Director-General of Munitions Production, instituted time-promotion to major, succeeded in having a Ministry of Supply established, and, after some flirtation with Liddell Hart's dislike of the continental commitment, succeeded in organizing a field force. In addition he had conscription introduced, organized anti-aircraft defence, set up conferences of higher commanders and made plans for the amalgamation of Sandhurst and the Royal Military Academy, Woolwich, which bore fruit after the war. These are a selection of his more important achievements at the War Office but many more could be added. The times were ripe, of course, for reform, because government and nation were very rapidly coming to accept the necessity for rearmament; some of the changes and developments had already been in train or were the brain child of others, including Liddell Hart and Churchill; it was, nevertheless, Hore-Belisha's vision and energy which had them adopted and implemented. He could have gone a lot further, of course, in theory, and he was not as strong for mechanization and the employment in key positions of officers recommended by Liddell Hart as the latter would have wished,[36] but in terms of practical military politics he went very far indeed, very quickly, perhaps further and faster than any other Secretary of State for War had ever done before. Naturally this upset a lot of people, but it made Hore-Belisha very popular with a lot more. His sudden decision to double the TA in March 1939 without consulting the Army Council and before the system was properly ready to absorb such an increase, followed a few weeks later by the introduction of conscription, caused a lot of criticism, but these moves were the product of his struggles with Chamberlain who was reluctant to introduce conscription which Hore-Belisha thought necessary. Doubling the TA was merely a temporary substitute for conscription and an attempt to deter Hitler.[37] Great credit must go to Hore-Belisha for fighting so strongly and courageously for these unpopular causes and Churchill himself recognized this.[38] Similarly his insistent demands for a Ministry of Supply to organize rearmament were made in the face of considerable discouragement from the Prime Minister.[39] In many ways the spring of 1939 was the high point in Hore-Belisha's career. He had successfully survived a revolt of junior ministers in December 1938 with the backing of the Prime Minister[40] and he may have been beginning to feel that he more nearly represented the national mood than did the latter. Indeed he asked Liddell Hart on 27 March 1939 whether he 'thought he was strong enough, with the country, to take a lead'.[41] One man, however, was certainly not impressed and that was Henry Pownall who became Chief of Staff to Gort in the BEF. In May 1939 he confided his view of the Gort-Hore-Belisha relationship to his diary: 'But the ultimate fact is that they could never get on — you couldn't expect two such utterly different people to do so — a great gentleman and an obscure, shallow-brained, charlatan, political Jewboy'.[42] In what senses an Old Cliftonian, ex-President of the Oxford Union, well-known journalist, inventor of the Belisha beacon and famous War Minister could be regarded as obscure, is itself obscure, unless, of course, Pownall intended obscure simply to mean not born into an acceptable race or social class.

The outbreak of war meant that Hore-Belisha had to appoint a C-in-C who necessarily then began to steal some of his power and limelight. He chose Gort and this was in the end his undoing. Told very briefly the story went thus. The Maginot line stopped at Givet and from there to the coast there were blockhouses at one kilometre intervals and a continuous anti-tank obstacle.[43] Shortly before the war, HQ 1 Division RE had made a study of the construction of concrete defences.[44] On 8 September, Ironside, by then CIGS, told the War Cabinet that the French were fully prepared against a possible turning movement through Belgium and Holland.[45] Hore-Belisha went to France on 20 September and on his return urged the War Cabinet that the strongest possible line should be constructed. He then arranged for Colonel A. Minnis of the RE together with Colonel J. French, a TA civil engineer, and Major S.A. Westrop, another TA engineer, to visit France to examine the problem of constructing a defensive line.[46] He wrote to Gort and told him about this. While this was going on, two generals, one of whom Liddell Hart thought was Pownall, had sought to enlist the support of the editor of the *Sunday Express* for the ousting of Hore-Belisha.[47] Pownall himself thought it strange that Hore-Belisha went to France to deal with a strategic matter and did not want him to get his 'feet into' that sort of thing.[48] On 28 September the BEF was allotted its sector of the line. On 29 September Pakenham-Walsh heard by accident that a construction force was to arrive at the end of October, but had a letter from the War Office later in the day announcing this and telling him that the force was to build a rear defence line and that the Secretary of State laid great importance on the scheme.[49] Minnis, French and Westrop arrived in France on 4 October; later in the month 'X' force itself began to arrive.[50]

There was very considerable confusion in the BEF about the tactical and even strategic purposes of the rear defence line. Pakenham-Walsh points out that the British sector was only twenty miles long and the French on either side showed no sign of building similar defences; Gort therefore wanted defences in depth.[51] Hore-Belisha was unhappy with the French proposals for an encounter battle in Belgium and believed that the Allies should stay put; such a strategy would have given some point to the pill boxes, but in the end Gort and Ironside agreed to move and Hore-Belisha failed to press home his opposition.[52] The design of the pill boxes themselves caused numerous problems, particularly as it was decided that they should be suitable for both French and British weapons, and also as a consequence of the widely divergent views of the various commanders.[53] A decision was not finally given by the C-in-C until 13 November and the designs were not completed until 16 November. The C-in-C's war diary talks about the need 'to avoid a repetition of the deplorable situation and delay'.[54] It was into this confusion that Hore-Belisha jumped when he began his second visit to the BEF on 16 November.

During this visit Gort and Pownall indulged in some rather school-boyish pranks in order to exploit Hore-Belisha's well-known dislike of physical discomfort. He saw only two pill boxes and spoke to Gort about this who told him about the design problems; he also discussed pill boxes with Pownall who wrote in his diary: 'The only minor moan that H-B made was that concrete fortresses were not springing up in all directions' since his men had been there for nearly three weeks.[55] On the way to Paris, where Gamelin appears to have told him either that the French could construct pill boxes in three days, or set them up in three days after the site had been prepared, or that the concrete took three days to dry, he told Kennedy that there were not enough pill boxes and that his engineer (French) had not been properly used.[56] In Paris he told Ironside that he was disappointed that the RE had failed to standardize pill boxes and that Gort had not used all the extra sappers he had been sent. Ironside told him that Gort had been 'put in by the King and must not be monkeyed about'.[57] Whether Hore-Belisha responded that he had chosen both Gort and Ironside himself is not recorded. He told de Guingand, then his MA, that they must see what could be done to accelerate the work. De Guingand never gained the impression that his discussions with Gort were carried out in a sense of criticism but were merely an exploration of ways and means of helping.[58]

Back in London, he gave the Army Council an account of the main impressions he had gained in France.[59] The views of some Dominion representatives who had recently visited France with Eden, that a great increase in pill boxes was required, were conveyed to him.[60] The next day he reported to the War Cabinet after Ironside had left the room that he had seen only two new pill boxes being constructed whereas Gamelin had told him the French could build them in three days. He hoped that great improvements would be made but 'generally speaking our defences were very strong . . . '.[61] On 22 November he wrote a friendly letter to Gort, full of thanks and praise but giving him his views on pill boxes and telling him about the views of the Dominion representatives and Gamelin. In the Commons that day he spoke about the Maginot gap and the necessity to improve the defences of the British line.[62] Meanwhile, Pownall arrived in London on 20 November where he saw Hardinge at Buckingham Palace and 'discussed with him pretty frankly the virtues and failings of Hore-Belisha at the War Office, of CIGS and various other generals'. He also saw Sir James Grigg the Permanent Under-Secretary at the War Office who he said hated Ironside and Hore-Belisha worse than ever. Grigg said that Gort need expect no support in trouble from them. He also visited Hankey and Horace Wilson and then flew back to France on 24 November, no doubt feeling that he had made good use of his time away from GHQ since he had by then firmly decided that Hore-Belisha would have to go because he was 'an enemy at our back' who had started Lloyd George tactics, this in spite of his opinion only a few days earlier that Hore-Belisha had only had 'a minor moan' in France.[63]

On the same day that Pownall made his return journey the Prime Minister mentioned the views of the Dominion representatives to Hore-Belisha, who subsequently saw French whom he found dispirited and who felt he was being treated as an outsider.[64] At 5.30 pm he chaired an Army Council meeting at which AG was the only military member present in person. Pakenham-Walsh and Collins were in attendance. Hore-Belisha conveyed the views of the Dominion representatives to the Council and indicated that the Prime Minister had mentioned the point to him that afternoon. Hore-Belisha 'admitted that his own impression tended to coincide with that of the Dominion representatives'. Pakenham-Walsh offered some explanations and said that 240 pill boxes would be required in all. Hore-Belisha then asked how construction could be speeded up as he wished to help: Pakenham-Walsh stated that plenty of steel and concrete were available, although there might be some difficulties with stone, and a standard design had been approved two weeks before. Hore-Belisha summed up the discussion by giving two reasons why they should do all in their power to hasten the work. The first was to give Britain's soldiers the best possible defence and the second was so that no one could say they had not done their very best. As Pakenham-Walsh was leaving, Hore-Belisha made his famous and contested concilatory remark.[65] He had also seen Pakenham-Walsh and Collins on 22 November and saw them again with French on 25 November.[66]

When Pakenham-Walsh arrived back in GHQ on 27 November he gave Gort a message from Hore-Belisha. There is nothing in the Army Council minutes about a specific message, but of course Pakenham-Walsh may have been given it at his meeting with the Secretary of State on 25 November. Pownall says that the message was to the effect that the 'Prime Minister, on the report of the representatives of the Dominions, the Secretary of State for the Dominions, and myself, has said in the War Cabinet that he is very perturbed at the reported weakness of the British sector of the line'.[67] Pakenham-Walsh merely states that Hore-Belisha asked him to tell Gort that the Prime Minister had expressed anxiety at a War Cabinet about the Dominions' representatives' report.[68] Gort was furious as well he might be, especially as the message was delivered by a member of his own staff,[69] and must have felt that his own position was in danger. Actually the pill box corner had been turned with the decision of 16 November and by 1 December thirty-two were under construction by 'X' force alone and the number increased fairly rapidly in spite of the winter conditions.[70] Gort had Pakenham-Walsh check out the message with Collins which he did; Gort was told that Hore-Belisha had had the Army

Council minutes amended and Pownall found out from Grigg that there was nothing in the Cabinet conclusions or confidential annex to imply that the message had been sent on the instruction of the War Cabinet or Prime Minister.[71] This is unsurprising because it was not so sent. The Prime Minister had told Hore-Belisha about the Dominion representatives on the morning of 24 November not in Cabinet on 21 November.[72] Pownall commented: 'We are now here all facing West'.[73]

On 28 November, the CIGS entered the lists and told the Prime Minister that he proposed to go to France and inspect the line. The Prime Minister agreed and asked Ironside to report to him on his return.[74] Hore-Belisha was not in favour of the visit[75] but Gort received a wire from CIGS's office telling him that Ironside was coming 'to inspect defences in BEF area on War Cabinet instructions'. Hore-Belisha was unaware of this and the War Cabinet had certainly not issued any such instruction. In France the situation must have looked ominous and Ironside himself went out primarily to sort things out. However, in France he met a barrage of complaints about Hore-Belisha and was convinced by the justifications which were put to him, which covered the facts that Hore-Belisha had asked to see men not works, that much construction was going on and that the plan was to advance into Belgium anyway. Liddell Hart believed that Ironside's 'trade unionism' then got the upper hand.[76] Certainly he returned convinced that the rage he found in France was justified and that Hore-Belisha would have to go. 'It is time', he told Kennedy, 'we had a better chap in the War Office.' He also told him a few days later that Gort was convinced 'Hore-Belisha was trying to unseat him'. On 29 November Pownall wrote to Grigg and also arranged through Munster for Ironside to see the Prime Minister on his return, but in fact this did not happen immediately. Instead he saw Hore-Belisha and told him about Gort's resentment. Hore-Belisha wrote Gort a conciliatory letter on 4 December but got no reply. 'The incident is closed', he wrote but this was far from the case.[77]

Later Ironside reported to the King and Prime Minister that pill boxes were being built as fast as possible.[78] In fact Munster had arranged for the King to summon Ironside on his return. 'One crushes a snake even if it does happen to be on the ground', Pownall wrote in his diary and then sent a list of Hore-Belisha's crimes to Ironside's MA and to Grigg. Hardinge received reports that there was resentment about Hore-Belisha in the BEF and on 4

December the King, accompanied by Hardinge, went to France where he saw Gort, Pownall and Pakenham-Walsh. Pownall noted that the King and Hardinge now realized that Hore-Belisha would have to go and gave them all the details of Hore-Belisha's 'disgraceful behaviour'. The King asked Pownall who should replace him and on his return spoke to the Prime Minister. On 12 December Hardinge wrote to Gort and told him that Kingsley Wood had said that the entire War Cabinet, less Hore-Belisha, had confidence in Gort while the next day Wilson and Bridges told the Prime Minister that Hore-Belisha's retention at the War Office would cause serious discontent in Whitehall.[79] On 14 December the Prime Minister summoned Hore-Belisha, told him that the King had asked him to see Ironside and also asked him if he had confidence in Gort. He only had to tell him if he wanted a change. Hore-Belisha said that he had complete confidence. He was next asked if he had instructed Ironside to go to France, which he denied, but added that he also had confidence in Ironside.[80]

The next day Chamberlain himself went to France where he too saw Gort, Pownall and Pakenham-Walsh. He questioned Gort about Pakenham-Walsh's message and read Collins' corroborative letter. Gort told the Prime Minister that they were not worried about the Ironside telegram, only the Pakenham-Walsh message and hoped 'that bolt hole is stopped for H-Belisha too'. He also told him that they did not have confidence in getting support from Hore-Belisha.[81] On his return he wrote to Gort to tell him he was impressed with the progress made with defence construction; Gort replied on 27 December with a most conciliatory letter about Hore-Belisha praising his reforms and concluding that resentment of misplaced criticism in the BEF had disappeared since Chamberlain's visit. He did add, however, that confidence and trust might fail at the critical moment if criticism of armies in the field were not couched in sympathetic language.[82]

However, Chamberlain had seen Hore-Belisha on 20 December, after a Cabinet meeting at which the former had stated that the defences already constructed 'appeared to him extremely formidable',[83] and had told him about the strong feeling about him in France. He advised Hore-Belisha to be careful but was, according to Hore-Belisha, extremely nice and expressed his complete confidence.[84] In his diary, however, the Prime Minister noted that he had not found the interview at all reassuring because Hore-Belisha 'did not and could not see where he had gone wrong and only thought he had been treated with great injustice and prejudice'. Chamberlain therefore came to the conclusion that he ought to be moved if a favourable opportunity occurred, because 'in wartime nothing could be worse than perpetual friction and want of confidence between the Secretary of State and the C-in-C in the field'.[85]

The favourable opportunity came quickly, because a new man was wanted at the Ministry of Information. Chamberlain decided to move Hore-Belisha and to replace him with Oliver Stanley. He summoned him for 2.45 pm on 4 January, but at the last minute Halifax opposed the move because Hore-Belisha was a Jew and 'his methods would let down British prestige'. Halifax suggested the Board of Trade and this was the proposal actually put to Hore-Belisha[86] who was thrown into confusion. Chamberlain told him there was prejudice against him, Hore-Belisha asked to time to think and was given till ten o'clock the next morning. That evening Chamberlain wrote him a very sickly letter asking him to think of his move as a sacrifice for his country. Hore-Belisha meanwhile saw Beaverbrook and Brendan Bracken and the latter arranged for Churchill to ring from Paris which he did, advising acceptance of the Ministry of Information, a significant error indicating foreknowledge. Later that night Hore-Belisha made his decision and wrote to Chamberlain rejecting the Board of Trade, and defending his action over the defences in France. On 5 January he saw Chamberlain, who then explained some of the prejudice. Hore-Belisha refused to change his mind and went back to the War Office to draft his resignation. In his resignation speech he did not make trouble because to do so would have necessitated giving information to the enemy.[87] When he heard the news Gort was depressed that he could be said to have been instrumental in the dismissal.[88] Pownall's comment was more forthright: 'A fine day's work for the Army and for the proper conduct of the war'.[89]

So virtually ended the career of one of the most active and imaginative of Secretaries of State for War. Why was such a concerted and persistent effort made by numbers of senior officers to have him removed? Undoubtedly there was resistance to reform but this related mainly to the pre-war period. In any case Hore-Belisha was not left wing; he came from the same public school as many senior officers and had a prosperous middle-class background. He did upset people by failing to consult them, notably over the doubling of the TA, or by riding energetically over their opposition, but this is a common characteristic of those who get things done. He certainly upset many officers by his early reliance on Liddell Hart, and his initial opposition to the continental commitment, but that ended long before the outbreak of war. The fact that he showed little strategic understanding was perhaps somewhat unexceptional in the late thirties in England. His questions about pill boxes in November 1939 were apposite since there had been delay and confusion and his messages and comments appear to have been deliberately misunderstood as criticism rather than support, but the whole Pill Box affair was steeped in irony since it was fundamentally irrelevant in the political and military context of 1939-40. Had Hore-Belisha fallen for continuing to oppose a move forward into Belgium he would have gone down in history as slightly more strategically respectable. He did interfere in matters which previous Secretaries of State had left to the military members of the Army Council, but such conduct was hardly heinous enough to explain the prejudice against him. He certainly had caused senior officers to be passed over or retired but the chief passer-over was Gort himself. Minney's statements, for which he offers no evidence, that 'the outbreak of war swept back into various positions of trust and responsibility senior officers who had been by-passed by the promotion of younger men', and that 'their hositility centred on Hore-Belisha . . . especially at the HQ of the BEF where many of these officers were now serving', are difficult to accept as sound judgements. He also states that Gort did not share these feelings but they determined to win him over.[90] The facts are that Gort himself, when he became CIGS in 1937, passed over, thanks to Hore-Belisha, Brownrigg, Dill, Brooke, Ironside, Kirke, Venning, Liddell, Finlayson, Wavell and May. Of the senior officers in the BEF, Brownrigg, Dill and Brooke might conceivably have felt resentment but would have felt it against Gort more than Hore-Belisha. Pownall, Lindsell and Neame had not been passed over and so could feel none on that score.[91] Resentment there was, but not for the reason Minney puts forward.

There is, however, one reason which could, and probably does, explain the violence of the campaign against Hore-Belisha which Pownall undoubtedly orchestrated in November and December 1939. This is that GHQ BEF began to fear that he intended to replace numbers of its senior officers from Gort downwards. Ironside suspected this, and was also warned about his own position by

Pownall;[92] Gort thought that Hore-Belisha intended to displace him; Pownall saw the enemy in the west not the east. Obviously fear was growing in GHQ that criticism would lead to removal. Pownall almost certainly decided to pre-empt the Secretary of State and used the informal networks open to him to do so. And faced with such an insidious onslaught Hore-Belisha was in the end defenceless because he did not fit, because he was a Jew and an outsider and because he had no substantial political basis of support in Parliament. The dislike and distaste many officers felt for him (crystallized in the Military Attaché's comment to Kennedy in Paris that he felt it was good for his soul to meet Hore-Belisha occasionally; 'he disliked him so much that it was a very good exercise in self-control'[93]) was not the cause of Hore-Belisha's downfall, but it greatly helped to motivate those who worked against him at the end. No ordinary Secretary of State would have generated such feeling, but Hore-Belisha was not one of 'them' and had actually more or less sacked an Army Council before. A man who could do that might surely to the same to a C-in-C and his principal staff officers if he had a mind to it? Cs-in-C in wartime, however, are generally in a stronger position than Army Councillors in peace — or so it transpired on this occasion, although Churchill later demonstrated that even Cs-in-C are not beyond political reach.

If there is any validity in this hypothesis what lessons might there be in its contemplation? An obvious one is that service ministries are different. Service ministers are wise if they take the social and institutional nature of the armed forces into account in their actions, as most do. If service ministers want to bring about substantial changes they either have to fit and govern by consent or they have to have a secure basis of power in the Cabinet and Parliament. Secondly, and of more general application, the fall of Hore-Belisha demonstrates that it never pays to underestimate the insecurity and the needs of others — particularly those who work for you. If you are ruthless others may in time retaliate with a similar ruthlessness. As his house magazine had commented many years before, what Hore-Belisha chiefly lacked was a better knowledge of the game. His reforms certainly helped to provide the social and administrative basis of Britain's wartime, and perhaps even more directly, post-war army, but that was his major contribution and in 1940 it was time for him to move on. It is doubtful anyway if he could have worked effectively under the next Minister of Defence.

NOTES

1. *Sunday Pictorial*, 7 January 1940.
2. *Daily Worker*, 8 January 1940.
3. R.J. Minney, *The Private Papers of Hore-Belisha* (London 1960), 279-80, 301-2.
4. *New Statesman*, 30 April 1960.
5. *Sunday Express*, 24 April 1960.
6. Conversation with General Sir Ronald Adam, 30 May 1978.
7. Chamberlain's private papers quoted in Ed. Butler *History of the Second World War*, Vol. II (London 1957).
8. Lord Woolton, *Memoirs* (London 1959), 157.
9. Imperial War Museum, letter from Haydon to Colville, 29 January 1970.
10. See Minney, op. cit., passim.
11. J.R. Colville, *Man of Valour. The Life of Field Marshal The Viscount Gort* (London 1972), 157.
12. These are held by Hore-Belisha's ex-secretary, Miss Hilde Sloane.
13. *Polack's House Magazine*, Winter 1908.
14. Conversation with Albert Polack, 15 February 1978. Albert Polack was the son of Hore-Belisha's housemaster and a contemporary at Polack's.
15. This account of Hore-Belisha's time at Clifton is based on interviews with Albert and Ernest Polack, and Colonel Crawford (Secretary, Old Cliftonian Society) at the school in February 1978 and on *Polack's House Magazine*, the *Clifton College Register* and *The Cliftonian*, July 1912.
16. This paragraph is based on Minney, op. cit., Liddell Hart's article in the *Dictionary of National Biography 1951-60, The Daily Mail*, 1 November 1957, and the Hore-Belisha papers in the Liddell Hart Centre for Military Archives, King's College London (LH Centre) especially 11/HB Misc.
17. See the author's, *Boney Fuller, The Intellectual General 1878-1966* (London 1977).
18. See Brian Bond's *British Military Policy between the Two World Wars* (London 1980).
19. Army Lists. I am indebted to Mr Timothy Ward of the HQ UKLF Military Affairs Reference Service library for the relevant research.
20. Ibid.
21. Ibid.
22. Colville, op. cit., 77-78.
23. General Sir Ronald Adam was very helpful to the author in an interview on 30 May 1978 in clarifying these matters.
24. Ian Macleod, *Neville Chamberlain* (London 1961), 284.
25. See Minney op. cit., 122-30, and Liddell Hart *Memoirs*, Vol. II (London 1965), 123.
26. LH Centre, 11/HB 1938/141b.
27. Specific evidence of his energy and drive can be found in the minutes of the Army Council, Public Record Office (PRO) WO 163/47-48.
28. PRO WO 163/48.

29. See Colville, op. cit., PRO WO 163/48 and 'The Pill Box Row' by Major-General R.P. Pakenham-Walsh in *The Royal Engineers Journal* 1960, 496-502.

30. There was no PR branch, for instance in the War Office until Hore-Belisha's time.

31. See Colville, op. cit., 111.

32. Liddell Hart Centre, 11/HB 1937/84b.

33. Ibid., 114b.

34. Ibid., 11/HB 1938/83b.

35. See PRO WO 163/47-48, WO 163/67-69 and WO 163/70-71 and 65-66.

36. Notably Pile and Hobart.

37. Adam, 30 May 1978.

38. Roderick Macleod, *The Ironside Diaries 1937-40* (London 1962), 83.

39. See Minney, op. cit., 185-200, Liddell Hart, op. cit., 229.

40. See Minney, op. cit., 161-66.

41. Liddell Hart Centre, 11/Hore-Belisha 1939/3.

42. Brian Bond (ed.), *Chief of Staff. The Diaries of Lietuenant-General Sir Henry Pownall*, Vol. I, 1933-1940 (London 1972), 203.

43. Pakenham-Walsh, op. cit., 497; Colville, op. cit., 157.

44. Pakenham-Walsh, op. cit., 497.

45. PRO CAB 65/1.

46. Author's conversation with Brigadier S.A. Westrop, 13 April 1978.

47. Liddell Hart, op. cit., 266.

48. Bond, op. cit., 238.

49. Pakenham-Walsh, op. cit., 497.

50. PRO 167/43, War Diary E-in-C BEF.

51. Pakenham-Walsh, op. cit., 498.

52. John Kennedy, *The Business of War* (London 1959), 30, 33.

53. Westrop, PRO 167/43; Pakenham-Walsh, op. cit., 498.

54. PRO WO 167/43 Appendix 1 to November 1939.

55. Bond, op. cit., 257.

56. Kennedy, op. cit., 38.

57. Roderick Macleod, op. cit., 164.

58. Liddell Hart Centre 11/HB Misc/34.

59. PRO WO 163/48.

60. Minney, op. cit., 259.

61. PRO CAB 65/2.

62. Minney, op. cit., 260-61.

63. Bond, op. cit., 258-59, 274.

64. Minney, op. cit., 261.

65. PRO WO 163/48.

66. Colville, op. cit., 157-65; Pakenham-Walsh, op. cit., 500.

67. Bond, op. cit., 259-60.

68. Pakenham-Walsh, op. cit., 500.

69. Colville, op. cit., 157-65.

70. PRO WO 167/1429, 'X' Force War Diary.

71. Bond, op. cit., 263 and Colville, op. cit., 157-65.

72. PRO WO 163/48.

73. Bond, op. cit., 262.

74. Roderick Macleod, op. cit., 165.
75. Liddell Hart Centre, 11/HB Misc/34.
76. Liddell Hart, op. cit., 268.
77. See Roderick Macleod, op. cit., 166-67, Kennedy, op. cit., 40, 43, Bond, op. cit., 261-63, 266 and Minney, op. cit., 263-64.
78. Colville, op. cit., 161.
79. See Bond, op. cit., 264-265, 267 and Colville, op. cit., 162-63.
80. Minney, op. cit., 266.
81. Bond, op. cit., 267-68; also see Colville, op. cit., 163, and Pakenham-Walsh, op. cit., 501.
82. Ian Macleod, op. cit., 285.
83. PRO CAB 65/2.
84. Minney, op. cit., 267-69.
85. Ian Macleod, op. cit., 285-86.
86. Ibid., 286-87.
87. Minney, op. cit., 266-86, and Liddell Hart, op. cit., 272-73.
88. Colville, op. cit., 166.
89. Bond, op. cit., 275.
90. Minney, op. cit., 230-31.
91. Army Lists.
92. Bond, op. cit., 263-64.
93. Kennedy, op. cit., 33-34.

8 George C Marshall and the Question of Military Aid to England, May-June 1940

David G Haglund

In a Foreword to the most recent biography of Harry Hopkins, W. Averell Harriman has put some words into the mouth of Winston Churchill. According to Harriman, if the British Prime Minister had been asked to pick the two Americans, apart from President Franklin D. Roosevelt, who were most responsible for stopping Hitler, he would have replied: 'Among the military, General Marshall, and among the civilians, Harry Hopkins'.[1] After the war, or even towards the end of it, it is possible — maybe likely — that Churchill would have said something of the sort; but if the question had been raised at the moment of Britain's darkest peril, June 1940, and if the Prime Minister had been aware of what was being said behind Washington's closed doors in the matter of sending military assistance to the Allies, his comment — at least his comment about Marshall — would assuredly not have been worthy of repetition in polite company.

It is not very well appreciated today that many members of the Roosevelt administration, during the dramatic late spring of 1940, were violently opposed to the policy of draining America of military hardware for the purpose of supplying Britain and (before she fell out of the war in June) France. No top official in Washington was more convinced of the unwisdom of sending increased aid across the Atlantic than the Chief of Staff, George C. Marshall. Yet a surprising 'White Legend' has grown up around Marshall's activities at this critical juncture, in somewhat the same manner that an obnoxious 'Black Legend' swirled about him in the early 1950s, when reactionary Senators Joseph McCarthy and William Jenner sought to smear the record of the then Secretary of

Defense, who was accused of being either 'soft' on communism or an outright 'fellow traveller'. While the Black Legend turned out to have a fortunately short life, the same has not been true of the legend of Marshall as the paladin, in May and June 1940, of further aid to Britain and France.

Ten years or so ago, Joseph Alsop, who had been an active interventionist in the summer of 1940, explained to an historian that only a few Roosevelt cabinet members 'and a very few far-sighted officers like General Marshall grasped the necessity for immediate aid to Britain'.[2] Alsop, who should have known better by the time he made this statement, was only echoing the conventional version of the role of the Chief of Staff in aiding Britain. This version had sprung from the pens of countless writers on the subject, not the least of whom was William Frye, whose 1947 biography of Marshall related that after Dunkerque, 'to Marshall, and to Admiral Harold R. Stark, the Chief of Naval Operations, the one immediate imperative was to prevent the fall of Britain'.[3]

Even the estimable Marshall biographer, Forrest C. Pogue, has given us an account of the Chief of Staff, vexed by the awesome problem of building an American army, yet still willing to share what little he had with the valiant British. At a time in May when Churchill was seemingly asking Roosevelt for the moon — the transfer of destroyers to the Royal Navy; a declaration of nonbelligerency; several hundred modern aircraft; a visit by the United States Navy to Irish ports; action to 'keep that Japanese dog quiet in the Pacific'; and anti-aircraft guns, ammunition, and steel — Marshall would only consent to part with a relative trifle, albeit a potentially invaluable trifle to the Home Guard in England. Vetoing any sale of fighters, the Chief of Staff did approve the transfer of supplies that were not as critical to American defence: 500,000 World War I rifles; 900 field pieces; 80,000 machine guns; 300 mortars; 25,000 Browning automatic rifles; 20,000 revolvers; and a limited supply of ammunition for these weapons.[4] The British were undoubtedly grateful for this assistance, yet it would be inaccurate to see in it, as Pogue does, evidence that Marshall was in agreement 'with Roosevelt and his supporters that heroic efforts must be taken to sustain Britain. . .'[5]

Marshall may indeed have been, at this time, in agreement with the President and his top advisers, but not in the manner that Pogue and others think; for to the leading civilian and military policy-makers in Washington, it was becoming apparent that Britain was as doomed as France, and that any further aid sent her way would only be wasted, and would greatly compound the dangers facing the United States. Only by examining carefully those perceived dangers can one really make some sense out of the reluctance of Marshall, his colleagues in the War Department, and — let it be noted — many of the President's close civilian advisers to part with precious supplies that might soon be needed to defend the Western Hemisphere.

Simply put, by the spring of 1940 Washington policy-makers were extremely anxious for the security of America's southern neighbours and, by extension (since even the staunchest isolationist would concede the hemisphere to be the legitimate sphere of American security interests), that of the United States itself. The fall of France, and the imminent collapse of Britain, portended what to observers in Washington had loomed as a nightmare ever since the end of 1937: the probability that Hitler, employing a combination of economic, political, and military means, would obtain control over several important republics of Latin America — republics that could ultimately be used as staging areas from which to launch an invasion of the United States.[6]

In an age before the advent of long-range bombers and nuclear warheads, what more likely menace could confront the United States than a European power's suborning, co-opting, or conquering any of several vulnerable states below the Rio Grande? Not only were far too many of the Latin neighbours — particularly in the distant reaches of southern South America — economically dependent upon a Europe that was rapidly turning into a Nazi fiefdom, but they were for the most part ruled by men who were not hostile to the basic tenets of the Nazi new order, and they contained within their boundaries large and unassimilated populations of emigrants (and their descendants) from Axis nations. This final point proved especially unsettling to the Roosevelt administration, for while it might be argued that even the 'American narrows' (1,600 miles of water separating Dakar and Natal) was not very narrow, and therefore no invitation to invasion, it was not possible to ignore the fact that millions of potential Axis sympathizers inhabited the southern portion of the hemisphere.[7]

Along with the vast majority of Washington officials, Marshall shared the preception of a hemisphere imperilled by the growth of Nazi power across the Atlantic. This sense of peril began to develop in late 1937, reached a peak after the Munich settlement in the early autumn of 1938, and then suddenly diminished the following September, when the British and French decided to stop caving in before Hitler. But the ending of the Phoney War in April 1940 spelled finis for the short-lived sense of complacency regarding the Western Hemisphere, as each German success during that first, frightening springtime of war made American leaders more apprehensive than ever that an eventual move against the Latin American republics was in the works, German protestations of innocence quite to the contrary.[8]

On 15 May Winston Churchill, still getting used to his new job as Prime Minister, cabled the request for aid discussed above. The following day, Roosevelt rejected the most important item on the British shopping list, the forty to fifty overage destroyers, and offered only limited hope that the other *matériel* sought would be forthcoming. Although the decision on the destroyers did not concern him directly, Marshall was in total accord with the President's action, as were also his civilian superiors in the War Department, Secretary Harry Woodring and Assistant Secretary Louis Johnson, men who rarely saw eye to eye on anything. But the question of selling fighters to England did concern the Chief of Staff directly, and led him to the office of the Secretary of the Treasury, Henry Morgenthau, the administration's foremost advocate of increased support for Britain. There Marshall explained to Morgenthau, two days after Churchill's entreaty, that 'we have got to weigh the hazards in this hemisphere of one thing or another'. Meeting the British request would only amount to 'a drop in the bucket on the other side, and it is a very vital necessity on this side and that is that. Tragic as it is, that is that."[9]

Even as the Chief of Staff was speaking, the 'hazards in this hemisphere of one thing or another' were growing more apparent to a frightened America, a jittery nation in which, noted one contemporary observer, a quickened solicitude for Latin America had 'broken out like a speckled rash'.[10] On 16 May, the day he turned down Churchill's request for the destroyers, President Roosevelt expounded upon one of the gravest dangers confronting the hemisphere: the 'treacherous use of the "Fifth Column",' which was widely thought to have played a major, and invidious, role in the recent string of German conquests in Europe. Warning the nation's law-makers that 'these are ominous days', Roosevelt asked for unprecedented outlays of money to rearm America — nearly a billion dollars for the two armed services, and whatever it would take to bring the capacity of American aircraft manufacturers up to fifty thousand planes a year. 'The clear fact is,' he concluded, 'that the American people must recast their thinking about national protection.'[11]

Although the President's invocation of the nefarious Fifth Column makes quaint reading today, it is important to remember that at the time he was lecturing Congress, many otherwise sober individuals were being caught up in the great anti-subversive mania that swept across the West. Secretary of State Cordell Hull, never known for excessive excitability, was certain that by late May Hitler's schemes in South America were being blatantly prefigured in Europe: 'We had before us the vivid examples of what Nazi "Fifth Columns" had accomplished during the invasions of Scandinavia, the Low Countries, and France, the full details of which were only then coming to our attention.'[12] In a fireside chat of 26 May, the President enumerated the new lineaments of the menace to the hemisphere: 'The Trojan Horse. The Fifth Column that betrays a nation unprepared for treachery. Spies, saboteurs and traitors...'[13]

A particularly revealing account of one man's paranoia during the German spring offensive is found in the diary of Assistant Secretary of State Adolf Berle. Shortly after the collapse of France, Berle recounted this 'shattering experience': he had conferred with a Hearst Newsreel executive who had given him details of a Nazi plan to seize New York after the capitulation of Britain. 'His story of the way the Fifth Column was already in control of New York was so graphic that it frightened me completely,' the Assistant Secretary confessed. 'Only after I got the FBI, which had heard the story in detail, to check, did I begin to pull myself together.'[14] That Berle could have been so worried about subversion in Manhattan strikes us today as incredible, and even a little amusing; but there was nothing incredible about the fear that American policy-makers had for the immediate future of several Latin American states, ostensibly menaced by their own Axis populations, and faced with a triumphant Hitler preparing to launch an invasion in support of local Nazi insurrections.

Even before the French withdrawal from the war, disturbing reports had been reaching the War Department from observers below the Rio Grande. 16 May, the day the Allied armies began their retreat from the Belgian cul-de-sac, the day the world learned of the enormity of the German breakthrough on the Meuse, was also the day that Army G-2 discovered from its attaché in Buenos Aires that 'the Argentine army, navy, the higher circles of society and the wealthy classes [are] definitely pro-Nazi and pro-Fascist'. Five days later, this same officer, Major M. A. Devine, Jr., informed the War Department that even the administration of the pro-Allied President, Roberto Ortiz, was 'honeycombed with Nazis', and that, in preparation for German landing operations, 'German nationals in South America have been ordered to buy up ranches with frontage on the South Atlantic both in Argentina and Brazil'.[15]

On 24 May word reached Washington from the French Foreign Office that a Nazi coup impended in Argentina. The plot was said to involve top Argentine generals, Chilean leftists (this was in the period of the Russo-German pact), and the thousands of Nazis who pullulated in southern Brazil. It would be set in motion immediately after the fall of France, simultaneously with the invasion of Britain. Not certain how much credibility to attach to this report, the White House was relieved when the American Ambassador to Argentina, Norman Armour, cabled on 5 June that for the moment at least, there was little danger of insurrection. However, Armour went on to explain that a highly-placed contact in the Argentine army had informed him that the situation could be expected to deteriorate rapidly should Italy enter the war — a contingency that was developing all the earmarks of a certainty. The Ambassador predicted that with Mussolini as an active belligerent, the 'three million Fascists in Argentina would be thrown into the Nazi camp, bringing the forces of totalitarianism in this country up to almost one-third of the total population'.[16]

As bad as things might appear to be in Argentina, they looked even worse in Uruguay. This small republic, tucked uncomfortably between the Latin 'superpowers' Brazil and Argentina, was considered by many to be the soft underbelly of South America, the most likely target for an invasion of the hemisphere. At the end of May it seemed that an invasion was on Hitler's drawing boards — an invasion launched not from German-occupied Europe, but from the German areas of southern Brazil. With wild stories of Fifth Column machinations making the rounds of credulous listeners in Uruguay, and with the forces of democracy crumbling in Europe, it was clear to Washington that it confronted a very dangerous situation in its own sphere of influence. 'The situation is deteriorating here,' cabled the American Minister in Montevideo, Edwin C.

Wilson, on 30 May. 'The government is well-meaning but weak, undecided and confused; things are drifting; people are climbing on the Nazi bandwagon; and an armed movement is a possibility.'[17] Alarmed, the President immediately ordered one of the Navy's fastest cruisers, the *Quincy*, to make full speed for the Uruguayan coast (where it would subsequently be joined by a second cruiser, the *Wichita*). This action was not enough to soothe the nerves of one State Department officer; Laurence Duggan, head of the Division of American Republics, worried that the cruisers would arrive on the scene too late, and wanted the Army to fly a squadron of bombers to South America. 'It is daily becoming clearer,' he told Under Secretary of State Sumner Welles, 'that the situation in Argentina, Uruguay and Brazil is deteriorating in the sense that a successful revolution backed by the Nazis is becoming a likely possibility.'[18]

It was not only high officials in Washington who were alarmed; everyone in the United States with eyes and ears was becoming aware of the growing political volcano below the Rio Grande. On 2 June the *New York Times* jolted its readers with this banner headline:

> 'Germans Bomb Rhone Valley and Marseille;
> Dunkerque Holds Out; Fighting Along Somme;
> U.S. Is Studying Nazi Threat in South America'

Commented a writer for the *Times* in the same issue: 'The belief [in administration circles] was general that, if they won the war, the Germans would physically invade South America; their present activity was described as boring from within in an attempt to set up totalitarian regimes.'[19]

From Brazil came further frightening tales. In the third week of May, the American military attaché in Rio, Major Lawrence C. Mitchell, informed the War Department that the regnant pro-Allied sentiment of September 1939 had all but disappeared from the Brazilian capital. Mitchell was appalled that so few Brazilians were taking seriously the possibility of either a Nazi invasion or a subversive rising, even though the 'presence of a million Germans in Brazil along with numerous German sympathizers can leave no doubt as to the existence of a potential "Fifth Column" undoubtedly already at work.'[20] In Washington, at least, people were taking seriously that which the attaché so feared: on 24 May

Roosevelt instructed Marshall and Stark to draw up plans for moving an army of more than a hundred thousand men to the strategic north-eastern bulge of Brazil. Three days later, his service chiefs presented him with POT OF GOLD, an invasion scheme based on the premise of the defeat of France and Britain.[21]

Although Argentina, Uruguay, and Brazil (which never did have to be invaded by the United States) manifested the most disquieting symptoms of Fifth Column infection, they were far from being the only Latin nations to cause consternation in Washington. As the President expressed it in a letter to his Ambassador to Chile, Claude Bowers, the administration believed that 'there is no doubt that in the event of a continued German victory in Europe, German agents in Latin American countries will immediately undertake activities with the view to overthrowing existing governments'.[22] For his part, Bowers, who had claimed firsthand experience with the Fifth Column in a previous posting as Ambassador to war-torn Spain, was certain that the initial blow against South America would land on Chile. He informed the State Department in late May that 'I have heard that there are ten thousand Germans in Chile who have actually been trained and drilled for war purposes. . . Let me reiterate with all possible emphasis my own conviction that these German agents count confidently on the assistance of the Fifth Column, so effectively used in Spain.'[23]

With a veritable litany of incipient doom reaching Washington, can it be any wonder that American policy-makers, confronted with the choice of sending further military equipment to Britain or hoarding whatever they had for the defence of their own nation, began giving very serious consideration to opting for the latter? It has become fashionable in recent years to imagine that Roosevelt, Marshall, and other stalwart champions of England stood out against the 'defeatist' counsel of such men as Joseph P. Kennedy, Ambassador to the Court of St. James, and gallantly plighted the fate of the United States to the survival of Great Britain. Nothing could be further from the truth; for in those dismal days of May and June 1940, the consensus of the administration was that England — brave as she might be — was finished, and that the United States would shortly be fighting the battle of its life in Latin America.

Two weeks before the British made their miraculous retreat from the Dunkerque beaches, Churchill once more implored the President to send him American destroyers and to declare nonbelligerency. The Prime Minister gave his assurance that his government would never surrender the fleet to the Germans, but added that future rulers might not be averse to the thought of making 'the best terms they could' for a defeated England. 'Excuse me, Mr President, putting this nightmare bluntly.'[24] Had Churchill wanted to instill fear in the White House, he could not have chosen his words with more precision; for among all the security concerns of the administration, 'this nightmare' of the British fleet passing into German hands was by far the greatest. If Roosevelt could have convinced himself that the probability of Britain's survival was high enough to justify the gamble, he would have done his utmost to comply with Churchill's request — just as he did do later that year, when it began to appear that the reports of Britain's death had been exaggerated. However, as of late May History had not done Washington decision-makers the honour of tipping her hand; consequently, plans were being formulated in the American capital that began with the *parti pris* of a British defeat.

Two days after Churchill's message of 20 May, the Army's War Plans Division presented Marshall with a memorandum on the 'imminently probable complications of today's situation'. The planners argued that the United States had no alternative to concentrating all its efforts on meeting the Latin American difficulties; to a quite limited extent, American interests in Europe and the Far East might be defended, but always upon the understanding that the protection of her hemisphere neighbours had the first claim upon the nation's resources. Armed with this memorandum, the Chief of Staff went to the White House the next day for a strategy session with the President, Welles, and Stark. According to Marshall's minute of this meeting, 'all felt that we must not become involved with Japan, that we must not concern ourselves beyond the 180 meridian, and that we must concentrate on the South American situation'.[25]

Washington's overriding concern with Latin America at the moment of the Allies' greatest peril was not without an element of sublime irony: for the better part of the past two years, the willingness of the administration to countenance measures leading away from isolation and toward support of the European democracies had grown in direct proportion to its perception of an increased threat to the security of the United States — a threat stemming mainly from the possible Axis domination of Latin America. The British and French had early perceived this phenomenon, and had done their best to hurry it along by highlighting the manifold dangers that Nazi expansionism posed to the hemisphere. This strategy had worked exceedingly well up to now, and had been of some importance in convincing the White House to campaign for the removal of the arms embargo the year before. The argument was, really, unanswerable, resting on the following quasi-syllogism: Hitler is out to dominate Latin America; Britain and France stand in his way in Europe; therefore American security interests demand that Britain and France be given aid. A fairly straightforward line of reasoning, this, and one to which the administration had subscribed, while at the same time remaining faithful to a coequal premise of American foreign policy, that the nation must remain isolated from war.

But there was a near-fatal flaw in this process of deduction, a *reductio* that threatened not only to demolish the prospect of further aid to the Allies, but also to establish the probability that the United States would find itself in a war after the British and French had gone down in defeat. This flaw, for which the seeming omnipotency of German arms — combined with the increasingly alarmed tenor of Allied requests for assistance — bore responsibility, was also the product of a simple, ostensibly unanswerable (if pinchbeck) syllogism: Hitler is out to dominate Latin America; Britain and France are beaten; therefore further aid wasted on their behalf only serves to further weaken American defences against the coming battle for Latin America. Put into this new perspective, Allied endeavours to depict the parlous consequences that a German victory must portend now became self-defeating. Thus, whether issuing from Paris or London, counsels for a greater American undertaking in the cause of stopping Hitler in Europe were bound to prove fruitless; indeed, to some American policymakers they even seemed insulting, as if the Allies were trying deliberately to drag the United States down with them, in a defeat for which they had only themselves to blame in the first place.

At the end of May the President confided to a delegation from the Conference on National Defense that the Allies were on the brink of extinction as independent nations. 'It is extremely serious for England and France,' said Roosevelt, speaking off the record, and sounding a theme that was shared by most of the men around him, including and especially the Chief of Staff. 'We are not saying so out loud because we do not want to intimate in this country that England and France have gone.'[26] What the President did say out loud was of a different order. On 10 June he addressed the graduating class of the University of Virginia, in Charlottesville, to whom he pledged that his administration would pursue 'two obvious and simultaneous courses: we will extend to the opponents of force the material resources of this nation; and, at the same time, we will harness and speed up the use of those resources in order that we ourselves in the Americas may have equipment and training equal to the task of any emergency and every defense'.[27]

This speech has often been interpreted as marking the end of isolationism and the beginning of full-scale material support of the Allies. Admittedly, it is easy to read into the President's words a strong hint of, at the very least, an incipient pro-Allied nonbelligerency; and it is tempting to argue, in a linear way, that the destroyers-for-bases deal announced on 2 September (which really did denote the end of Rooseveltian isolationism) was a natural sequel to the Charlottesville address. But to so argue would be to overlook the crucial determinant in the President's decision to proceed with massive aid to Britain: the ability of that nation to convince him that it really could carry on the fight, and that any *matériel* sent would not be wasted, or (much worse) later turned against the United States itself by the conqueror of Europe. It is simply wrong to conclude, as many writers have, that by 10 June this critical prerequisite, the survivability of Britain, had been met to Roosevelt's satisfaction; as the documents reveal, there was a great deal of controversy within the administration over the President's announced pair of 'obvious and simultaneous courses'. Many voices, particularly in the War Department, were raised in protest against what was considered to be an impossible promise; for by the most elementary arithmetic, it seemed that every gun sent to Britain was one less gun with which to defend the New World, when its turn came to be invaded.

The day France asked peace terms of Germany, 17 June, the Chief of Staff was meeting with his assistants to prepare a departmental policy memorandum for use in the struggle to keep American arms on the west side of the Atlantic. More than any other government department, the War Department was apprehensive that the failure to staunch what it considered to be a torrent — but what was, to the British, more like a trickle — of arms and ammunition to Britain would lay the hemisphere open to depredation. Working from an outline prepared by the WPD, Marshall and his aides, Brigadier General George V. Strong and Brigadier General

Frank M. Andrews, agreed on the following recommendation: that the United States should stay purely on the defensive in the Pacific; that it should conduct an immediate mobilization of national effort for the purpose of hemisphere defence; and, most importantly, that it should make 'no further commitments for furnishing *matériel* to the Allies'. This last stipulation was justified as a 'recognition of the early defeat of the Allies, an admission of our inability to furnish means in quantities sufficient to affect the situation, and an acknowledgment that we recognize the probability that we are next on the list of victims of the Axis powers and must devote every means to prepare to meet the threat'.[28]

Bolstered by these recommendations, Marshall later that day attended a meeting of the Standing Liaison Committee, where he hoped to be able to persuade Chief of Naval Operations Stark and Under Secretary of State Welles of the necessity to hoard military and naval supplies for the defence of the New World, in the New World. Of all the problems requiring the attention of America's armed forces, said Marshall, 'perhaps the most serious and delicate. . . and one which is now staring us in the face', was the creation of a network of Nazi satellite regimes throughout Latin America. Such regimes could be brought into existence by revolution, or they could eventuate as a simple consequence of the conversion to Nazism of an existing government. In either case, a strong American reaction would be needed; and Marshall wanted nothing less than the 'preventive occupation of the strategic areas in the Western Hemisphere wherein German or Italian bases might be established to menace the Panama Canal or the Continental U.S.'. As was, he hoped, apparent to all, the United States could not continue squandering resources on Britain. 'The essence of the problem is time. Consequently the definite suspension of French *or* British resistance should become the signal for the start of complete mobilization of all our national resources.'[29]

The Chief of Staff's testimony made a favourable impression on Stark, the official who would have to approve any waiving of destroyers from active service with the Navy — assuming, in the first place, that a way could be found to circumvent a federal statute seemingly prohibiting such a release. Welles was chary of Marshall's ideas on 'preventive occupation', but was otherwise in agreement with his analysis of the threat facing the nation. Of course, there were some men close to the President who took a radically different view; and if it had been up to Henry Morgenthau, the United States would have speedily granted Churchill what he so persistently asked for. But more authoritative figures than the Secretary of the Treasury were impressing upon the President the fact that all was lost in Europe. On 24 June, Marshall and Stark handed Roosevelt a joint memorandum entitled 'Basis for Immediate Decisions Concerning the National Defense'. The message contained therein was unequivocal: 'It is believed that to release to Great Britain additional war material now in the hands of our armed forces will seriously weaken our present state of defense and will not materially assist the British forces.'[30]

Unwilling to slam the door shut in Churchill's face, the President suggested a compromise, to which the service chiefs gave their reluctant assent: make further aid to Britain contingent upon that nation showing clear signs that it could survive until the beginning of 1941, by which date the United States would have had a chance to strengthen its hemisphere defences. Marshall reminded Roosevelt that the needs of the hemisphere must be the first priority, to which the latter responded that 'Yes, in general', he was in agreement with the Chief of Staff.[31] Thus was struck a compromise in the emotional dispute that was racking the administration: Marshall and Stark would agree not to foreclose the possibility of further aid, Roosevelt would agree to exercise the utmost caution with the nation's military hardware. All agreed that, from now on, Britain's fate would rest in its own hands.[32]

In a way, there was something diabolically clever about this proposition that Britain justify its sanctification by first arranging the preconditions that would make the sanctification unnecessary. It was the kind of problem that New England theologians had locked horns over during the seventeenth and eighteenth centuries: Britain would be 'saved' by the United States if it showed that it could save itself, the posterior proposition being taken as evidence that salvation was, indeed, deserved. Put plainly, the administration was applying to the question of continued aid to Britain the aphorism of Benjamin Franklin: 'God helps them that help themselves'.

This is not the place to recount the events of July that led to the cabinet decision of 2 August to transfer to Britain the World War I destroyers that Churchill had been trying to obtain since May. Suffice it to note that in July the British were able to provide the President with compelling reasons for approving additional military assistance to them. While Hitler pawed the ground on the other side of the Channel, making now placatory, now minatory, gestures in the direction of his island enemy, Churchill was busily showing the Americans that he and his nation had what it took to survive — at least until January 1941. The most effective show of British resolve came on 3 July, when units of the Royal Navy smashed the bulk of the French fleet while it rode at anchor in the North African port of Mers-el-Kebir.

By August, the President and the men around him, including Marshall, were willing to take the plunge and underwrite the survival of Great Britain. It has not been the purpose of this essay to portray the Chief of Staff prior to that watershed month as being indifferent to Britain's fate; he was anything but. But he was even less indifferent to his primary charge, the national interest of the United States; and he was, for two months, convinced that it would be suicidal to let emotion overrule interest, and to expend America's precious *matériel* in support of what to many observers looked like a hopeless cause. Marshall's and, *a fortiori*, the nation's dilemma at this time of tremendous uncertainty was pointedly suggested in a memorandum from Major Walter Bedell Smith, who wrote the Chief of Staff on 11 June, a day when the Army command was wrestling with the question of transferring five hundred 75-millimeter guns to the British, that 'if we were required to mobilize after having released guns necessary for this mobilization and were found to be short in artillery *matériel*. . .everyone who was a party to the deal might hope to be found hanging from a lamp post'.[33]

It would, of course, be silly to suggest that Marshall's position on the burning question of assisting Britain was influenced by considerations of personal safety; this would be patently unfair to the memory of the Chief of Staff. But it is equally unfair, both to Marshall and to ourselves, to let stand unchallenged the common view of him as one of the first and foremost advocates of all-out aid to England. Although never an 'isolationist' himself, it is clear that Marshall, for a short while at least, had something in common with those who would shortly rally a political movement around the slogan, 'America First'.

NOTES

1. W. Averell Harriman, Foreword to *Harry Hopkins: A Biography*, by Henry H. Adams (New York 1977), 15.

2. Quoted in Mark Lincoln Chadwin, *The Hawks of World War II* (Chapel Hill, N. C., 1968), 84.

3. William Frye, *Marshall: Citizen Soldier* (Indianapolis 1947), 276.

4. Richard M. Leighton and Robert W. Coakley, *Global Logistics and Strategy, 1940-1943*, United States Army in World War II: The War Department (Washington 1955), 33.

5. Forrest C. Pogue, *George C. Marshall: Ordeal and Hope, 1939-1942* (New York 1965), 46.

6. For the significance of the perceived security threat to Latin America, and its influence on the Roosevelt administration's decision to abandon its policy of isolation, see David G. Haglund, 'The Battle of Latin America: Franklin D. Roosevelt and the End of Isolation, 1936-1941' (PhD dissertation, Johns Hopkins University, 1978). The mood of alarm in the American capital during the months of May and June 1940 is captured in William L. Langer and S. Everett Gleason, *The Challenge to Isolation* (New York 1952), chaps. 14 and 15.

7. It is impossible to determine exactly the number of people with German, Italian, or Japanese blood living below the Rio Grande in 1940. Nevertheless, we can state with certainty that the President and his advisers were impressed that the figure was very large — at least five million in South America alone, according to the FBI. Not all of these were considered to be Axis sympathizers, but the point remains that a significant proportion were so considered. For the FBI estimate, see the Bureau's March 1942 report, 'United States Dependency on South America', Harry Hopkins Papers, Group 24, Container 144, Franklin D. Roosevelt Library (FDRL), Hyde Park, NY.

8. German leaders never tired of assuring Americans that they had no designs on any hemisphere lands. In early March 1940, Foreign Minister Joachim von Ribbentrop and Luftwaffe chief Hermann Goering told Under Secretary of State Welles, who was in Germany on a fact-finding mission, that no territory in Latin America would ever tempt the Reich. Sumner Welles, *The Time for Decision* (Cleveland 1945), 92-98.

9. John Morton Blum, *From the Morgenthau Diaries: Years of Urgency, 1938-1941* (Boston 1965), 150.

10. Hubert Herring, *Good Neighbors: Argentina, Brazil, Chile & Seventeen Other Countries* (New Haven 1941), 327.

11. Samuel I. Rosenman, comp., *The Public Papers and Addresses of Franklin D. Roosevelt*, 13 vols. (New York 1938, 1941-50), 9:198-205. (Hereafter *Public Papers*.)

12. Cordell Hull, *The Memoirs of Cordell Hull*, 2 vols. (New York 1948), 1:822.

13. *Public Papers*, 9:238.

14. Adolf A. Berle, Jr., *Navigating the Rapids, 1918-1971:From the Papers of Adolf A. Berle*, ed. Beatrice Bishop Berle and Travis Beal Jacobs (New York 1973), 326.

15. Military Attaché to Argentina, 16 May 1940, 2657-L-133/3; 21 May 1940, 2657-L-133/6; War Department Files, Military Intelligence Division, National Archives, Record Group 165. (Hereafter M/A and country, date, file no., MID).

16. Memorandum of conversation between Armour and his contact, Capt. Marcos A. Zar, 5 June 1940, Roosevelt Papers, PSF Diplomatic, Box 32, FDRL.

17. Wilson to Hull, 30 May 1940, Department of State, *Foreign Relations of the United States* (Washington 1862-), 1940, 5:1151-52.

18. Duggan to Welles, 31 May 1940, ibid., 1153.

19. *New York Times*, 2 June 1940.

20. M/A Brazil, 22 May 1940, 2657-K-123/4, MID.

21. Details of the POT OF GOLD plan can be found in Mark Skinner Watson, *Chief of Staff: Prewar Plans and Preparations*, United States Army in World War II: The War Department (Washington 1950), 96, 106.

22. Roosevelt to Bowers, 22 May 1940, in Claude G. Bowers, *Chile through Embassy Windows, 1939-1953* (New York 1958), 60-61.

23. Bowers to Welles, 25 May 1940, Roosevelt Papers, PSF Diplomatic, Box 36, FDRL. From nearby Mexico came even more startling reports. On 13 June FBI director J. Edgar Hoover told the Secretary of the Treasury that he had been reliably informed that 'approximately eleven thousand Germans between the ages of twenty-one and twenty-seven, and constituting a fully equipped fighting unit, have suddenly appeared in Mexico City'. Hoover to Morgenthau, 13 June 1940, in Unpublished Diary of Henry Morgenthau, Jr., 273:290-91, FDRL.

24. Churchill to Roosevelt, 20 May 1940, in *Roosevelt and Churchill: Their Secret Correspondence*, ed. Francis L. Loewenheim, Harold D. Langley, and Manfred Jonas (New York 1975), 97.

25. Marshall's minute of the 23 May conference cited by Stetson Conn and Byron Fairchild, *The Framework of Hemisphere Defense*, United States Army in World War II: The Western Hemisphere (Washington 1960), 32. For the WPD memorandum of 22 May, see Langer and Gleason, op. cit., 475.

26. Statement of 30 May 1940, in *Complete Presidential Press Conferences of Franklin D. Roosevelt*, 24 vols. (New York 1972), 15:412-13.

27. *Public Papers*, 9:259-64.

28. Strong to Marshall, 17 June 1940, WPD 4250-3, War Department Files, War Plans Division, National Archives, Record Group 165.

29. Marshall statement to SLC, 17 June 1940, ibid. (Marshall's emphasis.)

30. Marshall and Stark to Roosevelt, 24 June 1940, ibid. This memorandum had been composed on 22 June, the day France surrendered.

31. Marshall to Strong, 24 June 1940, ibid.

32. Marshall and Stark to Roosevelt, 27 June 1940, ibid.

33. Cited by Watson, op. cit., 312.

IV

The War at Sea

Owing to certain important reforms which had been carried out in the inter-war period, the British Navy was not unprepared when war broke out. Its unruffled confidence in ultimate victory was not, as Rear-Admiral Gueritz shows, an affectation but sprang from an inborn sense of invincibility. But it had some blind spots, the most important perhaps was its inability fully to recognize the impact of air power on naval strategy; the fact that the battleship was gradually supplanted by the aircraft carrier as the core of a modern fleet. The main task facing the navy was winning the battle of the Atlantic, the defeat of the U-boats. This battle was won after the Royal Navy had accepted, somewhat belatedly, air power as a co-equal partner. Another crucial factor was, as Vice-Admiral Schofield shows, Ultra, which explains the sudden reversal of the U-boats' fortunes in early 1943. Lastly, the formation of support groups to reinforce the escort of threatened convoys has to be mentioned.

9 Nelson's Blood: Attitudes and Actions of the Royal Navy 1939-45

Rear-Admiral E F Gueritz

On 1 August 1970 the issue of a free ration of rum, commonly called Nelson's Blood, to ratings in the Royal Navy was discontinued, and a custom which had originated soon after the capture of Jamaica in 1655 came to an end. Lord Nelson was no more associated with rum than any of his contemporaries, and the grisly association with the preservation of his body is based on a misunderstanding.[1] The significance of the nickname lies in the acceptance of Nelson as the embodiment of all the Royal Navy's traditions whether they originated with him or not. It is ironical, therefore, that some of Nelson's most important contributions to naval warfare became overlaid in the Royal Navy by a heavy layer of Victorian orthodoxy and social prejudice, to the detriment of British naval operations in the first world war. Some old sailors used to say: 'If 'e knew what was done in 'is name 'e'd be down off his pedestal to sort 'em out.' The purpose of this article is to review how attitudes had developed by the outbreak of the second world war, and to examine very briefly some examples of how actions may have been affected.

It seems remarkable that a nation with a strong maritime tradition should produce generations of naval officers addicted to an orthodoxy quite at variance with the character and practice of the great hero whose memory they venerated. It was for change in this attitude that Vice-Admiral Sir George Tryon strove, and literally died in vain, towards the end of the nineteenth century. He had recognized the baleful influence of orthodoxy and blind obedience, and sought to make his subordinates think for themselves.[2] The performance of the British fleets in the North Sea in the first world war bore distressing testimony to the wisdom of his appreciation. The courage and seamanship of the officers of those fleets are not in question, nor is the respect which they had for their Commander-in-Chief. It was this virtue which became the vice when it seemed to be accepted that the Admiral was omniscient, and that it would be presumptuous to give him information. Failures at Jutland were not confined to unwarrantable silence. There were also cases in which the Nelsonian injunction was ignored that '. . . no Captain can do very wrong if he lays his ship alongside that of an enemy'. There was no lack of courage but there was a great lack of initiative, and consequently orthodoxy triumphed over opportunity.

The contrast in the second world war was most marked. By a fortunate chance, certain men of genius had wrought a great change. One can, perhaps, date this phenomenon from the departure of Admiral Sir Roger Keyes from the Mediterranean, and attribute its development to the influence of Admiral Sir Ernle Chatfield (later Admiral of the Fleet Lord Chatfield) and Admiral Sir William Fisher[3] who became his successors as Commander-in-Chief. Certainly the restrictive effects of voluminous Fleet Orders and tactical instructions were quickly dispelled, training was made more realistic, and a proper emphasis was laid on training for night fighting.[4] Among the subordinate Flag Officers was Rear-Admiral A.B. Cunningham, who held the appointment of Rear-Admiral Destroyers, and himself made his name as a great wartime commander-in-chief in the Mediterranean. With his enormous experience of destroyers (he commanded HMS *Scorpion* for seven years, 1910-18) and the high standards which he expected, the destroyer flotillas of the Mediterranean must have been a fine school for initiative, quick-thinking and team work. There is no doubt that by 1939 there were a number of very experienced commanding officers and first lieutenants in destroyers. This was just as well, as it was upon them that fell the tremendous burdens of the first years of the war. There was a heavy toll among the less experienced and robust, as was evident in the RN hospitals of the time. Destroyer officers tended to be an exclusive professional group, contemptuous of their brothers in big ships and condescending, to put it politely, to newcomers to the 'boats'.[5] Commander Lord Louis Mountbatten was not fully accepted, and his invention, the Mountbatten Station Keeping Gear, was scorned by many 'old' destroyer captains.

Coincidentally, or so it seems, the resurrected spirit of the Nelsonian 'band of brothers' not only brought initiative and enterprise back into naval operations, but also a new sensibility in the handling of men, as was exemplified in the doctrine and practice pioneered by Commander Rorie O'Conor. By the outbreak of war, for example, the attitude adopted towards midshipmen had changed considerably. They were treated as young officers rather than as fugitives from a preparatory school, and the gunrooms in which they lived ceased to run as though Doctor Arnold had never lived![6] There may have been exceptions, but these tended to be in battleships where older ideas died hard. The change in attitude may have been due in some measure to the influence of the Special Entry scheme. Midshipmen trained under this scheme were older when they went to sea and had a wider educational background.[7] One lesson of the age of enlightenment in the 1930s was the emphasis placed on enemy reporting: the overriding duty of reporting the enemy, his strength and his movements.

There were, however, aspects of the Royal Navy's character which had escaped reform. The attitude to non-executive officers, Engineers and Paymasters, was considerably improved. The difference in their uniforms was now only that of the distinctive purple and white cloth between the gold rank stripes on the arms or shoulder straps. Nevertheless, the Seaman Branch retained its privileged position and certain prerogatives which caused ill-feeling until major reforms were enacted in 1955. Regrettably, this social prejudice extended to the Reserves. Officers and ratings who joined the Royal Naval Reserve (RNR) while serving in the Merchant Navy served for short periods of training in HM ships. On at least two occasions, groups of officers were accepted for transfer from the RNR to the RN. It would be gratifying to say that the public spirit of the Reserves and the welcome accession of strength represented by the transfers were recognized by officers in the fleet. The politest term which can be used about the usual attitude is 'patronizing'. Yet Merchant Navy officers had more practical sea experience by the nature of their profession than RN officers whose sea-time was restricted by fuel economices. (Shades of 1980-81.) Moreover, the attitude betokened a failure to appreciate that one of the main raisons d'être of a navy is the care of its merchant fleet. Lack of understanding of the virtues and the difficulties of the men who manned the British merchant fleet was inexcusable after the hard-won lessons of the first Atlantic war. Some progress was made by way of official training in Naval Control of Shipping just before the war: the Admiralty organization for such control was incomparably better than it had been in 1914 or even 1916. The underlying cause of inattention to the Merchant Navy was the failure to appreciate that fleet action was a means to an end, and not an end in itself. Anti-submarine warfare training was far more a matter of fleet protection than of convoy escort work.

The work of Chatfield, Fisher, Cunningham and others bore fruit in the first hard years of the second world war. Single ships or squadrons flung themselves at the enemy with little regard for the prospect of success but with complete certainty about the path of duty. There are examples in plenty: the Battle of the River Plate in December 1939, the forlorn hopes of destroyers such as *Gloworm* and *Acasta* in the Norwegian campaign, the sacrificial action of the armed merchant-cruiser *Jervis Bay* which saved Convoy HX 84. Or, one can add the actions against the battleship *Bismarck* in June 1941 (not least the excellent reporting by HM ships *Norfolk* and *Suffolk*) and the classic defence of Convoy JW 51B by a handful of destroyers and smaller escorts, pitted against a battle-cruiser and a heavy cruiser in December 1942. Any appearance of reluctance to engage brought censure, just or unjust. A shadow fell across the good name of HMS *Newcastle*, a Town Class cruiser, next on the patrol line in Northern Waters, when the armed merchant-cruiser *Rawalpindi* was sunk by the battle-cruisers *Scharnhorst* and *Gneisnau* in the autumn of 1939. A high-powered Board of Inquiry sat in Gibraltar in December 1940, under the presidency of Admiral of the Fleet the Earl of Cork and Orrery, to examine the conduct of Vice-Admiral Sir James Somerville in his action with Italian forces off Cape Spartivento, Sardinia. The treatment of Admiral Sir Dudley North, as Flag Officer Gibraltar, when a French squadron passed unmolested through the straits, remains a blot on the Admiralty's record.[8] The execution of an Admiral 'pour encourager les autres' may be desirable, sometimes essential, even if the execution has, in modern times, been metaphorical rather than literal. Nothing but harm is likely to result from an evident injustice to a subordinate in order to cloak the shortcomings of a superior.[9] It has been suggested that the First Sea Lord should have done more to restrain the Prime Minister from interfering in the operational conduct of the fleet. Men such as Admirals Cunningham and Somerville needed no urging to use their ships effectively. It is recorded that Admiral Cunningham 'could hardly forgive him [Churchill] for some of the insulting telegrams he received from time to time'.[10] Captain Stephen Roskill, with his close personal knowledge of Admiral Pound, has examined this question in the book already quoted,[11] and it has been an area of dispute between him and that other eminent scholar, the late Professor Arthur Marder. Great attention has been paid by well-qualified observers and authoritative writers to the question of Admiral Pound's health[12] and opinions differ about its significance. Discussion often centres upon the Admiralty's actions during the passage of the Convoy PQ 17 to Russia. It is not intended to rehearse the sequence of events or argue once again the rights and wrongs of the First Sea Lord's decision to scatter the convoy except in one respect. Convoys in the Mediterranean were escorted by heavy ships and were subjected to attack by surface forces, as well as by aircraft and submarines. They were fought through at great cost, and the same can be said of the Arctic convoys with the added comment that the weather frequently was appalling. In the Arctic deployments, heavy surface escorts were stationed in close or distant covering positions. In the case of Convoy PQ 17, a particular threat was posed by the German battleship *Tirpitz*. It seems strange that, instead of seeking to bring that enemy to action with our own heavy forces, the Admiralty's actions were diametrically the opposite. If it were decided to avoid risks of air attack on surface forces by limiting their movement to the east, this would be understandable, if contrary to the best traditions of eliminating the surface threat in battle. In any case, the order to scatter seems wholly inappropriate. Such an order was surely intended for use in the broad oceans against an immediate surface threat, and not in an area where air and submarine threats were equally real and dangerous to unescorted merchant ships. To withdraw all protection seems incomprehensible, particularly as this was the action of a distant command headquarters bypassing three levels of command: the Commander-in-Chief, Home Fleet, the Cruiser Force Commander, and the Escort Force Commander. What these men needed was the best possible information and the freedom to respond to the circumstances with which they were confronted, not in an office, but on the bridge. The Board Room in the Admiralty building has a weather gauge, a relic of the eighteenth century. Its sole purpose was to remind those sitting at the table that it was on 'storm-tossed ships' that success or failure would depend. The disastrous material consequences of the order to scatter are recorded. The losses which might have been inflicted by the *Tirpitz* could have been as bad, although other experience does not support such a proposition. What is unquestioned is the moral impact of the withdrawal of the escort forces. Perhaps the wounds have healed by now, but the damage done to relations between the Royal Navy and the men of its merchant fleet, and between the Royal Navy and the United States Navy, was deep and lasting. The accepted standard was voiced by Admiral Cunningham in his famous affirmation: 'It takes three years to build a ship but three hundred to build a tradition'. This was his view during the days of the evacuation from Greece, the defence of Crete, and finally the evacuation of Imperial forces from the island in the spring of 1941. He declared: 'Whatever the risks, whatever our losses, the remaining ships of the fleet would make an all-out effort to bring away the army', and 'We cannot let the army down'.[13] Stories of that period can be a source of pride for officers and men of the Royal Navy following, as they do, upon the catalogue of similar experience in the Norwegian campaign, at Dunkirk and elsewhere in France. The attitude which they fostered was again patronizing, that of a competent and self-righteous elder brother towards his junior who was frequently in some sort of scrape, and had to be picked up, dusted down with generous affection and sent on his way. They held a sneaking regard for the soldiers' courage and endurance coupled with tolerance for his unfamiliarity with shipboard life, and readiness to share such comforts as there were. As one period ended, so another was well under way.

Only the British would set up an Expeditionary Force Headquarters immediately after the precipitate withdrawal from a disastrous continental venture. This headquarters was established at Largs on the west coast of Scotland. Commando units were raised, and amphibious training started not only for commandos, but also for selected formations of the army proper. It has been said that it was possible to identify units which had been trained in amphibious operations by the fact that their officers and men had lost their child-like faith in the Royal Navy! The cause of this loss of faith was the natural consequence of familiarity with ships, boats and their watery environment, and also the effect of the realization that even sailors sometimes make mistakes! The most ordinary mistakes were those of navigation. The aids to navigation in small craft were primitive and were not helped by the close proximity to compasses of steel helmets and other metal objects. The crews with whom the soldiers trained were themselves under training. The system by which the officers and men were channelled into Combined Operations reflected another unreformed attitude of the prewar navy. This was, once more, a failure to appreciate the true role of a navy. Viscount Grey of Fallodon remarked that the army is a projectile to be fired by the navy.[14] It seems, however, that the Royal Navy, at least, neglected to carry out battle practice with that particular weapon system!

Naval vessels frequently acted as troop transports in emergency: the County Class cruisers were built with room for a battalion to be carried for short periods.[15] However, little money was laid out for the development, let alone the production, of the specialized vessels needed for modern landing operations. It has been said that the capture of Diego Suarez in Madagascar in May 1942 was the first successful British Combined Operation since Quebec in 1759. This is probably unfair, but in most respects the provisions for landing operations in 1940 were little better than those available at Aboukir Bay in 1801. Power boats had replaced some ship's oared boats, but many of the boats were less suitable for the purpose than those available to Abercromby's men. Even the Royal Marines gave visible evidence of the low priority which was accorded to their *per terram* task. The smartness with which the Royal Marines could adorn a ceremonial occasion, with blue uniform, white helmets and pipeclayed belts, was in strange contrast to their appearance when landing for field exercises. For these their khaki uniform, obviously dragged from the bottom of kitbags, would hardly have done credit to their forebears in the trenches on the Somme some twenty years before. Nor were the Royal Marines given their natural place as the first units of the new Special Service group. Army Commandos were formed, while Royal Marine battalions remained brigaded as infantry until 1942. Thereafter, Royal Marines Commandos were formed, and the balance of the men available manned landing craft flotillas and special support landing units. Thus the Royal Marines joined, very properly, the Royal Navy's effort to project power ashore.

The manning of the naval components of Combined Operations can be summarized as follows. Some enthusiastic and experienced yachtsmen, pre-war members of the Royal Naval Volunteer Reserve (RNVR), formed the cadre which provided leadership and skill. The bulk of the officers were appointed (selected would be too strong a word) from the mass production line of the training establishment, HMS *King Alfred*. Ratings were drafted from New Entry establishments and from the Patrol Service, which was based on the peacetime fishing fleet. The senior element was generally found from retired officers who were recalled to service and were found employment in the mushroom growth of landing craft bases. The organization quickly passed from the hands of a senior Royal Marines officer, General Sir Alan Bourne, into those of Admiral of the Fleet Sir Roger Keyes. It was not a happy arrangement. The navy was not disposed to look with great favour upon the eccentric activities of what promised to be a most irregular, if not piratical, crew. Admiral Keyes was not the person to oil wheels or to smooth ruffled feathers, and some of his appointees were worlds apart from the modern navy, let alone from its brand-new striking force. Some officers from the General Service of the Royal Navy volunteered for Special Service, and were appointed to Combined Operations. Many of these appointments were of comparatively short duration. The Royal Navy's appointing system rolled on its accustomed way, presuming with complete confidence that the war was only a break in the ordered pattern of the Royal Navy's life. Career planning must continue without thought of the possibility that it might be as well to hatch defeat of the Axis before counting the chickens of post-war appointments and promotions. It is hardly credible that an experienced senior beachmaster, recovering from wounds received ashore in Normandy, was told: 'to stop fooling around with his Combined Operations business and get down to some regular sailoring'.[16] At that time, the Walcheren operation had not yet taken place, and peace in Europe was eight months away. The war against Japan was at its height with amphibious operations pending in South East Asia and continuing in the Pacific. In spite of this, career planning took precedence over the use of knowledge and experience. This same spirit motivated the Royal Navy's approach to temporary promotions and the award of acting rank. Such benefits were dealt out lavishly among the ranks of RNVR officers, whose temporarily inflated status would not complicate the reversion to peacetime promotion patterns. This unruffled confidence in ultimate victory was not an affectation, but sprang from an inborn sense of invincibility. Disasters there might be, setbacks, reverses, critical struggles for existence but, in the end, the Empire and its navies would emerge triumphant. The same spirit was perceptible in operation orders which sent ships into night action against superior forces concluding with the injunction that 'ships are to return to harbour at 0900'.

However such confidence may be described, whether as optimism, arrogance or steadfast faith, it had its price-tag. There is the difficulty of encompassing the possibility of innovation. As

Field Marshal Kesselring remarked in his memoirs: 'Since then I have often observed this instinctive rejection of an innovation that has not broken down prejudice. It is remarkable how strongly the vis inertiae is able to exert influence on the best intelligence.'[17] Between the wars the impact of air power on naval strategy and tactics had yet to be appreciated fully in the Royal Navy. It is true that the pusillanimous attitude adopted towards Italy in 1935 stemmed partly from assessments of the vulnerability to air attack of the British Mediterranean Fleet. However, it seems that more energy and verbal ammunition was expended in Whitehall warfare between the navy and the Royal Air Force than ever went into the provision of effective air defence of the fleet, although Admiral Fisher declared in 1936 that great strides had been made. Chatfield, by then First Sea Lord, stated that: 'My personal view tends strongly in the direction that attack of ships at sea by aircraft will be unremunerative in a few years.'[18] Although the battle for the control of the Fleet Air Arm involved so much bloodshed in Whitehall, that arm of the service with its carriers had not achieved its rightful eminence in the Royal Navy's thinking. The big gun and the battleship still held sway, but the distinguished naval writer, Commander Russell Grenfell, ventured to suggest in 1937: 'When certain warships had become so large and expensive that there is an inevitable tendency to keep them in cotton wool, and when increasing numbers of other warships have to be devoted to their protection there are, perhaps, grounds for thinking that these particular vessels have outgrown their usefulness.'[19] At about the same time, Admiral Yamamoto in Japan was recorded as saying:

> These ships are like elaborate religious scrolls which old people hang up in their homes. . . . Military people always carry history around with them in the shape of old campaigns. They carry obsolete weapons like swords and it is a long time before they have become purely ornamental. These battleships will be as useful in modern warfare as a Samurai sword.[20]

Both in Japan and in the United States, the power of the aircraft carrier was appreciated to greater effect than in Britain, notably in the provision of up-to-date aircraft for the embarked squadrons. The lack of direct naval responsibility for procurement is blamed for the poor equipment of the Fleet Air Arm, but what sacrifices did the Royal Navy offer to make in those days of penurious budgets for defence? Later, there was a lack of industrial resources to meet all rearmament needs, and time was running out by the time the navy regained full control of the Fleet Air Arm in 1937. Nor was the personnel problem straightforward. By transfers from the Royal Air Force, promotions from the lower deck and the use of rating pilots, some progress was made in building up resources. A bigger step was the introduction of the Air Branch Entry by which officers were recruited expressly for flying duties. They were distinguished by the addition of the letter A in the curl of their rank stripes, and were restricted in the duties expected of them. Resources were increased by the creation of an Air Branch in the RNVR.

Two threads are distinguishable in the Royal Navy's attitudes towards the new influence on naval warfare. The first is the reluctance to recognize that the battleship was being supplanted as the core of a modern fleet by the aircraft carrier. This led to some mishandling of the available carriers and the consequent unnecessary and tragic losses. For example, the sinking of HMS *Courageous* was the result of her misemployment in anti-submarine operations. HMS *Glorious* was detached from the forces operating off Norway in 1940 to return to Scapa Flow in readiness for a court-martial. This was a deplorable reason for depriving the Allied forces of her services, and for imperilling a most valuable fleet unit. She was sunk by the battle-cruisers *Scharnhorst* and *Gneisnau* while on passage.[21]

The employment of a balanced force with a full range of air and surface elements came to be accepted in 1940, almost unconsciously, with the operations of Force H based on Gibraltar. This force, presumably inheriting its designation from one of the lettered hunting groups of the 1939 period, was an exemplar of the well-practised co-operative action which became commonplace in carrier task groups in the Pacific war and thereafter. It is interesting to reflect on the fact that the commander of this successful pioneering venture, Vice-Admiral Sir James Somerville, had, in fact, been invalided from the service before the war. He might well have adhered to conservative opinions, but he was, on the contrary, a most lively personality with a great gift of leadership. This stood him in good stead when he personally dragged the men of the Eastern Fleet out of a slough of low morale in the summer of 1942. The gift of appeal to all ranks and specializations was a key factor in a navy whose main striking power was increasingly dependent upon the skill and courage of young men, many of whom had no real naval background. The carrier aircrews were irked by traditional routines and ceremonial, disciplined in their own profession, but unimpressed by the rigid attitudes and conventions of the 'Fish-heads' (seamen officers) who ran their floating airfields. Needless to say, the Fish-heads were scandalized by the demoralizing behaviour of some of the aircrew in the squadrons which embarked. To an extent, specializations and sub-specializations within a service need their special ethos, some feeling of élitist separation. This must apply particularly to airmen and submariners, who need an extra element of self-discipline and professional responsibility. The dilution in the aircrew ranks increased inevitably with heavy casualties and great expansion of the air arm. With the dilution, the separation between the 'establishment' of the regular navy and its wartime reinforcements increased. Long-service officers and ratings were called 'the caretakers' by their 'hostilities-only' shipmates, and this term was not confined to any particular branch of the service. The second thread in the Royal Navy's attitudes related, therefore, to the difficulty of moulding the strength of tradition and customary discipline with the vital force of enthusiasm and new skills, the delicate balance between stifling orthodoxy and ineffective amateurism. Problems could, and did, occur in any ship or force, but in carriers, living conditions brought everyone into close propinquity and, at the same time, the flying task set the aircrew apart from their messmates. With good leadership at many levels a fine rapport could be achieved. The results of carrier co-operation were a source of pride and self-perpetuating efficiency of operations. In landing craft bases and assault forces, great care had to be exercised. Living and working conditions were often rough and ready, basic training had been sketchy, and the leavening of RN officers and ratings was lightly sprinkled. For the Normandy invasion a larger framework of organization was applied to direct the training, to oversee and execute administration, and to fit squadrons and flotillas into the great pattern of the assault and build-up. These squadrons and flotillas were a vital weapon in the armoury of Allied sea power. Their crews and the associated beach parties were very largely RNVR and hostilities-only officers and ratings. It would have been easy for them to have degenerated into an ill-kempt and incompetent rabble without sympathetic support and guidance from those with more experience and training.

Lord Nelson would have delighted in the offensive action which landing craft crews achieved. He would have revelled in the dash and courage of Fleet Air Arm crews and would certainly have enjoyed their respect. His humanity would have recognized and encouraged the enthusiasm of reservists of all kinds. He would have commended the fighting spirit of Cunningham and the sacrifice made by his band of brothers off Greece and Crete. He would have turned a deaf ear to the interference of the Admiralty. He might not have seen plainly that the defence of shipping and the projection of power ashore are truly naval roles, not distractions from the pursuit of the fleet action. As to how he himself might have performed as a Whitehall warrior, Lord Nelson's encounter with the Duke of Wellington in Whitehall one month before the Battle of Trafalgar was hardly promising!

NOTES

1. Nelson's body was transported to England after Trafalgar in a cask of brandy (not rum).

2. Richard Hough, *Admirals in Collision* (London 1959).

3. Admiral Fisher died suddenly in 1937 while serving as Commander-in-Chief Portsmouth.

4. Rear-Admiral Royer Dick, who was Chief of Staff to Sir Andrew Cunningham, has told the writer that at the Battle of Matapan he remarked that Chatfield's emphasis on night fighting was being rewarded.

5. The word 'boat' was formerly used colloquially to describe passenger ships, thus: 'P&O boat'. It was a solecism to apply the term to warships but, confusingly, jargon in the Royal Navy used 'boats' for submarines and collectively for destroyers, thus 'I served in the Boats up the Straits (of Gibraltar)'.

6. Captain O'Conor was killed while commanding HMS *Neptune* in 1941. His main published work was *Running a Ship on Ten Commandments*.

7. Special Entry cadets joined from their secondary schools by competitive examination from 17½-18 years of age.

8. Those two regrettable affairs are magisterially examined by Captain Roskill in *Churchill and the Admiral* (London 1977), chapter II.

9. The quotation originated from Voltaire's *Candide* and relates to the execution of Admiral The Hon. Sir John Byng in 1757.

10. Captain S.W.C. Pack, RN, *Cunningham* (London 1974), 126.

11. Roskill, op. cit., Appendix.

12. For example, Dr Hugh L'Etang, *The Pathology of Leadership* and *Fit to Lead?*

13. Pack, op. cit., 177.

14. Viscount Grey of Fallodon, *Fisher Memoirs*.

15. The writer travelled in a County Class cruiser carrying 500 survivors and 200 prisoners in addition to her complement.
16. Words spoken to the writer in September 1944.
17. Kesselring, *Memoirs* (London 1953), 17.
18. G. Till, *Air Power and the Royal Navy* (London 1979), 152.
19. Russell Grenfell, *The Art of the Admiral*, 244.
20. John Deane Potter, *Admiral of the Pacific — The Life of Yamamoto* (London 1965), 30.
21. Till, op. cit., 176.

10 The Defeat of the U-Boats during World War II

Vice-Admiral B B Schofield

> The Battle of the Atlantic was the dominating factor all through the war. Never for one moment could we forget that everything happening elsewhere, on land, at sea, or in the air, depended ultimately on its outcome, and amid all other cares we viewed its changing fortunes day by day with hope or apprehension.
>
> Winston S. Churchill

Sir Winston has recorded[1] that his first Admiralty Minute after taking office as First Lord in September 1939, was concerned with the strength of the enemy's U-boat fleet. 'There were now in 1939 two dangers to be considered', he has written,[2] 'the first the old one of submarine incursion; the second the new one of the air', and he was surprised to find that 'the new danger from the air' had been almost entirely ignored in regard to the defence of the main fleet base and he might well have added in the defence of shipping, since it was to prove a key factor in overcoming the U-boats. It is only within the last year that a fully documented study has been published which explains the reason for the Royal Navy's tardy acceptance of air-power as co-equal partner with sea-power.[3]

Fortunately the bitter lesson of World War I had not been forgotten and plans had been prepared to institute convoy should war break out with Germany and these revealed that an insufficient number of surface ships for escort duty were available and that Coastal Command of the Royal Air Force had an inadequate number of aircraft at its disposal to meet all the demands which would be made upon it.

The section of the Naval Staff responsible for implementing the plans drawn up for the protection of shipping in time of war was known as Trade Division and the late Admiral Sir Maurice Mansergh, my predecessor as director of that division, had the difficult task of making all the necessary arrangements for the Admiralty to assume responsibility for the control and movements of all shipping on the outbreak of war in September 1939. Since in peacetime merchant ships are controlled and operated entirely by their owners or their agents, a close liaison had to be established between them and the Admiralty. To this end a Shipping Defence Advisory Committee was formed comprising representatives of the Admiralty, the Board of Trade, the Chamber of Shipping, the Liverpool Ship Owners Association and Lloyds to consider all the factors involved in the protection of shipping in war. The full committee was a very large one and a smaller working committee presided over by the Director of the Trade Division met regularly once a month to deal with current problems and, once the war had started, to explain to particular shipowners the circumstances surrounding the loss of one of their ships. One month after the outbreak of war, a Ministry of Shipping was formed to deal with the problems of manning, bunkering, repairs, loading and discharge which were outside the Admiralty's responsibility but which nevertheless were closely connected with ships' movements. Later it became the Ministry of War Transport and embraced road and rail transport and storage facilities all of which were affected by the arrival, discharge and reloading of ships. As the war developed it became evident that the key factor in virtually every military operation was the availability of shipping. In consequence Trade Division steadily grew in size and when in March 1941 I relieved Mansergh as its director, the staff numbered 185; when in July 1943 I turned over to my successor it was twice that number.

It has to be admitted that the Admiralty underestimated the threat posed by the 57 U-boats possessed by the German navy on the outbreak of war. This was due in part to the ill-founded belief that Germany would observe the Geneva Convention to which she had subscribed regarding the provision to be made for the safety of the passengers and crew before a ship was sunk and in part to an over-optimistic belief in the efficiency of the newly developed asdic apparatus with which the majority of A/S ships were fitted. The fact that the commodore in charge of Germany's U-boat fleet (Karl Dönitz) was an advocate of night attacks by U-boats on the surface was overlooked and a surfaced submarine did not provide a target for asdic apparatus. As a result of this thinking, the allied A/S forces were not at first prepared to deal with such attacks and to make matters worse the few aircraft available to work with them were not equipped with a really lethal A/S weapon.

Because of the shortage of convoy escort vessels and the belief that the U-boats would confine their activities to the Western Approaches, it was decided that until the deficiency had been made up, transatlantic convoys would be escorted only as far as longitude 20° west when ships would disperse and proceed at their best speed direct to their destinations.

The Prime Minister, at his request, was supplied every week with full details of shipping losses, but due to a ruling given by his scientific advisor Professor (later Lord) Lindeman, ships originally in convoy but sunk after dispersal were counted as losses-in-convoy. This statistical error prevented for a long time a true comparison between the loss rate of independently sailed ships and those in convoy and was used by the advocates of independently sailed ships in the mistaken belief that imports would thereby be increased. The fact was that the loss rate of independently sailed ships with the exception of a very few capable of speed in excess of 20 knots, was consistently much higher than for those sailing in convoy, and it could be proved that, if due to convoy restrictions a ship carried only 85 per cent of her cargo capacity in a year, if sailed independently, because of the higher loss rate she would only carry 68 per cent.

The negotiated transfer of 50 overage United States destroyers to the British and Canadian navies in October 1940 in exchange for base facilities in the West Indies and Bermuda helped to relieve the surface escort situation but the shortage of aircraft persisted. The Prime Minister had no doubt about the fact that we should have to lean heavily on the United States for help in overcoming our deficiencies and his first meeting with President Roosevelt at Argentia Bay, Newfoundland, to which the First Sea Lord, Admiral of the Fleet Sir Dudley Pound had ordered me to accompany him, provided an opportunity to discuss with our future allies the problems with which we were faced in regard to the protection of our Atlantic convoys. The number of escort vessels we needed to give all convoys a through escort was given as 380, a figure which surprised the Americans by its magnitude.[4] The discussions between the British and American Chiefs of Staff summoned to the Argentia Conference were wide-ranging and although Roosevelt was urged by his military advisers to give priority to the strengthening of American defences and despite Germany's successes in Norway and France, the President, encouraged by Churchill, was prepared to gamble on Britain's survival. On 27 May 1941 in a broadcast he had announced that all measures necessary for the delivery of supplies needed by Britain would be taken (Lend-Lease). At the same time preparations were made to counter possible German plans to occupy Spain and Gibraltar as well as the Spanish and Portuguese Atlantic islands and the Vichy-controlled port of Dakar. But as the British decryption service intercepted information which indicated that Hitler was planning to attack Russia, the probability of any such action lessened and attention was again concentrated on events in the North Atlantic where an extension of German U-boat operations in the area south of Greenland emphasized the need to give our Atlantic convoys through escort.

When in April 1940 Germany had occupied Denmark, Britain had sent a token force to Iceland to forestall any attempt by the enemy to seize the island, and on 4 June 1941 the President decided, in view of its strategic importance in the protection of the Atlantic lifeline, to relieve us of that responsibility and on 7 July 1941, US Marines landed at Reykjavik.

The ground for what became known as the Atlantic Conference had thus been well prepared and was entirely favourable to the next step which was the establishment of a Mid Ocean Meeting Place (MOMP) in 26° west, to the east of which the Royal Navy would escort all the fast and slow transatlantic convoys and to the west of which the US Navy would escort the fast and the Royal Canadian Navy the slow ones. The first eastbound fast convoy HX150 comprising 50 ships with an escort of five US destroyers left Halifax NS on 16 September. Eight US escort groups each of five destroyers supported by four squadrons of flying boats based in Newfoundland were employed for this purpose. This was one of the important achievements of the conference; on the question of an increased procurement of aircraft to operate with the convoys, things did not go so smoothly, chiefly because it was not yet fully understood what a highly important role these were to play in bringing about the defeat of the U-boats.

One of the many factors which contributed to our success in the grim and hard fought Battle of the Atlantic was Operational Intelligence. It derived mainly from the interception and decryption of German cypher messages relating to the dispositions of the U-boats with which the German High Command hoped to sever our Atlantic lifeline and so starve us into surrender. The Director of Naval Intelligence on the outbreak of war, Admiral John Godfrey, had foreseen the need for a U-boat tracking room and had secured a barrister, Rodger Winn, to take charge of it. No better selection could have been made, since he possessed just the right sort of brain to pit against that of Karl Dönitz. Winn and his assistant Patrick Beesly were established in a room in the basement of the old Admiralty building, but moved in 1941 to one in the newly completed extension known as the Kremlin alongside one which housed the Trade Plot on which the movements of the Atlantic convoys were plotted, as well as those of independently sailed ships. This close cooperation was to prove highly satisfactory.

It was not until May 1941 that the cryptographers received the information which enabled them to break the current cypher in use by the enemy for communicating with the U-boats at sea and meanwhile, largely due to inadequate air reconnaissance, the OIC was starved for information. The German High Command, on the other hand, was being well served by its intelligence section through its ability, acquired before the war, to read British cyphers. Unfortunately, too, the mastery of the current German U-boat cypher was to last only two months before it was changed and a further period of 'darkness' supervened. In spite of these alternating In and Out periods and thanks to Winn's 'intelligent guesses' as he called them, on many occasions we were able to route our convoys clear of a line of U-boats which Dönitz, often acting on intelligence provided by the B-Dienst service, had established across their route.

Thanks to the technique of fuelling at sea underway which had been developed and to the additional escorts becoming available, by May 1941 it was possible to start giving the transatlantic convoys through escort for the whole voyage. This was a big step forward but we were well aware that the enemy shipyards were not idle and that despite the loss of some 39 U-boats from various causes, the total number operational was steadily growing. In 1940 we lost 471 ships (2,186,158 tons) to submarine attack and in 1941 the total was 432 ships (2,171,754 tons), a marginal improvement soon reversed following the entry of the United States into the war. Dönitz was quick to take advantage of the US Navy's complete lack of protection of the shipping sailing along that country's eastern seaboard and in consequence during the first six months of 1942 we lost 526 ships to U-boat attack and the total for that year reached the alarming figure of 1,160 ships (6,266,215 tons), a loss rate that could not be sustained indefinitely. More important than the loss of the ships themselves was the deplorable effect on the morale of the brave officers and men who manned them.

In mid-1942, the Admiralty invited Professor (later Lord) Blackett, a Nobel prize winner, and his staff of scientists to study the operation of the convoy system. His analysis showed that, contrary to popular belief, the larger the number of ships in a convoy, the smaller the percentage loss, since on the average a U-boat attacking a convoy only sank one ship. Further, that a convoy of 48 ships with eight escorts could be given the same density of protection as one of 24 ships with 6 escorts. He pointed out that larger convoys would enable the frequency of sailing to be reduced beside releasing escorts to form support groups which could be used to strengthen the escort of convoys under attack, a policy which Admiral Horton, C-in-C Western Approaches, was very keen to implement. Another factor which emerged was that the higher a convoy's speed, the smaller were the losses likely to be, provided it had adequate surface *and air* escort. As Dr Geoffrey Till writes in his penetrating analysis *Air Power and the Royal Navy*:

> Aircraft proved even more important in the defeat of the submarine in the Second World War than they did in the First. One obvious reason for this was the increased lethality of air attack. The development of new aerial weapons, increasing aircraft range and improved operational techniques rendered A/S air patrols much more directly dangerous to submarines than had been the largely scarecrow efforts of the First World War.[5]

Professor Blackett's analysis of convoy protection confirmed this belief, but in the face of competing demands from Bomber Command, the difficulty was how to obtain additional long range aircraft and fit them with the improved radar and weapons which made them the terror of the U-boats? Despite the Prime Minister's avowal that he regarded the threat to our shipping as the most serious of all those with which we were faced, he could not bring himself to insist that Bomber Command should forego deliveries of some new aircraft to enable Coastal Command to be reinforced. We were routeing our convoys as far north as practicable to take advantage of the air cover which could be provided from the airfields in Iceland and Newfoundland but there was still a gap of some 600 miles to the southeast of Cape Farewell (Greenland) in which air cover could not be provided. There was also an uncoverable area embracing the Azores and Canary Islands through which the Gibraltar, West and South African convoys had to pass and, as might be expected, it was to these uncoverable areas that the U-boats ultimately retreated and where they continued to operate with considerable success.

In October 1942, so desperate did the situation appear to me and my staff that I went to see the Director of Merchant Shipbuilding, Sir Amos Ayre, and persuaded him there and then to order the conversion of six tankers and six bulk grain ships under construction in a Scottish shipyard to be fitted with flat decks, which would not impede their normal use, but which would allow them each to operate six Swordfish A/S aircraft and so provide air cover throughout the voyage to the convoys in which they were sailed. These merchant ship aircraft carriers were christened the 'Mac ships' and all bore Scottish names; they flew the Red Ensign and proved very successful but they did not get the acclaim which they merited because by the time they were completed, US-built escort carriers were becoming available to work with the convoys.

The month of January 1943 was memorable for a number of events all of which played a part in bringing about mastery over the U-boat threat. On the German side, what Captain Roskill has described as 'the long smouldering conflict between Admiral Raeder and Hitler on the functions of maritime power and the employment of the German Navy, came to a head', and Admiral Dönitz was appointed Commander-in-Chief in his place, at the same time retaining his position as head of the U-boat arm. Meanwhile the Prime Minister and President Roosevelt decided that it was desirable for them and their Chiefs of Staff to have another meeting, which it was arranged should take place at Casablanca. Again the First Sea Lord bade me accompany him.

The future conduct of the Battle of the Atlantic was one of the main topics for discussion and although the Chief of Naval Operations on the US side, Fleet Admiral Ernest J. King, made clear his concern over the progress of the war against Japan, he agreed that the defeat of the U-boats must remain a first charge on our combined resources and he offered to arrange for a conference to be held in Washington as soon as possible at which all aspects of this great sea-battle including the allocation of both sea and air forces would be discussed. This took place the following March and to meet his dislike of mixed escort forces, each of the participating countries (Britain, Canada and the United States) assumed responsibility for certain specified convoy routes.

At the Casablanca Conference, the Combined Chiefs of Staff had agreed to the allocation of eighty VLR aircraft to cover the air gap to the south of Greenland, but delivery of these was well behind schedule. The matter was raised at the Washington Conference and as a result of enquiry by the President regarding the whereabouts of these aircraft, deliveries were speeded up.

Pressure by Stalin for the opening of a Second Front and the rapidly growing strength of the United States Army meant that planning for a return to the continent of Europe was being actively pursued and on 1 April 1943 I arrived in Washington as member of a small committee charged with examining together with our American allies whether, taking account of possible losses, new construction, the wartime needs of the United Kingdom, the feeding of India, and all other calls likely to be made of the total merchant ship tonnage available to the Allies, a sufficient allocation could be made to meet the demands which such a cross-channel operation would need. It was to be the largest combined operation ever undertaken and in the event called for the landing of close on one million men, 183,540 vehicles and 650,000 tons of stores. For this some 2,500 landing craft supported by 1,213 warships and 7,000 merchant ships were needed. Whilst I was in Washington seeking a solution to this problem, the crisis of the Battle of the Atlantic was reached. In true Wagnerian style, befitting the climax of such a long and dramatic struggle, victory was preceded by a number of unusual events. The weather in the North Atlantic during the first three months of 1943 was exceptionally severe and hampered both the attacker and attacked, but with the help of excellent information from the U-boat tracking room, our evasive routeing policy had increasing success. Thanks also to the strengthening of the convoy air and surface escorts, a heavier toll was being taken of the U-boats, a total of 55 being sunk during the first four months of the year. This period included what has been described as the greatest convoy battles of the war.

It had been evident for some weeks that we were moving towards a climax and the new German Commander-in-Chief found himself in January 1943 with a total of 393 U-boats at his disposal of which

212 were operational and, it seemed to him, in a position for a trial of strength. Unfortunately, just at this time not only did Captain Winn go sick from overwork, but a period of darkness in the field of Special Intelligence supervened. Fortunately neither of these disadvantages, severe though they were, lasted for long and by superhuman efforts on the part of all concerned, when the critical battles of March 1943 took place, both were functioning again. The issue was not decided as the result of one encounter but lasted for over six weeks, but as the toll taken of the U-boats steadily grew, their morale started to decline, which is not in the least surprising. By the third week in May, after the loss of 33 U-boats during that month's intensive encounters with the Atlantic convoys, Dönitz decided on a temporary withdrawal of his U-boats in the area 'to avoid unnecessary losses in a period when our weapons are shown to be at a disadvantage'. At one time in March, victory had seemed within his grasp, then almost suddenly, it eluded him.

The mystery of this sudden reversal of the U-boats' fortunes lay hidden for over thirty years, until, in fact, the ban on the wartime work of the Government Code and Cypher School at Bletchley Park was lifted with the publication in 1974 of F. W. Winterbotham's book *The Ultra Secret*. This was followed by an international conference in Germany which took place between 15 and 18 November 1978 at which all the factors which led to the defeat of the German U-boat offensive against Allied shipping during World War II were carefully analyzed and discussed. An account of the proceedings in the form of a 400-page book *Die Funkaufklärung und ihre Rolle im 2 Weltkrieg* was published the following year by the organizers Drs Jürgen Rohwer and Eberhard Jäckel. The conclusions reached during the conference showed plainly that a number of factors contributed to the Allied victory over the U-boats, of which the breaking of the cyphers used by the German U-boat command for communicating with the U-boats at sea was certainly an important one. Of equal importance was the long-delayed integration of air and surface escorts for the convoys which obliged the U-boats to alter their tactics. Their initial successes had been achieved by attacking on the surface at night in 'wolf packs' which allowed them to make use of their low silhouette and high surface speed, at the same time minimizing the chances of being detected by asdic. Another contribution to the Allied victory was the formation of support groups which could be ordered to reinforce the escort of a threatened convoy. Support groups which included an escort carrier were invaluable. On the purely technical side, the introduction of 10 cm radar and the fitting of HF/DF, together with the introduction of improved A/S weapons, and last but not least the intensified training of escort groups all assisted in tilting the scales in favour of the Allies. The fact that it happened so suddenly caused much heartsearching in the U-boat command, but the one factor which contributed more than anything to their undoing by providing the Allied direction finding stations and ships with information of the enemy's whereabouts was the number of radio signals and messages which U-boats in contact with a convoy transmitted without restriction, because as Dr Rohwer says, 'their presence was already known to the enemy'.[6] Over-attention to the countermeasures against radar led to the neglect of those needed to prevent the successful employment of both decryption and direction finding equipment.

It would be wrong to close this brief examination of the defeat of the German U-boats in World War II without reference to the courage and fortitude of the officers and men of the British mercantile marine and those of the Allies without which victory could not have been gained. Their loss rate, estimated at some 17 per cent, was higher than that of any of the three fighting services and on the British side alone totalled some 33,000, but there was never any shortage of volunteers to man the ships. In a paper submitted to the Admiralty in 1942, the late Admiral Sir Max Horton wrote:

> We are concerned now with a world war in which our existence must depend, as it always has done, on sea communications . . . If we are to hold our own during this vital year, and wear down the enemy before we are ourselves exhausted, it is essential that the whole of our naval and air strength should be concentrated and employed in the battle for sea power. If we lose our sea power, we lose the war.[7]

NOTES

1. Winston S. Churchill, *The Second World War*, vol. I, 131.
2. Ibid., 336.
3. Dr Geoffrey Till, *Air Power and the Royal Navy*.
4. See Theodore Wilson, *The First Summit*, 128.
5. Geoffrey Till, op. cit., 175.
6. Jürgen Rohwer, *The Critical Convoy Battles of 1943*, 200.
7. Rear Admiral W. S. Chalmers, *Max Horton and the Western Approaches*, 279.

V

Intelligence

The role of intelligence has been discussed more widely than any other aspect of the conduct of the war and this, mainly no doubt, in view of materials which have become accessible only in recent years. This applies to the role of Ultra and Magic and also to SOE whose main assignment was not to collect and transmit information but to engage in sabotage and help organize resistance in Occupied Europe. That Ultra was of great importance is not seriously disputed. But was it decisive? Mr Bennett notes that it played no part in the greatest command decision of the war in the West — the choice of time and place for the invasion of Europe—and he points out that on certain occasions, even in the last nine months of the war, information from Ultra was 'culpably neglected with unfortunate results'. But he also shows that in other instances information was not conclusive and that the passage of time makes it hard to understand the circumstances in which a commander's decision had to be made. Mr Lewin, on the other hand, stresses that it has now become indisputable that what uniquely distinguishes the second world war from the other wars is the conclusive effect on military operations of the many activities which are subsumed under the heading of 'Sigint' or signal intelligence. Mr Foot and Mr Wheeler try to assess the importance of SOE which has been a matter of lively controversies, and Mr Paul Kramer reveals for the first time details about a joint US/British Intelligence operation in Latin America well before America's entry into the war.

11 A Signal-Intelligence War

Ronald Lewin

Every large war has its salient characteristic. Between 1914 and 1918 the increasingly sophisticated use, by both sides, of unprecedented masses of artillery is the most striking feature. The Boer War demonstrated as never before that lightly equipped, highly mobile, guerrilla-type units with their own familiar country as 'a sea to swim in' can out-match the ponderous conventional armies of a major industrialized nation. The American Civil War brought into a new focus the strategic value of the railway and the telegraph, and disclosed, in its first burgeoning, the sterility of trench warfare. During the last decade, it has become indisputable that what uniquely distinguishes the second world war is the conclusive effect on military operations of the many activities which are subsumed under the heading of 'Sigint', or signal-intelligence.

A global war is so revolutionary in so many fields — social, political, economic — that to nominate Sigint as the supreme element in all that occurred between 1939 and 1945 would be grotesque. But from the strictly military viewpoint — that is to say, in terms of the way that the business of battle (in the broadest possible sense) was actually conducted — enough hard evidence has now become available for the detached student to be able to assert confidently that in the orchestration of war Sigint was the dominant theme, to a degree unequalled in any previous conflict. I say 'detached', because, as the first important books and documents on this subject entered the public domain, a number of those who had personal experience of certain operations during the war and were subjectively conditioned into believing that what they had observed was the whole truth, tended to write down Sigint as merely an incidental factor. Even those directly concerned with producing this special intelligence have sometimes been hesitant in recognizing the paramount quality of their contribution.

Ralph Bennett was one of the brilliant team, mainly composed of academics, who worked at Bletchley Park where the complex process was concentrated of deciphering, translating, evaluating and distributing the vast amount of information contained in the multitudinous radio messages transmitted by the Germans after they had been rendered 'secure' by encipherment on the famous Enigma machine. Though much else went on at Bletchley, this was the prime activity in which Bennett, a distinguished medieval historian and now President of Magdalene College, Cambridge, had a central role. Yet in his book *Ultra in the West* (1979)[1] he affirmed: 'Sweeping suggestions have been made that the revelation of Ultra would make it necessary to rewrite the history of the war. The evidence presented here does not altogether bear them out.' In this article I take a different stance.

For if we consider what is now known merely about the material derived from breaking the Enigma cipher (that broad swathe of intelligence which the British called Ultra although, as will be seen, this was not an exclusive application of the cover-word), we can assert, for example, that most of the significant volumes in the United Kingdom series of Official Histories of the Second World War are fundamentally misleading, inadequate and out-of-date: an exception, in this respect, being Professor Hinsley's history of British intelligence.

When he was composing his admirable group of narratives of the war at sea, Captain Roskill was prohibited from any reference to Ultra because the time was not yet ripe: yet from his grasp of the contemporary but still reserved documents he must certainly — and sadly — have known that his account of the Battle of the Atlantic, to take but a single instance, was emasculated because of his inability to record Ultra's vital and extensive role in the defeat of the U-boats. If we turn to the volumes on the Mediterranean theatre, we observe that in regard to crucial matters like the interdiction of the Axis convoys to North Africa, not to speak of many strategical or tactical issues in the African, Sicilian and Italian campaigns or the deception-schemes which permeate them, any references to Ultra are always veiled, usually minimal, and never correlated in explicit and documented detail with the way that operations developed. As for the volumes dealing with the Normandy invasion and the subsequent advance into Germany, it is sufficient to mention but one of many examples. The deception whereby the German 15th Army was held down supine and immobile in the Pas de Calais, an event on which the whole success of the Normandy landings depended, would have been inconceivable without the availability of Ultra intelligence: yet how and why the inconceivable became actual is absent from the relevant volume because, at the time they were compiled, the facts were unmentionable. If Ranke's dictum has any validity, that the historian's duty is to render an account of events '*wie es eigentlich gewesen*', then 'the revelation of Ultra' may be said to entail a rewriting not only of the official histories but also of most other major war-studies published before — and, in many cases, after — the pivotal year of 1974.

That year provides a datum-line because it was then that Group Captain Winterbotham published his recollections entitled *The Ultra Secret*. Written mainly from memory and certainly without access to the documents of the time, his book had inevitable limitations which may or may not have been increased by the fact that its text was in the hands of the authorities for a substantial period before it saw the light. Nevertheless, the world-wide interest it aroused was the beginning of a one-way process. Pandora's box was now gradually prised open, and the lid can never be clamped back in place. (The slightly earlier memoirs of the French intelligence officer General Bertrand, *Enigma*, singularly failed to have this effect.)[2]

In October 1977 the first considerable batch of the original Ultra messages distributed from Bletchley Park to command headquarters at home and abroad was made available to researchers in the Public Record Office, a concession which is being steadily, if slowly, extended. Others who, like Winterbotham, were intimately involved in the production or operational use of Ultra have been permitted to publish their own books — Patrick Beesly, Peter Calvocoressi, Ewen Montagu, Professor R.V. Jones, and, of course, Ralph Bennett among others.[3] By the first issue of Hinsley's *History of British Intelligence* an official imprimatur has been given to the publication of secret matter which, less than a decade ago, would have been officially unthinkable. There already exists, therefore, a sizeable corpus of documentary and first-hand evidence whose revolutionary implications for an interpretation of the war against Germany seem beyond question.[4]

But that was neither the whole war nor the whole story. By its dramatic, unexpected and — in its initial impact — breath-taking disclosure, the phenomenon of an Ultra intelligence derived from wholly German sources has so rivetted the attention both of historians and of the general public that few have turned their eyes further to the west, where the product of an equally sophisticated, elaborate and all-pervading system of signal-intelligence underpinned the American effort in the Pacific as effectively, and as decisively as did the output from Bletchley Park in the British — and later the Allied — conflict with Germany. Yet numerous clues existed. In the thirty-nine volumes of the *Hearings before the Joint Committee on the Investigation of the Pearl Harbor Attack*, published by the US Government Printing Office in 1946, an immense amount of information may be found — by way of personal testimony and formal documentation — about the cryptanalytical achievements of the Americans in their attack on Japanese signal-traffic before 7 December 1941. Roberta Wohlstetter's classic analysis, *Pearl Harbor: Warning and Decision* (1962), clarified and amplified this authoritative evidence. It was not to be supposed that the attack petered out amid the smoke and flames of sinking battleships on that dreadful day. Many indicators, in books like David Kahn's magisterial compendium *The Codebreakers* (1966), confirmed such an assumption. The thousands of declassified papers which have filtered into the various open archives of the United States and elsewhere during the last few years have turned the assumption into a certainty.[5]

Because the events at Pearl Harbor are generally interpreted as a prime example of the failure of signal-intelligence to avert disaster, there has perhaps also been a natural tendency to assume that American ability in this field can be discounted, with the result that further exploration has been at best tentative. But what happened in December 1941 was not, essentially, the consequence of a failure in signal-intelligence itself. This was the moment when the United States was hurled from the conditions and mentality of peacetime into the realities of war: only war, as Britain herself found, could teach the lesson that intelligence is a frail possession unless the means and the methods exist for evaluating it, processing it, and distributing it in a secure fashion to field commanders who can apply it constructively in action. None of these means or methods had been developed by the Americans, in any significant sense, before the attack on Pearl Harbor. Yet it is in this area that the fundamental causes of the catastrophe may be identified. People who live in glass houses should not throw stones: nor should the British, rightly proud of their Bletchley Park and an astonishing performance in the subtle manipulation of Sigint, forget that when their own country plunged into war, on 3 September 1939, such means and methods were no less deficient. 'My object all sublime/I shall achieve *in time*', is a principle, alas, that applies to the organization of signal-intelligence no less than in the Cloud-cuckoo-land of *The Mikado*.

Yet the record stands. By a supreme intellectual effort the cryptanalysts in the small unit at Pearl Harbor penetrated, in the late spring of 1942, the Japanese naval code, JN 25, which was most generally employed in the conduct of their Pacific operations. It was intelligence painfully assembled from such decoding — and *only* this intelligence — that warned Admiral Nimitz in sufficient time for him to anticipate a Japanese trap and place his carriers in the right position for his airmen, by their skill and sacrifice, to win the Battle of Midway in June 1942 and halt, for the rest of the war, the enemy's expansion into his Great East Asian Co-Prosperity Sphere. From time to time the code became impenetrable — as happened more than once, and on occasion dangerously, in the case of Enigma: Bletchley Park's inability to read the Atlantic U-boat cipher throughout some eleven months in 1942 was a calamity for the transatlantic convoys. Still, by and large the Americans continued to read the naval code with impressive regularity until 1945, and the direct influence of the information acquired from this source was so comprehensive that to produce a fully documented case-history, when all the details are available, will prove to be a monumental task. A subsequent mastery of the code used by the Japanese for the direction of their own convoys, which frequently supplied to the Americans their course, their daily noon-position, their cargo, the character of their escorts and other essential data, had a consequence so simple and yet so shattering that it can be summed up in a sentence: American strike-forces, primarily submarines, ultimately destroyed the Japanese merchant fleet — a victory which the Germans, for their part, were never to achieve over the Allies.

The Japanese army code proved more intractable and was not broken until 1943: even then it was a progressive business, for the code had many difficult technical features. However, by a considerable use of manpower and, even more to the point, by a massive injection of technology, the code was being read with a sustained fluency in time for the great counter-offensive launched by the Americans in 1944 over the central and south-west Pacific. Precise information about enemy locations, tactical moves, equipment, supplies and so on, in respect of the Japanese army and air forces, was now transferred from the realm of haphazard acquisition to that of a routine, incessant procedure.

For the specialist student and for the general public, there are infinite possibilities of confusion in the fact that, in American practice, all the intelligence obtained from breaking the Japanese army and navy codes was also known, *tout court*, as Ultra. It is probably going to take a long time before it is fully realized that the product of Bletchley Park had only a part-share in the name: an inevitable but regrettable consequence of the earlier release, by the British, of their own 'Ultra Secret'. Yet such is the case. The origins of this American nomenclature are to be found in the aftermath of the Midway battle, when the *Chicago Tribune* leaked the fact that effective code-breaking had made the victory possible. An urgent and apprehensive review of the security accorded to their secret intelligence, by the American Chiefs of Staff, initiated many adjustments of which one was an insistence on the use of Ultra as a universal cover-name for information acquired from Japanese coded signals. This decision is illustrated by the directive issued by Admiral King on 20 June 1942, to the Commanders-in-Chief of the Pacific and Atlantic Fleets, in which he laid down that all special intelligence of this nature 'should be passed without reference to its secret source and should contain, somewhere near the beginning of the message, the word ULTRA or the word ZEAL'. Zeal faded: Ultra survived until the end of the war.

In all the controversies over Pearl Harbor, however, it was not so much these naval and military codes that were an issue as the other form of high-level signal-intelligence which was christened Magic. Once again, concentration on German-derived Ultra — and the special agony of Pearl Harbor — have diverted attention from the vast scale and infinite variety of information acquired by the Americans from their reading of the Japanese diplomatic messages which were enciphered on the machine known as Purple — a distant relation rather than, as is often assumed, a descendant of Enigma. By assiduous team-work Purple was cracked in late 1940, and thereafter, until well after the Japanese capitulation, the world-wide signal-traffic of the Japanese diplomatic service was virtually an open book. Even the mass of decrypts reproduced in the eight volumes of *The 'Magic' Background of Pearl Harbor*, issued by the US Government Printing Office in 1977, is only a selection from material made available by the cryptanalysts before December 1941. The quantity and quality of the wartime intelligence obtained from this source alone may be assessed by a study of the 'Magic Summaries' regularly issued by the Military Intelligence Service between 1942 and 1945, which are now accessible in the National Archives in Washington. It will, perhaps, sufficiently illustrate the scope of Magic if one points out that during 1942 alone the texts were deciphered of signals exchanged between the Foreign Office in Tokyo and Japanese diplomatic posts in Berlin, Rome, Lisbon, Vichy, Madrid, Ankara, Stockholm, Buenos Aires, Hanoi, Helsinki, Sofia and Santiago.

When General George Marshall, in September 1944, wrote confidentially to Governor Dewey in a successful attempt to persuade him not to make the fumbling of signal-intelligence at the time of Pearl Harbor a stick with which to beat Roosevelt's back during the imminent presidential election, he went on record with these words: 'Our main basis of information regarding Hitler's intentions in Europe is obtained from Baron Oshima's messages from Berlin reporting his interviews with Hitler and other officials to the Japanese government.' But it is not only such conversations, in which the Führer and his associates spoke with great freedom to Ambassador Oshima and which were reported with equal freedom to Tokyo, that constitute the contribution of Magic to the waging of war against Germany. From meticulous descriptions of the construction and defences of the Atlantic Wall to the exact specifications for the latest jet aircraft, Magic offered a wide panorama of German plans and activities. As for the war against Japan, it may be safely stated without further elaboration that the Magic intelligence was invaluable — uniquely so, perhaps, in the very last months, when Japanese attitudes towards the possibility of surrender and Tokyo's desperate efforts to reach a protective accommodation with the Russians were revealed to Washington on virtually a daily basis.

The Japanese, by contrast, never penetrated any of the Americans' major communications systems. Security in the US army and navy was sometimes reprehensibly lax — though the British record is better, it is not always immaculate — but combined with the technical superiority of their cryptographic equipment it proved a sufficient safeguard. Nor was it until after the war that the Japanese, like the Germans, first grasped that the cover of their codes and ciphers had been 'blown'. Through both types of Ultra, therefore, and through Magic the Allies were able, as it were, to overhear the most secret conversations of their enemies about many of the main aspects of their military, political and economic business. This had never happened previously in the history of warfare.[6]

One outstanding reason for the British and American success was the high degree of integration displayed in their cryptanalytical agencies. At Bletchley Park the pre-war professionals of the Government Code and Cypher School blended with men and women hand-picked from the academic world or other realms of the intelligentsia, and a common product of Ultra intelligence was disseminated, as appropriate, to the operational commands of the army, the navy, and the RAF — as well as to the Pentagon and to all American commands in the Mediterranean and European theatres. The Admiralty's Operational Intelligence Centre was in direct and daily touch with its equivalent in Washington in respect of the shared battle against the U-boats. By 1944 the system of Special Liaison Units for handling in the field all types of Ultra had been unified, by an Anglo-American agreement, to work on identical lines and according to a single doctrine in every Allied theatre of operations throughout the world. The Americans, for their part, similarly combined their original professionals with a wealth of brainpower from their universities, the law and equivalent areas of civilian society.[7] At the main army centre, Arlington Hall in Virginia, as at the navy's OP-20-G in Washington or the Joint Intelligence Center, Pacific Ocean Areas at Pearl Habor,[8] the trend was increasingly towards harmonization, even though it would be unhistorical to imply that an absurd but traditional antagonism between the army and navy or the private policies of General MacArthur and his staff did not create formidable and sometimes unsuperable obstacles.

Nevertheless, the startling revelation of the Ultra secret — whether in its British or its American guise — has radically distorted the general view of the contribution of signal-intelligence to the operational conduct of the war. By many accounts, one would be led to assume that Ultra was the supreme tin-opener. This is only a half-truth. Its prevalence is largely due to two facts: first, too many of those who have expatiated about Ultra have an inadequate understanding of what really goes on in an army or air force command headquarters during a battle (in the words of the opening chorus of that breezy stage-show, *The Music Man*, they 'don't know the territory'); and, secondly, even the investigative historian is still inadequately equipped with source-material to enable him to assess that other form of signal-intelligence which distinguishes the second world war from all its predecessors.

This is the combination of a variety of forms of intelligence which the British and, later, the Americans subsumed under the broad heading of 'Y Service'. Roughly speaking, the elements involved were goniometric direction-finding, traffic-analysis, the breaking of tactical messages transmitted in lower-grade codes, and listening by skilled interpreters to the actual voices of the enemy, whether in the air war or during — for example — an armoured engagement. In one way or another, all these methods were employed with varying success by all the main combatants: as a generalization, it may be affirmed that the British and the Americans were more consistently and more extensively successful than their opponents, even though the Germans and the Japanese — and, on occasion, the Italians — could rightly claim notable results.

During the campaigns in the North African desert, for example, commanders and intelligence officers who worked at the highest level in the British 8th Army testify that whilst Ultra was frequently helpful and sometimes invaluable, the cumulative and constant flow of information provided by 'Y Service' was their sustaining daily diet. Even at Alamein, 'Y' counted for more than Ultra. We still know far too little about the precise quality and quantity of this information as it affected the battle on land, but of one thing we may be sure: the conduct of operations in North Africa will never be fully or properly understood until the 'Y' dimension can be accurately explored. As to its value in the air, the publication in 1980 of *The Enemy is Listening*, by Aileen Clayton, drew on her wide experience as one of the leading figures in the RAF's Mediterranean 'Y Service' and, for the first time, very considerably illuminated the critical importance of this intelligence source in every aspect of the aerial conflict.[9] On the German side, it has long been known that the tactical intercept-service of the Afrika Korps, under Captain Seebohm, provided Rommel with information of crucial significance for his decisions (due both to the unit's own skill and to a lamentable lack of signal-security in the 8th Army) until the unit was eliminated during the first Battle of Alamein in the summer of 1942: a wound from which Rommel never recovered.

Direction-finding, already a well-established practice in the first world war, was now developed on an unparalleled scale. A huge perimeter of listening-posts encircling the North and South Atlantic and the Mediterranean theatre from east to west fed the British with the locations (sometimes approximate but often precise) of German U-boats, commerce-raiders, contraband-runners and capital ships. The near-victory of the Germans in the Battle of the Atlantic will only be fully comprehensible when we have available complete traces showing the exact details, in the case of each transatlantic convoy, of how U-boat Command manoeuvred its submarine packs in the light of intelligence provided by direction-finding, combined with the lethal information which the B Dienst cryptanalytical unit acquired through its breaking of the code used by the Allies for signalling instructions to convoys: a flaw in the Admiralty's armour which was not detected and amended until 1943. The work already done by Professor Rohwer, the distinguished naval historian of the Bibliothek für Zeitgeschichte at Stuttgart, has demonstrated how illuminating such a comprehensive graphic representation might be. As for the Pacific war, both the Americans and the Japanese exercised this art on an elaborate scale.

Traffic-analysis was also universal, and perhaps at its most helpful when other systems failed: for it was not always possible to listen with a sufficient range to pick up the radio signals essential for direction-finding, or to establish so many listening-posts that the necessary intersection of bearings on a particular transmission could be achieved. Nor was it always possible to break the enemy's code swiftly and effectively. But by assessing the volume, the characteristics and the source of radio-signals which could not actually be decoded, the traffic-analysts were capable of extracting important evidence, especially as increasingly sophisticated skills enabled them to identify and interpret the specific call-signs which were transmitted at the beginning of such signals. From a wealth of instances one stands out. During the violent six-month campaign in the Solomons which followed the landing in Guadalcanal, a period of incessant naval action when, at times, battleships battered one another in night encounters at pointblank range and the famous 'Tokyo Express' ran like a commuter-train down the Slot of the Solomons, the Americans for many desperate weeks were unable to read the Japanese naval code and were compelled to conduct these complicated operations very largely on intelligence supplied by traffic-analysis.

Although the performance of the Russians at all levels of signal-intelligence is still impossible to assess, even a survey as superficial and selective as the contents of this article surely suggests, beyond question, that the contribution of signal-intelligence during the second world war constitutes a uniquely distinctive factor: that on the evidence already to hand most existing histories are not only out-of-date but, in important particulars, actually misleading: and that until many thousands more documents are declassified, and meticulous research has correlated them with existing conceptions of what actually happened, only a complacent military historian would dare to assert that what he has written is definitive or that he has presented an analysis of any of the main events in the second world war *wie es eigentlich gewesen*.

NOTES

1. Ralph Bennett, *Ultra in the West* (London 1979).

2. F.W. Winterbotham, *The Ultra Secret* (London 1974); Gustave Bertrand, *Enigma* (Paris 1973).

3. Patrick Beesly, *Very Special Intelligence* (London 1977); Peter Calvocoressi, *Top Secret Ultra* (London 1980); Ewen Montagu, *Beyond Top Secret U* (London 1978); R.V. Jones, *Most Secret War* (London 1978).

4. A useful and reasonably up-to-date list of books and articles on Ultra, and Sigint in general, will be found as an appendix on p. 464 of the German edition of the author's *Ultra goes to War* (London 1978) — *Entschied Ultra den Krieg?* (Koblenz/Bonn 1981).

5. Roberta Wohlstetter, *Pearl Harbor: Warning and Decision* (Stanford 1962); David Kahn, *The Codebreakers* (London 1968).

6. The author's detailed study of the American cryptanalytical attack on Japanese signal-traffic and the operational value in the Pactific war (and the German) of intelligence derived from this source — *The Other Ultra: Codes, Ciphers and the Defeat of Japan* — will be published in 1982 by Hutchinson in the UK and by Farrar, Straus and Giroux in the USA.

7. For a personal view, see *Deadly Magic* by Edward Van Der Rhoer (New York 1978).

8. The most authoritative account of the US navy's signal-intelligence activities is *Double-Edged Secrets: U.S. Naval Intelligence Operations in the Pacific During World War II* by Captain W.J. Holmes (Annapolis 1979).

9. Aileen Clayton, *The Enemy is Listening* (London 1980).

12 The SOE Phenomenon

Mark Wheeler

Midway through *Greenmantle*, John Buchan's second Richard Hannay adventure, the hero reflects on the failure of the American intelligence agent, John Scantlebury Blenkiron, to penetrate the secret of the Kaiser's nefarious plot to set the Muslim world alight: 'He had been the professional with the best chance. It would be a good joke if the amateur succeeded where the expert failed.' The joke comes off. Hannay and Sandy Arbuthnot, the gentlemen amateurs enlisted by the Foreign Office, both scupper the Germans' plans to raise a false prophet and save their ineffectual American colleague from his wounds and his ulcers.

During the second world war it was Britain which, having been ejected from the continent, sought to set occupied Europe ablaze. The organization so charged was the Special Operations Executive (SOE). It provided a host of young and not so young men reared on Buchan's tales with the opportunity to serve their country while living out their fantasies. One who served, Richard Usborne, has written that, 'Practically every officer I met in that concern, at home and abroad, was, like me, imagining himself as Hannay or Sandy Arbuthnot'.[1] Others have confirmed the prevalence of this self-image.

Another source of inspiration was T. E. Lawrence, though it is likely that it was Lawrence's demonstration of the possibilities of irregular warfare that particularly attracted SOE's progenitors, not the messianism that accompanied it or the voluptuary prose that succeeded it. Sandy Arbuthnot's own Lawrentian guise in *Greenmantle* (as the fancy dress leader of the Companions of the Rosy Hour) was perceived by Hannay as a dangerous aberration, the product of his friend's fascination with a woman (!), the uniquely evil Hilda von Einem. When the besotted Sandy encounters Hannay again after a period in the clutches of that she-devil, he remarks, 'It does me good to hear your voice, Dick. It reminds me of clean, honest things.'

These were the things to which the ostensibly (if self-deludedly) apolitical officers of SOE were also dedicated. Few of them would have identified such ideals with Lawrence. It is notable, too, that it has been SOE's many detractors, contemporary and subsequent, who have been most ready to point out the Lawrentian ethos which supposedly pervaded the organization, leading it wilfully into paths detrimental to real national interests (a conservative British critique), or embodying the perfidious machinations of English imperialism (a view of suspicious left-wing resisters). Lawrence might also be said to have offered the basis for a third criticism of SOE: that it, like he, was quite simply a failure.

But did the joke come off? Did the amateurs of SOE in the second world war accomplish feats comparable to those of their clubable inspirators? Did they show up the limitations of their jealous, narrow and professional rivals in SIS and the services? Did they confound the faint-hearted busy-bodies in the Foreign Office? Did they teach the Americans a trick or two? Did they help win the war? There were certainly notable successes — at the Gorgopotamos viaduct in 1942, at the Rjukan heavy-water plant and in Operation Animals in 1943, during Overlord in 1944 to mention but a few — but there were also dismal failures — in the Netherlands, with Mihailović, with the *Carte* network, with Maniu. If SOE can claim no triumph so significant as Ultra, it need be blamed for no disaster so wasteful as the strategic bombing campaign. If it can be accused simultaneously of promoting and vilifying certain communist-led resistance movements, it cannot be held responsible for their eventual fates. Either their victories and defeats were their own, or high strategy and high politics took over the hand.[2] As with the worth and effectiveness of European resistance to Nazism in general, the jury is still out on SOE. What is not in doubt is that SOE is a phenomenon, and perhaps one which is as much literary as military.

At its peak strength in the autumn of 1944 SOE employed some 10,000 persons. It has seemed with gathering pace in the years since that a remarkably large proportion of these has proved adept at exchanging the skills of parachuting and silent killing, the habits of reticence and secret ink, for the spinning of yarns of which John Buchan himself would have been justifiably proud. A conservative estimate would put the total number of books published on SOE at just under 200. What the ex-operatives of SOE have not abandoned is their desire to carry on by literary means the bureaucratic infighting and the rearguard defence of their organization's functions and achievements which proved necessary from its very birth in July 1940. The fortieth anniversary of that moment — one both ominous and exhilarating for a Britain that stood alone — had already (at mid-year) been marked by the publication of three books: Basil Davidson's *Special Operations Europe: Scenes from the Anti-Nazi War*, Patrick Howarth's *Undercover: The Men and Women of the Special Operations Executive* and David Stafford's *Britain and European Resistance, 1940-1945: A Survey of the Special Operations Executive, with Documents.*

The sub-titles of these books reflect accurately their differing intents. The first is a memoir combined with a sermon; the second is a collection of anecdotes about the accomplishments and eccentricities of SOE personnel; the third is a solid academic study, though one which is lucidly and excitingly written. The first two are very much in the tradition of works on SOE by its former officers. In varying degrees they emphasize the heroism, the muddle, the fun and the frustration of service in that body. Howarth retells the classic stories — not always uncritically — on a theatre-by-theatre basis. But he is basically at one with Bickham Sweet-Escott's pioneering *Baker Street Irregular* in his determination to defend SOE against all comers.[3] He does not appreciate the extent to which his adumbration of the double-barrelled pedigrees, public school values and merchant banking careers of his subjects provides grist for the mill of his radical ex-colleague, Basil Davidson.

It was Davidson who, as early as 1946 in *Partisan Picture*, castigated British policy for seeking to nobble the left, the only possible source of real European resistance. By 1971, reviewing F.W. Deakin's *The Embattled Mountain*, Davidson wrote of 'the nabobs of SOE London, most of whom were men of banking and commercial experience and attitude' who sought to restore the '*status quo ante bellum*' of kings and capitalism.[4] (This mild act of depreciation from inside seems to have caused as much offence to the guardians of SOE's grail as the not infrequent slurs from outside that the organization was infested by crackpots, communists and homosexuals.[5]) Davidson has returned to the charge in his new book, although it is not the work of history that might have been expected from a distinguished historian of Africa venturing to write again about his wartime experiences. It is instead a book about the futility of imagining that politics can be separated from resistance — a nice quotation from Smuts warning Churchill against letting politics 'loose among those peoples' of the Balkans and Italy serving as a leitmotiv — and the impossibility of expecting the Tory gamekeepers of the City to turn poachers of resistance and its concomitant, revolution. The argument may be wrong; it is more likely beside the point; but in Davidson's elaborately textured prose it is a joy to read.

Where Davidson does make a contribution to our understanding of the evolution of British policy towards resistance is in his hilarious account of Brigadier C.M. Keble's brief hold on SOE's Cairo base, and of his use of the German intercepts of which he was an accidental recipient to mount a campaign which eventually led to the dispatch of the first British missions to the Yugoslav Partisans in the spring of 1943. One reason for Keble's enthusiasm was his hope of gaining promotion to major-general if he were to contrive to place three brigadiers under him in the field. One reason he succeeded — in contacting the Partisans, not in getting further preferment — was that Davidson was able in January 1943 to make use of the friendship of his intelligence officer, F. W. Deakin, with the Prime Minister in order that Churchill should summon Keble to present the new evidence on who was actually fighting the Germans in Yugoslavia.[6] Davidson's story of the battles between the pro-Mihailović and pro-Tito elements in SOE Cairo rings true, even if his contention that London stood firm against any thought of working with the Partisans does not, and does the Foreign Office in particular a disservice. Nonetheless, as Davidson writes, 'All available experience shows that the only real pleasure to be got from war is to quarrel with your own side'.[7] SOE's quarrels, internal and external — and contrary to theory and the reiterated protestations of its defenders — were more often than not about politics. But where both Davidson and SOE's right-wing critics err is in assuming the dominance of a particular orthodoxy, save, that is, self-promotion.

Veterans of SOE have often asserted that its complete history can never be written. Such of its archives as remain in existence are closed and unlikely ever to be opened. The one official history of SOE's activities to appear, M.R.D. Foot's *SOE in France* (1966), aroused so much controversy (and so many actual and threatened law suits) that the decision was taken to publish no more.[8] An internally commissioned history produced soon after the war has been seen by only a few of the especially privileged old boys. The mania for secrecy which served SOE so ill during its wartime existence (principally by helping to deny it the full co-operation of the services on whom it had to depend to carry out its operations) has thus seemed likely to deny it its historical deserts as well. A second frequently voiced contention of the proprietarily inclined alumni of SOE is that no one outside their number should presume to write its history.

David Stafford, born in 1942 and an associate professor at the University of Victoria, has disproved both arguments. Though he modestly claims to have provided merely an interim assessment, Stafford has made impressive use of the materials which survive in the Cabinet papers, especially the minutes and memoranda of the Chiefs of Staff, in order to describe the origins, development and oft-mooted liquidation of SOE, as well as the shifting strategic objectives assigned to it during the war. His is a London-centred view, but this is precisely what has been lacking in the past. Of accounts of SOE operations in particular countries and regions there are plenty, including an increasing number based on documents in the Foreign Office files relating to SOE which, like the Cabinet papers used by Stafford, have escaped the capricious and counter-productive attentions of the weeders. Stafford could, therefore, have found much valuable material had he subjected the Foreign Office papers to a scrutiny as intense as he gave the COS files. He might also have found cause to modify his occasionally ill-judged assumption of inveterate hostility on the part of Foreign Office officials to all SOE's works. Had he gone further yet, and looked into the War Office files for the Middle East Headquarters — especially the military missions records in WO 202 — he would have discovered the partial archives of SOE Cairo. (Heaven knows how these got past the weeders!)

Cairo was the wayward base of Baker Street which played a large part in transforming SOE's Balkan operations and, in the process, gave first effect to the principal strategic change to overtake SOE. As Stafford demonstrates, this was the abandonment of the 'detonator concept', that counsel of illusion and despair which posited secret armies built up by SOE for use in 'grand finalé' risings whose success would need merely the guarantee of small British expeditionary forces. Sober calculation of the number of aircraft necessary to create and maintain such secret armies rendered the plan impossible even before American entry into the war made it unnecessary. SOE foundered for a while, but eventually grasped its new role of assisting the generals to make use of active guerrilla forces in the containment and deception of Axis divisions that might otherwise have been pressed into service on ever-broadening Allied fronts. The consequences of this alteration of SOE's strategic priorities were, of course, to be unfortunate for Mihailović's Četniks and the secret armies of Poland and Czechoslovakia. But it paid rich dividends elsewhere.

Stafford's achievement has been to reintegrate SOE in the war's grand strategy, to save it from the byways of genre literature. He has shown that the value of the documentary material available far exceeds what had previously been imagined. Future researchers will be indebted to him for providing the framework in which their detailed enquiries into particular aspects of SOE's work can proceed with less risk of isolation. He has also done something to restore the exile governments to the position of importance they deserve. What he did not need to do was to reassert the primacy of the people of occupied Europe. In its early days SOE's estimates of the potential for resistance of the various peoples of Europe were based on little more than national stereotypes: the plucky Poles and the doughty Serbs could be counted on; the French, the Italians, the Danes were more doubtful. SOE had, in other words, got little beyond Buchan, who had neglected even to provide an ending for the true hero of *Greenmantle*, the faithful Turk Hussin. SOE soon learned, and the memoirs of its officers rarely fail to give full credit to the resisters.

NOTES

1. Richard Usborne, *Clubland Heroes* (London 1974), 1.
2. Albania might be one exception. But it is, for example, impossible to credit assertions such as these by M.R.D. Foot: 'If it had not been for SOE we would never I think have heard much of Tito in Yugoslavia. If it had not been for SOE, Greece would certainly have been a Communist country for years. If it had not been for SOE, some of the most heroic stories in the tragic pages of Polish Resistance would never have been written.' (M. Elliott-Batemen (ed.), *The Fourth Dimension of Warfare*, Vol. I: *Intelligence, Subversion, Resistance* (Manchester 1970), 44.) Foot's argument is as exaggerated as is that which would damn SOE for having 'imposed' Tito on Yugoslavia, for having 'created' EAM/ELAS in Greece and for having 'betrayed' Poland.
3. Although written in the early fifties, *Baker Street Irregular* was not passed for publication until 1965.

4. 'With the Partisans of Tito', *Times Literary Supplement*, 3,634 (22 October 1971), 1302.

5. See Sweet-Escott's contribution to Phyllis Auty and Richard Clogg (eds.), *British Policy towards Wartime Resistance in Yugoslavia and Greece* (London 1975), 14.

6. *Special Operations Europe*, 107-28.

7. Ibid., 79.

8. *The Times* reported on 16 December 1980 that Charles Cruikshank had been commissioned to write an official history of SOE in the Far East, though the book would be published by Oxford University Press. A spate of letters followed, most promoting, a few deprecating the authorization of a similar volume on SOE's supposedly unsavoury Balkan operations.

13 Nelson Rockefeller and British Security Coordination

Paul Kramer

On 16 August 1940 (well over a year before Pearl Harbor) President Roosevelt, by Executive Order, created the Office of the Coordinator of Commercial and Cultural Relations between the American Republics (later changed to Coordinator of Inter-American Affairs),[1] and appointed young Nelson A. Rockefeller who was then thirty-two years old, Coordinator. The 'Rockefeller office', as it came to be known, immediately became a focal point of the first peacetime effort by a US government in what has since been termed operational intelligence.

The work involved in the creation of this office was conducted by James Forrestal, then serving as one of six Special Assistants to the President, and later to become Secretary of the Navy and, subsequently, America's first Secretary of Defense. Experience gained in operational intelligence became a factor, through Forrestal, in the founding of the Central Intelligence Agency.

American intelligence experts, as well as writers on the subject, have remained totally in the dark as to the work of the Rockefeller office in the intelligence field. Those who knew, for reasons we shall examine later, remained silent, and those who did not know, but who were experienced in other areas, preferred to describe themselves as the pioneers in the field. From the standpoint of intelligence history it has been as if Fremont, the 'Pathfinder', had never heard of Lewis and Clark, and they, in turn, either remained in ignorance of Daniel Boone, or preferred for reasons of vanity or pride, to ignore him.

Academia was also deluded. As late as 1963, a distinguished American historian wrote that 'in August 1940, an Office for Coordination of Commercial and Cultural Relations between the American Republics was established under the direction of Nelson Rockefeller although it was not until after Pearl Harbor that we began to send professors, tennis players and ballet companies to Latin America to prove that we were a cultured people.'[2] Like the Scarlet Pimpernel of fiction, the Rockefeller office was dismissed as all fripperies and frivolity.

In 1948 a Brookings Institution publication, although considerably nearer the truth, claimed that 'in the beginning the Coordinator was mainly interested in carrying out the responsibilities . . . of economic and financial cooperation'.[3]

In fairness to academia it should be pointed out that the key document for research has been the US Bureau of the Budget's Historical Report on War Administration.[4] Scholars have been captivated by it, and for two very good reasons. Nelson Rockefeller personally insisted that his top level assistants cooperate in the preparation of the study and made available to its authors the notes of the Rockefeller family historian who, in the early days of the office, had the run of incoming and outgoing baskets and personnel, so that he became a sort of unpublished Arthur Schlesinger of the 'Rockefeller administration'. But the real nature of the intelligence activities was withheld from the report's authors, as, of course, they were from the Congress and from most people in the executive branch of government.

It was not until the 1976 publication of *A Man Called Intrepid* about the work of Sir William Stephenson that the first reference to the intelligence activities of the Coordinator's Office appeared in print. Unfortunately, both Stevenson the author, and Stephenson the spy about whom the book was written, got the story wrong.

What really happened?

The first thing to remember are events surrounding the Rockefeller Office's creation.

When France fell in June 1940, wartime Britain, although beleagured and stripped of allies, had preserved and was continuing to expand its world-wide network of intelligence and cryptanalysis. Earlier World War I traditions of the *Zimmermann* telegram and the *Magdeburg* continued as an inspiration. The efforts and sacrifices of the small groups of dedicated and largely anonymous men during the lean years between the wars had preserved the basic structure and nurtured the concept that the intercept of enemy communications by cryptanalysis and other means, could, as was the case in 1914-18, supply Britain with important keys to ultimate victory, not only through contributions to British strategy and tactics, but also as an aid to British diplomacy.

There were historic parallels in the summer of 1940. Just as it had been in early 1917, America was neutral. As the *Zimmermann* telegram had in March 1917 left President Wilson bereft of the prop of public opinion which had previously sustained his struggle to keep the US neutral,[5] might not another intercept bring America in again on the side of Great Britain?

There were also differences. In February 1917, President Wilson was a neutralist who clung to the illusion that America could go about its business happily separate from other nations. In June 1940 President Roosevelt subscribed to no such view. He was pro-British and anti-Nazi. He regarded the possibility of a Nazi victory as a threat to America's future. But he was determined that only a united America should enter the war. Meanwhile, the 'American firsters' and the 'Fortress America' groups opposed US entrance. They were a force to be reckoned with in politics, in government and in business. 'Persons close to Roosevelt felt the non-interventionists had fought the President very nearly to a standstill late in 1941.'[6]

Under these circumstances, the goals of British intelligence were dual. On the one hand it sought to be ever on the look out for material that would, just as the *Zimmermann* telegram, destroy the props of public opinion on which American isolationists rested their cause. On the other, it had to use its material in such a way as to allow America, within the framework of existing neutrality, to pursue a course that could be independent of, although complementary to, the British goal of victory in the war.

This duality was not always fully understood. British intelligence in the period from June 1940 to 7 December 1941 thought in terms of using its information to help fight the war and bring America into it. The US often thought in terms of strengthening itself as a neutral and also helping Britain, not as an ally in a war, but as a friend whose victory over the Nazis would strengthen the US position in the world.

In the book *A Man Called Intrepid*, about the wartime work of Sir William Stephenson, the author has written:

> Nelson Rockefeller had persuaded Roosevelt to let him start a new agency in the unguarded vastness of South America — 'our soft underbelly' — where Stephenson operated a network, hampered by shortages of equipment and money. This new Office of the Coordinator of Inter-American Affairs acted covertly on information from BSC on Nazi sympathizers in sensitive jobs. Millions of Rockefeller dollars went into various schemes to discredit, depose, or in other ways damage the powers of Axis conspirators in South America. The FBI and the State Department were at loggerheads over who had jurisdiction in the region; it was easier for Rockefeller to show personal initiative and foot the bill than settle an argument about counterespionage in foreign lands. This also protected FDR's public stance of noninvolvement until America would demand to go to war.
>
> Hoover was right to feel uneasy. The surreptitious scope of the Coordinator, worked out by Rockefeller with Stephenson, foreshadowed the global agency under Donovan.[7]

By ignoring the dual nature of British-American intelligence cooperation before Pearl Harbour, one is left with an erroneous view.

Immediately after the fall of France there was unanimity of feeling within the Roosevelt administration that something had to be done about Latin America. Axis victories had cut off markets for Latin American agricultural and mineral goods. Traditional trade routes were in disarray. Nazi agents were seeking to establish a solid racial nucleus of German Aryans 'for the purpose of raising the German nation. . . to a dominating position'.[8] At the same time it was felt in Washington that with a powerful defensive military machine an evident need, many strategic materials that had traditionally been obtained from areas under Axis control, could be bought in Latin America. If this were done it would supply Latin America with needed foreign exchange to purchase manufactured and semi-manufactured goods. Financial pressures would be relieved, Latin American employment could be maintained and a fertile field for Nazi propaganda eliminated.

But if there was agreement that something needed to be done, there was total disagreement as to who should do it. Inter-agency feuding was intense, especially between the State Department and the Agriculture Department. Thus President Roosevelt asked James Forrestal, then an Administrative Assistant, to find a solution. Forrestal, who had been in the thick of the bureaucratic rivalry for control of Latin America, recommended a Coordinator's office and young Nelson A. Rockefeller as chief Coordinator. In fact, Rockefeller had applied for the job in the form of a memo on a hemisphere economic programme that had been submitted on 14 June to Harry Hopkins, an aide and confidante of Roosevelt. According to Paul Nitze, then an assistant to Forrestal and the one who drafted the executive order setting up the office, Roosevelt accepted the idea with the proviso that Will C. Clayton, a more mature and experienced businessman and a Democrat (Rockefeller was a Republican) be an assistant coordinator.[9]

The appointment thus evolved from a combination of Rockefeller interests and ambitions,[10] and the needs of the Roosevelt administration which felt compelled to do something about Latin America quite apart from the needs and objectives of a beleagured Britain. Furthermore, doing something about Latin America was within the traditional scope of Roosevelt foreign policy that ante-dated World War II.

Ever since Roosevelt's first inaugural address in 1933 when he had dedicated the country to the policy of the 'good neighbor', the idea had developed that US interests in Latin America could best be served by conference, mutual discussion and peaceful manoeuvre rather than by armed intervention. Marines had been withdrawn from the Caribbean rather than dispatched. Inter-American conferences had been held regularly, the last of which, a meeting of the foreign ministers in Panama in 1939, following the outbreak of war in Europe, had been called for the specific purpose of providing for hemisphere defence and the maintenance of the Latin American economy in the face of the dangers involved in world conflict. Another was called for July 1940 in Havana.

This special treatment not only contributed to Roosevelt's great personal popularity in the area, but also enjoyed almost universal support in the United States. Isolationists and non-interventionists, 'America firsters', and 'fortress Americans' who opposed favouritism for beleagured Britain could only support Roosevelt's friendship toward Latin America. 'Most America First spokesmen believed the US should fight if any part of North or South America were attacked.'[11]

Within the framework of his 'good neighbor' policy, Roosevelt enjoyed a freedom of action in Latin America he did not enjoy in his European policies. He was thus free to help Britain so long as that help was given within the scope of this established and highly popular policy toward Latin America. This is precisely what happened after Dunkirk and is why Rockfeller's office of the Coordinator of Inter-American Affairs became involved with the secret operations of British Security Coordination (BSC) in New York which was a focal point for all British intelligence activities in the western hemisphere. It was a successful marriage of convenience. As is always the case with marriages of convenience, the goals of the two partners were different. The one, Britain, sought to use BSC New York as a device for destroying Nazis and pro-Germans wherever they might be (and also to bring the US in the war on the side of Great Britain); the other, the US, sought to use BSC's assets — an intelligence network and mail intercept system and experience in fighting Nazis by means of operational intelligence — to further its own policy of western hemisphere unity and defence. Isolationists could thus work in comfort (as a number of them did) in the Rockefeller office so long as any affiliation with BSC New York was withheld from them.

By the last week of August 1940, the Rockefeller Office was in place, and had decided upon its first project. It was determined to create a voluntary programme by which American business would eliminate all Nazis and Nazi agents who represented their oganizations in Latin America. The programme at this time had to be voluntary. America was still neutral and there was no law or executive order that inhibited an American from trading in Latin America with a Nazi, or fascist. Behind the Rockefeller office was only the persuasive argument of hemisphere defence and solidarity, the commercial and financial power (not inconsiderable) of the Rockefeller family (which stood squarely behind Nelson Rockefeller in his work), their associates and friends, and their friends' friends. There was also the persuasive power of the Roosevelt administration and such facilities as it had which, at the time, were not great, in collecting intelligence on Nazi activity in Latin America. In actual fact this meant a handful of people maintained by the State Department in each of the other American republics plus a few FBI agents. In post-World War II terms, US government representation in Latin America at that time was minuscule.

The most immediate necessity was thus the development of an intelligence network to supply the Coordinator's office with all possible details of Nazi commercial activity. President Roosevelt personally moved toward the establishment of such a network. He instructed the State Department as well as the FBI to cooperate with the Rockefeller office. Sir William Stephenson of British Security Coordination, New York, also cooperated via the FBI by verbal arrangement. This evolved from conversations Stephenson had held with Roosevelt beginning in May 1940. With this support in line, on 30 August, but a fortnight after its creation, the Coordinator's office decided to send a special confidential mission south both to gather information and to arrange for a subsequent flow of intelligence. This mission was headed by Percy L. Douglas, on leave of absence from the Otis Elevator Company and a personal friend of Nelson Rockefeller. It also included John E. Lockwood, another Rockefeller friend and lawyer, George H. Butler of the State Department and Percy Foxworth, head of the New York office of the FBI, and BSC New York's ongoing liaison. Foxworth had a dual role on the trip in that he also laid the groundwork to extend the FBI network through Latin America. He enjoyed the confidence of both J. Edgar Hoover and the Rockefeller people. There was general agreement that his death in 1943 in a plane crash while arranging for the Roosevelt-Churchill meeting at Casablanca represented the loss of one of America's most able intelligence agents.

The mission began immediately to send back to Washington voluminous reports on Nazi commercial activity. Meanwhile information and intelligence began to pass to the Coordinator's office from its other sources. Information from all British sources went to British Security Coordination, headed by Sir William Stephenson, and coincidentally located in Rockefeller Center, New York. In those days the bulk of the mail originating in Latin America passed through Bermuda en route to Europe. Here British imperial censorship authorities had various methods of secretly examining letters in such a way that their recipients were not aware that they had been opened. From BSC New York this information was passed to Foxworth's office where it was incorporated with FBI information from its own sources and processed for transmission to the Rockefeller office in Washington, located at this time in the old State, War and Navy Building next to the White House, now the Executive Office Building.

Here the FBI material was always delivered by special messenger and labelled 'personal and confidential'. It invariably opened with the cryptic statement 'we understand from a confidential source believed to be reliable' or 'information has been received from a reliable confidential source' etc., and was dovetailed with the flow of information started by the Douglas-Lockwood-Butler-Foxworth mission.[12] Meanwhile John S. Dickey (later to become President of

Dartmouth) was brought to the Coordinator's office in Washington to set up mechanisms for correlating and processing the information that was coming in.

In Washington, the Coordinator, aided by Will Clayton of the Anderson Clayton Co., Joseph C. Rovensky, on leave from the Chase Bank, Berent Friele, on leave from the A.& P., and a few others (later to be rejoined by Douglas), began contacting American business to persuade them to drop Nazi connections in Latin America. Preclusive buying coups involving such items as industrial diamonds, wolfram and abaca were also suggested to the appropriate government agency.

It is noteworthy that the top echelon personnel in the Coordinator's office covered the broad spectrum of American business from banking (Rovensky) to industry (Douglas) to commodities (Clayton and Friele). When there were deficiencies such as in transportation, consultants were brought in.

The atmosphere in the Coordinator's office was casual and informal. Everyone was on a first name basis. Rockefeller had bought the Baker place four miles from his office in northwest Washington to house his wife and children and a sign was nailed to a tree beside the long curving driveway: 'careful, children at play'. This sign once mysteriously disappeared until it was produced at a conference by a consultant-house guest of Rockefeller who tossed it down on the conference table when his advice was sought on some point of procedure. In the early days, Carl B. Spaeth, the Assistant Coordinator and his wife also lived at the Foxhall Road house. A penny ante poker game was organized by Rovensky at his flat on 16th Street; lunch was often taken at the main dining-room of the Carlton Hotel, and Stamp, the Rockefeller driver, shuttled people about Washington in a black limousine. There were occasional weekend meetings at John D. Rockefeller Jr.'s house at colonial Williamsburg.

The informality, however, did not deflect from purpose. On 8 January 1941, the Coordinator announced in a press release that examination of the country-by-country reports made by the mission disclosed that:

1. U.S. business is frequently represented in Central and South America by firms and individuals now known to support objectives contrary to the best interests of the American Republics.
2. These representatives often use advertising appropriations of U.S. business

firms to force newspapers, and in some instances radio stations, to adopt anti-American editorial policies.

3. Many employees of U.S. companies or their affiliates in Central and South America are known members of local anti-American organizations.

4. Many anti-American firms, which formerly sold only European products, have now succeeded in obtaining agencies for U.S. business. These new connections are keeping them alive, and enabling them to maintain their trade contacts. In many instances, they openly declare they will return to their former lines at the expiration of the war.

5. Many of these agents who now represent U.S. firms are obtaining through this medium confidential trade information which is made available to anti-American powers.

6. Profits thus derived from representation of U.S. firms are being used to finance operations of propaganda agencies in Central and South America.

7. Many of the firms representing U.S. companies also serve as centers for distribution of anti-American literature and propaganda.

8. Many of the larger anti-American firms have established their own purchasing agents in the U.S. and with the goods obtained in the market remain in business.

9. Officers and employees of a number of firms, representing U.S. businesses, are officials of anti-American powers.[13]

This was in fact a declaration by the Coordinator of what specifically, on a voluntary basis, he was determined to destroy, and its net political effect was to equate anti-Nazism with a pro-hemisphere defence concept.

During the first half of 1941, US exporters dropped more than a thousand undesirable agency accounts in the other American republics. US concerns were also asked to investigate employees in their Latin American branch offices and to see that advertising allowances were not being used by agents to promote Axis propaganda. Later, it was decided to broaden the programme to include the examination of all consignees, not agents alone, and then to examine imports and ask US importers not to deal with undesirable purchasing agents in Latin America. Some 1,700 firms were contacted in this programme.

The Coordinator's office was not always successful in its voluntary anti-Nazi programme. General Motors was a case in point. Essentially this company adhered to the argument, later to be publicly espoused by one of its presidents over another matter, that 'what's good for General Motors is good for the country'. General Motors management at this time saw no reason to drop its pro-Nazi representation in Cuba, Chile and Bolivia so long as they sold more GM products than a potential replacement might be able to do.

Political concepts of hemisphere unity, GM felt, had nothing to do with the matter.

Such argument, however, ended on 19 July 1941, when President Roosevelt ended the voluntary programme and made it compulsory. A long detailed and specific 'Proclaimed List of Certain Blocked Nationals' was issued with whom the US was forbidden to deal in the interest of national defence.[14] Since the voluntary programme had thus become official policy, the Rockefeller blacklisting activities were transferred to the State Department's newly created division of World Trade Intelligence, and John Dickey, although retained on the Rockefeller pay-roll, transferred to the State Department to head it. This shift also involved a change in the flow of information from British Security Coordination, New York. With blacklisting official, rather than voluntary, the State Department, through John Dickey, could engage in direct contact on blacklisting with the appropriate economic warfare officials at the British Embassy in Washington, and no longer needed to be dependent on cryptic statements via the FBI from BSC New York.

July 1941 was also the month that saw the establishment of the COI, headed by General William J. Donovan, the predecessor organization to the OSS which, in turn, marked the loss by J. Edgar Hoover of the FBI's 'monopoly' in all US government dealings with the British Security Coordinator. To a certain extent, the transfer of the Rockefeller voluntary economic intelligence activities was all part of a mid-1941 reorganization of pre-Pearl Harbor intelligence. This was also the time when the Nazis broke with their Soviet Ally and attacked Russia.

Essentially July 1941 marked the close of the Coordinator's operations in the field of economic operational intelligence and the office went on to other activities largely in communications and health. A year had been gained, before Pearl Harbor, in which to strengthen and supplement British intelligence sources. British intercepts of Latin American communciations had been put to practical use in the elimination of Nazi economic activity in Latin America. Most important of all, experience gained among top level Americans in the problems and techniques involved became an invaluable asset. As a practical matter, it was as if several destroyers had been built and were operational and ready for war before it actually came. There was also a post-World War II effect. When James Forrestal, as the first Secretary of Defense, found the US without an operational intelligence arm with which to participate in the Italian elections of 1948, he revived the voluntary programme technique both to raise and channel and administer funds into Italy. And why not? Such an idea was not new. He had personally seen what the voluntary concept could do in Latin America in 1940 and 1941.

Whose idea was the voluntary blacklist? Sir William Stephenson and BSC's, President Roosevelt's, James Forrestal's, Nelson Rockefeller's? At this point it is impossible to say. Stephenson has claimed credit for it. Of equal significance, however, is that Franklin Roosevelt personally took a hand in implementing the idea, appointing the Coordinator and assuring him the tools with which to do the job. He not only saw to it personally that British, FBI and State Department information and cooperation were available, but followed through on this subject. For example, as late as February 1941, President Roosevelt, at Rockefeller's request, instructed J. Edgar Hoover and the FBI to make available to the Coordinator's office an FBI official in 'carrying out the Coordinator's program of contacting a limited number of executives of American business for the purpose of soliciting their cooperation in eliminating totalitarian agents who represent their organizations in the American republics'.[15] There was no palaver or cabinet discussion. Roosevelt simply ordered it and at the same time instructed his Appointments Secretary to send for Mr Hoover so he could talk to him personally about the matter.

This one year programme was not only successful in undermining totalitarian strength in the other American republics, but also in coping with the turmoil, the alarm over the suddenness of Nazi victories and feeling of helplessness over Nazi movement within Latin America.[16] At this time the Latin American countries were for the most part oligarchies. It did not take long for the ruling classes to see the effects of the blacklisting programme within their own communities. Persons close to the rulers were plunged into financial oblivion as a result and this had the effect, in a broader sense, of persuading those in power to turn to the US for aid and protection and relief.

There were also other areas of cooperation between BSC and the Rockefeller office outside of blacklisting. In 1940 radio station WRUL in Boston had a transmitting power — 50,000 watts — that was unsurpassed by any other station in either the Americas or Germany. It was privately owned, had a very large overseas listening audience and was potentially a valuable wartime propaganda asset.

Stephenson and BSC secretly subsidized it through intermediaries. The Coordinator's office did so directly in order to extend and expand WRUL's Spanish language broadcasts with the result that by Pearl Harbor the US had an overseas broadcasting service, comparable to the BBC in place.[17]

Other, more esoteric operational intelligence projects were developed. One of these involved the manipulation of the Latin American press, not through the control and sale of Canadian and US newsprint (this was already in hand) but by means of the purchase of advertising space. None of the Rockefeller people had previous diplomatic experience. Some were less inclined than they perhaps should have been to seek State Department political guidance on the newspapers they sought to manipulate. US diplomatic missions in Latin America were ignored. This caused friction. Sumner Welles, the Under Secretary of State, took the problem to the White House and, on 22 April 1941, the President wrote Nelson Rockefeller to take 'appropriate steps to institute arrangements for assuring that in all instances projects initiated by your Office shall be discussed fully with, and approved by, the Department of State, and a full meeting of minds obtained before action is undertaken or commitments are made.'[18]

This letter reflected the first conflict between operational intelligence and the State Department. President Roosevelt resolved it quickly, sharply and definitively. A precedent was established within the US government structure that was subsequently to be applied to the OSS and later, the CIA. To this extent the letter represents a milestone in the history of the development of US operational, as distinguished from informational intelligence. As a practical matter, too, the letter made Under Secretary of State Sumner Welles, via Lawrence Duggan, the Assistant Secretary for Latin America, the final arbiter in any operational intelligence projects that might have originated with BSC and Sir William Stephenson in New York and passed from him to Rockefeller where they could be treated as Rockefeller projects. Whether or not President Roosevelt fully understood this when he sent Nelson Rockefeller his 'clear it with Sumner' letter is not known, but the presumption is that he did.

From the standpoint of hindsight several questions arise.

How was it that the connection between the Coordinator of Inter-American Affairs and British Security Coordination, New York, remained a well kept secret for thirty-six years? The answer lies in both chance and circumstance. First of all, very few Americans knew of the actual connection, and of those who did, Roosevelt, Forrestal and Foxworth all died in office and did not write memoirs. Neither did Nelson Rockefeller, and in the interim between World War II and his death, he entered Republican politics. Reticence was the wisest course since many, but by no means all pre-war isolationists and American firsters were Republicans. Messrs. Lockwood, Douglas and Dickey would have been guided by Governor Rockefeller's reticence if they knew of the connection. J. Edgar Hoover is a special case although it is true that he, too, died in office and neither wrote memoirs nor cooperated in the preparation of an authoritative biography. Hoover clearly valued highly his pre-war connection with BSC New York[19] and his wartime intelligence network in Latin America which, to some extent, had its origins in the three-way association between BSC New York, the Rockefeller office and the FBI. He felt, after the war, and at the time of the founding of the CIA that his record entitled him to be placed in charge of all intelligence, both domestic and foreign; certainly, if not the world, at least Latin America from which the OSS had, during the war, been excluded. But Hoover lost this bureaucratic battle, and President Truman decided that Hoover should have the US, but the CIA should have all foreign countries. This caused intense feeling and bitterness in the FBI. FBI personnel experienced in Latin America, with few exceptions, refused to work for the CIA. The central records index at FBI headquarters was 'deindexed' and there was an 'auto da fe' of archives and files rather than turn them over to the 'enemy'. Hoover was not a man publicly to admit bureaucratic defeat. Why speak of the BSC-Rockefeller-FBI connection in which his Bureau had played such an active, and in fact resourceful and courageous part, when it could only serve as a reminder of how he 'lost' Latin America?

Finally, one must ask, did the enemy know? Was there a leak so that the Nazis, or the Japanese, or the Soviets found out? There is no direct evidence, but there are certain indications that they might have. Several foreign agents were found on the Rockefeller payroll. Why, one must ask oneself, waste a valuable spy on the Rockefeller office since its activities, other than the BSC connection, were largely unclassified? What were these agents after? A Nazi, a Japanese and several Soviet agents were caught by the FBI with Rockefeller office personnel help.

At this point one should perhaps refer to the Coordinator's secret fund. Future historians may come across references to it in the archives or in the Nelson Rockefeller papers, when and if they are made public. It was never significant; roughly $50,000 a year, although it is true that the Coordinator's office was one of the very few US government agencies before Pearl Harbor to have such a fund. Whether or not it was originally intended to use it in connection with the Coordinator's secret relationship with BSC New York, the author cannot say. He does, however, know that it was never used for this purpose. The only two projects funded out of this money in the pre-Pearl Harbor days originated with Under Secretary of State Welles, an indication, albeit indirect, of his power in the Latin American field. One project involved the bringing to the US, and *pari passu*, their removal from the body politic of Bolivia, of two malevolently pro-Nazi journalists named Cespedes and Quadros about whom Anzi Matiengo, the Bolivian Foreign Minister, had complained to Welles at a 1941 meeting in Rio de Janerio. Coincidentally, BSC was also very active in Bolivia in anti-Nazi work, and to this extent, the Welles project was supportive of it. The other involved the 'spontaneous' eruption throughout Latin America of birthday balls on behalf of polio relief in honour of President Roosevelt. For this, the Coordinator used a son of former President of Panama who later was to marry Dame Margot Fonteyn, the British *ballerina assoluta*. Even in its more secret operations, the Rockefeller office believed that a little frivolity was useful in concealing more serious intent.

The decision of Franklin Roosevelt to substitute the 'good neighbor' policy for earlier American traditions of armed intervention in Latin America has persisted. Only twice since 1933 have US presidents decided to send troops South to defend American interests. President Eisenhower made up his mind to intervene in Venezuela to rescue Vice-President Nixon from a frenzied mob, and only last-minute events rendered this unnecessary. President Johnson intervened in the Dominican Republic. But it should not be forgotten that in the interim operational intelligence was developed as a substitute for achieving US policy goals. The truth is that Roosevelt was the first to recognize that his non-intervention policy was unworkable without an intelligence substitute, and this occurred only seven years after he had first dedicated the country to the 'good neighbor' policy. Nazis and Nazi operations could not be eliminated from within Latin America without operational intelligence techniques. Diplomacy was not sufficient.

It was the British, through BSC New York, who indirectly introduced these techniques to an inexperienced America through the Office of the Coordinator of Inter-American Affairs and the FBI in 1940 and 1941. Unfortunately, the knowledge gained, in so far as Latin America is concerned, was largely lost. After World War II, an untutored and unpractised CIA in the Latin American field had to start all over again, almost from scratch. From the standpoint of a broad overview, one is bound to wonder if the Bay of Pigs as well as other Latin American fumbles was not derived from this. For it was as true, after the war, as it was in 1940, that there is a symbiotic relationship in so far as the US is concerned, between military and naval non-interventionism and the use of operational intelligence to achieve national goals.

NOTES

1. Federal Register, 22 August 1940 and 2 August 1941.
2. Wm. E. Leuchtenburg, 'Franklin D. Roosevelt and The New Deal, 1931-1940', in Arnold Offner, *America and the Origins of World War II, 1933-1941* (Houghton Miflin Co. 1971), 82.
3. Charles A. H. Thomson, *Overseas Information Service of the United States Government* (Brookings Institution 1948), 118.
4. *History of the Office of the Coordinator of Inter American Affairs*, U.S. Bureau of the Budget, Historical Reports on War Administration, 1947.
5. See Barbara W. Tuchman, *The Zimmermann Telegram* (Dell Publishing Co. 1963).
6. Wayne S. Cole, *America First* (University of Wisconsin Press 1953), 99.
7. William Stevenson, *A Man Called Intrepid* (Harcourt Brace Jovanovich 1976), 160.
8. Adolf Hitler, *Mein Kampf* (Munich 1934), 439.
9. 1979 conversation between the author and Mr Paul Nitze.
10. Governor Rockefeller once explained to the author that his family was at the time drawing millions of dollars annually out of Latin America via its dividends from Creole Petroleum. He thus felt obligated to put something back in.
11. Wayne S. Cole, op. cit., 97.
12. H. Montgomery Hyde, *The Quiet Canadian* (London 1962), 55.
13. Bureau of the Budget, *History*, 16-17.
14. Federal Register, 19 July 1941.

15. Roosevelt Papers, Franklin D. Roosevelt Library, Hyde Park, NY.

16. See Wm. J. Langer and S. Everett Gleason, *Challenge to Isolationism* (Harper & Bros 1952).

17. H. Montgomery Hyde, op. cit., 157.

18. Letter quoted in Charles A. H. Thomson, op. cit., 153.

19. From mid-1940 until mid-1941 J. Edgar Hoover and the FBI had a monopoly on official liaison with British Security Coordination, New York. Hoover's discretion in this was exemplary and President Roosevelt's confidence not misplaced. The risk to Hoover and the FBI was great for they drew much political support on the Hill from isolationist Congressmen who would have been the first to howl for Hoover's head had they known he had 'betrayed' them to Britain. Some were genuine isolationists; others were isolationist only because they felt that if the US were to go to war, it should do so against the Soviets, not the Nazis.

14 Ultra and Some Command Decisions

Ralph Bennett

'The historian is a natural snob. He sides with the gods against Cato and applauds the winning side', wrote Dean Inge half a century ago. *Victrix causa diis placuit, sed victa Catoni.*[1] It may seem strange to begin a discussion of Second World War intelligence with a classical tag and the 'gloomy dean' of the 1930s, but his remark neatly points up a familiar historiographical problem which has a double relevance to the task of assessing the place of Ultra in the making of command decisions. Since Ultra was perhaps the largest[2] and certainly the most reliable single source of intelligence about the enemy available to the Allies from the spring of 1941 onwards, it would clearly be useful to discover how much influence it had upon their conduct of the war. As this paper will show, however, no more than a partial and provisional estimate can yet be made. For the present at least, all talk of 'completely rewriting the history of the war' in the light of Ultra must be discounted, and even the eventual release of all the surviving Ultra material is unlikely to compel so drastic a revision.

By 1945, the Allies were the winning side. When the secret that the Enigma code had been broken was first let out[3] six years ago, there was an immediate tendency to attribute too great a responsibility for victory to it alone. This chimed in with — was perhaps really part of — a natural change in historical fashion a generation after 1945. The new fashion wanted to depose the heroes of the past and to replace the story of five years' uphill struggle with an insistence that the economic balance was so heavily weighted in favour of Britain, Russia and the United States that they were always bound to win, and with the assertion that the Allies should rather be blamed for the foolishness or timidity which (it was alleged) prevented them from gaining a quicker victory than praised for the determination which enabled them to triumph in the end. The chief recent sign of this fashion is John Grigg's *1943: The Victory that Never Was*, and it may also be discerned in Mr. Julian Amery's letter to *The Times* of 21 June 1980 about the proposed Anglo-French union of 1940.

In the present state of our knowledge, Ultra can probably contribute little towards tackling broad strategic questions such as are here raised, for scarcely half, even of the signals sent from Bletchley to field commands, have been released. A proper assessment of Ultra's strategic value will only be possible when the whole corpus has been thoroughly studied and compared with information obtained from other sources, notably the Y-service, prisoners of war and low-grade codes. (At this distance of time, it is not by any means easy to discover from which of these sources a field commander derived a particular item of intelligence, since most of the operational histories were written before the existence of Ultra could be publicly admitted.) Meanwhile, it is safe to assume that Ultra's best work was usually done at a level slightly below that of grand strategy, although it made periodical highly successful excursions into battlefield tactics.[4]

However, there is at any rate one exception to this general rule. The breaking of Triton[5] by the Naval Section at Bletchley Park in March 1943 brought the U-boats under control at last and so changed the balance of power in the Atlantic that the whole future course of the war in Europe may have hung upon it. The war at sea is outside my direct knowledge, however, and this paper is concerned solely with the land battle and the air above it, which alone were my business as a member of Hut 3 at Bletchley.

There is a second sense in which Dean Inge's warning may apply. The road to final victory lay through many lesser successes and several set-backs. In some of them, the value of Ultra to the field commanders is quite plain, in others — for a variety of reasons, some of which are obscure — it is strangely difficult to determine. But the need for caution in deciding Ultra's usefulness or otherwise is as great in the short term as in the long, and in almost every case demands a more detailed examination than has yet been undertaken. The contribution of a source unique in the history of warfare can only be measured the hard way. To say this is not to denigrate the importance of Ultra, but rather to plead that so exact a source demands an equivalent exactness of the historian, and to point out that Ultra's quality and quantity draw attention to something which, though by no means confined to this particular historical source, is a peculiar handicap in the evaluation of it. We know remarkably little about what the fighting commanders thought of Ultra and how it affected their decisions. Nor, so far as I am aware, are we likely to learn much more in future. As consumers, their appetites were rapacious, but they seldom explained their taste-preferences, and it is too late now for much market research. Exceptions, like the account Professor R. V. Jones has given of how Bletchley decodes helped to beat the beams and delay the V-weapons, are likely to remain exceptions.[6] The Ultra historian is therefore often compelled to guess in spite of the risks entailed, and to rely on inference where he longs for certainty; he must nevertheless hold fast to an austere resolve never to pass one off as the other.

Medievalists probably have to brave pitfalls of this sort more often than modernists, but we have not been conspicuously successful in avoiding them. Was the growth in the power of the twelfth-century French monarchy the result of conscious and deliberate policy on the part of a succession of Capetian kings, or was it accidental? What was in the mind of their contemporary, Frederick Barbarossa, when he asserted the Emperor's rights in Italy by force? The answers profoundly affect one's interpretation of several critical themes in the history of medieval Europe, but there is practically no positive evidence to provide them — despite which, reputable scholars have confidently presented pages and pages of inference as fact, and have explained actions as if the purposes behind them were as plain as the events themselves. Most of the explanations have taken the plausible but unsatisfactory form 'since this was the result, that must have been the cause' — the argument of the winning side. A practising medievalist, accustomed to demolishing arguments like these, therefore comes to modern military history with a ready-made scepticism of anything but conclusive proof of the relation between cause and effect, and with an innate distrust of any generalization which is not properly supported. The links between knowledge and action, between event and explanation, have to be demonstrated beyond all reasonable doubt. In the case of Ultra there is a real danger of an easy and uncritical descent into 'must have been', and the path is already well-trodden.

Even granted this necessary caution, a great deal more Ultra will have to reach the Public Record Office before the chief command decisions of the war can be classified with any certainty according to the part Ultra played in them. All that can be done at present is to indicate a few types and suggest some reasons why they differ. One differential, the incidence of which has not been much discussed but which will probably have a considerable bearing on the final conclusion, is variations in intercept policy. The progressive switch of resources from the Mediterranean to the west in the spring of 1944, for instance, is apparent from the most superficial comparison of the signals to the two theatres, but it is not so easy to see whether this is the reason why the value of Mediterranean Ultra seems to fall off that same spring. The theatre itself was deliberately downgraded, particularly after the capture of Rome, and it may be that with consequently reduced resources it was not always possible to determine which radio links were likely to give the best yield of high-grade intelligence or to monitor them regularly. Again, it is fair to surmise that coverage was never so complete anywhere as in Africa between the Gazala battles of June 1942 and the German surrender on Cape Bon a year later, but also to suppose that there was severe competition with the navy for intercept sets and that the military yield was reduced from time to time by the refractoriness of the army keys. Variations in the volume and value of Ultra depended mainly on three things: variations in intercept policy (about which little information is forthcoming),[6a] the success of the code-breakers (which advanced fairly steadily from early 1942 onwards), and the German use of landlines (which for practical purposes debarred Ultra from access to northwest Europe until the spring of 1944).

They also depended in the early days on the purveyors' and the consumers' inexperience of the medium, combined with a security consciousness which was sometimes misplaced — notably the fiction which represented Ultra information as the work of a superagent who could be in several places at once, with the result that some recipients (no doubt conditioned by their military training to distrust all intelligence not derived from battle contact anyhow) at first dismissed it altogether. Some of the 1941 signals, when we see them, will probably seem amateurish and clumsily drafted beside those of the summer before Alamein.[7] Both parties gradually became more sophisticated and began to settle into an easier relationship, but the two thousand miles which separated them were a distinct obstacle to mutual understanding and sometimes caused a dialogue of the deaf until exchange visits began in the spring of 1942. Things were already very much better by the time I went to Cairo in October to join another officer in signalling one easily-broken army/air cooperation key on the spot.

Because the signals cannot yet be inspected, comment on Ultra's influence on command decisions in the desert and Tunisia, in Sicily and at Salerno can be nothing but speculation at present.[8] It is, however, a safe reflection that some of these decisions will look very different when we see the evidence. One rediscovery to which I am particularly looking forward myself is the date of the Ultra signal which gave away Rommel's intentions at Alam Halfa, for this should settle the dispute whether Montgomery's defence plan was inherited from his predecessor or suggested to him by his opponent. The frequency with which we decoded and passed on the Africa Corps' tank strength returns is another. If, as memory suggests — but memory is not to be trusted — we did so regularly and often, then 8 Army must be supposed usually to have known pretty accurately where the balance of mobility and fire-power lay, but not always to have taken this knowledge into proper account. This in turn is likely to sharpen criticism of its conduct in some of the desert battles.

The Anzio landing (22 January 1944) is the first major action for which full Ultra coverage is yet available. Ultra can have played little if any part in planning, but in three respects it was evidently of great assistance during the weeks immediately before the operation. Kesselring told Jodl[9] early in January 1944 that he had no fear of an Allied landing, and Canaris (whom Kesselring subsequently blamed for giving him bad advice) shortly reassured his Chief of Staff, Westphal, that such a thing was out of the question for a month or six weeks.[10] Ultra had no access to either opinion, but by keeping touch with every German division in Italy and confirming that none of them was being shifted to coastal defence it arrived, if negatively, at the same conclusion as OKW — that between the Cassino front and mouth of the Tiber 'the coast was to all intents and purposes unguarded'.[11] That this should be so was the more remarkable in view of the number of Ultra reports by other authorities about expected landings on both coasts of Italy.[12] (Only one of them was anywhere near the mark: on 14 January Kesselring sent a single battalion of the Hermann Goering Division to watch the seaward approaches behind 94 Division's front.) Its effect was enhanced by what were admitted to be 'inconclusive' air reconnaissance reports which failed to spot anything sinister right down to the last day,[13] as well as by repeated misinterpretations of Allied shipping movements — the arrival of aircraft carriers in the eastern Mediterranean was taken to be a way of reinforcing land-based fighters, for instance, and no alarm was shown at the disappearance of landing-craft from Bizerta harbour.[14] Even the 10th Italian human torpedo flotilla, whose operational orders and after-action reports the Naval Section regularly intercepted at this time, saw nothing to awaken its suspicions off Gaeta or in the bay of Naples.[15]

As D-Day for Operation Shingle approached, Ultra performed a third priceless service by letting General Mark Clark know that his plan to press his attack on the Gustav Line hard enough to attract German reserves away from the neighbourhood of Anzio had succeeded. The GOC XIV Panzer Corps, General von Senger und Etterlin, phoned Kesselring on 18 January to ask for reinforcements to prevent his front from collapsing; after some hesitation Kesselring, believing that he had no reason to fear a landing behind it, ordered 29 and 90 Panzergrenadier Divisions up to 10 Army from Rome.[16] Barely 24 hours later, Ultra was reporting elements of 29 PG moving south,[17] with more unspecified reinforcements also on the way to von Senger's hard-pressed 94 Division, and by 0300 on the 20th it had discovered that 29 PG was to take over a section of 94 Division's front.[18] Both signals were of course sent with the highest priority. As the first troops went ashore on the 22nd, it became known that the unspecified reinforcements were 90 PG and that the staff of I Parachute Corps had come from Frascati to direct all three divisions.[19] Thus through Ultra the Allied command knew in advance that surprise was almost certain and that initial resistance would be light because the nearest reserves had been diverted elsewhere and were consequently not available to counter-attack the beach-head during its vulnerable first hours. Even if Anzio was in some respects a misbegotten scheme, this realization must add one more reason for regret that its early success was not more immediately and powerfully exploited.

However, we must not forget that Lucas, in command of the landing, did not receive Ultra because he was only a corps commander. Mark Clark did receive it, of course, at 5 Army headquarters, but security regulations forbade him to pass it on except under heavy disguise. Since apparently neither 29 nor 90 PG had been identified by contact on the Cassino front before 22 January, it is hard to imagine how, without betraying Ultra, Clark could have informed Lucas that both these divisions were by that time heavily engaged in the Gustav Line and therefore could not counter-attack him in the immediate future. Whether the knowledge that the road to Rome was open and the city almost unguarded would have been enough to stop Lucas feeling that the whole affair had 'a strong odour of Gallipoli'[20] and to prevent him from taking refuge behind ambiguous orders and refraining from a quick advance cannot be known. In any case, the German reaction to Shingle was only below expectation on the first day. By the afternoon of the 23rd it was more or less what had been foreseen, and Kesselring was quick to read Lucas's surprising passivity to mean that a large-scale expansion[21] of the beach-head was no longer imminent.

Information derived from Ultra offered better prospects of success than the landings achieved, then, but the reasons why the operation first stalled and then became hopelessly (if heroically) bogged down are to be found not in the performance of any source of intelligence but in the lack of an unequivocal definition of primary objectives and in the psychology of a tired commander. By way of contrast, Ultra provided little of high operational value to General Alexander for the offensive ('Diadem') of 11 May 1944 which broke the Gustav Line, joined up with the Anzio beach-head at last, captured Rome and took the Allies as far as Lake Trasimene before it petered out. Diadem is memorable not so much for what Ultra did as for what it has been wrongly credited with doing.

But first, its positive contribution to Diadem. A clutch of reports[22] from Kesselring and his senior subordinates in May and June repeatedly stressed the problems of supply and transport which plagued them. These reports confirmed to the Allied commanders that, once prised out of their fortifications, the German armies would find it immensely difficult to conduct mobile warfare on their way back to another prepared position, and no doubt thereby encouraged them to feel that one more big push might topple Kesselring's house of cards altogether and open the way not only to the Lombard plain but perhaps even to Austria as well. Until all the Italian signals can be studied in proper sequence it would be premature to attempt to assess whether, and if so how much, Ultra was responsible for Alexander's dream of advancing through the Ljubljana Gap into Hitler's homeland, but inasmuch as its gloomy reports about supply and transport were a regular feature of the Italian campaign it is safe to say that they probably fostered the belief that if only an Allied offensive could achieve enough momentum it might make it impossible for the Germans to stop anywhere south of the Alps.

To return to Diadem. On 8 May Kesselring 'once again' called upon the naval authorities in Italy to carry a larger proportion of the supplies he needed, since railways and roads were so frequently interrupted by air attack, and reiterated his conviction that the Italian front was 'decisive for the conduct of the war'.[23] By early June he was persuaded that the situation would improve only if more fighters and ground-attack aircraft could be allotted to the *Luftwaffe* in Italy.[24] (On only eight days during the previous four weeks of heavy fighting had *Luftflotte* 2 managed more than a hundred sorties of all types of aircraft, and had averaged about 70.[25] Ultra only missed its daily returns of total effort on four days in the month.) Recurring complaints of ammunition shortage are still more illuminating. By 11 June Kesselring had been forced to conclude that shortage of ammunition had deepened every successive crisis in the fighting, and he ordered corps and divisional commanders to adopt 'the most ruthless means' to overcome it, even to the closure of roads to all other traffic; he had evidently forgotten that less than a month earlier the chief quartermaster of 10 Army had pointed out that this was just what the units and formations for which he was responsible could not do, because they had too few lorries of their own to fetch supplies for themselves.[26]

Ammunition was not the only thing in short supply. On 6 May OKH curtly told the Hermann Goering Division that because fewer and fewer tanks and assault guns were coming out of the factories the division would have to lose the privileged status which OKL had granted it during the winter and that its establishment of weapons would be reduced to the same level as that of the *Wehrmacht* and SS divisions.[27] Next day Kesselring circulated an order from Hitler which drew attention to the 'excessively strained German manpower situation'.[28] After a fortnight's fighting Mackensen at 14 Army complained about low morale and almost everything else: the fighting power of his divisions had declined shockingly, partly through attrition and partly because there were not enough good NCOs; tanks and lorries often broke down on long journeys, he had too few anti-tank guns and he was 20 per cent under strength in radio operators.[29]

Just as before Anzio, there were enough divergent reports of expected new Allied landings to show that in this respect at least German intelligence was wildly inaccurate — or very gullible, for several of these rumours, notably those suggesting Civita Vecchia as the target, had been put about as part of the deception-plan known as Nunton.[30]

All in all, Ultra gave Alexander a good deal of useful information about the enemy as he planned and launched his offensive. Though very encouraging, it can hardly have been decisive for the success or failure of his operation. Diadem is therefore one of the cases where Ultra is unlikely to enforce the rewriting of history. It did, however, provide a curious forewarning of the future. In the course of it, the German rank-and-file fought with a skill and determination which gave the lie to what generals like Mackensen had been saying about them in Enigma messages. If this had been remembered eighteen months later, it might have served as a useful corrective to the facile conclusion, drawn by so many after the Falaise pocket battle and subsequently the source of so much error, that the war was over bar the shouting because the Germans could fight no longer.

Contrary to what has just been said, readers of Group Captain Winterbotham's *The Ultra Secret* have been led to expect that the Diadem battle narrative needs a great deal of revision. In four or five pages of his book Winterbotham claimed to quote (from memory, of course) from a dozen or more signals, most of them emanating from Kesselring or Hitler, in which every important reaction of the Germans to Diadem was starkly revealed. There appears to be no Ultra warrant for most of his claims.[31] Moreover, there was an interval of twenty-four hours or more between German and British times of origin on most days at this period — presumably a reflection of decoding difficulties or of delays in the retransmission to England of Mediterranean intercepts — which would, of course, have reduced the operational value of Ultra significantly.[32]

It would serve no good purpose to dwell upon every case where *The Ultra Secret* is misleading over Diadem, but a few examples may be quoted. While it is certainly true that Ultra showed that Kesselring was quite unable to decide where and when the Allies would strike next, the files contain no signal of 10 May to that express effect. Nor is there a signal of the 13th revealing that he had committed all his reserves by then, though it might have been possible to deduce as much from a close scrutiny of the many recent signals conveying corps and divisional locations. There is no sign of an order from Kesselring for a general withdrawal from the Liri valley shortly afterwards, nor of his asking and receiving permission to move back to the Caesar Line just in front of Rome. A signal of 3 June[33] does, however, by implication support the claim that Ultra showed Hitler agreeing to the evacuation of Rome; but it also says a great deal more, for it orders the formation of a new front as far south as possible — and Hut 3 could not despatch this signal until 9 June, by which time the whole world had heard about the Americans' triumphal entry into Rome!

The point that Winterbotham's book is completely unreliable as an Ultra source need not be laboured further, and indeed would scarcely be worth mentioning at all were it not for the fact that the contagion has spread. A volume of the United States official history (E. F. Fisher: *Cassino to the Alps*) was published three years after *The Ultra Secret*. Mr Fisher quotes it as his authority on about a dozen occasions[34] — usually, it must be admitted, in the most general terms. But in so doing he has cast over its inaccuracies the cloak of respectability which belongs to an official publication, and has very likely given further currency to errors which it would have been better to scotch at once, among them the legend that Bletchley could intercept, decode, and translate a German text and retransmit an English equivalent 'within minutes' of the original going on the air. (Between two and two and a half hours was the best Hut 3 could manage.) Gresham's Law applies to history as well as to coinage. The task of correctly assessing the usefulness of Ultra intelligence will be longer and more difficult unless the circulation of false coin can first be prevented.

Ultra played no part in the greatest command decision in the west — the choice of time and place for the invasion of Europe — and its chief value before 6 June 1944 was surely confined to revealing the dispositions the GAF intended to make in an emergency and to serving as an absolutely reliable check upon other intelligence about the order of battle of the German army. It was best on the panzer divisions (all of which it identified) and weakest on locations — for instance, it missed the late move to Caen of 21 Panzer, whose counter-attack on the first afternoon might have cut the bridgehead in two. Once the invaders were securely ashore, however, Ultra began to offer them a series of opportunities which could have been given by no other source. In several of these cases the cause-effect relationship between knowledge and action can be demonstrated quite convincingly if not positively proved.[35]

The air strike on 10 June which paralysed Panzergruppe West for a fortnight was the earliest and most spectacular of these cases, and the snuffing out of 17 SS's attack at Carentan three days later (also clearly the result of an Ultra warning) was decisive for the capture of Cherbourg by 1 US Army. By now Hitler had become sufficiently alarmed to order II SS Panzer Corps across from the Russian front to dislodge the invaders. There was no hint of this for several days, but ample Ultra evidence of it accumulated in time to enable Montgomery to prevent the new arrivals from interfering with Epsom, the battle for the crossings of the river Odon, and in particular to bring an attack by 9 SS Panzer Division to an abrupt halt on 9 July. In all three cases Ultra clearly prompted actions which had a most important bearing on the progress of the campaign. As the scale of operations grew greater during the following weeks, so did the scale of Ultra's contribution. A close scrutiny of the signals passed to western commands during Cobra, the American breakout at the end of July, and in the early days of what became the Falaise pocket, shows beyond reasonable doubt that Ultra was behind some of the most important decisions taken at this time.

All through the three weeks before Cobra the German commanders opposite 1 US Army were continually complaining about the heavy casualties they were suffering and about the material superiority of the Americans; more than one of them predicted that if (as they expected) an offensive soon opened on this part of the front it was bound to break through their fragile defence lines. The only serious effort von Kluge could make to support them was to transfer the Panzer Lehr armoured division from Caen to St Lô. Ultra knew of his decision within twelve hours of his making it on the evening of 7 July and thirty-six hours before the first tanks reached their destination; this, and the four hours' notice we gave of an order for the division to attack directly it arrived, was enough to ensure that Panzer Lehr came up against prepared defences and scarcely disturbed 1 US Army's equanimity at all.[36] By the time Cobra opened, then, Bradley had good reason to anticipate a victory almost as rapid and complete as he achieved, because he knew in advance that morale was low on the other side of the hill and that the enemy expected to be beaten.

The Cobra plan did not originally call for immediate exploitation eastwards, and Patton's first orders were to clear Brittany, not advance up the Loire valley. No very precise explanation seems to have been given of the reasons which led Bradley to abandon his more modest original intention on 8 August in favour of a bolder course, although there was still only a very narrow supply corridor through Avranches, but it is hard to escape the conclusion that he did so partly at least because he already knew from Ultra of the first moves in what we now call Hitler's Mortain offensive and was confident that he could ride it out and convert it into a chance to annihilate the German armies in France. There is no positive proof, but the evidence is persuasive enough to silence the sceptic. The first clear signs that a counter-attack was in the wind became available on 5 August (hindsight can now even detect them on the third) with the withdrawal of 2 SS Pz and 116 Pz from the line to concentrate under XLVII Pz Corps north of Mortain. Conclusive evidence for it was signalled during the evening of 6 August, and details of objective and troops engaged shortly after midnight. The attack was a little delayed, the warning was enough and the American lines held — but the enemy showed no signs of retreat. When Bradley took his momentous decision on 8 August, therefore, Ultra and the previous day's experience combined to counsel boldness rather than caution, for he could foresee that Hitler's foolish gamble would compound his own advantage and therefore already envisaged the destruction of Army Group B. This was surely the supreme moment of Ultra in the west, for if it was responsible for a stroke upon which we can now see that the triumphant progress of the next few weeks largely depended, then its contribution to victory was great indeed. Bradley's judgement was soon proved right by the signal forecasting a renewal of the attack on 11 August, but if he had hesitated after the first phase there might never have been a Falaise pocket and the swift advance across northern France in the next three weeks.[37]

The weakness at the western end of the front which opened the way for Cobra showed how successfully the German command had been induced to believe that the main Allied thrust would come in the east. To the obvious topographical considerations which suggested this there had been added the repeated British attacks round Caen, and some of the most useful Ultra signals during the first six weeks were no doubt those which showed the panzer divisions concentrating in the same area to counter them, together with intelligence appreciations which revealed the intensity of Rundstedt's fear that they presaged a deadly thrust from Caen towards Paris. The other half of the deception plan sought to propagate the notion that a large Anglo-American army group in southeast England was preparing to pounce on Calais as soon as the Normandy landings had distracted the attention of OB West sufficiently. Signals like the group in late June which showed 116 Pz being kept away from Normandy to meet this threat are therefore likely to have been taken into account when command decisions were made. Another and very much larger group — German digests of deductions drawn from their Y-service intercepts and intelligence appreciations based upon them, which make up a considerable proportion of the signals issued during the middle six months of 1944 — proved the success of the deception plan still more convincingly. In other respects these signals may now be of mainly academic interest, but this cannot be established until they have been properly investigated. Because I did not know either the real or the notional Allied order of battle, *Ultra in the West*[38] touches only lightly upon this group of signals; Mr Cruickshank, who is familiar with both, did not make much use of Ultra when he wrote *Deception in World War II*. The official history of deception which is now being prepared will presumably show whether the Germans' errors were ever of such a size or kind that they could directly affect an operational decision by the Allies — and will perhaps also reveal how many of the breaches of signals security which gave the Y-service its chances were deliberate and how many culpable.

Thus until the liberation of Paris, the receipt of all major items of Ultra intelligence in the field was followed by action so evidently dependent on it that the relationship cannot be doubted, and there are no examples to the contrary. From the moment when the great advance came to a halt in early September, however, striking instances of the disregard of Ultra on matters of first-rate importance begin to accumulate. On 1 September Eisenhower took over the duties of Land Force Commander, directly controlling operations in a way he had not done before; SHAEF itself was similarly without experience of operational command. That the one change accounts for the other would be a more tempting hypothesis if it fitted all the facts, was not obviously an over-simplification, and did not involve thinking the unthinkable — a 21 Army Group commander without a will of his own. There is some support for the theory that after Falaise many at all levels of authority believed the war to all intents and purposes already won, and therefore suddenly relapsed into a state of euphoria. A collective fit of midsummer madness which lasted long enough to explain why the significance of some Ultra items was overlooked in November is scarcely credible, but there appears to be no acceptable alternative.

The contrast between the two periods is sharp and sudden. After Mortain, the influence of Ultra can still be traced in the early stages of the Germans' efforts to escape from the pocket, but then gradually fades from view in the fortnight's mobile warfare which followed (a great many signals were sent at this time, but the speed of the advance probably meant that most were out of date by the time they were delivered). On 5 September, the day after the capture of Antwerp docks, came an item so obvious (it now seems) that hindsight can scarcely believe that the news that Hitler planned to render Antwerp useless to the Allies by holding on to both banks of the Scheldt was even needed to prompt the measures necessary to foil him.[39] Yet this explicit warning — repeated two days later in an even more swiftly decoded instruction from Hitler to 15 Army in Holland — was completely disregarded, with the consequence that a pardonable momentary oversight by an armoured division exhilarated but exhausted by its long drive across France and Belgium was soon converted into a strategic mistake of such magnitude that its repercussions were felt almost until the end of the war. Montgomery's dream of an immediate advance to the Ruhr or Berlin in force great enough to kill the German bull with a toreador's thrust before it could turn at bay in its homeland was militarily feasible only if his 40 divisions could be supplied through Antwerp.[40] Yet for ten days he made no effort to ensure that he could use the port, and by then it was too late. If, in all the flurry and excitement of seeming victory, ordinary logistical prudence deserted the planners, Ultra was there to remind them in good time. Why its warning went unheeded is incomprehensible. Both Montgomery and Eisenhower continued to issue orders which either directly stated or indirectly implied that the approaches to the port were of only secondary importance, although both friend and foe (Ramsay and Hitler) had pointed out their error.[41] Within a few days the defence of Breskens and Walcheren had been organized and the Allies condemned to an autumn and winter of impotence and frustration.

Whatever the reason for the aberration — and it plainly had a great deal to do with the sudden emergence of a plethora of strategic options and the necessity to re-adjust sights from the short range of the bridgehead battle to the far longer range of a final victory on German soil — the atmosphere in which the mistake over Antwerp was made was to all intents and purposes still the same at the time of the decision about Arnhem: Comet (the lesser operation out of which Market Garden grew) was first contemplated on 3 September, when 11 Armoured Division was still racing towards Antwerp. The similarity extends into the field of Ultra. The main distinction is simply that the evidence was a shade less compelling in the later case, but the process of thought which could dismiss as unimportant the confirmation which Ultra's strong hints that 9 and 10 SS Panzer Divisions were near Arnhem gave to Dutch Resistance reports and to one probable interpretation of air photographs was surely very much the same as that which paid no heed to Hitler's explicit declaration of intent about Antwerp.[42] The evidence for the movements of 9 and 10 SS was not conclusive, mainly because it was not right up to date when 1 Airborne Division was briefed, but the authority of Army Group B was behind some of it. Unless there had been a very recent high-level change of plan — which was improbable now that Student and 1 Para Army had managed to stabilize the front — the Ultra evidence was therefore not likely to be misleading. Market Garden was not an operation planned entirely in relation to tactical opportunities and intelligence about the enemy, however. There are slightly sinister undertones of excessive haste, Anglo-American rivalry and even desperation about it; the possibility that there were tanks at Arnhem was the one awkward fact that would not fit the desired pattern, so the best thing was to sweep it under the carpet.

This hypothesis, unappealing in itself, has at least the merit of partly explaining away the problem the Ultra historian has to face over Antwerp, Arnhem and the Ardennes — that almost all the officers who received Hut 3 signals were by this time thoroughly experienced at their job and had in the very recent past shown themselves fully capable of estimating accurately the value of every item of intelligence that came their way. Only one of them, Strong, is known to have demurred at Market Garden,[43] but it is inconceivable that others did not do the same. Their masters overrode them, as they were fully entitled to do, but their masters were at fault when they allowed both their subordinates and posterity to believe that the tanks at Arnhem were a surprise.

Browning, in command of the airborne troops, was on the Ultra list and may have had the Ultra evidence about 9 and 10 SS in mind when he told Montgomery, 'I think we might be going a bridge too far', on 10 September, for most of it had been transmitted by the sixth. He was evidently no longer paying any heed to it two or three days later, for he advised Major Urquhart 'not to trouble himself'[44] about the air photographs. Montgomery had reacted in the same way to Strong's and Bedell Smith's warnings on the twelfth. Wisdom after the event must not misconceive the way military decisions are made by demanding that an operation of this size, from which immense strategic advantage could be expected if all went well, should have been cancelled because of a single piece of intelligence. It is entitled to suggest, however, that because tanks could so easily overrun unprotected infantry and because without the last bridge the whole operation was pointless, this single piece of intelligence clearly held the key to success or failure, and therefore deserved much more serious consideration than it received.

The same four weeks of rapid advance and abrupt check saw the broad front strategy applied for the first time, and this offers a kind of inverse parallel to Arnhem on a larger scale. Some of the British objections to Anvil/Dragoon, the extremest example of it, were proved sound by Hitler's prompt[45] order to evacuate the south of France (reported at once by Ultra) and by the Americans' failure to cut off significant elements of 19 Army although Ultra revealed the intended timetable of its laborious march up the Rhone valley. More importance, however, attaches to the signals which show that it was not only Blaskowitz (commanding Army Group G) who was nervous about his escape route through the Vosges, but that others were equally concerned about the immediately adjacent area to the northward — from Trier and the Mosel valley to Dijon, the rendezvous for the columns retreating from the south-west, and Belfort, where 19 Army reached comparative safety on 6 September. Thus the very area where Patton was pressing forward with or without permission as far as his artificially restricted resources allowed was shown by Ultra to be even more sensitive than south Holland or Aachen, where the sacred soil of the Reich was just coming under attack. Rundstedt admitted it when, even before the fall of Paris, he transferred XLVII Panzer Corps thither straight from Mortain and the pocket, and Hitler demonstrated the competition for scarce reserves between two widely-separated danger-spots when he moved 1 Parachute Army to the Albert Canal over much the same route in the opposite direction shortly afterwards. At this moment Patton was a greater menace than Montgomery. It was no doubt as politically impossible to give the Americans a monopoly of petrol and glory as the British, and the logistical problem entailed by a switch of direction from north to south would have been formidable; but simply from the point of view of intelligence about the enemy it was evident throughout September that the southern part of the front might yield more quickly to pressure than the northern and that it would be easier to 'bounce' a Rhine crossing up the Mosel or through the Saarland than at Arnhem.

The first of Ultra's many hints of a forthcoming offensive in the Ardennes came in late September,[46] but all were overlooked. None was explicit, and there was almost no indication of date, but cumulatively they amounted to a long series of reminders that something large and unexplained was going on. The length of the time-scale — just three months elapsed between the decoding of the order for the setting-up of 6 SS Panzer Army and the launching of the offensive — was perhaps the biggest handicap to the elucidation of what should have presented itself as a mystery demanding solution, for it required the evidence to be pieced together after the fashion of a PhD thesis rather than that of a normal military intelligence task. The clearest indications were of place, and it is astonishing (particularly in view of Eisenhower's reported remark that Allied lines were so stretched south of Aachen that 'we may get a nasty little Kasserine if the enemy concentrates in one place')[47] that the arrival of so much armour opposite the weakly-held Ardennes front and the constant air reconnaissance of the area behind it was not seen to contradict the prevailing theory that the Germans would counter-attack further north and then only when the Allies struck out for the Rhine.

The mythology of the Ardennes, like that of Arnhem, took shape long before Ultra could be mentioned openly. Nor is it easy today to superimpose Ultra upon analyses of the intelligence digests of the period before 16 December like Pogue's,[48] which could not mention it. In this mythology only Strong (whose account does not carry much conviction) at SHAEF and 'Monk' Dickson, the G-2 of 1 US Army, are held to have foreseen the attack. Colonel Dickson came quite near the truth in November but veered away from it later, and his opinion is in any case said to have been discounted partly because of an alleged reputation as an alarmist and partly because he was on bad terms personally with his superiors. But Dickson had been receiving Ultra since the Tunisian campaign of 1942, and in cooperation with Bradley had become skilled in the operational use of it. How much did Ultra shape his opinions and add steel to his expression of them? Alternatively, why did it not do both of these things to greater effect? Were there really no other Ultra officers, apart from these two, who saw anything from any intelligence source to jolt them out of their equanimity? And what was the real reason why the commanders did not listen to such warnings as they received? It can hardly be put down simply to cocksureness, and they were all experienced enough by Christmas 1944 to distinguish the one risk it was too dangerous to run from the many which had to be accepted if all action was not to be paralysed. These are questions which it may already be impossible to answer because few of those who could do so are still alive, and if this is the case then the release of the Ultra signals has made the mystery of the Ardennes more rather than less difficult to understand.

This reflection throws into sharp relief the chief obstacle confronting any retrospective Ultra criticism of the conduct of the war: namely, that the historian's temper is vastly different from that of the man of action, and that the passage of time makes it even harder for him to recreate in imagination the circumstances in which a commander's decisions have to be made and the sense of urgency which propels most of them. A commander always has to take calculated risks, but his calculations can never be exact and it is all too easy for the historian to expose the looseness of his arithmetic afterwards. Out of fairness to those who bore tremendous responsibilities in the past, the historian must never forget this. This said, however, there do appear to be several occasions during the Second World War when Ultra was culpably neglected with unfortunate results. It is almost certain that the release of more signals will show up new cases in the desert in 1941 and 1942. Inexperience in the handling of Ultra and a failure to comprehend fully either its peculiar nature or its potentially decisive value may perhaps explain some of the earlier cases — as, on a favourable construction, it does Pound's behaviour over Convoy PQ17, for instance — but the mistakes made in the last six or nine months of the war are not so easy to pardon.

NOTES

This paper was presented to the Anglo-American Conference on the History of the Second World War held at the Imperial War Museum, London, 28-31 July 1980.

1. W. R. Inge, *Outspoken Essays* (second series 1922), 169; Lucan, *Bellum Civile*, i, 126.

2. Working from the slight statistical evidence available and from our recollections, Mr Peter Calvocoressi (*Top Secret Ultra*, 6 and note) and I arrived independently at the figure of not less than half a million separate items produced between spring 1941 and the end of the war. My own service in Hut 3 covered just the same period.

3. By Group Captain Winterbotham in *The Ultra Secret* (1974), which was published before any Ultra documents had been released and was therefore written from memory.

4. Some examples are given below on p. 141.

5. See P. Beesly, *Very Special Intelligence* (1977), 152-185.

6. R. V. Jones, *Most Secret War* (1978).

6a. But now see Aileen Clayton, *The Enemy is Listening*, which was published after this paper was written.

7. Cf. F. H. Hinsley, E. E. Thomas, etc., *British Intelligence in the Second World War*, i, 393-394, 420.

8. When the signals become available, I hope to publish a study of Ultra in the Mediterranean.

9. P. E. Schramm, *Kriegstagebuch des OKW*, iv, 122.

10. M. Blumenson, *Salerno to Cassino*, 319.

11. Schramm, op. cit., iv, 124-125.

12. Public Record Office, DEFE 3/129 etc., VLs, 3531, 3624, 3771, 3805, 3855, 3925, 4423, 4427, 4255.

13. VLs 3857, 3863.

14. VLs 3540, 4161, 4441.

15. VLs 4072, 4129, 4158, 4213, 4240, 4379, 4400, 4430, 4434.

16. Blumenson, op. cit., 318-319.

17. 18/1 VL 4302 1904/19. (This formula means that a German message which originated on 18 January was transmitted at 1904 hours on 19 January as VL 4302. The same formula, sometimes with a more precise time of origin, is also used in later footnotes.) On 29 PG, see also VL 4308.

18. 2300/19 VL 4331 0304/20.

19. 20/1 VL 4464 0159/22, VL 4476, 1300/21 VL 4506 1802/22.

20. Blumenson, op. cit., 355, 426.

21. Ibid., 365 (23 January).

22. KVs 3451, 3886, 4328, 4370, 4652, all dated between 3 and 18 May.

23. KV 3378.

24. KV 6745.

25. KVs 3291, 3391, 3514, 3715, 3854, etc. At the same time, the Allied air forces in Italy were flying an average of 435 sorties every twenty-four hours (excluding anti-shipping operations and attacks on ports). (C. J. C. Molony, *The Mediterranean and Middle East*, v. 689.)

26. KVs 7965, 4328.

27. KV 3623.

28. KV 3482.

29. KVs 5761, 5796.

30. KVs 3652, 3791, 3884, 4424.

31. *The Ultra Secret*, 113-118. Similar misapprehensions can easily multiply. Mr. Nicolson interviewed General Mark Clark in 1970 (Nigel Nicolson, *Alex*, 233). Clark told him, 'We had broken the German code and read the messages from Hitler to "drive us into the sea and drown us".' What code? Clark did not say. When Mr. Lewin quoted this passage (*Ultra goes to War*, 285), he took the code to be Ultra. So did I — until recently I sought in vain for a remotely similar signal in Ultra. However, there was a Hitler order timed 0045 on 26 January to mount a counter-attack and 'break and bridgehead into bits and throw the enemy into the sea' (Schramm, op. cit., iv, 132). This order may have been transmitted in another code broken by the Allies; alternatively, Clark may have seen it as a captured document after the war and have come by 1970 to believe that he had seen it as a decode in 1944.

32. See, for instance, KVs 3652, 3693, 3720, 3791, 3886, 3951, 3960, 4365, etc.

33. 3 June KV 7169 2039/9.

34. E.g. on pp. 20, 42, 541.

35. Full references for this and the next two paragraphs will be found in my *Ultra in the West*, chaps. 2, 3 and 4.

36. 2300/7 XL 1196 0654/8, 0215/10 XL 1492 1403/10. Compare Blumenson, *Breakout and Pursuit*, 137-138.

37. The Ultra battle-narrative is in *Ultra in the West*, 112-122. For Bradley's decision, see Omar Bradley, *A Soldier's Story*, 372-376. Bradley represents the decision as his own, but, of course, as Land Force Commander, Montgomery was still technically his superior, although he and Bradley had both commanded Army Groups since 1 August.

38. Pp. 52-53.

39. P.m./3 September XLs 9219, 9248 1835/5; *Ultra in the West*, 141-143.

40. It has been suggested that either Amsterdam and Rotterdam or Hamburg were 21 Army Group's real objectives, and that this explains the neglect of Antwerp. Neither suggestion is at all convincing; both depend, for instance, upon a successful outcome to Market Garden (which was then still in the first stages of planning), for all three cities are east of the Rhine.

41. See, for instance, L. F. Ellis, *Victory in the West*, ii, 21-27; J. Ehrman, *Grand Strategy*, v, 524-529.

42. The Ultra evidence about Arnhem is set out in *Ultra in the West*, 143-151.

43. K. W. D. Strong, *Intelligence at the Top*, 149; C. Ryan, *A Bridge too Far*, 139-141.

44. Ryan, op. cit., 142.

45. 0940/17 August, XLs 6753, 6919 1408/17.

46. 18 September HP 1378 1626/27; *Ultra in the West*, 180-190. The parallels with 1940 can be pursued in extraordinary detail. Not only was Corap's 9 Army as ill-advisedly weak as Hodges' 1 US Army in 1944, but long before *Sichelschnitt*, the GAF had regularly reconnoitred the same Meuse crossings in the Ardennes as they did later before *Wacht am Rhein*, and the French Deuxième Bureau knew in March 1940 of German troop concentrations in the same part of the Rhineland as SHAEF

knew from Ultra in November 1944 (Alistair Horne, *To Lose a Battle,* 198, 233). But since it is unlikely that anyone in authority at SHAEF in 1944 had also been at GHQ four years earlier (or would have noticed the parallels if he had!), these can only be items in a historian's collection of curiosities.

47. Forrest C. Pogue, *The Supreme Command*, 295; Strong, 153-154.
48. Pogue, op. cit., 361-372.

15 Was SOE Any Good?[1]

Michael R D Foot

The Special Operations Executive was a British secret service formed in 1940 and dissolved in 1946. Its tasks were to deal with sabotage, subversion and resistance to the occupier during the six years' world war. Notoriously the start of that war in September 1939 caught the British imperfectly prepared. Three small governmental bodies, still sometimes confused with each other,[2] and all recently formed — one confidential, one secret, and one very secret — were starting, hardly before time, to examine problems of subversive activity. They were:

(1) EH, named after Electra House on the Embankment where it worked under Sir Campbell Stuart (so it was also sometimes called CS). He had been prominent under Lord Northcliffe at a similar task in 1918.[3] EH was a part of the Foreign Office and studied propaganda.

(2) MI R, previously known as GS(R), a tiny branch of the military intelligence directorate of the War Office. Originally it consisted of one major and one typist; the major could research on any subject he chose. The current head, J. C. F. Holland, wounded in Ireland during the Troubles,[4] was at work on methods of irregular warfare, and had by this time got some support from the chief of the Imperial General Staff and a few companions, including (Sir) Colin Gubbins, who had been a cadet at Woolwich with him and had also, after surviving the western front, fought in Ireland in 1919-20.[5] Several others he had chosen from courses for young reserve officers held ostensibly on current affairs, actually on theory of guerilla, during vacations at Cambridge.

(3) Section D of MI 6, the inadmissible secret intelligence service (SIS),[6] was founded just after the German-Austrian Anschluss of March 1938. Its head, Major Lawrence Grand — like Holland a regular engineer by training and eventually a major-general — had long been seconded from regimental work, and had numerous friends in the City of London, some of whom he recruited.[7]

The German victories in the spring and early summer of 1940

pointed clearly enough to the need for some such body to be effective. Everyone concerned in the business said (then and thereafter — it remains a *leitmotif* of survivors' conversation), that of course we had never done anything of the kind before; forgetting MO 4 Cairo that had run T. E. Lawrence (for what that was worth — still something of an open question), forgetting Pitt's flooding of revolutionary France with false assignats, forgetting how Walsingham framed Mary, Queen of Scots. The educated classes had got out of touch with their country's history. This sort of underhand dealing was by 1939 usually regarded as inadmissible among gentlemen; ten years earlier Henry L. Stimson had suppressed the American 'black chamber', the deciphering staff, with the remark that 'gentlemen do not read each others' mail'.[8] That there were few, or no, gentlemen in the Nazi High Command was a point that the British High Command only took in slowly.

By July 1940 it was beginning to do so. Churchill the new Prime Minister was, as a duke's grandson in the male line, a gentleman down to his toenails, but his mother had been American, a daughter of one of the great New York financial tycoons who set more store by money than by manners. The chiefs of staff, true to their own *Kaderfamilie* origins, remained entire gentlemen, but it was they who on 25 May 1940 sounded the first note of alarm. They envisaged already that the western front was broken, and that France as well as Belgium was in process of collapse; in which case in their view subversion would be the only stick left, however feeble at first, with which the British could hope eventually to beat Germany; in which case again, it was indispensable to have a single authority to direct it.[9] Lord Hankey, long ago the Secretary to the Committee of Imperial Defence, promoted in the middle of the previous great war to be the first Secretary to the Cabinet also, undertook as his last important political activity the welding together of EH, MI R, and section D. He saw the heads of section D and MI R together on 13 June, and attended the decisive meeting in the Foreign Office on 1 July. Lord Halifax presided; Cadogan his permanent secretary, Gladwyn Jebb, Cadogan's private secretary, Menzies the new head of SIS, Beaumont-Nesbitt the director of military intelligence, and (Sir) Desmond Morton, who handled secret matters for Churchill, were also present, and so were two ministers, Lord Lloyd, the Colonial Secretary (an old friend of T. E. Lawrence's) and Hugh Dalton, the Minister of Economic Warfare.[10]

Dalton had been, in his own phrase, 'much involved' in the discussions. 'Many alternatives [he said] were canvassed, both of plans and persons. My own idea had been that Attlee, who, as Lord Privy Seal, had no departmental duties should take charge and that I should be his Chief of Staff. He, on the other hand, wished me to take it, and steadily used his influence to this end.'[11] At Halifax and Hankey's meeting, 'after some discussion of the multiplicity of bodies dealing with sabotage and subversive activities, there was a general feeling, voiced by Lord Lloyd, that what was required was a Controller armed with almost dictatorial powers'.[12]

Dalton wrote to Halifax next day, in an often quoted but still re-quotable letter,

> We have got to organize movements in enemy-occupied territory comparable to the Sinn Fein movement in Ireland, to the Chinese Guerillas now operating against Japan, to the Spanish Irregulars who played a notable part in Wellington's campaign or — one might as well admit it — to the organizations which the Nazis themselves have developed so remarkably in almost every country in the world. This 'democratic international' must use many different methods, including industrial and military sabotage, labour agitation and strikes, continuous propaganda, terrorist acts against traitors and German leaders, boycotts and riots.
>
> It is quite clear to me that an organization on this scale and of this character is not something which can be handled by the ordinary departmental machinery of either the British Civil Service or the British military machine. What is needed is a new organization to co-ordinate, inspire, control and assist the nationals of the oppressed countries who must themselves be the direct participants. We need absolute secrecy, a certain fanatical enthusiasm, willingness to work with people of different nationalities, complete political reliability. Some of these qualities are certainly to be found in some military officers and, if such men are available, they should undoubtedly be used. But the organization should, in my view, be entirely independent of the War Office machine.[13]

Hankey took the meeting's conclusions to Neville Chamberlain, the Lord President of the Council, who passed them on to Churchill, who in turn saw Dalton on 16 July and entrusted him with charge of subversion: 'And now, set Europe ablaze!' — a good phrase, even though while Dalton was still responsible for burning it up Europe was too damp to do more than smoulder.

On 19 July Chamberlain signed a most secret paper, treasured by SOE as its founding charter and still unavailable to the casual researcher at the Public Record Office. The war cabinet approved Chamberlain's document on 22 July, and a few hours later he went into hospital; he never lived to do anything of importance again. It is a nice irony that the man whom two generations have reviled for not standing up to Hitler firmly enough did in the end help to forge a clandestine weapon designed to bring Hitler down.

For Chamberlain's most secret paper laid down that 'a new organization shall be established forthwith to co-ordinate all action, by way of subversion and sabotage, against the enemy overseas. . . . This organization will be known as the Special Operations Executive.' The war cabinet's only comment — which perhaps explains some reluctance in making the paper available — was that 'it would be very undesirable that any Questions in regard to the Special Operations Executive should appear on the Order Paper' of the Commons.[14]

Not only was SOE to be outside parliamentary control, it was to remain secret and inadmissible, while other departments were expected to assist it. With such a start, it could hardly fail to be unpopular. Bureaucrats detested it anyhow, because it was new and therefore upset the accustomed order of things; as if Hitler had not made upsets enough already. A particularly absurd case of obstruction may be quoted from the War Office, where the director of staff duties' minions tried to insist as late as the winter of 1943-44 that travel abroad, even on operations, by army officers employed by SOE was not to take place until that director had been satisfied that the security of the impending invasion of north-west Europe would not be imperilled by each projected journey.[15] There were dozens of other examples during the war, and the history of SOE since then has been much troubled by authors who did not understand what it had been, and — sometimes unintentionally — misrepresented it as a sort of monster.

It was most unpopular of all in SIS. Senior men in the intelligence service loathed it, because the new body broke the old one's monopoly of clandestine activity in foreign countries. Senior men in SOE loathed SIS in return, because it was always placing minor (or where possible major) obstacles in SOE's way; not quite with the savage obscurantism of Chiang Kai-shek's Tai Li, surely the stupidest secret police head of the war,[16] but quite maddeningly enough. For a long time, for example, SIS prevented SOE by various means from operating at all by sea into Brittany out of Cornwall. This was partly because SIS wanted to keep Brittany peaceful for its own agents and those of its protégé MI 9, the escape service; partly it was out of sheer inter-secret-service spite. At last, as late as June 1943, SOE's and SIS's private navies in Cornwall were amalgamated

> and it came as a source of great surprise [according to another SOE section historian] to more than one Officer (and to some of the more intelligent Ratings) to discover that — contrary to what they had been educated to believe — the principal enemy was Hitler and not their opposite number in the sister organization. Nothing but good came of this amalgamation at the same Base, and the personnel of the two Organizations at Helford worked thereafter in the closest co-operation, with the discomfiture of the Hun as their sole objective.[17]

The SOE-SIS antagonism has been aptly summed up in one of the most recent studies: SIS 'never fully accepted the SOE-SIS divorce of 1940, and its subsequent behaviour only too often resembled that of an embittered ex-spouse'.[18]

There was moreover a major inter-departmental — as opposed to inter-secret-service — battle about the control of propaganda, which SOE in the end lost, and lost with it that third of its original membership who had worked in Electra House and come from the Foreign Office. This was not the Foreign Office's grandest period, and some of its middle-rank officials seem rather to have enjoyed inter-departmental wrangling; moreover, from the constitutional nicety that SIS could be regarded for some purposes as a Foreign Office fief, they felt themselves enlisted on whatever side was going to cause most trouble for SOE. The Electra House group finally split off again in August 1941 to form the Political Warfare Executive. Charles Cruickshank's *The Fourth Arm*,[19] the best available history of PWE, only touches lightly on the battle, which might one day be worth a detailed study.[20]

Service civilian and secret departments alike were worried and perplexed by SOE. It luxuriated in a wealth of cover names — MO 1 (SP), using War Office writing paper, NID (Q) at the Admiralty, AI 10 at the Air Ministry were only a few of them. Universal Export, made notorious in Ian Fleming's novels, came close to a fourth, used by it for trade. Harris, the chief of Bomber Command, once launched a gibe at 'the amateurish, ignorant, irresponsible and mendacious Ministry of Economic Warfare'[21] which may really have been meant for SOE, for which that ministry provided convenient Whitehall cover. Portal, the chief of the Air Staff, put in a counterword at once: it was 'an unworthy and inexcusable travesty of our conduct of the war to suggest that our policy is determined on that kind of basis'.[22]

(Sir) Dingle Foot, the under-secretary who answered for MEW in the Commons after Dalton had been kicked upstairs to the Board of Trade in February 1942 and Lord Selborne who had become the new minister, took care never to visit SOE's headquarters at 64 Baker

Street. (The brass plate on the door read 'Inter-services Research Bureau', another cover name; it accounted for the constant flow of people in army, air force, or occasionally naval uniform who passed in and out.) Dingle Foot could therefore reply to occasional tiresome parliamentary questions about what on earth went on there with the bland statement that he had never been there, and could therefore tell the house nothing.[23]

'Amateurish' was SIS's favourite gibe against SOE. The accusation came a trifle oddly from the body that had been completely taken in by the *Sicherheitsdienst* in the autumn of 1939,[24] and had had its networks in western Europe cleaned up in the summer of 1940.[25] If SOE was 'ignorant', it was partly because SIS kept it starved of information; 'irresponsible' was frequently the Foreign Office's gibe, at a time when diplomats were not notable for the daring of their decisions. 'Mendacious' was a common, even if sometimes an unfounded, charge from several other departments, which found that the organization seemed to change its collective mind uncomfortably often — a necessary consequence of any attempt to act in an original way through a group of other departments set firm in their existing tramlines. In London SOE had few of the attributes of an established government office — it had for instance no central registry and no central filing system, its unlisted telephone lines (200 of them) were on three separate London exchanges, and there was no head office at which an inquirer could call to seek elucidation of a puzzle: SOE's officers went out instead, or saw people in furnished flats in Bayswater or South Kensington. Yet in spite of all this passion for secrecy, some of the staff formed the habit of dropping in at a night club near their actual place of work — at 1 Baker Street, now a Kuwaiti bank — and one young agent under training, taken there by his intensely secure mentor, met in this club four people whom he afterwards identified at a glance when on duty in occupied Europe.[26]

In Cairo tensions could be still worse than among the *prime donne* who were to be found giving tongue, or keeping too silent, in London. In London it was not unknown for people in SOE — as in many other bureaux, PWE and the Ministry of Information conspicuous among them — to engage in office politics instead of pursuing the public weal and the war effort. Cairene heat seemed to intensify this tendency. Seven changes in command there in five years[27] could hardly in any case assist continued policy. Bickham Sweet-Escott, an occasional visitor though never posted there, remarks that, 'Nobody who did not experience it can possibly imagine the atmosphere of jealousy, suspicion, and intrigue which embittered the relations between the various secret and semi-secret departments in Cairo during that summer of 1941, or for that matter for the next two years'.[28] It would be interesting to know what the exact pecking order was between the various services involved — MI 5, MI 6, MI 9, the Y service, the Government Code and Cipher School, the Radio Security Service, the Home Defence Executive, the W committee, the XX committee, the London Controlling Section and any others that may yet be hiding under the blankets of security. These blankets are irritatingly thick where SOE is concerned. To pretend that Baker Street was more secret than Bletchley Park — the centre where the GC and CS deciphered the Germans' and Italians' most secret traffic — can only heighten the impression that SOE had something exceptionally nasty to hide. If it had, then it was completely concealed from the present writer when he had access to most of SOE's surviving archives that bore on France, and on general SOE policy, in the early 1960s.

Right from the start, SOE was obsessed by problems of personality. Even before it was founded, Grand and Holland got on badly; Grand thought Holland over-careful, Holland thought Grand rash. A keen observer traced the two strands of feeling through much of SOE's subsequent history. Grand was dismissed as soon as SOE got under way, in the early autumn of 1940, and Holland left also, because a regimental command fell vacant and as a professional soldier he thought he ought to fill it. He had in his two years at the War Office initiated the deception and escape services, as well as a large proportion of SOE, had founded the commandos, and had picked Gubbins to command the stay-behind parties who were to do what they could to harass the *Wehrmacht* after the Germans landed in England.[29] Dalton secured Gubbins for SOE in November 1940, and he became director of training and operations under the symbol 'M'; eventually he was executive head ('CD').

The first executive head was Sir Frank Nelson, a former conservative MP and an India merchant, who had recently been consul in Basle — 'traditionally an SIS position', in David Stafford's phrase.[30] Dalton's aide Gladwyn Jebb claimed much later that at meetings of SOE's council at which he and Nelson had both been present, he took the chair himself.[31] Certainly his knowledge of the Whitehall machine was superior to Nelson's. Between them they achieved a task which Grand had begun — indeed Grand's work on this was probably the most important thing he ever did. The task was to explain to a very few very senior people in other departments (such as the Treasury, the Board of Trade and the Colonial Office) that there was a new equal to them in the government machine, which was operating in deadly secrecy to cause confusion to the King's enemies by unconventional and even ungentlemanly means. Nelson burnt himself out in the effort, and by the spring of 1942 had to retire, a broken man (he died in poverty in 1966).[32] He was succeeded by Sir Charles Hambro the banker, who had become his second-in-command after distinguished work in Scandinavia.[33] Selborne appointed Hambro on the ground that a man who could run the Great Western Railway could run anything.[34] By this time SOE was beginning to show some results.

Its total strength has never been established, and probably now never will be. It appears to have contained about 10,000 men and 3,000 women. Most of the women were cipher clerks or home station wireless operators, but a few of them were staff officers of distinction and a very few highly accomplished and gallant ones were agents operating in France or Yugoslavia. (On these few there is a large popular literature, almost all of it worthless and much of it about the wrong people.) SOE was divided into 'facilities' sections (wireless, finance (extremely efficient), tailoring (inefficient), training and so on) and 'country' sections which covered most enemy-occupied areas and the whole of the neutral and allied world as well. There were large subordinate staffs in New York,[35] Cairo, Kandy, Brisbane, Algiers (when available) and Bari (when available — working into Poland and the Balkans). Efficient wireless links enabled London to control the outlines of SOE's policies 'in the field', but all the details had to be left to the men on the spot, who in turn frequently had little or no idea of what the agents they had sent forward into occupied territory were doing, or even of which side they were on.

In the current climate of opinion there is likely to be interest in traitors in SOE. The Gestapo often used with success against captured agents the statement that they had a traitor in SOE's headquarters in Baker Street. Agents ought to have been able to spot that this is a routine interrogator's device, and need not have any factual basis; the present writer's researches indicate firmly that it was a lie.[36] The Gestapo could be mendacious as well as SOE.

Of Russian influence there are more signs. A junior staff officer in London was convicted in 1943 of communicating secret information to a foreign power; newspaper reports indicated that the foreign power was our current gallant Soviet ally, and D. F. Springhall, a member of the central committee of the Communist Party of Great Britain, was arrested and sentenced on similar charges at the same time. James Klugman, also an eminent British communist, was first a sergeant, then a major on SOE's Balkan planning staff in Cairo. He made no particular secret of his views, had been up at Cambridge with Philby and Blunt, and had some influence on SOE's support for Tito. This support, according to a very recent and well-informed account, derived from a staff accident. Brigadier C. M. Keble, SOE's chief of operations (and later one of the transient local directors) in Cairo, happened to be already privy to Ultra decrypts from Bletchley Park, and against exceptionally strict orders passed them on for analysis to two of his subordinates, Basil Davidson and (Sir) F. W. D. Deakin.[37] As no one in authority but Keble knew he had broken the taboo, both Davidson and Deakin were later allowed to go on their distinguished forays into occupied territory (Deakin and Tito were wounded by the same bomb). Meanwhile their analysis of what the German security forces were saying to each other made it clear which, from the Allied point of view, was the better bet as between Tito and Mihailović. SOE did not find it at all difficult to support communists against monarchists in Yugoslavia, while across the frontier in Greece it went along with Myers and Woodhouse, its own successive chiefs of mission, and supported monarchists against communists.[38] Of this more shortly. Klugman's influence, if any, on the complexities of SOE's policies in Albania — lavish promises to two divergent resistance groups, the communist one of which was provided with warlike stores used to destroy the other, which got nothing — remains obscure.[39]

SOE's high command at the London end nevertheless remained in perfectly firm and loyal hands. Gubbins, another *Kaderfamilie* character, whose clandestine career had begun with an evasion from Germany disguised as a schoolboy in early August 1914 — within a fortnight he was a gunner subaltern on the western front[40] — was totally loyal to the crown and would never willingly have endured a traitor near him. He had been in Russia with Ironside in 1919, and understood communism with unusual clarity of view. Jebb called him SOE's 'mainspring', and he suceeded Hambro as its working head in September 1943.

How much actual use was SOE in the winning of the war? The question remains open, and until recently has been little debated; Stafford's book should help to ventilate it more.[41]

Bomber Command's total dead were four times as many as SOE's apparent total strength. Former members of Bomber Command get understandably upset when anyone tries to suggest that a great deal of their effort was wasted, and that many of the tasks on which expensive aircraft carried almost irreplaceable aircrew could have been much more cheaply performed by half a dozen discreet agents on the ground, introduced clandestinely with a few pounds of plastic explosive and exact knowledge of where and how to use it. There are a few specific instances of the value of sabotage as a superior instrument to mass bombing — only a few. Vemork and Montbéliard are the two outstanding ones. Vemork probably deterred the Germans from trying to make an atomic bomb, a really world-shaking operation. Montbéliard showed that one team of brave men could do what several squadrons of bombers could not: put a tank turret factory out of action for the duration.

The official British staff doctrine was always, 'We are sure of our artillery and aircraft; we know exactly what they have and have not done. You saboteurs may provide us with a bonus, but it will be a bonus, not a certainty.' The size of the bonus secured in France at the end of the first week of June 1944, when on Eisenhower's orders the whole of French Resistance mobilized, and brought the country's railway and telephone system to a virtual standstill as well as blocking most of the main roads, was much larger than any staff officers outside SOE had foreseen, but SOE got little credit for it. Being a secret service, it could not attract the propaganda resources lavished on the comparatively photogenic bomber commands of the RAF and the USAF, and the public remained unaware of its existence till the end of the war. Most of the sources on which a proper assessment of SOE's military value could have been made have probably by now been destroyed. It still might be worth somebody's effort to attempt the task. (One small point is clear, in an age when many people will translate RAF to themselves as Rote Armee Fraktion rather than as Royal Air Force: it was not SOE that disturbed the childhood slumbers of the Baader-Meinhof gang.)

SOE undoubtedly had great political importance in some but not all of the countries where it tried to operate, as did the American Office of Strategic Services, ancestor of today's CIA, set up in June

1942 to combine the tasks of SOE and SIS under a single chief. By stimulating, indeed in one or two cases by originating, local resistance movements, SOE enabled the populations of occupied territories to take a real share in the way their countries were governed after the war. Above all it provided opportunities for variety, for keeping political options open. Wherever the Red Army conquered, it was followed close behind by the police of the NKVD (now the KGB), who imposed their will and their system and allowed no freedom of choice or open options at all. Suitable regimes, from the Kremlin's point of view, followed everywhere except in Finland — once bitten, twice shy — and in Austria, where the population had no wish to go the way of Russia. In Yugoslavia the Kremlin fell out with Tito's arrangements; it was thanks to SOE's past support of him that Tito was able to stand up to Stalin and assert the real strength of his local communist party, which had been forged in real battles with SOE's real guns against really awful Axis occupiers and even more atrocious Croat Ustache separatists. In Greece, if it had not been for SOE, the communist-dominated left-wing resistance movement would almost certainly have imposed its will on the country from an extreme minority standpoint, under the leadership of the man who called himself Ares. (Ares fell out in the end even with his own followers, who decapitated him and left his head on a stake.[42]) In France, the communists might have dared to try to seize power in the confusion of the late summer of 1944, had they had any orders from Moscow (they were dreadfully Moscow-bound, even then), and had there not been small arms for half a million men distributed round the rest of France by SOE — with half an eye on counter-balancing just such a coup. Even in the Netherlands, where the German security services brought off astounding professional successes against SIS and SOE in turn, SOE was eventually able to set up some well-placed and well-armed parties who smoothed the way back to her throne for the much-beloved Queen Wilhelmina.[43] In Norway, wartime politics revolved round SOE's efforts. In China it could do little — OSS barred it out, and even OSS found it hard to work in a country where the only efficient anti-Japanese forces, Mao's communists, were at daggers drawn with Chiang Kai-shek's Kuomintang. And in Burma SOE achieved one of its most remarkable coups: it turned round Aung San's *milice*-type internal security force, which deserted the Japanese at a critical moment in the spring of 1945 and made the reconquest of Burma a lot less bloody, and politically a lot less complicated, than it might have been. The official Burmese government-in-exile at Simla was not best pleased, but the days of Sir Reginald Dorman-Smith were passing. In Malaya SOE learned to work with the communist underground workers, with some odd consequences in the 1950s. Sir Gerald Templer who managed to put down the main communist rising there, with the help of a Special Air Service unit that found out how to parachute straight into jungle, had learned his way round subversive warfare when at Gubbins's invitation he had spent six months on SOE's governing council in London after being wounded (by a grand piano blown out of a lorry in front of him) in Italy in the autumn of 1943.

Liddell Hart used to say that Clausewitz had been right to distrust irregular forces.[44] In their view the social impact of letting people have their own heads militarily, untrammelled by discipline, was bound to be bad. Liddell Hart and Clausewitz are two big names in the theory of war, and only a brave man or a man very sure of his facts will try to contradict either of them lightly. But surely in this case they did exaggerate?

At this point the historian has to abandon his documentary sources, somewhat sparse in any case for the handling of SOE,[45] and fall back on insight, sympathy and common sense. For millions of people in north-western and south-eastern Europe, life in the early 1940s was harrowed by the daily recollection of how disgracefully their armed forces had done against the Germans at the time of invasion, when *Blitzkrieg* had swept them swiftly into oblivion. This was exceptionally painful in France, consciously *la grande nation*. To have the least toe-hold in resistance gave back to millions of people the self-respect they had lost at the moment of national disaster, and SOE was one, one of the largest, of several bodies which provided opportunities and arms for taking part in the resistance struggle.

The attitude of mind encouraged by SOE, to take nothing for granted, to be ready to flout any constituted authority if it was constituted by the wrong side, was not one that encouraged legality, nor in the early days of occupation did it look 'realist'. But was it wrong? Did it not rather encourage people to retain their self-respect, or rather to regain it, when they could play some part however minute in getting rid of the occupying forces that had inflicted on their country so shameful a defeat? At the end of the war

SOE tried to get back the arms it had distributed, mainly by air (Bomber Command never gave up more than four squadrons of aircraft for parachute deliveries: one of the great brakes on SOE's activity). Only in one case did it wholly succeed — a tribe in north Burma handed back not only all the weapons that had been dropped to it, but all those that with their help had been captured from the Japanese as well. Were the surviving caches of arms and explosives a serious stimulus to later social unrest?

There was once a caïque captain who was caught by the Royal Navy smuggling sten guns (still in the cases in which SOE had dropped them) into Cyprus. He remained silent throughout his trial, was found guilty, and was asked if he wished to say anything in his own defence before he was sentenced. Silently he handed up to the judge a king's commendation for brave conduct, signed not by George II of the Hellenes but by George VI. So SOE must admit a share in the blame for subsequent troubles, but surely not a large share. Others deserve more: television for example, hardly as worked in the west a medium to discourage the display of violence; the KGB, ever active at the task of keeping the pot of unrest against capitalism simmering (the Russians are supplying arms to both sides in Northern Ireland, just in case that pot cools down too far); the innate disposition in mankind to make difficulties and to disobey orders, which anthropologists take back to the species' hunting instincts and theologians take back to the Garden of Eden and original sin.

The present writer at least would answer the question at the head of this article with an emphatic Yes.

NOTES

1. The Political Studies Association of the United Kingdom provided a chance to discuss a previous version of this paper at its Exeter conference in 1980, and the writer is grateful to it for the opportunity. Neither the Association, nor all the many friends and acquaintances with whom he has discussed the subject over many years — and to whom he expresses his lively gratitude — nor any government or university is in any way responsible for the views of a private scholar which follow.

2. E.g. in Mark C. Wheeler's otherwise interesting *Britain and the War for Yugoslavia, 1940-1943* (Boulder, Colo. 1980), 24, 251.

3. See his *Secrets of Crewe House* (1920) and *The Times* obituary, 15 September 1972.

4. *Who Was Who 1951-60* (1961), 533; Joan Bright Astley, *The Inner Circle* (1971), references and snapshot; talks with his friends. *The Times* and the *Dictionary of National Biography* both missed him.

5. *The Times* obituaries, 12, 17, 19 February 1976; Sir Peter Wilkinson in *The Gunner* (spring 1976). See also Gubbins's remarkable articles in *RUSIJ* xciii, 210 (May 1948) and in M. R. Elliott-Bateman (ed.), *Fourth Dimension of Warfare* (Manchester 1970), 83.

6. F. H. Hinsley et al., *British Intelligence in the Second World War*, i (1979) xiii, say that SIS means 'Special or Secret Intelligence Service'.

7. *The Times* obituary, 27 November 1975.

8. Cf. David Kahn, *The Codebreakers* (1966), 360.

9. PRO, CAB 66/7, WP(40)168; and see comments in P.M.H. Bell, *A Certain Eventuality* (1974), 31-38.

10. M.R.D. Foot, *SOE in France* (1968), 7-8, quoting MI R files 6 and 10, which are still not publicly available.

11. Hugh Dalton, *The Fateful Years* (1957), 367.

12. Foot, loc. cit., from MI R file 10.

13. Quoted in Foot, op. cit., 8, from a copy on MI R file 10; version, undated, in Dalton, *Fateful Years*, 368.

14. Quoted from the unavailable paper in Foot, op. cit., 8-9.

15. Ibid., 11, quoting an SOE section history (also unavailable).

16. See M.R.D. Foot and J.M. Langley, *MI 9* (1979), 264-267.

17. Foot, op. cit., 66.

18. David Stafford, *Britain and European Resistance 1940-1945* (1980), 209.

19. 1977.

20. PWE's papers fill 545 items in FO 898 at the PRO.

21. 28 December 1944, in Sir C. Webster and A. N. Frankland, *The Strategic Air Offensive*, iii (1961), 88.

22. Ibid.

23. E.g. 391 H.C. Deb. 5s. 2312; conversation with him, 1974.

24. Hinsley et al., op. cit., i.57 & n.; L. de Jong, *Het Koninkrijk der Nederlanden in de tweede wereldoorlog*, ii (The Hague 1969), 80-110.

25. De Jong, op. cit., ii, 110-115.

26. Conversation with him, 1967.

27. Listed in M.R.D. Foot, *Resistance* (1977), 159.

28. B. Sweet-Escott, *Baker Street Irregular* (1965), 73. This book had been written some ten years earlier, but was refused clearance till the impending publication of *SOE in France* was announced (693 H. C. Deb. 5s, 29-30, 13 April 1964).

29. See David Lampe, *The Last Ditch* (1968).

30. Stafford, op. cit., 36.

31. Conversation with him (as Lord Gladwyn), 1974.

32. *The Times* obituary, 13 August 1966.

33. *The Times* obituary, 29 August 1963; see also R. Barker, *Blockade Busters* (1976), 12, 35, 75, 78.

34. Letter to the present writer, 1962.

35. See H. Montgomery Hyde, *The Quiet Canadian* (1962).

36. Foot, op. cit., 125.

37. B. Davidson, *Special Operations Europe* (1980), 116-128.

38. See E. C. W. Myers, *Greek Entanglement* (1955) and C. M. Woodhouse, *Apple of Discord* (1948).

39. See Julian Amery, *Sons of the Eagle* (1954) and *Approach March* (1973).

40. Information from his widow, through Joan Astley, who is writing his biography.

41. He prints in an appendix the chiefs of staff's directives to SOE, which are freely available in the Public Record Office.

42. C. M. Woodhouse, *The Struggle for Greece* (1976), 140-141.

43. Philip Johns, *Within Two Cloaks* (1979), ad fin.

44. Clausewitz, *On War*, IV, xxvi; B. H. Liddell Hart, *Defence of the West* (1961), chap. vii; conversations with (Sir) B. H. Liddell Hart, 1960.

45. But not half as sparse as the custodians of SOE's surviving papers seem to think. Almost everything of political importance is to be found somewhere in the huge, largely unexplored rag-bag of FO 371. See, for two telling examples, Elisabeth Barker, *British Policy in South-East Europe* (1976), and Mark C. Wheeler, *Britain and the War for Yugoslavia, 1940-1943*.

VI

The State of the Alliance

Roosevelt and Churchill made the unilateral aid programme to Russia a tool to overcome Soviet distrust and thereby to establish a partnership that would outlast the war. For Roosevelt this remained the basic tenet of his policy almost up to his death. Given the importance of the goal, says Mr Langer, it is difficult to fault them for trying to achieve it. But it was bound to fail because it was based on unrealistic assumptions regarding Soviet intentions and also the character of the Soviet regime. But doubts in this respect crept in only during the last year of the war, up to that date — even in summer 1944 — the general consensus in the British Foreign Office was optimistic, and, as Graham Ross shows in his contribution, there was the belief that further improvement in relations seemed quite likely. True, from time to time a pessimistic position paper would be composed, but these were of no influence. The general belief was that Russia's energies in the post-war period would be absorbed by the needs of economic recovery and that for this reason, if for no other, Stalin would welcome continued co-operation with Britain and the United States. The attitude towards the Soviet Union in important sections of the press was even more friendly. E. H. Carr, the leading historian and editorialist of the London Times, *who had advocated accommodation with Germany in the 1930s, was now the main spokesman for co-operation with the Soviet Union: there must be no ganging up against Russia, and Western leaders were berated for not making due allowance for the obsessive — but psychologically understandable — nature of Soviet preoccupation with security. Coverage from the Soviet capital was quite uncritical; Ralph Porter, the* Times *correspondent subsequently settled in Moscow. Anglo-American policy in Yugoslavia during the war is surveyed in Hugh De Santis' article.*

16 Foreign Office Attitudes to the Soviet Union 1941-45[1]

Graham Ross

This article is in no sense an attempt to summarize the course of Anglo-Soviet relations during the second world war. It seeks rather to trace the evolution of assumptions within the Foreign Office about two problems in particular — what was the best way to handle the Russians and what were their post-war aims? The main source is the large number of minutes and memoranda written by officials and by the Foreign Secretary at the time. This has the benefit of showing what a fairly small group thought and was prepared to put on the record, while avoiding too much reliance on hindsight. Sir E.L. Woodward in his five volume history of *British Foreign Policy during the Second World War* uses some of this material. But limitations of space meant that he had to concentrate on the substance of British policy rather than the thinking behind it and he tends in any case to be discreet about differences of view and emphasis between individuals.

There was never, of course, a monolithic Foreign Office view of the problem, nor did London and the Moscow Embassy always see eye to eye, especially when Cripps was Ambassador. But the evidence shows certain consistent assumptions. Soviet suspicions could only be allayed by a policy of cautious reasonableness that gave the Russians as little cause as possible for legitimate complaint. Such a policy might take some time to work, but the hope was that it would have a cumulative effect which would make post-war collaboration possible if not easy. As for Soviet aims, it was obvious that she would seek a degree of influence in Eastern Europe and the Balkans. The problem was — how much and of what kind? If the Soviet Union was interested mainly in security, then a sphere of influence in Eastern Europe would not necessarily threaten British interests. But she could easily become uncooperative, especially if she thought her allies were not being firm enough in their treatment of Germany. That seemed likely to be one of the major tests that the Russians would apply in assessing American and British intentions. These assumptions were linked to a nagging doubt in the Foreign Office about the United States. Even if she did not repeat the retreat into isolation that had occurred after Versailles, she might rapidly disengage from European affairs. Even in the summer of 1945 it was far from clear that she would line up in support of Britain against Russia. This made it all the more important to retain the goodwill of the Russians, however frustrating and exasperating they might be. The alternative of confrontation with a hostile Soviet Union was something which the Foreign Office wanted to avoid and, indeed, did not like to think about. This was to lead to a serious clash with the Chiefs of Staff, as will be described later.

One set of minutes in July 1944 sums up well the basic approach to Russia. Our own policy must be directed to co-operation, wrote Cadogan on 4 July, if it failed it must not be our fault. Eden agreed:

> It is all very difficult, but at least we are convinced that we are trying to operate the right policy. The Russians may make it impossible. If we fail it should not be through our fault, nor through an undue display of weakness . . .

Christopher Warner, Head of the Northern Department, added that if the Americans pulled out of Europe, the Russians would then see themselves as our main collaborator in European affairs.[2]

This is not to suggest that the Foreign Office view of Russia remained static or that a simple formula appeared overnight. Prior to the German attack on the Soviet Union, British policy was on the whole reserved. Despite the urgings of Cripps, Eden did not wish to go out of his way to cultivate Russia and until she changed her attitude towards Germany there was little possibility of an understanding with her.[3] In the wake of the German invasion Churchill and Eden proclaimed British support for the Soviet Union, but the press of events left little time for detailed reflection on the new situation. Matters were brought to a head by Stalin's letter to Churchill of 8 November which made clear that Russia wanted clarification of British aims and intentions. Warner was inclined to try for postponement of discussion. The Russians might well be suspicious of Britain, but in trying to reassure them there was the danger of being pushed from one concession to another. A meeting in Cadogan's room on 18 November also came to the conclusion that Britain should avoid being tied down by the kind of treaty Stalin was likely to want. The best course would be some general statement of an intention to co-operate and to treat Russia as an equal.

Two points are worth noting from this discussion — the general belief that Russia's main concern was security and the British interest in encouraging federations in Eastern and South-Eastern Europe. The first was to remain a fairly consistent assumption; the second was to take up a good deal of Foreign Office energy over the next two years.[4]

The immediate result was Eden's visit to Moscow in December 1941, during which Stalin presented him with precisely the kind of demands which the meeting of 18 November had feared. Eden returned without having committed himself, but Stalin's aims were now clearer and the check to the German offensive removed any danger of an early Russian defeat. It was therefore necessary to ask what Britain should do next. Orme Sargent produced a minute on 5 February 1942 in which he speculated on the possible course of the Russo-German war. In the event of an early German defeat, Russia would be left in a dominant position in Europe, which led him to the conclusion that Britain should sign a treaty with her while the going was good. Cadogan and Eden agreed. All three men had some fears about the possibility of Russia making a separate peace, especially if no formal alliance were signed.[5] Shortly afterwards, the Foreign Office received three telegrams from Baggallay, then Chargé at the Moscow Embassy. Though primarily concerned with problems facing the British Military Mission, his comments raised the wider issue of how best to handle the Russians. It was no doubt right, said Baggallay, to help them as much as possible, but as a result they were getting all they wanted and giving nothing in return. He was pessimistic about the chances of overcoming Soviet suspicion and self-interest. In commenting on these messages, both Bruce-Lockhart and Strang agreed on the depth of Russian suspicions and on the need for patience. Cadogan, however, pointed out that the Russians had brought many of their difficulties on their own heads. The one specific suggestion for action came from Warner, who thought that the Foreign Office needed to clarify its ideas on dealing with the Soviet Union. Indeed, he proposed the formulation of an agreed doctrine to be followed by all departments who had contacts with the Russians. The latter resented being treated as something peculiar. The answer was to be more businesslike and to consult them more, whatever the difficulties. Although Eden liked the idea of an agreed doctrine, the proposal was abandoned; but one can see how the discussion helped to bring Foreign Office ideas into focus.[6]

There was also the question of ultimate Soviet aims. On 3 April we find Strang writing that whatever Britain said, a victorious Russia would almost certainly have a predominant influence in Rumania and a powerful one in Czechoslovakia. Just over a month later, Roger Makins assumed that the general aim of Soviet policy was to obtain exclusive influence in Eastern Europe. If so, said Dew, it was all the more important to sign a treaty and obtain some formal standing in the area. How should we deal with such a Soviet policy? enquired Sargent, to be given the answer by Strang that if Germany were crushed and Russia were involved in the final victory then we could *not* counter her predominance in Eastern Europe. This led Sargent to the 'distressing conclusion' that there would have to be a Germany strong enough to counteract Russian predominance.[7]

All roads seemed to lead to the Anglo-Soviet Treaty signed on 26 May 1942 while Molotov was in London. It is easy with hindsight to overlook the satisfaction of the Foreign Office at obtaining what looked like a good basis for post-war collaboration apart from its short-term advantages. It might even be used to balance American influence. Warner wrote on 9 July: 'I hope we shall try to avoid a position in which (1) we face the Russians with too cut and dried agreed Anglo-American ideas and (2) are completely debarred from bilateral exchanges of views with the Russians.'[8] The Soviet Union clearly had strong reservations about federations in Eastern Europe, but their general attitude on post-war planning remained cautious and negative as Clark Kerr pointed out in a despatch on 25 November. While home on leave, he gave a talk to the Dominion High Commissioners on 3 December 1942, in which he said that he had no idea of the lines on which the Russians were thinking about a post-war settlement but that he had no illusions that negotiations with them would be easy.[9]

If the treaty was going to lead to closer collaboration, then the logical next step would be some kind of approach to Russia about post-war problems. This was set in train by a despatch from George Rendel, Ambassador to the Yugoslav government, on 19 December 1942. In an analysis of possible developments in South-Eastern Europe, he foresaw that Bulgaria would fall under Soviet influence and this might have consequences elsewhere in the area. His answer — an approach to Turkey — found little favour in the Foreign Office. On the contrary, an approach to Russia about the Balkans in particular and post-war problems in general seemed to be the answer. Warner for example, on 2 January 1943, doubted whether Russia was seeking unlimited expansion, but felt that the only chance of preventing the Balkans falling completely under her control was to get her agreement to three-power collaboration there as elsewhere.[10]

Accordingly, Clark Kerr was instructed to approach Molotov. He was to touch on the treatment of Germany and seek elucidation of some passages in a speech by Stalin of 6 November 1942 in leading up to the need for an agreed three-power policy for Europe as a whole. Indeed, Britain would propose that at some point the three allies should hold consultations. He was also to explore the Soviet attitude on federations. The Ambassador saw Molotov on 20 February and at first the conversation seemed to be going well. Unfortunately it got bogged down on the question of what Stalin had meant in his speech of 6 November. Molotov seemed increasingly uneasy so Clark Kerr decided to end the talk for the time being and to write to Molotov to make clear the nature of the British enquiry. As it turned out, this proved to be a tactical error. It provoked a reply from Stalin which came to Churchill's notice and the latter enquired of Eden what had brought the matter up. On discovering that the Foreign Secretary had made an approach to Russia without consulting him he 'emitted a series of most vicious screams of rage', in Warner's phrase, and ordered that the whole idea be dropped. This in fact was what happened and a telegram drafted by Sargent in an effort to revive the *démarche* was not used. Instead, Clark Kerr was instructed on 1 March to leave well alone and not to explore the Soviet attitude further. Warner thought that perhaps a great opportunity had been missed. That may have been the case, but there is some room for doubt. In a second conversation with Clark Kerr on 25 February, Molotov had been somewhat rambling and unwilling to proceed until he knew the attitude of the United States. Moreover, Stalin in his reply had suggested bilateral talks to reach binding agreements. As Jebb pointed out on 27 February, this was rather ahead of the Foreign Office's idea, which was to have tripartite meetings of experts to see if they could recommend agreed policies. It was to become clear at the Moscow Foreign Ministers' Conference in October 1943 that the Soviet Union had come out against federations. On the other hand, it is certainly true that Anglo-Soviet relations were soon to be complicated by the break of relations between Moscow and the London Poles. This increased the difficulty of attaining the objectives set out in Clark Kerr's instructions — to treat the Soviet government as partners and discuss plans with them as a matter of course.[11]

Russia's relations with her allies went through a bad spell in the summer of 1943, but the Moscow and Tehran meetings seemed to restore cordiality. Writing to Clark Kerr on 28 September, Warner thought that the forthcoming meeting of Foreign Ministers would be a test of Russia's future attitude. Everything she did was open to an optimistic or pessimistic interpretation and Warner himself seemed inclined to the latter. Yet he was still unhappy lest any appearance of a joint Anglo-American front antagonize the Russians — a view shared by G.M. Wilson. Despite the apparent success of the conferences, Warner regretted that more had not been discovered about Russian intentions in Eastern Europe. Nor had Britain made sufficiently clear what she understood by co-operation. Sargent thought the Russians were trying to establish an exclusive sphere of influence in Eastern Europe. Eden, however, did not feel that this was quite fair. The Foreign Secretary was pleased by the creation of the European Advisory Commission which he hoped was going to meet a long-felt need. In that sense he could claim to have set up a piece of machinery for the kind of tripartite consultation envisaged at the beginning of 1943.[12] That it never quite functioned as originally hoped was as much the fault of the Americans as the Russians.

During 1944, it became clear that the defeat of Germany was only a matter of time and post-war problems began to assume greater significance. Attitudes within the Foreign Office tended to fluctuate between doubt and hope. On 31 March Eden was worrying about the situation in Italy where he feared the communists would swallow up the Badoglio government. By 3 April he was confessing to fears that Russia had vast aims which might include the domination of Eastern Europe and even the Mediterranean. Despite these worries, he was at almost the same time urging caution on Churchill. In reply to a minute from the Prime Minister, he agreed that personal messages to Stalin should be given a rest, but he refused either to assume that Russia had abandoned a policy of co-operation or to agree that the time had come for a showdown with Stalin. He took a reassuring line when Churchill began to worry about the implications of the Russo-Japanese economic agreement of March 1944 and he rejected a suggestion in May that Clark Kerr be recalled for consultations.[13] Foreign Office doubts had to be kept within the family and there was in any case some feeling that Churchill tended to overreact in his dealings with Stalin.[14]

At the end of April two papers were produced within the Foreign Office on future Soviet behaviour, one pessimistic and one optimistic. The pessimistic paper attracted little attention then or later. Ivor Pink of the Economic and Industrial Planning Staff had asked W.H. Young on 5 April whether any lessons could be drawn from Soviet policy in Iran about their possible behaviour in a zone of occupation in Germany. Replying on 1 May, Young painted a gloomy picture of Soviet suspicion and obstruction. The Russians had taken what food they needed in northern Iran and denied that they had any surplus, thus leaving the British and Americans to feed the rest of the country. Appeals to sentiment or to the spirit of allied solidarity only aroused their suspicion. Young concluded that there was little chance of the Russians in Germany parting with food surpluses for the benefit of the whole country. Within the Foreign Office only Viscount Hood and G.M. Wilson seem to have looked at this paper.[15]

The optimistic paper, dated 29 April, dealt generally with possible post-war developments in Soviet policy. Eden found it 'remarkable'. Its basic assumption was that Russia's post-war energies would be absorbed by the tasks of economic recovery. She would therefore welcome continued co-operation with America and Britain. Friction was more likely to arise over the treatment of Germany than from ideological differences. (Eden had his doubts on this point.) An American withdrawal from Europe would make Anglo-Soviet co-operation more difficult but not impossible. If, however, the Russians did decide against co-operation, they were more likely to be passively difficult than expansionist, but this would certainly mean a period of uneasy relations.[16] Commenting on this paper in a despatch of 31 August, Clark Kerr made three assumptions. Complete victory over Germany would relieve Russia of any serious threat to her security; the regime would have its confidence considerably increased; the theory of world revolution had been discarded. But he then entered a caveat. Russia had retained her freedom of action and still possessed 'a morbidly developed sense of inferiority' which would need careful handling, although he was careful to emphasize that Britain should not always take the line of least resistance. This despatch met with rather a lukewarm reception in London; Warner in particular felt that the analysis had not been given a proper framework.[17]

Despite some reservations, therefore, the general Foreign Office view in the summer of 1944 was hopeful. It seemed reasonable to seek ways in which post-war relations with Russia could be improved. In a minute of 10 August, Wilson thought the Russians were likely to want military conversations and staff talks even if a new international organization were set up. Orme Sargent agreed that there should be some consideration of ways to revise and strengthen the 1942 treaty. The trouble with bilateral staff talks was the difficulty of finding suitable subjects which did not impinge on the interests of others or on the arrangements being discussed at Dumbarton Oaks, and this particular idea was dropped at the end of October. Meanwhile, Wilson put the case for a revision of the treaty in a paper of 24 September. Its military clauses would lapse at the end of the war and if something specific did not replace them then at the very least Britain and Russia might drift apart. Britain was interested in creating a security group in Western Europe; the Russians would probably do the same in Eastern Europe. A clash between the two groups must be avoided. In any case, Russia was unlikely to put complete trust in the new international organization so that strengthening the alliance would help to prevent her playing a lone hand. Wilson wanted the Americans involved in some way and speculated whether the combined Chiefs of Staff could be turned into a tripartite body. Sargent and Eden both liked the proposals but both foresaw difficulties. The British military, Eden commented, got on so badly with the Russians. So nothing came of this idea either. The type of arrangement which Churchill and Eden in fact made with the Soviet Union was the famous 'percentages agreement' of October 1944.[18]

'Our military get on so badly with the Russians.' The Foreign Office had been critical of the Military Mission in Moscow almost from its inception in June 1941, and suspected the service departments of being anti-Russian in general. Nevertheless, the system of having Foreign Office representatives chairing predominantly military committees worked reasonably enough until 1944, with Cavendish-Bentinck chairing the Joint Intelligence Committee and Jebb the Post-Hostilities Planning Sub-Committee. A warning signal appeared in February 1944 when Jebb reported that the Chiefs of Staff did not like the assumption of four-power co-operation as a basis for post-war planning. They believed that Russia would have her own sphere of influence after the war — a belief likely to undercut briefings for discussion of the proposed new international organization. It was also, of course, contrary to the trend of Foreign Office thinking mentioned above.[19]

Trouble really began when the sub-committee was reorganized, with effect from 20 May, as the Post-Hostilities Planning Staff. It was now charged with making a number of studies of post-war strategic problems. A reasonable task no doubt, but the PHPS would obviously have to make some kind of assumptions about Russia and America. On 23 May, Warner was worried that they might get a directive which would give their papers an anti-Soviet approach. Neville Butler produced a different worry on the same day. It would be unsafe to assume that the United States would support Britain against Russia. Jebb on 7 June tried to defend his service colleagues by pointing out that they could not be expected to ignore completely the idea that Russia was a potential enemy. Indeed they did not; his minute accompanied a paper they had produced about their basic assumptions. Britain's relations with Russia were more likely to deteriorate than those with the United States. 'Soviet long-term intentions must of necessity remain a matter of guesswork.' Although the PHPS were willing to assume the continuation of three-power collaboration, they also wished to assume that Britain disposed of sufficient forces in association with America to deter Russia from advancing her interests to the detriment of her allies.[20]

This provoked an outraged reaction from Orme Sargent on 9 June. Not only were the PHPS acting outside their terms of reference but their report was tendentious and contrary to British policy as conducted by the Foreign Office. That policy was certainly not based on the assumption that Britain would have to deter Russia by force of arms in the foreseeable future. The sharpness of Sargent's criticism was somewhat blunted by his definition of that last phrase. He argued that it was difficult to plan more than two years ahead — a point with which Cadogan agreed.[21] This conceded, by implication at least, that at the end of two years Britain and Russia might be at odds. Jebb now found himself caught in a crossfire. He had to explain to Cadogan in a long and rather defensive minute that the Vice-Chiefs of Staff had held an off-the-record discussion with the PHPS which he had been unable to prevent. He tried to explain Foreign Office objections to the 'basic assumptions' mentioned above, but made little headway. In effect, the service view was that it was necessary to consider the worst possible eventuality. In any case, said the Vice-Chiefs, adding insult to injury, strategic planning ought not to be unduly influenced by political considerations. There was now an open difference of approach. Sargent continued to press his idea of laying down assumptions for two years. Cadogan did admit that the worst might happen, even though Britain wanted to maintain three-power co-operation. It might break down and the new international organization might not work. But he remained unhappy with the approach of the PHPS, who were in danger of trying to plan on the basis of too many possibilities, some of them conflicting.[22]

More trouble arose over a paper on security in Western Europe, which particularly provoked the wrath of Christopher Warner. It did say that the proposed Western grouping must not prejudice the Anglo-Soviet alliance, but this was not enough to satisfy him. He preferred the emphasis to be the other way round — that it would be possible to fit the Western block into the alliance. Moreover, it was important to make clear the Foreign Office view that the most important way of securing collaboration from Russia was to demonstrate our intention to go on holding Germany down. On the other hand, the PHPS paper assumed that Britain might at some time wish to combine with Germany against Russia in rather vaguely defined circumstances. In Warner's view, such an ill-defined policy could easily turn into one of building up Germany soon. There might be a danger from Russia, Warner admitted, but he did not wish to endorse loose talk about it. Cadogan was again forced to admit that Russia might cease to co-operate and one could not ignore 'that ominous possibility'. That being so, the Foreign Office was open to the charge of merely following the negative line of refusing to discuss possible Russian hostility, and this was a point that both Jebb and Cavendish-Bentinck made. They argued that the degree of anti-Soviet feeling among the Chiefs of Staff was exaggerated. The later assumed that Germany would be impotent for some time and that no conflict was likely between Britain and the United States. But they were equally sceptical about the possibility of American help if we encountered trouble in Europe. Hence their interest in having Germany on the British side or in the British sphere of influence. The arguments, however, failed to carry much weight with the colleagues of Jebb and Cavendish-Bentinck. Building up Germany would simply provoke a Soviet reaction and the Russians could always beat Britain at that game.[23]

It was the dispute with the Chiefs of Staff which helped to produce the proposals already mentioned for staff talks with the Russians and for strengthening the 1942 treaty. Apart from what could be seen as their substantive merits, they would also provide a means of counter-attacking the COS and rebutting the charge of Foreign

Office negativism. In his minute of 10 August Wilson took a more balanced view of the argument than some of his colleagues had done. He pointed out that the military saw Russia as the only possible threat to Britain in Europe and wanted to organize against the threat now. In the view of the Foreign Office this would render inevitable the very danger which the Chiefs of Staff wanted to avoid. But the differences were of degree not of principle. The Foreign Office and the services agreed in wishing to ensure that in any future war the Soviet Union was on Britatin's side. Where the COS would perhaps have disagreed with Wilson was his belief that 'the Anglo-Soviet Treaty is one of the corner-stones of our whole foreign policy . . .'. The idea of staff talks as a riposte to the military found support from Warner, Ward and Roberts. 'Interesting and suggestive' minuted Warner on 11 August. J.G. Ward felt that it 'offered a definite objective for our counter-attack against the Chiefs of Staff and their wild acolytes in the PHPS'. He hoped that we would not be deterred from building up the Anglo-Soviet alliance through 'excessive deference to America'. Roberts agreed that the Foreign Office had hitherto adopted too negative an attitude in trying to discourage the Chiefs of Staff from considering the possibility of a hostile Russia. As it turned out, the proposed counter-attack came to nothing; instead the upshot was to be retreat. On 18 August Sargent sent Eden a minute explaining the background to the dispute and saying that arrangements were in train to dissociate the Foreign Office from the preparation of PHPS papers. Eden spoke to Ismay about the dangers of indiscreet talk by the services, but this seems to have had little effect. By 1 September Wilson was reporting that the anti-Russian attitude of the services was becoming more widely known and was beginning to attract the attention of journalists. It appears from a later minute of 24 September that a number of temporary officers serving in the War Office had been in touch with him. Meanwhile, the Foreign Office went ahead with its decision to 'bring the boil to a head' and end its membership of PHPS, though it would still have the right to be represented at meetings. Eden made a challenge to the views of the COS by putting a paper on the dismemberment of Germany to the Armistice and Post-War Committee.[24]

This resulted in a meeting between Eden and the Chiefs of Staff on 4 October. They put the need to consider the worst possible case when dealing with the future of Germany. Britain could be confronted by a single German state allied with Russia. Against this,

Eden argued the danger of going too far in assuming possible differences with Russia. The immediate problem was preventing a German resurgence and indiscreet talk would simply increase Soviet suspicion. To this the Chiefs of Staff replied that Britain had as much right as the Russians to make long-term plans. It was agreed that Eden and the COS would withdraw their respective papers on dismemberment of Germany now, before the APW Committee and the COS would restrict the circulation of papers in which Russia was mentioned as a potential enemy. But there was no agreement about what assumptions on Russia were permissible in strategic papers dealing with the post-war situation. Eden had contemplated sending a minute to Churchill about the dispute but did not do so. Nor does it appear that he had any informal discussion with the Prime Minister about it.[25] The Foreign Office lost this particular battle. Its suggestions for improving relations with the Soviet Union were not tried out; it withdrew from the PHPS and failed to prevent the latter from producing yet more papers on post-war strategy; no directive came from the Cabinet or the Prime Minister to prevent contemplation of the awful fact that Russia might be hostile. But it is interesting to see how much store the Foreign Office was still setting on maintaining co-operation with Russia and how little faith it still had in the United States as a post-war collaborator in Europe. That Germany would be a major test of Anglo-Soviet co-operation was clearly true, yet Foreign Office officials do appear to have reacted rather sharply when the services expressed an opposite view.[26]

After the Yalta conference the pace of events began to quicken and the optimism of 1944 to ebb. Both in the Moscow Embassy and in London there were reassessments of Soviet policy, though these on the whole took place independently of each other. Reports from Moscow were not in themselves the cause of the reappraisals that took place in the Foreign Office. In a despatch of 27 March 1945, Clark Kerr assessed developments since Yalta and found them disturbing and disappointing in many ways. In Rumania Russian conduct had been the sheerest power politics because the Soviet Union knew that Britain and America were unlikely to make it a test case. She was under special temptation to press ahead in Eastern Europe while she had a relatively free hand. The Russians were in a confident mood and to them co-operation meant accepting spheres of influence. Nevertheless, the Ambassador thought Russia was pursuing a policy of limited objectives, none of which immediately endangered British interests. Wilson, on 19 April, generally agreed and pointed out that in the light of Churchill's visit to Moscow the Russians had every reason to think that we accepted Rumania and Bulgaria as part of their sphere of influence.[27]

Ever since December 1944, there had been some disquiet in the Foreign Office about Soviet attitudes to UNRRA. The Russians seemed anxious to keep its representatives out of Eastern Europe and to use it for what they could get out of it. Clark Kerr was asked for his views and the result was a rather gloomy message on 12 April. There was little evidence that the Russians had prepared plans for relief in Eastern Europe and they were unlikely to release supplies in areas under their control for the relief of Western and Southern Europe. Given the present trend of Soviet policy, it was important for Britain to strengthen her position in these two areas. 'It is regrettable to have to contemplate a Europe divided in this way but we must recognize the fact that the Russians are not prepared to treat the problem as a whole except on the basis that all help goes from west to east.' A realistic policy of strengthening those countries where our influence remained strong was likely to change the Russian attitude. After all, they were likely to need economic assistance from Britain and America. This was a commonly-held view at the time and logical enough on the assumption made in the Foreign Office paper of April 1944 that Russia would have to devote much of her energy to reconstruction. Clark Kerr's opinion did not, however, have any great impact in London. Most of the minutes on his message were concerned with the practical problems of reconstruction rather than the wider political implications.[28]

The evidence continued to come in that the Russians were seeking to build up their position in Eastern Europe. Benes visited Moscow in March and was well received. A *Pravda* article, commenting on his visit, referred to the desirability of forming a defence bloc against Germany, including in particular Czechoslovakia and Poland. At the end of June the Czechs were to cede sub-Carpathian Ruthenia to the Soviet Union, to the annoyance of the Foreign Office which nevertheless found itself unable to do anything about it. In April it was Tito's turn to come to Moscow to sign a treaty and an economic agreement. Frank Roberts, now in Moscow, commented that the Soviet Union did not see a network of bilateral treaties as incompatible with three-power collaboration. But the leaders of Russia, hard-headed and unused to compromise or concession, were determined not to tolerate rival influences in neighbouring countries.[29] Roberts followed up with a letter to Warner commenting on and enlarging upon Clark Kerr's despatch of 27 March. He argued that it would be wrong to see the difficulties since Yalta as just a passing phase, but equally wrong to regard Russia as a power potentially as dangerous as Germany. The Kremlin was run by tough, tricky personalities who were still orthodox Marxists. But there was no essential conflict between Britain and 'these hard-headed realists' provided she demonstrated her firmness to the Russians. They were organizing Eastern Europe regardless of British wishes; Britain should ensure that her part of Europe was the stronger.[30]

By 10 July, Clark Kerr found some improvement in the atmosphere in Moscow but also some worrying features. There had been agreement over the Polish question and voting in the Security Council. There was a provisional agreement on Trieste and the Reparations Commission had begun its work. But the Soviet government had not given way substantially on any issue affecting its vital interests. It had reacted sharply to the more open criticism appearing in the British press and was on the whole more irritated with Britain than with the United States. The latter had 'taken fright' as he saw it at the widening gulf between her allies and had therefore sent Hopkins to Moscow. It was likely that America and Russia would come closer together which might push Britain into a more modest role than she was entitled to play. The most worrying area was Greece and Turkey. Russia's far-reaching demands on the latter implied a threat to British interests in the Middle East. It was a 'melancholy truth' that the Russians were still uncertain how far we would go to protect our friends and when in doubt they were dangerous.[31]

On the eve of the Potsdam conference, therefore, the Moscow Embassy could be said to have reached a position of qualified pessimism. There was little to be done about Eastern Europe, but Britain needed a more sharply-defined policy. It was not assumed that collaboration with the Soviet Union was as yet completely out of the question. What changes of view had meanwhile been taking place within the Foreign Office? To answer that question we must look once again to the indefatigible Orme Sargent.

He produced a long minute on 2 April, which, if not quite a recantation, certainly cast some doubt on the validity of the Foreign Office approach. He wondered if the time had come to change tactics in dealing with the Russians. Until the Second Front was opened we had been in a weak bargaining position, so our attitude had to be defensive not to say apologetic. In 1944 it had looked as if Russia might occupy the whole of Germany and it was right to propitiate her. Unfortunately, as Sargent had to admit, this policy had brought little response from the Russians, but he argued that had we adopted a more assertive line, things might have been even worse. Now that the military position had changed, the Soviet Union had responded with a growing truculence and seemed determined to give nothing away until she had to do so. Had the time come for some plain speaking over Germany, Austria and Eastern Europe? He rejected the idea of striking a bargain by recognizing Russia's exclusive interest in certain countries, on the grounds that Britain could not in this way abandon the interests of small states and her own right to be involved in the whole of Europe. How Russia would react to this new approach was not certain. Britain would have to show that plain-speaking did not mean the end of cooperation. Anything, however, would be better than the present uncertainty. Cadogan shared Sargent's fears but was more particularly concerned about the Polish question. If there was a reasonable settlement, then we might not need a general showdown. Roosevelt's death and the need to work with a new President seems to have led to the abandonment of the idea. Churchill, of course, was to press for an early meeting of the Big Three.[32]

What is unclear is the precise nature of the showdown that Sargent envisaged. He presumably was not thinking in terms of military threats; at any rate he does not make clear what pressures he hoped to employ. He was critical of a similar idea from O'Malley, Ambassador to the London Poles, who wrote to him on 22 May. O'Malley wanted a showdown with the Soviet Union at the next Big Three meeting, even at the risk of precipitating a crisis. The collapse of Germany meant that there was now 'an armed and brittle peace' which would lead to growing tension in an already divided Europe. Trying to deal with the Soviet Union by moderation and concessions had been a failure. Sargent thought O'Malley had proposed 'truly desperate remedies', since Britain could not pursue such a policy without American support and it was going to be difficult enough to obtain that for the more moderate British policy of standing up to the Russians while maintaining collaboration. The United States saw herself as an independent mediator who would not be dragged into an Anglo-Soviet quarrel. Eden agreed with this and no answer was sent to O'Malley.[33] Yet Sargent's own proposal of 2 April had been open to the same objection; 'moderate' or otherwise, a policy of firmness towards Russia would depend on American backing. Sargent himself had not been as sharp in criticizing previous British policy, but there was less difference between the two men than his comments implied.

Worry about Soviet intentions continued. Molotov's opening speech at San Francisco seemed to hint that although Russia was prepared to collaborate, there were limits to the concessions she would make and that she might pursue an independent policy.[34] A Research Department paper prepared by Toynbee examined developments in Iran, Finland, Hungary, Rumania and Bulgaria. In all five cases Russia wanted satisfactory and subservient governments and had gone to great lengths to circumscribe Anglo-American influence. But she was more interested, the paper assumed, in her own security, than in pushing the interests of local communist parties.[35] On the other hand, examples of outright Soviet bad faith proved hard to find when Eden asked for a list before leaving for Potsdam. In Rumania and Bulgaria there had been alleged violation or evasion of agreements, but the majority of complaints arose from a complete lack of Soviet co-operation.[36]

The last major consideration of policy towards Russia prior to Potsdam appears in a stocktaking paper on Britain's position in the light of victory in Europe. Written by Sargent on Eden's request, the first draft appeared on 11 July and was revised at the beginning of August to take account of various comments. In an annexe, he added a revised version of his minute of 2 April and a minute by Bruce Lockhart of 11 April. The latter had on the whole shared the views of Sargent's original minute. The only way to check Russia was by bolder yet still friendly diplomatic action by both Britain and America. The moment was ripe because Russia was faced with great problems of reconstruction which she could not hope to solve without Anglo-American aid.

In the final version of his main paper, Sargent saw three problems which had not existed in 1918. Soviet troops were in occupation of Eastern Europe, there was the general need for economic rehabilitation throughout Europe and the task of administering Germany. Both the United States and the Soviet Union thought that Britain was now a secondary power — a misconception to be opposed. The Soviet Union sought maximum security and did not want another war in Europe. Now was the time for a diplomatic trial of strength, which would affect Germany and indeed the whole of Europe. The Soviet Union would have the advantage of being able to exploit the economic crisis. Britain would need the wholehearted co-operation of the United States and it would be difficult to induce her to resist Russian penetration. Cadogan and Eden both found it a good paper. The former agreed on the need to speak firmly to the Russians and to show no subservience. But he did wonder if she would be so dependent on Anglo-American aid for reconstruction. This had not been clearly proved, a comment with which Eden agreed. Troutbeck was worried about Germany — prosperous or poor she would present a problem. If the right elements could not be found for an all-German government, Britain might have to settle for partition as the best of a bad job.

Jebb favoured a tough bargaining line with the Russians. Crude bargaining was the only kind of negotiation which they understood, and there was no need to over-estimate their strength or be afraid to stand up for British interests. But he wondered if it was wise to meddle in Soviet preserves. Beyond a certain point the Russians would not understand interference in Bulgaria or Finland. E. J. Passant of the Research Department raised the question whether Russia saw Eastern Europe as a protective cordon or a jumping-off point for further expansion. This was a worrying point because it was doubtful whether the Americans would be willing to maintain adequate forces in Europe over the next five years. This led him to the conclusion that Britain must collaborate with Russia in the effective demilitarization of Germany and show that this was mean to be permanent. Butler and Warner agreed on the need to secure American support, the former pointing out the need to convince the Americans that Britain was supporting some principle, the latter that without American support Britain would make little impression on the Russians.[37]

The Foreign Office was therefore not in total despair, though much of the optimism of earlier years had disappeared. The Americans were still regarded as unreliable allies, strong indeed but of uncertain intentions towards Europe. Britain was becoming conscious that she was no longer quite on the same level as her two allies, yet illusions persisted. Sargent in his stocktaking paper spoke of the need for an independent policy and for living 'beyond our political means at times'. This still left the question of how Britain could hope to influence the Soviet Union. The main instrument mentioned was economic aid for reconstruction. Yet if the Soviet Union refused to yield to pressure, what then? One has to remember that this is still the pre-atomic age. Few of the officials quoted in this article would know about the programme to develop a bomb which was soon to change the international situation. But equally, the Foreign Office on the eve of Potsdam was still in a pre-Cold War era. The Soviet Union might seem a difficult colleague with whom unpleasant compromises might have to be made, but she was not yet seen as an impossible collaborator. She was seen as a state pursuing her own interests in a crude and overbearing way, not as the leader of an ideological crusade.

NOTES

1. The author wishes to acknowledge the help of the British Academy in making a grant which enabled much of the material for this article to be collected.

2. FO 371/43143; minutes on two despatches by Dana Wilgress, the Canadian Ambassador in Moscow. Eden's is dated 6 July and Warner's 9 July. All Crown Copyright documents are quoted by permission of Her Majesty's Stationery Office.

3. FO 317/29464; minute by Orme Sargent of 28 March 1941; Eden minute of 15 April and Eden to Cripps 16 April. See also FO 317/33026, review of the Soviet Union for 1941. Sargent was Deputy Under-Secretary.

4. FO 371/29471; undated minute by Warner. FO 371/29472; minute by Dew, dated 21 November. Present at the meeting were Cadogan himself, Law, Sargent, Strang, Harvey, Ronald and Dew. *Stalin's Correspondence with Churchill and Attlee* (New York 1965), 33.

5. FO 371/32905; Cadogan minute 7 February 1942, Eden minute 8 February.

6. FO 371/32897; Baggallay telegrams of 12 and 13 February, minuted by Warner on 16 February. FO 371/32876; another minute by Warner, also dated 16 February and comments thereon by Bruce Lockhart and Strang on 20 February, Cadogan minute of 28 February, Eden minute of 1 March, underneath which Warner has written, 'It was later decided to proceed with this'.

7. FO 371/30834; Makins minute of 7 May, Dew minute of 9 May, Strang minutes of 12 and 14 May, Sargent minutes of 13 and 14 May. Makins was Head of Central Department, in which post he was soon succeeded by Frank Roberts.

8. FO 371/31513.

9. FO 371/35338. DO 121/12.

10. FO 371/33154.

11. Prem 4. 30/1; Eden to Clark Kerr 4 February 1943, Clark Kerr to Eden 21 February and 26 February, Churchill to Eden 26 February and Eden to Churchill 1 March. FO 371/35338; minutes by Jebb and Sargent 27 February, Foreign Office to Moscow 1 March. FO 800/301; Warner to Clark Kerr 16 March.

12. FO 800/301; Warner to Clark Kerr 28 September 1943. FO 371/37028; minutes by Warner and Wilson 15 September 1943. FO 800/302; Warner to Balfour, 25 January 1944. FO 371/34340; minute by Sargent of 29 November 1943 with undated marginal comment by Eden. Prem 3. 136/3; Eden to Churchill, 27 November 1943.

13. FO 371/43304; Eden minutes of 31 March, 3 April and 5 April. Churchill minute of 1 April. FO 371/41823; Churchill to Cadogan on 23 April, Eden to Churchill on 27 April. Prem 3. 66/7; Churchill to Eden 4 May, Eden to Churchill 9 May.

14. FO 800/302; Wilson to Clark Kerr 19 March and 15 May 1944.

15. FO 371/40171. Hood on 21 April found Young's views 'interesting and depressing'.

16. FO 371/43335 with undated comments by Eden.

17. FO 371/43336; Warner minute of 28 September 1944.

18. FO 371/43306; Warner to Jebb 11 October, Jebb to Warner 18 October, Warner and Wilson minutes of 25 October, minutes by Sargent and Eden on 30 September.

19. FO 371/40740; Jebb minute of 9 February 1944.

20. Ibid. for minutes by Warner, Butler and Jebb. CAB 81/42 and CAB 81/45 for PHPS papers.

21. FO 371/40740; minutes by Sargent and Cadogan, both 9 June.

22. FO 371/40741A; Jebb minute of 15 June, Sargent minutes of 18 and 28 June, Cadogan minute of 28 June.

23. Ibid.; Jebb minutes of 17, 25 and 28 July, Cavendish-Bentinck minutes of 16 June and 18 July, Warner minutes of 17, 24 and 29 July, Cadogan minute of 18 July, Mason minute of 29 July, Roberts minute of 31 July.

24. FO 371/43306; Warner minute of 11 August, Ward minutes of 15 August, 2 September, 15 September and 18 September, Roberts minute of 18 August, Wilson minutes of 1 September and 24 September, Eden minute of 25 August.

25. FO 371/43306; Warner minute of 8 October. Woodward, Volume Five, 205-10 puts more emphasis on the APW committee than on the PHPS. *The Memoirs of Lord Gladwyn* (London 1972), 132-36 passes lightly over his role in the PHPS. FO 371/43336 for an account of Eden's meeting with the COS.

26. See CAB 81/46 for PHPS papers produced between January and June 1945.

27. FO 371/47941.

28. FO 371/41197; minutes by Camps 4 December 1944, Hoyar Millar 6 December and Wilson 9 December. FO 371/51318; Clark Kerr to the Foreign Office 12 April 1945. There is an interesting echo here of W.H. Young's comments on Soviet Policy in Iran, *vide supra*.

29. FO 371/47076; Clark Kerr to Foreign Office, 16 April 1945. FO 371/47078; Sargent to Cadogan on 6 July, Foreign Office to Clark Kerr 8 July. FO 371/48928; despatch from Roberts 21 April.

30. FO 371/47882; Roberts to Warner 25 April.

31. FO 371/47883.

32. FO 371/47881; Orme Sargent minute of 2 April, Cadogan minute of 4 April.

33. FO 371/47882; O'Malley letter of 22 May, Sargent minute of 31 May. Wilson thought on 30 May that O'Malley was simply reflecting Polish views.

34. FO 371/47862; minutes by Hill 3 May and Wilson 4 May.

35. FO 371/47987; paper dated 20 July.

36. FO 371/47964; covering letter from Lawford to Dixon, 20 July. There were

separate briefs on various other Soviet shortcomings, e.g. in EAC.

37. FO 371/50912; Cadogan minute of 11 July, Eden minute of 12 July, Troutbeck minute of 19 July, Jebb minute of 20 July, Passant minute of 21 July, Butler and Warner minutes of 30 July.

17 The Times and Appeasement: The Second Phase

Alan Foster

Few historians of British foreign policy in the 1930s have resisted the temptation to comment upon the role played by *The Times* during that decade in the support the newspaper offered for the official policy of the appeasement of Germany. Far less remarked upon has been the same newspaper's advocacy of the appeasement of the Soviet Union in the 1940s, as the harmony of the wartime Grand Alliance gave way to the discord and antagonism of the early years of the Cold War. The relative neglect of this second phase of commitment by *The Times* to policies of appeasement in Europe is surprising for a number of reasons, three of which I should like to pursue in this article.

In the first place, *The Times'* advocacy of a sympathetic policy towards the Soviet Union in the 1940s, following as it did so closely upon the heels of a similarly conciliatory line towards Nazi Germany in the earlier decade, tended to invite from its critics charges of inconsistency or worse which have served to mask a striking continuity of vision about the external world on the newspaper's part. Secondly, the repeated pleas by *The Times* for a greater degree of understanding of Russia by the western powers led the newspaper to expound a philosophy of international relations which is of intrinsic interest when found in a journal, which, sometimes to the intense embarrassment of British ministers, was so often in these years assumed by foreigners to enjoy a special relationship with all British governments. Thirdly, any student of *Times'* leaders on relations with Russia at the onset of the Cold War cannot but be struck by the number of occasions when the newspaper, in support of its general thesis that the western powers shared the guilt for the deterioration of relations with the Soviet Union, anticipates the main features of the arguments to be put forward in support of a similar thesis a generation later by the revisionist historians of the Cold War's origins.

The substantial continuity of view which links *The Times'* support of policies of appeasement through the two decades under consideration can best be illustrated in the formulation of one simple proposition. This was that British governments should 'disinterest' themselves in Eastern Europe.

How did *The Times* arrive initially at such a position? The explanation for this must be sought in the newspaper's reflections on the Versailles treaty. According to the consequent analysis of that treaty and its outcomes, the Versailles settlement rested upon a series of illusions. The first of these was that tranquillity in Europe could be secured by the general extension of representative democracy. Post-war experience had in fact confirmed the wisdom of Mill's conclusion of a century earlier that a high level of cultural and economic development was the essential prerequisite for the successful operation of representative institutions. Of nowhere had this proved more true than Eastern Europe, where attempts to transplant parliamentary institutions native to Western Europe had met with almost universal failure. Moreover, the newspaper no more than other sectors of informed opinion in the thirties, believed that the first world war had really been a struggle between democracy and authoritarianism as Allied propaganda had come in time to claim. As for the conviction that democracies were necessarily pacific, this must remain an act of faith.

The second great illusion upon which Versailles had been constructed had been the belief that a stable European order could be created through the universal application of the principle of national self-determination. This principle raised problems of a general character everywhere, but given the racial confusion of Eastern Europe in particular was little short of a recipe for permanent turmoil in that region.

The third great illusion to inform the settlement was the hope that a stable new European system could be fabricated without the participation of either Germany or Russia.

This constituted a reasoned and considered perspective on the problems raised for British policy-makers by developments in Eastern Europe between the wars. To a large extent it reflected much common ground in, for example, the willingness of inter-war British policy-makers to enter into, in concert with other powers, security commitments guaranteeing the Western European frontiers established at Versailles as contrasted with their extreme reluctance to enter into identical agreements with reference to those Eastern European frontiers similarly established. *The Times*, however, was prepared to draw the logical conclusions from this reluctance. As no vital interest of Great Britain was at stake in Eastern Europe and as she lacked the political will and the military resources for decisive intervention in so distant an area, then she should not necessarily feel compelled to oppose the predominance in that region of another great power. Though the putative ultimate beneficiary of this advice, if taken, might have changed in the interim, this was to remain the position of *The Times* on Eastern Europe in the 1940s for, as the newspaper repeatedly argued, British foreign policy was not and should not be based upon ideological considerations but upon national interest assessed in a rational and enlightened manner.

A few years ago Professor W.N. Medlicott suggested that the term 'appeasement' should join the term 'imperialism' as terms which henceforth no serious scholar should employ on the grounds that they had been used to cover promiscuously what were often quite discrete attitudes and policy positions.[1] He may or may not have had in mind *The Times* when he wrote these words, but certainly any study of the special character of that newspaper's support for appeasement in the 1930s, and of its distinctive attitude towards Eastern Europe should induce hesitation in those tempted to easy generalization. To suggest, for example, that 'what united the appeasers was a common belief in the principle of self-determination'[2] is either to forget or to misunderstand the position of *The Times* for reasons already indicated above. In its support for the Munich settlement *The Times* might indeed point out that given its substantial minorities, Czechoslovakia was not defensible in terms of the doctrine of national self-determination, but this by no means meant that the newspaper itself subscribed to that doctrine in any unqualified manner. Manifestly it did not. In advising against the blank rejection of Hitler's demands, *The Times* was arguing that a proper deference be paid to the realities of power in Eastern Europe.[3]

Another familiar generalization about the appeasers is that which claims 'the appeasers drew their strength and sustenance from a hatred of Russia and of communism'.[4] In view of the reputation the newspaper was to acquire in the forties for its pro-Soviet sympathies, this is a difficult charge to sustain against *The*

Times. And a reading of *Times*' leaders written in the thirties reveals no obsessive concern with Russian expansionism. For *The Times* followed most other informed opinion of the period in regarding Stalin's triumphant emergence from the Kremlin power struggles as signalling, among other things, Russia's transformation into a cautious, defensive power on the international scene which henceforth would give priority to domestic development. The rise of Stalin was widely welcomed in the western press at the time for precisely these reasons. *The Times* opposed the construction of a general anti-German alliance in the 1930s, which perforce would have included the Soviet Union, not because of a preoccupation with the superior danger supposedly presented by Russia but because of a general theoretical objection to the emergence in Europe of two opposed alliance systems which might end in a repetition of the catastrophe of 1914.

The second world war broke out over Poland and many commentators, including Churchill, have seen in Allied disagreements over Poland the seeds of the Cold War.[5] These facts make *The Times'* treatment of the Polish Question a specially instructive example of its attitude to Eastern Europe as a whole and the supreme illustration of that continuity of view about that region which characterizes the newspaper in the thirties and forties.

When Chamberlain announced the unilateral British Guarantee to Poland in the Commons in March 1939 the unqualified nature of that Guarantee surprised the Prime Minister's supporters as much as it did his critics. The unease that *The Times* felt at seeming acceptance by Britain of such a sweeping security commitment in Eastern Europe, in apparent contravention of all previous policy, found immediate expression in the controversial leader that Geoffrey Dawson wrote on the morrow of the statement.[6] Here Dawson stressed that Chamberlain's statement repaid the closest scrutiny for this would show that Britain had guaranteed the independence of Poland but not her territorial integrity. There was no blanket endorsement of the status quo, for on the British side there was a recognition that problems still existed in which adjustments were still necessary and Dawson added, somewhat ominously for the Poles, 'The relative strength of nations will always and rightly be an important consideration in diplomacy'.[7] This leader cause Beck to delay his imminent departure for London until the Foreign Office had issued an official statement repudiating *The Times'* interpretation of Britain's new obligations and, as the Czech precedent was in every mind, caused the Polish ambassador, Raczynski, to proclaim emphatically to Orme Sargent, 'We want no Runcimanism in Poland'.[8]

This initial reserve of the newspaper about accepting an unlimited obligation to Poland set the tone for the future. Amidst the clash of arms and during the gallant but doomed resistance of the Poles there were no further references, however oblique, to the negotiability of Poland's frontiers and *The Times* followed the rest of the press, the *Daily Worker* apart, in denouncing the Soviet occupation of the eastern territories of Poland. Yet in regard to the latter, the newspaper reflected some of the ambivalence of official British policy. Whilst condemning aggression whatever its source, Halifax had distinguished in the Lords between German and Russian action in Poland on the grounds that the latter had not actually initiated the war. He had further noted that Soviet forces had advanced only up to the Curzon Line.[9] Although there were no further 'Curzon Line' arguments available to be invoked in mitigation of Soviet conduct when Russia subsequently moved against the Baltic states and Finland, *The Times* was for the next two years to maintain a broad distinction between German and Russian expansion in Eastern Europe. This led it continually to suggest that Soviet expansion, whatever overtly aggressive form it assumed, was fundamentally reactive and defensive in character. Russia was seeking security through pre-emptive moves which would allow her to resist from the most forward positions the perceived threat from Germany. *The Times* took it as axiomatic that a ruler as experienced and cunning as Stalin would place little credence in Hitler's public professions of goodwill. These being the wellsprings of Soviet actions, the lesson for Britain was that she must on no account alienate Russia as a potential future ally through quixotic action over Eastern Europe.

The events of 22 June 1941 were to simplify matters. Looking back, *The Times* was to find in these events confirmation for its interpretation of the sources of Soviet conduct and, incidentally, a degree of retrospective justification for that conduct itself. Russia's fears had proved well-founded. When, six months later, the United States followed Russia into the war, *The Times* was to repeat in leader after leader one simple message. This was that ultimate Allied victory was assured so long as harmony between what the newspaper liked to call 'the Great Allies' prevailed. Conversely, it would be a primary German objective to shatter that harmony. At all costs this objective must be frustrated.

The Poles were soon to learn what the implications of this simple message for a lesser ally might be. As the Russians first contained, and then rolled back the invading German armies, those Russo-Polish differences which had been buried under the first impact of the German attack began to surface again. With every step that the Russian troops took towards the 1939 frontiers of Poland, the settlement of these differences became more urgent. There was little attempt at impartiality on the part of *The Times*. Although Russia's claims against the Poles were at no time fully or explicitly stated, the newspaper supported concessions to the Soviet Union by Poland on what it understood to be the two key issues. In the first place, the Polish government-in-exile must publicly accept the Curzon Line as the international boundary between the two countries. Secondly, that government must purge itself of those reactionary and militaristic elements which the Soviet authorities found so objectionable. According to *The Times* these latter blemishes on the democratic legitimacy of the Polish government were a consequence of that government's dubious origins, successor as it was of the 'regime of the colonels' and ultimately of the Pilsudski military dictatorship. At no time during the war was *The Times* to subject the democratic credentials of Britain's Soviet ally to the same searching scrutiny. By its discreet silence in the latter case it demonstrated an altogether more charitable understanding of the complexities of history.

The Poles proved obdurate on both points. The Russians broke off diplomatic relations with the Poles over the latter's reaction to German radio's broadcast of the news of the discovery of the mass graves of Polish officers at Katyn, although as *The Times*' Moscow correspondent noted,[10] this event merely provided the occasion for a move long contemplated from the Russian side. According to *The Times*, in seeming to support publicly German proposals for an international enquiry into the affair, the Poles had fallen headlong into the German trap and had demonstrated to the whole world their political gullibility, their diplomatic ineptitude and their Russophobia.[11] Yet the newspaper was not primarily concerned with the rights and wrongs of the Katyn affair, but was much more concerned with the pattern of post-war Eastern

Europe, on which subject it had long since proclaimed its own position that there could be no return, after the defeat of Hitler, to the pre-war situation where the states of the region had suffered from a lack of 'leadership'. That leadership could come from only one source and this fact should be openly acknowledged in advance by all the major parties involved to preclude dangerous misunderstandings:

> If Britain's frontier is on the Rhine, it might just as pertinently be said — though it has not been said — that Russia's frontier is on the Oder. . . . The sole interest of Russia is to assure herself that her outer defences are in secure hands; and this interest will best be served if the lands between her frontiers and those of Germany are held by governments and peoples friendly to herself. Everything goes to show that she will be in a position after the war to shape the settlement on lines consistent with this conception of what her security demands. But it will make all the difference to the future of Anglo-Soviet friendship whether they are freely approved and welcomed by Britain in advance, or whether they are grudgingly accepted as a fait accompli after victory has been won.[12]

Given this vision, the intransigent Poles could be little more than an embarrassment. At the time of the Warsaw Rising, *The Times* paid tribute to the heroism of the insurgents but at the same time it rebuked the Polish government-in-exile for imperilling Allied understanding by failing to integrate its military plans with those of the Soviet High Command. The suggestion that the Russian forces had been held back outside Warsaw to allow a war of mutual destruction to be fought between Germans and Poles was a 'malicious and unfounded rumour'.[13] On no account should the western powers permit themselves to become embroiled with the Soviet Union over Poland. Moreover they should avoid applying double standards for:

> Both Great Britain and the United States have shown themselves to be sensitive traditionally to the direct intervention of any other power in certain regions that they have considered vital to their security. It would therefore be all the more unreasonable if they were blind to an equally legitimate sensitiveness of Russia towards independent action by other powers anywhere in the territories that lie between her frontiers and Germany. The long and tragic record of the nineteenth century shows that the attempted intervention of western powers in relations between Poland and Russia, however well intentioned, has rarely brought credit to those powers or — what is more important — advantage to the Polish nation.

Two months before Yalta, *The Times*, in an important leader, returned to the spirit of Geoffrey Dawson's controversial leader on Chamberlain's announcement of the Guarantee to Poland in subjecting the obligations assumed by Britain under the Anglo-Polish Mutual Security Treaty of 25 August 1939 to the closest scrutiny.[14] Indeed this time the scrutiny was so close that it enabled the leader writer to read between the lines of the published treaty. According to the published document that treaty was directed against aggression by 'a European Power'. According to the leader writer the treaty was directed against Germany and German aggression alone and did not therefore commit HMG to restore Poland within its 1939 frontiers. What the leader writer was more than hinting at, of course, was the existence of those secret protocols to the treaty which the British government was eventually to release to cover its embarrassment in the aftermath of the Yalta debate. Earlier in 1944 *The Times* had departed from its standard practice in publishing in its correspondence columns an anonymous letter[15] drawing readers' attention to a little remembered Commons reply by the then Minister of State at the Foreign Office, R.A. Butler, in the charged circumstances of October 1939, to a question on the sensitive issue of the diplomatic implications of Russian aggression in eastern Poland. In this reply Butler had given every indication, short of outright revelation, of the existence of the secret protocols of the Anglo-Polish Treaty limiting that treaty's application specifically and exclusively to the case of aggression by Germany.[16] Therefore, before Yalta *The Times* was arguing that only a misplaced sense of honour bound Britain to the London Poles, the great majority of whom 'were blindly faithful to a fatal and discredited tradition'.[17] Moreover, the newspaper put aside contractual niceties in declaring that 'the British government and British peoples . . . obligations . . . are to the Polish people as a whole, and not to any one group'.[18]

Unsurprisingly, *The Times* received the news of the Yalta accords with rapture as exceeding its highest expectations and found 'the most remarkable achievement of the Crimea Conference' to be 'the agreement upon the future attitude of the three Powers to Poland'.[19] At Yalta Churchill had objected to documentary references to the Polish government-in-exile as the 'émigré' Poles[20] on the grounds that to Anglo-Saxon ears this suggested a government in flight from popular rejection. Yet after Yalta and before the British withdrew official recognition from that government we find *The Times* referring Molotov-fashion to the 'émigré Polish government'.[21] Long before the shift in diplomatic recognition to the new Warsaw government came about the newspaper was advocating such a move as the only logical outcome of the London Poles' failure to reconcile themselves to the changes in regard to Poland agreed at Yalta. One could not save those who would not save themselves. When the shift in recognition came, the Polish government-in-exile was warned against abusing British hospitality by indulging in 'mischief-making' and 'wrecking' activities.[22] Ordinary Polish servicemen were advised to join Mikolajczyk in returning home, as all patriotic Poles should do, to help build the new Poland and at the same time repeatedly warned against the malign influence of their own officer class in shaping their decision.

The Polish Question has been dwelt upon at some little length for reasons previously indicated. Given its attitude to Eastern Europe, *The Times* had never been happy with Chamberlain's original commitments to Poland and as these obligations threatened in the course of the war to provide new embarrassments for Britain, the newspaper led the movement of those who believed that Britain again should disengage herself from all East European entanglements. In propagating this message in the 1940s, the newspaper was led to expound a philosophy of international relations which was global in its implications to which I should like now to turn.

Inevitably *Times'* leaders of the war years devote most of their space to the pressing issues of the hour, but from the beginning they expound a clearly articulated and coherent philosophy of international relations and proclaim that the war is not being fought to restore the status quo ante in Europe. They advance a model for a stable new European and world order. This philosophy and that order are to a great extent historically conditioned and that favourite journalistic phrase 'the lessons of history' is much invoked. What were these lessons and what guidance did they offer statesmen concerned with the construction of the post-war world?

Two of these lessons have already been touched upon in this article. Inter-war experience had, according to *The Times*, demonstrated that no stable European order could be built simply by applying the twin Wilsonian principles of national self-determination and of representative government. These had proved particularly inappropriate in Eastern Europe. The inter-war 'sovereignty' of many of the states of that area had been little more than a polite fiction of diplomacy given their military and economic weaknesses. Moreover, inter-war experience had suggested that representative institutions transplanted from Western Europe could not confidently be expected to flourish in the thin soil of Eastern Europe. The likely post-war choice in Eastern Europe, in practice, *The Times* suggested, would be between rival forms of authoritarian rule. It is important to bear this last point in mind when considering the relative equanimity with which the newspaper was to meet the extension of communist rule throughout Eastern Europe in the aftermath of the second world war. The two greatest needs in post-war Eastern Europe would be for what *The Times* liked to term 'leadership' and 'organisation'.

The third lesson of history that the newspaper derived from the catastrophe of the world war was that henceforth international relations must be anchored firmly in the realities of power and not clouded and confused by the illusions of idealists. The great illusion of the 1930s had been that collective security could be achieved through the League of Nations. Men had attempted to build a new world order on the basis of the equal rights and responsibilities of each sovereign state. An international system had been built upon a polite fiction of diplomacy. Inevitably in these circumstances collective security had meant collective insecurity. In the real world, states differed widely in their resources and in their ability to mobilize those resources for military and other purposes. The real world of states was not a democracy but an 'aristocracy of power'.[23] Henceforth, any new international system must temper idealism with realism and the rights, duties and responsibilities of states must be aligned with a state's effective power to control and influence events. Unsurprisingly, such attitudes expressed in the newspaper's leader columns alarmed some readers[24] as strikingly reminiscent of that doctrine of realpolitik which supposedly Britain was at war to oppose. Therefore *The Times* was all the more insistent in its self-imposed task of educating public opinion out of its illusions. The beginning of all wisdom in approaching international relations lay in the unsentimental intellectual acceptance of the fact that the world is as it is and not as we would have it be.

The fourth lesson which could be garnered from twentieth-century history was that stability could no longer be secured in Europe through the maintenance of a balance of power. In view of

Britain's history, this lesson was of particular relevance to the statesmen of that country. August 1914 had shown that any equilibrium based upon the countervailing power of two great alliance systems, sustained by massive arms expenditure, with Britain providing the fine balance, was inherently unstable. The character of modern war, once a diplomatic balance collapsed, meant that the ensuing conflict would be so costly in blood and treasure that there could be no real victors.

These were the lessons to be garnered from twentieth-century experience and they were all of a negative character. For the positive lessons of history one had to look further back to the nineteenth century for that century provided a successful model on which to base an international order. That nineteenth-century prototype was provided by the Concert of Europe. A new Concert was what was now required, but a Concert intelligently modified to suit the changed circumstances of the mid-twentieth century. This meant in the first place that the new Concert would be, in the words of a *Times'* leader, not so much 'a Concert of Europe as a Concert of the World'.[25]

From this model springs *The Times'* essential division of the powers of the world into two categories, viz. the great powers and the small powers.[26] The great powers alone disposed of those orders of resources and military strength which could maintain world peace or launch world war. Furthermore, because of the terrible cost of such war, given the destructive potential of modern technology, the great powers in the post-war world would have a common interest in the preservation of that peace. For the great powers to realize fully this community of interest in practice it would be necessary for each of their number to feel confident in its own security.

How was this confidence to be instilled? According to the newspaper, by the rational division of the world into spheres of influence within each of which the predominance of the security interests of one of their number would be freely acknowledged by the other great powers. In an important sense, as *The Times* put it on one occasion, 'zones of influence exist, were bound to exist and will continue to exist'.[27] What would characterize the new international system, however, would be the universal recognition of non-overlapping, clearly demarcated spheres of influence. In this way friction between great powers on matters of vital interests would be avoided.

At the same time not all of the globe would fall within those areas judged by one great power or another to be vital to its own security. In these uncontested regions the great powers must practise consultation and seek to coordinate their policies. Particular prudence would be called for as minor powers would understandably seek to gain great power backing in pursuit of their own aims. At all costs the great powers must avoid a situation arising in which they would be set upon a collision course with each other through the rash espousal of the conflicting claims of rival clients amongst the lesser states.

A programme such as this when put forward in a newspaper of the standing of *The Times* could hardly be expected to pass without comment from readers. And rightly or wrongly, foreign readers in particular tended to assume the existence of a relationship of special intimacy between the newspaper and those responsible for the making of British foreign policy. The representatives of the governments-in-exile in London who spoke for the smaller European powers felt especially alarmed. From their perspective it seemed that the second world war itself was being fought to prevent Germany from being able to impose its will upon the lesser states of Europe. Less directly interested readers were to regret what they discerned as the adoption by *The Times* of the language of realpolitik. Was this not, after all diplomatic euphemisms were set aside, the very philosophy of international relations which Great Britain had gone to war to oppose? We find, therefore, *Times'* leaders of the war years defending the newspaper against charges of 'Hitlerism' and allegations that it was preaching power politics. The newspaper set about educating its critics out of that condition of naivety that alone made the formulation of such an indictment possible. Power, it explained, was the necessary if not the sole ingredient of all politics. There was no such thing as 'powerless' politics.[28] The open and universal use of the expression 'the powers' in international politics was simply testimony to the fact that this general truth was more honestly acknowledged and could therefore be more starkly expressed in discussions of international politics than in other aspects of politics.

Having expounded its philosophy of international relations *The Times* was not remiss in drawing all the logical conclusions that flowed from that philosophy. If each great power was to be freely conceded its legitimate sphere of influence in the post-war world by its fellow great powers, then there could be no gainsaying the fact that Eastern Europe must fall within the Soviet sphere. As early as

August 1941 *The Times* had concluded that the chief lesson of the inter-war period for the states of Eastern Europe was that in any new post-war order they would have to accept the 'leadership' of a great power.[29] As neither Great Britain nor the United States could or should seek to exercise predominant influence in the area, this in the nature of things must mean the leadership of either Germany or Russia. And, as Hitler's Germany by its aggressive conduct had demonstrated that its ambitions ran beyond a legitimate regional predominance to continental mastery and perhaps to global power, post-war leadership in Eastern Europe must mean the leadership of the Soviet Union.

It is of the greatest interest that *The Times* should adopt this position so early in the war on the eastern front as the Soviet Union was still staggering from the opening German onslaught. Much later in the conflict, after the tide had turned in the east, many other sectors of British opinion were to come to a similar conclusion, at least temporarily, that it would be wise to accept in the east the results of the arbitrament of arms. However, their reaction could be viewed, in part at least, as governed by expediency. They were counselling the acquiescence of a war-weary Britain in the somewhat mixed results of a war from which she had emerged in the ranks of the victors. The position of *The Times* was quite different. It anticipated events and it was able so to do because its views on Eastern Europe sprang from a considered and deliberate philosophy of international relations. This philosophy dictated that Great Britain must 'disinterest' herself in Eastern Europe.

As relations between the wartime allies began rapidly to deteriorate once the war itself had been won, *The Times* at no time absolved the Soviet Union from its share of guilt in contributing to this sad process. It found the vitriolic language of Soviet diplomacy unpalatable. It suggested that the Soviet Union's perfectly legitimate sensitivity over its own security showed signs on occasion of degenerating into paranoia. Yet what was to characterize the attitude of the newspaper was its insistence on the shared, indeed, the equal guilt of both sides. Thus towards the end of a leader arguing the need for a restoration of the wartime conditions of harmony and trust among the Allies, in which it had surveyed the varied contentious issues which had come to divide them, *The Times* concluded

> If relations are to be improved, if suspicions are to be exorcised, Russia has a large contribution to make. But an equally large contribution is required from the U.S. and Britain.[30]

This was very even-handed justice. On what precise counts did the newspaper indict the policy-makers of the western powers?

The general charge was one of inconsistency against the western powers, inconsistency tinged with hypocrisy. These powers were showing themselves decidedly unenthusiastic about the prospect of Soviet predominance in the Balkans and in Poland. Indeed from time to time they interfered to show their disagreement with Soviet plans for the post-war organization of Eastern Europe, action which could only excite the hopes of anti-Soviet elements in that region. And all of this was done in an area which was manifestly one of the utmost sensitivity for Soviet security. At the same time Britain was asserting for herself a primary role in the settlement of Greece and together with the United States effectively excluding Russia from any significant participation in shaping the post-war destinies of Italy, France or the Low Countries. As for the United States alone, she was clearly intent on fashioning a Japanese settlement exclusively according to her own ideas. To none of these schemes of the western powers had the Soviet Union made any noisy objections, until, that is, it became clear that the western powers would seek to deny to the Soviet Union what they claimed for themselves, i.e. predominance in regions where they held their own security to be at stake. To the Russians this smacked of double-dealing and a refusal to accept the Soviet Union as an equal amongst the great powers when she had made the greatest sacrifices of all in the defeat of the common enemy. *The Times* could see no logical distinction between Britain's claims to a preponderating influence in the Middle East and the Low Countries or America's claims to exercise a similar influence in the Pacific and in the western hemisphere as a whole and Russia's aspirations in Eastern Europe. Moreover, the newspaper repeatedly said so. On a number of occasions the analogy was made with the Monroe Doctrine. Following Franklin Roosevelt, the latter was characterized as a 'good neighbour policy'. All the Soviet Union was claiming in Eastern Europe, *The Times* explained to its American readers, was the world's acceptance of its right to play a similarly concerned role in Eastern Europe.[31] Setting aside all necessary obfuscations of language, it is of the greatest interest that at the very outset of the Cold War we find *The Times* advocating the voluntary acceptance by the western powers of something akin to the Brezhnev doctrine a generation before that doctrine received a formal formulation by the Soviet rulers.

In the months that followed Potsdam, *The Times* was to return to this theme repeatedly. By that time, however, western policymakers had provided the leader writer with new evidence of their refusal to treat the Soviet Union as an equal and act towards her in a free and open manner. In regard to the development of the atomic bomb, the newspaper found the behaviour of the western powers on political and scientific grounds to be myopic and irrational. Conversely it judged Soviet suspicions to be legitimate.

> No decision taken now by any power or any group of powers is likely to restrain the number of nations possessing the skill and resources to develop the use of atomic energy. . . . But what is done now may have incalculable diplomatic consequences in fostering or allaying suspicions between the great nations of the world . . .[32]

The Times advised that,

> The control of the latest and deadliest of weapons fully and frankly shared between the principal governments of the United Nations must take its proper place as part, even though the weightiest part of the control of all weapons. This control cannot be separated from the general business of the planning of peace and the prevention of war and the responsibility for it must rest in the same hands.[33]

Churchill's speech at Fulton is conventionally taken to mark the first public declaration of the Cold War from the western side. In that speech Churchill had deliberately singled out for condemnation attempts to gain security in Europe by counselling the adoption of a policy of 'appeasement' towards the Soviet Union. The response of *The Times* to the Fulton speech is therefore of particular interest. The newspaper echoed Churchill's criticisms of Soviet policy but then proceeded to temper these with a strong plea for western understanding of the obsessive nature of Soviet preoccupations with security together with an insistence that Russia alone was not responsible for that deterioration in inter-Allied relations that had undoubtedly occurred. In a variety of ways the western powers, perhaps unintentionally, had sown the seeds of distrust in Russian minds. And it concluded

> Most of all, perhaps, the policy which has retained for the U.S. the exclusive exploitation of the atomic bomb has aggravated an existing state of insecurity in

> Soviet minds that may not be intelligible to Westerners who forget by how narrow a margin the Soviet Union escaped catastrophe. It has fortified the belief in an attempt to build up a reservoir of military power against the Soviet Union and it has troubled their pride, never more conspicuous than in the hour of victory and exultation.[34]

Much earlier *The Times* had commented adversely on the failure of the Attlee government to dissociate itself from American policy on this crucial issue.[35] This acquiescence could only contribute to the impression being gained by Russia's rulers that the western powers were intent upon concerting their policies against the Soviet Union. And this was a direct contravention of the first principles of that revived Concert of Europe which *The Times* had expounded as its model for a new international order. For that model had stipulated that whereas there should be some kind of formal or semi-formal institutionalization of that 'aristocracy of power' which would be an inevitable feature of the post-war world, the newspaper had been insistent that the experiment could only succeed if all the member states of that aristocracy were treated as equals. This meant in particular that there be no 'ganging up' against one of their number by the others. Within the aristocracy of power, in short, democracy of conduct must prevail.

Such in broad outline was *The Times'* critique of western policy which it offered to sustain its general thesis that the Soviet Union enjoyed no monopoly of guilt for the deterioration in inter-Allied relations. When this critique is brought forward to be examined in the context of the varied arguments advanced subsequently by the revisionist school of American historians of the Cold War's origins, it takes on an obvious renewed interest in that it prefigures many of the attitudes they were to adopt. Yet a number of points need to be made here. In the first place to claim that all of the positions taken by the revisionist school on the Cold War's origins can be found anticipated in the leader columns of the contemporary *Times* would be to claim too much. However, though licence allows one to speak of a revisionist 'school' that school, like most historical schools, reveals a significant degree of differentiation of attitude and argument upon closer scrutiny. The contemporary line adopted on international relations by *The Times* at the Cold War's inception was relatively simple in itself and was lucidly expressed. Not surprisingly, it does not anticipate all of the shades and nuances of the later debate.

The second point is more important. It concerns a difference of moral perspective. The revisionist school has sought to portray the Cold War as an old-fashioned power struggle masquerading as something else behind a weight of rhetoric on one side about freedom and on the other side about socialism. Infusing their whole thesis has been something more than an indictment of western hypocrisy. This has been a profound puritan distaste for the world of power politics as such, a yearning for a different kind of world in which, perhaps, the great issues will be decided upon their merits and not upon the disposition of military force. Nothing could be more different from the moral or amoral perspective from which *The Times* viewed the international scene in the 1940s. As has been previously indicated, *The Times* constantly argued for realism and maturity in politics. Power was the necessary though not the sole ingredient which informed all politics and differentiated political behaviour from other forms of human activity. On a number of occasions the newspaper found it necessary to defend itself against the charge that it was preaching 'power politics' by distinguishing between its own realism and what the usage of the time tended to term 'Prussianism' or 'Hitlerism'. One can find no trace in these leaders of a moral revulsion from the world of actuality nor any evidence of anguished yearnings for the creation of a new order where the swords will be transformed into ploughshares. Rather, the newspaper found it necessary to suggest that it was specially incumbent upon democratic statesmen not to pander to the wishful thinking of such substantial sections of their electorates in these matters. As we have seen, the model which *The Times* took for its own conception of a sound and practicable post-war international order was provided by the system established at the Congress of Vienna. Conversely, when the newspaper was in need of a negative model, illustrative of how such an order could not be achieved, it invoked the Versailles settlement. More specifically it used the part played by Woodrow Wilson in the shaping of that settlement to illustrate the dangers that democratic statesmen ran in awakening a body of unrealizable aspirations in the peoples of the world through irresponsible moralizing. Innocence and cynicism about the role played by power considerations in international politics were equally dangerous and each had played its part in bringing about the war. The supreme quality in statesmen and peoples which alone could offer Europe and the wider world the promise of post-war tranquillity was realism in the conduct of foreign policy. For these reasons, whilst it is substantially true that we can find many of the arguments advanced by the revisionist school prefigured in the leader columns of *The Times* a generation earlier, it would be erroneous to deduce from that any coincidence of basic values still less any shared moral vision. *The Times* was advocating a more general, a more open, a more businesslike acceptance of just those canons of international conduct which the revisionist historians would seem to deplore.

In the war years *The Times* was to acquire a reputation on the back-benches, and not only on the Conservative back-benches, for having become a left-wing newspaper, an up-market edition of the *Daily Worker*. In part, this exaggerated reputation was a consequence of the line that the newspaper took on domestic affairs. For here *The Times* adopted a highly progressive approach giving, for example, the warmest of welcomes to the Beveridge Report whilst leader after leader expounded on the bankruptcy of laissez-faire and propounded the need to embrace 'planning' and full-bloodied Keynesian demand management in the post-war world. The newspaper stopped short only at the advocacy of the widespread extension of public ownership. Readers had recently been reminded of the radical past of 'The Thunderer' by the published volumes of Stanley Morison's authorized history. Barrington-Ward's Tory radicalism could be seen as reviving this tradition. Even Geoffrey Dawson had been known to confide that he had always regarded *The Times* as an organ of the left, though not, he had hastily added, of the extreme left.[36] There was a marginal area of overlap between the newspaper's re-awakened domestic radicalism and its foreign policy line which did not fully square with non-ideological approach to British foreign policy which *The Times* had proclaimed through the thirties and forties. This was the espousal from time to time of the 'convergence' thesis according to which all that separated the Soviet Union from the liberal democracies was a difference of choice of the preferred path to the common destination of 'democracy', the former having chosen the economic road whilst the latter had chosen the political road.[37] In the thirties, there had been no similar talk about the common aspirations of British and German societies, *The Times* on that earlier occasion being much more inclined to argue that each state had a perfect right to construct its own version of heaven — or hell — without outside interference and that what suited Britain might very well not suit Germany and vice-versa.

To return, however, to the foreign policy field, the figure who at the time was credited by the cognoscenti with the responsibility for the pro-Soviet line the newspaper was taking was E.H. Carr, Assistant Editor of *The Times* from January 1941 to July 1946. The ease with which this assumption was made sometimes proved offensive to the *amour propre* of the Editor, Barrington-Ward, but the latter's biographer has not found this contemporary belief to be substantially incorrect, roundly stating in reference to Carr that, 'it is clear that the main strategic thinking on foreign policy was done by him'.[38] Barrington-Ward's confidence in Carr meant that he largely confined his own interventions in the leaders dealing with Eastern Europe to matters of presentation rather than of content, tempering the full ruthlessness of Carr's message by the substitution of language more diplomatic than Carr's own chosen vocabulary. Just how ruthless this message in essence was is indicated by Carr's pronouncement in the privacy of an office memorandum that Russia should be given 'a free hand in Eastern Europe'.[39] This stark message could hardly be conveyed to the readers in unvarnished form but the more judicious language in which the leader columns clothed the same message failed to disarm the critics, who merely found, in the many euphemisms this process involved, confirmation of that traditional penchant of Printing House Square for compounding its many sins with a dash of mendacity.

Yet what is important about Carr's personal role in the context of this article is that Carr was not recruited to *The Times* for any views he may or may not have had on communism or on the Soviet Union. He was first brought to the attention of Barrington-Ward, then Assistant Editor, by the ubiquitous Tom Jones in the thirties as a man with a useful Foreign Office and academic background who might offer powerful intellectual support for the line the newspaper was then taking on Germany, in short as an exponent of appeasement.[40] On this basis, Carr made contributions to *The Times* in the later thirties and it was at this time that Barrington-Ward resolved to recruit him to the staff of the newspaper when the opportunity arose, a project which did not reach fruition until Barrington-Ward himself succeeded Dawson in the Editor's chair. Carr's support first for the appeasement of Nazi Germany and then for the appeasement of communist Russia testify to the non-ideological character of his approach to international relations and give to his journalism and published works on contemporary international history a degree of symmetry, for Carr can be seen as both the spiritual precursor of the British revisionist historians of British foreign policy in the thirties and as the precursor of the American school of historians of the Cold War's origins. *The Times'* Diplomatic Correspondent of the forties has recorded his embarrassment at having constantly to fend off the charge that the newspaper, having led the campaign for the betrayal of the peoples of Eastern Europe once, was intent on repeating the performance.[41]

The tone of any great newspaper, however, is something which cannot be entirely established by any one man. The leaders on British military intervention in Greece in December 1944, composed on the basis of reports from the Athens correspondent, Geoffrey Hoare, were for the most part written by Donald Tyerman, and it was these which sparked off Churchill's angry attack on *The Times* in the Commons. Churchill certainly held Carr and Barrington-Ward responsible for those leaders.

An important contribution to establishing the tone of the newspaper was made by Ralph Parker, the Moscow correspondent. Parker's reports merit attention because whilst the newspaper's leader columns tended to warn the western powers against applying double standards in seeking to deny to the Soviet Union those regional security safeguards which they claimed for themselves, the Moscow correspondent reproached some sections of western opinion for precisely the opposite transgression, viz. for applying to Russian politics those same exacting standards that they invoked when dealing with the liberal democracies. According to Parker, this was completely to ignore the circumstances in which the Bolsheviks had come to power and the standards of popular culture to which they were heirs. When this argument for relative values found expression in, for example, a totally uncritical *Times* report of the politically educational function of public executions (in which the death agonies of the condemned were filmed for general distribution) it proved too much for some readers like Arthur Koestler to stomach.[42] After the war, Parker's connection with *The Times* was to be severed, but he was to grow even warmer in his enthusiasm for Russia's experiment in socialism[43] and join that long line of foreign correspondents who have gone completely 'native', settling premanently in Moscow from whence he continued to represent a variety of western newspapers and journals until his death twenty years later.

Although for obvious reasons his connection with *The Man-*

chester Guardian is better known, a significant part in expounding *The Times'* line on Eastern Europe and its views on the Polish Question in particular was played by Lewis Namier in the articles supportive of that line and those views that he contributed during the war years. From very different points of departure — a firm Tory, a committed Zionist, a believer in the principle of nationality, an active anti-appeaser in the thirties and still one of Churchill's warmest admirers — Namier had reached substantially the same conclusions as to the qualities desirable in a post-war settlement as Carr. Though a Tory, Namier had never been among those Tories who were obsessed by the Bolshevik bogy, as his record of political journalism from 1918 onwards makes plain. Moreover his *Times* articles in support of a Russo-Polish boundary settlement on the basis of the Curzon Line came with special authority from Namier, given his intimate personal knowledge of the area under dispute and his claim to have been the original author of that Line[44] when he was serving with the Political Intelligence Department of the Foreign Office during the first world war and its aftermath. Something of the special character of Namier's views on Eastern Europe at that time can be garnered from the fact that Headlam-Morley, writing to Namier from Paris, felt constrained to discount some of the latter's advice on the grounds that Namier appeared to regard Polish imperialism as a greater threat to European peace than Bolshevism.[45] Inter-war experience had demonstrated for Namier that one or other of the two regional Great Powers must inevitably enter the power vacuum that Eastern Europe constituted, whether or not the smaller nations of that area continued to enjoy formal political sovereignty. For British policy-makers, therefore, this raised one simple question: whose predominance in Eastern Europe best served or least harmed Britain's national interests? For Namier there could be but one answer to this question. Germany had demonstrated by her two bids for power in the twentieth century (always for Namier the 'German' wars) that Germany's ambitions extended far beyond legitimate regional predominance to continental mastery and ultimately to world dominion. As, like Vansittart, Namier held the German people collectively responsible both for the world wars and the barbarous methods by which the second in particular was waged, he had no faith that a post-war German nation could be rapidly rehabilitated through a change of office-holders and formal constitutional changes to forget its dreams. On no account should a misplaced sense of national honour over the Polish Question lead British policy-makers to balk the explicit and unqualified acceptance of Russia's leading role in Eastern Europe. Poland must be compelled to accept the political logic of its geographical position. The unqualified nature of Namier's own acceptance of Russia's position in Poland can be appreciated from the fact that when, in the process of preparing some of his wartime journalism for hardcover publication in 1947, he included his *Times* articles (which, given the then impersonal character of the newspaper, had been anonymous on first appearance), he did so with the affirmation that their 'underlying contentions seem to me as valid then as now',[46] and with a renewed plea for that more systematic division of Europe into spheres of influence which alone could prevent a further deterioration in Great Power relationships. This was, of course, some considerable time after Russia had failed to honour the Yalta promises of free and unfettered elections in Poland. As Namier wrote, 'The destiny of nations is written on the globe'.[47]

It has been the basic contention of this article that a fundamental continuity of view on the problems of Eastern Europe provides the connecting link which unites the advocacy by *The Times* of politics of appeasement in the two decades under consideration. Yet though *The Times* might preach the same message, the world which received that message in the forties was much changed and was still changing fast. As E.H. Carr has himself reminded us in explaining the attitude the newspaper adopted towards Russia in the forties, that attitude must be understood in the context of the times.[48] In the first place, *The Times* proved no more prescient about the rapidity of Britain's decline from Great Power status than most other opinion leaders. Secondly, given the precedent of 1919, it would have been quite irresponsible in planning for the peace to assume confidently that the United States would be prepared to accept permanent post-war security commitments in Europe. What had to be avoided at all costs was a situation in which Britain faced alone an alienated Russia across a devastated Europe.

In addition to these changes in the external world, the position of *The Times* in the domestic world of British politics between the two decades was much changed. Barrington-Ward's friend and colleague Stanley Morison liked to distinguish the newspaper from all others as the newspaper of Britain's ruling class.[49] As a Marxist this was a consistent view for Morison to hold, although it was by no means a view held exclusively by Marxists. Yet, in the forties

Barrington-Ward was at no time to establish those relations of easy intimacy with Downing Street that Dawson had enjoyed with Baldwin and Chamberlain. Churchill's distrust of *The Times* was too deep-dyed to be easily expunged and the wild cheering from the Tory back-benches which met his attack on the newspaper in the Greek debate in the embarrassed presence of the Editor and Chief Proprietor gave some indication of its standing with Britain's natural party of government at large. When the first majority Labour administration succeeded the coalition, *The Times*, despite its newly acquired left-wing reputation, could hardly have expected its influence to grow, but it was an entirely new experience for its editor to find himself summoned to the Foreign Office to be denounced by the new architect of Britain's foreign policy for his newspaper's lack of patriotism. When Ernest Bevin followed this by partially exonerating the Editor himself from this general indictment with the insulting suggestion that Barrington-Ward was not perhaps in full control of the 'pink intelligentsia'[50] at loose on the newspaper, the pattern of the future must have been clear. Whilst *The Times* would retain its capacity for embarrassing British governments as the Cold War unfolded, its influence over the formulation of official policy would be minimal.

NOTES

1. *International Affairs*, XXXVIII (1962), 84-85.
2. M. Gilbert, *The Roots of Appeasement* (1966), 159.
3. According to *The Times*, the rise of Hitler placed Europe in the dilemma of having to yield to extremism what had been denied to moderation. That she must do the right thing, albeit for the wrong reason, and yield, the newspaper had no doubt. See *The Times*, 28 June 1933, 'Germany's Day of Mourning'.
4. A.P. Young (S. Aster, ed.), *The X Documents: The Secret History of Foreign Office Contacts with the German Resistance* (London 1974), 204.
5. W.S. Churchill, *Triumph and Tragedy* (London 1954), 332.
6. *The Times*, 1 April 1939, 'A Stand for Ordered Diplomacy'.
7. Ibid.
8. Quoted in H. Dalton, *The Fateful Years* (London 1957), 239. For the ambassador's own account see E. Raczynski, *In Allied London* (London 1962), 14.
9. House of Lords Debates, 28 October 1939, Vol. 114, cols. 1565-6.
10. *The Times*, 30 March 1943.
11. *The Times*, 28 March 1943, 'Russia and Poland'.

12. *The Times*, 10 March 1943, 'Security in Europe'.
13. *The Times*, 31 August 1944, 'Cross Purposes'.
14. *The Times*, 16 December 1944, 'Frustration'.
15. See the letter to the Editor signed 'Diplomaticus', *The Times*, 12 January 1944.
16. House of Commons Debates, 19 October 1939, Vol. 352 col. 1082.
17. *The Times*, 1 December 1944, 'A Retrograde Step'.
18. *The Times*, 16 December 1944, 'Frustration'.
19. *The Times*, 28 February 1945, 'Yalta and Beyond'.
20. A. Polonsky, *The Great Powers and The Polish Question* (London 1976), 244, footnote 3.
21. *The Times*, 22 June 1945, 'The Trials in Moscow'.
22. *The Times*, 6 July 1945, 'The New Poland'.
23. This phrase was coined by Vansittart to characterize a view of the management of international relations of which he disapproved. See his letter to the Editor, *The Times*, 28 October 1945.
24. For example, Barrington-Ward's old friend, the educationalist Kurt Hahn. See Golo Mann, 'Kurt Hahn's Political Activities' in H. Rohrs (ed.), *Kurt Kahn* (London 1971).
25. *The Times*, 4 November 1943, 'After the Conference'.
26. *The Times*, 23 March 1943, 'Great and Small Nations'.
27. *The Times*, 14 July 1945, 'The Unity of Europe'.
28. *The Times*, 3 January 1945, 'The New Congress'. See also the leader 'The Rule of Law', *The Times*, 12 April 1945.
29. *The Times*, 1 August 1941, 'Peace and Power'.
30. *The Times*, 29 November 1945: 'Conditions of Confidence'.
31. *The Times*, 3 January 1945, 'The New Congress'.
32. *The Times*, 8 October 1945, 'Policy and the Atom'.
33. *The Times*, 9 October 1945, 'Peace and the Atom'.
34. *The Times*, 14 March 1946, 'The Three Powers'.
35. *The Times*, 29 November 1945, 'Conditions of Confidence'.
36. C. Cockburn, *In Time of Trouble* (London 1957), 199.
37. See for example the leader of 7 November 1941, 'Britain and Europe'.
38. D. McLachlan, *In the Chair: Barrington-Ward of The Times* (London 1971), 221.
39. Ibid., 222.
40. This account of the circumstances of Carr's recruitment to the newspaper, which is substantially McLachlan's, was confirmed by Professor Carr in a personal interview with the writer on the 26 March 1980.
41. I. McDonald, *A Man of The Times* (London 1976), 86.
42. Koestler's objections to this kind of reportage were first published contemporaneously in the New York press, but subsequently put out between hard covers. See A. Koestler, 'Soviet Myth and Reality' in his collection *The Yogi and the Commissar* (London 1945).
43. See for example Parker's *Moscow Correspondent* (London 1949).
44. A claim Namier made twice publicly in the presence of the Polish ambassador. Interview with Count Edward Raczynski, 31 March 1980.
45. Sir James Headlam-Morley (A. Headlam-Morley, ed.), *A Memoir of the Paris Peace Conference 1919* (London 1972), 36.

46. L.B. Namier, *Facing East* (London 1947), 96.

47. Namier's views on Poland smack of a geo-political determination and he himself acknowledge one of the few lasting influences of his brief attendance as a student at the LSE to have been the lectures of Halford Mackinder. It is of interest, therefore, to note in passing that Mackinder argued a precisely opposite case to Namier's, i.e. that it was a British interest to preserve a tier of independent states in Eastern Europe free from either Russian or German domination. See H. Mackinder, *Democratic Ideals and Reality* (New York 1941), 154.

48. *The Times Higher Educational Supplement*, 7 July 1978, 'A Profile of E.H. Carr'.

49. N. Barker, *Stanley Morison* (London 1972), 473.

50. McLachlan, *In The Chair*, Appendix 2, 280-81, 'Interview with Ernest Bevin 11.3.1946'.

18 The Harriman-Beaverbrook Mission and the Debate over Unconditional Aid for the Soviet Union, 1941

John Daniel Langer

In the middle of September 1941, three months after German armies invaded the Soviet Union, British and American delegations journeyed to Moscow to promise Stalin a long-range, large-scale aid programme. The principal negotiators — Lord Beaverbrook for Britain and W. Averell Harriman for the United States — spent three days in talks. Then, with Soviet Foreign Commissar Vyacheslav Molotov, they signed the 'First Soviet Supply Protocol.'[1] That document established a uniquely generous unilateral basis for allied aid to Russia. By doing so, it provoked high-level dissent within both the British and American governments. The mission that Harriman and Beaverbrook led touched off a debate over Soviet aid policy that continued for the rest of the war.

The original decisions to assist the Stalin regime preceded Harriman and Beaverbrook's trip to Moscow. In fact, the basic decision preceded even the Nazi invasion of Russia — Operation Barbarossa — without which the question was purely theoretical. On 15 June, the British Prime Minister, Winston Churchill, cabled President Franklin D. Roosevelt that 'should this new war break out, we shall, of course, give all encouragement and any help we can spare to the Russians, following the principle that Hitler is the foe we have to beat.'[2] Churchill had argued as early as May 1939 that an alliance with Russia was a practical necessity. Since then, Germany had conquered most of Europe. The Anglo-Soviet alliance that had, in 1939, offered a means of defending Poland held out, in 1941, a hope of saving Britain itself.[3]

Roosevelt answered Churchill's cable with a presidential promise that the United States '. . . would immediately support publicly "any announcement that the Prime Minister might make welcoming Russia as an ally".'[4] His readiness to follow the British lead may have stemmed, in part, from a disinclination to challenge Churchill's major policy decisions from his side-line position as leader of a neutral country. In addition, that first aid decision offered real advantages to the United States. Roosevelt was under tremendous pressure to authorize increased naval activity in the Atlantic. The navy was already taking measures against German submarines that made a fiction of American neutrality. Any additional step might goad Hitler to respond by declaring war. With Barbarossa, a Russian aid programme rose — temporarily — as an alternative to risking war on the Atlantic. Finally, promises to Russia had a potential restraining influence on Japan that warfare against U-boats could never have matched. Increased activity in the Atlantic might have had just the opposite effect by requiring the transfer of ships away from the Far East.[5]

Neither Churchill nor Roosevelt harboured any fondness for the Soviet regime. The Prime Minister had sought to destroy it at the end of the first world war. The President, after granting American recognition, had watched the Russians renege on the concessions he had exacted in return. More recent events accentuated old grievances. By signing his non-aggression pact with Hitler in August 1939, Stalin had collaborated in the outbreak of the second world war. He had then absorbed various of his small neighbours. When he finally attacked Finland, Britain contemplated war with Russia as well as with Germany. Americans, although unwilling to express their opposition in deeds, condemned Russian aggression with a vehemence and unanimity uncharacteristic for the time. American and British relations with Russia could not have been much worse when Churchill and Roosevelt first decided to send aid. Their willingness to overlook the past testified to their desperation for the future.

In Washington, State Department experts were unable to forget.

Citing past experience with the Moscow regime, they urged the administration to '. . . make no approaches to the Soviet Government', to treat any Soviet approaches 'with reserve', and to '. . . exact a strict quid pro quo for anything which we are willing to give the Soviet Union.'[6] When Operation Barbarossa began, on 22 June, War Department officials joined their colleagues at State in counselling against extensive aid. Experts estimated that the Nazis would crush the Soviets within weeks or months. Aid would be wasted. Instead, they advised Roosevelt to step up the Battle of the Atlantic.[7]

As early as June 1941, then, the contestants in the aid debate had drawn up sides. Politicians adopted a generous policy against the advice of experts — both military and diplomatic. The division reflected the different responsibilities of the men on either side of the issue. The concern of the military was least ambiguous. Professional officers looked to the strength of their own forces as their country's ultimate source of security. With military hardware in short supply, they felt that they deserved an unchallenged first call on the nation's production.[8] Diplomats lacked the same kind of organizational loyalty. Like elected officials, their duty was clearly to serve no interest smaller than that of the nation as a whole. More than politicians, however, they tended to define the national interest narrowly. Their business was that of bargaining; their job, to secure the greatest possible advantage for the lowest possible price. 'Give and take' and 'quid pro quo' were well-worn expressions in the diplomatic vocabulary.

The discourteous and secretive behaviour of the communist regime reinforced the inclinations of both soldiers and diplomats. While Barbarossa forced them into the western camp, the Soviets remained unwilling to confide in their new allies. At a time when other countries had to justify their aid requests with detailed statistics, the Russians refused to share not only economic data but military intelligence which could only have strengthened the common cause.[9]

To their hostile secrecy, the Soviets added what seemed to be a consistent and deliberate rudeness. That habit was Russian rather than Soviet; it had hampered relations between the czars and more 'civilized' governments years before the revolution. Under Stalin, it manifested itself in a multitude of small, studied discourtesies or 'pinpricks'. Visa applications, customs inspections, and even routine maintenance problems became sources of friction which the Kremlin manipulated.[10] When western diplomats complained to

Stalin, the dictator made excuses. He told British Ambassador Stafford Cripps that the cause of the problem lay in '. . . the preoccupation of the Soviet Staff with the actual conduct of the war.'[11] To Cripps' successor, Sir Archibald Clark Kerr, Stalin admitted that '. . . his "people" were rough and rude and unfamiliar with the requirements of collaboration with foreigners and that they had moreover been so strictly schooled and disciplined in secrecy that they found it almost impossible to amend their habits in that respect.'[12]

Although such explanations were not altogether disingenuous, it was impossible to believe that the Soviets were doing their best to cooperate. They refused, for example, to allow allied military attachés to visit the front.[13] Their reason could only have been suspicion or ill will. Men who worked with the Soviets in Moscow had to endure that suspicion or ill will — and the unending frustrations to which it gave rise — every day. Meanwhile, they saw aid negotiators like Harriman and Beaverbrook fly into town for a few days and fly out again with major agreements in their pockets. Almost to a man, they concluded that Stalin was taking advantage of their governments while deliberately abusing their own patience.

As originally conceived, the Harriman-Beaverbrook Mission promised to correct that pattern of Soviet behaviour. The idea came first from the British Ambassador to the Soviet Union, Sir Richard Stafford Cripps. A product of the British labour movement, Cripps had long advocated Anglo-Soviet cooperation.[14] Experience as a diplomat in Russia had not altered his basic views but had convinced him — as it had a generation of professional diplomats — that generosity was no way to win Soviet confidence. Cripps proposed a three-cornered supply conference as a way to force the Soviets to release data that the British and American embassies, acting independently, had been unable to obtain. In a draft cable sent to Stalin, he emphasized the importance of a full exchange of information.[15]

The occasion that prompted Cripps' suggestion was the arrival in Moscow of Roosevelt's friend and adviser Harry Hopkins. A social worker rather than a diplomat, Hopkins had administered the New Deal's relief programmes. In the middle of 1940, he had moved into the White House to function as a presidential assistant. The American aid programmes — first for Britain and then for Russia — quickly fell into his jurisdiction.[16] In July 1941, he flew to the

Soviet Union to convince Stalin '. . . that we mean business on a long-term supply job.'[17]

Never having dealt with the Soviets, Hopkins was not concerned with the problems that plagued day-to-day relations. He was a visiting fireman interested only in getting supplies moving as quickly as possible. That objective made him an improbable confidant for Cripps. Still, the ambassador chose Hopkins to hear his hopes for a supply conference and to receive the cable he drafted for Roosevelt and Churchill's signatures. Any one of several reasons might explain Cripps' choice. First, Hopkins had ready access not only to Roosevelt but to Stalin and Churchill as well. More than any other individual, Hopkins was in a position to discuss the conference with each of the big three and to promote agreement between them. Second, Cripps may have feared that Hopkins was about to give away too much for too little. He may have talked of a future conference in order to dissuade Hopkins from making immediate commitments. Finally, Cripps may have failed to understand Hopkins' position as an advocate of an unconditional policy. Such a misunderstanding would have been impossible later in the war. By his reaction, however, Hopkins demonstrated that the lines were not yet clearly drawn between a generous policy on one hand and a quid pro quo approach on the other.

Sometime after his conversation with Cripps, Hopkins went to the Kremlin to meet Stalin. There, he adopted the supply conference proposal as his own and emphasized those points that Cripps himself held most dear. He told his host that a three-cornered meeting should deal with '. . . the relative strategic interests of each front, as well as the interests of our several countries. . .' The United States would have to have '. . .complete knowledge, not only of the military situation in Russia but of type, number and quality of their military weapons, as well as full knowledge of raw materials and factory capacity.'[18]

Cripps based his proposal on a real willingness to curtail aid if Stalin refused to make minimal sacrifices for it. In making the idea his own, Hopkins may not have shared that willingness. He had good reason to expect the Soviets to agree to his demands: Stalin had abandoned his usual secrecy by treating him to detailed descriptions of the Nazi-Soviet war and he had offered to have his airmen show American experts '. . . everything about the Russian equipment . . .' and had agreed to pool Soviet tank, plane and gun designs. Responding to Hopkins' remarks about a supply conference, Stalin assured his guest that he 'would be glad' to share any information.[19]

With those promises ringing in his ears, Hopkins left Moscow for the first meeting between Roosevelt and Churchill. At the Atlantic Conference, he reported that the Soviet Union was not in the desperate straits that military analysts had predicted.[20] With his optimism, Hopkins confirmed the decision that Roosevelt and Churchill had already made.[21] On 13 August, the President and the Prime Minister telegraphed the conference proposal to Moscow. Stalin immediately welcomed the idea and promised '. . . to take all measures in order that this conference should take place as soon as possible.'[22]

As Hopkins had done, Roosevelt and Churchill made the Cripps proposal their own. If Hopkins may not have shared Cripps' intention, Roosevelt and Churchill certainly did not. They had decided to mount a large Russian aid programme and for neither was that decision contingent upon small signs of Soviet gratitude. The Prime Minister actually instructed his delegation 'not [to] disclose speculative figures of our . . . production when none are given of theirs by the Russians.'[23] Both men picked representatives who were more interested in dispensing supplies than in trading statistics.

To head the British half of the mission, Churchill named his Supply Minister, Lord Beaverbrook. A conservative with little regard for party loyalty, Beaverbrook had often expressed views that his colleagues must have regarded as unduly 'pro-Soviet'.[24] By July 1941, he had already emerged as a champion of aiding the Soviet Union.[25] From the time of his appointment, Beaverbrook set out to arrange in the shortest possible amount of time for the greatest possible amount of aid.

Beaverbrook's logical American counterpart was Harry Hopkins. His poor health, however, ruled out a return to Russia.[26] Instead, Roosevelt chose W. Averell Harriman, the American Lend-Lease Representative in London. Son of railroad tycoon E. H. Harriman, Averell Harriman was a Democrat and an associate of Hopkins from New Deal days. Having directed the British aid programme, he attributed his selection to his familiarity with the supply situation, his working relationship with Beaverbrook, and to the fact that he '. . . clearly understood . . . [Roosevelt's] own objectives.' Actually, his relationship with Hopkins may have outweighed all other considerations. Harriman belonged to the 'Hopkins shop'.[27] By naming him, Roosevelt did as much as he could — short of sending Hopkins himself — to concentrate Russian aid decisions where he and Hopkins could make them.

In his enthusiasm for Russian aid, Beaverbrook quickly encountered opposition within his own government. Most British officials sided with Cripps and insisted that aid should flow to the Soviet Union only after the Soviets had paid for it with adequate concessions. Members of the embassy staff in Moscow actively seconded their chief. The military attaché, Lieutenant General F. N. Mason MacFarlane, advised a fellow officer in London that Beaverbrook should be '. . . very firm about insisting on obtaining maximum information both on Russian production and resources, as also on the Russian General Staff appreciation of the military situation, before they agree to any form of long-term or even short-term supply policy.'[28]

If Cripps and his staff were too far from Whitehall to make themselves heard, they had allies closer to home. Two days before the mission was to leave for the Soviet Union, Churchill called a meeting to hammer out final decisions about how much Beaverbrook could offer the Russians. As talk began, '. . . it was clear that Churchill, Eden and Beaverbrook were the only ones on the positive side for aid.' After the Prime Minister made it clear that '. . . in his view, an offer — a fair offer — of supplies . . . must be forthcoming . . . the battle became one of what, and how much.' It became no less bitter, however, and eventually '. . . the atmosphere of reason and debate seemed to deteriorate.'[29]

The argument failed to sway Beaverbrook. On his way to Moscow he outlined his thinking: 'They were not going to Moscow to bargain but to give. . . The Mission must not only offer supplies. It must offer them in such measure that the Russian leaders would be satisfied and encouraged.'[30] He communicated the same attitude to his staff. On 26 September one member of the mission wrote that 'we are sent to Russia to give the greatest amount of aid which the United Kingdom can offer . . . In a sentance [sic], this is our purpose.'[31]

American officials never debated the purposes of the mission so explicitly. Diplomats in Moscow 'were concerned lest too much be promised with not enough strings attached.'[32] Unlike Cripps, however, the American ambassador refused to make an issue of such views. He certainly shared them. Laurence Steinhardt had taken great pride in initiating a 'tit for tat' policy to combat Soviet pinpricks. By August 1941, however, he hoped for a favourable reassignment. With his diplomatic career depending on the President's regard for him, he maintained a prudent silence on matters of substance.[33]

In Washington, there was no room for debate. Harriman's appointment shut opponents of the President's policy out of any role in the organization of the mission. On 18 August the State Department officer in charge of Russian matters wrote to Steinhardt that he did not know who would represent the United States at the upcoming conference: 'I do not even know as yet what will be the subjects to be discussed.'[34] The mission was a Lend-Lease show. Arrangements for it included a decision by Hopkins that Harriman '. . . be given a designation that will make him senior . . . to the Ambassador to the USSR.'[35] The mission's cables were to go directly to the White House. The delegation included three important Lend-Lease officials (Harriman, General James H. Burns, and Colonel Philip Faymonville) but only one representative from State (Edward Page, Jr., a young career officer with experience in the Soviet Union).[36]

The lengths to which Hopkins was willing to go to exclude other agencies — and his reasons for doing so — became clear in his handling of Faymonville. A Russian expert of long standing, Faymonville had developed a reputation as a Soviet sympathizer that made him unpopular in the War and State Departments but that qualified him, in the eyes of Burns and Hopkins, to handle Russian aid.[37] In organizing the Harriman-Beaverbrook Mission, Hopkins decided to send Faymonville to Moscow with it. He told an assistant that 'Colonel Famonville [sic] will remain in Moscow indefinitely as our representative.'[38] The colonel was so controversial a figure, however, that Hopkins kept that plan secret. Officially, Faymonville went to Moscow as the secretary to the American delegation. Only on 2 October when the mission was about to come home, did Hopkins cable Harriman that 'it is understood that Colonel Faymonville. . . will remain in Russia.'[39] Over loud protests, Faymonville did remain in Russia until late in 1943. He represented the Lend-Lease organization and enforced its policy over the complaints of the American Embassy staff. Admiral William Standley, a member of Harriman's delegation and, shortly thereafter, the American Ambassador to the Soviet Union, called Faymonville's presence in Moscow an 'unfortunate by-product' of the mission.[40] Hopkins undoubtedly viewed it as one of the mission's most important accomplishments.

On policy matters as on organizational ones, the mission followed Lend-Lease and the President. The essential function of the conference, as FDR had Hopkins emphasize to Churchill, was '. . .to communicate to the Russian Government the definite aid to be furnished . . . prior to July 1942.'[41] Obtaining information from the Russians was an afterthought. Harriman, according to one member of the delegation, described the mission's purpose as to 'give and give and give, with no expectation of any return, with no thought of a quid pro quo.'[42]

The mission that arrived in Moscow at the end of September 1941 was not the mission that Stafford Cripps had suggested in July. Neither delegation cared to press the Soviets for information or cooperation. Cripps, however, was unwilling to let his own strategy die quietly. As Beaverbrook reported later, the ambassador 'suggested' that the British delegation insist on a full exchange of information. Over his dissent, 'it was decided . . . that this information could be obtained, if at all, only after long arguments and delays which might have prejudiced the success of the Conference.'[43]

While not in Moscow to bargain, mission members were ready to accept whatever cooperation or information the Soviets provided. Negotiation quickly taught aid officials what diplomats had long known: Stalin's promises notwithstanding, the Soviets made no unnecessary concessions. On his second full day in Moscow, a British delegate complained that '. . . we are up against this wall of secrecy and feel it much. I got evasive replies to my questions . . .'[44] General Burns was equally discouraged:

> Any hope that he had entertained concerning finding out something about the Russians' capacities were soon dashed. Their secrecy went so far that at one point they asked for a certain amount of a highly specialized explosive. Burns asked for details on exactly what type and composition they wanted. They refused to be too specific, he said, because they believed it would reveal details of some of their new shells and cannon![45]

The middle-level members of the British and American missions tasted, for a few days, the frustration that allied diplomats in Moscow endured all the time. Harriman and Beaverbrook did not. Neither one became concerned with the aspects of Soviet behaviour that bothered their subordinates. Like Hopkins before them, they dealt not with tight-lipped bureaucrats but with Joseph Stalin. They worried more about the dictator's current mood than about his government's consistent attitude.[46]

It was Stalin's idea to crown the discussions with a formal protocol. The western delegations had no authority to give written commitments and explained that none had been needed at a comparable stage of previous Anglo-American negotiations. Molotov retorted that 'you didn't have a conference.' 'A conference must terminate with a protocol.' Eager to satisfy their hosts, Harriman and Beaverbrook eventually decided to sign a carefully hedged agreement.[47] By outlining a comprehensive and long-term aid programme, the first Soviet Supply Protocol put Russian aid on a unique footing. No other Lend-Lease recipient enjoyed the benefits of such a consolidated schedule. The First Protocol named seventy things — from 'Aeroplanes' to cocoa beans — that the allies would supply. Nowhere did it broach questions of repayment. Technically, the document did not commit the United States or Britain any more than it committed the Soviet Union. The supplying countries, for example, did not promise to deliver anything to Russia; they would make items available '. . . at British and USA centres of production . . .' and '. . . help with the delivery.' That promise was, itself, firmer for some entries than for others. In response to a request for 300 tons of magnesium alloys per month, the protocol recorded only that 'the quantity of possible deliveries will be cleared up in London and Washington.' The agreement qualified even the specific commitments by remarking that a change in the military situation would force the three countries '. . . to decide what adjustment of the present arrangement is necessary.' As Harriman told Stalin, '. . . the materials listed in the protocol were not a definite commitment but were what we would make every effort to supply.'[48]

In spite of its loopholes, the First Protocol improved relations between the Soviet Union and its new partners. According to Harriman, 'Stalin made no effort to conceal his enthusiasm. It was my impression that he was completely satisfied that Great Britain and America meant business . . .'[49]

At the end of the conference, Stalin held the first of the long, opulent banquets that became a trademark of wartime diplomacy in Moscow.[50] A more important indication of his attitude was his decision, shortly after the conference, to send Maxim Litvinov to Washington to replace Constantine Oumansky as his ambassador.

Litvinov symbolized collective security and Soviet-American friendship. His appointment signalled Stalin's satisfaction as nothing else could have.[51]

Stalin had good reason to be pleased. His optimism about the military situation had impressed his guests. Harriman recalled years later that his '. . . determination and confidence were infectious. When Beaverbrook and I got home, we reported our belief that Russia would hold out.'[52] Stalin may also have guessed that his allies would not construe their obligations under the First Protocol as narrowly as the actual wording of the agreement allowed. In fact, Churchill and Roosevelt both came to regard the document as a binding commitment rather than a statement of intent. On his way to meet Roosevelt in December 1941, the Prime Minister wrote: 'Neither Great Britain nor the United States have any part to play in . . . [the Nazi-Soviet war], except to make sure that we send, without fail and punctually, the supplies we have promised. In this way alone shall we hold our influence over Stalin . . .'[53] Later in the same month, Roosevelt ordered Secretary of War Henry L. Stimson to begin meeting the protocol provisions by 1 January. Any deviation would require the President's personal approval.[54] By that time, the Japanese attack on Pearl Harbor had given the President the kind of military excuse that the protocol explicitly recognized as sufficient to justify a re-evaluation of the entire supply situation. Instead of falling back on that excuse, Roosevelt pushed his subordinates to meet the Russian commitment in spite of their other problems. In March 1942, with American shipments falling substantially behind schedule, he stated his wish '. . . that all material promised under the Protocol be released for shipment at the earliest possible date regardless of the effect of these shipments on any other part of our war program.'[55]

Critics in both the British and American governments knew that the First Protocol was not the binding agreement that Churchill and Roosevelt made it. Citing the tight supply situation and continuing Soviet intransigence, they argued against meeting the schedules. In London, Beaverbrook fought with the service chiefs for strict adherence to the protocol amounts.[56] Dissent reached into the Foreign Office as well. Christopher Warner noted his opinion that '. . . our tactics, in so far as they have been consistent at all, have been wrong . . .' He agreed with a cable from the Moscow embassy that Britain should adopt '. . . a less sentimental approach, a more matter of fact and businesslike one.'[57]

In Washington, Navy Secretary Frank Knox argued against furnishing critical machine tools to Russia because '. . . the United States should require a justification statement describing the proposed uses for the tools . . .' William L. Batt, a supply expert who had served on the Harriman-Beaverbrook Mission, replied that '. . . the Russian Government is not asking for an excessive amount of tools, and. . . it is necessary to relax some refinements of procedure in granting tools to a people actively resisting aggression.' Batt's remarks had little effect. Even in the face of a message from Hopkins saying that prompt shipments were essential and represented presidential policy, Knox persisted in his opposition.[58] Nor was he alone. On 23 February Batt complained about American handling of some Soviet requests. He told the director of Lend-Lease that 'it needs the strongest man you can get in the country. Everyone around here is thumbs down on Russia.'[59]

The agreement Harriman and Beaverbrook signed in Moscow crystallized the aid debate. Prior to the supply conference, critics of the generous policy had had no concrete targets to attack. After it, they had not only the terms of the protocol itself but the increasingly obvious failure of the Soviets to respond to western good will. Lord Alan Brooke, chief of the Imperial General Staff, expressed his impatience '. . . with our attitude of giving *everything* [the] Russians ask and getting *nothing* in return.'[60] In the United States, Stimson noted that 'I am rather discouraged. He [Roosevelt] is entirely in the hands of people who see only their [sic] side of the other nations. . .'[61] Beaverbrook had faced such criticism squarely in his refusal to accept the advice that Cripps pressed on him. The Americans faced it only when the results of the conference gave them no choice. After the Soviets repeatedly refused to honour American requests, Lend-Lease officials adopted the position that the requests were unimportant.

The issue came to a head after the supply conference closed. At the end of October, Hopkins learned '. . . that American technicians who are ready to go to aid in the erection and care of airplanes and tanks are to receive no visas.' He immediately wired his representatives that 'it was understood that technicians would be welcomed when Harriman and I had our talks in Moscow. That these technicians should precede the equipment is believed essential . . . The matter is extremely urgent. . .' Hopkins believed that the difficulty was no more than a simple 'misunderstanding.' Accordingly, he asked Steinhardt to '. . . consult Molotov at once in order to clear it up.'[62] He apparently thought it would be as simple as that.

Two weeks later, on 11 November, the American Red Cross Representative in Moscow relayed another disappointment to Washington. Allen Wardwell, who had spoken for the Red Cross at the supply conference, had asked the Soviets to accept '. . . a continuing mission here with an office so as to keep in constant touch with [the] situation.'[63] Wardwell's deputy now reported the Soviet response:

> . . . it had been decided by the Soviet Government that it was not necessary to have such a delegation. . .
>
> He [Andrei Vyshinski] maintained. . . that no privileges were expected by others making offers of gifts and that the President, when he made a grant from Lend-Lease of one billion dollars, did not insist that privileges of observation and supervision be allowed to special representatives.[64]

Hopkins could no longer attribute Soviet actions to misunderstanding. As he told General Burns: 'it is perfectly clear that the Russians do not want technicians in the Soviet Union.' His reaction was to '. . . hope the Red Cross will not insist on personnel' and to ask Burns to make the State Department understand '. . . that we are not insisting on technicians.' He wanted to avoid '. . . a lot of conversations. . . that will only irritate the Russians over something that is not really important to us.' Thereafter, the Lend-Lease position was unambiguous. On 21 November an aid official cabled Faymonville that, in regard to the technician issue, 'the United States authorities have not the slightest desire to insist on supplying such services.'[65]

Hopkins had not forgotten the problem. Journalist Raymond Clapper made the following notes at a press conference Hopkins held on 18 May 1942: 'have favorable report on Russia. They have fighter planes surpassing anything else. Said, however, we know almost nothing — Russians won't tell anybody anything. Secrecy hangover from revolutionary technic.'[66]

The Lend-Lease organization had decided to deal with Soviet sensibilities by catering to them rather than fighting them. The decision reflected a rethinking of the purpose of Russian aid which had started during the Moscow conference. Gradually, a rationale developed which converted Soviet behaviour from an irrelevance to a positive reason for generosity. Beaverbrook wrote that 'the one way to break down the suspicious attitude which had given rise to

Russian secrecy was to make clear beyond a doubt the British and American intention to satisfy Russian needs to the utmost in their power. . .'[67] Harriman reported that 'I left feeling that . . . if we came through as had been promised. . . the suspicion that has existed between the Soviet Government and our two governments might well be eradicated.'[68] Churchill regarded aid as the only way to '. . . hold our influence over Stalin. . .'.

Churchill and Roosevelt still had immediate reasons to insist on a generous policy. They may have viewed aid as a payment for their inability to meet Stalin's requests for a second front. Until the invasion of Normandy, the Soviets complained that they were bearing the major burden of the fighting. Aid was one thing the West could offer for the other side of the scale. Similarly, they may have hoped that aid would propitiate Stalin enough to keep him from dealing with Hitler. Fears of a separate peace waxed and waned through the war. Aid was a way to stave off that possibility. Only the more long-range problem of overcoming Soviet suspicion, however, could have prompted Roosevelt's order that protocol schedules be met '. . . regardless of the effect . . .on any other part of our war program.' General James Burns expressed the President's thinking in a memorandum for his signature:

> I am convinced that sincere and lasting friendship between the Soviet Union and the United States is of vital importance to victory in this war and to the future peace of the world.
>
> I am also convinced that such friendship can best be achieved by a general policy of generosity. . .[69]

The dispute over Russian aid followed the same course on both sides of the Atlantic. In London, as in Washington, soldiers and diplomats lined up against politicians. Soviet behaviour confirmed each side in its view. Critics of the aid policy felt that the Soviets would never trust a non-communist state. Generosity was wasted. 'Straight oriental bartering or trading methods' might at least win Stalin's respect.[70] To those who favoured the generous approach, Soviet actions taught the opposite lesson. To them, Soviet behaviour proved the importance of achieving close relations before distrust poisoned the peace of the postwar world.

Roosevelt and Churchill made the unilateral aid programme a tool to overcome Soviet distrust and thereby to establish a partnership that would outlast the war. Roosevelt, in particular, believed in that goal so strongly and so consciously that he defended his aid policy against mounting criticism until he died. In his approach to the Soviet Union, he did not, as he has so often been charged, let short-run military considerations dominate long-range political ones. As early as 1941, he had begun to worry about the requirements not only of victory but of peace thereafter.

The advent of the cold war marked the failure of the generous approach. The wartime coalition never developed into anything more than that. At the same time, the course of the cold war showed the wisdom of General Burns' assertion that '. . . sincere and lasting friendship between the Soviet Union and the United States is of vital importance. . . to the future peace of the world.' Given the importance of the goal, it is difficult to fault Churchill or Roosevelt for attempting to achieve it.

NOTES

1. US Department of State, *Soviet Supply Protocols* (Wartime Agreements, Department of State Publication 2759, European Series 22; Washington: United States Government Printing Office, n.d.), 3-12.

2. Winston S. Churchill, *The Second World War*, Vol. III: *The Grand Alliance* (Boston 1950), 369.

3. For Churchill's views, see his *The Second World War*, Vol. I: *The Gathering Storm* (Boston 1948), 362-63, 365, 373-76.

4. Churchill, *Grand Alliance*, 369; John Gilbert Winant, *Letter From Grosvenor Square: An Account of a Stewardship* (Boston 1947), 203.

5. For a similar explanation of Secretary of State Cordell Hull's early support for aiding Russia, see Raymond H. Dawson, *The Decision to Aid Russia, 1941: Foreign Policy and Domestic Politics* (Chapel Hill 1959), 117. See also William L. Langer and S. Everett Gleason, *The World Crisis and American Foreign Policy: The Undeclared War 1940-1941* (New York 1953), 445-46, 451, 459-63; and James MacGregor Burns, *Roosevelt: The Soldier of Freedom* (New York 1970), 89-92, 98-101, 104-06. The respite that FDR achieved was significant. Although American troops occupied Iceland early in July and the navy began to convoy allied shipping there and back, it was not until September, in response to the *Greer* incident, that U.S. destroyers got orders to shoot at German submarines 'on sight'.

6. Departmental memorandum in Hull to Steinhardt, 14 June 1941, *Foreign Relations of the United States: Diplomatic Papers* (cited henceforth 'FRUS'), 1941, Vol. I, 757-58. For discussions of the State Department position, see Dawson, *Decision to Aid Russia,* 115-18; and George C. Herring, Jr., *Aid to Russia 1941-1946: Strategy, Diplomacy, the Origins of the Cold War* (New York 1973),

26-29.

7. For discussions of the War Department position, see Dawson, *Decision to Aid Russia*, 112-15; and Herring, *Aid to Russia*, 13.

8. For the supply situation at that time, see Mark Skinner Watson, *Chief of Staff: Prewar Plans and Preparations* (in *United States Army in World War II: The War Department*; Washington 1950), 299-330. See also the entry for 4 August 1941, Vol. 35, Henry L. Stimson Diary (cited henceforth 'HLS D'), Henry L. Stimson Papers, Manuscript Department, Yale University Library, New Haven, Connecticut (quoted in Herring, *Aid to Russia,* 13).

9. For discussions of the Soviet penchant for secrecy, see Joan Beaumont, 'A Question of Diplomacy: British Military Mission 1941-45', in *RUSI* [Journal of the Royal United Services Institute for Defence Studies], 118:3 (September 1973), 74; and John R. Deane, *The Strange Alliance: The Story of Our Efforts at Wartime Co-operation with Russia* (New York 1947), 48-50. Stimson's reaction was typical: 'they are keeping a veil of secrecy about all of their movements and it is awfully difficult to help people who do that.' Entry for 24 November 1941, Vol. 36, HLS D.

10. The consistency of czarist and Soviet behaviour was the point of the 'plagiarized' cable that George Kennan put together from old dispatches of Neil S. Brown, the American Minister to Russia from 1851 to 1853. See William C. Bullitt to Hull, 4 March 1936, *FRUS, The Soviet Union 1933-1939,* 289-91. For detailed American catalogues of Soviet pinpricks, see *FRUS, Soviet Union,* 837ff; *FRUS,* 1940, III, 244ff; and *FRUS*, 1941, I, 866ff.

11. Cripps memorandum of 20 September 1941, on talk with Stalin of 19 September, document N5585/3/38, Foreign Office General Correspondence, Classification FO 371 (cited henceforth FO 371), Public Record Office. This and subsequent quotations from Public Record Office material are reproduced by permission of Her Majesty's Stationary Office.

12. Standley to Hull, 10 April 1942, relaying Clark Kerr's account of a recent meeting with Stalin, *FRUS*, 1942, III, 437.

13. See entry for 29 July 1941, Vol. 34, HLS D; and William H. Standley and Arthur A. Ageton, *Admiral Ambassador to Russia* (Chicago 1955), 285.

14. Colin Cooke, *The Life of Richard Stafford Cripps* (London 1957).

15. The cable — as sent by Roosevelt and Churchill — is available in *FRUS,* 1941, I, 822-23. For Cripps' authorship, see Robert E. Sherwood, *Roosevelt and Hopkins: An Intimate History (*revised edition; New York 1950), 331. For a later report on Cripps' views as expressed during the conference, see A. J. P. Taylor, *Beaverbrook* (New York 1972), 491.

16. For Hopkins' background and his role in the aid programme, see Sherwood, *Roosevelt and Hopkins,* 38ff, 267-69.

17. Hopkins to Roosevelt, 25 July 1941, printed in Sherwood, *Roosevelt and Hopkins,* 318.

18. Hopkins' remarks to Stalin are from his reports to Roosevelt and are available in Sherwood, *Roosevelt and Hopkins,* 341-42; and in *FRUS,* 1941, I, 812-13.

19. Hopkins' reports to the President in Sherwood, *Roosevelt and Hopkins,* 327-30; for *FRUS*, 1941, I, 802-14.

20. In spite of his trip to Moscow, Hopkins' judgement was in no way expert. Robert Sherwood has argued that he drew his confidence from the nature of Stalin's requests — raw materials that showed the Soviets were planning on a long-term

basis. *Roosevelt and Hopkins*, 344. Hopkins himself told a different story. Asked how he had decided that the Soviets would survive, he replied, 'I had a hunch where I wanted to come out and then I looked around to find some reasons to justify the hunch.' Quoted in Louis W. Koenig, *The Invisible Presidency* (New York 1960), 331-32.

21. The aid question was not a major subject of discussion at Argentia. If Elliott Roosevelt is to be believed, the British provoked some exchanges by arguing that it would be wiser to stockpile material in the United Kingdom than to send it to Russia where the Nazis would capture it. *As He Saw It* (New York i946), 30, 33-34. A more reliable clue to Churchill's position is his claim to have chosen Beaverbrook — before the conference began — '. . . to deal for us with the whole question of American supplies to Russia.' *Grand Alliance,* 430. Beaverbrook was strongly in favour of aid (see note 25 below). Theodore A. Wilson touches briefly on these discussions in his *The First Summit: Roosevelt and Churchill at Placentia Bay 1941* (Boston 1969), 70, 140, 144. His treatment relies heavily on Elliott Roosevelt's account.

22. The official text of the cable appears in Steinhardt to Hull, 18 August 1941. For its delivery, see Steinhardt to Hull, 15 August 1941. *FRUS*, 1941, I, 822-23, 820-21. See also Dawson, *Decision to Aid Russia,* 178-79.

23. 'General Directive by the Prime Minister and Minister of Defence', 22 September 1941, DO (41)12, War Cabinet, Defence Committee (Operations), Classification CAB 69, Public Record Office.

24. Beaverbrook opposed British intervention in the Russian Civil War in 1919, minimized the Zinoviev letter scare in 1924, and advocated an Anglo-Soviet alliance in 1939. Taylor, *Beaverbrook,* xii-xiii.

25. Taylor, *Beaverbrook,* 477-82; Kenneth Young, *Churchill and Beaverbrook: A Study in Friendship and Politics* (London 1966), 199-205.

26. Sherwood, *Roosevelt and Hopkins*, 347-49, 359.

27. Harriman was one of 'Hopkins' tame millionaires.' Sherwood, *Roosevelt and Hopkins,* 111. His own views are from his *America and Russia in a Changing World: A Half Century of Personal Observation* (Garden City 1971), 16; from W. Averell Harriman and Elie Abel, *Special Envoy to Churchill and Stalin 1941-1946* (New York 1975), 76; and from an interview he gave Marvin D. Bernstein on 19 July 1954. Professor Bernstein generously allowed the author to see his notes from that and other interviews.

28. Undated extracts from Mason MacFarlane's letter appear in box 20/4 of the papers of Lord Beaverbrook (cited henceforth 'Bb MSS'), the Beaverbrook Library, 33 St Bride Street, London EC4.

29. Harold Balfour, *Wings Over Westminster* (London 1973), 167. Churchill later wrote that 'the Service departments felt it was like flaying off pieces of their skin' to send equipment to Russia. *Grand Alliance*, 452-53.

30. Beaverbrook quoted in Taylor, *Beaverbrook,* 487 (Taylor's ellipsis).

31. 'Lord Balfour's Moscow Diary 1941', Bb MSS.

32. Charles Thayer memorandum of 29 September 1953, quoted in Harriman and Abel, *Special Envoy*, 85.

33. For Steinhardt's background and views, see Joseph E. O'Connor, 'Laurence A. Steinhardt and American Policy Toward the Soviet Union, 1939-1941' (unpublished Ph.D., University of Virginia 1968). See also his letter to Harriman of 2 December 1941, item 537, Personal Letterbook, box 79, Laurence A. Steinhardt

Papers (cited henceforth 'LAS MSS'), Manuscript Division, Library of Congress. He became Ambassador to Turkey, a very important post at the time.

34. Henderson to Steinhardt, file 'G-I 1941', box 33, LAS MSS.

35. Undated memorandum Burns to Hopkins on the 'Mission to the USSR', file 'Book 4: Harriman-Beaverbrook Mission', box 306, Harry L. Hopkins Papers (cited henceforth 'HLH MSS'), Franklin D. Roosevelt Library, Hyde Park, New York. The British, concerned to have their mission parallel the American one in organization, found that decision 'rather tiresome' and 'entirely contrary to our custom'. See minutes on papers N5109/3084/38 and N5164/3084/38, FO 371.

36. Marvin D. Bernstein and Francis L. Loewenheim, 'Aid to Russia: The First Year' in *American Civil-Military Decisions: A Book of Case Studies* (edited by Harold Stein, University of Alabama Press, 1963), 112. Page was so subordinate a member that he is not listed in secondary accounts. See letters between Hull and Harriman of 9 and 10 September 1941, documents 121.861/21A and /29, Department of State Central Files, Record Group 59 (cited henceforth 'RG 59'), National Archives.

37. For Faymonville's background see Demaree Bess, 'The General Called the Turn' in *Saturday Evening Post*, 215:9 (29 August 1942), 12, 101-02; and Standley and Ageton, *Admiral Ambassador*, 238. For his entry into the Lend-Lease organization, see Bernstein and Loewenheim, 'Aid to Russia', 103.

38. Unsigned memorandum on 'Meeting with Harry Hopkins', 12 September 1941, file 'Hopkins, Harry', box 135, Edward R. Stettinius, Jr. Papers (cited henceforth 'ERS MSS'), Manuscript Department, Alderman Library, University of Virginia, Charlottesville, Virginia. See also Burns' memo to Hopkins cited in note 35 above.

39. Hopkins to Harriman, file 'Harriman (Outgoing Cables, 1941-1942)', box 157, HLH MSS. For the surprise which the permanence of Faymonville's position in Moscow occasioned, see Thurston to Hull, 15 November 1941, 121.861/68, RG 59; and Standley and Ageton, *Admiral Ambassador*, 74-75.

40. For the protests, see Marshall to Hopkins, 10 October 1941, file 'Book 4: Harriman-Beaverbrook Mission', box 306, HLH MSS (part of which is printed in Sherwood, *Roosevelt and Hopkins,* 395); and Standley and Ageton, *Admiral Ambassador,* 237.

41. Hopkins to Churchill, 10 September 1941, item 401/10, 206-08, Records of the Prime Minister's Office: 'Operational Papers', Classification PREM 3, Public Record Office.

42. Harriman quoted in Standley and Ageton, *Admiral Ambassador,* 63. William McChesney Martin and Douglass Brown, both of whom worked in the aid programme at that time, were unable to vouch for the remark's accuracy as a quotation but agreed that it fairly represented the mission's policy. Personal interviews, 21 August and 10 October 1974.

43. See Cripps' memo for Beaverbrook, 27 September 1941, box 20/3, Bb MSS; and Beaverbrook's report, W. P. (41)238, War Cabinet Memoranda, Classification CAB 66, Public Record Office.

44. Entry for 30 September 1941, Balfour Diary, Bb MSS.

45. Marvin D. Bernstein, unpublished notes from interviews with General Burns, July and August 1954.

46. Harriman has recalled making a protest about Soviet treatment of members of

his mission. Still, his own account — with its emphasis on Stalin's on-again-off-again cordiality — tends to confirm this impression. Harriman and Abel, *Special Envoy*, 87-94, 96.

47. Harriman and Abel, *Special Envoy*, 91, 97.

48. Department of State, *Soviet Supply Protocols*, 3-12; Harriman, *America and Russia*, 20.

49. Harriman's report to Roosevelt quoted in Sherwood, *Roosevelt and Hopkins*, 391.

50. For accounts of the banquet, see Harriman and Abel, *Special Envoy*, 98-101; and Standley and Ageton, *Admiral Ambassador*, 72-74.

51. Steinhardt to Hull, 29 October 1941, *FRUS*, 1941, I, 652-53; Cordell Hull, *The Memoirs of Cordell Hull* (2 vols; New York, 1948), II, p. 981.

52. W. Averell Harriman, 'From Stalin to Kosygin: The Myths and Realities' in *Look*, 31:20 (3 October 1967), 56.

53. Churchill, *Grand Alliance*, 646-47.

54. Roosevelt to Stimson, 28 December 1941, *FRUS*, 1941, I, 865.

55. Roosevelt to Donald Nelson, 17 March 1942, file 'Requirements — Russia — First Protocol — January-June 1942,' 135.6, War Production Board Paper, Record Group 179, National Archives. The letter has been widely quoted; see, for example, Herring, *Aid to Russia*, p. 60.

56. Beaverbrook memorandum 'Controversy Over Russia,' 3 March 1942, box 20/2, Bb MSS. A. J. P. Taylor quotes a stronger version in *Beaverbrook*, 493.

57. Warner minute of February 16 on cable Baggallay to Foreign Office, 11 February 1942, N927/5/38, FO 371.

58. Minutes of 26 November and 2 December 1941 in [U.S.] Civilian Production Administration, Bureau of Demobilization, *Minutes of the Supply Priorities and Allocations Board: September 2, 1941, to January 15, 1942* (Historical Reports on War Administration, War Production Board Documentary Publication No. 3; Washington: United States Government Printing Office, 1946), 30-31, 33.

59. Memorandum of phone conversation, file 'Batt, William,' box 124, ERS MSS.

60. Brooke paraphrased by Alexander Cadogan in *The Diaries of Sir Alexander Cadogan, O. M., 1938-1945* (edited by David Dilks; New York, 1972), 446 (italics in original).

61. Entry for 15 October, 1941, vol. 35, HLS D.

62. Hopkins to Faymonville and Steinhardt, 28 October, 1941, file 'Book 4: Harriman-Beaverbrook Mission (folder 1),' box 306, HLH MSS. A rephrased version appears in *FRUS*, 1941, I, 848.

63. Entry for 4 October 1941, Allen Wardwell Diary, Allen Wardwell Papers, Archive of Russian and East European History and Culture, Columbia University, New York. Wardwell was the same Allen Wardwell who served under Raymond Robins in the Red Cross Mission to Russia of 1917-18.

64. Nicholson to Davis, 11 November 1941, file 'Hopkins Memoranda', box 18, Records of the President's Soviet Protocol Committee (cited henceforth 'SPC MSS'), Franklin D. Roosevelt Library.

65. Hopkins to Burns, 14 November 1941, and Spalding to Faymonville, 21 November 1941, file 'Hopkins Memoranda', box 18, SPC MSS.

66. Raymond Clapper notes in file 'Pers Memo May, 1942', box 23, Raymond Clapper Papers, Manuscript Division, Library of Congress.

67. Beaverbrook quoted in Taylor, *Beaverbrook*, 487.

68. Harriman's report to Roosevelt quoted in Sherwood, *Roosevelt and Hopkins*, 391.

69. Unsigned, undated 'Draft For the President's Signature', file 'Book 5: Aid to Russia', box 310, HLH MSS. The hand-written draft is in Burns' writing and was probably written in the summer of 1943. Roosevelt did not sign it.

70. The phrase is Steinhardt's, Steinhardt to Henderson, 20 October 1940, *FRUS*, 1940, III, 408. For almost identical expressions, see Standley to Hull, 10 March 1943, *FRUS*, 1943, III, 510; and John R. Dean to George C. Marshall, 2 December 1944, file 'Russia', box 5, President's Secretarial File, Franklin D. Roosevelt Library.

19 In Search of Yugoslavia: Anglo-American Policy and Policy-making 1943-45

Hugh De Santis

Before the winter of 1942-43, when the allies focused their attention and energies on repelling the German offensives in North Africa and Russia, neither the United States nor Britain exhibited much interest in Yugoslavia. Intelligence reports, of course, had kept both Washington and London informed of the activities of the Četniks, the resistance movement that had formed following Germany's invasion of Yugoslavia in April 1941. Četnik leader Dragoljub (Draza) Mihailović, a Serb, colonel in the Yugoslav army, and later minister of war in the exiled Yugoslav government in London, had established contact with British officials in Cairo during the summer of 1941. Messages from the Special Operations Executive in Cairo, the supersecret intelligence service created in July 1940 to stimulate resistance to the Axis, suggested that Mihailović was not vigorously attacking the enemy. Neither at this time nor, for that matter, later on did SOE perceive that Mihailović's inactivity stemmed in part from his fear of provoking further German reprisals against the Serbs. In any event, preoccupied with the North African campaign, and influenced by the presence of the exiled Yugoslav government, officials in London screened out information that conflicted with their policy of support for Miahilović and continued to supply the Četniks with arms.[1]

At this stage of the war, Yugoslav affairs received scant attention from officials in Washington. In the first place, the Balkans did not figure prominently in American military planning. Furthermore, the United States had never developed any significant interests in the region. More importantly, American policy-makers across the broad political-military spectrum were wedded to the belief that the

Author's note. The views expressed in this article do not necessarily reflect the policies of the State Department.

tenets of the Atlantic Charter enunciated by President Roosevelt in 1941 heralded the millenium of a new world order. Optimistic expectations of a post-war world based on the principles of political self-determination, free trade, and the lawful resolution of international disputes pervaded the State Department. The élite corps of professionals General William Donovan recruited into the Office of Strategic Services, the American intelligence counterpart to SOE set up in June 1942, shared the State Department's commitment to the Atlantic Charter ideals. Having recognized the Yugoslav government-in-exile, the United States duly extended moral — but not material — support to Mihailović. For the most part, however, policy-makers in Washington viewed developments in Yugoslavia with apollonian detachment.[2]

Neither Washington nor London had any idea of Josip (Broz) Tito's existence before 1943, and only fragmentary knowledge of the resistance movement he had created. Called to arms by Moscow after the German attack on the Soviet Union, the Partisans had successfully incited anti-Nazi uprisings in Serbia, Montenegro, Bosnia, and Herzegovina. Unlike the Germans, who early on learned of Tito's identity and who sought to suppress the Partisan movement, the British and Americans tended to attribute all guerilla activity in Yugoslavia to the Četniks. In January 1943, W. J. Gallman, the American minister to the Yugoslav government in London, identified the Partisans, 'who have come into prominence in the last six months', as leaderless guerilla bands operating in Croatia and along the Dalmatian Coast. Having learned from the British that they were also attacking the Četniks, he concluded that the Partisans, 70 per cent of whom he believed to be communists, were acting with encouragement from Moscow.[3]

By the winter of 1942-43, the tide of battle in Europe had changed. The Anglo-American invasion of North Africa urged by Prime Minister Churchill turned back the German thrust into the eastern Mediterranean and paved the way for the allied landings in Italy. The Herculean Soviet defence of Stalingrad, the effects of a bitter Russian winter, and the Red Army's surprise counter-offensive produced equally gratifying results in the east. As the military situation improved, the British began to pay closer attention to Yugoslav affairs. On 25 December 1942, Colonel S. W. Bailey parachuted into Yugoslavia to confer with Mihailović. A former mining engineer in Yugoslavia, Bailey joined the congeries of bankers, businessmen, journalists, engineers, and armed forces volunteers who comprised SOE. Like his colleagues, he tended to be pro-Serb and anti-communist. Although Bailey did not have a high personal regard for Mihailović, he sympathized with the Četnik leader's predicament in fighting a guerilla war without adequate military support from Britain. No friend of the Partisan cause, Bailey did not contribute to the speculation voiced earlier in the year by some SOE officers over the issue of alleged Četnik collaboration with the Italians.[4]

Meanwhile, in London, tensions were building between the Foreign Office and the exiled Yugoslav government. Foreign Minister Anthony Eden, George W. Rendel, the British Ambassador to Yugoslavia, and others in the Foreign Office had grown weary of the incessant quarrelling among Yusoglav leaders and, a fortiori, of their inability to define any war aims. The British found the Yugoslavs 'rude, arrogant and absolutely uncooperative'. The Yugoslavs reciprocated this disaffection. The government of Slobodan Jovanović complained to the Americans about London's insensitivity to its plight, which irritated the British all the more. At this point, however, the British were not prepared to disavow Mihailović or his resistance movement simply because they held Yugoslav politicians in low esteem.[5]

Constantin Fotić, the Pan-Serb Yugoslav ambassador to the United States, provided the State Department with a steady stream of commentary on the exiled government's problems in London. For their part, American officials did not have to contend with the unremitting squabbles that exasperated the British. They were concerned, however, about the increasing friction between Yugoslav-Americans of Serbian and Croatian descent created by the stories of Ustaši (Axis supporters in Croatia) atrocities in Serbian-American newspapers and by articles suggesting that the Partisans, and not the Četniks, were assuming the burden of fighting the Axis. The State Department found Serbian and Croatian propaganda harmful to the war effort and potentially damaging to American national unity. Cavendish Cannon, the Balkan desk officer, observed that one third of the American public was composed of first- or second-generation foreign stock, which made it dangerously susceptible to foreign propaganda. Officials in the department also suspected that the Partisans were receiving material assistance from the Soviets (though, much to their chagrin, the Partisans were not). No less anti-communist than their British counterparts, career diplomats strongly encouraged military aid to Mihailović, in which effort they were buttressed by Fotić. 'Then there would be point in saying with emphasis to the USSR', noted Cannon, 'that we want one war, not two, in Serbia, and Mihailović is its leader.'[6]

Beginning in February 1943, when Churchill visited Cairo and met with SOE officials, British policy toward Yugoslavia entered the first phase of a metamorphosis that would culminate a year later in Tito's replacement of Mihailović as the beneficiary of British political and military assistance. During this phase, which extended through May, British policy-makers, while continuing to support the Četniks, decided to establish a separate mission with the Partisans. This policy shift entailed considerable deliberation and reflected the lack of consensus that existed in London in support of the pro-Mihailović policy.

The SOE personnel with whom Churchill conferred in Cairo advised him to continue backing Mihailović, but to extend assistance to the Partisans as well. In their judgement, this would serve to unify all resistance elements on behalf of the military effort, which was still the primary consideration, and guard against the possibility of a serious rift between the British and the Soviets over their support of rival factions within Yugoslavia. Believing that a communist-controlled Yugoslavia would almost surely evolve if the British, through their own inactivity, drove the Partisans into Russian arms, the Foreign Office cautiously advocated the same approach. The Foreign Office's decision was facilitated by its general disrespect for the exiled Yugoslav government and by Mihailović's intemperate accusation that King Peter and Prime Minister Jovanović were virtual prisoners of the British. Moreover, Mihailović's statement that the Partisans, Croatians, and Ustaši were his real enemies made it difficult for Eden to justify to the British public the wisdom of backing the Četniks. Almost fanatically anti-communist, SOE-London, which competed with the Foreign Office for primacy in the foreign-affairs establishment, argued that British aid to the Partisans would result in precisely the situation that Eden wished to avoid. The resulting bureaucratic friction between SOE and the Foreign Office, both of which withheld information from one another, hardly contributed to a cohesive policy. To complicate matters further, British military leaders contended that political considerations should not be permitted to impinge on the prosecution of the war. They therefore recommended exclusive support for Mihailović.[7]

Confronted with this mélange of multiple advocacy, Churchill was of two minds. On the one hand, his doubts about Mihailović's military effectiveness intensified following the Četnik leader's vituperative outbrusts in February. On the other hand, just as Roosevelt had little faith in the State Department, Churchill had no great confidence in the Foreign Office. But in the end, partly because he liked and respected Eden, and partly because a paralysis of policy would have been most disadvantageous at a time when plans for the invasion of Italy were moving forward, Churchill sided with the Foreign Office. Thus in May, Captain F. W. Deakin of the SOE, along with a staff of military and intelligence officers, departed from Cairo to join Partisan forces in Yugoslavia. Fundamentally, however, Churchill's decision to render aid to all resistance elements had more to do with his ad hoc style of policy-making. 'Psychologically, British foreign policy tends to be based on practical politics rather than logic', he had stated at the end of 1942, 'on trial and error rather than systematic planning.'[8]

The American Embassy in London informed Washington of British plans to establish contact with the Partisans at the end of February. Anthony Drexel Biddle, the new American ambassador to the exiled government, pointed out in March that British actions aimed to impress on Yugoslav political leaders, now bitterly divided between those who favoured a federated Yugoslavia (such as the Under-Secretary for Foreign Affairs Ilija Jukić) and the Pan-Serbs (such as Justice Minister Milan Gavrilović), the importance of subordinating their differences to the cause of national unity. However, reports from Yugoslav expatriates transmitted by the American diplomatic mission in Istanbul suggested that the Partisans aimed to impose communism on the country. Incoming OSS cable traffic added more themes to this communications pastiche. OSS commands in London and Ankara attributed London's decision to assist the Partisans to the propaganda of the Free Yugoslav radio station, the effect of Russian military power on British thinking, and Soviet pressure in London.[9]

Though suspicious of Anglo-Soviet intrigues in the Balkans, and concerned about the potential repercussions of the Četnik-Partisan controversy on Serbian- and Croatian-Americans, State Department and OSS officials in Washington preferred to avoid entanglement in Yugoslav internal affairs. Influenced in part by Fotić's impassioned representations to Roosevelt in May, they reaffirmed their support for Mihailović and the Yugoslav government, even if its leaders were 'low-grade politicians'. Much more significantly, Washington policy-makers had formed a broad consensus in support of the Atlantic Charter ideals. Seduced by the vision of a peaceful, prosperous, and secure future world, they were predisposed to compartmentalize political divisions in Yugoslavia as temporary aberrations that would be reconciled by the allies at the end of the war. Even as the OSS, with the president's approval, decided in May to send liaison officers to the Četniks and the Partisans, Washington remained committed to the Yugoslav government, pending its legitimation by the popular will, and to Mihailović. Furthermore, so long as policy-makers perceived the Soviets to be faithful comrades-in-arms, reports of Moscow's putative aid to the communists in Yugoslavia, while not ignored, had little effect on America's globalistic policy of principle.[10]

The second and crucial phase of the British initiative in Yugoslavia extended from May to the Cairo and Teheran conferences in November. Deakin's reports had convinced SOE-Cairo and the British military that the Partisans were shouldering the brunt of the fighting in Yugoslavia. Deakin also gave substance to the rumours of Četnik-Axis collaboration, which had a profound effect on British policy-makers in London, particularly since SOE officers attached to Mihailović's forces had reported that the Četniks were not actively engaging the enemy. Significantly, British intelligence failed to notice that the Partisans had also made contact with the Germans and Italians.[11]

Meanwhile, in London, Serb-Croatian dissension within the Yugoslav government, catalyzed by King Peter's untimely announcement of his impending marriage, led to the fall of the Jovanović government and the elevation of Misa Trifunović as prime minister. This arrangement proved to be no more enduring. In August Peter replaced Trifunović with a government headed by Dr Božidar Purić. But despite these recurrent cabinet crises, which further alienated the Foreign Office, and the analyses from Yugoslavia and SOE-Cairo, the Foreign Office and SOE-London doubted the political wisdom of redirecting British support to the communist-led Partisans, as the military had recommended. Confronted with mutually irreconcilable policy alternatives from officials in the field and in London, Churchill settled for the time being on the compromise position of providing assistance to both guerilla movements.[12]

With the fall of Mussolini in July and the approaching surrender of Italy, developments in Yugoslavia assumed increasing importance to Churchill. As he would later do at Cairo and Teheran, the prime minister pressed Roosevelt at the first Quebec Conference in August to accept a British offensive in the Balkans in tandem with the allied cross-channel invasion of northern France. Although strategic objectives were prominent in Churchill's thinking, Washington's 'atavistic suspicions' of British political objectives in the Balkans, as recent studies have termed them, were not baseless. Churchill's fundamental objective in the Balkans was to maintain political control in Greece, which would safeguard British security in the eastern Mediterranean and, in turn, preserve its strategic interests in the Middle East. Because he admired Greek resistance in 1941, because of his commitment to monarchical principles, and probably for personal reasons as well, the prime minister also wanted to restore King George II to the throne. If the Soviets, who were marching toward the Balkans, became the dominant influence in Yugoslavia, the British position in Greece and the eastern Mediterranean would be jeopardized. Considering the evidence attesting to Mihailović's military ineffectiveness and the seemingly irremediable divisions within the Yugoslav government, it was inevitable that Churchill would turn his attention to Tito. Before setting on a course of action, however, he decided to send a personal emissary to the Partisans, 'a man of daring character, with Parliamentary status and Foreign Office training', to make a final assessment of the situation.[13]

It is arguable that Churchill had made his decision to back the Partisans before Brigadier Fitzroy Maclean parachuted into Yugoslavia; for in September, the same month Maclean arrived at Tito's headquarters, King Peter and the Purić government took up residence in Cairo. Ostensibly, this move, which London welcomed with alacrity, facilitated the eventual return of the government to Yugoslavia. But its probable underlying intent was to remove the major political obstacle to Churchill's support of the Partisans. In any event, Maclean's analysis of Yugoslav internal affairs, which arrived in London in November, removed whatever doubts, if any, that might have existed in Churchill's mind. The Partisans were not only the dominant military force everywhere in Yugoslavia save Old Serbia, Maclean reported, they had also established an effective political organization. Bent on exterminating the Četniks, they had thus far reserved judgement on the status of the monarchy. To be sure, they were overwhelmingly communist in their political outlook, Maclean went on to say, and they would likely retain ties with Moscow after the war. Continued British backing of Mihailović, he added, would only prolong the civil war in Yugoslavia, which, in any case, would be decided in favour of the Partisans. Ralph Stevenson, the new British Ambassador to the Yugoslav government in Cairo, reinforced Maclean's assessment on purely military grounds. 'The Partisans will be the rulers of Yugoslavia', he wired the Foreign Office. 'They are of such value to us militarily that we must back them to the full, subordinating political considerations to military. It is extremely doubtful', he concluded, 'whether we can any longer regard the Monarchy as a unifying element in Yugoslavia.'[14]

Washington stayed abreast of developments in British-Yugoslav relations through OSS channels in Cairo. Idealistic, committed to the Atlantic Charter, and influenced by their more experienced British cousins, OSS officers defended London's decision to back Tito. Their cables stressed the Partisans' military contribution to the common cause and London's concerns about Anglo-Russian competition in the Balkans. They portrayed the Yugoslav government as reactionary, 'a clique of discredited politicians associated with previous dictatorial and Pan Serb regimes'. In the most dramatic of the OSS analyses, written at about the same time as Maclean's report, Major Linn Farish extolled the military and political accomplishments of Tito's forces, belittled the inactivity of the Četniks, and urged the despatch of military supplies to the Partisans. Almost certainly influenced by Maclean, Farish extended warm appreciation to the brigadier and his staff for their assistance and courtesy. Farish's fellow officers, impressed by the Red Army's military effort, dismissed Soviet ideological expansion in the Balkans. Even if Stalin were so inclined to foment revolution, one report stated, he would not risk alienating the allies and reducing to hypocrisy his commitment to the Atlantic Charter principles.[15]

American diplomats in Istanbul, however, held the view that Britain's growing preference for Tito reflected its desire to keep pace with Soviet machinations in the Balkans. London recognized that it 'cannot impose its will on Moscow as regards the Balkan situation' by supporting Mihailović 'because Tito is supported by the

Soviets'. Indeed, Serbian refugees told Burton Berry, head of the US mission, and his staff that the Partisans planned to liquidate Serbian business, professional and political leaders and to impose communism on the country. Still, American diplomats noted that Tito appeared to enjoy the support of Serbian refugees in Egypt. Moreover, they had thus far seen no evidence of Soviet expansionism. Consequently, they were inclined to overlook much of this internal unrest as traditional Balkan divisiveness.[16]

The contradictory messages from the field left policy-makers in Washington with two impressions: that Britain and the USSR were planning to divide Europe into spheres of influence and that the Soviets were intent on communizing Yugoslavia. Some officials in the State Department favoured an Anglo-American invasion of the Balkans to ensure, by dint of American military presence, that the Atlantic Charter principles would not succumb to power politics. But Secretary of War Henry Stimson and the Joint Chiefs of Staff vetoed this idea as strategically impracticable. Furthermore, Roosevelt did not believe that Stalin desired to exert control over the Balkans, and it was his voice that carried at the first Quebec Conference, where he and a reluctant Churchill agreed only to supply guerilla forces with military equipment and to engage in minor bombing and commando raids. The State Department's preferred alternative was to form a league of Eastern European states and to work toward a federalized Yugoslavia along the lines of the Serb-Croatian political accommodation, or *Sporazum*, of 1939. Despite their concern about Soviet ideological aims in Yugoslavia, officials at the State Department did not recommend any change in Washington's policy in the Balkans. The cost entailed in adopting either a policy of ideological confrontation or spheres of influence — the dissolution of the globally idealistic policy of principle — was simply too high a price to pay.[17]

American policy received reinforcement at the Moscow and Teheran conferences in October and November, when the Soviet Union announced its commitment to the formation of the United Nations. Influenced by Major Farish's report, Roosevelt did advocate aid to the Partisans at the Teheran Conference, but without removing Washington's political recognition of the Yugoslav government. Churchill's plan to invade the Balkans never materialized. Economically debilitated by four years of war, and increasingly dependent upon United States manpower and matériel, Britain's power to influence wartime strategy had run its course. By the end of 1943, the idea of equal partnership in Anglo-

American relations had given way to American pre-eminence. As the conversations at Teheran made clear, the 'Roosevelt-Stalin axis' had become the core of the grand alliance.[18]

Churchill was acutely sensitive to his country's diminished stature. For this reason, British policy toward Yugoslavia in the final phase of its transformation, and in the disillusionment that followed, demonstrated an impulsiveness that reflected the prime minister's desperate attempt to secure Britain's position in the Balkans. By the end of 1943, Tito had demanded recognition of the provisional government (AVNOJ) that the Partisans had established in November at Jajce. Having learned from Maclean, whose personal entrée into the prime minister's office had virtually eroded SOE-London's policy-making role, that Tito would never accept the return of King Peter as long as Mihailović remained part of the cabinet, Churchill directed the Foreign Office early in 1944 to request the King to dismiss the Četnik leader. But Eden questioned the prime minister's decision. For one thing, he feared an adverse public reaction if the case for Mihailović's perfidy could not be unequivocally made. For another, he was not convinced that Tito enjoyed popular support throughout Yugoslavia. The British diplomatic mission in Cairo voiced even stronger objections. Ambassador Stevenson contended that the Partisan movement was clearly revolutionary and that Churchill's proposed action would simply 'increase Tito's arrogance'. General Sir Henry Maitland Wilson, Supreme Allied Commander in the Mediterranean, argued that the Četniks had not demonstrated a complete lack of military value. His view was shared by Colonel Bailey of SOE-Cairo, who further defended Mihailović against his detractors' charges of trafficking with the Axis. At least, Stevenson recommended, Mihailović should be permitted to retain his position as a guerilla leader. But since the prime minister had concluded that political and diplomatic objectives in the Balkans outweighed purely strategic considerations, he screened out these conflicting messages. Now personally committed to the Partisans, he took matters into his own hands.[19]

On 22 February 1944, Churchill expressed regret before the House of Commons that some of Mihailović's commanders had collaborated with the enemy. However, 'a new and far more formidable champion' had appeared, he stated, one who had been fighting the Axis since 1941 and who had amassed a force of more than 250,000 men. Tito was 'an outstanding leader', in Churchill's words, 'gloriously fighting for freedom.' Now Britain had to extend its efforts to help Tito 'and his gallant band'. The following day a Russian military mission led by Lieutenant-General N.V. Korneyev arrived in Yugoslavia. Since they had not brought any military supplies, Maclean suspected that their real purpose was to expand Moscow's political influence. The foreboding perception of Soviet control of Yugoslavia hastened the prime minister's decision. Although he continued to state publicly that Britain could not 'obtrude its ideas' on the King, Churchill was privately determined to separate Peter from 'his present fatal millstone advisers'.[20]

In March, Eden and Ambassador Stevenson independently requested King Peter to reform his government without Mihailović. By now the Foreign Office had come to terms with the new course Churchill was resolutely charting. A policy memorandum prepared in April concluded that Britain's abdication of its responsibilities in the Balkans would be detrimental to Anglo-Soviet relations. Moreover, unrest in the Balkans could spread to adjacent areas in the Middle East 'which are of vital importance to the British Empire because of our lines of communication through the Mediterranean and Red Sea and to the oil supplies in Iraq and Persia'. On 17 May the King dismissed Purić and his cabinet and announced the formation of a new government led by Dr Ivan Šubašić, the governor of Croatia. While these developments were taking place in London, Yugoslav Communist party theoretician Milovan Djilas met with Stalin in Moscow. The Soviet leader urged the Partisans to compromise their differences with the new government. In June, Tito stated his willingness to work with Šubašić in forming a government of national unity. Despite the absence of material aid from the Russians, the Yugoslav communists remained ardent adherents of Marxist-Leninist orthodoxy, more so even than the Soviets themselves.[21]

Although Churchill's role in the policy process dramatically altered the course of London's relations with Yugoslavia, British policy was fundamentally episodic. In April, at the same time that the prime minister was eulogizing Tito and exerting pressure on King Peter to reform the Yugoslav government, he took steps to prop up the monarchy in Greece — and thus to stifle communist influence — by ordering the British military to suppress the mutinous Greek armed forces in the Middle East. But in Churchill's mind, the ad hoc character of his policies was a virtue. As he told the House of Commons in May: 'In one place we support a king, in another a Communist — there is no attempt by us to enforce particular ideologies.' In both countries, however, Churchill was hedging his bets. To ensure British influence in Greece and Yugoslavia, the prime minister was already formulating a plan to divide the Balkans — much as the British and Russians might have done in the nineteenth century — into spheres of influence. Late in May and again in June he solicited Roosevelt's approval to make overtures to the Soviets concerning wartime responsibilities in the region.[22]

Partly because the messages transmitted to Washington from the field contained conflicting information on the situation in Yugoslavia, through the first half of 1944 American policy-makers preferred to remain spectators before this unfolding Balkan drama. At first, OSS officials in Cairo accepted SOE-Cairo's view that Tito had not indoctrinated the rank and file of the Partisans with communist ideology and that the Partisan movement was more a Yugoslav rather than a communist phenomenon. Their early telegrams urged American support of Tito to avoid the impression that Washington backed the 'reactionary, anti-democratic' forces of Mihailović. Since the Partisan movement represented 'the wave of the future in southeastern Europe', one despatch stated, 'we should consider whether our Allies should ride the crest and relegate to us the trough or whether we by our own absence of alertness should find ourselves there in the eyes of the Balkan people themselves, who are still exceedingly well disposed toward our country.' But by June the tenor of OSS cables had changed. In contrast to his strong endorsement of the Partisans at the end of 1943, Farish now concluded that Tito, like Mihailović, had concentrated his military resources on winning the political struggle within Yugoslavia. Influenced by the views of Yugoslav military officials and businessmen, American diplomats in Istanbul tended to portray Mihailović, rather than Tito, as the commanding political figure in Yugoslavia.[23]

As far as policy-makers in Washington were concerned, Churchill hoped to achieve 'by flattery' what he perceived the Russians to have accomplished by indoctrination. But despite Moscow's political and moral support of the Partisans, a State Department memo pointed out, the Soviets had maintained formally correct relations with the exiled government and left it to the Yugoslav people to work out their own political destiny. As career diplomat Harold Shantz wired from Cairo in July, 'It should be within the realm of possibility to have Balkan governments friendly to all powers'. Carried away by the success of the Normandy invasion and by the Red Army's progress in the east, American policy-makers believed that the Soviets would remain faithful to the liberal-democratic world order enunciated in the Atlantic Charter principles. Furthermore, policy planners in Washington felt that neither the Četniks nor the Partisans could claim to be representative of Yugoslav opinion. They therefore recommended continued recognition of King Peter and the exiled government and proposed that 'enlightened attention' be given to the Sporazum of 1939 as a political model for post-war Yugoslavia.[24]

A second reason for Washington's guarded reaction was its growing apprehension of an Anglo-Soviet condominium in the Balkans. Early in 1944 the American Embassy in London had informed the State Department that Churchill's decision to back the Partisans presaged the emergence of historical Anglo-Russian rivalry in the region. By spring, Washington's concerns of a great power confrontation in the Balkans had given way to the equally alarming prospect of an Anglo-Soviet agreement to divide the region into spheres of influence. An OSS cable from Cairo pointed out in June that the most important objective of the British was to secure their position in post-war Greece and the eastern Mediterranean. Secretary of State Cordell Hull told Roosevelt that Churchill's proposal to divide wartime responsibilities in the Balkans departed from the principle adopted by the allies at the Moscow Conference in repudiation of spheres of influence. State Department officials further feared that it might set a dangerous precedent that could impoverish American plans for a general security system in the United Nations. To entangle the United States in the Yugoslav internal struggle for political supremacy or to acquiesce in a great power division of influence in the Balkans would ultimately vitiate reconstruction of the post-war world on the basis of the Atlantic Charter principles.[25]

In mid-June, while the foreign-affairs establishment in Washington reaffirmed the policy of principle in Yugoslavia, Roosevelt secretly agreed to Churchill's proposal to discuss wartime arrangements in the Balkans with the Soviets. Although he espoused the ideals of the Atlantic Charter, Roosevelt was not adverse to realpolitik. Quite the contrary, the post-war security system he envisioned, as symbolized by his concept of the 'Four Policemen', rested on the assumption that the allies would maintain order in their respective spheres of influence. Given the paucity of American interests in the Balkans and Eastern Europe, Roosevelt accepted the pre-eminence of Britain and the Soviet Union there. But in order to mobilize American support for the war effort, he never publicly revealed his realpolitik strategy. Nor did he disclose his aims to officials in the foreign-policy establishment, who logically argued the incompatibility of balance-of-power politics and the Atlantic Charter principles. Indeed, Roosevelt reinforced their view by reminding Churchill that American acceptance of Anglo-Soviet wartime arrangements in the Balkans did not imply support for post-war spheres of influence. The effect of the president's silence was to perpetuate a dual policy of realpolitik and principle. According to Roosevelt's timetable, resolution of this dichotomy would await allied discussions at the end of the war.[26]

In the meantime, however, Churchill conjured up visions of a post-war communist government in Yugoslavia. Tito helped to magnify the prime minister's apprehensions by cleverly fending off Britain's overtures to make peace with King Peter and to incorporate the Partisan national committee into the new Šubašić government. In June and again in July, Tito reneged on his agreement to meet with Šubašić in Italy. Clearly annoyed by the lack of pay-off for his Yugoslav policy, Churchill flew to Italy in August to discuss matters with Tito. Once again, Tito evaded a decision on the King. However, not wishing to jeopardize continued British support, he assured the prime minister that he had no intention of creating a communist state. For the moment, Tito had mollified Churchill.[27]

But Churchill's suspicions revived soon thereafter. In mid-September Tito secretly visited Moscow to meet — for the first time — with Stalin. Conversations between the two were cool, particularly on the subject of King Peter, whom Stalin, intent on maintaining good relations with Britain and the United States, advised Tito to reinstate. Churchill learned of Tito's journey to Moscow in October during the course of his own private talks with Stalin. Having vainly appealed to Roosevelt at the second Quebec Conference to launch an invasion of the Balkans, and been equally unsuccessful in his efforts to gain Tito's adherence to a united Yugoslav government, Churchill travelled to Moscow in a last-ditch attempt to recoup his political and military investment in Yugoslavia. News of the Partisan leader's unannounced trip infuriated the prime minister. Aside from Tito's discourtesy, Churchill felt that the Yugoslav had opportunistically flaunted the support the Partisans had received from London. Stalin sympathized with the prime minister's anger and his desire to establish a Yugoslav government of national unity. Indeed, two days earlier he had accepted Churchill's invitation to divide military responsibilities in Yugoslavia on a fifty-fifty basis. Neither Churchill nor Stalin misunderstood the implicit political ramifications of the percentage deal.[28]

On 1 November Tito and Šubašić reached agreement on a unified Yugoslav government to be composed of twelve members from AVNOJ and six from the royal government. They further agreed to form a three-member council of regents which would represent the exiled King in Yugoslavia. While formalization of the concept awaited Peter's approval, the Tito-Šubašić agreement brought to an end the British initiative. Unhappy with the disproportionate influence the merger accorded Tito, the prime minister and the Foreign Office accepted the outcome with a sense of resignation. In November Churchill put pressure on Peter to sign the agreement. But the King understandably balked at accepting a regency, which 'would practically amount to abdication'. Frustrated by the King's attitude, Churchill openly expressed his mistrust of Tito. 'He is nothing but a Communist thug', the prime minister stated, 'but he is in power and we must reckon with that fact.' When King Peter implied that the British were responsible for his predicament, Churchill rejoined, 'Would you have been better off if you had followed Mihailović?'[29]

Although Roosevelt reacted impassively to the Anglo-Soviet agreement to divide responsibilities in the Balkans, the State Department viewed Churchill's and Tito's manoeuvring suspiciously. Throughout the summer of 1944, department officials in Washington and diplomats in the field anticipated with considerable apprehension that Britain's action would indirectly commit the United States to a spheres agreement in derogation of the principle of political self-determination. As Lincoln Macveagh, the ambassador in Greece, observed, British policies were anachronistic: 'perfect for the eighteenth century, impossible for the twentieth'. In the State Department's view, the British 'would seem to be overestimating their strength when they believe that they can prevent Russia from establishing [a zone of influence] in the Balkans'.[30]

The department's misgivings about Tito's objectives mounted during the waning months of 1944. Certainly Fotić, who remained in Washington even after being relieved of his duties by the Šubašić government, made every effort to impress upon the department the gross injustice of Britain's support for the Partisans. Yugoslav officials in London and the King reiterated this point. In November Bogoljub Jeftić, the Yugoslav ambassador in London, explained to Hamilton Fish Armstrong, the editor of *Foreign Affairs* and a former member of the US Advisory Committee on Postwar Foreign Policy, that Churchill and his emissaries in Yugoslavia were completely ignorant of Yugoslav affairs. Fearful of Soviet influence in the Balkans, the British had naively played into Tito's hands without recognizing that the majority of Serbs remained loyal to Mihailović and most Croatians preferred Vlatko Maček, head of the Croatian Peasant party. While Churchill and the Foreign Office were now disillusioned about Tito, Jeftić added, they seemed resigned to perpetuate their policy and the present civil war. King Peter similarly told Armstrong that the Tito-Šubašić agreement did not represent the sentiment of the Yugoslav people. In his view, Šubašić had simply acquiesced in a government that favoured Tito. Like Jeftić, he urged the United States to 'show an interest in the final settlement in an area where wars have often begun, including two wars which brought American soldiers overseas and left thousands of them buried there'.[31]

OSS officials in the field shared the department's concerns. To be sure, the reports of Major Charles Thayer, who had formed a close relationship with Maclean, took a decidedly pro-Tito cast. Without minimizing Tito's 'fervent devotion' to Moscow, Thayer averred that the Partisans dominated Yugoslav political life and that popular support for the King was negligible. Nevertheless, he did not believe that Tito's assumption of power necessarily meant that 'he intends to govern entirely without reference to the desires of the people of Yugoslavia'. Other OSS officials in the field, however, gave credence to the views of Yugoslav informants who cynically scorned Britain's policy of trying to co-opt Tito as a fiasco and who suggested that the Yugoslav people would ultimately rise up and defeat the Partisans and their communist programme. Lieutenant-Colonel Robert McDowell, an army intelligence officer who served with the OSS between April and November in Mihailović's area of operations, reported that the peasantry revered Mihailović. Thayer's colleagues in Cairo also expressed pessimism about the viability of democratic government in Yugoslavia. They contended that Tito, who '[did] not appear to be a stooge for Stalin or anybody else', was nonetheless determined to be the sole ruler of the country. In their opinion, free elections would only take place under allied supervision.[32]

American diplomats in Caserta and Cairo attacked the injudiciousness of British policy in the Balkans. Writing from Cairo in November, Emil Kekich noted that political analysts of Yugoslavia on both sides of the Atlantic had commented 'that the British either have no policy at this late date toward Yugoslavia . . . or that the policy incomprehensively contains little of substance beyond temporary expediency of doubtful value'. He pointed out that the British strategy of limiting Russian influence in the Balkans had acquired 'a halo of practicality' in its assumption that Russia's wounds of war would militate against her playing the game of power politics. Kekich foresaw the likelihood of a joint Anglo-American initiative in Yugoslavia which would have been unnecessary, in his view, had London demonstrated more self-confidence in its relations with Tito and Moscow. As for Tito, American diplomats now perceived him to be an agent of Moscow. Alexander Kirk observed from Caserta that Tito would avail himself of every opportunity 'to enhance the prestige of the Soviet Union', adding that 'we should not close our eyes to the potentialities of a revolutionary and authoritarian regime' led by 'an able and ambitious leader who had shown a not inconsiderable capacity for cynicism and international blackmail'. Impervious to the rule of law in the lives of men and nations, the 'very asceticism' of the Partisans 'can make these men dangerous'. Believing that the United States faced a fait accompli 'of serious potentialities for both good and evil', he recommended that Washington 'hold the Yugoslav rulers to the spirit of the democratic principles they so glibly voice'.[33]

In contrast to the policy divisions between the field and London in 1943, the information provided by American intelligence and diplomatic officers abroad intensified Washington's suspicions of the Partisans and reinforced the globalistic policy of principle. Consequently, policy-makers in Washington ignored those messages that advocated support for Tito and gave hope of a democratic Yugoslavia. Furthermore, the analyses from Cairo and Caserta coincided with the assessments of diplomatic and military personnel who witnessed developments elsewhere in the Balkans.

By the end of 1944, American officials in Sofia and Bucharest similarly expressed concern that Soviet-influenced elements threatened to subvert the Atlantic Charter principles. 'As matters go [in Bulgaria]', warned Maynard Barnes, chief of US diplomatic mission in Sofia, 'certainly will they go in Yugoslavia.'[34]

Having served as midwife to the provisional government Tito and Šubašić agreed to form, Churchill understandably requested Washington's recognition of it, especially after Peter, under Churchill's threat of expulsion from Britain, had signed the agreement late in January 1945. But Britain's political initiative met the same unreceptive response from the United States as had its proposed landing in the Balkans. Preferring to let the Yugoslavs work out their own form of government in accord with the principle of self-determination, Washington withheld recognition until the viability of the new coalition could be determined. The Southern European division of the State Department pointed out that only half of the country was under allied control. A second reason adduced in support of the decision was Washington's mistrust of Tito. Cyril Black, a Yugoslav expert in the department, pointed out that Tito sought to preserve Yugoslav independence through a regional protective political-security system. A promise of security from Moscow and minimal political and economic rights would be far more attractive to Tito than Britain's 'hypothetical "Europe" of small, independent states', which reflected London's antiquarian attachment to its pre-Munich policy and its 'deep-seated inability to understand a foreign point of view'. In a memorandum to the president, Charles S. Cheston, acting director of the OSS, noted that Tito's willingness to work with Šubašić was purely a tactical manoeuvre to gain allied recognition. In his view, Tito was neither likely to modify his objectives in exchange for recognition nor incapable of militarily suppressing internal opposition to his rule. Finally, officials in Washington concluded that Britain's request for recognition was 'in large part a design to prepare a facade of "Allied" action' to conceal its political manoeuvring with Moscow to carve up south-eastern Europe. The American government, therefore, refused 'either to exert pressure on the King to "play his part" or to declare in advance that we will make no reservations in our recognition of the new regime in Yugoslavia'.[35]

At the Yalta Conference, Washington's policy of principle, as opposed to the power-political policy Roosevelt carried in his head and artfully concealed from view, received added sustenance from the pious-sounding 'declaration on liberated Europe'. This declaration, a compressed version of the Atlantic Charter principles, became the post-Yalta symbol of America's globalistic policy and the political yardstick against which developments in Yugoslavia (and elsewhere in Eastern Europe) were to be measured. One will never know how US-Soviet and, therefore, US-Yugoslav relations would have evolved had Roosevelt lived. Clearly, however, the policy of principle could not survive compatibly with Moscow's objective of politically dominating that part of post-war Europe which fell under Soviet military control. The Soviet-engineered coup in Romania in March, a harbinger of what was to come elsewhere in Eastern Europe, provided early evidence that the American initiative to gain Stalin's adherence to the Yalta declaration had little chance of succeeding.

The deterioration of US-Soviet relations after Yalta gradually altered Washington's perceptions of Moscow's post-war aims and transformed the American initiative into the policy of ideological confrontation. As developments abroad diminished the intrinsic value of the policy of principle, hence policy-makers' commitment to it, officials in Washington began to pay closer attention to incoming traffic from the field. Unschooled in foreign affairs and totally unaware of Roosevelt's attachment to balance-of-power politics, President Harry Truman placed especial importance on the analyses of American diplomats in Eastern Europe and the Balkans. Exposed to the daily acts of political reprisal by the Partisans and the more insidious intimidation and outright terrorism of the secret police, officials in the Belgrade Embassy held out little hope for the future of democracy in Yugoslavia.

For a time, officials in Washington tried to compartmentalize the information from Yugoslavia, which contradicted the policy of principle. Colonel Franklin Lindsay, who had replaced Thayer in Yugoslavia, returned to Washington convinced that the Tito régime had become entrenched through the ruthless suppression of all democratic opposition. Still, like the State Department, he nurtured the hope that the Yugoslav people would ultimately bring about a democratic form of government. The November elections laid these ebbing hopes to rest. While American officials in Belgrade and Washington could not conclude, as had the British, that the elections revealed Tito's popular support, neither could they perceive any value in adhering any longer to the policy of principle. The policy of confrontation toward Yugoslavia that emerged in Washington during the winter of 1945-46 — and toward the whole of Eastern Europe — provided a new cognitive structure that gave meaning to the unsettling developments policy-makers confronted. Significantly, however, the policy of confrontation was just as globalistic as its idealistic antithesis. Consequently, the reality of developments in a specific country — such as the nationalistic imperative of Tito's communism — tended to be ignored or denied to preserve the intrinsic value of the new policy. Since Washington believed that Tito was a Soviet puppet, a perception that the traffic from the American Embassy in Belgrade strongly underscored, the United States similarly adopted this policy in its relations with Yugoslavia.[36]

The British, for their part, having no more cards to play in Yugoslavia, resigned themselves to the inevitability of Tito's domination. Churchill had played the game of political brinkmanship with Tito and he had lost. As he told King Peter, he regretted the situation in Yugoslavia, but he was powerless to alter the course of events. Convinced, following the Romanian coup, that the Soviets 'had become a mortal danger to the free world', he, along with the Foreign Office, supported Washington's confrontationist policy toward Moscow. Apprehensive of Tito's 'aggressive pretentions against Italy', which London, like Washington, attributed to Soviet instigation, he joined ranks with the Americans in May to force Tito's withdrawal of Yugoslav troops from Venezia-Giulia.[37]

During 1946 Britain and the United States found themselves joining together in a common ideological cause that mirrored the remarkably close military association they had formed at the start of the war. In a way, the war they had fought to defeat the disrupters of world order had not ceased; only now it would be fought — in Yugoslavia, as elsewhere — with ideas rather than arms. In March, ironically only three days after Washington had, *faute de mieux*, recognized the Yugoslav government, Churchill, now a private citizen, publicly endorsed the emerging US policy of confrontation by calling attention to the 'iron curtain' that had fallen across Eastern Europe and the Balkans. Although this policy would not be formally enunciated until the following year, at this juncture Washington had already written off Eastern Europe.

NOTES

An earlier version of this article was presented at a symposium of American and Yugoslav historians in Plitvice Lake, Yugoslavia, 3-7 August 1980.

I am grateful to Michael Doyle, Paul Costolanski, A.W. DePorte, and Dušan Biber for their critical comments on the original manuscript.

1. Walter Roberts, *Tito, Mihailović and the Allies, 1941-1945* (New Brunswick, NJ, 1973), 28, 70; Milovan Djilas, *Wartime* (New York 1977), 94; Mark C. Wheeler, *Britain and the War for Yugoslavia, 1940-1943* (New York 1980), 65.

2. See Hugh De Santis, *The Diplomacy of Silence* (Chicago 1980), ch. 4; also see R. Harris Smith, *OSS* (Berkeley 1972), ch. 1.

3. Vladimir Dedijer, *Tito Speaks* (London 1953), 147; Gallman to secretary, 5 January 1943, 860h.00/1435, National Archives, Record Group 59 (hereafter NA, RG59). Milovan Djilas has stated that the Yugoslav communists would have begun to resist without Moscow's directive. See *Wartime*, 4-5.

4. G.H. Seton-Watson, 'Afterword: Thirty Years After' in Phyllis Auty and Richard Clogg (eds.), *British Policy Towards Wartime Resistance in Yugoslavia and Greece* (London 1975), 284-86; Sir Ernest Llewellyn Woodward (ed.), *British Foreign Policy in the Second World War*, Vol. III, (London 1971), 289; Roberts, op. cit., 89, 120.

5. OSS report 27302, 20 January 1943, National Archives, Record Group 226 (hereafter NA, RG226). See Wheeler, op. cit., ch. IV.

6. Cannon memo to Atherton, 7 May 1942, 800h.00B/72½; Cannon memo to Dunn and Atherton, 25 June 1942, 800h.00/1402½; Cannon memo to Dunn and Atherton, 6 August 1942, 800h.00/1408, NA, RG59.

7. Woodward, op. cit., 289-90; Elizabeth Barker, 'Some Factors in British Decision-Making over Yugoslavia, 1941-4', in Auty and Clogg, op. cit., 22-23; Djilas, op. cit., 229-30; Matthews to secretary, 23 March 1943, 760h.61/63, NA, RG59.

8. Barker, op. cit., 21; Churchill Mansion House speech, 10 November 1942, Box 2, H. Freeman Matthews-John D. Hickerson Files, NA, RG59.

9. Matthews to secretary, 24 February 1943, 860h.61/63; Biddle to secretary, 30 March 1943, 860h.01/458; and Berry to secretary, 26 May 1943, 860h.00/1497, NA, RG59; OSS reports 35419 and 33004, dated 26 February and 25 March 1943, respectively, NA, RG226; OSS bulletin 16, 16 April 1943, Box 72, Map Room Files, Franklin D. Roosevelt Library, Hyde Park, NY (hereafter FDR Library).

10. Welles memo of conversation with Fotić, 29 April 1943, 860h.01/484, NA, RG59; Political Subcommittee of the Advisory Committee on Postwar Foreign Policy, P minutes 206, 12 February 1943, Subcommittee on Security and Technical Problems, ST minutes, 7, 3 February 1943, P minutes 54, 1 May 1943, and T minutes 44, 19 March 1943, boxes 55, 57, 59 and 79, Harley Notter Files, NA, RG59; Cannon memorandum, 24 March 1943, Box 31, Records of the European Advisory Commission, NA, RG43; OSS report 33004, 27 March 1943, NA. RG226.

11. Roberts, op. cit., 118-23; Djilas, op. cit., ch. 3.

12. Roberts, op. cit., 119.

13. John Ehrman, *Grand Strategy* (London 1956), 112; F.W. Deakin, 'The Myth of an Allied Landing in the Balkans during the Second World War (with particular reference to Yugoslavia)', in Auty and Clogg, op. cit., 114; Seton-Watson, op. cit., 293; see also John O. Iatrides, *Revolt in Athens* (Princeton 1972); Winston Churchill, *Closing the Ring* (Boston 1951), 465.

14. Winant to secretary, 29 July 1943, 860h.01/503, NA, RG59; Woodward, op. cit., 296-99; Churchill, op. cit., 468.

15. R&A report 1563, 26 November 1943, NA, RG59; *U.S. Department of State, The Conferences at Cairo and Teheran*, 606-15; OSS report 959, 19 June 1943, NA, RG59; see Smith, op. cit., 28-35.

16. Fraleigh to Berry in Berry to Cannon, 22 November 1943, 741.60h/24; Berry to secretary, 20 August 1943, and 16 September 1943, 874.00/764 and 874.0111/397, NA, RG59.

17. Interview with Foy Kohler, 13 September 1976, Coral Gables, Fla., see H-Policy Summaries, H-95 and H-99, 12 November 1943, Box 153, Notter Files.

18. Christopher Thorne, *Allies of a Kind* (London 1978), 273-84.

19. Roberts, op. cit., 189-90, 194-95, 200-01; Stevenson to Foreign Office in MacVeagh to secretary, 12 December 1943, 860h.01/636; MacVeagh to secretary, 31 December 1943, 860h.01/603, NA, RG59.

20. OSS Report 63271, 22 February 1944, NA, RG 226; Churchill, op. cit., 476.

21. Foreign Office memo, 'British Interests in South-East Europe', 17 April 1944, Box 14, Matthews-Hickerson Files, NA, RG59; Milovan Djilas, *Conversations with Stalin* (New York 1962), 74.

22. Iatrides, op. cit., 34-55; C.M. Woodhouse, 'Summer 1943: the Critical Months', in Auty and Clogg, op. cit., 117-18; Herbert Feis, *Churchill-Roosevelt-Stalin* (Princeton 1967), 338-43.

23. OSS bulletins 82, 92, and 99, dated 3 December 1943, 21 December 1943, and 29 January 1944, May Room Files, Box 73, FDR Library; OSS report 52519, 4 January 1944, NA, RG226; Berry to secretary, 9 March 1944, 860h.01/798, 5 April 1944, 868.01/818 and 17 July 1944, 860h.00/7-1744, NA, RG59.

24. State Department memorandum, 19 March 1944, 740.0011 Stettinius Mission/37944; Shantz speech on US policy in the Balkans, 29 July 1944, 870.01AMG/8-144; Cannon memorandum, 19 May 1944, 711.60h/33, NA, RG59.

25. Norden to Dunn and Matthews, 19 January 1944, 860h.01/1-1944, NA, RG59; OSS report 81864, 23 June 1944, NA, RG226; Matthews to secretary, 29 May 1944, 870.01/5, NA, RG59; unsigned memo, 'American Policy Toward Spheres of Influence', May 1944, Box 17, Matthews-Hickerson Files, NA, RG59; Matthews to Stettinius and Kohler to Cannon, 6 June 1944; Cannon draft memo for Roosevelt, 12 June 1944; and Cannon to Kohler, 14 June 1944, 870.00/48. NA, RG59.

26. See De Santis, op. cit.

27. Dedijer, op. cit., 227-29.

28. Ibid., 234; Anthony Eden, *The Reckoning* (London 1965), 542-47; Churchill, *Triumph and Tragedy* (Boston 1953), 230-34.

29. Woodward, op. cit., 357; Donovan to secretary, 21 November 1944, 860h.01/11-2144, NA, RG59.

30. Iatrides, op. cit., 125; Cyril Black to Cannon and Hohenthal, 16 September 1944, 860h.01/9-1644; Cannon to Henry Labouisse, 20 September 1944, 840.50UNRRA/9-2044; Cannon draft memo to secretary, 18 August 1944, 860h.01/8-1844; and Hohenthal to Cannon, 27 November 1944, 860h.24/11-2744, NA, RG59.

31. Armstrong memos of conversations with Jeftić, 10 November 1944, and King Peter, 2 December 1944, Box 16, Records of the European Advisory Commission, NA, RG43.

32. Thayer to Col. Ellery Hungtington, Jr., transmitted by Carmel Offie, 13 November 1944, 860h.01/11-1344; OSS reports 107407, 109576, 116126, and 109475, dated 6 December 1944, 27 December 1944, 7 February 1945, and 29 December 1944, NA, RG226; Kirk to secretary, 5 November 1944, 860h.01/11-544, NA, RG59.

33. Kekich to secretary, 27 November 1944, 741.60h/11-2744; Kirk to secretary, 29 November and 9 December 1944, and to Dunn, 11 December 1944, 860h.01/11-2944, 860h.01/12-944, and 860h.01/12-1144, NA, RG59.

34. Barnes to secretary, 1 December 1944, 871.01/12-144, NA, RG59; see Hugh De Santis, 'Conflicting Images of the USSR: American Career Diplomats and the Balkans, 1944-1946', in *Political Science Quarterly*, 94 (Fall 1979), 475-94.

35. Woodward, op. cit., 363; Black to Cannon and Hohenthal, 16 September 1944, 860h.01/9-1644, NA, RG59; Cheston to Roosevelt, 31 January 1945, Map Room Files, Box 73, FDR Library; Cannon to Hickerson, Dunn, and Grew, 27 January 1945, 860h.01/1-2745, NA, RG59.

36. Lindsay memo to Cannon, 24 September 1945, Box 14, Matthews-Hickerson Files, NA, RG59.

37. Woodward, op. cit., 382; Eden, op. cit., 605; Churchill, *Triumph and Tragedy*, 457.

VII

The Last Phase

During the last two years of the war, Nazi leaders constantly hinted at horrible retaliation that would be visited on Britain in response to the air raids on German cities. This was a major theme in Nazi propaganda, but it proved to be less than successful. Many Germans doubted the capacity of their leaders to retaliate in the first place, others expressed the belief that retaliation would come too late to have much effect. Thus, as Gerald Kirwin shows, when the bombing of London was resumed by means of missiles, the propagandistic effect was both shallow and of short duration.

The idea of dismembering Germany was first mooted by President Roosevelt at the time of the Tehran conference. Stalin supported the idea for a while, whereas the British, as emerges from Frank King's essay, showed no enthusiasm at all. Subsequently, the Soviet Union withdrew its support and came out in favour of four-power control. In Washington President Roosevelt was supported only by Harry Hopkins and Sumner Welles; the other policy-makers doubted the wisdom and feasibility of his concept.

20 Waiting for Retaliation – A Study in Nazi Propaganda Behaviour and German Civilian Morale

Gerald Kirwin

In the second half of the second world war the promise of retaliation (*Vergeltung*) against the United Kingdom was a theme of increasing importance in Nazi domestic propaganda. The military setbacks following Stalingrad were accompanied by a sharp increase in the intensity of Allied bombing of Germany. The raids themselves constituted the most immediate and visible proof of enemy superiority and of the fact that the tide had turned. Virtually all attempts by Nazi propagandists to offset the negative effects of this development — its stress on the high losses in enemy aircraft, the increase in German armament production, the promise to rebuild the devastated cities after 'final victory', the strengthening of the 'defence will' of the German people — failed miserably. What is more, since May 1941 the air war had become a very one-sided affair and the Luftwaffe, tied up in Russia, was unable to launch more than the occasional light raid on British targets. Unable to conceal this inability to strike immediate hard blows at the enemy, all the Nazi leadership could do was promise all-out retaliation at some time in the future. It was encouraged in its hopes by the development of new and revolutionary long-distance missiles at Peenemunde and supposed that these would be ready for employment by the end of 1943. But the success of the promise of *Vergeltung* ultimately depended on its realization. The German people, however, had to wait until June 1944 until words were backed up by action, and it is this long waiting period which is the subject of this study of Nazi propaganda behaviour and German civilian morale.

Although predictions of retaliation had been made throughout 1942, care was taken not to give any clues as to the date operations would begin. In a speech in October 1942 Goebbels informed his listeners that the defeat of the Soviet Union was the necessary precondition[1] and this was repeated by Göring on 30 January 1943.[2] Retaliation was, however, at this time to be understood as the resumption of conventional raiding in the style of the 1940-41 blitz. In the spring of 1943, the word *Vergeltung* took on a clearly different meaning. It now came to stand for something vague and indeterminate, but nevertheless terrible and decisive in its effect. Soon its very mention sufficed to conjure up mystical and even apocalyptic visions of the future. These very hazy qualities were to enable the building-up of such fantastic hopes in the months to come, that the point was soon reached when it was regarded as the very guarantee of final victory.

As the British stepped up their blitz on Germany in the spring and early summer of 1943, retaliation was increasingly viewed by the German masses as a question of utmost urgency. Even if the Nazi propagandists at times would have preferred to remain quiet, they were forced by circumstances they could not control to take up the theme time and time again. The promise of *Vergeltung* now became an essential component of Goebbels' propaganda repertoire. At times it must have appeared the only theme left fit to still the growing anxieties of the German people. German propagandists must certainly at first have found it the easiest theme to use, since, by directing popular attention to a future time, it did not require any immediate basis of fact. As early as April 1943 Goebbels assured his readers in *Das Reich*:

> By day and night we are working on the possibility of repaying the British terrorists in kind. We are certainly not looking on at the British air war with folded arms.[3]

In a speech in the Berlin Sportpalast two months later, the minister assured his audience: 'One day the hour of retribution will come'.[4] The earlier condition concerning the prior defeat of the Soviet Union was quietly abandoned, presumably because the prospects of its fulfilment would not seem good enough to the population dispirited by Stalingrad and the general news from the Eastern Front.

It would certainly seem that during the spring of 1943 promises of retaliation did much to assuage the widespread anxiety and bitterness of the inhabitants of raided towns. Above all, they considered an all-out counter-blow to be the most effective way of putting a stop to the enemy attacks.[5] They were encouraged in their hopes by the many rumours circulating, according to which new revolutionary weapons including rockets, were being tested at Peenemunde.[6] But many drew the wrong conclusions from these official forecasts and thought that the blow was imminent. When it turned out that this was far from being the case, disappointment set in. All further promises made by the leadership managed only to irritate rather than encourage the downcast population.

At the end of May, the SD was already reporting the first doubts.[7] Although most people continued to believe the blow would fall later that year,[8] the constant repitition of a promise that had not as yet borne fruit became a source of great annoyance.

> All the talk about the coming retaliation is slowly becoming superfluous. The time has now come for action. This opinion is to be found among all parts of the population.[9]

At the end of June the Weimar SD reported: 'One no longer wishes to hear anything concerning *Vergeltung* from Dr. Goebbels.'[10] Sarcastic comments were heard in south-west Germany to the effect: 'We cannot prevent the enemy from continuing his destructive attacks with fair words and empty threats.'[11] Nevertheless, despite growing impatience and nagging doubts, by the early summer of 1943 the promise of retaliation had become the most important favourable factor determining morale. Its rising significance was, without doubt, tied to the negative turn in Germany's military fortune.

> In regard to this question, the conviction is very often being expressed that, whereas there is no chance of developments in eastern and southern Europe ending successfully, only the destruction of the aircraft-carrier England can bring about a final decision in our favour.[12]

The German people was said to be divided in its opinion of *Vergeltung*. Whilst a minority was reported as doubting whether the Reich was at all capable of launching a massive attack, the majority was apparently convinced that it would come by the beginning of autumn at the latest. The constant repetition of the same promise, although irritating and tiresome, led many to draw the conclusion that the leadership could in no case afford to run the risk of destroying its own credibility by making false predictions. All sorts of fantastic rumours were spreading across the land at lightning speed. There was talk of large guns capable of bombarding the British Isles, of missiles, rockets and even atom bombs. Many people allowed their fantasies to run wild and even thought that the blow could easily be followed up by a military invasion which, in turn, would mean 'the early defeat of England'.[13]

Such high hopes, accompanied by burning emotion, would inevitably prove a great problem once it was realized that the attack was not imminent. This was indeed to be the case. The emotional cry for revenge increased with the surge in the intensity of Allied bombing. *Vergeltung* was rapidly becoming a question of individual survival. More and more it was regarded as the one effective way of putting a stop to the enemy raids.[14] As German towns continued to be pounded without the announcement so many Germans were yearning for, doubt and scepticism grew still further. The fear was uttered that, by the time the blow fell, all the most important German towns would be razed to the ground.[15] SD Schwerin reported the growing belief that, if retaliation did not start before August or September, it would be quite superfluous, for by that time 'the English will have decisively paralysed our armaments industry'.[16] After the heavy attacks on Hamburg at the end of July, the fact that *Vergeltung* had not been mounted was reported to be 'making many despondent despite all good will, as well as shaking their faith in final victory'.[17] The utmost importance that had come to be attached to retaliation by the summer of 1943 was expressed in the extremely dangerous view that an immediate blow was now the only means left of winning the war. Without it the war was utterly lost.[18] Even the frank reporting of enemy bombing at this time only served to support this attitude by making the heart-felt cry for retribution even more voluble.[19]

By July, the propaganda leadership had come to realize that it would have to go cautiously. *Vergeltung* had become such a burning issue that a serious 'boomerang effect' was to be expected if policy did not radically change. A Nazi Party report had already warned at the beginning of the month that, unless retaliation came that year, 'trust in the leadership will reach zero point'.[20] This view was underlined in an SD report from Schwerin at about the same time. The leaders would lose all credibility if operations did not begin soon.[21] As the propagandists themselves had learned that operations could not begin for some considerable time, they now opted for a policy of cautious reserve. Although not wishing to relinquish the theme entirely, they certainly wished to avoid giving the impression that the blow was imminent and that *Vergeltung* itself was the only means left of winning the war. Far from improving morale, constant repetition would, in the long run, succeed only in doing irreparable harm by arousing hopes that could never be fulfilled, thereby undermining the bond between the leaders and the governed. On 6 July the retaliation theme became the prerogative of members of the government. The press was forbidden to discuss it unless it was mentioned in speeches of ministers.[22]

Of course, it was too much to expect that such great hopes could be simply damped by a change in propaganda policy. The seed once sown would continue to grow. This was recognized in a party directive of 1 July. It was admitted that people were becoming 'impatient' and that they wished to know when retaliation would begin. Party speakers were instructed to give the following answer:

> Do you want a big or a small retaliation? If you think a revenge blow, which would merely aim now at paying back the enemy for what he has done to us, is enough, then the weapons at present available would be sufficient for this purpose. If you want a revenge which overshadows all that we are now having to go through and which would really constitute the punishment the enemy has rightly deserved for his vile attacks, and if you want a revenge that is truly fantastic, then you will still have to wait.[23]

This cautious line was to continue throughout the weeks that followed. Although the policy of almost complete silence had in the meantime been somewhat relaxed, party representatives were reminded in September:

> It is wrong to name a date for the *Vergeltung*. There must be no unnecessary talk about details, extent and form of retaliation. It must be clearly pointed out to the population that it should avoid any unnecessary gossip about this or that retaliation measure, as well as any unnecessary gossip about new weapons etc., so that the enemy is not wantonly provided with valuable clues. The *Volksgenosse* must be content with the knowledge that retaliation will come.[24]

As if in urgent need of an ersatz theme, the Nazi propagandists returned to an old stand-by, the Luftwaffe raids on Great Britain. The German newspapers were told to pay more attention to these 'conventional' attacks on 18 August, 'since the impression ought not to be created that absolutely nothing was happening against England'.[25] This was none too easy a task because, in fact, very little indeed was happening in the skies of England at this time. Throughout the whole of 1943 the German Luftwaffe dropped a mere 2,240 tons of bombs on the British Isles, whilst the RAF and USAF dropped over 200,000 tons on the Reich.[26] Nazi propagandists were careful, however, not to portray these pinprick raids as 'retaliation', as directives issued to the press at the beginning of the year show.[27] They did not wish to arouse new hopes which would inevitably backfire on them once the German population realized that the attacks were of no more than nuisance value. But this did not rule out the fullest possible exploitation of Luftwaffe achievements. The British authorities were even accused of trying to disguise the damage and losses inflicted.

> They would very much like to depict the situation as if they sky were merely reserved for the British and Americans and as if both had only to drop sufficient bombs at random in order to overwhelm Europe. The drone of German engines over British ports and factories does not harmonise with this tune at all.[28]

Although such reports had appeared intermittently since the beginning of 1943, they were to become more frequent that summer when the retaliation theme was being played down. The essentially manipulative purpose of these accounts had been detected by American propaganda analysts during a short lull in the RAF bombing offensive at the beginning of June:

> An empty sky over Germany delivers German propagandists from their irksome efforts to blow up feeble counter-raids against Great Britain. The immediate drop in attention paid to retaliatory raids proves better than anything else the propagandistic nature of previous raids and raid accounts.[29]

As Allied planes returned in force and as the *Vergeltung* theme became inopportune, the hard-tried German civilians were once again reminded of this 'forgotten' theatre of war.

The response to these blown-up reports was not always a very positive one. Most Germans appear to have recognized them for what they were and to have reacted with impatient irritation.[30] The cautious wording, in particular, was a source of aggravation, as a report from Schwerin shows: 'Many speak of the frequent accounts of attacks on selected targets in the Greater London area in the OKW-Report only with bitterness.'[31] It was thus clear that this type of propaganda would always remain a very poor second-best and would never succeed in diverting attention from that which had come to be the very embodiment of such deeply felt hopes and emotions — the 'retaliation'.

Throughout the dark summer of 1943 doubts about *Vergeltung* grew. The propaganda reticence did not go unnoticed. But the morale picture, and with it the attitude to retaliation, seemed to undergo a radical change with Hitler's radio address at the beginning of September. At one stroke, lurking doubts gave way to a new-found confidence. It should, however, be added that the new trust in *Vergeltung* cannot be seen apart from the overall more positive view of developments that accompanied news of successful German counter-measures in Italy. In exploiting this 'proof' of Germany's might, Hitler managed to create a mood of virtual exhilaration which, however, soon abated and gave way to a more realistic appraisal of the situation. (In fact, the RAF attack on Peenemunde on 17 August had put paid to all chances of an early start to *Vergeltung* operations.) Many ascribed great importance to the fact that it was Hitler himself who promised retribution: 'People believe these words of the Führer unconditionally because they consider it quite impossible that in this darkest hour of the war the Führer would feed them with cheap hopes.'[32] Many let their imaginations run wild and conjured up visions of England being destroyed within a space of a few hours.[33] It is interesting to note the persuasive power Hitler still possessed at this later stage of the war. The effect, however, proved to be only temporary and after a few days a decline in belief in *Vergeltung* was once again registered.[34] This phenomenon was to be observed again after the Führer's next address in November. Not only were all doubts reported as having suddenly disappeared, but many people were said to be believing — naturally quite wrongly — that the attack was imminent.[35] According to the SD: 'One promise from the mouth of the Führer weighs heavier than all the declarations made in the press, on the radio and at party rallies.'[36] Hitler's speech in September gave Goebbels and his propagandists the cue to take up the retaliation theme yet again. Perhaps they had fallen victim to the illusion that the day they longed for so much was not far off. On Harvest Thanksgiving Day (3 October), the minister remarked:

> The English are under an exceedingly fatal delusion if they imagine they are faced with only a rhetorical or propagandist slogan with no reality behind it. England will one day make acquaintance with this reality. . . . English and American trees will not grow into the sky. Our German technicians, inventors, engineers and workmen will see to that.[37]

Although not as effective as his master, Goebbels also seems to have been able to throw the doubters onto the defensive, if only temporarily so.[38] At the end of October, his rhetoric took on an even more confident tone: 'The day of radical retribution against Britain is drawing slowly but surely nearer.'[39]

The promise of *Vergeltung* had become a drug for so many Germans. Their attitude to it might be a very negative one but they were unable to dispense with it. This would help to explain the fact that, although repetitious promises were so often the source of intense irritation and exasperation, the German people somehow needed those words they so violently criticized. All speeches of party dignitaries were scrutinized word for word in order to detect some direct or veiled reference, and there was great disappointment when little or nothing of relevance was found.[40]

In the autumn of 1943 the attitude to retaliation swayed to and fro between outright pessimism and over-enthusiastic optimism. The reaction to Hitler's promises in September and November indicates quite clearly the *willingness* to believe. But the higher hopes were raised, the greater was the disappointment and deep feeling of depression that followed on realizing that *Vergeltung* was not imminent. Nevertheless, despite all outward pessimism which expressed itself in bitter attacks on the leadership, belief in the secret weapons was never given up completely. To have done so would have meant for many giving up all hope of a favourable end to the war. Retaliation had become the very key to victory. Again and again the Nazi leaders succeeded in rekindling the flame of faith which had seemed to have been extinguished for ever. What was really nothing more than wishful thinking constituted the sole source of comfort in these dark days of wartime Germany. As the weeks and months drew on, visions of the coming blow became more and more fantastic until *Vergeltung* came to represent the panacea to all Germany's difficulties. An SD report of October 1943 commented on this dangerous trend and described the change in attitude that had taken place since the early months of that year:

> Initially, *Vergeltung* had been ascribed great, but not decisive, importance for the course of the war as a whole. But thoughts about *Vergeltung* have undergone an important change during the past few months. The entire development of the war since Stalingrad has meant that the *Volksgenossen* are under the impression that the enemy encirclement of Germany and the occupied areas is becoming tighter and tighter and that this development will inevitably lead to a crisis. A 'miracle' seems the only way out of this crisis. And this miracle, which constitutes the decisive turn of the tide, is expected from *Vergeltung* today by the majority of *Volksgenossen* — in the areas affected by the air war by almost the entire population. Especially in the case of those *Volksgenossen* whose confidence in victory has a positive effect on others and fortifies the hearts of many who are faint-hearted and fickle, belief in victory is principally based on the hopes attached to the future employment of new weapons and war instruments. These hopes extend far beyond the mere halting of the terror raids. This is the least people expect of *Vergeltung*. It is supposed that the counter blow will rather result in England being 'knocked out' of the war within the space of a few days

> or weeks. People imagine that the tremendous damage wrought on the larger English towns will secure the conditions necessary for the occupation of the island which will, in turn, lead to an armistice with England. It is then argued that America would then have no particular interest in carrying on the war. Our entire force could then at last be directed at Russia, the result being the early collapse of Soviet offensive power.

The same report went on to remark that the longer the delay, the greater the expectations. It concluded by explaining that *Vergeltung* had come to stand for something much more than the bare word at first seems to imply. It was 'the decisive chance to gain victory, without which one can no longer believe in a good end to the war'.[41] Talk of retaliation reached a new height during the first week of heavy bombing of Berlin at the end of November. The very simple and credulous hope was described at the time as 'an important element for the good bearing of the people'.[42] This was not without its inherent dangers and once again the SD pointed out that retaliation was a question of confidence in the government. Should the oft-repeated forecasts not materialize, such bitterness and disillusionment would result that all efforts of the leadership to remedy the situation would be bound to fail.[43]

Although not as cautious as it had been the previous summer, German propaganda did try to damp any over-enthusiastic optimism. Newspaper readers were informed in October that, though their impatience was quite understandable, they had to appreciate the supreme importance of the need to prepare the blow thoroughly so that its effect would be decisive.[44] But, at the end of the year, the propagandists themselves seem to have been convinced that the time of *Vergeltung* was rapidly approaching. Their utterances were marked by a somewhat more confident tone. In the last days of November, Goebbels delivered a particularly fiery speech in bomb-shattered Berlin:

> In Germany there is no demand more passionate than to pay back the criminals on the Thames in full measure for what they have been doing and are still doing to us. The German people can rest assured. Day and night this retaliation is being prepared with feverish energy . . .[45]

Perhaps the best evidence that German propagandists were allowing this false illusion to guide them in their choice of words is a remarkable article by Schwarz van Berk published in *Das Reich* on 5 December. Although professing to mute fantastic conceptions of *Vergeltung*, he presented such a glowing picture of its effects that many concluded that the start could only be a few days off. At the same time as endeavouring to soothe the widespread impatience, he made some very hazardous statements:

> The question of the date of *Vergeltung* is no longer dependent on its technical completion but on the purpose it is intended to have. *Vergeltung* will be employed in an energetic form at the moment which is psychologically suitable so that it can influence the course of this war. It would be a useless start merely to repay ruins with ruins. The purpose of the undertaking will be expressed in quite different and surprising effects — both psychological and political. . . . The *Vergeltung* is not to be stopped or hindered by any manoeuvre of the enemy or by any operation he might venture. The ball is rolling. For us *Vergeltung* is not just a question of triumph of arms or merely of a chastisement which is being demanded by our people, but a question of putting a stop to the unrestrained mass-murder with one extremely drastic blow. For a peaceful observer it might seem that the time is not far off when mankind can blow up half of the world.[46]

In the days preceding the Christmas holiday, the German press appears to have thrown all caution to the wind. The reader was informed that retaliation was not simply a matter of bringing about 'only a breathing space but a turning-point'. The aim was not merely to destroy a few British cities but to eliminate the 'island' as 'a jumping-off point for all kinds of terror operations'. No doubts were left as to its vital strategic significance: 'When considered together with other plans the Anglo-American General Staffs apparently intend carrying out from the island base, this view then appears of paramount importance for the course of the war.'[47]

Up to then, the propagandists had never ventured to make such confident predictions. They certainly convinced many that the long-awaited blow would come in the form of a very welcome Christmas present.[48] Schwarz van Berk's article, in particular, was reported to have created lively interest and to have increased speculation on the form and the effects of the new weapon. Above all, news of its launching was expected any day.[49] This conviction was demonstrated in the precautions many people were rumoured to be taking to meet an expected Allied counter-blow. 'It is being said that in west Germany the population has been instructed to furnish itself with requisites for a 60 hour stay in the air-raid shelter — this, namely, is the time the *Vergeltung* will last. When they leave the shelter, the war will be over.' An increasing tendency to tie retaliation to the end of the war was also noted. More cautious people were said to be expecting the attack in the spring and to believe that it could prove decisive only if accompanied by a German landing in England. It would be wrong, however, to suppose that *all* Germans shared this optimism in the last days of 1943.

> Quite a few *Volksgenossen* even doubt in *Vergeltung* completely. They regard it as nothing more than a splendid propaganda manoeuvre of the German leadership, the purpose of which is to frighten the population of England and to make the Anglo-American leadership carry out their incomplete invasion plans prematurely.

So-called 'opponents' were reported as viewing the whole *Vergeltung* propaganda as a clever attempt by the leaders to maintain popular support and to secure the population's willingness to carry on a war that could no longer be won.[50]

Of course, retaliation was not imminent in December 1943. The high hopes that had been raised were dashed yet again. Already on Christmas Eve, many were very disappointed that Goebbels had not even mentioned it in his traditional radio address and interpreted it as a conscious attempt to damp any excessive optimism.[51] The old doubts re-emerged and, according to an SD report, it was just those people who shortly before had believed so ardently that the strike was imminent who were now being plagued with pessimism.[52] There was a growing tendency to regard it all as one gigantic bluff. Less radical minds feared that it would either come too late or would be rendered impossible by Allied landings in northern Europe.[53]

The propagandists, as well as the German leadership as a whole, realized that it would not be enough to return to a policy of enforced silence. Something would have to be done to prevent a crisis of confidence in the German leadership. It would be necessary to give the German people immediate visible proof of the Reich's ability to strike back at the enemy. As a means of bridging the gap to the beginning of all-out *Vergeltung*, it was decided to resume conventional bombing of the United Kingdom, in particular London, in force. All planes that could be spared were brought to northern France until the Luftwaffe commanded a front-line force of 150-200 bombers. In the months January-March London was once again the target of repeated attack which, however, never reached the intensity of the 1940-41 blitz. In these three months, a total of 2,350 tons of bombs were dropped in fifteen major attacks, thirteen of which were aimed at the British capital.[54]

Nazi propaganda portrayed the raids as by far the heaviest of the war and did not hesitate to exploit them to the full. Even the *OKW*-

Bericht played its part in this propaganda drive. On 2 February, for example, it claimed that on the nights of 21-22 and 29-30 January, 900 bombers had been dispatched against London, of which 750 had reached the target and dropped over 1,000 tons of high explosive and incendiary bombs.[55] According to British accounts, however, in the first raid only 27 enemy aircraft actually reached London and of the 161 planes sent in the second attack only 15 dropped their bombs within the capital's boundaries.[56] On the German radio on 21 February, Rudolf Semmler exulted in the 'thousands of bombs' that were raining down on London: 'They are only a weak foretaste of what is to come. London and other cities will now pay for Cologne, Essen, Hamburg, Berlin and all the other towns delivered cynically to British terrorism.'[57] About two weeks later, Goebbels was making the over-confident forecast 'that very soon every Anglo-American raid on a German town will be paid back by a German raid on an English town'.[58] It was a promise that could not be kept. German radio listeners were encouraged in the belief that the attacks on London were at least as heavy as the Allied attacks on German cities. American analysts saw this propaganda quite correctly as an attempt to give the population new confidence in Germany's aggressive potentialities in the critical pre-invasion period.[59] Unrestrained exaggeration and downright dishonesty were to become increasingly the typical characteristics of propaganda treatment of these attacks. Of course, the German public would be dissatisfied with any accounts that did not allow the conclusion to be drawn that the British civilian population was suffering at least as much as they were. Often the reality contradicted propaganda claims quite dramatically. On 22 March, for instance, an article appeared in the *Völkischer Beobachter* entitled 'Hull Harbour is Burning'. In the attack of 19-20 March, however, most of the German bombs had been dropped quite harmlessly on east Lincolnshire and north Norfolk and not a single bomb had landed on Hull.[60] Similarly, heavy and destructive attacks were claimed to have taken place on Bristol on the nights of 27-28 March, 23-24 April and 14-15 May. In fact, the attacks were scattered and Bristol remained virtually unscathed.[61] To make their assertions sound plausible, Nazi propagandists accused the British authorities of endeavouring to cover up the effects of the Luftwaffe raids by enforcing an unusually harsh censorship.[62] So as to disguise the minimal effects the raids were, in fact, having, the press was forbidden to publish Reuter figures of British air-raid casualties for the month of February.[63] In line with this policy, German papers were advised on 26 February: 'Care is to be taken when publishing enemy press statements on the effect of German air raids in England that no information is given that would allow the drawing of incorrect comparisons.'[64] The Germans were thus to be deprived of any opportunity of comparing the Luftwaffe raids with those of the Allied air forces. The sensitivity of the German propaganda treatment of the 'Baby Blitz' is further demonstrated in the ban on any mention of the lack of good air-raid shelters in London[65] and the visits of Churchill and the King and Queen to the areas worst hit by the attacks.[66] It was feared that German civilians would draw their own 'inappropriate' parallels. It must be remembered that, despite all Goebbel's promptings, Hitler repeatedly refused to visit blitzed towns.

Despite the propagandists' relief at hearing the news of the resumption of raids on Great Britain, they were nevertheless in a quandary when depicting the importance of the event. They naturally wished to make the most of the raids but they did not wish to give the impression that this was the real thing or a replacement for the real thing. They knew all too well that this would have caused great despondency. The decision was therefore taken that the press, though giving prominence to the attacks, should refrain from using the loaded word *Vergeltung*.[67] It would suffice when the idea was conveyed that at last something was being done to answer the Allied pounding of German towns and that the air war had again become 'a two-sided affair'.[68]

The reaction to this propaganda was a very mixed one. Although the renewed raiding of Britain was generally welcomed, there was a marked tendency to see it as the mere prelude to *Vergeltung*, as a kind of warming-up operation.[69] At the same time, quite a few people, especially the inhabitants of Germany's bomb-battered towns, feared that the enemy would retaliate by stepping up his attacks on the Reich still further and that they, in the long run, would be the ones to suffer most.[70] The RAF raid on Berlin on 15 February was, in fact, interpreted by many as the enemy's reply to the Luftwaffe bombing in London. Some people were of the opinion that it would be advisable to refrain from launching such attacks until the Reich was in a position to deliver one devastating blow at the heart of the enemy which would destroy for ever his capability of mounting raids on Germany.[71] The direct effect on their own lives became the criterion for judging the wisdom or efficacy of bombing Britain.

The raids do not seem to have had a very great influence on morale. Although they were naturally better than nothing, the Schwerin SD summed up the general disappointment in the words: 'People want to see something more . . .'.[72] From Koblenz it was reported that few positive results were expected from the raids.[73] As the Allied bombing offensive continued as if nothing had happened, the attitude to official treatment of the Luftwaffe raids became increasingly critical and by March it was becoming downright hostile. First suspicions that press and radio coverage was guilty of exaggeration were reported in an SD report of 22 February from Koblenz,[74] but four weeks later criticism was taking on a much harsher tone. SD Linz reported: 'The clumsy attempt by the press at playing up the frequent German raids on London, while dismissing the damage caused by enemy raids as insignificant, has a most provoking effect and is leading to a further diminution of trust in German news reporting.'[75] Many people even confessed to have unearthed the propaganda intention and dismissed the raids on London as 'appeasement' tactics.[76]

The renewal of the blitz on London was quite insufficient to distract people's attention from that theme that was uppermost in their minds and which for many had become the very incarnation of all their hopes. Despite a marked tendency by the more optimistically inclined to believe that *Vergeltung* would come with the launching of the Allied invasion,[77] the SD reports gave a definite impression that the number of doubters was rapidly increasing in the first few months of 1944. According to a report from Frankfurt-on-Main in February: 'Large parts of the population no longer believe in *Vergeltung* but regard it as merely an invention of German propaganda.'[78] In April SD Schwerin made the even more sweeping comment: 'In general, it can be observed that, for the most part, the population has lost its belief in *Vergeltung* which had once been so firmly anchored.'[79] In fact, the mood appears to have been very depressed indeed at this time. Belief in retaliation seems to have reached an all-time low and to have become the object of bitter reproach expressed in the form of political jokes.[80]

Never do doubt and pessimism regarding retaliation appear to have been greater than at that very moment when the launching sites in northern France were eagerly awaiting the order to commence operations. On 6 June — D-Day — the Frankfurt SD reported:

> The absence of retaliatory measures in the face of the present air terror is seen by many *Volksgenossen* as a tacit admission of our own inability ever to launch a *Vergeltung*. After all that the leadership has said, written, promised and failed to realize, it is possible, in view of the present course of the air-raids on the Reich, to speak of a crisis of confidence among a broad section of the population.[81]

It therefore seems that the long predicted crisis of confidence had begun. But, exactly one week later, the first two V-1 missiles landed on the London area. For the propagandists it must, at first, have appeared that they had been saved at the very last moment.

The initial mood of euphoria on hearing the news of the start of operations,[82] however, soon gave way to a spirit of dejection and intense disappointment as it was realized that the new weapon was having no effect whatsoever on the course of the war and that the enemy was even able to step up his attacks on the Reich.[83] Nazi propagandists could do precious little to counter this feeling of having been let down. The time of waiting for *Vergeltung* had been long and the longer it became all the greater were the hopes tied to it. And in 1944 these hopes could no longer be met. Retaliation had been, however, the only propaganda theme able — if only temporarily — to bolster German civilian morale in the dark months after Stalingrad. It was essentially the substitute for military success which in better days had been regarded as the fundamental guarantee of future victory. But it, too, was ultimately dependent on realization in the form of action.

NOTES

1. Wiener Library Press Cuttings. *Danziger Neueste Nachrichten*, Goebbels' speech in Gotenhafen, 22 October 1942.
2. Imperial War Museum (IWM), BBC Daily Digest of Foreign Broadcasts, 30 January 1943.
3. Ibid., Goebbels, *Das Reich*: 'Mood and Bearing', 9 April 1943.
4. Ibid., 5 June 1943.
5. Bundesarchiv (BA) R58/182. RSHA, Meldungen aus dem Reich, Nr.379, 29 April 1943.
6. BA NS6/415. Partei-Kanzlei, Auszüge u. Berichte der Gauleitungen u. a. Dienststellen, 18.4-1.5.43.

7. BA R58/183. RSHA, Meldungen aus dem Reich, Nr.387, 31 May 1943.

8. BA R58/185. RSHA, SD Berichte zu Inlandsfragen, Betr: Stimmen aus der Bevölkerung zur Sportpalastkundgebung am 5.6.43, 10 June 1943.

9. BA NS6/406. SD Ab. Weimar to Partei-Kanzlei, Betr: Allgemeine Stimmung und Lage, 22 June 1943; see also ibid., SD Ab. Halle/S., Betr: Stimmung u. Haltung zur Lage, 6 July 1943.

10. Ibid., SD Ab. Weimar to Partei-Kanzlei, Betr: Allgemeine Stimmung u. Lage, 29 June 1943.

11. BA NS6/411. RSHA to Partei-Kanzlei, Betr: Meldungen aus den SD (Leit-) Abschnittsbereichen, 2 July 1943.

12. BA NS6/vorl.243. SD Halle/Saale, 13 July 1943.

13. BA R58/186. RSHA, SD Berichte zu Inlandsfragen, Betr: Verbreitung zahlreicher Gerüchte über neue Waffen u. Abwehrmittel, 1 July 1943.

14. BA NS6/vorl.244. SD Hauptaussenstelle Schwerin, 7 September 1943.

15. BA R58/186. RSHA, SD Berichte zu Inlandsfragen, Betr: Meldungen über die Terrorangriffen auf Köln u. Aachen und ihre stimmungsmäßigen Auswirkungen, 22 July 1943.

16. BA NS6/407. SD Hauptaussenstelle Schwerin, Betr: Allgemeine Stimmung u. Haltung, 6 July 1943.

17. BA NS6/vorl.244. SD Hauptaussenstelle Schwerin, 3 August 1943.

18. Ibid., 10 August 1943.

19. BA NS6/407. SD Hauptaussenstelle Schwerin, Betr: Aufnahme u. Auswirkung der Propagandalenkung in Presse u. Rundfunk, 29 June 1943.

20. BA NS6/415. Partei-Kanzlei, Auszüge aus Berichten der Gauleitungen u. a. Dienststellen, 27.6-3.7.43; see also ibid., 20-26.6.43.

21. Same source as in footnote 16.

22. BA ZSg.109/43. V.I.-Nr.163/43, 6 July 1943.

23. Hoover Institution Microfilm Collection, Reel 16. RPL, Hauptamt Reichsring, Rundschreiben 102/43, 1 July 1943 (available in Wiener Library-90/Doc.V).

24. BA NS6/vorl.358. Fernschreiben an alle Gauleiter, Betr: Führungshinweis der Parteikanzlei (Bormann), 9 September 1943.

25. BA ZSg.101/42. Slg. Brammer, Vertraulich, nicht zum Ausdruck bestimmt, 18 August 1943.

26. See Frankland Webster (ed.), *The Strategic Air Offensive Against Germany 1939-45*, Vol. II, 224; and O'Brien, *History of the Second World War — Civil Defence*, 437.

27. BA ZSg.109/40. V.I.-Nr.17/43, 18 January 1943; BA ZSg.109/41. Tagesparole des Reichspressechefs Nr.56/43, 4 March 1943.

28. IWM. BBC Daily Digest of Foreign Broadcasts, 18.30 *Zeitspiegel*, 26 May 1943.

29. National Archives (NA) NNR-71-550(904) Roll 1. Records of the Foreign Intelligence Service, Central European Radio Analysis — A Weekly Report on Nazi Propaganda, No.22, 11 June 1943.

30. BA R58/185. RSHA, SD Berichte zu Inlandsfragen, Betr: Meldungen über Entwicklungen in der öffentlichen Meinungsbildung, 24 June 1943.

31. BA NS6/vorl.244. SD Hauptaussenstelle Schwerin, 10 August 1943.

32. Ibid., 14 September 1943; see also BA R58/188. RSHA, SD Berichte zu Inlandsfragen, Betr: Meldungen zur Führerrede u. den Ereignissen in Italien, 13 September 1943.

33. BA R58/188. RSHA, SD Berichte zu Inlandsfragen, Betr: Entwicklung der Stimmung seit der Befreiung der Duce, 23 September 1943.

34. BA NS6/vorl.244. SD Hauptaussenstelle Schwerin, 28 September 1943.

35. NA T81/Roll 119 (140738). EAP 251a/23, Kreisleiter Maintaunus-Obertaunus to Gauleiter Hessen-Nassau, 29 December 1943.

36. BA R58/190. RSHA, SD Berichte zu Inlandsfragen, Betr: Meldungen zur Führerrede vom. 8.11.43, 11 November 1943.

37. IWM. BBC Daily Digest of Foreign Broadcasts, 3 October 1943.

38. BA R58/189. RSHA, SD Berichte zu Inlandsfragen, Betr: Entwicklung der Stimmung vor u. nach der Kundgebung zum Erntedankfest, 7 October 1943.

39. IWM. BBC Daily Digest of Foreign Broadcasts, Goebbels, *Das Reich*, 29 October 1943.

40. BA R58/191. RSHA, SD Berichte zu Inlandsfragen, Betr: Meldungen zum Luftkrieg u. zu den Reden von Reichsminister Dr. Goebbels u. Staatssekretär Backe . . ., 2 December 1943.

41. BA R58/189. RSHA, SD Berichte zu Inlandsfragen, Betr: Was verspricht sich die Bevölkerung v. der 'Vergeltung'?, 18 October 1943.

42. BA R58/191. RSHA, SD Berichte zu Inlandsfragen, Betr: Zusammenfassender Bericht über Stimmung u. Haltung der Berliner Bevölkerung während u. nach den Großangriffen Ende Nov. 1943, 20 December 1943.

43. Ibid., Betr: Meldungen zur Entwicklung in der öffentlichen Meinungsbildung, 2 December 1943.

44. Weiner Library Press Cuttings. *Stuttgarter NS-Kurier*, 21 October 1943.

45. *Völkischer Beobachter*, Norddeutsche Ausgabe, 29 November 1943.

46. *Das Reich*, 'Die Ungeahnten Folgen', 5 December 1943.

47. Wiener Library Press Cuttings. *Münchner Neueste Nachrichten*, 19 December 1943.

48. BA R58/191. RSHA, SD Berichte zu Inlandsfragen, Betr: Zusammenfassender Bericht über Stimmung u. Haltung der Berliner Bevölkerung während u. nach den Großangriffen Ende Nov. 1943, 20 December 1943; Ibid., Betr: Aufnahme der aktuellen Ereignissen in der Bevölkerung, 9 December 1943.

49. Ibid., Betr: Meldungen zur Stimmung u. Haltung, 16 December 1943.

50. Ibid., Betr: Meldungen über Gerüchte u. Kombinationen zur Vergeltung u. Invasion, 27 December 1943.

51. Ibid.

52. BA R58/192. RSHA, SD Berichte zu Inlandsfragen, Betr: Meldungen über die Entwickling in der öffentlichen Meinungsbildung, 20 January 1944.

53. Ibid., Betr: Gedanken u. Wünsche der Bevölkerung zum Jahreswechsel — Aufnahme der militärischen Ereignisse, 6 January 1944.

54. O'Brien, op. cit., 439.

55. *Völkischer Beobachter*, Norddeutsche Ausgabe, 4 February 1944.

56. O'Brien, op. cit., 440-41.

57. IWM. BBC Daily Digest of Foreign Broadcasts, 12.30, 21 February 1944.

58. Ibid., Goebbels, *Das Reich*, 'The Interim Balance of the Air War', 3 March 1944.

59. NA NNR-71-550(904) Roll 2. Records of the Foreign Intelligence Service, Central European Radio Analysis — A Weekly Report on Nazi Propaganda, No. 59, 24 February 1944.

60. O'Brien, op. cit. 442.

61. See *Völkischer Beobachter*, Norddeutsche Ausgabe, 28 March, 25 April and 16 May 1944. The raids were also reported in the Bristol *Evening Post*.

62. Ibid., 7 and 11 February 1944.

63. Staatsarchiv Koblenz 662,5/28. RPA Koblenz, Rundschreiben 111/21/44, 18 March 1944.

64. BA ZSg.109/48. Slg. Oberheitmann, V.I.-Nr.50a/44, 26 February 1944.

65. Ibid., V.I.-Nr.4/44, 3 March 1944.

66. Ibid., V.I.-Nr.50a/44, 26 February 1944.

67. BA ZSg.109/48. V.I.-Nr.44/44, 19 February 1944; see also BA ZSg. 109/47. V.I.-Nr.19/44, 22 January 1944; Ibid., V.I.-Nr.26/44, 30 January 1944; Ibid., Tagesparole Nr.26:/44, 31 January 1944.

68. Hessisches Hauptstaatsarctiu archive (HSta), Wiesbaden Abt.483/3304. RPA Frankfurt/M., Rundspruch Nr. 40, 'Rundfunkparole', 5 February 1944.

69. HSta Wiesbaden Abt.483/5737. SD Ab. Frankfurt/M., Betr: Presse-propaganda, 22 February 1944.

70. Ibid.

71. BA NS6/vorl.244. Chef der Sicherheitspolizei u. des SD an Leiter der Partei-Kanzlei (Bormann), Report on effects of Berlin raids of 15.2.44, 25 Feburary 1944.

72. Ibid. SD Hauptaussenstelle Schwerin, 1 February 1944.

73. HSta Wiesbaden Abt. 483/5737. SD Ab.Koblenz, Betr: Öffentliche Führungsmittel — Presse, 29 February 1944.

74. Ibid., 22 February 1944.

75. BA NS6/vorl.243. SD Ab. Linz, 21 March 1944.

76. BA R58/193. RSHA, SD Berichte zu Inlandsfragen, Betr: Zur Aufnahme der Führungsmittel, 23 March 1944.

77. HSta Wiesbaden Abt.483/5737. SD Ab.Koblenz, Betr: Öffentliche Führungsmittel — Presse, 18 January 1944; HSta Wiesbaden Abt.483/5738. SD Ab.Frankfurt/M., Betr: Presse-Propaganda, 17 January 1944.

78. HSta Wiesbaden Abt.483/5737. SD Ab.Frankfurt/M., Betr: Bund-funkbericht, 16 February 1944.

79. BA NS6/vorl.244. SD Hauptaussenstelle Schwerin, 11 April 1944.

80. Wiener Library Press Cuttings. *Die Weltwoche*, Zurich, 12 May 1944; Ibid. *Arbeiter Zeitung*, Schaffhausen: 'Streiflichter aus Deutschland', 20 May 1944.

81. HSta Wiesbaden Abt.483/5739. SD Ab.Frankfurt/M., Betr: Stimmung u. Meinungsbildung, 6 June 1944.

82. See HSta Wiesbaden Abt.483/5737. SD Ab. Frankfurt/M., Betr: Stimmung u. Meinungsbildung, 17 June 1944; see also HSta Abt.483/5739. SD Ab. Frankfurt/M., Betr: Stimmung u. Meinungsbildung, 20 June 1944; also BA NS6/411. RSHA to Parteikanzlei, Berichte aus den SD (Leit-) Abschnittsbereichen, 26 June 1944.

83. See BA NS6/407. SD Ab. Schwerin, Betr: Stimmung u. Meinungsbildung, 27 June 1944; see also ibid., 11 July 1944; also ibid., Betr: Vorstellungen u. Wirkung der V1-Waffe in der Bevölkerung, 25 July 1944.

21 Allied Negotiations and the Dismemberment of Germany

Frank King

During a pre-conference meeting between Winston Churchill and Josif Stalin at Tehran, the Prime Minister said Prussia should be weakened and separated from the rest of Germany and that Bavaria, Austria, and Hungary should be encouraged to form a confederation. Stalin felt this inadequate and wanted a closer look at the economics of the problem. During the conference itself, on 1 December 1943, Franklin Roosevelt took the initiative in proposing the fragmentation of Germany, which he said 'could be done in 3 or 15 ways'. He then suggested a plan whereby Germany could be divided into a combination of autonomous parts and jurisdictions under international control. Churchill thought the Prussians should be singled-out for especially harsh treatment. Stalin approved in general of Roosevelt's approach, but he stolidly opposed Churchill's notion of creating Danubian and other confederations because they would only present themselves later on as convenient prey for the Germans. He preferred to see Austria and Hungary restored as independent countries. Roosevelt, who had spent part of his student days in Germany, replied that 'Germany had been safer when she was divided in 107 small principalities'.[1]

On the President's initiative, the task of working out the details of this decision was given to either a sub-committee of the European Advisory Commission (EAC), which had been established during the October meetings of the foreign secretaries in Moscow, or a special three-power committee. Later, it was understood that the matter of dismemberment had definitely been passed along to the EAC. Churchill at this time also told the War Cabinet it had been decided at Tehran that 'East Prussia and Germany east of the River Oder are to be alienated forever and the population shifted. Prussia itself is to be divided and curtailed. The Ruhr and other great centres of coal and steel must be put outside the power of Prussia.'[2]

On this particular topic, Cordell Hull, Anthony Eden, and their civil-service planners had a greal deal in common. As the result of appreciating the complexities of this problem, they were ambivalent; and their conversations and plans never emphasized the importance of dismemberment as one of the possible solutions to the dangers of a resurgent Germany. What both departments were partial to was moderate decentralization, which was a milder and more conventional policy. When Eden, Hull, and their advisers had talked about this topic at Quebec in August 1943, none of them had favoured forced dismemberment.[3] A thoughtful expression of this rather guarded viewpoint was contained in an uncirculated paper which George F. Kennan, the first political adviser to the American delegation in the EAC, wrote in March 1944:

> If . . . we attempt to dismember the Reich, without centralizing at some point outside the boundaries those activities which obviously call for centralization in the modern world, we will have set ourselves in opposition to the whole trend of technological progress. We will have endowed the 'Reichsidee' with the charm of all forbidden fruit. We will have revived for the campfires of romantic German youth an old and outworn mysticism. We will have set a premium on the earliest possible destruction of our own arrangements.[4]

Nevertheless, during the EAC's first month of operation in January 1944, Sir William Strang, the leader of the British delegation, took the initiative in trying to have the question of German partition placed on the commission's agenda. When he suggested the establishment of a sub-committee to study the subject, since the Foreign Office was undoubtedly interested in plumbing the views of its allies on this important issue, both John G. Winant and Feodor T. Gusev readily agreed; and the latter recommended the appointment of two representatives from each delegation to serve. Strang, who was impeccably prepared for the moment, then produced terms of reference which broke the larger question into its more manageable parts. Somewhat overcome, neither Winant nor Gusev was ready to accept this procedural guide on such quick inspection; and so they agreed to postpone the whole question until another meeting.[5]

When that time came the following month, however, Gusev, the Soviet Ambassador in Britain and leader of the Soviet delegation to the EAC, said his delegation was preoccupied with drafting and negotiating the surrender terms for Germany and had neither the proper materials nor the expertise to pursue the dismemberment issue. Kennan, deputizing for Ambassador Winant, said his delegation was willing to discuss the topic but admitted it had no materials or instructions on this subject from Washington.[6] At this inconclusive point, there was nothing more to be done. From this time until after the Yalta conference, for very nearly a year, not one of the three governments attempted to raise this issue again. Inescapably, the only explanation for this curious lapse is that the topic, at least in the EAC, was overtaken by others — such as the terms of unconditional surrender and the drafting of the agreements concerning the zones of occupation in Germany and the administration of Berlin, the armistice terms for Bulgaria, and the creation of control machinery for Germany — which were unanimously felt to be of greater importance.

Nearby the commission, however, attitudes concerning partition continued to develop. Arkady A. Sobolev, the Minister-Counsellor of the Soviet Embassy in London, told Kennan and H.M. Gladwyn Jebb, the chief British planner and Head of the Economic and Reconstruction Department of the Foreign Office, that 'it would be impossible to carry out the dismemberment of Germany in the early stages. Further, it would be highly undesirable to try to do so, seeing that the only way of dealing with the Germans properly would be to make use of the central administrative machine.'[7] Within a few weeks, in April 1944, Pierre Viénot, a representative of the French Committee of National Liberation, and Strang had an interesting conversation during which the French diplomat commented that 'any particularist tendencies which might manifest themselves in Germany should be encouraged'. With this there was no serious argument in either the State Department or the Foreign Office. Viénot also thought there would be important political and economic advantages in linking the Rhineland-Westphalia region with Western Europe rather than dismembering Germany intrinsically. Strang replied, accurately, that the Belgians had similar thoughts.[8]

While the consensus in Clement Attlee's influential Armistice and Post-War Committee still supported the notion of dismemberment, a steadfast minority led by the Secretary of State for War, Sir P. James Grigg, by August 1944 began to see the policy as a worrisome problem. This faction argued that dismemberment and other harsh measures might very well provoke internal resistance within Germany that would require just what the British increasingly realized they lacked, manpower. The Tehran agreements still remained official policy, but increasingly members of the War Cabinet agreed with their civil servants that the partitioning of Germany, contrary to early unexamined assumptions held by Churchill and others, was going to be costly.[9]

Ironically, just at the time when British interest in dismemberment was seriously flagging, the Americans were undergoing a jolting upsurge of concern. This time it was not just Roosevelt on his own but an appreciable number of energetic persons who were prepared to push the issue. It all began in mid-August 1944 when Eden told Henry Morgenthau, the Secretary of the Treasury, Harry Dexter White, his chief assistant, and Winant, while all three were in London, about the Tehran discussions. Armed with this information, Morgenthau and White were fired on their return to Washington into producing their own plans for the post-war treatment of Germany which were infused with the severe tone taken by Roosevelt, Churchill, and Stalin at Tehran.[10] When the President learned from Morgenthau about the seeming indifference and inadequacy of the EAC and the State Department to deal with dismemberment, this made his well-known aversion to both even more pronounced.

By early October 1944, Strang had become convinced, as Winant was to become by early 1945, by a number of signals in addition to Sobolev's warning in March, that the Soviets were not fixed in their policy. As he warned his Foreign Secretary, who was preparing for his crucial trip with Churchill to Moscow, 'There are indications that, in spite of what Marshal Stalin said at Tehran, the Soviet Government are opposed to dismemberment.' Unfortunately, this brilliant solo lead, which crossed the conventional wisdom and anticipated the official Soviet pronouncement by some five months, was not pursued by Eden, Churchill, or the Foreign Office.[11]

During the Yalta conference, Stalin said the time had come for a 'definite decision' to be taken since 'the exact form of dismemberment had still to be decided'. He also reminded the conference of his preference — as expressed at Tehran and more recently during his discussions with Churchill and Eden in Moscow — for the consideration of international economic controls. While Churchill thought the subject was too complicated to be solved during the short space of the conference, he then restated, at great length, the points he had made at Tehran. Roosevelt, with perception, if not levity, observed, 'The only difference between Marshal Stalin and the Prime Minister was that Marshal Stalin wanted to add to the surrender terms a statement to the effect that Germany would be dismembered.' Without presenting a specific plan, the President again put himself on record as 'decidedly in favour of decentralisation and therefore of dismemberment'. He then proposed that the Foreign Secretaries should prepare a plan for studying dismemberment within twenty-four hours and a final plan for the partition of Germany within thirty days. All three leaders agreed with this, as they did with the proposal supported by Roosevelt and Stalin that article twelve of the European Advisory Commission's surrender instrument be amended to include provisions for the decentralization and possible dismemberment of Germany.[12]

The official Soviet account of this discussion in English, written almost completely in paraphrase, changes its emphasis. Roosevelt is reported as having said the zones of occupation might serve as 'the first step in the dismemberment of Germany'. Stalin, in contrast, only cautiously agreed with the President and Prime Minister about the principle of dismemberment itself and the need to have the details worked-out. Roosevelt is also supposed to have said that dismemberment was the only viable policy because recent German history had witnessed the creation of a centralized authority which was impervious to decentralization; and that if Germany were partitioned then 'each of her parts would have an administration subordinate to the corresponding Allied Command'. In short, of the three leaders — according to Soviet records — Stalin was the least enthusiastic about dismemberment. All authoritative records of the Tehran and Yalta conferences are in agreement that Stalin, unlike Roosevelt and Churchill, never proposed a specific or even general dismemberment plan for Germany.[13]

When the Foreign Ministers met the following day, Edward R. Stettinius proposed that the word 'dismemberment' be added to article 12(a) of the surrender terms. Vyacheslov M. Molotov agreed, but Eden hedged by arguing the matter had not yet been studied. At one point, with Strang at his elbow or nearly so, he precisely stated, 'It was not our fault that the E.A.C. had not completed a study of dismemberment as had been agreed at Tehran'. The following day, Molotov, who had the immediate benefit of Gusev's counsel, discreetly called for the creation of a dismemberment committee in London — since Roosevelt had already asked for a special three-power reparations commission to meet in Moscow — composed of Eden, Winant, and Gusev. Stettinius, who had not included anyone from the EAC group in London in his delegation, feared the result would be to lessen the prestige of the EAC. Eden then addressed the obvious point, namely that the French, who had become full members of the EAC in mid-November 1944, would thereby be left out. After this anxious sparring was over, however, both Eden and Stettinius accepted Molotov's proposal. This was made more agreeable after Molotov suggested the subject could be referred to the four-power EAC contingent on the three powers agreeing on the proper procedure. Eden hoped aloud that this special committee, on which he would serve as chairman, would go beyond procedure; and he then produced terms of reference for the committee which were little more than a redraft of the crumpled terms Strang had put before Winant and Gusev nearly a year earlier. These were quickly accepted; and thus the questions of timing, boundaries, and the relations between the separate parts of Germany all became suitable for study. It was also agreed that Eden's special committee would decide when the EAC would be consulted. During the third plenary session, these arrangements were accepted by Roosevelt, Stalin, and Churchill. They also agreed, the latter under protest, that the surrender instrument would be changed so that Germany could be — at the discretion of the allies — dismembered.[14]

The Foreign Office reacted to the news of these decisions with aggrieved shock. The two ranking members remaining in London, Richard K. Law and Sir Orme Sargent, wrote Eden on 9 February that the exclusion of the French from the dismemberment and reparation committees was 'due merely to prejudice and ignorance' on the part of the Americans, 'but in the case of the Soviet Government it almost looks as though it might be part of a considered policy of weakening Western Europe, both politically and militarily'. To them the cumulative effect of the Americans' attitude was nothing short of foreboding: 'To declare that U.S. troops will not stay in Europe longer than 2 years and at one and the same time veto the participation of France in the settlement of German affairs is to upset the balance between Eastern and Western Europe to Russia's advantage.'[15]

In the wake of the Yalta decisions and the prevailing gloom of the period, Sir John Anderson, the Chancellor of the Exchequer, prepared what Sir Llewellyn Woodward has described as 'the most decisive document submitted to the War Cabinet on the treatment of Germany . . .'. In Anderson's view, nothing could be done in the fields of reparations and dismemberment which would entail cost to Britain. Dismemberment in particular would be undesirable because it would provoke internal German resistance with 'heavy commitments' resulting. More important, for nearly the first time, Anderson consciously put a price on certain foreign policy outlooks and considered Britain's post-war economic problems. The cost accountants, at least when it came to dismemberment were beginning to gain the edge over the policy planners and diplomats. 'If certain trends in the Yalta discussions are allowed to develop into firm conclusions without substantial modification, the result might well prove beyond the financial strength of this country and of the Commonwealth which looks to us for help and would impair our capacity for proper leadership in Europe.'[16] Weakness was beginning to tell, and limits had to be established.

With the passing of time, confidence, among all three governments, in dismemberment as a feasible remedy simply waned. Early in March, Strang informed his fellow civil servants on the Official Committee on Armistice Terms and Civil Administration about the nebulous situation. According to recent remarks he had made to Strang, Gusev was more interested in seeing four-power control established in Berlin than in dismemberment. Eden, for his part, felt 'no decision had been reached at present on the method and time for giving effect to the policy of dismemberment'.[17]

Late in March, Winant reported to Stettinius, James C. Dunn, H. Freeman Matthews, and Roosevelt that the dismemberment committee had held only one uneventful meeting on 7 March. Since then, on 26 March, Gusev had written a letter which stated his government interpreted the Yalta decisions as meaning that dismemberment was not obligatory but an option only if other means of making Germany harmless could not be found. Winant concluded that the USSR was 'not committed in principle to a policy if dismemberment'. Shortly thereafter, Roosevelt informed his Secretary of State, after reading Winant's report, that 'I think our attitude should be one of study and postponement of final decision'.[18]

On 8 May 1945, Stalin proclaimed to the peoples of the USSR that their country 'does not intend either to dismember or to destroy Germany'. Later in the month, when Harry Hopkins was in Moscow on his last diplomatic mission of the war — this time for President Harry Truman — he asked Stalin if his position had changed since Tehran and Yalta. Stalin said it had, because his request at Yalta for a decision on dismemberment had been 'turned down'; and, during the subsequent dismemberment committee meeting in London, Eden and Strang had spoken of dismemberment as only a last resort, and Winant had not objected to this. As a consequence of this, Stalin said he had assumed both of his major allies were opposed to the policy. When Hopkins said this was not so, Stalin pledged he would 'keep an open mind' on the subject.[19] This proved to be unnecessary, for since Roosevelt's death on 12 April there had been no one left with real power in Washington or London who was eager to promote the dismemberment of Germany.

During mid-August, the British Embassy in Washington asked the new Secretary of State, James F. Byrnes, if the London dismemberment committee should be declared moribund. The issue of dismemberment had not been raised during the spring months or at the Potsdam conference, and the committee had met only twice, on 7 March and 11 April, and had had no proposals submitted to it. Three weeks later, the State Department concluded that the committee had completed its task.[20] In this odd manner, the matter came to an end.

Looking back at this particular feat of inter-allied diplomacy, several observations seem to be in order. First, considering the early and firm unanimity reached by Roosevelt, Churchill, and Stalin on this issue, it is not inaccurate to describe this as an example, especially on the British and American sides, of bureaucratic erosion. The technicians who worked close to this problem realized that the implementation of this policy threatened to be exceedingly difficult. Second, the guidance from the top was sporadic and uncertain. Given this and the opposition from the bureaucrats below — a factor not to be lightly discounted — it is not surprising that little headway was made on this issue after Tehran.[21]

It is interesting to note that the Soviets from near the beginning seemed willing, at least from the evidence at hand, to follow the policy leads furnished by the Americans and the British. Considering the lack of reinforcement, the USSR's constancy was rather surprising. Later, as one would expect, when the United Kingdom and United States failed to lead, the Soviets pursued their own interests and had their own second thoughts. The Soviets came to this point, as one would suspect, for a number of reasons. As Gusev made clear in September 1944, the determining factor, which influenced a number of issues, was 'under what conditions the defeat takes place'. If there were a central authority to work with, then the allies could force it to co-operate, for instance, in demilitarization, the transfer of various parts of the civilian population, the repatriation of foreign conscripts, and, in general, in the fulfillment of the terms of unconditional surrender. Much of the evidence suggests, moreover, that the Soviets feared that the Germans would surrender well before they were helpless. In these circumstances, dismemberment would have been both unwise and impossible. Later, in March 1945, the Soviets simply could not see any strong separatist movements in Germany or popular support for partition.[22] Neither, it should be added, could the British and Americans. Finally, the Soviets fully understood, by Yalta if not earlier, the fundamental juncture between the extraction of reparations and unified allied control of Germany at the centre.[23] The British, on the other hand, could see the cost of dismemberment primarily in terms of economic hardship and manpower expenditures to themselves. The differences revealed the anticipated vulnerabilities of the two countries.

The American position was dissimilar. Initially, Roosevelt was the most conspicuous supporter of dismemberment, but, with the exception of Hopkins and Sumner Welles, he had no loyal supporters for this policy within his administration.[24] Later, when Morgenthau and the Treasury Department came forward with their programme for the economic disarmament of Germany, dismemberment again gained a sort of currency. But, by that time it had become fashionable in Washington, primarily because of the influence of the Supreme Headquarters of the Allied Expeditionary Forces, to think about dismemberment only in terms of the zones agreed upon and the decentralization of political control. The end of this was that by Yalta none of the Big Three believed in the policy as originally discussed. Although the legacy of Tehran and the pledges made there were strong enough to bring about the creation of Eden's dismemberment committee, which was merely a truncated version of the EAC, it was only a pro-forma gesture. The result was that in the United States and Britain, if not the USSR, the larger conception, which was certainly not without merit, was lost.

NOTES

1. CAB 66/45, WP (44) 8, record of a conversation between Churchill and Stalin at Tehran on 28 November 1943, and record of a plenary tripartite meeting on 1 December 1943.

2. CAB 66/45, WP (44) 33, unconditional surrender, note by Churchill, 15 January 1944.

3. RG 59, records of H.A. Notter, box 19 file: First Quebec Conf. August 1943, memo of conversation between Hull, Eden, Cadogan, Dunn and Atherton on 20 August 1943.

4. George F. Kennan Papers, Seeley G. Mudd Manuscript Library, Princeton University, box 3, file: 1944 March to mid-December, letter (memo) from Kennan to Winant, March 1944.

5. FO 371/40613, U 520/104/70, minute for Cadogan from Strang, 19 January 1944, minute by Strang, January 1944, telegrams from FO to Washington and Moscow Embassies, 22 January 1944.

6. FO 371/40580, U 1379/3/70, EAC (44) 3rd meeting, minutes of a meeting on 18 February 1944 dated 19 February 1944.

7. FO 371/40623, U 2260/104/70, record of a conversation by Jebb, 14 March 1944.

8. FO 371/40634, U 3688/104/70, record of a conversation by Strang, 17 April 1944. For evidence that the Luxembourgians had had similar ideas for quite some time see RG 59, Leo Pasvolsky Office Files, box 4, file: January-March 1943, memo of conversation by Welles with Hugh Le Gallais and Pierre Dupong, 9 February 1943.

9. CAB 87/66, APW (44) 14th and 15th meetings, minutes of meetings on 23 August 1944 and 31 August 1944.

10. Harry Dexter White Papers, Seeley G. Mudd Manuscript Library, Princeton University, box 7, memo of conversation by White with Eden, Strang, Morgenthau, and Winant, 15 August 1944.

11. FO 371/40581, U 7671/3/70, Strang's brief for Eden on the work of the EAC, 4 October 1944. For Winant's vigorous confirmation of Strang's assessment, see *FRUS, 1945*, III, Winant to State Dept., 26 January 1945, 396-97. Even earlier than Strang, the distinguished historian William L. Langer, the Chief of the Office of Strategic Services Research and Analysis branch, predicted, quite rightly, that the USSR would be more interested in reparations than the partition of Germany. See RG 43, Mosely Records, box 3, file: 133 I, memo by Langer, 'Russian Aims in Germany and the Problem of Three-Power Cooperation', dated 11 May 1944, copy to Winant, 18 May 1944.

12. CAB 66/43, WP (45) 157, records of the Malta and Yalta Conferences, record of the meeting on 5 February 1945. For the American version, see Truman Papers, Naval Aide File, box 7, file: Byrnes Notes (Naval Aide 7), notes of meeting on 5 February 1945.

13. 'The Crimea and Potsdam Conferences of the Leaders of the Three Great Powers', *International Affairs*, 6 (June 1965). Moscow 1965, record of second sitting on 5 Feburary 1945, 96-99. Cf. *FRUS, Malta and Yalta*, second plenary meeting (Bohlen minutes), 5 February 1945, 620-22.

14. CAB 66/63, WP (45) 157, records of meetings of the foreign secretaries on 6 and 7 February 1945 and annex I, Eden's suggested terms of reference for the special dismemberment committee and the record of the 3rd plenary session on 7 February 1945. Bohlen thought that Churchill had simply switched his position between Tehran and Yalta, and that by early 1945 he wanted a united Germany and France to serve as counterweights to the USSR. See Charles E. Bohlen, *Witness to History, 1929-1969* (New York 1973), 183.

15. PREM 4, 78/1, part 2, communication from Law and Sargent to Eden, 9 February 1945.

16. Sir Llewellyn Woodward, *British Foreign Policy in the Second World War*, Vol. I (London 1970), viii. CAB 66/63, WP (45) 146, reparations and dismemberment, memo by Anderson, 7 March 1945. For an interesting discussion of the relationship between these topics, see CAB 65/51, WM (45) 35th conclusions, minute 3, confidential annex, 22 March 1945.

17. FO 371/40815, U 1715/356/70, ACAO/M (45) 8, minutes of a meeting held on 7 March 1945.

18. Roosevelt Library, President's Secretary's File, box 44, file: Germany 1944-45, communication from Winant to Stettinius, Dunn, and Matthews, 29 March 1945; ibid., memo from FDR to Stettinius, 6 April 1945.

19. *FRUS, 1945*, III, message from Hopkins to Truman, 30 May 1945, 317-18, and note 7, 317.

20. *FRUS, 1945*, III, communication from British Embassy to Byrnes, 18 August 1945, 367-68, and Byrnes' reply.

21. As an example of this bureaucratic resistance, see RG 59, State Decimal File 1940-44, box 2558, memo by Riddleberger for Hull, 4 September 1944.

22. RG 43, Mosely Records, box 16, file: January-September 1944, minutes of informal EAC meeting on 11 September 1944; Roosevelt Library, President's Secretary's File, box 44, file: Germany 1944-45, communication from Winant to Stettinius, Dunn, Matthews (and FDR), 29 March 1945.

23. For some very shrewd insights into this matter, see Lloyd C. Gardner, 'America and the German "Problem", 1945-1949', in Barton J. Bernstein (ed.), *Politics and Policies of the Truman Administration* (Chicago 1970), 114-22.

24. Sumner Welles, *The Time for Decision* (New York 1944), 349.

VIII

Central Asian Side-show

*Waziristan was not one of the main battlefields of the second world war; at the time, the place mainly attracted movie-makers (*Bengali Lancers, Khyber Pass*). Yet the Faqir of Ipi was not just a colourful figure and the area was eventually to become of interest to the great powers. But this happened only three decades later. Though German help was given even after the tide of the war had turned, Berlin could not provide decisive assistance to the fighters for Pakhtunistan in their endeavour to expel the British.*

22 One Man against the Empire: The Faqir of Ipi and the British in Central Asia on the Eve of and during the Second World War

Milan Hauner

Among the enemies of the British Empire on the eve of the Second World War the Faqir of Ipi was unique. He was the most determined, implacable single adversary the British Raj in India had to face amongst its own subjects; and yet, he was also the most anachronistic one. He utterly disregarded the logics of the international situation and unwittingly started a campaign when he had the least chance of attracting international support against the British. As a guerrilla leader he was uncompromising, unyielding, obstinate and unscrupulous in the choice of combat methods against his opponents. These included traditional methods of tribal warfare such as ambush, kidnapping and mutilation. His hatred of the British bore no relation to *raison d'état*, though he was usually supported with money and military hardware by the Afghan authorities, especially so after the Partition, when he became the symbol of independent Pukhtunistan. The decision to attack was always his own; like the truces which he decided when his casualties had passed the accepted norm and it became necessary for him to retreat once again into the inaccessible hideouts of Waziristan. There he would wait for another opportunity to open hostilities, thus keeping the British army on the North-West Frontier fully mobilized. At one point nearly 40,000 British and Indian troops were reported to be in the field trying to capture him, while he remained elusive as ever, always succeeding in evading the tight net put around him. And yet, his own force of armed tribesmen probably never exceeded one thousand men, armed with rifles and a few machine-guns, and occasionally one or two pieces of antiquated cannon; he was always short of ammunition, had no radio communication, and relied for all his intelligence on the traditional network of informants and messengers. The British on the other hand had modern artillery, tanks and aircraft. When he died in 1960, *The Times* of 20 April described him as 'a doughty and honourable opponent...a man of principle and saintliness ...a redoutable organizer of tribal warfare....' But only with a tinge of irony could the obituary claim that 'many retired Army officers and political agents...will hear the news with the tribute of wistful regret'. A wry smile and a curse perhaps would have been a more accurate description.

Today, the name of Ipi is hardly remembered outside Muslim central Asia, and among the Europeans only by a handful of surviving administrators and soldiers who served on the Frontier. The Faqir of Ipi had of course a number of distinguished precursors in the region like the Hadda Mullah, a Mohmand leader in the 1890s, or the Powindah Mullah, whom Lord Curzon called 'a first-class scoundrel', because of the unprincipled methods of warfare he perfected amongst the Mahsuds.[1] Even the foremost authority on the region, Sir Olaf Caroe,[2] whose official correspondence in those days was, of course, full of the Faqir's name, does not mention him in his postwar historical study on the Pathans.[3]

The purpose of this article is not to pursue a tempting sentimental exercise in reviving the exploits of no doubt one of the most fascinating guerrilla leaders in a region which has today again become so topical since the recent Soviet invasion of Afghanistan, nor is it my intention to dwell on the parallel which the Faqir of Ipi might strike with an equally anachronistic religious fanatic, at the moment in control of Iran, namely Ayatollah Khomeini. However, the case of the Faqir of Ipi could be of great interest to historians since it opens the back door to an amazing story of guerrilla activities against a major power which were taking place in parallel to the main ideological conflict — at least as far as our Eurocentric approach still prefers to see those events — from which the Second World War emerged. From the Faqir's Islamic fundamentalist view of the world, terms like fascism and anti-fascism, must have been utterly irrelevant. The Pathan tribesmen were simply carrying on their centuries-old struggles for tribal independence, to keep their valleys free from foreign occupation, and accepted the Faqir as their supreme religious authority as one endowed with divine rights. Whether Hitler or Stalin were about to conquer the rest of the world, or the British about to quit India, did not concern them in the least, unless Nazi or Soviet troops entered their living space.

Whatever the struggle led by the Faqir of Ipi against the British might have looked like from the narrow perspective of the tribesmen, who had never accepted a state authority above them nor were they anxious to form a government of their own, their daring exploits were bound to attract the attention of the Great Powers interested in weakening or defeating the British Empire. Already during the First World War Imperial Germany had despatched Werner Otto von Hentig and Oskar von Niedermayer to Kabul with the purpose of winning over the Afghan government for a subversive scheme against British India, which was to be largely carried out by the Frontier tribes.[4] The mission failed but the idea persisted. The Axis powers, for instance, made several attempts to exploit the lonely 'freedom hero of Waziristan'[5] for their own purposes. It cannot be entirely ruled out that the Soviets might have harboured similar intentions, though the outside world has found only a few indications of their immediate schemes.[6]

The most notorious area of tribal unrest in the British Empire on the eve of the Second World War was Waziristan, situated in the southern tip of the non-administered Tribal Territory between the Indo-Afghan border, known since 1893 as the Durand Line, and the North-West Frontier Province of India. These tribal districts have been one of the few regions in the world whose inhabitants have cherished a strange anarchic independence from the constraints of 'civilized' governments. Even when the British succeeded in forcing their way through almost every tribal valley, they were never able to administer the tribes, let alone to disarm them. Although the British established many fortified outposts in the area, improved communications by bringing railways and roads closer to their cantonments, appointed political agents who were capable of conversing fluently in the local languages with the tribal *maliks* (chiefs) and *mullahs* (priests), this brought no permanent solution. It had been one of Lord Curzon's great ambitions to bring the Frontier under full control gradually by means of his 'Close Border Policy', which consisted of replacing the permanent British military presence in the Tribal Territory by local militia, thereby leaving it as a sort of 'marshland' to go its own way. However, this policy was no more successful than the previous 'Forward Policy' of conquest, as it did not prevent the tribesmen from raiding across the administered border. Sir Kerr Fraser-Tytler, who served during this period as a young subaltern in a Frontier Cavalry Regiment, and later during the crucial years of 1935-1941 as British Minister in Kabul, recalls his frustrating experience in fighting the tribes:

> And always there were the raids, the sudden alarm, the long dust-choked ride through the stifling heat of a July night, clattering out on to the stony glacis of the frontier hills, and away forty miles before dawn only to find as often as not that the birds had flown, leaving a trail of death and destruction behind them.[7]

The grievances of the border tribes were believed to be essentially economic — though from the tribesman's own point of view the motivation would be translated into their fundamental moral codes (*Pukhtunwali*), which imply retaliation and blood feud (*Badal*) in settling old disputes. And retaliate they did. The Pathan hill tribes rightly complained that the British, by pushing their control closer and closer to their areas, cut them off from their traditional recourse to raiding in the fertile valleys running down to the river Indus in the administered districts, which were populated mostly by the people who spoke the same language — Pashtu (Pukhtu). Because the hills were too poor to maintain their inhabitants and, if there was no alternative source of income, their only choice was to carry out raids or to starve. Following the established practices of the Mughal and Afghan governments, the British first satisfied themselves by paying allowances in cash to the tribal *maliks*, which for instance for the year 1940 amounted to nearly one million Rupees for the whole Tribal Territory.[8] Theoretically, these were paid for services rendered, such as road and camp protection by the local tribal levies called *khassadars*. These were untrained men, many either young boys or old men in the last stages of decrepitude, selected by their local *maliks*. They were used alongside with other irregular or auxiliary forces such as the Frontier Constabulary or the Scouts, before the military were called in. The *khassadars*, however, proved unreliable, 'more often than not keeping out of the way of the raiding gangs they are supposed to deal with', complained a British intelligence officer.[9] They were distrusted by the military who almost invariably insisted on the withdrawal of all *khassadars* from any area in which military operations took place. As a result of their dealings with the authorities on both sides of the Indo-Afghan border, the Wazirs and other Pathan tribes had, rightly or wrongly, come to the conclusion that the shortest cut to lucrative allowances was not through loyal service, but by occasional demonstration of their nuisance value. In particular the Wazirs, in the barren and inaccessible country athwart the Durand Line, were in an admirable position to play this game.

It is certainly no exaggeration to describe the Pathan tribes as the largest known potential reservoir of guerrilla fighters in the world.[10] The British statistics of fighting strength and armament among the trans-border tribes in the NWFP (meaning cis-Durand Line and excluding Chitral), corrected up to 1 April 1940, produced 414,000 fighting men armed with 233,562 breech-loading rifles or carbines; the corresponding figures for Baluchistan up to 1 April 1941, accounted for over 100,000 men and almost 18,000 rifles.[11] Thus, on paper there were more modern rifles among the tribes and certainly more fighting men than in the entire Indian Army. As a result of this challenge, a vast proportion of the Indian Army had to be permanently posted on the Frontier, which made them unavailable for other tasks. At the outbreak of the Second World War the Indian Army formed the largest segment of British imperial troops: 187,000, of which 140,000 were Indian.[12]

Furthermore, between the two world wars the Frontier offered practically the only combat experience to young and adventure-seeking British officers facing the boredom of a monotonous service in India.[13] It was the Frontier where the young Churchill had gained his first experience of direct fighting during the 1890s.[14] Sending troops on punitive expeditions against rebellious villages and bombing them from the air developed into something of a favourite sport, which received the full support of strong military commanders in India. Fraser-Tytler criticized the 'Forward Policy' as adopted on the Frontier after 1929 for giving undue preference to the military over the civilian point of view.[15]

Thus, as continuous friction with the Afridis, Mohmands and Wazirs mounted during the 1930s, British 'Forward Policy' on the Frontier was turning into a more rigid one and dominated entirely by military criteria. Here British imperial policy found itself between two extreme options: a more reasonable one which dictated a retreat to the Indus, and a more aggressive one which demanded the incorporation of all Pathans by pushing steadily forward to the Hindu Kush; but under the circumstances it chose the more difficult middle course.[16]

Throughout the 1930s public opinion in Britain and in the world became increasingly aware of the military escalation on the NWF of India — though public outrage was confined to intellectual circles and cannot be compared, for example, with the recent anti-Vietnam campaign in the United States. The British government was criticized at home and abroad for the 'uncivilized' pattern of warfare applied against civilian populations in the form of air bombing, in spite of the fact that this rarely happened without due warning in the form of leaflets dropped on the chosen target. The outspoken C. F. Andrews, a Quaker and a friend of Gandhi, made an eloquent plea for a drastic revision of British policy by stating his case in a nutshell: 'We cannot stand out boldly for disarmament in Europe while carrying on war in Asia'.[17] He proposed that troops should be withdrawn from the Tribal Territory and civil methods of administration applied to help to come to terms with the tribes. Needless to say, Soviet and Nazi propaganda relished exploiting the issue of British involvement against the tribes whenever it suited their aims.

In 1939 the Marquess of Linlithgow, the Viceroy, himself participated in the preparation of a comprehensive document on Frontier policy. Although strongly favouring at least a partial disarmament of the tribes, he admitted that as yet no way had been found to eliminate the gun factories in Waziristan, and that this would also be impossible to implement in view of the international situation. Lord Linlithgow's recommendations amounted in fact to no more than a very slight modification of the existing 'Forward Policy'. Thus, the military dispositions, involving the presence of large numbers of regular troops in advanced positions in the unadministered Tribal Territory, remained substantially unaltered when the war broke out.[18]

It is not easy to provide the basic biographical data on the Faqir of Ipi: his life has always been shrouded in mystery. He was born as Mirza Ali Khan sometime between 1892 and 1897, into the Bangal Khel clan of the Madda Khel section of the Tori Khel Wazirs, which belong to the greater Utmanzai branch concentrated in Northern Waziristan. He first went to religious schools on the British side of the border, and, eventually, to a place near Jalalabad, where he became a *murid* (pupil) of the Naqib of Chaharbagh, at the time the most famous and influential religious leader in Afghanistan. In 1923 Mirza Ali Khan performed the *Haj* to Mecca and thereafter settled down in the village of Ipi, situated near the British military road connecting Bannu and Razmak. There he gradually acquired the reputation of saintliness among the clan of Daurs, but not attracting as yet the attention of the authorities as a potential agitator.[19]

In March 1936, however, came the turning point in the Faqir's career. The incident was the trial case of the so-called 'Islam Bibi', which concerned an alleged abduction and forcible conversion to Islam of a Hindu girl, still a minor. The case aroused considerable local excitement in which the Daurs joined in at the Faqir's instigation. The British retaliated by sending two columns converging in the Khaisora river valley. They suppressed the agitation by imposing fines and by destroying the houses of the ringleaders, including that of the Faqir of Ipi. However, the triumph was not theirs. The subsequent planned withdrawal of the troops was credited by the Wazirs to be a manifestation of the Faqir's miraculous powers. He succeeded in inducing a semblance of tribal unity, as the British noticed with dismay, among various sections of Tori Khel Wazirs, the Mahsuds and the Bhittannis, who were usually at logger-heads, thus well preparing the ground for his bold challenge which was soon to follow. He continued to ride on the wake of the 'Islam Bibi' case which, upon appeal, had been lost for the Islamic party, and he gradually added, measure by measure, a long catalogue of local Muslim grievances under the slogan 'Islam in Danger'.[20]

Thus, after eleven years of relative peace in Waziristan, a major rebellion began to flare up. In the early autumn of 1936 the Faqir of Ipi openly adopted the role of champion of Islam. There were, however, other long-standing reasons for the rapid spread of unrest on the Frontier. Since the early 1930s a radical Muslim movement in the NWFP, the *Khudai Khidmatgaran* (Servants of God), more popularly known as the 'Red Shirts', had made, rather unexpectedly since the NWFP was overwhelmingly a Muslim province, a common cause with Mahatma Gandhi's Congress Party. The Red Shirts, organized on a paramilitary basis under the charismatic leadership of Abdul Ghaffar Khan, called upon the tribesmen across the administered border to help the Congress to free the subcontinent from the British yoke.[21] During 1930-1931 the garrison of Peshawar had to quell an internal uprising in the city and to fight off an Afridi invasion, stirred up by the arrests of the Red Shirt leaders. Furthermore, the recent constitutional changes following the Government of India Act of 1935 which granted self-government to the eleven provinces of British India, indicated to the tribesmen that British authority over India was withering away in favour of a distant but still disquieting perspective of a possible Hindu take-over. Paradoxically, in September 1937 the NWFP became, thanks to the agitation of the Red Shirts, the only Muslim province with a Congress government.[22]

For all intents and purposes, British and Indian troops in

Waziristan were to remain on active service continuously for the next twelve months. The Faqir had successfully avoided all traps and remained constantly on the move over the rugged but familiar terrain, in which a modern army with its cumbersome equipment and long supply lines proved all too slow and inefficient. The elusive Faqir earned himself the nickname 'The Scarlet Pimpernel of Waziristan', as a contemporary couplet testified: 'They sought him here, they sought him there, those columns sought him everywhere.'[23] Although his tactical moves still remained entirely unpredictable, he pursued his major political aim with single-minded determination: stirring up the maximum trouble for British authorities, forcing them thereby to withdraw beyond the administered border. Soon, a number of Waziri *mullahs* were to demand a complete British evacuation of Waziristan.[24] India's Northern Command, despite substantial numbers of troops at their disposal, must have felt frustrated by their inability to design any coherent pattern of operation against the Faqir. The 1937 campaign was soon bogged down and fragmented into numerous separate operations none of which could dislodge the Faqir.

The fame of the Faqir's miraculous powers spread quickly. He attracted a large number of followers who brought in food and money, which helped to some extent to keep his *lashkars* in the field (a self-supporting tribal levy, capable of action without replenishments for about twenty days). As the tribesmen flocked under the Faqir's banners in a genuine belief in his claims to divine support, Indian intelligence considered it important to analyze their credulity and superstition as an important strategic factor. Here are some of the miraculous powers commonly attributed to the Faqir of Ipi:

> Firearms would not harm his followers, provided they were true *ghazis*, i.e. followers of Islam, and not mere plunderers and adventurers in search of private gain; his followers had only to cut off trees and the Faqir would turn the sticks into rifles; a few loaves of bread in a basket covered by a cloth, would suffice to feed a multitude; gas, if loosed by the troops, would be dissipated by divine breezes; divine power would turn bombs dropped from aircraft into paper (an opportunist miracle which must have appeared on the verge of fulfilment when aircraft were employed to drop leaflets. . .)[25]

Fantastic as such stories may appear today, they were widely believed in tribal areas and even reached distant bazaars in India.

Throughout 1937 the tribal raids into the administered territory continued, seemingly undeterred by military action. Meanwhile intelligence sources tried to track down the Faqir himself. They found him hiding in a Mahsud village in the Shaktu river valley with the delightful name of Arsal Kot, which was then promptly flattened by air action — but without causing much harm to the Faqir as he had moved into the safety of a cave nearby. Here he was visited by many tribesmen, mostly those who were neither receiving British allowances nor profiting from the *khassadari* system and had therefore little to lose. The Faqir also sent letters to all quarters, including the Mohmands, Afridis, and the Kurram Wazirs, as well as to tribes in Afghanistan proper, urging them all to join in the *Jehad* against the British.[26] In September 1937 he wrote a letter to Jawaharlal Nehru, then the President of the Indian National Congress, addressing him as 'the leader of the liberty-loving people and the distinguished Head of the Indian Nation'.[27]

However, despite all the Faqir's extraordinary appeals to Muslim tribesmen, they failed in their main purpose due to the inability of the tribes to combine their considerable fighting power in any common cause under a unified command, even though the Faqir's *lashkars* achieved quite a few stunning successes by blocking British lines of communication. In retaliation, the British set out to take Arsal Kot but, of course, found the nest empty. The Faqir had fled further south in an attempt to seek refuge among the Bhittannis. This, however, the British prevented by extensive air bombing and by sending in troops. But the ubiquitous Faqir yet again managed to elude them. After failing to bribe the Faqir by offering him land outside Waziristan to help him to settle peacefully elsewhere,[28] the British attempted to get the Afghan government to assist in the capture of the Faqir. But, as could have been predicted, these attempts failed as well.[29] Meanwhile, the Faqir moved westwards. He was to hide for the rest of his life among the Madda Khel Wazirs. They continued to shelter him despite British reprisals. He occupied inaccessible caves in the mountain cliff at Gorwekht, barely a mile from the Afghan territory into which he could easily slip should the British ever attempt to dislodge him from his eagle's nest.

Some voices alleged that the Faqir's incredible capacity to throw in his *lashkars* whenever he liked was largely due to his receiving Italian money and arms. On 16 April 1937, for instance, the *Daily Herald* claimed on its front page that 'Mussolini was behind the revolt on the NWFP'. The British Minister in Kabul could find nothing to substantiate this wild claim.[30] But the rumours continued. The *Sunday Chronicle* of 26 February 1939 implied that a radio link between the Faqir of Ipi and the Italians had been established, and added, for good measure: 'Meanwhile Hitler is active in Kabul. . . where more and more German airmen are being sent as instructors.' Again, Fraser-Tytler refuted these rumours, but, on the other hand, he did admit that the Italian Minister at Kabul, Signor Pietro Quaroni, was using unscrupulous methods to spread extremely bellicose anti-British propaganda among Indian visitors.[31]

But there was another unusual incident which occurred in 1938 on the Frontier, known as the Shami Pir affair, and in which the Axis powers were believed to be implicated. When by December 1937 nearly 40,000 British and Indian troops pulled back to their cantonments, the situation was no better than it had been at the beginning of the campaign twelve months earlier.[32] While the Faqir of Ipi was still left at large, a major threat of extraordinary dimension was developing in Southern Waziristan which might have brought down the ruling Afghan royal house of Yahya Khel. The story is worth telling, especially as it was connected with the appearance of Muhammad Saadi al Keilani, otherwise known as the Shami Pir — the holy man from Syria. His arrival was seen by many as playing the counterpoint to the actions of the Faqir of Ipi. The Keilani family claimed direct descent from the Prophet and spiritual leadership of one of the most important Islamic fraternities: the Quadiria. Muhammad Saadi, then a young man of thirty-seven years of age, had studied in Germany where he had married a daughter of a senior police officer from Potsdam. He was also, through his extended Afghan lineage, first cousin of ex-Queen Souriya, Amanullah's wife. During the latter's rule, he had visited India and Waziristan where he spent some time among his religious adherents. Thence he proceeded to Kabul where he stayed as a guest of the Foreign Minister and Amanullah's father-in-law, Mahmud Tarzi, whose sister had been the wife of Keilani's grandfather. Although King Amanullah had treated him in public with marked affection, there is little evidence — though Indian intelligence had a vested interest in proving the contrary — that Keilani maintained other than family contact with Amanullah's family in exile in Rome after the King's resignation in 1929.[33]

By the end of 1937 Keilani decided to visit India again, ostensibly for the purpose of collecting money (*shukrana*) from the Quadiris, which was customary among religious leaders. Since the British authorities saw nothing objectionable in these activities, he was granted a visa to India and arrived at Bombay on New Year's Day. Towards the end of January 1938 he entered NWFP and in March went further to Southern Waziristan. Until June he preached on religious matters, spent his time settling disputes amongst the tribes, and did his best to unite the Wazirs and Mahsuds. He gained a very large following and was deeply revered as a saintly person, the Shami Pir, like his counterpart the Faqir of Ipi in the northern half of Waziristan. Almost immediately upon his arrival on the Frontier, the Afghan government became deeply suspicious of his activities and alleged that he had come to stir up pro-Amanullah and anti-Yahya Khel propaganda, but Major Barnes, the Political Agent for Southern Waziristan, who had met Keilani several times, was not able to corroborate these suspicions.[34] However, on 13 June the Pir summoned against British wishes a *jirga* (tribal assembly) of some 3,000 tribesmen.

He openly denounced the ruling Afghan King Zahir Shah as a usurper and acclaimed Amanullah as the lawful king of Afghanistan.[35] This announcement, as Fraser-Tytler admitted in his annual report, unleashed a wave of fanatical enthusiasm which ran through south Waziristan with such electrifying effect that the tribesmen, predominantly Mahsuds, flocked in to join the Pir, who on the 23rd set out on his march to Kabul. It did not bother the Mahsuds in the slightest that less than ten years earlier they had played a leading role in installing Nadir Shah upon Amanullah's throne. They wanted to be kingmakers again. For four days the downfall of the Kabul government seemed very possible. The Pir's appeal, however, did not reach wider Amanist circles inside Afghanistan and his supporters failed to establish contact with the Ghilzai insurrection right across the Durand Line.[36] 'It was only with the most determined use of force combined with cajolery', writes Sir Olaf Caroe, a man with probably the best insight into the affair, 'that the Government of India were able to secure the Pir's surrender and removal, and the break-up of *lashkars* already on their way to Kabul'.[37] Fraser-Tytler, writing about the extraordinary incident long after the war, recalls that 'it was a very narrow escape from a disaster of the first magnitude. . .'.[38] 'The use of force' meant straightforward air bombing by the RAF of the Pir's *lashkars* before they could reach the Afghan border, and the word 'cajolery' — though Caroe does not elaborate further as if the details were too painful to reveal — suggests a handsome bribe of

£25,000, offered to the Shami Pir on condition that he discontinue his activities and return to Syria at once. Hence, although the British authorities were rather slow in recognizing the threat, they were nevertheless extremely quick to meet it. Already on 25 June the Pir had agreed to the deal and was flown out of the country shortly thereafter.[39]

The Shami Pir affair left many people completely baffled as to the British scheme behind his activities. The German Minister in Kabul, Dr. Hans Pilger, admitted for instance to his British colleague, that he was totally at a loss to account for British policy on this occasion: was the Shami Pir a British agent introduced to Waziristan to raise the tribes against the Afghan government which, nevertheless, everyone assumed was pro-British, in the face of a potential Soviet aggression? Or was he somebody else's agent? Whose then?[40] As for Caroe, who was in charge of India's external relations during the war, he remained deeply convinced that the Shami Pir's activities had been part of a more sinister Axis intrigue designed for the whole of the Middle East, of which the Grand Mufti of Jerusalem appeared to have been the chief exponent and which Indian intelligence failed to discover. It was not only the Shami Pir's family connection with Amanullah which worried Caroe so much. Another deeply intriguing pointer for him was the Keilani brotherhood in the Muslim world and he wondered whether there were not definite contacts between the Shami Pir and Rashid Ali al Gailani of Iraq, who, as Prime Minister, was to attempt in the spring of 1941 to ally his country with the Axis.[41]

Such conjectures were to be put forward frequently during the war, particularly after the British learned that the German Foreign Office and the *Abwehr* had contacted the Shami Pir. However, there is precious little evidence to show that he had been recruited by the Germans at any stage prior to or during the war to work for them for the restoration of Amanullah to power in a pro-Axis Afghanistan. Although the Shami Pir had visited Germany before the outbreak of the war in 1939, and took refuge there for the rest of the war after Syria had been recaptured by the Free French with British assistance, he denied to his British interrogators after the war that he had resumed contacts with Amanullah or had ever met Ghulam Siddiq Khan, the ex-King's most active supporter, in Berlin. Sometime in June 1939 for instance, British intelligence learnt that the Shami Pir had admitted in the course of a private conversation that the German authorities had expressed their displeasure at his failure to carry out the restoration of Amanullah to the Afghan throne.[42] Indeed, it is conceivable that the Pir might have been contacted during this time by von Hentig, who was the head of the Oriental Section in the Political Department of the Wilhelmstrasse till the outbreak of the war, and was rightly regarded by the British as the most competent and therefore dangerous expert on the Islamic countries.[43] But in 1939 Hentig certainly did not include Keilani in his secret plan for the restoration of Amanullah to power, which the Wilhelmstrasse and the *Abwehr* had hoped to put into effect with Moscow's help, following the conclusion of the Nazi-Soviet Pact.[44] By the end of 1940 the Pir was again contacted by the Germans at his home in Syria. There were rumours that he had been promised the Afghan throne if he would be prepared to go to India at once and to conduct his mission successfully. In January 1941 he was again visited by the *Abwehr* agent in Syria, Rudolf Roser, in the company of von Hentig, who was said to have been putting pressure on the Pir to go to Afghanistan to help to stir up a pro-Amanullah rebellion. Again the Pir refused.[45]

With the failure of the Shami Pir incident of 1938, the Axis missed its last chance on the eve of the Second World War to exploit the tribes against either government. Further, during the war, even in the early stages when the Axis held the military initiative and had sympathizers among the Muslims, such unique opportunities as the rising in Waziristan under the Faqir of Ipi in 1936-7, and the Shami Pir incident in the following year, never presented themselves again.

Let us now return to the Faqir of Ipi — still the main protagonist on the Frontier — who remained rather inactive during the Shami Pir agitation. There are some striking points of similarity and dissimilarity between these two men. First of all, it remains but a speculation that the two religious leaders could have combined their powerful charisma and organizational talents in raising both parts of Waziristan for a common purpose. While the Faqir needed Afghan assistance, or at least friendly neutrality, for his activities against the British who were, after all, his chief enemy, the Pir ventured in an opposite direction: he agitated for the overthrow of the existing Afghan government in favour of Amanullah's restoration. This he did, it appears, without the ex-King's explicit instructions, let alone direct involvement. For this he required at least some British connivance, if open support was ruled out. Although the Pir was later to claim that he had gained the Faqir's active support for his venture, Indian intelligence denied this resolutely.[46]

Thus, given the specific conditions prevailing on the Frontier, it could not be argued that the Syrian adventurer prevailed against the local religious fanatic. During the war, however, the Faqir, though quick to explore unscrupulously any opportunity which could guarantee him Axis supplies of money and arms, proved extremely furtive whenever Axis agents tried to establish a direct communication with him via their diplomatic missions in Kabul. He did not want to be harnessed into any anti-British scheme which would not be of his own doing. As far as the reports of the Faqir's alleged support for Amanullah during the war are concerned, these must be taken with a pinch of salt.[47] Although one can never be certain whether his loyalty to the Yahya Khel in Kabul would have resisted the temptation to join the pro-Amanullah forces had they been present in sufficient strength and had they been supported by the majority of the Waziri tribes, as long as Amanullah was physically absent and the German intrigues insignificant, there was no reason to expect the Faqir to change sides too hastily.[48] Moreover, had the 'godless' Soviets been a party, alongside the Germans, in a pro-Amanullah coup, one cannot imagine the Faqir working hand in glove with them and the ex-King, whose radical reforms of the 1920s he must have loathed. In any case, the last chance for the Axis to gain the Faqir's collaboration expired in the summer of 1941, at the height of German influence in Afghanistan and prior to the formation of the Anglo-Soviet alliance.[49]

Things might have looked different had that great intriguer, Hentig, replaced Pilger as the head of the German Legation at Kabul. Immediately after Barbarossa commenced, the Nazi Foreign Minister Ribbentrop issued instructions to Hentig to go to Kabul. His task was not only to observe and report on, but to support actively 'the national independence movements in Iran and Afghanistan, particularly in so far as these are connected and cooperate with one another'.[50] Hentig was further instructed to ascertain British strength and position both in India and Afghanistan, to coordinate all German agents and experts available at the time in Afghanistan, with the purpose of using them, if necessary, against the government in power. He received specific orders to establish direct links with the Frontier tribes and their leaders —

among whom the Faqir of Ipi was seen as the most important. Fortunately for the Allies, Hentig never reached Kabul due to combined Anglo-Soviet diplomatic pressures on the Afghan government, which also brought about, later in November following the events in Iran, the expulsion of Axis nationals from Afghanistan.[51]

It was in fact Pietro Quaroni, the Italian Minister at Kabul, and not his German colleague, who became the driving spirit in establishing direct contact with the Faqir of Ipi. Already in June 1939 he was reported to have declared in front of two Indian visitors that the Frontier tribes should be worked up and, in the case of war, led against the British: 'We could not defeat Great Britain in a war in those areas, but seriously injure her, and we possess adequate instruments for the purpose.'[52] One month later, Quaroni told the Germans in Kabul that the Axis powers should coordinate their political activities in Afghanistan with a view to using Amanullah as well as promoting unrest among the tribes on the Frontier in the event of war with Britain.[53] But how the Axis would have used Amanullah and the Faqir of Ipi at the same time has never been explained in detail. On the other hand, Quaroni played a crucial role in helping Subhas Chandra Bose, a former President of the Indian National Congress and the most serious rival to Gandhi and Nehru, to acquire an Italian passport when he was hiding in Kabul in February 1941. Bose was then able to reach Berlin via the Soviet Union and became the most prominent Asian revolutionary to collaborate with the Axis both in Europe and in Asia.[54] Quaroni summed up his conversation with Bose as follows:

> If in June 1940, that is at the time when the defeat of England seemed certain, we had a ready organisation like the one Bose proposes now, it could have been attempted to liberate India, and it might have been possible. Politically and militarily India is the corner-stone of the British Empire. Last year's chance is gone, but a similar one could come this year also; one should be ready to take full advantage of it. . . . Our enemies, in all their wars, the present one included, have always largely used the 'revolution' weapon with success: why should we not learn from our enemies? Two things are necessary to make revolutions: men and money. We do not have the men to start a revolution in India, but luck has put them in our hands; no matter how difficult Germany's and our monetary situation is, the money that this movement requires is certainly not lacking. It is only a question of valuing the pros and cons and to decide on the risk.[55]

Bose indeed assigned the Tribal Territory an important role to play in his comprehensive 'Plan for Cooperation Between the Axis Powers and India', which he submitted immediately after his arrival in Berlin. Isolated attacks, such as those carried out by the Faqir of Ipi, were to become part of an ambitious scheme to combine propaganda and subversion against the British Empire at its most vulnerable spot. In his single-minded obsession with ousting the British from India, Bose was convinced that the mere appearance of a small force of 50,000 soldiers with modern equipment on the Frontier would have been sufficient to turn the British out of India.[56] However, the Axis proved incapable even in following up Bose's more modest suggestion to set up a strong propaganda centre on the Frontier with a radio transmitter and printing equipment — though these were available at Axis legations in Kabul — let alone to airlift commando troops to Afghanistan.

According to Quaroni's own extremely detailed testimony made to the British after the Italian surrender in 1943, it had taken the Axis agents a whole year after the outbreak of the war to establish direct contact with the Faqir of Ipi. Because of procrastination both in Rome and Berlin, it was not until March 1941 that Quaroni's proposal to send the first payment to the Faqir was accepted.[57] The holy man from Waziristan had a quite definite idea how he should charge the Axis for his real and potential capabilities. Through his intermediaries, the Axis legation in Kabul received the following price list: £25,000 paid every other month to keep the pot boiling; to double the sum if tribal unrest should be extended to other areas; in the event of a general uprising on the Frontier the price would have to be tripled, not counting supplies of weapons and ammunition which the Faqir also required urgently.[58] The German Minister in Kabul admitted that to keep the tribes in the field against the British was a sheer question of money. But even if the Faqir's annual requirements amounted to around half a million Reichsmark,[59] it would have been quite a cheap price considering the cost which the government of India had to spend on each punitive expedition into the Tribal Territory. It was not so much the problem of forwarding foreign banknotes to Kabul, which the Axis did not find difficult as long as the Soviet territory remained open for traffic to and from Afghanistan, but that of converting pounds sterling and US dollars into a convenient currency like Afghanis or Indian Rupees which the Faqir's men could use.

Indian intelligence, suspecting that links between the Axis and the Faqir had existed for some time, first received concrete evidence in June 1941, after the arrest of the interpreter to the Italian Legation in Kabul while he was visiting his relatives in Baluchistan. According to his statement, several Italians had visited the Faqir between 1939 and 1941 with supplies of money and weapons, including machine-guns and a wireless transmitter and receiving set.[60] He also supplied the British with the names of Afghan officials and army officers collaborating with the Italians and with the Faqir, which were then used by the British and Indian governments to bring more pressure to bear upon the Kabul authorities.[61] When Quaroni was confronted with this statement, it infuriated him that the British 'could have swallowed the most palpable rubbish' and made themselves 'ridiculous in Afghan eyes by using it as evidence'.[62] The only European to have visited the Faqir during the war was Enrico Anzilotti, the Secretary of the Italian Legation, who did so alone and in disguise as a Pathan tribesman in June 1941. Anzilotti reported that the Faqir was in principle ready to start action against the British on the Frontier, but required money, weapons, and ammunition. He repeated the terms of cash payments and the Faqir's wish to have a wireless transmitter with a trained operator.[63]

The Germans, too, wanted to establish their own link with the Faqir. But unlike the Italian improvisation theirs had to be on a truly grandiose scale. The establishment of contact with the Faqir, furnished with a transparent code-name Operation Feuerfresser (fire-eater), was to be followed by Operation Tiger, a full-scale uprising among the Frontier tribes scheduled for September 1941 when Barbarossa was expected to be completed. The plan had been hatched by *Abwehr II*, responsible for sabotage and subversion, whose commander stipulated Tiger's task as follows: (a) to incite the Frontier tribes, mainly the Mohmands, Afridis and Wazirs; (b) to damage important military installations in North-West India; and (c) to supply weapons to the tribes so as to enable them to attack field fortifications prepared by the British in the Frontier passes.[64] *Abwehr* officers were despatched to Rome to contact Amanullah, and to Sweden in order to consult the last survey maps of India with Sven Hedin, the famous explorer and authority on central Asia.[65] Meanwhile, in Kabul, preparations for the full-scale uprising on the Frontier (*Grossaufstand*) were in full swing. The chief *Abwehr* agent there, Lieutenant Witzel, who under the cover-name 'Pathan' was to be in charge of contact arrangements with the Faqir of Ipi, was full of optimism. He had already started giving sabotage instructions to members of the 'Bose-Organization' in Kabul;[66] it did not occur to him at the time that the main recipient of his sabotage instructions, and indeed of most of the Axis money, was at the same time spying for the Soviets.[67]

Thus, in mid-July, shortly after Anzilotti's successful return, the impatient Germans could wait no longer. Off to Gorwekht they sent their two specially trained agents, accompanied by a dozen tribesmen carrying ammunition and money. They never reached their target, falling into a trap set up by the Afghan authorities in the Logar valley just south of Kabul. In the ensuing exchange of fire with an Afghan patrol waiting in ambush for them, Professor Manfred Oberdörffer was killed and Dr Fred Brandt wounded, the tribesmen arrested and everything confiscated. Oberdörffer was a specialist in tropical medicine and had participated in several expeditions to Africa and Asia, Brandt was a lepidopterist. Both had nonetheless been fully trained agents of the *Abwehr* with a very definite task to perform. The *Abwehr* experts in Berlin thought that if the two men posed as 'leprosy experts' and collected insects and butterflies en passant, they would appear entirely harmless and inconspicuous on the Frontier.[68] To save face in the eyes of ever watchful British and Soviet diplomats, and in order to preserve the policy of strict neutrality during the war, the Afghan government ostensibly criticized the conduct of the German Legation for their direct involvement in the Logar incident. But privately the German Minister received an apology from the Afghan Premier, who was quick to reassure him that his government, in the event of German troops approaching, was ready, as Pilger had reported to Berlin, 'to let all of Afghanistan take up arms on our side. . . about 500,000 men including the tribes'. But he begged Pilger repeatedly to abandon all such ventures like the recent incident. Such attempts were all bound to fail given German ignorance about the country and its people and given the vast British spy network.[69]

In spite of the fact that the Logar incident amply demonstrated that German intelligence was incapable of mounting even a small-scale operation in Afghanistan, let alone a major one on the Frontier, Axis activities with the Faqir through intermediaries went on for some time. Axis legations still had some money to spend. Besides, their staff had to be engaged, in the eyes of Berlin and Rome, in some meaningful activities to justify their presence in Kabul. In view of the pending Anglo-Soviet invasion of Iran and, possibly, of Afghanistan, Ribbentrop in Berlin readily agreed to spend as quickly as possible the balance left over from the original sum of one million Reichsmarks in hard currency and gold, which had been earmarked for subversive activities in Afghanistan and India. About half-a-million Reichsmarks was still left unspent. This equalled about two-and-a-half million Afghan Rupees. The other half-a-million had already been brought to Kabul during 1941 before the Allied occupation of Iran by five couriers from Germany. Such funds enabled the German Legation in Kabul not only to send regular payments to the Faqir of Ipi but also to finance their schemes in India until the end of the war whereas their poor Italian partners could afford nothing of this sort.[70] However, despite receiving Axis money, the Faqir still failed to launch a 'large-scale' operation against the British which he had been promising for some time. Since 1941 Indian intelligence had been haunted by repeated rumours — which were also partly self-generated as it later transpired — about two German mechanics working with the Faqir of Ipi. They were reported to be spending their time sketching the countryside, presumably in connection with the preparation of a landing-ground for Axis warplanes, and counterfeiting Indian and Afghan banknotes.[71] By February 1943 Indian intelligence estimated that the Faqir must so far have accrued about half-a-million Afghanis paid to him through the Axis legations.[72] During that and the following year, however, the British were able to acquire a fairly accurate picture of the Faqir's strength, his gun factory and other hiding places. They were satisfied to learn that the Faqir had no wireless transmitter nor any receiver, but only a simple radio set. Nor were any Europeans in Gorwekht, nor had there been any let alone those mysterious Germans.[73] As for the notorious Faqir of Ipi, during the dramatic months of 1941 he remained in seclusion at Gorwekht, despite German intentions to induce him into action. He continued to display an intriguing unawareness of the world situation. In one of his letters to *mullahs* in Southern Waziristan, which came to the knowledge of Indian intelligence, the Faqir stated, while continuing to vilify the British, that no help should be given to the Germans as they were opposed to Islam.[74]

But in the following spring, symptoms of growing tribal unrest became clearly discernible in Waziristan as the Faqir persisted in his attempts to fine Wazirs engaged by the British in defence works and threatened local contractors with religious sanctions. It is important to realize that these seasonal job opportunities were the only ones available to the tribesmen, already suffering from the economic constraints imposed by the war on both sides of the Frontier.[75] In May, the Faqir besieged the fortified outpost at Datta Khel with approximately 500 tribesmen, supplemented by machine-guns and a few primitive pieces of artillery. The British sent in a relief column supported by light tanks and aircraft, but the convoy failed to reach its objective because of road blocks. Two additional infantry brigades had to be sent in and it was not until August that the road to Datta Khel could finally be opened and repaired.[76] What worried the British was not just that the Faqir had recruited a substantial number of Afghan subjects to his ranks but, even more, that the Axis legations had re-established direct contact with him — despite the fact that in the previous autumn over 200 Axis nationals had already been expelled from Afghanistan, leaving behind only a skeleton staff at both legations.[77]

Meanwhile, in August 1942, a major internal upheaval flared up in India. The Congress-inspired rebellion was not only the most important rising to occur within the entire British Empire, but within the entire United Nations coalition during the war. 'The Quit India Movement', wrote Lord Linlithgow to Churchill, was, 'by far the most serious rebellion since that of 1857, the gravity of which we have so far concealed from the world for reasons of military security.'[78] One would have expected the Axis powers, as long as they still possessed strategic initiative, to make a maximum effort to exploit the crisis in India, 'when the British position was never so weak and that of the Axis never so favourable'.[79] Since I have treated the complex reasons for German indecision elsewhere,[80] I shall confine myself to dealing with events directly relevant to our main theme.

During the August Rebellion in India the only noticeable increase in Axis activities was through their radio propaganda. But apart from broadcasting, no concrete assistance was forthcoming from the Axis. Was it conceivable at all to despatch for instance to the North-West Frontier a mixed unit of German and Italian paratroopers, supplemented with a limited number of ex-Indian prisoners-of-war who were willing to fight for the Axis? The *Abwehr II* had already discussed such plans in August 1941 but decided to postpone action till German troops advanced nearer to India.[81] But in the spring of 1942 there was already some uncoordinated fighting going on in western India, which had tied up British and Indian troops and thus given the Axis planners ample time to initiate some kind of direct military assistance before the

August riots. As mentioned earlier, in Northern Waziristan, the Faqir of Ipi besieged Datta Khel and was appealing to the Axis for financial assistance and ammunition which could have been dropped by airplanes.[82] Further south, a fanatical sect of Hurs, dacoits from Sind, stepped up terrorist actions against railway lines, frequently interrupting traffic between Karachi, Hyderabad and Lahore, and in June martial law had to be proclaimed over the area. The atrocities committed by the Hurs during the train-wrecking continued well into the spring of 1943, when their savage leader Pir Pagaro was then finally caught and sentenced to death.[83] In addition, unprecedented landslides, following exceptional floods in Upper Sind and Baluchistan during July 1942, resulted in a further interruption of the important strategic railway lines connecting the port of Karachi, the main American base in India at the time, with the approaches to Afghanistan and the NWFP.[84] Although the train-wrecking by the Hurs had no political motivation, the German Legation in Kabul was led to believe that these actions had been directly instigated by Bose's underground organization in India, and that the Faqir of Ipi had been co-ordinating with Pir Pagaro.[85]

Mainly because of their preoccupation in quelling the rebellion in India, British pressure on the Afghan government during that period almost ceased. It cannot altogether be ruled out that an internal crisis in Afghanistan, aided by Axis intrigues, might have given ex-King Amanullah one more chance. The India Office feared that continuous Axis intrigues among the tribes and with the pro-Amanullah elements in the country 'might undermine and bring about the downfall of the present Yahya Khel regime whose continued stability is so obviously in our interests to promote'.[86] There were indications that the Amanists in Axis Europe wanted to set up an Afghan government in exile. The prime mover behind this scheme was not the ex-King himself but his brother-in-law and former Foreign Minister, Ghulam Siddiq Khan. He was in contact with the Grand Mufti in Jerusalem, with the ousted Iraqi Premier, Rashid Ali al Gailani, and especially with Subhas Chandra Bose, the most important Asian exile in Berlin. Had an Afghan government in exile been established in Germany, Bose was convinced — ignoring Hitler's fundamental opposition on this issue — a 'Government of Free India' would soon follow suit, thereby striking an incalculable blow to Allied propaganda. Fortunately for the British, the Axis had no clear concept of how to accommodate under one roof its support for Amanullah's restoration with that for the Frontier tribes and the Faqir of Ipi.[87] After the outbreak of the Congress Rebellion, Amanullah made it known to the Italians that he was now ready to broadcast and use his name in the Axis press to encourage his supporters in Afghanistan, as well as fellow Muslims in India, to rise in revolt against the British. He was afraid that the British, after eliminating the Congress as negotiating partners, might go ahead with the disastrous scheme of Pakistan. Amanullah was said to be particularly keen to offer his good offices for influencing the Pathan tribes who neither recognised the Kabul government nor the Axis powers, but were seemingly ready to fight for the ex-King. But the Italians declined his offer as they were in perfect agreement with the Wilhelmstrasse that the moment was not propitious enough to antagonize the existing Afghan government in favour of Amanullah.[88]

It was not earlier than December 1942, when the main thrust of the Congress Rebellion had already been suppressed, that the chief *Abwehr* agent in Kabul, Lieutenant Witzel, produced his most comprehensive scheme yet for an all-round military action to be staged on the Frontier.[89] The idea was, in fact, the same old one which had been tried unsuccessfully by the Germans during the First World War: namely that of using the armed tribesmen to tie up as many British troops as possible in North-West India — thereby facilitating the expected Japanese advance on India from Burma. The scheme was equally as bold as it was naive, for it anticipated strong pro-Axis feelings among the tribes, of whom Witzel calculated that about 400,000 armed men would potentially be available against the British. Witzel's key man whom, needless to say, he never met, was the unapproachable Faqir of Ipi, being already in contact, so he claimed, with other guerrilla leaders such as Hassan Khan in Baluchistan and Pir Pagaro in Sind. In order to prepare for a major uprising (*Grossaufstand*) in these three areas, Witzel estimated that at least one million Rupees, 25,000 Sovereigns, and 200 kg of gold would be required. Necessary ammunition was to be supplied by air. Witzel calculated that in order to supply a fighting force of 50,000 tribesmen in Waziristan with 250 cartridges each, 525 tons of ammunition would have to be flown in. His calculations were wrong, for the cargo would have amounted to 5,000 tons and this would have to be transported over a distance of 4,000 kilometres. This the *Luftwaffe* was in no way fitted to carry out. Leaving aside such speculation as what the Afghan government's reaction might have been to such massive violation of their airspace, the basic strategic premise for the Axis operation in India rested upon an assumed penetration of the Caucasus by German troops. But by the end of 1942, this was definitely doomed. Yet, with whatever scepticism we may approach late German schemes for an Axis-instigated major tribal uprising, whose most striking feature was its overestimation of inter-tribal cohesion — not to mention a remarkable disregard of such broader military factors as logistics — one wonders even today what might have happened in central Asia during the second half of 1942, if at the height of the German military triumph even a few Axis planes had landed or paratroopers been dropped on the Frontier.

How seriously was the Axis threat to the stability of Afghanistan and to India taken by the British? Although the Axis connection with the Faqir of Ipi was vastly exaggerated by Indian intelligence, British diplomats in Kabul saw it more realistically. Thus, the new minister, Sir Francis Wylie, summed up his appreciation in October 1942:

> There was a healthy little disturbance in North Waziristan a couple of months ago fomented by Ipi. Simultaneously the Germans were advancing towards the Volga at a terrific pace. If Pilger and Quaroni were really dangerous men and if they had unlimited resources and really close contacts with Ipi, what better chance of doing something nasty and incidentally of tying up quite large formations of British-Indian troops were they likely to get or at what more suitable juncture?... The Axis Legations (a) undoubtedly had some money though probably not enough to foment large trouble either in internal India or on the Frontier; (b) that whatever they had in the way of resources they had so far succeeded in giving us very little trouble — after more than three years of war — compared with the not inconsiderable fears which we harbour about their activities and the high potentiality which we are inclined to accord to these activities.[90]

A year later Quaroni admitted to his British interrogators that he himself had already realized during the summer of 1941 that the Axis plans to use the Faqir of Ipi were a sheer waste of time and money. The most propitious time, he maintained, to start action against the British on the Frontier would have been in the autumn of 1940. But the Germans in Kabul, whom he characterized as to a greater or lesser degree incompetent, had wasted their time in slowly collecting information, in working at cross purposes, and in spending most of their time sending mutual denunciations secretly to Berlin. Quaroni gave four reasons why it became impossible to start a general revolt on the Frontier by using the Faqir after the outbreak of the Russo-German war: (a) the Faqir's authority was too circumscribed; (b) even with unlimited supplies of arms the Faqir could not gather more than 10,000 adherents; (c) he and his men would be useless outside their mountain fastness; (d) the Faqir relied on arms which could no longer be supplied by land after Hitler had attacked Russia whence previously arms could have been smuggled through as 'factory machinery'. As regards the idea of sending warplanes to the Faqir, Quaroni believed that it had been technically feasible since the Italians possessed at the time long-distance planes which could have taken off from their base at Rhodes. However, this idea had been rejected allegedly in deference to the Faqir's own view that, whilst the planes would not bring him much material help, they would inevitably attract the attention of the British, who would proceed unmercifully to bomb the Faqir's headquarters and all surrounding villages.[91]

During 1944 the Frontier remained unusually quiet, the peace being occasionally disrupted by the customary raiding and by British retaliation in the form of air bombing. Although German intrigues with the Faqir continued, they were entirely harmless. Nevertheless, one might still ask why the Germans continued to pursue those futile activities when the prospects of a decisive military breakthrough in favour of the Axis powers had vanished by the end of 1942? The answer lies partly in a strong tendency to survival which is characteristic of all bureaucratic institutions, even if these activities are no longer useful. In order to justify their presence in neutral Afghanistan, Axis diplomats and agents displayed feverish bogus activity which, of course, nobody in Berlin could verify. Although it was clear to all participants in the game at both ends that a second major upheaval in India was no longer possible, that there was not the slightest chance of inciting the Frontier tribes through direct Axis assistance, they carried on their activities, be it in Kabul or at the receiving end in Berlin, as if such an opportunity was ever very close. On the British side we can observe a similar bureaucratic phenomenon in the desire to show off in 'successfully tracking down German agents', particularly among members of Indian intelligence, civilian or military, watching the Frontier from Peshawar or Quetta. They would have been even more frustrated had they known about the true 'Great Game', which was the double-crossing of Axis plans through the exploits of the multiple agent Rahmat Khan — a closely guarded top secret by the IPI (Indian Political Intelligence). It would have been otherwise incomprehensible why the Allies did not insist after November 1941 on the expulsion of the remaining Axis 'diplomats' from Kabul.[92]

The end of the war did not stop the Faqir of Ipi from resuming his activities against the British who were, in any case, ready to quit India soon. Thus the year 1946 again saw the British in action in Waziristan and the Faqir making yet another attempt to unite the Mahsuds and the Wazirs.[93] After Partition the Faqir turned into the most vehement tribal opponent to the Pakistan takeover of the British heritage. He allied himself with the Red Shirt leader Adbul Ghaffar Khan for an independent Pukhtunistan, thus transferring his old hatred of the British to the new Pakistani authorities — regardless of the fact that they shared with him the same creed. In 1948 the Faqir succeeded at last in taking Datta Khel. Although the Pakistani authorities did not want to and could not afford to imitate the British 'Forward Policy' on the Frontier, they carried on the tradition of air bombing in order to disperse the Faqir's *lashkars*.[94] The Faqir is known to have made a series of overtures to Pandit Nehru, whom he allegedly addressed as 'King of India'[95] — but to no avail. Apart from receiving constant encouragement and material help from the Kabul government, who referred to the Faqir of Ipi as the 'President of the National Assembly for Pukhtunistan',[96] he increasingly became suspected of being in receipt of Soviet assistance — though this allegation still needs to be substantiated by hard evidence. However, in 1955, that is when the Faqir was still alive and fighting, the Afghan Prime Minister Prince Daud, who was known as a strong advocate of Pukhtunistan, received official backing for his policy from the visiting Soviet Premier Bulganin and Party Secretary Khrushchev. The Kremlin leaders then referred to Pukhtunistan and overtly stated that the Soviet Union stood for a 'just settlement of the problem'.[97] Although it may appear that particularly since the 1979 invasion of Afghanistan, Russia has been nearer to the 'just settlement' of the Frontier problem than at any time in her history, one should not forget Lord Curzon's dictum: 'I do not prophesy about the future. No man who has read a page of Indian history will ever prophesy about the Frontier.'[98]

NOTES

Abbreviations in the text and footnotes

BA-MA	Bundesarchiv-Militärarchiv, Freiburg i.Br.
CAB	Cabinet Papers (archives in the Public Record Office London)
FO	Foreign Office London (archives in the Public Record Office)
GFO	German Foreign Office (as classified in G. O. Kent, *A Catalog of Files and Microfilms of the German Foreign Ministry Archives, 1920-1945,* vol. 3, Stanford, Cal. 1966)
GOI	Government of India
IO	India Office London
IOR	India Office Records (archives in London)
NWF(P)	North-West Frontier (Province)
WO	War Office London (archives in the Public Record Office)

I wish to thank Prof. R. E. Frykenberg, Univ. of Wisconsin-Madison, for his valuable comments.

1. Major-General J. G. Elliott, *The Frontier 1939-1947. The Story of the North-West Frontier of India* (London 1968), 165-174, 228-331.

2. Entered the ICS (India Civil Service) in 1919. Pol. Officer in the NWFP since 1923 and from 1933-4 Chief Secretary to its Governor. From 1934-7 Deputy Secretary in the For. and Pol. Dept. of the GOI. Between 1937-8 British Resident in Waziristan and Agent to the Gov. General in Baluchistan. From 1938-9 Revenue Commissioner in Baluchistan. From 1939-45 Secretary of the External Affairs Dept., GOI. From 1946-7 Governor of the NWFP.

3. Sir Olaf Caroe, *The Pathans, 550 B.C.-A.D. 1957* (London 1958).

4. W. O. von Hentig, *Mein Leben eine Dienstreise* (Göttingen 1962), 91-199; O. von Niedermayer, *Im Weltkrieg vor Indiens Toren* (Hamburg 1942); see also the recent critical investigation by R. Vogel, *Die Persien- und Afghanistanexpedition Oskar Ritter v. Niedermayers 1915/16* (Osnabrück 1976).

5. This is an allusion to a title of a pamphlet published in Nazi Germany by E. Tewes, *Der Freiheitsheld von Waziristan* (Aalen 1940).

6. There is some scanty evidence that in 1937 the Soviets through their Naval Attaché offered advice and assistance to Afghan military cadets in Turkey who had requested it for the Faqir of Ipi (N 3943/14/97, FO 371/21065).

7. W. K. Fraser-Tytler, *Afghanistan* (London 1967), 190-191.

8. WO 208/773: Tribal allowances in the NWFP.

9. Ibid.: Tribal cooperation in the NWF.

10. This has been surprisingly ignored in the recent literature on the guerrillas. The recent massive and authoritative book by Robert B. Asprey (*War in the Shadows. The Guerrilla in History*) is a telling illustration of this negligence. Even recent publications by authors in India and Pakistan on this subject are no exception, e.g. B. N. Majumdar, *The Little War* (New Delhi 1967); M. Akbar Khan, *Guerrilla Warfare. Its Past, Present and Future* (Karachi w.d.).

11. WO 208/773 & 774.

12. Compiled from: The Royal Institute of International Affairs, *Political and*

Strategic Interests of the United Kingdom (London 1939), 284-285; B. Prasad (ed.), *Defence of India: Policy and Plans.* Official History of the Indian Armed Forces in the Second World War 1939-45 (New Delhi 1963), 35-37, 118-120; CAB 68: W.P.(R)(39)5.

13. See reminiscences of Field-Marshal Sir Claude Auchinleck, who served as a brigade commander on the Frontier during the 1930s, in C. Allen (ed.), *Plain Tales from the Raj* (London 1977), 197.

14. W. S. Churchill, *My Early Life 1874-1908* (London 1969), 107-167.

15. Fraser-Tytler, op. cit., 269.

16. Ibid., 270.

17. C. F. Andrews, *The Challenge of the North-West Frontier. A Contribution to World Peace* (London 1937), 10.

18. Memorandum by the Viceroy on Frontier Policy, 22 July 1939, IOR L/P&S/12/3265.

19. Note on the Faqir of Ipi, 24 June 1937, WO 208/773.

20. Ibid.; Activities in Khaisora Valley. FO 371/20313-20314; Activities of the Faqir of Ipi: IOR L/P&S/12/3236-3237, 3192-3193, 3249, 3217-3219; Waziristan 1933-1938: WO 106/5446, FO 371/24766; see also Elliott, op. cit., 271-289; A. Swinson, *North-West Frontier. People and Events 1839-1947* (London 1967), 327-332; G. N. Molesworth, *Curfew on Olympus* (London 1965), 115-120.

21. R. Coupland, *The Indian Problem 1933-1935* (Oxford 1943), 127; id., *Indian Politics 1936-1942* (Oxford 1943), 121-123; Swinson, op. cit., 305-320; J. W. Spain, *The Pathan Borderland* (The Hague 1963), 165-173; Caroe, op. cit., 431-434.

22. Ibid.; cf. also the unpublished PhD thesis by S. Rittenberg, 'The Independence Movement in India's North-West Frontier Province, 1901-1947' (Columbia Univ. 1977).

23. See the *News Review* of 8 June 1939, which estimated that the cost of the thirty months' effort to capture the Faqir must have been in the region of £10 million. Cf. also Elliott, op. cit., 273.

24. N 4935/14/97, FO 371/21065.

25. Intelligence Report on NWF, 24 June 1937, WO 208/773.

26. N 5642/14/97, FO 371/21065.

27. J. Nehru, *A Bunch of Old Letters* (Bombay 1960), 251-252.

28. N 5820/14/97, FO 371/21065.

29. FO 371/22234-22238. The Afghan Prime Minister Muhammad Hashim Khan admitted to the British Minister in Kabul that it was quite impossible for the Afghan government, for usual reasons of religion and loss of face with their own people, to cooperate with the British in armed operations against the Faqir of Ipi (IOR L/P&S/12/3236).

30. IOR L/P&S/12/3249; see also N 3281/14/97, FO 371/21065; and the *Daily Express* of 17 May 1937.

31. FO 371/23630 and IOR L/P&S/12/3249.

32. Thirty-six battalions of infantry, almost the entire air force, and substantial artillery and auxiliary units were deployed in Waziristan. Cf. Operations in Waziristan, December 1937-December 1938, by Gen. R. A. Cassels, C-in-C India, 13 April 1939, WO 106/365; see also Spain, op. cit., 185; Swinson, op. cit., 328-331; Elliott, op. cit., 278-281.

33. Caroe's letter No. 7989 of 25 August 1945 to IO with enclosure, IOR L/P&S/12/3258; Afghanistan-Annual Report 1938, FO 371/23630; Diary of Mil.

Attaché-Kabul, FO 371/22248; IOR L/P&S/12/3255-3258; CAB 24/278: C.P. 188.

34. Ibid.; Interrogation of Shami Pir in October 1945 by Lt.-Col. H. O. de Gale, FO 371/45216; Comments by Dep. Director Intelligence, Peshawar, NWFP, February 1946, IOR L/P&S/12/3258.

35. Ibid.; Report from Brit. Consulate-Damascus, 26 August 1939, IOR L/P&S/12/1656.

36. Afghanistan-Annual Report 1938; Kabul to FO, 27 February 1941, IOR L/P&S/12/1778.

37. Caroe, op. cit., 407-409.

38. Fraser-Tytler, op. cit., 266-267.

39. Cf. IOR L/P&S/12/3255-3258. Sir George Cunningham, Governor of NWFP, reveals in his diary (entry 29 June 1938) that he himself had to draw a cheque for the Shami Pir from his own bank (cf. IOR MSS. Eur. D.670).

40. Kabul to FO, 16 March 1939, IOR L/P&S/12/1758.

41. See footnote 33 above.

42. Ibid.; and further FO 371/23614-23619; IOR L/P&S/12/3257.

43. See footnote 4 above.

44. IOR L/P&S/12/1656. The German-sponsored Amanullah Plan of 1939/40 is discussed in detail in chapter II-4 of my book *India in Axis Strategy. Germany, Japan, and Indian Nationalists in the Second World War* (Stuttgart 1981).
1981).

45. See Hentig's manuscript 'Aufzeichnungen 1934-1969' vol. 2, chapter 'Reise nach Syrien', 9, Institut für Zeitgeschichte, Munich. Hentig does not disclose the true nature of his political mission to the Shami Pir and reveals no more than trivialities. For the British view: IOR L/P&S/12/256, 3257-3258.

46. Note on the case of the Shami Pir, prepared by the Intelligence Bureau, GOI, in IOR L/P&S/12/3258.

47. E.g. GOI to IO, No. 2704 of 25 July 1940, WO 106/3651.

48. Peshawar Weekly Intelligence Summary, No. 41 of 9 October 1939.

49. Ibid., No. 39 of 25 September 1939.

50. GFO 329/195546-8; see also Hentig, *Aufzeichnungen,* 1957, vol. 2, 41-42.

51. See chapter III-3 in Hauner, *India in Axis Strategy* (under footnote 44 above).

52. See footnote 31 above.

53. Report by Dr. Georg Ripken, head of the German trade delegation in Kabul, 7 November 1939, GFO 617/249899-910.

54. See chapter II-8 in Hauner, *India in Axis Strategy.*

55. Extracts from Quaroni's report of 2 April 1941, as reported in S. C. Bose, *The Indian Struggle 1920-1942* (Calcutta 1964), 415-418.

56. GFO 195/139137-43.

57. As compiled from IOR R/12/1/131, L/P&S/12/1805; FO 371/34931, 34932, 39936; WO 208/30.

58. GFO 617/249975, 195/139145-9.

59. GFO 617/249926, 249956-7, 249958. After the war Hentig claimed that the money had never reached the Faqir (cf. Hentig, *Aufzeichnungen,* vol. 2, 36).

60. IOR L/P&S/12/3249, R/12/1/131.

61. IOR L/P&S/12/1778.

62. E 8036/1757/97, FO 371/34932.

63. GFO 617/249975. It was only symptomatic of Italo-German relations that the *Abwehr* denied the claim of their more successful partners that Anzilotti had visited

the Faqir of Ipi. The Germans accused Quaroni of keeping the money for himself (cf. R. Schnabel [ed.], *Tiger und Schakal.* Deutsche Indienpolitik 1941-1943. Ein Dokumentarbericht, Vienna 1968, 198-199).

64. BA-MA/RW 5, OKW/Ausland/Abwehr, Lahousen Tagebuch, 118, 138.

65. Ibid., 138-139.

66. GFO 617/249956-7.

67. The agent's name was Rahmat Khan. He was a member of the Kirti Kisan Party in the Punjab which was known as crypto-communist. In January 1941, he escorted S. C. Bose from Peshawar to Kabul. For more details about this extraordinary double-agent of the Second World War, see M. Hauner, *India in Axis Strategy.*

68. Lahousen, op. cit., 118, 138; GFO 329/195561-3, 4748H/E233441-9; IOR L/P&S/12/1572 & 1778.

69. GFO 617/249988-90; cf. also GFO 329/195554-63.

70. GFO 617/250004, 329/195539.

71. Army & Air Headquarters Intelligence Weekly Summary of NWF & Afghanistan, No. 30 of 29 July 1941, No. 37 of 19 September 1941, and No. 45 of 14 November 1941.

72. Ibid., No. 2 of 15 January 1942, No. 11 of 20 March 1942, No. 13 of 4 April 1942; Kabul Weekly Intelligence Summary, No. 2 of 16 January 1943, No. 5 of 5 February 1943, and No. 7 of 19 February 1943.

73. IOR R/12/1/122.

74. GOI to IO, No. 5889 of 27 October 1941, WO 208/26; cf. also 'Indien Nachrichten', No. 1 of 5 November 1941, GFO 41/28568.

75. General Headquarters India Weekly Intelligence Summary of NWF & Afghanistan, Nos. 18-24 from 8 May to 19 June 1942.

76. CAB 68/9:W.P.(R)(42) 29, 33, 38, 43; FO 371/34928.

77. Kabul to GOI, No. 221 of 19 June 1942, FO 371/31324; GFO 195/139669-71. On the expulsion of Axis nationals from Afghanistan, see M. Hauner, *India in Axis Strategy*, chapter III-3.

78. N. Mansergh and E. W. R. Lumby (eds.), *The Transfer of Power 1942-1947. Constitutional Relations between Britain and India* (London 1971), vol. 2, No. 662.

79. Two memoranda by F. J. Furtwängler, member of the 'Sonderreferat Indien' at the GFO Berlin, dated 26 September and 9 October 1942, GFO 1313/350076-80, 350069-73.

80. In this article I have concentrated on the German side only; the Japanese factor has been analyzed in my forthcoming book.

81. Lahousen, op. cit., 175-176, 190; Schnabel, op. cit., 98-99, 142; GFO 195/139273; cf. GFO document of August 1941 entitled 'Die indische Nordwestgrenzprovinz', GFO 1314/350132-204.

82. GFO 1065/312851, 312904, 312966; 195/139919-21, 140043-5; cf. also *The Times* (London) of 10 July and 13 August 1942.

83. WO 208/786 & 795, 106/3712; CAB 68/9:W.P.(R)(42) 29.

84. Ibid.; Molesworth, op. cit., 237-243; the *Manchester Guardian* of 20 March 1943.

85. Lahousen, op. cit., 226.

86. G. E. Crombie, Principal in IO Pol. Dept., to R. T. Peel, Head of IO Pol. Dept., 22-24 December 1941, IOR L/P&S/12/1789.

87. GFO 617/250184-8, 329/195476-7.

88. GFO 86/62917-63.

89. GFO 195/140047-64.

90. Comments on Peshawar Intelligence Summaries on Events in Afghanistan by F. Wylie to D. Pilditch, Director of Intelligence Bureau, Delhi, 21 October 1942, IOR L/P&S/12/1928.

91. E 8036/1757/97, FO 371/34932; see footnote 57 above.

92. See footnote 67 above.

93. FO 371/52290; India Command Fortnightly Intelligence Summary, No. 12 of 7 June 1946, in WO 208/761A.

94. IOR L/P&S/12/3241.

95. The *Dawn* (Karachi) of 28 June 1948.

96. Spain, op. cit., 237-243.

97. The *Dawn* (Karachi) of 18 December 1955; R. T. Akhramovich, *Afganistan posle vtoroi mirovoi voiny* (Moscow 1961), 146, 171; M. R. Arunova, *Afganistan — spravochnik* (Moscow 1964), 215; see also R. D. Hicks, 'An Analysis of Afghanistan-Pakistan Tensions 1947-57' (M.A. Thesis Stanford 1958), 93-95.

98. Lord Curzon of Kedleston, *Speeches as Viceroy and Governor-General of India 1898-1905* (London 1906), 43.

Notes on Contributors

Peter Baldwin is a Teaching Fellow in the History Department at Harvard University and is the author of articles on Max Nordau and on Weimar Jewry in the journal *Central European History*, June 1981.

Ralph Bennett is the President of Magdalene College, Cambridge. He is the author of various publications on medieval European History and of *Ultra in the West* (1979), and is currently working on a book on Ultra and Mediterranean strategy.

Hugh De Santis is the special assistant for West European regional affairs (Bureau of Intelligence and Research) at the US Department of State. He received his PhD from the University of Chicago in 1978. He is the author of *The Diplomacy of Silence* as well as a number of articles on international relations.

Michael R. D. Foot is the editor of *The Gladstone Diaries* (1968-74) and the author of *SOE in France* (1966), *Resistance* (1977), *Six Faces of Courage* (1978) and, with J. M. Langley, *MI 9* (1979). He is currently working on a history of England from 1815 to 1916.

Alan Foster is a Senior Lecturer in Politics at the Thames Polytechnic. He has had papers published in the fields of comparative politics and political education and is currently involved in research into 'The British Press and the Origins of the Cold War'.

Rear-Admiral Gueritz is a consultant to the Royal United Services Institute for Defence Studies. He is also President of the Society for Nautical Research and sets naval questions for the television series, *Mastermind*.

David Haglund is Assistant Director of the Institute of International Relations, University of British Columbia. He has recently finished a manuscript entitled 'Latin America and the Transformation of American Strategic Thought' and is now engaged in a research project on Canada and the international politics of oil.

Milan Hauner is currently at the History Department, University of Wisconsin-Madison. He is the author of *India in Axis Strategy*.

Germany, Japan and Indian Nationalists in the Second World War (Stuttgart 1980).

Gerhard Hirschfeld is at present a Research Fellow at the German Historical Institute, London. He is the author of *Die Kollaboration mit der deutschen Besatzungsmacht in den Niederlanden während des zweiten Weltkriegs* (forthcoming), and is currently working on 'Corporatism in Britain in the Inter-War Period'.

Frank King is co-editor, with Robert D. Craig, of the *Historical Dictionary of Oceania,* published by the Greenwood Press (Westport, Connecticut).

Gerald Kirwin is at present lecturing at a college in Mülheim/Ruhr, West Germany. He was a postgraduate student in the Department of Politics, University of Reading and in 1979 was awarded a PhD for his thesis, 'Nazi Domestic Propaganda and Popular Response, 1943-45'.

Paul Kramer after twelve years in intelligence, both as a civilian and a naval officer, left to become a businessman. He is the author of *The Last Manchu, Latin American Panorama* (with Robert McNicoll) and *The City in American Life* (with Frederick Holborn).

John Daniel Langer has taught American diplomatic history, American history and Russian history at Yale University and at Bennington College, Vermont.

Walter Laqueur is Director of the Institute of Contemporary History and Wiener Library in London, and Chairman of the International Research Council of the Center of Strategic and International Studies in Washington. He is co-editor of the *Journal of Contemporary History* and of the *Washington Quarterly.* His works in the field of modern history and international affairs include *Weimar, Guerrilla, Terrorism* and the recently published *The Terrible Secret*. His first novel, *The Missing Years*, was published in 1980 and its sequel, *Farewell to Europe* in 1981.

Ronald Lewin is a Fellow of the Royal Historical Society and a Fellow of the Royal Society for Literature. His publications include *Rommel as Military Commander, Montgomery as Military Commander, Slim the Standard-bearer* (the official biography of Field Marshal Lord Slim; W. H. Smith Literary Award 1977), *Ultra Goes to War* and *The Chief*, a study of Field Marshal Lord Wavell. His current book, *The Other Ultra: Codes, Ciphers and the Defeat of Japan* is due to be published in 1982.

Mark M. Lowenthal is a Specialist in National Defense with the Congressional Research Service, Library of Congress, Washington. He is the author of numerous articles and of a novel, *Crispan Magicker*. Dr Lowenthal works primarily in the areas of intelligence and national security policy formulation, and recently completed his third novel.

Graham Ross is a Lecturer in International Relations at Leeds University. He is the author of 'Operation Bracelet: Churchill in Moscow, 1942' in Vol. 2 of D. Dilks (ed.), *Retreat From Power* (London 1981). He is currently working on two books: *The Great Powers and the European State System 1914-45* and *The Foreign Office and the Kremlin: Documents on Anglo-Soviet Relations 1941-45*.

Patrick Salmon is a Lecturer in History at the University of Newcastle upon Tyne and is currently working on a study of British and German economic and political relations with the Scandinavian countries in the 1930s.

Vice-Admiral Schofield is a Fellow of the Royal United Services Institute for Defence Studies. His publications include *The Loss of the Bismarck* (1972), *The Attack on Taranto* (1973), *Operation 'Neptune'* (1974) and *The Arctic Convoys* (1977).

Philip M. Taylor is a Lecturer in International History at the University of Leeds. He is the author of several articles on the subject of British propaganda in the twentieth century, and his first book, *The Projection of Britain; British Overseas Publicity and Propaganda, 1919-39* was published in 1981. He is currently working on a book concerning British propaganda during the First World War with M. L. Sanders of Middlesex Polytechnic, to be published by Macmillan later this year.

Major-General A. J. Trythall is Director of Army Education in the Ministry of Defence. Previous publications include *Boney Fuller. The Intellectual General 1878-1966* (London and New Brunswick 1977) and articles in the *RUSI Journal*, the *Army Quarterly* and the *British Army Review*. He is at present engaged in the preparation of a book on 'Innovation in the Military Bureaucracy'.

Mark Wheeler teaches Balkan history at the University of Lancaster. He is the author of *Britain and the War for Yugoslavia, 1940-1943* (New York 1980).

A Mother Dimension

Mink Elliott

www.minkelliott.com

We shall not cease from exploration
And the end of all our exploring
Will be to arrive where we started
And know the place for the first time

***TS Eliot* (no relation!)**
Four Quartets

1

‘Well, *I’ve* got wrinkles on my *cankles*!’ Kate declared.

Georgia nearly spat her Pinot Grigio out, managing to regain a little wine-soaked decorum just in time to nod enthusiastically and splutter, ‘Okay, okay! You win!’

Kate had, once again, trounced the competition in the Who’s Looking Oldest? game – although, to be honest (as Kate always tried to be these days – what with trying to be a good role model for the kids and everything), it was never really much of a contest.

Everyone knew that Kate, with a penchant for anything with astronomical levels of fat, sugar and salt and three kids under her undo-up-able belt, looked way older than her best friend, childless Georgia.

Georgia slapped her (thin, long) thigh with mirth, but the two men seated at the table looked nervously at each other. Was it okay for them to laugh at Kate’s revelation? Would that render them insensitive? Insulting? Sexist? And what the hell were cankles, anyway? They slowly nodded at each other, as if to give the go-ahead, and haw-haw’d loudly, shrugging their shoulders and pouring more wine into their own glasses.

Kate herself cackled, safe in the knowledge that even though she may, indeed, have calves like Doric columns, there were, as yet, no wrinkles on them. She had, earlier that day, seen a line encircling each thick ankle, and had been suitably mortified. But she was relieved to find it was merely the mark left by the too-tight, short sports socks she'd been wearing as she'd tried (in vain) to tackle that Davina McCall exercise DVD in her front room again.

She looked fondly at Georgia, remembering how the pair had fared so differently years ago when they decided to adopt the French Women Don't Get Fat approach to eating and drinking. It was written by the CEO of Veuve Clicquot and advocated walking everywhere, turning the TV off, quaffing (expensive, French) champagne, munching buttery croissants and popping a couple of squares of dark, organic chocolate into a perfectly-lipsticked mouth every now and again. It was all about being sophisticated and indulging yourself every so often, pushing the pleasure principle, the idea that a little bit of what you fancy does you good.

Of course Georgia, who already looked like a French noir movie star by the time she was three years old, had no trouble staying slim and looking all leggy and louche and glamorous, whatever she did. The French woman diet involved very little change for her.

Kate, on the other hand, just a few centimetres shorter than George, her 10-year-old son, had always been a complete stranger to such things as 'moderation', 'control' and 'self-restraint'. And there was always such good telly on! And she just didn't like dark chocolate – was that a crime?

An image of her chubby arm with its fat fingers opening a battered old fridge full of Veuve Clicquot and Kit Kats flashed into Kate's head.

'Podgy, pissed and poor,' she muttered to herself, as if she were introducing three new Dwarves to Snow White.

She pulled Declan, her sleepy eight-and-a-half-year-old, to her breast and ruffled his hair.

'You must get back to bed now, Darling,' she breathed her alcoholic fumes all over his soft, warm, Johnson & Johnson's-smelling, thick hair and pulled away, slightly ashamed by their sharply contrasting aromas.

She quickly planted a dry kiss on the top of his head as the boy lazily left her embrace and whined as he wandered towards his father. Kate followed her son with her eyes, her gaze falling onto Seamus, who was sitting opposite her at the other end of the table. She felt herself sway slightly in her seat and her head swam – but her eyes stayed glued to her husband.

And then she felt something stir within her, confusing the very core of her being.

Was it lust?

Nah, couldn't be. Sure, she'd felt a vague attraction to all the guys on Horrible Histories from time to time – who hadn't? But that had been mere maternal murmur compared to this rambunctious rumbling.

No, the sexual part of her life was well and truly over, she thought to herself. After all, it had been 33 months, four days and seven hours since the last time she remembered feeling anything truly sexy. Not that she'd been keeping count or anything. Much.

An excessive amount of red wine?

Possibly, considering she'd been off alcohol for nearly two years, due to a sickly pregnancy and a punishing (but immensely satisfying) breast-feeding schedule. This *was* her first foray back into the adult world of dinner parties since she found out she was pregnant all those months ago, so perhaps she was merely suffering from the Lightweight's Lurgy – getting all hot and bothered after only a few sips.

But she didn't feel drunk, exactly – or even a little bit tipsy...

Oh God, Kate O'Reilly thought to herself. I'm having a hot flush, aren't I?

She sat bolt upright, heat spreading through her body. It was as though molten lava, starting first at her scalp, was working its way down, coursing thickly through her veins.

It *must* be the menopause, she reasoned, because it simply *couldn't* be lust.

Then again, she thought, it's been so long, you wouldn't know what desire was if it came up and tore your knickers off.

Her fingertips tingled and she imagined tiny sparklers attached to them as she watched her husband laugh and haul their son onto his broad shoulder in an outstandingly manly, heroic fireman's lift.

'Back to bed for you, Big Man,' chuckled Seamus

as Declan struggled valiantly in mock protest.

It's funny, really, Seamus thought to himself as he went upstairs: he never thought he'd see the day when he'd voluntarily leave a party in favour of the kids. Like all his old mates he rarely saw these days, it had taken him quite some time to come round to the whole kid/family thing. And, if he was being honest, he'd never really wanted so many kids – two would have been perfect. Even just the one would have suited him fine.

But he'd mellowed over the years, got a bit less selfish and, he congratulated himself, become quite the model dad in the process. He enjoyed it – and he was good at it. He'd even go so far now as to say that sometimes he *preferred* hanging out with George and Decko – even Baby Jane when she wasn't throwing up or soiling yet another nappy – over just about anything else.

Except golf, of course. Which reminded him - he'd better get an early night tonight if he was to be any cop out there on the golf course tomorrow morning.

Kate watched Seamus trudge through the doorway and slowly climb the stairs, like the giant carrying Jack back up the beanstalk.

'Fe, fi, fo, fum,' she murmured, instantly regretting saying it out loud. She shook her head slightly, wondering when – if ever - she was going to stop seeing the world through a fairy tale lens.

Her hot flush – if that's what it was - got a smidge

hotter. But it couldn't be. Surely it couldn't be the menopause yet. She was only 44. Peri-menopausal perhaps? In a little less than one month's time she would turn 45 and even *that* was still too young for The Change. Wasn't it? Even if her own mother had started it at 45? God, where *was* her mum when she needed to ask her about all this sort of stuff?

Kate fanned her face and tried to compose herself.

'Sorry about that, Kevin. Kids, eh?' she said. 'Do you have any?'

Kevin stared at Georgia who looked away quickly, her eyes studying the slightly nauseating orange/brown/beige swirly carpet to her right. For a strong, smart, fiercely independent and spectacular-looking woman in her early 40s, she suddenly seemed vulnerable and fragile. Even the tiniest bit anxious.

But only to the well-trained eye. Only Kate would have noticed those flickers of fragility in Georgia – because she'd known her for what sometimes felt like forever. They'd been best friends practically since the moment they first met, a million years ago, at Reception.

As they got older, they only seemed to get closer. Kate even named her eldest boy, George, after her. And if Georgia had ever had kids, she probably would have called them Kate - girl or boy.

'Nope,' grinned Kevin. 'Well...none that I know of, anyway.'

Georgia looked up and exhaled, her relief audible.

Kate got up to open a window and asked her

guests: 'Is it just me or is it really hot in here?'

'It's just you,' replied Georgia. 'It's only the beginning of June, remember. And one warm evening does not a summer make. No need to break out the Pimm's just yet. Although...'

A wicked smile crept across Georgia's full, scarlet lipstick-drenched mouth and she half-winked at Kevin across the dining table.

Kate watched as Kevin's Adam's apple bobbed up and down a bit and heard him swallow loudly. He'd barely been able to take his eyes off Georgia all night and now he looked not only smitten and mesmerised, but a tad nervous, too.

'Now, there's an idea,' Kevin said in the Sean Connery-James Bond voice he used when he was desperately trying to sound cool. 'Why don't I wander down the High Street and get some? You girls see if you can rustle up some mint, cucumber and oranges and I'll be back in a jiffy.'

Kate raised an eyebrow at Kevin's (quite frankly rubbish) Scottish accent – and being referred to as a 'girl'. She cast her eyes in Georgia's direction and saw that she was positively beaming, coming over all wide-eyed and Noddy-esque in her emphatic approval of the man's plan.

Kevin stood up and grabbed the cagoule off the back of his chair, turning quickly to face the front door lest either Kate or Georgia see him blush.

Jiffy? He asked himself incredulously. Who under 75 says 'jiffy'?

He refused to let his choice of old fogey word take the spring out of his step, though, and fairly bounced out of the front door before Kate had the chance to say: 'No, no – it's already late! I'm dead on my feet as it is and I've got the school run in the morning and the mother's group's coming over at 10 and the place is a tip and...'

Kevin looked up into the bright night sky and casually draped the anorak over his right forearm. It *was* warm, Kate was right. And he was having the best time he'd had in ages. It certainly beat staying up to be lulled into a lonely sleep by the strains of The Shipping Forecast, any day.

But why had it taken Seamus so long to introduce him to Georgia, he wondered. Surely he must have known how desperate – no, no – what did his counsellor say? Not desperate, just keen. Yes. Surely Seamus must have known how *keen* Kevin was to meet Miss Right. Or even Miss Wrong. Just the chance to meet any misses at all would have been a dream come true, let's face it.

Mind you, he reminded himself, Seamus *had* been stupefyingly sleep-deprived the whole time – ever since the baby – Alison? Sarah? No, no – Jane, that was it. Baby Jane. Ever since Baby Jane had come along and made a new Daddy of an old man again, Seamus had barely made it into work, let alone been in any fit state to sort out his best mate's love life.

Now he thought about it, maybe that was one of the real reasons the bank had made Seamus redundant.

He was always late, after all – and when he did make it in, he was spacey and distracted. He'd been caught sleeping under his desk so many times, they probably had no choice but to let him go, even if they'd cited 'infra-structure restructuring' as the official reason for his job no longer existing.

Kevin sucked the dank outside air deep into his lungs and thanked God he wasn't in Seamus' size 10s.

Crivens, though. Was she gorgeous or what? Georgia that is – not Baby Jane, he giggled to himself. But did she – *could* she – fancy him? She was way out of his league, obviously. He knew that, he wasn't a complete cretin. But he could've sworn he was getting some sort of vibe off her – and it didn't feel like the usual revulsion. No, she definitely didn't find him totally repellent because he knew without a doubt what that felt like. Women could be so cruel. But hey! She did wink at him just now, didn't she?

Calm down, Kev, calm down –just keep your cool, he pep-talked to himself breathlessly and broke into a run.

*

'Fresh mint?' Kate's muffled laugh came from deep inside a kitchen cupboard. 'He'll be lucky. Closest we've got is some Colgate upstairs. Oh, hang on - do you think this dried basil,' she squinted, bringing the Sharwood's jar closer to her eyes, 'ah... best before March 2010, will do?'

She clambered down from the kitchen chair and checked the fridge's crisper drawer. She let out a gasp when she spied half a tomato wrapped in cling film, a couple of curled-up outer leaves of an iceberg lettuce, something yellow, shrivelled and furry on a small polystyrene platter, and one small cucumber.

'A-ha! I'll chop this little beauty up and we'll feel like we're front row at Centre Court any minute now,' she said grasping the cucumber with her right hand, its jellied mush oozing forth between her fingers.

'In a *jiffy*, you mean,' Georgia said as she glided in, putting the near-empty pasta bowl on the kitchen table and twirling to face Kate as though it was all part of a carefully choreographed ballet – The Dance of The 1950s Housewife or something.

'Yeah,' Kate snorted, chucking the liquefied cucumber mess into the bin with a thud.

'It's just like the old days, this,' Georgia went on as she pirouetted and plie-ed, gently placing three empty wine bottles in the recycling bin. 'You know, getting drunk together, not a care in the world, fancying the new boy, hoping to get a snog...'

Georgia broke off as Kate silenced her with her hand and a 'shoosh!' It was nearly 11 p.m., and all the kerfuffle with Declan and Seamus having to go through the whole bedtime routine all over again must have woken Baby Jane, because she was crying and screeching away upstairs like a deranged chimpanzee.

'I'd better go and –' Kate began.

'No, no,' Georgia grabbed her by the elbow. 'Let Seamus deal with it. He's much better at getting her back to sleep than you – and besides, when was the last time you and I had a good chat, just us two, no husband, no kids, no –'

'I can't remember,' sighed Kate and plonked herself down into a kitchen chair.

'Exactly.'

'God, they really were the good old days, you know – young and free, able to do what you wanted when you wanted – when you didn't have to arrange a spontaneous night out three months in advance and you'd spend hours just kissing the face off your boyfriend ...'

'Speaking of, how are you and Seamus getting along lately?'

'Good, good,' Kate nodded, her eyes wide all of a sudden, as if she'd just remembered she had a husband. 'No sex, still – but good. I suppose. I mean, he's great, really – nice guy, not bad looking, super with the kids. But – '

'But what? You've just described the perfect man!'

'I know, I know,' said Kate softly, rubbing moisturiser into her rough hands, concentrating on the latest age spot to have joined the rest on her right hand. 'Don't get me wrong, I love him, I really do – love the bones of him. I just don't know if I'm *in* love with him anymore.'

Georgia locked eyes with Kate and raised her chin in a gesture that said 'go on, tell me more' in the pair's silent body language, finely honed over the last 30-odd years.

‘I can’t help craving some more excitement, something a little more high-octane than this,’ Kate’s hand swept before her, knocking over a plastic bottle of Daddies Sauce. ‘I mean, where’s the drama? Where’s that giddy, sudden rush of blood to the head? Where are the butterflies? And feeling like if you don’t see them soon you will just *die*?’

‘That’s only for 15-year-old kids, like Romeo and Juliet. Or 24-year-olds.’

Kate slumped back, contemplating the frightening prospect of never experiencing the dizzy, heart-popping feelings of being madly in love ever again.

A sneaky smile scudded across Georgia’s face.

‘Or 44-year-olds...’

Kate didn’t hear Georgia, she was too busy remembering what it felt like when she was hopelessly in love: with her long lost ex, Tom.

She hadn’t seen him in the flesh for God knows how long, but she hooked up with him regularly in her dreams – about three or four times a week, these days. Sometimes she’d tell herself that this made her, officially, Mrs Normal, three times a week being the national average, and all.

She would wake up all flushed and giggly, bursting with energy and full of girlish glee – even if it was 2 a.m. and Baby Jane’s squawks had just jolted her into consciousness.

‘Earth to Kate O’Reilly, come in, Kate,’ Georgia said into her cupped hand, making her voice sound as though it was coming through a tannoy.

'Sorry, I was miles away,' Kate apologised.

'No change there, then. Yet another trip down memory lane, I'll bet. Kate, Darling, you really do have to do something about this little dwelling on the past problem you've got. You're missing all the good stuff in the here and now – your gorgeous kids, your wonderful husband. You're so lucky, you know. I'd give anything to have what you've got.'

'But you're still so fantastic-looking!' Kate tried to jump up out of her seat, but her bum was a bit too firmly wedged into it. 'You've still got what they call a midriff – not a mummy tummy like I have! And you still have your career! I'd love to be working in an office again – the banter, the money...*And* you can go anywhere you want and do anything you want at a moment's notice –'

'Ach,' Georgia dismissed Kate with her hand. 'Too much drama and far too much freedom. Endless uncertainty. All I want is a little contentment. All I want is the husband and the kids.'

'The handbrakes, you mean. No, no – the hand*cuffs*,' Kate said as she rolled her eyes up to the ceiling. 'But anyway – what's wrong with escaping back in time for a little while every now and again? It doesn't hurt anybody and you get to re-live the good times, say all those things you never thought of at the time so you can floor everyone with your razor sharp wit...'

'If your present's tense, the past can look perfect,' Georgia interrupted.

'Exactly,' said Kate. 'Even though it's not particularly tense anymore, not now Jane's nearly one – it's more, well, *dull*, I suppose. Beyond boring in fact.'

'Give me this kind of boring any day,' tutted Georgia.

'What? You'd swap your amazing Marylebone mansion flat for a semi in the 'burbs? Complete with net curtains, cracked lino and stained carpets?'

'Well, obviously I'd Farrow and Ball all the walls into submission, bin the nets, invest in some plantation shutters, rip out those grotesque carpets, put floor boards down –'

Kate raised her eyebrows in mock offence and put her hand to her chest.

'Well, I never!' she said, sounding a little more at home in her Hyacinth Bucket voice than ever before.

Georgia laughed and the two friends looked around the room, their mouths simultaneously turning down as their eyes were drawn to a large, mysterious dark brown spot right in the middle of the heavily-crevassed kitchen floor.

2

'Where's Kev? And what are you two up to?' whispered Seamus as he peered around the kitchen door jamb.

'You will always find us in the kitchen at parties,' Georgia sang along with Gold Radio (The Greatest Hits of All Time) softly playing all the best bits from the 70s, 80s and 90s.

'Yes you will still find us in the kitchen at parties,' Kate joined in, swaying over to Seamus. 'Remember? You used to love this song!'

'Don't know it – must've been before my time,' he teased.

'Even the music was better back in the day,' Kate continued to plead her case with Georgia. 'God I miss the 80s.'

'The 80s? Nah. Back then I was too young,' grinned Georgia.

'Too young? There's no such thing!' Kate squealed.

'No, the 90s were more my decade,' Georgia stared off into the middle distance, her grin fading fast, only to be replaced by an apologetic grimace.

Kate nudged Seamus in the ribs, their married shorthand for *quick! Say something to cheer her up!*

Because even after fifteen or so years of seeing a psychiatrist, Georgia had still not fully recovered from her trauma. Sometimes, when they were alone together, the best friends wondered whether she ever would.

'Oh! Uh...yeah! Now you're talking,' said Seamus, slapping Georgia awkwardly on the back. 'Oasis, Britpop, football...'

'Must admit, I never really go there in my daydreams,' mused Kate. 'I usually just hang around somewhere near 1988, when I was 18. Maybe you should try my favourite era sometime, Georgie.'

Just then the doorbell rang, wrenching the time travelling threesome out of the past and plunging them slap bang back into the present.

'Oh, shoosh!' said Kate, her mummy reflex going into overdrive.

'So you're shooshing *the doorbell* now?' Seamus said, raising his eyebrows as he headed towards the front door.

'I'll bring the rest of the stuff in,' Georgia mouthed, tip-toeing off behind Seamus.

Kate could hear Seamus, Georgia and Kevin talking and laughing as she carried on clearing up in the kitchen. And despite herself, she even managed to resist several times going into the living room and asking them to keep it down.

Because it was so nice to have a few moments alone so she could hear herself think without demands being placed on her left, right and centre. Shame then, she thought, that all she could think about was *housework.*

But if she could just get a bit of a head start on tidying the place up, she sing-songed to herself, sounding just like her dear, departed mother, then it wouldn't all seem so insurmountable tomorrow morning. Because if there was one thing she'd learnt in this life as a mum (and she counted herself lucky that she'd learnt *anything*, her mummy brain being the consistency of impenetrably dense cotton wool for well over 10 years, now), it was that if you started the day behind schedule, you'd never catch up. And before you knew it, you'd be greeting the coiffed-to-perfection mothers' group with bird's nest hair, red eyes, tear-stained cheeks, an unchanged, pooey baby on your hip, an embarrassingly filthy house behind your back and your hideously unflattering peasant skirt tucked into your saggy, baggy, so-old-the-elastic's-perishing maternity knickers.

Just as she was wincing at this, the memory of the last time she hosted the mums' group meeting, Georgia re-appeared with a stack of plates and two tall glasses of Pimm's.

'Sod the oranges and the mint – all you need's a bit of lemonade and this stuff's simply divine, Kate!' Georgia whispered conspiratorially.

'Go on, then.' Kate didn't bother to struggle getting her Marigolds off, she simply grabbed the fuller glass and downed the whole drink in one.

'Rough day?' Georgia looked surprised.

Kate wiped her mouth on the forearm of the pink rubber glove and stifled a burp, smiling.

'It's like *Revenge of the Nerds* in there,' Georgia jerked her head in towards the front room. 'Two computer geeks comparing gigabytes and hard drives or whatever.'

Kate laughed. Having people round for dinner was so much more fun than falling asleep on the couch to the *Emmerdale* credits, she thought to herself. It felt good to have Georgia here, so happy, so full of beans. And booze. On a school night!

Kate couldn't remember the last time she'd thrown caution to the wind. Ever since she'd had the children, she'd always done the sensible thing: she did what was best for her kids first, her husband second and herself last. *If* she featured in the consideration equation at all. She knew it was the same for all her mummy friends, but she'd never dared admit to them that sometimes she wished she only had herself to think about and look after again. Not all the time, of course, just sometimes.

Still, that's what she had her healthy addiction to nostalgia for – those times when she wanted to escape, but couldn't, tied to the house and the kids as she was. It didn't hurt anyone's feelings, it didn't give her a hangover, she didn't need expensive regression therapy or embarrassing stints in rehab - and it was free. She didn't need to leave the house, change her clothes, remember her keys or even check that her handbag was packed with stuff she might desperately need but actually never did (nappies, wipes, pouches of baby food for emergencies, a change of baby clothes, at least two furry lint-covered dummies and a couple of pounds of stray, sticky sultanas).

Her obsession with the past was her safety harness, her private Prozac, her coping mechanism of choice. Because when being a wife and mother weighed her down, made her feel trapped and overwhelmed her, all Kate needed to do was take a quick journey back through her personal history - to where the music was better, her social circle was wider, her self-esteem higher, her hair thicker and her waist much, much thinner - and voila! All was right with her world again.

Or at least it would be if only she could shake the nagging feeling that she made some seriously bad decisions back then and maybe even married the wrong guy. And then there was the eventual flatlining, the depressing come down when Kate 'came to' and realised that there was not a damn thing she could do to change it. In real time, at any rate.

'So what do you think of Kevin, then? Georgia asked. 'Cute, eh?"

Kate thought Georgia should've gone to Specsavers, but she didn't say it, because she herself was having to hold jars and bottles far away from her face these days, when reading the miniscule print on the labels.

And also, just in time, she remembered that if he hadn't clumsily caused a commotion, due to his unfortunate propensity for tripping over himself at every turn, she probably wouldn't ever have noticed Seamus when she'd first met him. He was so *vanilla*, camouflaged completely by his environment, blending in perfectly with the background like a speccy, geeky chameleon. Especially when she compared him to her stand out, loud, proud and super-attractive Tom.

Even with her failing eyesight, though, Kate could see that Kevin was not particularly cute. Not that he was some kind of grotesque gargoyle or anything, but he was no Bradley Cooper, either.

He was a really nice guy - friendly and definitely warm, yes, Kate'd give him that. Knew a lot about computer programmes, too, if what Seamus said about him was correct. He was probably a brilliant dancer, a Perrier-Award winning comedian, Michelin-starred chef, uber-knowledgeable about wine and the last of the red-hot lovers, too. But cute? Nah. Not really.

'But he's so not your type!' Kate deftly avoided answering the cute question.

'What's my type? Total and utter bastard?'

'Well, um...'

'Not anymore it isn't. No way. He's sweet, smart, the right age, he's single, hasn't got kids, he's good looking and correct me if I'm wrong, but I think he fancies me!'

'Well, of *course* he fancies you, but –'

'So I'm going for it. This could be my last chance for happiness, Kate. Come on, then. Let's go back in there and put some tunes on. Hey! Have you still got my green 12-inch of *Too Shy*?'

*

At 1:45 a.m., Kate waved Georgia and Kevin off at the door. The weather had turned seriously nasty and

Kevin's cagoule was chivalrously sheltering Georgia from the deluge as they made their way to the waiting mini cab.

Kate wearily tramped upstairs to join Seamus in their bed.

'Finally off to Noddington,' she sighed, ruefully noticing that she even talked to *herself* like a child these days. But at least she didn't do it all the time, she consoled herself. No, sometimes she changed the destination... and said 'Bedfordshire' instead.

She carefully placed a large glass of water on her bedside table (that would remain untouched until 5 a.m. when Baby Jane woke up, screaming the house down), and lay back on her pillow, completely submerged and delightfully drowning in the delicious, welcome waves of nostalgia crashing about in her head.

She imagined her younger self in the mid-1990s. It wasn't her usual decade of escape, but made for a rather nice change, she thought. And they say a change is as good as a holiday, don't they? In her mind's eye she was the picture of youthful loveliness: enthusiastic and full of energy; hopelessly romantic and optimistic. And thin!

The sound of Seamus snoring didn't irritate her at all, for once – she barely even registered him, so preoccupied was she, snuggling cosily into her warm past. She closed her eyes and smiled as she remembered her high-heeled Spice Girls sneakers and almost being in the target age range for Top Shop.

Seconds later, amid images of loose-fitting combat trousers and pig tails looking cute and sexy (as opposed to try-hard and mutton), she hopped onto the Snoozeville Express and was out like a light.

3

'Face like a Picasso portrait,' Kate mumbled to her reflection in the bathroom mirror the next morning. 'And eye bags like that belong on a bloodhound.'

It was always a shock, seeing herself like this. Seeing herself at all, actually, was a bit of a surprise. Because over the past ten years, she'd grown accustomed to avoiding her image whenever she could – shop windows on the High Street, all mirrors, other people's sunglasses – she steadfastly refused to look at any reflective surface, anywhere she could catch an unwitting glimpse of her portly, ageing self.

'That'll teach you to look,' she told herself. 'You should know by now it's just not worth the grief and inevitable disappointment.'

She scraped her ever-thinning bob back into a small, split-ended ponytail and smiled at the one thing she looked forward to about getting older: wearing a wig. At least then her hair would do exactly what she wanted it to do – and neither rain, nor humidity – not even gale force winds would mess up her 'do. What joy it would be – such sweet relief.

She brushed her teeth. They were all still her own – a fact she often cheered herself up with (even if they could do with a bit of Hollywood-style whitening to erase all the years of enthusiastic smoking and tea-slurping she'd indulged in before she had kids and became sensible). She snorted with derision as she remembered the hot flushes she'd had last night.

'Lust?' she gargled. 'Ha! Chance'd be a fine thing.'

As Baby Jane toddled up to her mummy's knees and grabbed hold of them, Kate jutted out her chin and inspected it. Seamus used to say she reminded him of Reese Witherspoon, so strong was her jaw-line when she was younger.

'Bet Reese wouldn't be seen dead with chins like this, though,' she muttered when she noticed that overnight one or two (OK, three or four) new hag hairs had sprung forth and the few that were already in residence had turned a most alarming grey. Or, on closer inspection and a bit more worryingly, *white*.

'Looks like Santa might be coming a little early this year,' she grinned down at Baby Jane. Picking her child up, she made a bold move, going ear-to-ear with Baby Jane, looking straight into the mirror and talking to their image. 'You don't mind Mummy letting off a bit of steam, do you Precious? Having a little drink like big girls sometimes do?'

Baby Jane laughed and roughly pushed her palm up into her mum's chin, making Kate's head fly back. She bit her tongue in the process and put Baby Jane down.

'On th-econd thoughth, maybe you do mind,' Kate managed a smile at her youngest. 'And you're right, I'm far too old for that sort of caper. Half-day coach trips with all the other OAPs, stopping at the nearest Wetherspoon's for lunch is more my speed these days:

yes, I'll have a luke-warm, milky Horlicks, with a splash of prune juice and a dash of menopause, a packet of Steradent and a large bowl of salt and vinegar regret, please...'

Baby Jane squealed and clapped her hands.

'Come on you,' said Kate, scooping her up one more time. 'Let's go downstairs and make you some breakfast, shall we? What would you like this morning, hmmm?'

*

Honestly, she thought to herself, where *do* these people come from? All those Facebook friends of hers posting pictures of their idyllic holidays in rustic France, their marvellously photogenic, beautiful kids with their Boden floral dresses tucked into their knickers trying to catch tadpoles in sun-dappled streams while they themselves, all impossibly young- and good-looking, were snapped sipping wine and laughing easily, relaxing under the shade of nearby willow trees in shabby-but-effortlessly-chic straw hats.

'I mean,' she said aloud, 'are they for *real*?'

This innocent-enough question had formed a crucial part of her morning routine, lately. Every day for the past three weeks at around about seven a.m., Kate would fire up her laptop, lose herself in severe Facebook Envy and, soon after, ask the ether the same old question.

Not that she was *always* spying on her old friends, checking out what had happened to them over the years, scrutinising every photo for signs of ageing, weight gain and general decrepitude. No, she often looked up old boyfriends, too. Tom, mainly. Well, always Tom, if truth be told.

But she always drew a blank – nothing ever came up. No articles about the lads' mag he used to edit, no entries in Wikipedia about him, no nothing. It was as though he'd completely disappeared, been wiped from the face of the earth, all trace of him gone.

So if she wasn't tending to one of the kids, making food or watching old music videos from the 80s on YouTube, she'd find Tom again by simply retreating into her own memory banks (the only banks you can trust these days, she was, perhaps, a little *over*-fond of saying), as she spoon-fed Baby Jane.

Both Georgia and Seamus said she was obsessed with nostalgia and she should 'build a bridge and get over it' (one of Georgia's favourite phrases that she thought made her sound young and cool). Seamus said she should 'draw a line under it and move on' – which was about as down-with-the-kids as Seamus was ever going to get.

But Kate could do neither of these things. Not when revisiting old events and conversations was the only way she could keep an (albeit tentative) grip on her sanity. Not when her Groundhog Day reality of domestic drudgery was really doing her head in. Not when her here and now was nowhere *near* as attractive or fun as her there and then. And definitely not when desperate times called for desperate measures.

Times like right now when George and Declan

were fighting, punching each other hard over the kitchen table; when Baby Jane was sitting in the middle of the kitchen floor, covered head to toe in super-sticky, but-at-least-it's- organic strawberry jam; when Seamus was about to leave her to it while he went out to play golf.

'Is who for real? he asked.

'Oh, no one, Shay,' she sighed.

Looking up from the lap top, she saw Seamus sticking his shiny, newly-shaved bald head round the door, his hands unwittingly wiping off several days' worth of honey and Nutella and God knows what else from the door jamb.

'I'm off out for a quick round of golf, OK?' he asked, although he didn't really expect her to be okay with it. His top lip curled as he inspected his fingers, all gooey with unidentified gunge and made for the front door.

Considering her hangover and the fact that Kate and Baby Jane had been up since five a.m. for the seventh morning running, she was a little slow to respond, sleep deprivation being second only to waterboarding as the most effective brain scramblers known to the torture industry.

But not so slow that she didn't wonder whether he should be keeping his head down and seriously looking for work now that he was unemployed. He'd signed up for volunteer work all over the shop as soon as he'd got his marching orders from the bank. It was almost as if being retrenched had restored his joie de vivre –

he seemed so much more... *awake* now. He'd always been banging on about working for various charities, ever since Kate could remember. Which was all very noble and true and brave and everything, but it wasn't exactly going to pay the bills and put food on the table for the family, now, was it?

Kate felt the sharp sting of selfishness nip at the nape of her neck. She loved Seamus' Boy Scout streak, really she did. And the fact that he seemed happier now than he had for ages should have made *her* happy, too, she knew that. But she couldn't help panic a bit when she remembered how much a standard weekly grocery shop for a family of five cost.

She got up and assumed her usual position at the kitchen sink, filling it up to wash baby bottles. And in that very instant, an enormous black cloud engulfed the house, plunging the kitchen into darkness, the lights flickering on and off. In the time it took George to repeatedly press play on the remote and the theme tune for *Sorry I've got No Head* to start up, thunder rolled right over their house, rain pelting the windows, threatening to smash them.

'Isolated showers, yeah right,' Kate muttered, echoing the prediction of last night's weather forecast. But the violent storm had been raging for hours - its on-again/off-again nature no doubt to blame for unsettling Baby Jane and making her wake at such an ungodly hour. Well, *that*, Kate said to herself, and the fact that the poor little mite was obviously teething, what with those toxic poos, nasty nappy rash and consistently high temperature.

'It's positively *torrential* out there!' cried Kate over her shoulder as she scrubbed and rinsed yet another Avent teat. 'You'll catch your death, Shay!'

But it was too late. Just as the word 'death' bungee-jumped off her lips, she heard the front door slam. Or, rather, felt the door slam – suddenly, she found she couldn't hear anything except rain pounding their roof.

Kate's heart sank when she realised she'd have to get the kids ready for school and soothe the inconsoleable Jane all by herself. Again. She stared down at her grubby, pale pink, dog-eared bunny slippers and said in a sing-song voice to the baby: 'If you see a little bunny with a red nose and runny, don't think it's funny, because it's snot.'

She giggled to herself, wondering whether she had lost her marbles for good or whether it was a temporary blip; one which would probably last – ooh - only about another 18 years or so.

George shot her an appalled glance, one which looked a lot like it was saying 'You're so pathetic, Mum.'

Kate clocked George's expression and wiped her wet, dish-pan hands on her pilled, positively *Medieval* it was so old, fleecey dressing gown.

'Ahem!' Kate pulled herself together, strapping Baby Jane into her high chair and addressed what was left of her brood. 'Porridge will be ready in a sec. Anyone for toast in the meantime?'

Of course, she got no reply. George merely turned the TV up, Declan fell off his chair clutching at his tummy, laughing uproariously and Jane's cheeks got that little bit redder with every octave her already-high little voice went up as she caterwauled and desperately tried to extricate herself from the straps of her high chair.

'You poor little love,' Kate cooed, immediately trying to undo the intricate system of pulleys, levers and buckles she'd just done up.

As she carefully put Jane back on the floor, Kate wondered whether this morning – or any time today, this week, this month – she might be able to have a super-speedy shower. Maybe Jane would sleep for two hours after lunch and – oh! What was that? Was that a couple of pigs flying by the kitchen window?

'MUUUUU-UUUUUM!'

The boys chorused their favourite whiney refrain just as the din outside ratcheted up with even more ferocity. She turned to shoot daggers at the cacophony coming from the kids.

'What's happening now?' she demanded as she half-stomped/half-collapsed towards the kitchen table, finding it hard to breathe in the steamy room.

'He knocked over my milk. On purpose!' cried George as he punched his little brother.

'OWW! I did not! OWW! Mum! He gave me a dead arm!' protested Declan.

'WAAAAAAAAAH!' Jane weighed in on the debate, standing up, but quickly falling over as she skidded in the sticky mess on the lino.

Suddenly the stink of teething diarrhoea wafted up through the fug and invaded Kate's nostrils, attacking her sensitive nose, leaving her shocked and awed and very nearly sick.

'Pwoar!' Kate shouted and tried to smile as she looked down at Jane. But just as she bent down to pick her up, she smelled something else - something burning.

'Oh, shhhi -!' she gasped, and ran (ambled, really) to the stove, grabbing the saucepan off the hob and throwing the whole acrid thing, bubbling and hissing, into the sink.

'Did you burn the porridge *again*?' groaned George loudly.

'But Mum! I can't go to school unless I have porridge! Will I have to stay home today? I'll have to stay at home with you, Mum!' shrieked an excited Declan, bouncing up and down in his chair.

'WAAAAAAH!' bawled Baby Jane.

Not having the faintest clue what to do next, Kate did what any self-respecting mum at her wits' end would do – she took a deep breath and turned up the radio. As The Talking Heads' *Once In A Lifetime* blared out, she steadied herself, leaning both arms on the kitchen sink and stared out the window at the water cascading down next door's brick wall.

She let her chins fall onto her chest and closed her eyes until the noise from her offspring was completely drowned out and all she could hear was David Byrne singing about how this was not his beautiful house and nor, indeed, was this his beautiful wife. Too right, she agreed as she opened her eyes and spoke the words, shaking her head slowly.

Then, just as she was girding her loins, about to turn around and face her feuding family, a massive bolt of lightning flashed and split the sodden sky outside. It lit up the whole kitchen, making everything look over-exposed - exactly like her Facebook profile pic ('over-exposure's better than surgery or even PhotoShop for making wrinkles and other blemishes completely disappear', she would often tell Georgia).

Kate shut her eyes tight and found herself wondering for a nano-second whether a nuclear bomb had gone off and whether she and her kids would shortly be flung against the melting walls by the sheer force of the blast and fried alive by the accompanying intense heat.

She heard, somewhere in the distance, in a kitchen far, far away, the muffled screams of three terrified children as the cracking thunder retreated.

Then she smelled perfume – and she knew it wasn't her Air Wick Spring Sensations thingy – that had stopped filling the room with fragrance long ago and she hadn't had a chance to replace it for at least six months now. And it's not like Seamus or the kids would ever do it.

No, it was a posher aroma... something by Chanel that always reminded her of Georgia. And there was something else, too. There was a different feeling in the air and, although not remotely cold, Kate felt a shiver run up and down her spine.

She flipped her eyes open. At once she saw a vase full of deep red and vibrant orange gerberas in front of a spotless window, looking out over sunny, blue-skied but unmistakeably London rooftops. A gleaming tap with a small shower head looked down on a bright white ceramic double Belfast sink and a stainless steel Zanussi dishwasher (sans grubby finger marks) sparkled to the left of her crotch. Kate's eyes sprang up to the window sill once more and focused on the Roberts radio/CD sound system.

'Way-HEY!' she heard the familiar voice of Chris Evans say, seconds before he started banging on about football over the end of *Once In A Lifetime.* When, finally, the fast-talking DJ took a breath, so did Kate.

Panic started to rise in her throat – the kids! Where were the kids? She turned around, wide-eyed, frantically searching the room expecting to see George, Declan and Jane all huddled together in the middle of the kitchen floor, shaking with fear and crying out for their mummy. But instead she saw a fresh-faced, Cristalle-scented Georgia sitting down at the heavy oak table, on a particularly thick, expensive-looking bench.

'I'm just saying that once a woman has a baby, her career's over,' stated Georgia, matter-of-factly. 'Simple as that.'

'Oh, do wake up and smell the skinny cap, Georgie,' grinned Steve as he placed one bowl of Honey Nut Cornflakes in front of her and another in front of himself. 'It's 19*96*, not 19*56*. Right, Kate?'

Georgia and Steve both looked up expectantly at Kate, as they chewed their, by all reports, ludicrously tasty cereal.

Kate thought she might hyperventilate. Georgia looked even more gorgeous than she did in her old photos. And her brother, Steve! He looked wonderful – all young and smiley and happy and full of potential. Just the way he always was in her mind's eye, the only place she ever saw him since they fell out over...she couldn't for the life of her remember what, now.

She wondered briefly whether it was April the 1st and someone was playing an elaborate joke on her. Or whether it was a fancy dress 'come as you were' surprise birthday party for her. Nah, couldn't be – it was May, a month away from her 45th birthday. Wasn't it?

She scratched her head and began to entertain the possibility that maybe she'd had a stroke - or had contracted late on-set narcolepsy and this was all one, big, crazy dream.

Her eyes darted all over the place, trying to take it all in. Where was she? Why was she...*how*?

'Am I... *dead*?' she said out loud, her voice wavering as she grasped the table edge and felt her forehead prickle with sweat.

She must have died, she thought - died of exhaustion and frustration at trying to be the perfect wife and mother, probably. Yes, that's it – she'd died and gone to Heaven. Which was one good thing, she supposed.

'Oh, come on – it wasn't that big a night, you lightweight!' scoffed Georgia. 'It was only a few gentle Sunday drinks, nothing more nefarious than that. Now get a shift on, Kate – we'll be late for work if you don't.'

'Uh...um,' Kate stammered.

She went to put her hands on her hips, but there was nothing there. She looked down – her side-shelves had all but disappeared and her nipped-in waist had come back! She saw her slim legs encased in khaki combats and a flat belly proudly exposed by a long-sleeved crop top with a pink and white tie-dyed love heart on the front. Her boobs were proud and perky. Her bingo wings no more.

Her hands darted up to her throat and she felt for her chins. There was only one. And her neck felt smooth, too.

Kate laughed the kind of nervous laugh you involuntarily come out with when you're on a rollercoaster – when you're scared witless, but hopelessly excited and exhilarated too.

'It's 1996? Oh. My. *GOD*!' Kate's breaths were getting shorter and more shallow with every word. 'Is it? Is it really 1996?'

'Take some brotherly advice, Katie my love, and leave the E's well alone!' said Steve through a particularly crunchy mouthful as he nodded towards the wall where their kitchen calendar was hanging.

Kate's eyes followed the direction of Steve's nod

and sure enough, in big, black, bold type, on a stark white background it said:

JUNE 1996

She put her soft, liver spot-less hands over her mouth to stifle a yelp.

And then she fainted.

4

'Kate? Kate!' Georgia fell to her knees next to her best friend's prone body. 'Wake up, Kate!'

Steve joined Georgia on the kitchen floor and slapped his sister's face. Not too hard, but with enough impact to leave a small, reddening mark.

Regardless, Kate lay motionless.

'Kate? I'm sorry, Sweetie. This hurts me more than it hurts you, believe me...here goes!' This time Steve slapped Kate's face really hard.

'OWWW!' Kate complained crossly. She sat up, rubbed her palm across her cheek and angrily addressed her brother. 'What did you do that for?'

'Because that's what they do in the movies and it always seems to work...I'm sorry, Darling, but you fainted –' Steve spoke quickly.

'And we didn't know what else to do!' chimed in Georgia. 'Are you OK? How do you feel? Are you all right?'

'I'm fine,' Kate said, slowly unknitting her brow. 'Of course I'm fine. Just feeling a bit, um, woozy, that's all.'

Georgia and Steve helped her up and walked her into the living room, plonking her onto the perfectly shop-distressed leather couch.

'You gave us all a bit of a fright there,' said Steve, relief spread all over his handsome face. 'Don't do it again.'

'No, don't,' Georgia said as she rubbed Kate's back. 'Hey! You're not pregnant, too, are you?'

'What?' Kate muttered, her head feeling sore and fuzzy, the cogs of her brain whirring thickly as though submerged in a sea of treacle.

'That'd be right,' Georgia sniggered. 'Always stealing my thunder. But you can tell me all about it later, at lunch. Come on, let's go!'

'Hang on,' Kate said slowly as her eyes were drawn to the Jenga blocks, lying casually about on the coffee table and the coir carpet underneath. She was about to say, in her best super-authoritative voice (that was always duly ignored): 'Clear up those blocks before I count to ten' when she realised that her kids were nowhere to be seen and the rest of the house was spotless. The kind of spotless you have when you don't have children - *cleaning lady once a week* spotless.

Spotless the way their shared flat in West Hampstead usually was in the mid '90s.

The penny started its long and winding drop. Had she really been transported back in time? Simply because she had wished for it so hard and for so long? She'd tried positive thinking before and it had never worked. Why now? Why her? Why -

Her speeding heart thudded audibly in her chest.

Where are the kids? And what about Seamus?

'I've changed my mind!' Kate said out loud to Steve and Georgia's blank stares.

She hadn't really ever wanted to be without the kids and Seamus. And she hadn't really meant all those things she'd said and secretly thought about them in the heat of too many moments to mention. Yes, she'd clung onto her child-free past as though her life depended on it – because sometimes it felt like it seriously did. But that didn't mean she actually, physically, *literally* wanted to go back in time to when she was young, free and single.

Did it?

No! She loved her family to bits – what would she do without them? She felt the blood racing through her veins and her heart pounding. What would she do without Baby Jane's make-it-all-worthwhile hugs? George's funny and oh-so-endearing tales of his adventures in young manhood? What would she do without Decko's take on the world as he sees it, one where his Mummy is still Number One and the only girl he can ever imagine loving so much? And what the hell was she going to do without Seamus' calming, supportive and yes, now she thought about it, sexy presence? Eh? Where was he now? Now that she needed him the most?

She hugged herself, rubbing her upper arms in an effort to provide some much-needed comfort, as Seamus might do if he were here. And just at that moment, when she felt like bursting into tears, she realised she could nearly completely close her fingers around the top of her arms.

That stopped her in her tracks.

She was shocked. She was stunned. She did it again and again, her French-manicured fingers showing no signs of the arthritis she had sworn she was about to be riddled with as her middle fingers almost met her thumbs on both arms. Her eyes nearly fell out of her skull, she found what she was seeing so impossible to believe. It was just too amazing!

'HA!' she squeaked at her flatmates. 'Look at *that*!'

'What?' Steve and Georgia chorused, looking more and more puzzled.

Slowly, Kate felt the fog of her mind - like the fug of the family kitchen, and the melee that was her mummy brain – lift a little. Instinctively, she felt calm in her heart – as though she'd just been told that the kids were all right. It was as though her mother's intuition had finally found her and she just *knew* they were all OK - unharmed and happy.

She didn't know where it came from, but the thought of this cheered her up no end. Instantly she felt so much lighter. And not just because she'd obviously just shed the better part of four stone in seconds flat, but because no one was hanging off her, making constant, unreasonable demands, expecting her to drive them to football, wipe their bottoms and make their dinner and then steadfastly refusing to eat it before chucking it all over the walls with glee. She felt virtually weightless and positively fizzing with energy when she thought of it like that...

But how long was she was going to be in 1996 for? Would she ever return to 2014? Had she ever *been* in 2014? Maybe *that* had all been one long, weird dream (or nightmare, depending on her mood) and she hadn't left the 90s in real life, yet.

And how would she ever understand the quantum physics involved in time travel when she had to take her shoes off if she was counting past ten?

Maybe she was doomed to roam different time planes, surf different dimensions for the rest of her suddenly quite exciting life.

'Like Dr Who,' she said breathlessly.

She'd been banging on about her past, utterly obsessed with nostalgia for so long, it took a few seconds for it to dawn on her that no matter how she got here, the important thing was that she was here – and this was her chance to put everything right. This - right here, right now – was her dream come true!

When she finally got it, she made the snap decision to make the best of it and enjoy it. Now she was on a mission. She set her Witherspoon jaw to 'determined' and felt little sparks fly off her fingertips, just as she had the night before.

She grabbed the Size 10 cropped, faded blue denim jacket that was flung over the back of the couch behind her and grasped it to her lap.

'Typical,' she dared herself a wry smile as she surveyed the familiar room around her. 'My Tardis is a kitchen sink...and it's taken me back to the wrong sodding decade. I wanted the 80s!'

Steve and Georgia swapped a lingering, highly concerned glance.

They looked so sweet and innocent - like they

were *pretending* to be adults.

'Listen Lady,' said Steve, wagging his index finger at Kate. 'I'm the one they voted Most Likely To Become Seriously Unhinged, so don't even *think* about pissing on my chips, all right?'

'Yeah. What on *earth* are you on about, Katie?' Georgia asked, the worry in her voice making it waver slightly.

'Nothing, nothing,' Kate stood up far too quickly, feeling the blood suddenly drain from her head and rush madly to her high-heeled Spice Girls sneakers-shod feet. 'We'd better get a move on and get to work, though. God knows I may not have much time left!'

5

DING!

Kate felt a vaguely familiar flutter in her heart as the lift doors opened up to her on the ground floor of PGT&B, the magazine publishing house where she used to work.

The owners of PGT&B liked to think that everyone shared their joke in telling anybody who asked that those four initials stood for the company's core values - Profit, Good Times & Banter. But seriously, they would then calm down, slowly taking their red noses off and folding up their floppy shoes, it was actually the initials of The Four Horsemen (as the founding bosses often referred to themselves), Peter, Glenn, Todd & Ben.

As soon as Kate stepped into the mirrored lift with the bright red carpet, she had to steady herself, grabbing hold of the stainless steel bar that went all the way round the reflective walls at ribcage-height. She took a few deep breaths as she saw how slim, young and pretty she was and then the memories bombarded her, slamming her up against the walls with their invisible, centrifugal force.

This lift! THIS lift! *The* Lift! This is where it all happened – or at least where you *heard* about everything that had happened. Especially on Monday mornings when the excited gaggle of sales people, editorial, PR and management would huddle together, squeezing into the tiny box as Friday night's exploits, debacles and degradations were discussed.

She remembered the icy stab of hurt she'd endured – for four slow, clunking floors – as she'd listened to Tamsin bray about stealing Tom away from her at her birthday drinks the previous Friday night.

Kate had been the first one to get into The Lift that fateful Monday morning and as it filled up with weary workers beginning yet another week at the grindstone, she'd ended up buried right up the back in a corner, squashed and unseen by the clear-skinned, blemish-free Tamsin who forced her way in to the already packed to capacity lift.

'I tell you,' Tamsin loudly told Lucy, the new receptionist on the PR floor. 'He was like an animal! Honestly, it was as though he hadn't had it for *months* or something! Whoo! God – he is so gorgeous, though, there was no way I could say no...'

'But doesn't he have a girlfriend?' Lucy whispered.

'Shhh!' came Tamsin's giggly reply. '*Had* a girlfriend, you mean. But keep it under your hat – she works here, you know, in PR.'

Kate shut her eyes tight at the memory and winced. Two seconds later, when she opened her eyes again, the pain was gone. All that was left in its place was mild surprise that even now, even after all these years, she could still dredge up and actually feel that painful sting of humiliation.

No wonder she didn't like Mondays. Or lifts.

Before they'd get to the fourth floor, Tamsin would have waxed lyrical about, among other things, how fantastically pert Tom had said her breasts were, how wonderful her flat stomach was, how gorgeous and endless her slender legs were, how charming and amusing she was and how her face had that innocent yet slutty quality that he and the punters loved. When the lift finally went DING! and the doors opened at the fourth floor, Tamsin stepped out, saying:

'He's going to get me some glamour work in *LASHED.* Says I'm every schoolboy's dream. *Wet* dream more like!'

Kate couldn't move once she'd heard all that. She'd stayed in the lift and was forced to go up nine more floors, then go down to the basement, then languish about, slumped in the corner of the lift on the ground floor for a while before her boss, Archie, rolled in, reeking of alcohol and an obscenely late night.

'All right, Kate?' he'd said cheerfully. 'Kate?'

'Hmmm?' Kate's eyes eventually came unstuck from the bright red nylon carpet and rose to meet his.

'Bit late this morn – soz! It's those *LASHED* boys – no idea what "quiet Sunday afternoon bevvie" means, eh?' Archie chuckled.

'Hmmmm,' Kate had nodded slowly as she stood up.

Amazing, she mused. It was remarkable how clearly she could recall the details of that painful morning. As she stood in The Lift now, she could actually, physically feel exactly how she'd felt all those years ago.

Of course, in her nearly 45-year-old mind, she cringed when she remembered that her boyfriend, the man she thought was The Love of Her Life, The One That Got Away, her Mister Right, sometimes seemed solely responsible, as Editor of Lad Mag extraordinaire, *LASHED,* for making it okay for young boys to ogle women openly and say 'hilarious' things like: 'Cor! Out of 10, I'd give her one!'.

Imagine Baby Jane at the mercy of that kind of attitude. Imagine George or Decko cockily saying: 'Grab your coat, Love – you've pulled,' to some poor girl in a smoky, leery pub. She felt decidedly uneasy at the thought.

But on the other hand... Tom was so charismatic! So quick-witted! So handsome! And she had simply been caught up in the madness of those heady times – swept away on the tide of being *sort-of* close to the thick of it; *almost* where it was at, on the periphery, the outer of the in-crowd, the warmer part of the cool Britannia set.

That was the only feasible excuse she could offer herself for turning a blind eye to (for surely she never did any *condoning*) the misogynistic, boorish and boring bad behaviour of her boyfriend and his cronies. She couldn't have gone along with all their shenanigans because she thought it was all harmless fun – a bit of an old-fashioned seaside postcard kind of a giggle, could she?

Well, yes, she conceded as she looked around The

Lift in wonder, she could have. She really, truly, very possibly in all likelihood could have.

She shuddered.

But that was her then and this was her now. Or, rather, that was her then and *this* was her then, too. Except with an older, more experienced, wise(ish) mind. Kate frowned at how confusing this time slip business was becoming already – and she'd only been back in 1996 for five minutes.

She brightened visibly when she reasoned with herself that this was her chance to set the record straight on the old sexism score; put things right and strike a blow for feminists everywhere, in all decades – for the suffragettes that were and the fantastic females to be! For Baby Jane and the boys!

Just as soon as she'd slept with Tom again.

'WHAT?' Kate's inner Germaine Greer sat bolt upright and glared at her.

'Oh, come on!' Kate tried to reason with her. 'What harm could it do? Turn the tables and use the *man*, for once, I say. And Seamus won't know – nor will the kids. It might even be *good* for me to reawaken that long-forgotten part of myself. I mean, I haven't had sex for so long, I can't even tell the difference between feeling saucy, having a hot flush and being a bit tiddly, for goodness' sake!'

'Fair point,' said her inner Germaine, and lay back down again.

And at that, Kate thrust her nose in the air and confidently strode out onto the fourth floor.

Lucy looked up from the magazine draped over the switchboard, stopped twirling her hair and smiled.

'Are you Kate?' she asked, all bright-eyed.

'Yes,' replied Kate in kind, now that her own eyes weren't so bleary anymore and had regained quite the youthful shine to them.

'Some guy's been calling for you all morning...Tom? From the third floor? Here,' she said as she handed Kate five slips of paper with While you were out...written at the top in red.

Kate beamed. She felt excited, proud – yes, even a little smug. Because even though the receptionist didn't know who Tom was just yet, she would soon. And she, like most of the other girls at PGT&B would be as envious as all hell of Kate. Lucky Kate.

'Ooh, lucky me!' Kate giggled.

'And there's something for you on your desk, too,' Lucy jerked her head to the left, towards a sea of carrels, people bustling about, glass offices and...Tamsin.

'Lucky me,' said Kate again, suddenly deadpan.

She walked over to her desk, dropped her bag on the floor, hung her denim jacket on the back of her chair and gasped when she saw the spray – nay, shower, storm, *tsunami* – of lilies virtually taking up her whole desk.

She plucked the card out from the flowers. It read:

Say you will – please, please,
PLEASE say you will.
Oh, go on – you know you want to
T xxx.

Kate surmised that the florist – for reasons known only to them - who wrote the card must have put that full stop after the kisses. Because Tom would *never* have dictated that – he was a stickler for grammar and punctuation, you see, and would often correct Kate on her, by comparison, more casual approach to detail: things like apostrophes in the wrong place, an over-liberal use of exclamation marks and other faux pas of the pen. At first Kate thought it endearing – something pernickety about the man who seemed so comfortable and cool with everything being lackadaisical – or lax-a-daisical, as Kate once said, only to be reprimanded sharply by Tom.

She smiled to herself, secure in the knowledge that this time around, if he tried to correct her the next time she said 'pacific' when she meant 'specific' – even if accompanied by his famously sexy, disarming grin – she would surely lamp him.

Tom wanted Kate to move in with him – he'd been asking her for months. But even though she wanted to – really, badly wanted to – two things were holding her back.

Since her brother, Steve, had split up with his long-time girlfriend and lost his job, he'd been living with her and Georgia, with Kate basically paying his way. Until he got his act together, Kate felt as though she couldn't leave him – and she was pretty sure Tom wouldn't want them to move in as a job lot. So she was kind of stuck there.

She was also a bit hesitant because, well, she could never put her finger on it, really. The first time round, she called it instinct and intuition – like she had some sort of sixth sense that something wasn't quite right about them living together and that she would somehow, most likely have her heart smashed to smithereens by Tom. Naturally, she now *knew* he was a cad and bounder of the highest order – despite being fantastic in the sack – and, if her calculations were correct (iffy at the best of times, not much of a chance with time travel added into the mix), in about a month's time, at her 27th birthday do, Tamsin and Tom would run off together and Kate would have to relive that horrible lift scene all over again.

But wait, thought Kate – that's it! That's why he took off with Tamsin –because she refused to move in with him! Maybe if Kate agreed and they *did* move in together, maybe Tom would be faithful and they could live happily ever after. Or even just for a little while, to give her some closure on the relationship that had haunted her for years. And to have sex with him in the flesh – not just in her dreams? Well, that would be great! Wouldn't it?

A picture of George, Declan, Baby Jane and Seamus – the one on her iPhone wallpaper – all tumbling over each other and mugging for the camera, suddenly flashed in front of her mind's eye and pulled her up sharply, as if she suddenly remembered she had a husband, three kids and a whole other life.

She heard a strange ringing in her ears – a brutal, masculine sound that she couldn't quite place. It wasn't the gentle harp sound of her iPhone (a sound that she often missed, actually, it being far too soft and serene to penetrate the ear-splitting chaos usually surrounding her) – nor was it a tinny, irritating ringtone – like some hideously awful novelty pop song involving an Ibiza backing track and a maniacal frog on a motorbike or something. It was just her ordinary work phone, buried somewhere beneath all those flowers.

6

'He's dumped me!' cried Georgia as soon as Kate picked up the receiver.

'What?' replied Kate. 'Who?'

'SIMON!' Georgia shouted back, followed by some small coughs, signalling the beginning of a hysterical sob session.

Ah, sighed Kate inwardly, Simon. Kate knew this was going to happen because:

Simon was always making passes at any female who moved (including Kate) as though the seriously gorgeous Georgia wasn't enough for him and he could do better. Or more.

She'd already lived through the whole episode once before, 18 years ago, so she knew exactly what was going to happen. And that's when it really hit her – this slightly strange feeling that she was cheating or something – like she had hidden knowledge and a secret super power. Which she sort of did.

'Shh, shh. Come on, shh. Calm down, now, Sweetheart,' Kate soothed, sounding like her mother. No, hang on a sec! She sounded just like herself, her *real* self – her 2014 self. Kate looked around her and wondered whether anyone had heard her. But of course they hadn't – they were all still too busy throwing spit balls up onto the ceiling, having sword fights and 'bantering' loudly to be heard over the banging tunes that were blasting from the office radio.

There was silence for a second on the end of the line, though – Georgia was shocked by the motherly, warm, comforting tones of her best friend. Not that Kate didn't show *potential* to be like that – she would be a great mum one day, everyone said it - it was just that Georgia never really gave Kate much opportunity to hone her sweet mothering skills.

Georgia was normally so in control, so fearless, so unfazed, that merely hearing her cry, imagining her vulnerability, made Kate want to climb down the phone line, draw Georgia close to her (not-so-mumsy and ample now) bosom, stroke her hair, tell her everything was going to be all right, make her some pink milk, settle her down with a duvet in front of the telly, get the old lady from next door to watch her, get in the car, hunt that Simon down, yell at him until he cried and promptly disembowel him on the spot. All that and *still* be on time to pick up the boys from football and whip up their favourite lasagne for tea.

'I mean, how COULD he?' continued Georgia. 'In my condition! And you wanna know the worst bit?'

Georgia didn't wait for Kate to answer.

'He did it by fax. He sent me a sodding *fax!* My secretary brought it to me – so she read it, probably photocopied it and stuck it up in the staff room by now and...oh, Kate! What am I going to *do*?'

'What did it say?' Kate said.

'What does it matter? I can't bear to read it again – especially not over the phone. Can you get out? Can you meet me somewhere?'

Kate scraped pens, papers and coffee mugs off her A5 desk diary and was surprised to see a pretty packed schedule. She'd become so accustomed to keeping all the kids' appointments in her head or on the backs of envelopes stuck to the fridge, she panicked a tiny bit when she could see no mention of J (Baby Jane) D (for Decko), or G (George, yes) and dentists, doctors, playdates, concerts, practice .

She was so used to the days drifting in and out with no shape or form to them – apart from, of course, distinctly kid-shaped form. So used to putting the kids and their needs first was she, that she couldn't even remember the last time she'd actually had an appointment anywhere for herself. An appointment, a meeting – even an organised (months in advance) cup of tea in a nice cafe – never happened for Kate. Now more than ever, it was clear that she came last on the family list of priorities.

But not today. Not Monday the 3rd of June, 1996. Nope, today she was back at (paid) work!

She shook her (thick, beautifully, professionally highlighted, with not a single wisp of grey) Rachel-from-*Friends* hairdo and ran her index finger down the diary page.

'Can we meet up after work?' Kate asked, putting on her best business voice, which meant she sounded distant and cold all of a sudden. 'It's just that I've got a meeting with Archie right now – ooh, ten minutes ago, actually – then I've got a client lunch and then, straight after that, I have to go to a launch...the launch of some teen soap or something –'

'You're so important, yeah, yeah, I get it,' sniffed Georgia. 'I might actually call it a day here, cry off with a migraine. I can defo feel some soul searching on the Southbank coming on.'

Kate imagined Georgia looking all wistful and contemplative, sitting on one of those benches, staring out at the river, a well-thumbed old Virginia Woolf paperback classic in her lap, her hands pulling her coat collar up around her ears as black storm clouds gathered overhead.

'Ha! All dark and dramatic? Doesn't sound like you,' Kate snorted.

'It's the perfect day for it!' said Georgia, suddenly getting excited.

Kate looked out one of the windows to see a duck egg blue sky, the weak sun valiantly trying to break through some light cloud cover.

'So where's this launch on, then? I could do with a drink or 10. I take it there'll be plenty of free booze laid on there?'

Kate told her where it was and what time she would be there.

'You just hang on in there,' Kate said, all soft and mum-like again. 'We'll sort this out soon – don't do anything stupid until you see me. Understand?'

'So I can do something stupid *after* we've met up?'

'No!' Kate giggled girlishly and hung up.

She grabbed her diary, found a pen and walked

(with ease, despite the hollow plastic heels of her Spice Girls sneakers) over to Archie, the head of PR at PGT&B. He was in his glass office (or cage or cell as he sometimes referred to it), sitting on his big leather swivel chair behind an oversized desk, as if to physically emphasise, with the use of office furniture, how big and crucial to the company Archie was.

'Ah! Young Kate,' Archie said by way of greeting.

How sweet those words sounded.

Kate beamed back at Archie. She got on well with him, always had, from the moment she'd met him at her interview for the job. They'd hit it off straight away and had made it a priority to try to always see the funny side of any situation, always have a laugh together. Kate trusted and respected Archie and, even though he was a good five years older than her, she sometimes nearly felt *equal* to him, in a professional capacity, if not an earning capacity – she was, after all, constantly bumping her head on the glass ceiling at PGB&T. But Archie had often told her that her ideas were as good as his – usually much better, in fact - and he needed her to make him look good.

He was almost attractive, she thought. There was nothing particularly handsome about his face – but neither was there anything hideous or offensive. His eyes twinkled when he smiled and his Scouse accent really was very cute – nearly sexy, even. But looking at him now, swamped by the chair and desk (he was only 5'7" - at a push), she felt not the sudden, hot rush of sexual desire, more the slow, warm, gooey spread of maternal feeling: all she wanted to do to Archie was wipe his nose, smooth his hair down and kiss his cheek.

'Good weekend?' he asked her.

Kate didn't have the faintest idea.

'Yeah, yeah,' she said, trying to sound confident. 'You?'

'Well-bladdered. Started Friday afternoon, as you know, and just went nuts from there. I've said it before and no doubt I'll say it again – that feller of yours is an insane party machine!'

'I know!' she grinned.

'But he's gone and got himself and his mag in a bit of bother, now, Kate – and I want you to help me fix it. It's damage limitation time and we need to work fast.'

'Why? What's happened?'

'Nothing we can't handle – just some strumpet from a small, feminist publishing outfit called Medea Media having a go at him, saying he's to blame for the poor self-esteem young girls are supposedly suffering from these days. Poor body image yada yada yada –'

'What? You mean *my* boyfriend? The one at the vanguard of the new lad revolution, propagating the absurdly sexist myth that the only thing women have to offer the world is a cracking set of boobs? Or nothing at all if they are flat, can't afford surgery, plain or – imagine! – interested in other things apart from male attention/objectification?'

Kate crossed her arms in front of her chest, widened her eyes, interrogating cop-style and, chuffed with herself for calling it exactly as she saw it, waited for Archie to close his mouth and take that stunned look off his face.

'Erm, no. Not exactly,' he eventually managed. 'Oh, come on, Kate! Whose side are you on?'

But just as Kate opened her mouth to speak, she was silenced by the tower of boxes outside Archie's office falling to the floor with the almighty crash and scream of glass breaking.

'Oops!' a tall, lanky, speccy young man bent over and tried to pick up bits of shattered brown bottle now being carried down the corridor on a frothy tide of room temperature beer. 'Sorry, I-'

'There goes breakfast,' Archie grimaced.

Kate furrowed her brow and stared at the scene of devastation. There was something eerily familiar about this hapless guy: his awkward presence, as though he was too big for himself. It was as if occupying any amount of space was too much for him and made her cock her head to one side, like a dog trying to understand what a human was saying. The fact that he'd drawn a whole office's attention to himself and his clumsiness made him appear all the more uncomfortable in his own skin. Kate could tell by his body language that he wanted to run and hide, wanted the ground to swallow him up whole, to instantly disappear. And when he looked up, ever so briefly, mumbling apologies, coughing nervously and smiling twitchily, she got it.

It was Seamus!

Kate couldn't help herself and jumped out of her seat a bit, letting out a squeal. She quickly composed herself, putting a hand over her mouth, and shook her head affectionately.

'It's all right, Kate,' laughed Archie, 'there's plenty more in the fridge.'

Kate couldn't take her eyes off Seamus. He actually had hair – thick, jet black hair. After all the years they'd spent together, Kate always pictured Seamus with a could-have-been-hot-in-his-day bald pate – she'd forgotten that he used to be quite hirsute. His coke-bottle-bottomed John Lennon glasses still did absolutely nothing for him – she'd been right to insist he bin those soon after they got together, and she congratulated herself on her once-wise fashion advice.

'Dress sense of a total dork,' she used to say to him – and, once again, as she could quite plainly see now, she had been right. He was wearing a cagoule over a Liverpool shirt, jeans that were way too tight (leaving little to the imagination) and all-black trainers.

It's not that that, in and of itself, was even so bad, really – it's just that amidst the sea of designer-label-wearing, uber-trendy men who worked at PGT&B, Seamus really stood out.

God! How on earth did they *ever* get together, Kate asked herself. He was so not her type!

'Hello? Hello!' Archie lifted himself out of his seat by his short arms in a bid to regain Kate's attention.

'Sorry, Archie,' said Kate, turning around to face him again. 'But shouldn't we help Seamus?'

'Who?' said Archie, pulling his chin into his neck and frowning.

Kate gulped. She shouldn't know what this geeky guy's name is, either.

'Ah, that's me,' said Seamus, standing up, but somehow staying hunched over, as if he was trying to minimise himself. 'There's no need, I can do it myself. I...I...I just came up here to introduce myself. You're Archie? Is that right?'

Both Kate and Archie nodded fast in an effort to encourage Seamus and make him hurry up.

'Ah, well, I am, as the lady said, Seamus,' he shot a quick glance down at Kate and blushed. 'And I'm heading up PGT&B's new IT Department. Which is...actually...made up of only me at the moment. But I just wanted to say hi and give you my extension, so if you have any computer problems – or any machine-related problems – anything at all, just, ah, give me a ring.'

'Right,' said Archie, standing up and shaking Seamus' hand. 'And this is Kate, my senior PR adviser and guru of all things grey-matter related.'

Kate stood up in slow motion, giving the moment the time and gravitas she knew it deserved. She imagined herself in black and white, in 1940s garb, at a steamy railway station like in *Brief Encounter*. At exactly the same time as she stepped up on tippy toes and craned her neck in an attempt to look deep into Seamus' eyes, as if she was being filmed in close-up, all Bambi-eyed and innocent yet blessed with a knockout, sexy, full, pout, Seamus also bent down quickly, muttering something about too many wires left lying loose on the carpet and the very real tripping dangers they posed.

CRUNCH!

Seamus' forehead collided with Kate's nose in a headbutt of epic proportions.

'YOW!' Kate cried.

'Oh, God! I'm so sorry,' Seamus said, sounding like he was on the verge of tears himself. 'Ah, um – where's the first aid box?'

Archie ran out of the office and came back in seconds flat, brandishing a load of ice wrapped up in a tea towel.

'There you go, Kate, put that on your face. You'll be all right. Just hurts like hell, doesn't it?'

'Mmmmfff,' Kate grunted.

After flapping around for a few minutes, virtually tripping over himself with 'sorries' and 'oh my Gods', Seamus made his exit from the scene, leaving Archie and Kate alone in the office once more.

'I'll be fine,' said Kate. 'I don't think it's broken. With any luck, I won't look too horrendous for my client lunch later.'

Or for my first meeting with Tom, she thought. He must be roaming these corridors somewhere, prowling like a panther, stealthily coming up behind her seated at her desk and putting his hands on her shoulders to massage them masterfully, as he always used to.

'Right, right,' said Archie as he watched Kate lost in thought. 'Just take it easy for a while – you might have a bit of concussion. Cancel all this morning's meetings and phone calls and just take it easy, please Kate. I'll bring you a tea, you go back to your desk and don't force anything, just casually come up with something brilliant to quieten *LASHED*'s critics.'

'Thanks, Archie,' she said, wondering whether she would, if she'd been in his shoes, have offered her his reclining seat, pulled down the blinds and told her to rest for a while in his quiet office.

And as she got up to walk back to her desk, Archie close behind her, heading for the kitchen, he said softly:

'Oh! And your teen mag? It's in freefall, dying a reasonably fast-paced death. If we can't pull something big out of the bag fast, it's going to have to fold. Sad, but you know. Business is business. So. Two sugars?'

7

Kate leaned back on her chair, closed her eyes and dabbed at the bridge of her nose with the tea towel that was really just a soggy, dripping cloth with a tiny bit of blood on it now. Her top had caught most of the water, mainly on her chest.

'Phwoar!' she heard behind her as she suddenly felt two big hands on each of her breasts. 'Guaranteed first place in any wet t-shirt contest anywhere!'

That voice... Those sleazy-coming-from-anyone-else-but-dead-sexy –coming- from-him words...Those hands...

Kate got ready for her knees to go weak at this point and she imagined her pins looking like long(ish) tubes of green jelly.

Typical, she thought. Bloody typical! You spend 18 years mooning over some man and when you get to see him again, finally, in real life, not just in your desperately bored housewifey fantasies, you've got a black eye, a throbbing, bloody nose and a splitting headache!

It was always the way, she reminded herself. Like, when you've got to get to the shops for some milk, but you've got the flu and you feel lousy and you can only find a pair of battleship grey, grubby trackie daks to wear and your hair's pulled back off your wrinkly and simultaneously spotty face in a greasy ponytail and who decides to start working behind the till at your local corner shop without telling anyone? Only George

Sodding Clooney!

The radio, with impeccable timing, struck up those distinct few chords of Alanis Morrisette's *Ironic* and Kate had to agree. *Yes it is, Alanis. It most certainly is.*

She took a deep breath and opened her eyes. Kate suddenly realised that Tom's touch was *anything* but masterful – he was actually hurting her. As he brought his hands up to her shoulders, he kneaded her neck and (oh-so-satisfyingly hollow, protruding) collar bones - and all she wanted to do was wriggle away, get out from under his ham fists.

'Well, *technically*, Alanis,' Tom took his right hand off Kate's (grateful because it was now quite sore) shoulder and she imagined him wagging a finger at the radio, 'it *isn't*. All those things you list aren't ironic at all – the rain on your wedding day, the free ride when you've already paid – they're merely slightly annoying. I think you'll find, my dear, that, in typically American style, you just don't *get* irony. All those things you're banging on about are, quite frankly, just a bit of a pisser.'

Someone, somewhere laughed – an admiring, brown-nosing kind of a laugh. More of a giggle, really. It was probably Tamsin.

Spurred on by his audience's appreciation, Tom took his left hand off Kate's other poor shoulder and took a bow.

'Thankyou, M'Lud,' he said. 'Case closed, I believe.'

Kate felt a little sick. But not because of Tamsin

making a show of herself (or Tom, for that matter, making a show of *him*self), but because the downright hugeness of this moment was overwhelming her – with disappointment. For so long she'd planned and prepared what she would be wearing, what she would say, how she would dazzle Tom with her brilliance when next they would meet – but when it came to the crunch, she couldn't think of a single witty thing to say.

Even though she'd rehearsed thousands of hilarious opening lines and perfected her air of nonchalance and aloofness and means-nothing-to-me-either-way-ness to a tee over the years, here in her 'office', sat at her little cubicle, she could barely breathe, let alone be fabulous.

She forced a smile. A twitchy, nervous, constipated-looking smile, but a smile nonetheless.

'All right, Lover?' Tom's hot breath filled her ear as she swivelled her chair around to face him.

She gasped.

Tom was just as gorgeous as she remembered – if not more so. And he was so young! So baby-faced! She felt a jolt of shame, as though she was guilty of robbing the cradle, but it passed as quickly as it appeared. And it was replaced, with lightning speed, by a tingling sensation. An all-over body tingling, that was rather pleasant, truth be told, and getting hotter with every second. Definitely *not* a hot flush, she thought to herself.

Tom completed the chair's twirl by putting his

hands on her knees, now in front of him. He pushed his right knee roughly between Kate's tightly crossed legs, nudging them apart.

'Tom!' shrieked Kate, shooting glances to first her left and then her right.

'Sorry, Babes – just can't help myself around you – you make me so- oi! What happened to your face?'

'Oh, this?' she put her hand up to her blackening eye. 'Nothing, nothing – just a bit of an accident, that's all. Bumped heads with the new IT guy.'

'I see. What you might call a close encounter... of the *nerd* kind,' he said, looking over in Tamsin's direction, his tongue planted firmly, smugly in his cheek.

Tamsin duly brayed like a donkey.

'Thanks for the flowers,' Kate said, still embarrassed by his insistent knees between hers. She wasn't used to such public displays of...these blatant shows of...of what, exactly? Sensuality? A deep affection and really close connection between two consenting adults? *Ownership?*

She was suddenly confused. Well, not *suddenly* at all, really – she'd been completely dazed and discombobulated ever since she arrived back in 1996, a few hours ago. But now she was feeling as though a rug had been pulled out from under her, Tom-wise. She hadn't remembered him as being such a caricature, such a stereotypical *lad*. Nor did she remember him as being such a crap massager, either. And she was surprised how, after years of nursing a broken heart, she'd made Tom less handsome in her memory than he was in real life. Because surely when you were as obsessive as she was about the past and the people in it (particularly the ones who'd made her cry) – you'd accentuate, really exaggerate the good stuff.

Or maybe, she thought, the bad stuff would eventually overshadow the good and cast a pall over everything about them. Maybe, though, it was a coping mechanism, and the only way she could handle the rejection was to make him plainer in her mind, more anonymous, more everyday, less special.

And then *again*, she smiled looking up at him, maybe she was so intoxicated during their time together (both literally and figuratively), that actually, she had very little clue what he was really like.

'Oh, well how about tonight,' Tom cooed. 'You, me, the moonlight...couple of packs of Marlboro Lights. Bit of champagne. Or a gallon if you're a woman after my own heart. Which I know you are, Doll-Face. Kensington Roof Gardens. Six of the clock. It's a date. Be there.'

And God! Did he really used to talk like that? Doing a really bad impression of Roger Moore as James Bond? And in such short, sharp sentences. Kate couldn't tell whether she found it offputting or beguiling and quite charming, in a schoolboy, affected kind of a way.

She settled on nonplussed in the end.

'Ah!' she eventually said. 'I can't! I've got to meet Georgie. She's having a bit of a rough time and...well, I need to talk her down, I suppose.'

'Bring with, my love,' he purred, lifting an eyebrow as he looked down at her.

'Oh, no – she needs some serious one-on-one –'

'Girl-on-girl action?' he leered.

'No –'

'I like it! Come on, it'll be fun! Just you, me, Georgie, most of the *LASHED* lads, Archie, probably – come on!'

'Hmf,' Kate scoffed. 'Intimate.'

'It's a party for a new champagne called...I dunno, some or other bullshit about bubbles...but who cares? It's Monday night! And besides...we are young, dee-doo-dee, something 'bout teeth, nice and clean...' he sang the last bit from that old Supergrass song that Kate instantly recognised.

'We'll see,' she said, pursing her lips and sounding like a parent considering whether or not to let their child have any ice cream.

As soon as the words left her lips, she felt like a fraud. She always *had* felt a tad fraudulent at work, never fully believing that she could get paid quite well just to have fun and think up daft ways of promoting things and planning parties. But now she felt like a total impostor; a dag in disguise, mutton in lamb's clothing – a beige, non-descript old bag squeezing herself into bright, young Miss Selfridge designs.

Honestly, she thought to herself, it wasn't easy flitting about between the past and the future. She was starting to feel decidedly schizo what with one minute being all young and firm and full of future potential and a sexiness she never even *knew* she'd once had – and the next minute falling into the all-too familiar territory of feeling fat, frumpy, harried and fighting off an unbearably strong urge to grab Tom's hand as if she were about to cross a busy road with him and steer him to safety.

It was getting bloody hard, actually.

She tried to correct her slightly authoritarian, scolding tone with what she thought might be a coquettish smile. She wasn't 100% sure how to go about this – having never really been a naturally gifted flirt - but she gave it a go anyway, slowly raising the left hand side of her mouth up to greet her nice, sharp cheekbones and looking up at him with her watery eyes from behind her furiously batting lashes. And instead of Tom asking her whether she was all right and did she need a blanket and a good lie down, as if she was having a stroke, it worked.

'You little MINX!' He growled playfully and touched her cheek in a surprisingly tender gesture, before he turned around and sauntered off.

Kate swivelled back to face the flowers, puffed her cheeks out to exhale and closed her eyes once more.

8

'Thought you'd never get here!' slurred an already-sloshed Georgia.

'Couldn't get a taxi for love nor money,' replied Kate. 'Didn't wait for me, then, before you got stuck in?'

Georgia handed one of the two balloons of red wine she was holding – the one with the least liquid in it – and the friends clinked glasses as they surveyed the scene.

The launch for *More Than Just Cows*, a teen soap, set in Guernsey, was well under way in an all-white warehouse-y loft, up the dodgier end of Caledonian Road in North London. The usual suspects were there – the scribes from rival magazines, PR people from TV stations, the young, unknown actors themselves and a handful of hangers-on who had no obvious connection to the soap or, indeed any reason to be there apart from the free bar and the off-chance that they might get to rub shoulders with someone famous off the telly.

Liggers, as they were starting to become known. And Georgia was doing a great impression of the biggest one there.

'Oh, thanks love,' Georgia said as she raised her glass to the 12-year-old waiter who'd just filled it to the brim. 'Got any Pringles?'

The boy, who was probably frightened out of his wits by this Amazonian woman actually looking him in the eye (sort of) and paying him some attention, pointed, silently, to a long table in front of a big projector.

The table was a veritable smorgasbord; cocktail sausages, crisps (Wotsits, Pringles, Walkers – you name 'em), sausage rolls, prawns, tzatziki, tuna pate, houmous, a selection of both white (hardly any left) and wholemeal (tons left) M&S mini pitta breads, small boxes of New York-style Chinese take-away noodles, half-sized spring rolls, dinky won tons, and a humungous bowl of Smarties. It was a spread so scrummy that in 2014, it wouldn't have lasted five minutes before Kate had hoovered up every last morsel ('I just hate waste and can't bring myself to throw all this food out!' She was fond of saying – especially when it came to her kids' leftovers and they'd had fish and chips for dinner). But here and now, she felt happier and more in control (diet-wise) by giving the scoff a swerve and concentrating on the wine.

She looked down at her flat tummy and couldn't resist running her right hand across it, as though she still couldn't quite believe it was hers and there wasn't more to it. There was a slight roundness to it –what one might call a sensual swell if they were so inclined – but nothing even vaguely resembling the deflated, stretch-marked bag of skin hanging over her pubic bone that it would one day become. And just underneath the waist band of her combats was the spot where one day a caesarean scar would languish, getting redder and thicker and more jagged with every baby she had. Kate continued to stroke her own belly, making the most of how tight and taut and *young* it felt to her touch.

'Could we have some shoosh please, ladies and gentlemen?' came the plea from a strawberry blond guy near the projector, accompanied by three short hand claps.

The buzz of the crowd slowly died down, much to the surprise and immense pleasure of the young man.

'Great! Thanks! Um, right. First off, we'd like to say thankyou all so much for coming – we know it's Monday and you'd probably all much rather be sat at your desks clock-watching till six tonight –' he paused to give people time to get the joke and politely guffaw, 'but we figured we'd give you a break from all that strenuous paper shuffling, get you out for a civilised drink or two (Georgia raised her hand high in the air at this and went 'Woo-hoo!' garnering titters from the young waiters and a slightly concerned look from the MC) before the football – yay for Euro '96! - gets underway this weekend and, er, take you on a trip to the island of Guernsey. Where, as you will soon see, there's so much more to life as a teenager than just cows and grass.'

Everyone milled about taking their seats in front of the huge cloth screen up against the opposite wall. Even Kate, who knew this poor soap was going to barely see its first series through before it was taken off air, if she remembered correctly, felt quite excited to see the first episode again. It was as though she was really embracing all the promise and potential, the courage to fail and the enthusiasm to succeed that being young (again) gave you automatically. As far as Kate could see at this very moment, *that* was what youth was all about.

She shuffled her tiny bum back into the seat next to Georgia and held her wine glass at its base in her lap.

'Oh! And stick around for a little bit afterwards, People – there'll be the chance to win a trip to the lovely Guernsey for you and a friend if you do. Now, is everybody sitting comfortably? Yes? Roll 'em, then!'

The show was neither great nor dismal – not that Kate got to see much of it. After approximately just three minutes, Georgia nudged Kate hard in the ribs, demanding she join her in the next room for a chat and a much-needed cigarette.

Kate bent over as she walked and apologised repeatedly in a whisper for causing a black shadow against the lush, green countryside on the projector screen.

Georgia didn't bother with any of that. Instead, she stopped half-way, looked to the screen, waved at it with both hands, fingers splayed and said: 'How do you do a shadow bunny again? Or a fox – yeah! How do you do a fox?'

Kate grabbed her by the elbow and got her into the smaller adjoining room and opened the windows while Georgia grabbed two chairs, virtually throwing them at the wall underneath.

'I don't remember you being so rubbish at holding your liquor,' Kate mused out loud.

'Me? Rubbish? How dare you?!' Georgia frowned back at her, looking seriously offended. 'For your information, I've been drinking since I got off the phone to you this morning and I think I'm handling it all pretty well, actually, thangyouvermuch!'

'But what about the baby?' Kate asked, trying not to show her shock and harsh judgement towards a pregnant woman knocking it back like a sailor on shore leave.

'Yeah, well,' Kate said, sparking up a cigarette.

It was all Kate could do not to grab it out of Georgia's mouth, throw it out the window and say: 'That's QUITE enough, young lady! Now go to your room and THINK about what you've done until I say it's time to come out! You're not too old to put across my knee, you know!'

'I've been thinking about that. And if Simon doesn't want it – or me – then I don't want it, either. So consider it gone!' Georgia left her cigarette to dangle out of the corner of her mouth and slapped her hands together, like she was finished with the whole ugly business.

'You mean, you –'

'Yep, that's right! I've booked myself in at an abortion clinic for two weeks' time and that's the end of it.'

Kate was shocked to see her best friend so hard-hearted, so laissez-faire. Not that she felt strongly about abortion one way or the other – she firmly believed it was a woman's right to choose (her own mum had always left her dog-eared copy of *Our Bodies, Our Selves* lying around when Kate was a kid, after all) – but in this instance, she knew something Georgia didn't and she simply *had* to stop her.

'Georgie, I think – no, I *know* – you're making a mistake. A huge mistake. Cancel the appointment, please. Hmm? Will you? Or at least postpone it until we've had a chance to talk about it some more.'

'No need. I know what I want – my brilliant career. And Simon. I can't have those if I have a baby, so something's got to go. And besides, I'm far too young for nappies and sleepless nights. I DO NOT want this baby. Why can't you get it through your thick head?'

'Can we at least talk about it? When you're, you know, not feeling quite so raw? You only just split from Simon a few hours ago!'

'No point!' Georgia said, taking another ma-hoosive slug of wine. 'No more discussion, no more debate needed. And anyway, why's it so important to you what I decide?'

Kate looked out the window at the rows of North London chimney pots and pressed her lips together, exhaling through her nose.

How could she possibly tell Georgia the truth? How on earth could she explain to her that if she went through with the termination, she would be scarred for life and never – even with extensive operations and painful, heart-breaking and eye-wateringly expensive IVF treatment – be able to get pregnant again.

She couldn't, she decided. Not without giving herself away as a traveller from another time in the future. And Georgia probably wouldn't believe that, anyway. God knows, Kate was having a hard time getting to grips with it herself.

She'd have to come up with something sneaky, something that Georgia, who was as smart as a whip (but who made increasingly dumb choices about men) wouldn't suspect. And it had to be something that Georgia thought was all her own idea. Somehow, Kate would have to plant the seed of doubt in Georgia's mind and let her think that she decided against going ahead with the abortion all by herself.

She needed to think. And she needed to think fast. She looked at Georgia French drawing a large amount of smoke up her nose.

Kate hadn't smoked for...ooh! About a million years, since she first found out she was pregnant with George. But she had missed it, from time to time. And she had never quite managed to disabuse herself of the teenage myths surrounding smoking, like, it made you look cool and helped you concentrate. And it was so sexy! Thinking of it like that again, like her old, younger self did, she momentarily wondered why she'd ever bothered to give them up.

'Gimme one of those, will you?' She growled, simultaneously pulling one of Georgia's cigarettes out of its flip-top pack.

'Got a light?' She looked up at Georgia.

'Of course,' smiled Georgia. 'And even though you never have any fags or lighters on you at the beginning of a night, what's the bet you end up with several lighters and a full pack of Marlies in your bag by tomorrow morning?'

It was true, Kate giggled, remembering their old ritual. Every morning after a big night, the two friends would go through their pockets and handbags for evidence – clues to help them piece their evening together.

Kate inhaled deeply. Then spluttered. Then coughed. And then, amid a whirlwind of hacking and barking, as though she was in the throes of a particularly nasty case of croup, she vomited. All over the loft's recently-done lime-washed floor boards.

'Oh dear!' Kate heard someone say. 'Looks like everyone's a critic!'

Kate looked up, wiping her mouth on the back of her hand. That voice belonged to the strawberry blond MC guy, who, by now, had attached a big, Cheshire Cat kind of a grin to his face, just above his ginger goatee.

Georgia, who'd moved behind Kate and was holding her hair back off her face (in the way that only true best friends will do in times of crises like these), said:

'Sorry about this. She's not usually so, um, she's not normally this delicate.'

'Oh, that's all right,' said Blondie. 'Don't worry about it – I'll get someone to clean it up later.'

All three of them studied the pool of shame at Kate's feet. It was mainly liquid – Kate hardly eating anything at her client lunch and staying well away from the buffet table here.

'Ah,' the MC dragged his eyes away from the floor, briefly shut them and gulped hard. He spoke and pointed to the door to the larger room. 'Er, in there, we've been busy watching the first episode and drawing the winner out of a hat for the trip to Guernsey.'

He opened his eyes, raising his chin high in an attempt to make sure even his peripheral vision didn't clock Kate's humiliating puddle.

'And someone called Kate Henderson from PGT&B is the lucky girl. Would either of you two be...'

'Way-hey!' cheered Georgia as she looked at Kate. 'Look at you, Sweetie – one eye all bloodshot and watery, the other a deep purplish shade of black – you *need* this holiday! And quite frankly, so do I – when do we depart, my good man?'

'Whenever you want – as long as it's the 14th-16th of this month. I've got all the details in here, if you want to take a look...'

'Great,' sniffed Kate. 'That's brilliant - thanks so much!'

Georgia hooked her arm into Kate's, pulled her along back into the other room and gasped in horror when she saw that the crowd had halved – and what was left of it, were fast making for the door.

'Oh!,' she whined, adding a small stamp of her foot to complete the overall picture of a tantrumming three-year-old. 'We can't leave! We can't go home yet - not now we've got some serious celebrating to do! Where to next, Katie?'

'Well,' said Kate, straightening herself up after signing some travel documents on the buffet table. 'I really don't feel very much like going on anywhere, to be honest. I've got a splitting headache and look at me! I look like I've gone ten rounds with Frank Bruno.'

Georgia laughed.

'Don't be silly - you look great! And anyway. What else are you going to do? Go home, microwave a meal for one and settle down to a boring night in troughing Hob Nobs, watching Question Time and sipping Horlick's?'

Kate sighed. That was *exactly* what she wanted to do. What a great idea, she thought - the perfect evening, in fact. She pictured herself, snuggled up on one of the leather couches at their flat, a throw over her legs, biscuit crumbs in her tea – and the gentle buzz of the telly the only noise in the place. She couldn't help but wistfully stare into the middle distance as she imagined the scene; no kids running up and down stairs, having sword fights and dead arm competitions, no babies waking up and screaming the house down, no washing up to do, leftovers to eat, clothes to sort for the next day...

'Earth to Kate...Kate? KATE!' Georgia yelled in her ear. 'You all right?'

'Oh, yeah, sorry. Just knackered, really, that's all. Tom wanted me to bring you to some do at the Kensington Roof Gardens, but I'm just not up for it tonight, Georgie, sorry. I'm ab-so-*lutely* shattered.''

'Awww, poor you,' Georgia said, almost sounding sympathetic and able to see sense, ready to call it a night. 'Luckily, I've got a little something here in my purse that can help with that. Come on, I'll show you when we get to the loos at the Roof Gardens. We'll easily get a cab from here... '

'What?' asked Kate, unable to figure out what her best friend was on about. Georgia grasped the shoulder of Kate's crop top and dragged her to the warehouse exit.

'To Kensington!' Georgia cried. 'And don't spare the horses!'

9

Kate opened her one good (albeit a bit bleary) eye on Tuesday morning to the sound of an old tramp with emphysema squeaking and wheezing away somewhere in her room.

She jerkily lifted her head and peered under her duvet, even though she didn't really think she would find anything there, and then very slowly, very gently, lowered her throbbing head back down onto her pillow.

'Ooh,' she winced, 'ow, ow, ow!'

Upon realising that the invisible old man with chronic lung disease was actually *her*, she reached an arm across to the bedside table for her Ventolin.

A few puffs later, she could breathe again.

'Guess that's another reason I don't smoke anymore,' she muttered.

Propping herself up on her hand, she looked over at her bedside table and almost fainted with relief when she spied (eventually, that is – it took a while for her eye to focus) a pint glass filled to the brim with cool, clear water.

Kate licked her lips, sat up and grabbed the glass. Slowly bringing it to her mouth, she closed her eye, anticipating the delicious almost sweet taste of the water and savouring this, her last moment of dry, cracked dehydration.

One gargantuan gulp later and both her eyes shot open – even the puffy, bruised black one. She scanned the room in seconds flat for a half-way decent receptacle, found none and so was forced to spit a whole mouthful of neat vodka out onto the coir carpet next to her bed.

Luckily, she didn't then throw up for real – diced carrots and specks of mini party food being absolute murder to get out of those deep carpet crevices and grooves.

'ARGH!' she croaked.

It took Kate a while to regain her composure. But when she did, she was horrified.

What on earth had she been playing at last night? Who did she think she was?

In her head, she sounded like her own mother, telling her off the first time she ever drank too much Babycham when she was 15 and was sick all over her bedroom. Her mum had been pretty cool about it after that, encouraging Kate to have a small glass of wine with her evening meal, in an effort to a) not make drinking such a big deal to the young girl and b) keep her at home and not out on the town with the 'rougher elements' of their small village at the end of the Central Line.

I could really do with Mum, now, thought Kate. She would love to hold her mum close, snuggle in to her warm, soft chest and hear her soothing voice offering her brown bread and honey sandwiches, as if they alone could cure the world of all its ills.

But ever since Paris (her dad) and Blue (her mum) had died in a chartered aeroplane flying over the

Bermuda Triangle at the stroke of midnight on December 31, 1999, Kate had missed them like crazy.

She'd never really got over their death/disappearance (for the bodies were never found) and she would often comfort herself with the thought that they had somehow scammed an insurance company and were now blissfully happy lying on a couple of sunloungers on a beach somewhere in the Bahamas.

Because at least they'd be alive, then – and one day, when she had the spare money and time, she would be able to set sail for the Caribbean and track them down.

God, she missed them. Her mum, especially – particularly once she started having kids. Everyone else seemed to have motherly advice coming out of their ears, wherever they turned – their own mothers, their partner's mothers – everyone else seemed to be lousy with mothers.

But not her. For Kate, there was no one she could ask for help when George came along. Even Seamus' mum was a non-starter – she'd left her husband and Seamus when he was five – and no one had heard from her since. Then, with the advent of Decko 18 months later, when Kate desperately needed to know how to divide your attention between two young boys equally, so as to avoid any jealous rages, she would often find herself screaming, wanting to jump into the gaping black hole of uncertainty her mother had left behind her.

If only she could...

Kate sat up, stiff as a board, mouth agape.

'OW!' she groaned, rubbing her head. 'Its 1996! Nineteen ninety fucking SIX!'

'Shut up!' came the chorus from the other bedrooms in the flat.

But Kate didn't hear them – she was like a woman possessed.

She leaped out of bed, ignoring all the protestations coming from her head, heart, forearms (for some unknown reason), legs (particularly her calves) and back. She flung her bedroom door open, raced towards the kitchen, backtracked immediately to get her slippers (that coir stuff can be really rough on your delicate tootsie toes, you know) and positively crashed into the phone on the wall.

'Number, number – what's their bloody number?' Kate mumbled frantically. 'GOD! You'd think it would be indelibly printed on my brain, it being the number we grew up with, the first set of numbers I ever managed to memorise when I was six, oh, for the love of –'

She stopped herself pfaffing about and coolly, calmly sat on the stool by the kitchen bench. She exhaled slowly, deliberately and picked up the receiver.

'Now think. Think!'

She stared at the phone for a few seconds and then noticed the red light flashing on the small, black box next to it.

'Ha,' she laughed softly. 'Answering machine! God – remember when your phone and answering machine were two different things?'

'Yeah,' said Steve, shuffling into the kitchen with his trademark sleepy drawl. 'Like it was yesterday. Because – *der* – it *was?*'

'Oh, Steve! What's our number? I mean at home,' she pleaded with her brother. 'Quick! What's Blue and Paris' number?'

'Mum and Dad, you mean?' Steve's voice was muffled as he peered into the fridge.

He made a point of not calling them their hippie, off-their-faces-for- a-week-in- a-commune-in-Camden names – ever. He resented their 'me' generation ideals and blamed them and their laissez-faire attitude towards parenting (by which he meant *him*) for all his problems. Even the ones that patently had nothing to do with his parents. Like groceries.

'Oh, bollocks,' he sighed wearily as he emerged from the fridge, pulling himself up to his full height. 'Plenty of full-fat, but not a drop of skimmed left. Typical, I suppose. I blame the parents, you know.'

'Yes I *do* know,' smiled Kate.

'Well, it's true!' he grinned back at her. 'They never taught us to plan ahead, to make provisions for the future...and now look at us! Scrounging a living, foraging around in the steaming rubbish dumps of West Hampstead , never knowing where our next trip to Ibiza is coming from...'

'Go to the shop, you lazy bugger!' Kate threw one

of her slippers at him and felt the merest twinge of recollection in the pit of her stomach.

As she watched Steve lollop out of the kitchen, the twinge grew larger until Kate could actually decipher it. She frowned when she remembered that it always used to nark her somewhat that Steve was so blasé about Blue and Paris. And always so spoiled, as though having his university fees, his rent and food, his *life*, pretty much, paid for him by Kate and her parents was his God-given right and nothing to be thankful for or appreciative of. He never even looked as though he was trying to pull himself out of the doldrums he'd been languishing about in for ages.

She half expected some all-seeing, all-knowing, pesky 1996 radio to start playing *Driftwood* by Travis at this point – the song that always made her think of Steve and his aimlessness. But it didn't. Mustn't have come out yet, thought Kate to herself, because when it did, and for several years afterwards, you couldn't move for hearing it.

Then she made a mental note to make sure she remembered to thank her parents for all they'd ever done for her, all they'd ever given her and everything they ever were to her and her brother, the second she got them on the end of the line.

'Now, what was our number...0208 something – no, hang on! It was still 0181 in 1996! Well remembered, Katie – even with the mother of all hangovers, you've still got it! Now wait, hold on, it's coming back to me, it's coming, it's coming...'

The radio seemed to spring to life all of a sudden, even though it must've been on all night, and Kate felt as though she was going to burst with happiness when she heard:

'...it's coming, football's coming home. It's coming home, it's coming home, it's coming, football's coming home...'

It was Frank Skinner and David Baddiel singing their Euro '96 hit, *Three Lions*. And whenever she heard it, in either 2014, 1996 or even if she lived to hear it in 2096, she knew she would always immediately feel the unbridled optimism and the endless enthusiasm of that one month when Euro '96 was a national obsession. Even *she* had been into it, despite never really paying too much heed to football in her life before. It seemed like everyone became a football fan that June and England really *did* seem like they were going to win it.

If only poor old...

Oops, she stopped her train of thought. Better not spoil it for anyone. There'll be plenty of time for crying into our beers later.

Kate shook her head, as if to force herself to re-focus and concentrate on more pressing matters.

She shut her eyes tight and tried to picture the numbers and after a while, they appeared, as if by magic. She hastily punched them into the phone's keypad, her fingers trembling ever-so-slightly.

It rang.

And rang.

And rang.

Don't be out! You *can't* be out! It's only eight in the morning! Oh, please, please! Don't be out *now*! Come on...come on!

'Eight five zero two,' a voice, not unlike Joanna Lumley's, came on the line.

'MUM!' Kate cried.

'DARLING!' Blue replied. 'Good. You got my message, then?'

'What? No – what was it?'

'To give me a ring, of course. I called your flat hundreds of times last night, but Steven kept answering, so I had to hang up every time. I left a message for you at work yesterday afternoon, because you were out, *all afternoon*, so I imagine that's where you are now, hmm? At work?'

'No, no – I'm ah, still at home –'

'Oh dear, Sweetheart,' said Blue.

Kate had forgotten that her mum was always so full-on about work – as though Kate was lucky to have a job, and that she shouldn't take it for granted or take the mickey in any way. Blue never failed to understand, though, that as a sales person at PGT&B, it actually *was* Kate's job to go on endless lunches with clients and colleagues. Kate could never make her see that her job – and the magazines she publicised – depended upon her schmoozing and boozing: getting paid to become a total and utter lush.

'What was it this time, hmm? Another client lunch, I suppose?'

'Well that, yes – and the launch for a new teen soap, where I won a trip to Guernsey,' said Kate proudly.

'How? By drinking your own body weight in tequila, I bet. And after that? I must say, Honey Bunny, you sound awfully rough. Have you got any Alka-Seltzer? Beroccas?'

'After that, I...I..can't quite remember, to tell the truth,' said Kate, racking her brains for something – *anything* – that might give her a clue as to what on earth she'd got up to last night.

She looked around the kitchen and saw an overflowing ashtray on the table surrounded by several cans and bottles of European beer. Four, actually. Four overflowing ashtrays and a cagoule lying on the floor.

'Four ashtrays and a cagoule,' she unintentionally said out loud, her head really pounding at the sight of all this undeniable debauchery. 'Ha! Sounds like a good name for a movie!'

'I see,' Blue said. 'Well, regardless of your social life, we really need to talk. About Steven. Can you come to the house - no, no – I'll come and meet you. In Carnaby Street somewhere. I'm coming up to London tomorrow – can you meet me tomorrow at, say one?'

It seemed like forever to wait.

'Not today?' Kate sounded disappointed.

'No, no – I forgot, Ickenham council meeting. I simply have to be there, otherwise they'll have me de-frocked or something.'

'Ooh-er, missus!' said Kate, keen to keep her

mum on the line.

'I see. Tomorrow at one, then? And don't tell your brother – he can't know I'm in London and not seeing him. Understand?'

'Yes, Mum.'

'Until tomorrow, then. Now get some rest, Sweetheart – and take some of that Echinacea I gave you. Fantastic at warding off colds, apparently.'

And with that, she hung up.

Just like that. One *click* and she was gone again.

But only momentarily. Kate would see her mother again tomorrow – if she wasn't propelled back to 2014 in the next few hours – and she bit her lip in an effort to stop herself screaming with delight.

A few minutes later, Kate made her way to the kitchen table to make a start on clearing up. Even though the mere sight of all those dog ends and overturned cans of lager made her want to heave, she figured someone had to do it – and she was used to clearing up after people, anyway. What was one more disgusting bombsite of a mess to contend with when you had three kids and a husband?

'Three kids and a husband – another good name for a movie!' She said.

'Or not,' said a groggy Georgia behind her. 'Urgh. Somebody shoot me. Please.'

'Mornin'!' chirruped Kate, trying to hide the fact that she, too, felt like death warmed up. Without the warmed up bit.

'Oh, GOD! Why did I ever let you drag me to

Kensington?' said Georgia, slumping down at the kitchen table, her head resting on her outstretched arm.

'*Me* drag *you*? I think it was the other way around, Lady! And what did you spike my drinks with?'

'Nothing,' said Georgia, sitting up. 'Although you were a veritable Hoover in the toilets, if you know what I mean...'

'No, I – oh, Georgie! Please say it isn't so - not drugs! I haven't done anything like that for a million years – I HATE it!'

'You've got a funny way of showing it! You made Liam look like a lightweight!'

'What?'

'You went berserk! Mind you, it was quite funny. And I think Liam quite fancied you, actually.'

'Liam who?'

'Blimey, Kate! You really don't remember? Gallagher! Liam Gallagher!'

'Liam Gallagher was there? Last night?'

'Der! You got on like a house on fire, you did. Not that Tom was too pleased to see it. Mind you, I think he was probably miffed that it wasn't *him* making Liam laugh all night – not merely that you were talking to him, getting all cosy and stuff.'

'We were?'

'Yeah, looked like a fun couple for a little while, there. Before you got us kicked out -'

'Typical,' Kate mumbled. 'The one time I actually get close enough to Liam Gallagher to actually have a chat, I can't remember a single thing about it!'

‘I wouldn’t worry about it, Katie,’ Georgia closed her eyes and yawned. ‘It’s hardly like he would’ve said anything particularly erudite, is it?’

‘You’re probably right. So how did I get us booted out, then?’

‘Busting your best Dirty Dancing moves on Liam,’ Georgia said, smacking her lips and shaking the packet of Crunchy Nut Cornflakes into a bowl. Kate eyed Georgia’s breakfast jealously (the same way she did with the kids’ Frosties in 2014) and started to salivate. But there was no way she would ever allow herself any of that sugary treat – why, her hips would never forgive her! Or her back fat.

‘Is that all?’ Kate said, hoping this would be her cue to feel relieved. Because there was never any harm in dancing, was there? It’s not like they lived in that town in *Footloose*, where dancing was banned and the work of the devil or whatever.

‘In the Gents,’ Georgia added.

Kate groaned. She wasn’t sure she wanted to hear anymore. No, no, scratch that – she was. She *was* sure she didn’t want to hear anymore.

Imagine if Seamus and the kids had seen her! Imagine if Blue and Paris had seen her! She was mortified.

‘In fact,’ Georgia went on, ‘Liam asked me to take you home – he was quite chivalrous, come to think of it. Seemed more protective of you rather than wanting to take advantage of you or anything. Which was rather unexpected, I must say.’

'Oh, great,' Kate moaned, burying her head in her hands. 'Was it...was I...were *we* always like this?'

'Like what?'

'You know, ridiculously embarrassing. And grotty. And out of control.'

'You mean out there, up for it and always on the lash?'

'Yes... I think...?'

'Dunno. But I think Tom's really led *you* astray. Things have really ratcheted up a few notches since you started going out with him, that's for sure. But you've always been a bad influence on me, Kate. Ever since we started at infant school together. That's what my mother always says, anyway.'

Kate didn't remember being the ringleader of their exploits, the instigator of their mischief. But now that Georgia mentioned it, maybe she was sometimes guilty of egging her best friend on, goading her into doing things she wasn't 100% sure were the 'right' or the 'good' thing to do.

'Hey! That's not entirely fair,' she grappled with the moral high ground that was fast disappearing beneath her feet. 'You were the one who got me so wasted last night I can't remember any of it! And it involved Liam Gallagher?! You've robbed me of my one decent memory of probably the closest brush with fame I'll ever have!'

'You weren't exactly a shrinking violet when it came to Neil Morrissey, either, you know...'

'WHAT?'

‘You kept poncing ciggies off him. Not that he minded – he just kept nicking Clunesy’s packets.’

Neil Morrissey? *Clunesy*? This was worse – a hundred times worse than Kate first thought.

‘STOP! I don’t want to hear anymore. Let’s just forget it ever happened and we’ll never mention it again. OK?’

‘Mention what again?”

‘Atta girl,’ said Kate, brushing the hair off her face and shaking her head as though she could erase any remaining memory she might have of the previous evening with a few short, sharp tosses of her mane.

‘That’s it for me,’ she continued, refreshed. ‘Never again.’

Georgia snorted as though she’d heard this refrain many times before – which she had, not least from her own lips. But unbeknownst to Georgia, Kate really *did* mean it this time and would, in an unprecedented move, actually stick to her vow. She’d forgotten how hopeless she was at taking the emotional battering and horrendous embarrassment their mornings-after would invariably bring. And since she’d had the kids, the biggest a night got was usually one family block of Cadbury’s Dairy Milk too many in front of *Location, Location, Location*. Dancing with pop stars and smoking with celebrities was nothing but a dim, distant memory now she was a mother of three. Or at least it would be if she could remember any of it.

And so now, with her muzzy head quite a bit clearer (her 26-year-old self’s hangover lasting only a few hours in the morning – as opposed to the three days she would spend out of action with an ice mask over her eyes when she was 44), she sat opposite Georgia and looked longingly at her friend's bowl of cereal once more.

'Oh, sod it,' she said, grabbing the packet and filling a bowl to the brim with its crunchy, nutty, sweet, carby tastiness. She splashed on lashings of creamy, cold, fantastically full-fat milk.

'Do you remember whose that is?' Georgia jerked her head towards the rogue cagoule on the end of the pew.

'Of course I don't,' Kate said through a mouthful of sheer bliss. 'Hmmm – joy. These are delicious!'

'God, you are absolutely dreadful,' said Georgia. 'When we got kicked out of the Roof Gardens, we tried to get a taxi home, but couldn't. Then we bumped into some technical guy from your office, who was just driving past on his way home from work – must've been about 11 or so – and he rather gallantly put it over your shoulders. You said it felt weird having your fat mummy tummy exposed and he wanted to help keep you warm. As well as preserve what little was left of your dignity, I suppose.'

'Really?' said Kate. 'What was his name?'

'I can't remember. He was quite a nice guy, though – gave us a lift home in his Skoda. Came in for a quick drink – our way of saying thankyou.'

'Was it...was his name Seamus?'

'That's the fella!'

'And he only came in for a quick drink, did he? I mean, I didn't try to snog him or drag him into the loos or...'

'No, no - not that I'm aware of.'

'Thank God for that,' said Kate rolling her eyes to the ceiling. 'For a second there, I thought you were going to say I'd disgraced myself even further...'

At this, Georgia arched an eyebrow and laughed unconvincingly. Then she turned to look behind her just as an impossibly tall, lanky guy in a Liverpool shirt hopped into the kitchen, pulling on his black trainers.

'I can give you a lift to work too, Kate, if you can be ready in the next ten minutes,' coughed Seamus, his face reddening as he studied his shoelaces.

10

She hadn't felt jealous – really jealous – when it came to Seamus and another woman, for – God! Come to think of it, Kate didn't know if she'd *ever* thought that Seamus might have fancied someone else.

But sitting here in his Skoda, the floor littered with empty (she'd checked) Quavers packets and various unidentifiable wires and plugs, she felt herself turning a most unattractive shade of green.

'So,' she said, breaking the silence that had hung heavily in the air between them ever since they bade Georgia farewell. 'I see you're getting to know not only your colleagues at work better, but getting to know their best friends even better!'

Seamus stole a lightning fast glance at his passenger.

'Hmm?' he hummed as he negotiated the morning traffic.

'Georgia,' Kate said accusingly. 'My best friend? The woman with whom you shared a *bed* with last night with?'

Kate momentarily panicked about whether she'd used 'whom' correctly and overdone the 'withs' in that last sentence. She'd never said 'whom' before in actual, real-life speech and half-expected Tom to pop out from the back seat, telling her how wrong she'd got it and how she had, quite unnecessarily, doubled – trebled, even, the 'withs'.

'Who?' asked Seamus, concentrating hard on the

road ahead. '*Me*?'

'Well I don't see any other dirty stop out here!'

Kate heard herself for the first time that morning and swallowed hard. Trying to rein herself in, she gave herself a brief but strict talking to.

Steady on! He doesn't know he's married to you in the future – barely even knows who you are, yet! You'll scare him off if you carry on like this, so go easy with the wounded wife routine, will you?

'But I didn't! I slept on her floor,' said Seamus.

'Details, details,' Kate couldn't help herself.

'Look,' Seamus said, yanking on the handbrake at a set of red traffic lights. 'I don't know what you're suggesting – or why it matters to you so much, but just for the record, Georgia tried to kiss *me* last night. I declined with thanks, fending off her advances in the most gentlemanly way I knew how.'

Kate stared back at him, her mouth agape.

'Well,' he went on 'we'd all had too much to drink and I barely know either of you and it didn't feel all that romantic to me and I know it sounds strange and you'll probably think I'm a real pratt, but –'

'Yes?' Kate folded her arms across her chest.

'...I'm just not that sort of guy.'

'Yeah, right!' scoffed Kate. 'You mean human?'

Kate couldn't imagine there was a man alive who wouldn't be bowled over by Georgia's striking beauty. She believed that every man who ever saw her wanted to bed her (as was commensurate with what she'd seen over the years) and couldn't quite comprehend what

Seamus was saying.

She felt confused. This was not how it had been the first time round, had it? All straight men were crazy about Georgia, weren't they? And all men were only ever after one thing, weren't they? She felt as though she were blindly weaving her way through a veritable rabbit warren of reality and perception, fact and fiction, making her feel more like Alice in Wonderland than ever.

'I am sorry about your eye, you know,' he said wearily, as though he'd already said it a thousand times.

Kate grunted.

The lights turned green and Seamus jerked the car into first and bunny hopped for a few metres before he spoke again.

'So are you watching the match on Saturday?'

'What match?' asked Kate.

'England v Switzerland, of course!' laughed Seamus. 'Where have you been?'

Kate felt her shackles rising. She felt exactly as she did when Seamus would come home from work and, finding the house in a right state with dirty plates and clothes strewn everywhere and Baby Jane bawling her eyes out, say: "What exactly do you *do* all day?'

'Well, how am I supposed to know?' Kate felt like answering him. 'I've only been back in the 90s for a day! You try to remember a football tournament's schedule on top of everybloodything else!'

But she didn't. She let her annoyance pass,

quickly, and then a wave of excitement washed over her.

'Oh yeah! It's the first one, isn't it? What do you think of our chances?'

As soon as she'd asked this question, she regretted it. Not because she knew exactly how it all turned out, so it was kind of irrelevant to her, but because she knew that once you got any guy banging on about football, they couldn't shut up. It was as though there was no room left in their heads for feelings and emotions – their brains were packed to capacity with boring stats and 'interesting' facts.

Note to self: remember to never even get him started on Fantasy Football league tables.

'Hmm,' she said, trying to sound as though she'd been listening. 'Still, I wouldn't ever discount the Germans. Best for us to not get complacent and keep on our toes at all times, give it our all no matter who we're playing.'

Seamus looked at her as though she were mad (a look she knew very well, it having not changed in 20 years) and said:

'Do you like football?'

'Yeah, I suppose so,' she thought of Georgia, whose ex, Simon, was obsessed with football, making Georgia pronounce it 'a sickness' – and their sex life on weekends, as a result, DOA. 'But this time it's special, really, isn't it? I mean, a chance like this only comes once in a lifetime.'

Seamus shot her an admiring glance and smiled,

nodding his head in agreement.

Kate leaned over and turned up the radio, which was, oddly enough, playing *Once In A Lifetime.*

'Curiouser and curiouser,' Kate said as she sat back and began to enjoy the ride.

*

'So, Kate,' Archie yelled out across the office. 'Got anywhere with Medea? Or that, um, other matter we spoke about yesterday?'

'Hang on a sec,' Kate called back, organising her bag and hanging her optimistically lightweight trench coat over the back of her chair.

In all the flurry of debauched activity yesterday, she'd clean forgotten all about the media storm brewing between Medea and *LASHED.* And as for *Mad Fer It!,* well, she didn't have a clue how to reverse her favourite teen mag's fortunes.

Kate looked at the phone. She was one of the lucky ones, Archie had told her, to be getting a new whizz-bang machine that was an answering machine and phone in one. State of the art technology, she believed it was called.

But she hadn't received it yet – she imagined Seamus would deliver it to her, hook it up, tell her how it worked and then somehow fall over in some way that would make her other eye black, too. A matching pair.

There were some hand-written messages sitting next to the phone and she looked up to see Lucy, the receptionist, smiling politely at yet another person walking in who looked past her, totally ignoring her, too important to take the time to say hi.

Kate told herself off for not having formally introduced herself to Lucy. It wasn't like her, she thought. Because she'd always made a point of being nice to everyone. Not in a 'you never know who'll you'll bump into on the way down' way, but just because she was generally, overall, for the most part, a really nice person.

She picked up the messages and strode over to reception.

'Hi there,' she breezed, holding out her hand 'I'm Kate. I don't think we've been properly introduced.'

'No, I, ah, hi! I'm Lucy,' the girl said shaking Kate's hand. 'Have I done something wrong?'

'No, not at all,' laughed Kate. 'I just wanted to thank you for taking these messages for me.'

Lucy looked puzzled. Then embarrassed. 'Just doing my job,' she said, warily.

'And doing it well, too. Thanks again, Lucy. I'll see you later.' Kate turned around and, immensely pleased with herself, as though she'd just wiped out third world debt or fed the poor, sick and hungry for a year, heard herself say, just as her mother always had, 'good manners cost nothing' as she headed back towards her desk.

'Oh, Kate?' Lucy called after her. 'The guy who called this morning – you're holding the message in your hand – was that Liam Gallagher? It sounded like him, but is it really *The* Liam Gallagher? From Oasis?'

'I very much doubt it,' scoffed Kate as she looked down at her hand. 'When did this Liam call?'

'At about 8:30, I think. I wrote it on the paper there, see?'

Kate did see.

8:25am Tuesday June 4

When can I see you again? Call me on my paging service – I gave you the number last night.

Liam Xxx

'Oh, come ON!' Kate said aloud, looking frantically at the ceiling. 'This has GOT to be a dream. I mean, as IF!'

'I know!' squealed Lucy. 'I thought the same thing! It can't be the real one – he doesn't get up before two in the afternoon!'

Kate stared at Lucy.

'Or...at least...that's what they say in this fortnight's *Mad Fer It!,*' she said, sounding slightly scared and holding up her copy of the magazine, fairly festooned with pictures of Mr Gallagher. 'It's a special edition...um...their We Love Liam issue...'

'Yeah,' Kate nodded, calming down a bit. 'Just a joke I expect.'

She slumped down in her chair and looked crossly at the message.

'What paging service number?' she muttered as she picked her mini black leather rucksack off the floor and rummaged through it.

Kate marvelled momentarily at how little there was in there – save for a few lighters, lots of loose tobacco and broken cigarettes, her purse, her puffer, her favourite Rimmel Raspberry Fool lipstick and wet/dry compact, a packet of Extra (sugar free) chewing gum, a small, travel sized perfume bottle and, as always, her keys in the special secret zipped compartment. It was really light.

These were the days, she thought – when her handbag wasn't overflowing with wipes, nappies, sultanas (both in and out of their box), iPhones (both real and toy), car keys, house keys, crayons, markers, random bits of dog-eared paper with shopping lists and notes to herself scribbled on them, unused but grubby and suspect-looking tissues (she always grabbed four upon leaving the house, contributing to the mini mountain of Kleenex growing daily in her bag), spare pairs of pants (for the boys), tampons and pads (for her), big jars of Vaseline, smashed about tubes of Savlon, half-eaten lollipops stuck to the cloth lining, long-forgotten receipts...

Kate tutted thinking of all the rubbish she carted about with her back in 2014, emotional and otherwise. Her problem was always trying to be prepared for every eventuality and emergency while constantly being blindsided by the completely unexpected. She sighed. And immediately felt like crying.

Could it be that she was missing the noise and clutter of home? Missing the kids' cute, Marmitesmeared faces? She wanted to hold them all close to her right now, vowing that she'd never, ever, EVER shout at them again, ever. Even if she'd had no sleep and George wouldn't get off his Playstation and get dressed and Decko was transfixed by the telly and Baby Jane was pooing up a storm three minutes before they were due to leave for the school run. Nope, not her. The second she got back to them – hoping, now, that it would be soon - she would become the perfect mum, unflappable, in control but not stern, warm and funny, stylish and slim – she would really be the kind of mum she'd always wanted to be and everything, as a direct result, would be fantastic.

Kate felt the need to slope off to the toilets for a quiet little power weep. Then she would get back to putting the magazine world to rights.

But as she pulled her hand out of her rucksack, a beer coaster came flying out as well, a soggy corner hitting her square in her bruised eye.

'Ouch!' she exclaimed as she bent down to pick the coaster up off the floor. She turned it over and read what had been scrawled on the back in thick, pinky-red (Raspberry Fool, anyone?) lipstick:

LG

6781235 #6660

X

She flipped the coaster over and over again so many times, she looked as if she were fanning herself.

'Hey Hot Stuff!' she heard Tom's confident desert-booted swagger approaching. 'Where did you get to last night? I was looking for you everywhere!'

Out of the corner of her eye, Kate clocked Tamsin's head popping up out of her cubicle, like a meerkat coming up from underground and standing to attention on a mound of dirt, its sharp eyes, excellent ears and cute button nose sensing predators.

'Oh,' she laughed nervously, stuffing the coaster back in her rucksack. 'Ah, nowhere. I mean, home. I was in no fit state to be seen in public, I'm sure you'll agree.'

Weirdly enough, Tom, who rarely noticed how anyone else was looking or behaving, his focus usually being solely on himself, did agree.

'Too big a sesh for such a little girl, eh?' he said, perching his bum on the side of Kate's desk and stroking her hair.

How *did* he get away with being so patronising, Kate wondered, as she started to melt under his touch, annoyed with herself for being such a cliché and fancying him like mad despite his reprehensible behaviour.

'Now, listen, Reese,' he said, crooking his index finger and gently holding it under Kate's chin, as if her head was a budgie and it was sitting on his finger. 'I'm in a bit of hot water with some slappers at Medea – can you sort it out for me? I'm up to my nuts in it this week and just haven't got the time. Yeah?'

Kate nodded.

'Archie's already briefed me,' she said softly.

'Good. Great. Excellent!' Tom said, slapping his

hands on his thighs and standing up. 'I've got to check out some flats tomorrow. Round lunchtime. Come with?'

He got up, backed out of the office and shot her with his right index finger as he winked and made a *nyick, nyick* clicking sound with his tongue.

Kate pondered the Tom question. Just how did he do it? How did he manage to be so creepy and downright sleazy and still so damned sexy? And how did he still look so good, so GQ model-esque when the only working out he ever did was the occasional shag (after which he would always give himself a mark out of 10 – usually 11 – as though he was both Olympic gymnast and judge) and 'taking care of himself' meant he was...what was the office radio playing now? That Pulp song...yes, yes, that's it. How did Tom look so hot when taking care of himself merely meant that he was always sorted for Es and whizz, as he might say. As he would *definitely* say.

Kate heard Tamsin swoon. Or was that her?

She shook her head and got down to work, drafting a document to fax to Medea and flicking through the latest copy of *LASHED* on her desk for inspiration.

She laughed at a few of the magazine's jokes – and when she felt she had the kernel of an idea, she started writing, stream-of-consciousness-style on her Apple Mac.

She went on and on about how, contrary to Medea's first impressions, *LASHED* is, in actual fact, a celebration of womanhood. And how far from being a tacky skin mag, *LASHED* is ironic and leading the way for women to be taken seriously and loved for all the things they are (sexy AND smart) in an increasingly man's world. It's tongue in cheek, she wrote, and aimed at the intelligent young male, featuring only equally-intelligent females in their 'Thinking Man's Crumpet' pages (where a scantily-clad TV celebrity would pose, sprawling about on a round bed, her glossy-lipped mouth about to tuck into a jam-covered crumpet. A small Q&A would accompany the pictorial, with such edifying questions as Which do you prefer - blueberry or strawberry jam? And: Thongs or your boyfriend's boxers?).

Kate couldn't believe she was coming out with such drivel. But once she started, she couldn't seem to stop. She pointed out that, contrary to Medea's accusations, *LASHED* loved women – all women - in all their wonderful forms - which is why they often featured women who were shorter than 5"11 – and sometimes models who had real boobs! They were not shy about interviewing powerful, non-pin up women occasionally, too (even though Kate couldn't find any examples) which was more than many women's magazines were doing, virtually ignoring their local sisters in favour of their Hollywood, perma-tanned, perma-vacuous counterparts.

Yes, *LASHED* was pro-women. From her beautiful body, whatever its shape or size (unlike teen and women's mags who foisted hideously unrealistic-looking girls on their reading public and had the audacity, the chutzpah, to call them role models – now that was anti-women! That was misogyny in action right there!) to her sharp, fascinating mind, to her cracking sense of humour, *LASHED* was on our side (and our front and our back) – and all about equality. And, in the end, wasn't that what Medea Media was all about, too?

The more she went on, the more she almost started to believe it. Maybe the lads at *LASHED* were feminists in louts clothing, after all – and doing a great job of highlighting the inequality of the sexes, bringing the struggle up to date and shoving it into the spotlight. Hmm. *Maybe*.

Kate was really getting a true sense of how, in this heady, intoxicating atmosphere of New Labour and spin and summer and football and foreign lager, how *male*, how full-on bloke-centred it all was. And how seductive it was, too – how loads of women (condescendingly called ladettes) wanted a piece of that action, too - some of that control and power. And what was so bad about that?

Blue's face landed with a thud at the front of Kate's mind. A bony finger wagged at her and Blue looked disapproving. She said:

'You don't get to be equal to men by *acting* like them, Darling. We need to be tough, not rough. Drinking like a demented school boy and having sex with people whose names you don't even know is not the way to fight for our rights. It might be a double standard – and a lot of fun – but, my Dear, it's our minds that will win the war in our favour in the end. So think, don't drink! Think, don't drink!'

Kate blinked her mother's image out of her head and stared at her document. Was it convincing? Would they buy it? Really?

Kate thought hard and in her final paragraph, promised Medea Media free advertising for their titles (including the worthy, serious *That's Ms To You!* and the softer, more mass market *Millie* – a reference to the old 'rad fem' *Viz* cartoon character, Millie Tant) for a year, as a gesture of goodwill, should they decide not to take matters any further.

She was sure they'd go for it – Medea was small and, word had it, about to go bust any second now. Free advertising in the nation's number one men's magazine? Which, statistics proved, was read by more women than the leading women's magazine? And where a quarter of a page advertising space would set them back 1000 pounds? They would definitely go for it.

She ran it by Archie, who read it fast and then, with a wry smile, said:

'So glad I asked you to do this. You know what Tom wanted to say? He wanted to ask them whether they needed a good seeing to, because if they did – the whole of Medea Media – he knew just the mag to give it to them.'

Kate shook her head in mock disbelief, because of course she believed it – it was starting to become all-too clear what Tom's true colours were, what was on his unevolved mind 24/7.

'Please don't ever leave me – you make me look too good!' Archie beamed, handing the document back to her.

She smiled back at him, but her lips were tight and she sucked on them through her teeth.

Standing at the fax machine, Kate wondered why she just didn't feel as chuffed with herself as she would have done 18 years ago upon hearing Archie's fulsome praise. In fact, she rubbed her tummy, wincing, she felt a bit seedy – even grottier than when she'd first awoken this morning.

When she'd finished, she took herself off to the loo and studied herself in the mirror.

Had Kate really decamped to the other side? The dark side? Was she fast becoming a traitor to the cause? She felt disappointment seeping through her (tightly-closed, dewy, youthful, really rather beautiful) pores. Was this really tearing the lads' playhouse down, as she promised herself she would do only yesterday?

Oh, bollocks! This was all getting too much! The 90s were far too much responsibility – it was like having the family without the fun – what sort of a break from reality was this? All she wanted was to dance *to Girls Just Want To Have Fun* in her bright, day-glo gear and big hair - with nothing to lose any sleep over except which fluoro shade of nail varnish to wear!

'I didn't even want the 90s!' she said out loud. 'It's all mixed up! That was Georgia!'

She wondered whether Georgia was stuck somewhere in the 80s, her hair super-sized, her waist tiny in an ankle-length white tube skirt, bobby socks and a belted XL white shirt with big, black capital letters saying CHOOSE LIFE on it, dancing to WHAM!

'That should be me,' she muttered to herself, realising that however hard she tried, the corners of her mouth just wouldn't turn down.

'Too much elasticity still in the skin, I expect,' she said, turning her head this way and that, trying to locate the loose stuff, the jowls that she constantly self-lifted in her bathroom mirror back home in 2014 whenever she was passing. 'Smooth, unlined, no wrinkles, no adult acne scars, no hag hairs, no moles or skin tags – you never knew you had it so good, did you? And those bright blue eyes with their whole life ahead of them -'

She heard a toilet flush, which made her jump – she thought she'd been in there alone. Seconds later, one of the cubicle doors opened and Tamsin walked out, smoothing her sprayed-on pencil skirt down over her non-existent hips.

'Don't forget your kookiness and your oh-so pretty chin, Reese,' she giggled, washing her hands and pouting at herself.

Kate felt her temperature escalate rapidly. She was acutely embarrassed and watched, agog, as a deeply unflattering shade of crimson crept up her face, rising all the way from her perky décolletage to her frown-line-free forehead.

Tamsin smiled sweetly at Kate as she turned tail and left the loos. And although Kate was mortified her rival had heard her, she managed to spot a rather nasty crop of whiteheads making itself at home just to the left of Tamsin's cute, button nose.

Which cheered her up no end.

11

'So much for the Sisterhood,' Blue said, when Kate told her all about Medea the next day at lunch.

'I know, I know,' said Kate. 'But what can I do? It's my job to put a positive spin on these things.'

'I understand that,' said Blue, licking the chocolatey froth off her cappuccino spoon, 'but you don't have to go quite so over the top, do you? I mean, surely they'll see through all your claptrap and want to use such a high profile, controversial magazine like *LASHED* to highlight their plight, illustrate their point, so to speak.'

'They could do that in a negative way, of course,' said Kate. 'But in these days where magazines are folding faster than a Chinese laundry, I think I made them an offer they simply can't afford to refuse.'

'You bribed them?'

'Not exactly. I made it more worth their while to use *LASHED*'s profile to better theirs in a positive way. For Medea to be seen to be in bed – so to speak – with *LASHED*. I think it might work and both parties would benefit.'

'Hmm,' Blue sounded unconvinced and peered at the menu over her half-moon glasses.

Kate shrugged her shoulders. She knew her position was fairly indefensible – especially to a die-hard feminist like Blue – but she was stuck between a rock and a hard place on this one.

And quite frankly, Kate thought, she didn't give a

damn. Not at this particular juncture, anyway, what with her beautiful mother sitting before her, no doubt ready to impart pearl after pearl of wonderful wisdom.

'So where's Dad?' Kate asked, gnawing on a Grissini.

She always pictured her parents as a pair, almost as if they were joined at the hip, with never a problem or harsh word between them their whole married life.

'Playing golf,' Blue said without looking up, as though it was no big deal that Kate didn't get to see her father today, even though it had been 14 years since they'd met up. 'He said to send you his apologies and oceans of love, though. He expects to see you on Sunday for lunch at ours, of course, but he thought today might be nice, just you and me. He's thoughtful like that.'

'Yeah – as long as it fits in with his tee times,' Kate chuckled.

'Of course, penne alla tonno is always a good choice,' Blue muttered. 'But why do they have to drown it in pesto sauce? Can't they just keep things simple? Someone should come along and show these ridiculous chefs how to strip food down to its essentials, get back to the basics...'

'What? Like Jamie Oliver?'

'Who?'

'Oh, no one,' Kate shifted uneasily in her seat, instantly realising she was in a time slightly before *The Naked Chef* and all the Jamie Oliver hype had hit. 'One day soon someone will come along and do just that, though – you mark my words. And he's going to blow us all away.'

But Blue wasn't listening, caught up as she was in the Carluccio's conundrum of which dish to order.

''But anyway, anyway, anyway!' cried Kate, clapping her hands together with glee and jumping out of her seat a little bit. 'You haven't changed a bit! Oh, it's *so* good to see you, Mummy!'

Mummy?Where did that come from?

'Thankyou, Dear,' said Blue, running her index finger down the menu. 'Neither have you – except I don't think you've called me Mummy since you were about seven years old.'

A waiter came and took their order (Sea Bass for Kate, keen to preserve her svelte figure and Carbonara for Blue, for whom carbs had never been a problem) and a stern, serious look came over Blue's kindly face.

'We need to talk,' she said, clasping her hands in front of her on the table.

'About Kevin?' Kate spluttered.

'Who?' replied Blue, getting visibly agitated. 'Honestly, Kate, I can't keep up with all your friends, all those pop stars and TV presenters. I don't know who they are and to be perfectly honest, I –'

'No, no, I...it's the name of a hugely successful book, which...oh, never mind. I'm sorry. Go on.'

'Steven,' Blue sighed. 'Your little brother. What on earth are we going to do about him?'

'Well, it's interesting you should mention little brothers,' said Kate. 'I've been dying to ask you this for years – just how did you and Dad manage to pay us kids the exact right amount of attention so that we didn't get jealous of each other? How did you guys do the whole parenting thing so well?'

'I – well, thankyou, Kate – but I'm not so sure we did.'

'Don't be so modest, Blue! You're the perfect mother, everyone can see that!'

'That's sweet of you to say, Darling, but I think the proof is always in the pudding. And if you prod our Number Two pudding –'

'Hmph! You said Number Two!' Kate blurted out, wishing George and Decko were here to appreciate the hilarity.

'I'm not sure he worked out so well. Not yet, anyway. Seems we've made mistake after mistake with him and before it goes too far, before he does something stupid we'll all regret, I wanted to sound you out.'

'About what?'

'An intervention.'

'A what?'

'An intervention. It's when-'

'I know what an intervention is, I just can't see how that will make Steve any better,' Kate said, dimpling her chin and shaking her head. 'In fact, an intervention might be just the thing to tip him over the edge, cement in his mind how little you really know of him and how completely hopeless and incompetent you really think he is.'

'Well he is!'

'No, he isn't – not in the way you think he is. He just needs to get back on his feet, that's all – he's just a little down at the moment. He might need an encouraging – not bullying – shove in the right direction. He needs a bit of help to get him back on his feet – his own two feet, I might add – again.'

'Well, we did something right, I suppose,' said Blue, 'We always wanted you and Steve to be close, to defend each other and look out for each other. None of us are getting any younger and we won't be around forever, you know.'

'I know,' said Kate, softly as she watched her mother. It may have been a little unnerving for Blue, but Kate couldn't waste a single moment of drinking in her mother's presence, as though it were the very elixir of life itself.

'Darling,' said Blue through thin, hardly-moving ventriloquist's lips as she glanced swiftly sideways, checking whether anyone else was looking. 'You know you're staring...'

'Hmmm,' Kate replied, unable to tear her eyes away from Blue, as though she was lost in a trance.

Their main meals arrived and the pair were silent. Blue pushed her food around her plate, taking small, uninterested bites every now and again and Kate continued to freak her mother out, watching her every move, an unsettling, beatific grin plastered to her face.

'Darling,' Blue sing-songed, getting annoyed with her daughter.

This prompted Kate to come back into the room, to come out from under the spell her mother had unwittingly cast.

She coughed a small 'ahem' and, looking down, smoothed her napkin on her lap.

'I think I might have a way of forcing – gently – Steve to sort himself out,' Kate said after a while.

'You do?' Blue looked at her expectantly.

'Well, as you know, Tom – you know Tom - Tom is crazy-keen for us to move in together and I know you think it will be a total and utter disaster and I know you think he's a misogynist, an arrogant pig and not even that good looking...'

Kate paused to give her mother the chance to refute any of the above. But Blue was simply nodding and listening intently.

'...and I think I'd be a fool and regret it forever if I didn't give it a go.'

Kate waited for Blue to put her hand onto her chest and gasp, but instead she looked at her pasta and pursed her lips as she always did when she was concentrating hard. When, eventually, Blue did look her in the eye, Kate grasped the edges of her chair and took a deep breath, as if in preparation for the full force of Blue's acid tongue.

'Darling,' Blue began softly, making Kate relax her vice-like grip of the chair. 'I think you might be right.'

'What?' said Kate, incredulous.

'I think it's just what you need, in order to see this

Tom character for what he really, obviously is. And if you moving in with Tom forced Steve to get a job and pay his own way in the West Hampstead flat with Georgia, he'd have to step up to the mark, wouldn't he?'

'Well, that's what I've been thinking –'

'And you know what else?' continued Blue. 'I suspect that if you *didn't* move in with Tom, you'd forever blame me for talking you out of it. And you'd somehow resent Steve, too, for needing you too much and thus preventing you from getting on with your own life.'

God, she was good. She was right! *That's* what Kate and Steve had fallen out about all those years ago – Steve's dependence on her and Kate's overgrown responsibility gland getting in the way of her doing exactly what she wanted with little or no regard for anyone else.

'So you think it's a good idea?' asked Kate, a little perplexed by her mother's reaction.

'As long as you think it'll make you and Steve happy,' she smiled.

At that, Kate shook her head and welled up.

Just as she'd remembered, her mother was always putting the happiness of her kids before her own. And even though her day dreams might paint quite a different picture – fantasies involving old boyfriends, old situations, her old life – Kate's main priority, too, was to be a good mum. Frustratingly, it was an ambition she often felt she would never realise. At least not to the dizzying heights of perfection her own mother did.

'Typical,' Kate murmured. 'Perfectly selfless. Just perfect.'

'What was that, Sweetheart?' Blue asked. 'I think my hearing's going, you know.'

'Oh, nothing,' said Kate. 'It's just that, well, were you always so good at this, Mummy?'

There was that word again. *Mummy*. Kate couldn't help herself. It was as though she so desperately needed Blue, so keenly felt the need for connection with her, the first person she'd ever truly loved and trusted and respected, who always had her best interests at heart, that to call her by any other name would merely put more distance between them. And Kate couldn't bear that.

'At what, Dear?'

'Being the perfect mum.'

'Oh, come on, Darling,' Blue looked around again, but more as though she was searching the room for someone this time, rather than being embarrassed. 'I'm far from perfect.'

'But you are!'

'No, I'm not.'

'Are too!'

'No, Darling. I really am not.'

'Are too!' Kate said again, thumping her fist down on the table, as though these were the final words on the matter and she had won the 'am not/are too' battle she often had with her own kids (even though, back in

2014, it was usually about burnt biscuits or being late for school, as opposed to being the perfect mother. Come to think of it, her kids had never accused her of that – not even once.).

'You've got the perfect marriage to that handsome devil, Paris – or Daddy as I keep wanting to call him - and a spotless, lovely house. You've got two beautiful – if I say so myself – and reasonably well-adjusted kids...well, one reasonably well-adjusted kid...You're still travelling the world, making new discoveries all the time, lecturing when you feel like it, doing what you love with the man you love. What's *not* perfect about that?'

'We all have our dark sides, Sweetie – the bits we'd rather other people didn't see.'

'But not you!'

'Yes, Kate, even me.'

Blue looked slightly beyond Kate and almost imperceptibly nodded at something in the distance. Not too far in the distance, of course – Blue could only see about a metre clearly in front of her. Further away than that, and it was all a blur.

'And you should watch that tendency of yours to never take off those rose-coloured glasses, Kate. I've always said it – you're too absolute, too black and white. But life's not like that, Sweetheart,' Blue said, eyes twinkling as she reached over the table to hold Kate's hand. 'There are grey areas, messy problems that can't be fixed, people who'll let you down. And I fear I may be one of those, because at this level of adoration, I can only disappoint you in the end. No one can live up to those lofty ideals you have. Certainly not me! And I don't want to be around when you discover my feet of clay!'

Blue laughed, a little too loudly, and Kate joined in, not believing a word her mother had said.

After a tiramisu (for Blue) and a coffee (for Kate), they stood up and put on their near-identical Burberry trench coats. Blue adjusted the blue and gold Hermes scarf that was permanently attached to her coat's collar and Kate fluffed up her own hair. Quite unnecessarily, really, her 1996 thick 'Rachel' always had the appearance of a slightly teased, hairsprayed 'do.

'You'd better get back to work,' Blue said, giving Kate the distinct impression that she was being hurried.

'Oh, it's OK, I can take my time.'

'Well, I can't,' Blue said quickly. 'I've – ah – I've got to get back to Ickenham. There's council stuff and a public lecture to prepare – time waits for no woman!'

Kate felt Blue's hand on the small of her back as she was chivvied out of the restaurant by her mother.

Standing out the front of Carluccio's, Blue proceeded to shoo Kate away.

'Go on, Dear,' she said. 'I'll settle the bill, you go back to work.'

Kate didn't move, so surprised was she that her mother, on this most momentous of occasions, seemed to really want to get rid of her.

'But –' Kate began.

Blue tutted and put her hands on Kate's shoulders,

kissing her continentally, on both cheeks.

'Go on! Away with you, now! We'll see you on Sunday!'

Kate reluctantly turned and began to walk back to her office. She'd only gone a couple of steps when she glanced back over her shoulder, just in time to see Blue taking off her coat, draping it over her arm, fluffing up her own hair and smoothing down her pants (which, as Kate had commented on earlier, made her look young and zippy and showed off her model figure nicely). Kate watched, transfixed once more, as her mother pointed her chin to the sky, laughed at something blindingly funny and, with arms outstretched, as though she were greeting a much-loved, long-lost old friend, went skipping lightly straight back in to Carluccio's.

12

Kate stood at the doors to The Lift, chewing her lip and making grooves in the carpet with the right toe of her sneakers.

It had been so great to see her mum again – she looked so wonderful, full of life and radiant, vitality emanating from her every pore. And even though she'd seemed a bit distracted at the end, Kate had basked in the warm glow of motherhood Blue had always brought with her to the table.

But she wasn't just a great mum – though that in itself was a major achievement and worthy of constant applause – she was a great *person*. With a lot to offer the world. And a full and satisfying life.

That's what never losing your identity to your kids does for you, Kate thought. An image of her bedraggled self, baby on hip, pilled dressing gown hanging crookedly over her frumpy nightie, thin, straggly hair and an arse the size of Cuba flashed into her mind.

She had officially become one of those women who had nothing else to get up for other than tending to three kids. Not that there was anything wrong with that, *per se*, she reminded herself – Mother being the most noble, true and brave profession she could think of.

It's just that when the kids grew up and moved away (which, Seamus often promised her, they would one day), what would they leave behind in their wake? A fat, exhausted, old woman with no job, that's what. And no idea what had happened in the world while she'd been away, out of every loop going, missing in child-rearing action.

She'd only been back in 1996 for three days, but already she'd had enough. She'd seen nearly everyone she wanted to and even though there was still a small amount of unfinished business with Tom that needed seeing to, right now, she wanted to go home.

Because – and this made her take a small step back at the ferocity of the realisation – she missed those kids like crazy! Their cute faces, the funny things they came out with (that she had to restrain herself from boring Georgia with on a daily basis) and their soft, warm hugs which always made her melt, even when she was about to lose her temper and let fly, shouting and stamping her foot, in that hopelessly ineffectual way she had.

And she even missed Seamus, with his grumpy old man frown and his propensity to choose golf over being with the family at every turn.

She gave a little snort when she remembered that she used to wish Seamus was more like her dad – because, take away the bad moods and the baldness, what did she have? Her dad!

She pictured Seamus in a CHOOSE GOLF t-shirt, dancing to *Wake Me Up Before You Go-Go* and giggled. He was never much of a dancer, her Seamus. Which was hardly surprising, really, considering the act of putting one foot in front of the other and actually *walking* posed too much of a problem for the hapless Seamus sometimes.

Kate smiled. He may be an awkward, uncoordinated old bugger, but he was *her* awkward, uncoordinated old bugger. Or at least he was in 2014, she suddenly remembered.

'How am I ever going to get back there?' she asked her (rather cute, actually, if she said so herself) reflection in the mirrored lift doors.

She straightened up and admired her form for a few seconds before the doors opened with a DING!

"Finally,' Kate muttered as she stepped into The Lift, standing in the opposite corner to the boy already in there.

It took her a few seconds for it to dawn on her that that was no boy standing nervously opposite her – it was the young Seamus!

'Hello there!' she said, buoyed by seeing not only a younger version of herself, but also the gangly, baby giraffe that was Seamus, whose face was fast turning red with embarrassment.

But embarrassment at *what*?! Honestly, she thought to herself, he really had to sort that shyness out if he was ever going to get anywhere.

And those clothes! What on earth *did* she ever see in him? And how did they ever get together, when he was so...so...so beige, he was bordering on the invisible?

Her mind flipped through its mental Facebook

page for pictures of parties they'd been to together, their wedding, the births of their kids – but she couldn't seem to locate any.

Oh God. It's like Back To The Future when Marty's family start to disappear in that photo, as though they never existed!

Not being an expert in quantum physics – or any kind of physics at all, for that matter - Kate started to panic. How did she get here? How would she get back? Where was her family? Were they disappearing? Were they ceasing to exist? What were they doing? They couldn't possibly manage without her! Could they?

'Oh, hurry up,' she said, looking at the illuminated numbers above the closed doors. 'Why does this bloody lift always take so bloody long?'

'Actually,' Seamus' small voice piped up, as he pushed his glasses back up to the bridge of his nose with his forefinger 'it's quite speedy, considering. I mean, *technically* it takes no time at all, when you think about the incredible feat of modern machinery that it is.'

Kate's first impulse was to say: 'Oh, what would you know?', as her fearful panic reached its zenith. But she was so stunned that Seamus had actually spoken, her head enjoyed a few seconds of quiet, giving her just enough time to have an idea.

Seamus, IT...Google, that's it! I'll Google time travel and work out a way to get back. Ha! Too easy!

Kate's fast-beating heart calmed down somewhat. Her fear started to subside at the thought of the internet and a wave of sweet relief washed over her.

But as soon as she dared to feel a little bit relaxed about her situation, she heard the sickening screech of metal scraping against metal, so loud and shrill, she swore it would make her ears bleed.

Kate covered her head and screamed as the sound of slow grinding, gigantic gears and the cranking of similarly large cogs was followed swiftly by an almighty jolt. The Lift suddenly dropped down and stopped dead, leaving Kate (who must weigh eight, eight-and-a-half-stone, tops) suspended in the air for a few moments before landing back down square on The Lift floor with a satisfyingly small thud.

Seamus rushed over to her and she felt those familiar big arms envelop her. She instinctively turned her head to face his chest and felt the strap of something scratch her cheek.

She opened her eyes to the frightening sound of silence just in time for The Lift's lights to go out.

Seamus' grip tightened around her as she breathed in sharply.

'It's OK,' he said, sounding as though he knew what he was talking about.

'Is it?' asked Kate, who had always doubted Seamus' authority.

'Call reception or someone – the police? Fire brigade!' Kate said, freeing herself from Seamus' embrace.

'What with?' Seamus replied. 'We only have a handful of mobile telecommunication devices and they're all with management.'

Kate's mind raced as she pictured the first mobile phone she ever bought herself . It had been the size of a house brick and she'd felt acutely self-conscious every time she was on a bus and Georgia called her to tease her about having one. She couldn't remember the ring tone, but it was loud, she knew that. And when it rang, people would tut and stare at her crossly, making her put her hand over the mouthpiece and whisper, so as not to inspire her fellow passengers' wrath any further.

'Of course, of course,' Kate said, feeling her way around The Lift walls. 'There must be a phone in here somewhere, mustn't there? Health and safety and all that...A-ha!'

'Well I'm not sure it works, wherever it is,' began Seamus as Kate's fingernails jimmied the small metal door open. 'We've been having some problems with the – '

She fumbled for the phone inside, put the handset up to her ear and hissed an exasperated 'shhhh!', waving Seamus and his words away with her left hand in the darkness.

A few seconds passed. Thirty seconds passed. Fifty-eight seconds passed. And then *Kate* nearly passed out with frustration.

'ARGH!' she thundered, sounding exactly as she did in 2014 whenever she discovered that Baby Jane had done a poo in the bath. Or when, in a rare and exhausting fit of domestic goddessery, she'd cleaned the front room only to discover an ancient nest of sultanas taking root in the orangey-brown, swirly carpet. 'There's no dial tone. It doesn't bloody work!'

She beat the metal box on the wall with the receiver a couple of times until she felt Seamus' cool hand upon hers.

'That's not going to help anybody,' he said, his voice so thick and deep and controlled, like the guy who does those voiceovers for movies: 'In a world where lifts break down at the most inopportune times, comes the surprise hit of the summer, *Elevator!* Because in a trapped lift, no one can hear you scream...'

Except in an English accent.

Kate very nearly swooned.

She heard Seamus somehow locating the hook and replacing the receiver on it. She heard the metal door close and felt a frisson of desire.

There was something undeniably sexy and *Fifty Shades of Grey* about the whole situation. Here she was, trapped in The Lift with zero visibility, a virtual stranger (who would, one day, be her boring old husband – but she, quite rightly, didn't want to think about that right now, the mere thought of which could blunt the sharpest of exciting sensations, dull the brightest spark of potential pleasure, let's face it) who sounded like George Clooney only smoother, more viscous, and a dormant – if not dead - libido fairly leaping out of its slumber, grinning like a lunatic. She thought she might have heard the high-pitched whirring of her imagination in overdrive as Seamus slipped his hand into hers.

She let out a gasp, taken completely unawares by the strength of this unfamiliar lustful feeling.

She imagined how his back muscles would ripple when he took her in his arms and dipped her as though they were ballroom dancing or on the cover of an old Mills and Boon book. She pictured him as the white, floaty shirted hero in tight breeches and herself as the helpless damsel in distress in dire need of rescuing and, maybe some quick bodice ripping if there was time.

This wasn't like her. Or, at least, it wasn't like her in 2014. Maybe it was the raging hormones of the young that meant they constantly saw and smelled and felt sex everywhere, in every possible circumstance. Then again, maybe it was the preserve of the middle-aged, bored housewife whose inner life was her *only* life worth speaking of, her fantasies running away with her every time she was doing the washing up and her eyes glazed over, the drudgery of her real life too tedious to bear.

She was always on at the kids to turn the telly off/stop playing those computer games/give her back her iPhone, so that they could give their imaginations a chance. She worried all the time about how kids today (or tomorrow, depending on which decade she was talking in) had it all laid on, how they didn't even have to *read* anymore, for goodness' sake, to escape into another world, a world different from their own.

Maybe that was Kate's problem, though – perhaps she could do with a little more playing with a DS than trying to keep the house clean. Maybe then her daydreams and obsessions with the past would fade into the background.

Speaking of, Kate thought to herself, maybe it was her imagination that had been responsible for getting her into this mess in the first place. And, if it was, maybe it could get her out of here, too...

Seamus helped her sit down on the floor of The Lift, lowering her gently.

'We could be here for some time,' those molasses-drenched vocal chords wove their magic once more.

'Yes,' Kate whispered, weakly.

Something big swung down from where she imagined Seamus' waist was and hit her head.

'Oh!' she exclaimed, capable of nothing more.

'Sorry!' Seamus said, his voice going up an octave and sounding more unsure than before as he scrambled to contain the wayward object.

Kate pictured a musket hanging from his belt and fanned herself with her hand, the euphemistic possibilities of such swashbuckling attire making her come over all unnecessary.

But then the lights flickered on and a harsh, badly-dressed reality stood above her.

It wasn't a musket or a whip or anything even remotely resembling anything phallic or masterful that had struck her head a few moments ago – of course it wasn't! It was one of those big, square-shaped, nylon record bags that guys in the media or the record industry used to wear over one shoulder. A kind of precursor to the smaller, more compact man-bag.

And it was the bag's thick strap that had scratched her face when Seamus had pulled her close to him.

But why was he wearing it? It was so not an accessory that Kate would ever have associated with Seamus.

'It's been hanging around the music mags' offices for ages,' Seamus said apologetically, once he noticed that Kate was staring at his bag. 'I...I didn't think anyone would miss it.'

The banality of her situation came crashing down on her and Kate blinked to put it into focus, to put everything back into perspective.

'Looks good,' she smiled, reaching for his hand, so he could help her up. 'Very trendy. But what else are you wearing?'

'Um, just jeans and a rugby shirt – it's a Harlequins one, see?'

He pulled at the insignia on the left side of his shirt and tried to see it himself, which gave him several chins and made him stick out his big bottom lip like a fish, gulping for air.

This was not how a romantic hero should look, Kate thought to herself.

'You know,' she began, 'you'd actually be quite cute if you sorted yourself out.'

'Excuse me?' Seamus blinked at her, all wide-eyed and innocent.

'Sartorially, I mean,' said Kate. 'Quite a catch, in actual fact.'

And in that moment, she got it. She hatched a plan in her head to get back to 2014 as soon as humanly possible – and ensure that a handsome, debonair Seamus was waiting for her when she arrived.

'Who do you go shopping with?' Kate asked, knowing full-well what the answer was.

'Just myself,' Seamus replied. 'If I ever go shopping, that is. My mum sometimes sends me stuff from catalogues, though, and –'

'And what do you know about time travel? I mean, is it possible to be transported back into the past? Or is it just a figment of my – I mean, *our* – imagination? Like, can you manipulate the universe, the time/space continuum to go into the future?'

Kate thought she sounded quite knowledgeable herself, saying 'time/space continuum' – a phrase she plucked out of the ether, having never said it before in her whole life.

'Like, you mean get The Lift working again? Like it was a short while ago? In the past?' Seamus struggled to get what Kate was going on about.

'Yeah, well, it'd be a start,' said Kate. 'You're a technical genius, aren't you? Can't you fix it for us?'

'Yes and no,' Seamus smiled. 'Well, no and no, to be really honest. Not a *genius*, anyway. I'm good – but I'm not *that* good!'

Kate met Seamus' grin with her own.

'There's not much I can do from the inside,'

Seamus carried on. 'It looks to me that everything's fine here – apart from the phone. It's something on the outside that needs fixing.'

'You said it!' squealed Kate. 'I've got a proposition for you. How's about I help you develop your own stylish wardrobe, tell you what suits you and what girls like to see on guys – and you help me find out all I can about time travel. You're the IT whizz, you can Google up a storm for me!'

'*What* up a storm?'

'Google! T'interweb? You know...?'

But Seamus clearly didn't.

Kate had that sinking feeling again. Just like she'd had a few hours ago when she'd mentioned Jamie Oliver to her mum.

'Oh, don't tell me! It hasn't been invented yet, right?'

'What hasn't? I'm sorry, Kate, but I haven't got the faintest idea what you're talking about!' said Seamus, his brow knitting, creating the crease that would one day be so deeply etched in his face, you'd swear he'd been *born* looking cross.

'I'm thinking of pitching a new mag to the powers that be,' she said, looking wildly around her for inspiration. 'Um, a sci-fi one, given the...ah...popularity of The X-Files and stuff...and -'

Another jolt upwards made both Kate and Seamus hang onto the silver bar in The Lift, terrified of what was going to happen next.

The Lift kept moving for a few seconds until

DING!

The doors flew open, the little bell pinging continuously as though there had never been a problem from *its* end, everything had been working just fine all along and now it was impatient to see to its other customers, thankyou very much.

Tom, Archie, Tamsin and Lucy whooped in delight (although Tamsin's whoop was more sarcastic than delighted, it has to be said, accompanied by some bored eye-rolling and a fast exit) as soon as the dinging stopped.

'Way-hey!' boomed Tom. 'I knew my punching the buttons would get things moving again! How are you, Kate? Are you all right?'

Kate beamed and he pulled her to him, kissing her.

Now *that's* what a romantic hero should look like, she thought to herself. And that's exactly how one should kiss, too, she added.

She was vaguely aware of Seamus slipping away from the group as she closed her eyes, her body going limp with desire.

And as she melted into Tom's embrace, she heard Seamus putting to some fourth-floor funster the most-asked question in the world of computer technical support: 'Are you sure it's turned on?'

'Quite sure,' Kate mumbled to herself. 'Quite, quite sure.'

13

When Kate, Georgia and Steve arrived at O'Flaherty's just before three o'clock for the first match of Euro '96, the atmosphere was electric.

In fact, Oasis' *She's Electric* was playing loudly while young lads in England shirts sang along and spilled their European lagers over each other, due to their slightly over-enthusiastic sideways arm swinging in time to the music.

'What are you drinking?' Steve shouted at Kate.

'WHAT?'She yelled back.

Steve mimed drinking a pint and Kate shook her head.

'JUST A LIME AND SODA FOR ME,' she grabbed Steve by the lapel and bellowed into his ear.

'All right, all right!' he pulled away, wiping imaginary saliva off the side of his face. 'Georgia?'

'I'll have whatever you're having,' she said, just as the music stopped. 'On second thoughts, better make it a double.'

A baby-faced, shirtless hooligan (as Kate saw him) caught Georgia's eye (who saw him more as an excited, ripped football fan, roughly the same age as her) and she smiled lasciviously.

'But what about the baby?' asked Kate, instantly regretting it.

'Oh, for God's sake, Katie, let it go, will you?' Georgia said, irritated by Kate's little reminder. 'I'm here to have fun. And anyway, I'm far too young for that sort of thing – can you imagine giving all this up?'

Georgia swept her hand out in front of her as she said 'all this', as if she was presenting a gold dinner service to an audience of aghast onlookers. Kate looked around and sniffed snootily as though she smelled something nasty and pooey.

'Like a shot,' she said.

But even as she uttered those words, she knew she was lying. Because she clearly remembered when she was pregnant with George, all she longed to do was have her old life back for one (or maybe two) nights, just to reiterate how much she was looking forward to and desperately in need of a drastic change in her life.

Then, when George was born, and Kate was finally free to go out on the town, to drink too much and act like a seven-year-old on a massive sugar bender, it was always the last thing she felt like doing.

Sleep became her desert island, luxury item of choice and had remained thus for the past 11 years. She longed for the little bit of space, the small amount of breathing time sleep afforded her. And now, looking around her at the rowdy pub, she felt exactly like she used to when she'd pick George and Decko up from nursery school – like she was trapped in a loony bin and couldn't wait to make good her escape.

With her kids, of course.

'You may not want it now – but what about the future? You don't know how you'll feel five *minutes* down the track, let alone five years!' Kate continued.

'Give it a rest, Kate,' said Steve as he deposited

their drinks down on the soggy coasters adorning the already soaking wet, sticky round table. 'Let's just have a laugh and watch some football, eh?'

Kate nodded, reluctantly agreeing to drop the subject.

'For the time being, anyway,' she mumbled under her breath, just as *Three Lions* was cranked up to 11 behind the bar.

The first half of the match was extremely exciting, even Kate had to admit that. And despite the fact that she knew how the whole tournament was going to end, she somehow couldn't help but get swept up in the joy of the moment, the sheer bliss of being a part of it all. The expectation was huge, the bonhomie was palpable (particularly for Georgia who would be snogging the shirtless lad by the time the full-time whistle blew) and the camaraderie was contagious.

It was half-time and Kate could feel herself loosening up. She decided to let herself go with the flow, get with the spirit of things, relax and have a nice time - forget about trying to get back to her family in 2014. Just for this afternoon.

This was no easy task for Kate, who had, over the years, become one of the biggest control freaks she'd ever known. She was the last person she'd have expected to turn out this way and could find no other cause for this strange phenomenon than the kids. Or, rather, the sometimes overwhelming burden of care and responsibility the kids brought with them.

Kate heaved a sigh, imagining all her worries and

anxieties about her parenting style, how her family was actually faring without her and how the hell she was going to get back to 2014 to be little bubbles of air, like you'd find in a mint Aero, carried away on the breath expelled from her lungs.

Time to let the good times roll, thought Kate.

'Oh, go on, then,' she said to Steve. 'I will have that pint, after all.'

'I'll get it,' came a voice, dripping in honey from behind her.

'Seamus!' she shrieked, nearly giving herself whiplash as she turned around to see who it was. 'What are you doing here?'

'The flyers at work said everyone was welcome, the more the merrier –'

'Of course, of course,' Kate spluttered. 'I didn't mean that how it sounded, I'm just surprised to see your face, that's all.'

And she was. Like a goldfish swimming past a portrait in a sunken treasure chest and being shocked to see a human face at the bottom of his bowl, she was constantly surprised to see Seamus' face. Particularly when he looked so youthful and happy and...and actually quite handsome.

'And you, Georgia? What would you like?' Seamus asked, ever the gentleman.

'Oh, you are a sweetie,' said Georgia, going all gooey and sickly sweet. 'And a man after my own heart. I'll have a gin and tonic. Double. Mother's ruin, right Kate?'

Georgia laughed and nudged Kate in the ribs. Kate threw her head back and pretended to find this hilarious.

Once Seamus was ensconced at the bar (which was three-deep in punters with raging thirsts), Kate glared at Georgia.

‘Who *are* you? Coming on to every man you see like that? What’s got into you?’

Georgia’s smile faded and she turned to face Kate.

‘Take a chill pill, Kate. And when you’ve calmed down, would you mind telling me just when you decided to go all po-faced and judgemental and boring on me?’ Georgia asked. ‘And once you’ve told me that, would you mind giving me my old best mate back? Please?’

‘Sorry,’ Kate said, looking sheepish. ‘I don’t know what’s going on, really. Stress at work?’

‘Yeah? Well, why don’t you talk to me about it rather than wag your finger at me all the time? You’re not my mother, you know!’

No, thought Kate, she wasn’t. But she was *a* mother and she took her role as mum very seriously. More seriously, indeed, than she’d ever imagined she would, to be honest. And it seemed to her now that it was her job to be a moral compass, defender of the truth and disher-out of justice to whomever she saw fit, whenever she saw fit and wherever she saw fit. Because she was so used to doing it to the kids, she could no longer help herself in company. It was like her default setting had been re-calibrated since she’d had children and now it was stuck on 'stern, dull, predictable and prone to being a shouty old bag' where once it had been permanently fixed on 'fun, spontaneous, always up for a laugh and predisposed to being a giggly young dolly bird'.

She simply hadn't realised how difficult it would be to shake off her mumsy persona. She'd always pictured herself slipping straight back into carefree, fun-loving, up-for-whatever mode whenever she was daydreaming about the past and fantasising about feeling unshackled and untethered.

But now her fantasy had become a reality, she was stumped. How should she act in such a bizarre situation? As a mum-of-three, she was well aware of the consequences she would suffer for throwing caution to the wind; horrible hangovers (the physical side of which lasted for four days, the emotional battering lasting forever), the inevitable weight gain from too many fry-ups and the potential for a knock on the door from Social Services any minute. But as a good time girl in her late twenties, she was obliged to make the most of her time in the sun and go for it. Even if 'it' was a woolly, nebulous thing, usually involving copious amounts of alcohol and playing tonsil hockey with total strangers.

As soon as Seamus returned with the drinks, much to the threesome's delight, Kate made up her mind.

'I really am sorry,' Kate addressed her best friend. 'Let's forget about it and get hammered, shall we?'

'That's more like it,' Georgia said, putting her arm

around Kate's back and singing along with Baddiel and Skinner.

'So where do you stand on the Blur v Oasis debate?' Steve asked Seamus, valiantly trying to make small talk.

'Oh, I don't really,' said Seamus. 'I mean, I like them both. Maybe Oasis slightly more?'

'Is that definitely maybe?' Steve grinned.

'Leave him alone,' said Kate, putting a protective arm around Seamus' rock-hard shoulders.

'Are you in the Oasis camp, Kate?' Seamus asked. 'Seeing that you know Liam so well...'

'What?'

'You know, the other night. I think you were asleep, but as I drove you home, Georgia told me the pair of you were getting to know each other quite well at the Roof Gardens.'

'Much to my chagrin,' Tom laughed, his voice piercing the invisible membrane of budding friendship encasing the table as he bent down to kiss Kate. 'But I took it on the chin. I look at it as though the missus was doing my work for me, buttering him up good and proper, so we can make him our cover star and feature the band in our upcoming Best of British issue.'

'Yeah,' Tom carried on, pulling up a stool and muscling in between Kate and Seamus. 'It's going to be a corker. We've already nearly sold out all the available advertising space and pre-orders are up 110%'

'One hundred and ten per cent?' Seamus sounded

confused, staring at his coaster. 'I'm pretty sure no such percentage exists. I mean per cent means, literally, by a hundred, and you can't have 110 in every hundred, can you? No, I think you'll find there really is no such number.'

Oh, God, thought Kate. Not now. Not here.

'Who brought Poindexter?' Tom chuckled.

'Leave him alone,' Georgia said, making Kate narrow her eyes and wonder whether her best mate was going to try to snog her husband-to-be again.

Inside, Kate was also confused. She knew she was going to end up with Seamus, but she still fancied Tom like mad, even if he was, to be frank, a bit of a dick sometimes. What on earth was she going to do?

Sitting there, mulling over her quandary, she pictured herself and Georgia and Tom and Seamus playing the starring roles in a *Mad Fer It!* photo love story, all pained expressions, sideways glances, tortured souls and slightly off-centre speech bubbles.

But how long would she have to wait before finding out who was to be The One? Would she have to wait for the next fortnight's issue?

And now with the undeniably sexy Liam in the frame...

'That's IT!' Kate squealed. 'I think I know how to save *Mad Fer It!'*

'Always talking shop, you lot,' said a disappointed Steve, rolling his eyes to the ceiling and tutting.

'No, wait!' cried Kate. 'What if I asked Liam to be in a photo love story?'

‘He’d never do it,’ laughed Tom. ‘Never in a million years.’

‘Yeah,’ agreed Seamus. ‘You’ve got more chance of getting Noel to apologise to Damon from Blur. More chance of getting those two to kiss and make up and admit that their “rivalry” is all made up to spark media interest.’

‘It is?’ asked Tom, as though this was news to him.

For a hard-bitten, no-prisoner-taking, uber-laddish editor like Tom, he could be quite dim sometimes.

‘Of course it is!’ Georgia weighed in. ‘Maybe not a hundred per cent made up –’

‘And definitely not one hundred and ten percent made up –’ Seamus interrupted, a wry smile spreading across his (really rather fetching, Kate was surprised to note, again) face as he leaned towards Georgia.

‘But a large chunk of the so-called competition between them positively *reeks* of media manipulation,’ Georgia went on.

‘You know, Seamus,’ Kate said slowly, staring at him as though he’d just recited a poem he’d written for her, the whole pub melting into the background, her focus, her personal spotlight shining only on him. ‘I think you’ve just saved *Mad Fer It!* from folding!’

14

'Daddy!' cried Kate as soon as Paris opened the front door.

She flung her arms around his neck and nearly knocked him over with the force of her unconfined joy.

'You look exactly the same!' she said, studying his face for a few seconds and then hugging him hard again.

'Not quite so tight,' Paris managed to say, despite greatly reduced lung function courtesy of Kate's crushing hug.

'Sorry,' she giggled. 'But it's been...oh, it just feels like so long since I last saw you! So much has happened since then, Dad, and I've been desperate to talk to you and Mum about a million things and –'

'It was only last Sunday!' Paris coughed. 'Tom...nice to see you. Do come in.'

Paris extended his hand for Tom to shake, but Tom didn't see – his Aviator sunglasses were too dark.

Paris retracted his hand, placed it on his trim, button-down-shirted tummy and ran his other hand through his thick thatch of grey/white hair.

'Right, right,' he said, not knowing what else to say. 'So come in, come in. Blue's in the kitchen, I'm out in the back garden, working on my swing. Care to join me, Tom?'

'Nah, you're all right,' said Tom, chewing furiously on some gum, 'think I'll have a quick chat with your missus, find out what's cooking in your average, middle class suburban kitchen.'

Tom, who always put on a fake, exaggerated Cockney accent when he was nervous, left his sunglasses on and brushed past Paris and Kate. Paris was visibly irritated by this, humming his disapproval, but Kate couldn't stop admiring Paris.

'You look so well!' she said, the love and adoration showing in her eyes.

'Hmm?' Paris looked down at his daughter and his body spasmed a tiny bit, as though he'd forgotten she was there and was startled to see her. 'Oh, thankyou, Beautiful. You're looking as lovely as always, yourself.'

Kate didn't move, even though her father was giving her back her hands which were gripping onto his forearms so tightly, her knuckles had turned white.

It was as if she couldn't let go, as though her heart was controlling the muscles in her hand and she was holding on for dear life.

Which she kind of was, really. She'd missed her mother and father so badly since they disappeared, it had become a physical ache. And even though she'd got to the stage where she had accepted they'd gone (but where?) and she could just about live with her loss in 2014, there was no way she was going to let go of her precious parents now she'd found them again.

Steve ambled up to the front porch and muttered a recalcitrant 'Hi Paris,' without even looking at his father, and slowly lolloped up the stairs, Kate and Paris feeling the exhausted, heavy-hearted pain of each step.

Paris jerked his head in the direction of the garden and finally managed to extricate himself from Kate's grip, walking off down the hallway towards the back of the house.

The house. *This* house!

Kate couldn't get the grin off her face.

She held onto the knob at the end of the banister as if to prepare herself for possibly fainting from delirium due to too much happiness and closed her eyes. She inhaled deeply and steadied herself, the near-intoxicating smell of lamb roasting in the oven, with sprigs of rosemary and garlic inserted into the fleshy bits of the joint, nearly bowling her over. She'd always loved her mother's lamb – so had Steve – even when she went through that 'difficult, rebellious phase' (from the age of nine onwards, her mother would say) and wanted to be with friends and boyfriends more than family, she always made it home for Blue's Sunday lamb roast. She craved the smell, the taste and the overall feel of home so much, that even when she went vegetarian and moved into a flat with Georgia, she'd never miss a Sunday lunch at Blue's.

Apart from when Blue and Paris were otherwise engaged, of course. And they had cancelled quite a few roasts, now Kate thought about it. It was always a sick colleague in Oxford they had to go and see – or visiting academics in Leeds.

Kate frowned and cocked her head to the side, opening her eyes. There had always been something rushed, something so last-minute about these little trips away of her parents' that for some reason she couldn't quite put her finger on, their excuses never quite seemed to ring true.

Despite the fact that Kate would more often than not console herself with ready-made packaged food from M&S (the houmous, the vine leaves, the tuna linguine! Her mouth started to water at the memory), she always felt an emptiness in the pit of her stomach when the Sunday roast in Ickenham didn't eventuate.

'But it's happening today!' she said out loud, pulling her shoulders back, thrusting her nose in the air and marching towards that heavenly aroma.

'I dunno,' said Tom, his accent getting thicker by the minute. 'maybe it's because –'

'You're a Londoner?' Kate piped up, mocking him and pretending to pull out invisible braces from her chest.

'Nah, nah,' Tom shot Kate a cross glance. 'Me muvver died when I were a nippah and me elder sisters brought me up, didn't they?'

'Really, Tom? I never knew that,' said Blue. 'It's no wonder then, that you're so in touch with your feminine side and get along with women so well.'

Kate tittered. Her mother's sarcasm never missed its mark.

Blue turned to put the roast back in the oven and, as she did so, winked at Kate and poked the inside of her cheek with her tongue.

'I didn't know that either, Tom,' said Kate, putting her hand on his shoulder. 'You never said...'

‘Well, she didn’t exactly *die,*’ he said, looking sheepish. ‘She left us. Dad took off wiv some tart and Mum did the same. We never ’eard from eiver of ’em again. So they’re both dead to us, me and me sisters. It’s like we could only ever depend on each other, so we got very close. And to this day, me sisters are still me best mates.’

Kate gave Tom a kiss on the cheek, even though he was sounding more and more like Sid James with every sentence. She knew he was extremely close to his sisters, but never exactly how they’d got that way. And all of a sudden, she softened to him. Could this revelation signal a whole new side to Tom? Was the caring, sensitive part of his personality emerging, leaving the bravado and laddish persona to simply, effortlessly fall away, much like a centrefold’s bra might at a *LASHED* photo shoot?

Kate looked past Tom and Blue and saw her dad standing in the middle of their back lawn, staring off into space.

‘Are you OK, Dad?’

Paris gave a mini start again, as though he was being woken from a particularly deep sleep.

‘Oh, hello Darling,’ he said, rocking back and forth on his heels. ‘You caught me. Just indulging in a spot of daydreaming. It’s my favourite hobby, you know. Even takes priority over golf – which is really saying something.’

‘Really?’ said Kate. ‘I never had you down as a dreamer.’

'Oh, your old man's quite nostalgic, Katie,' he chortled. 'Not a day goes by when I'm not lost in thoughts of the past, what I'd do differently, what I'd change if I had the chance again.'

So that's where she got it from!

'But I always keep one eye firmly fixed on the future, too,' her dad went on. 'Because I truly believe the best is yet to come. What about you, Darling?'

'You really are a man after my own heart, Daddy – sorry, Paris – because ooh, I just love a good daydream, me,' Kate rubbed her hands together with glee. 'So what were you thinking about?'

'Your mother, actually.'

'Ha! You old saucepot – I don't want to hear any more!'

Her father laughed thinly, his care-worn face twitching back into its usual expression of concern within seconds.

'Dad?' Kate put her arm around her father.

'Oh, I'm all right,' he smiled. 'No, really – I'm fine. But tell me – what are we going to do about that brother of yours, hmmm?'

'I am here, you know,' came Steve's voice from on high.

Paris and Kate looked up to see Steve leaning out of his old bedroom window, having a cigarette.

'Ahoy there!' said Kate cheerfully, shielding her eyes from the sun's glare with a lazy salute. 'Why don't you come down and join us? Lunch is nearly ready and Tom's regaling Blue with tales of his lost childhood.'

'*Fassss-cinating,*' said Steve, the smoke snaking out of his mouth and back into his nostrils at the long, drawn-out 's' sound.

Paris and Kate both shrugged their shoulders and sighed simultaneously, exchanging 'what-can-you-do?' glances and walked back into the house.

'So, yeah, it's all gone a little bit tits up – sorry - *Pete Tong* if you know what I mean,' Tom was holding forth.

'No, I'm afraid I don't,' said Blue.

'It's like this wild beast that can't be tamed! I lost control of it ages ago. I tell you, it's got a mind of its own and goes where it wants to go. And there's not a damn thing I can do about it!'

'Talking about your love-making prowess again, Tom?' Steve smirked, flopping into a chair at the dining table.

Tom didn't skip a beat.

'So what started out as a joke, one big schoolboy prank, has now grown into a multi-million-pound publishing phenomenon. Which is pretty cool, yeah – but my sisters can't stand it and are threatening to disown me if I don't drastically change it and make it more like, I dunno, *National Geographic* or something. Either that or I have to get another job.'

'You talking about *LASHED*?' asked Kate. 'Wow, so the pressure's really on, eh? And how come you've never told me any of this before? Not even a hint of it?'

'Oh, I don't know,' Tom said, sounding more and more like the insecure young man he was fast revealing himself to be. 'Didn't fit with the image of the mag, really. Can you imagine the headlines? *Grubby Mag Ed in Bullying By Feminist Sisters Shocker!'*

'Yeah,' said Kate. 'Filthy Rag Ed Is Big Girl's Blouse!'

'Or *Porn Mag Ed Beats Chest in Bare Breast Fem-Fest!*' Steve joined in, suddenly brighter and warming to the theme.

'That's not bad,' chuckled Tom. 'I didn't know you had an eye for a good headline, Steve. That one sounds like a double page pictorial spread, with me the caveman filling in a sexy sex sandwich!'

Kate and Blue groaned.

'It's like a *LASHED* editorial meeting in here! Only without the drugs!' Tom beamed.

'So much for your inner feminist-sympathiser, new age guy coming to the fore, Tom!' laughed Paris.

'Yeah – you couldn't keep it up, could you?' Blue smiled.

'Fnarr, fnarr!' said Steve and Tom in unison, nudging each other in the ribs.

Kate shook her head and rolled her eyes, fondly.

'That nice guy is in there somewhere,' she said, tapping Tom's head with her forefinger. 'It's just a matter of teasing it out.'

'Now enough of all that – the lamb is ready. Let's have a civilised lunch, shall we?'

Kate laughed. And wished she'd brought Tom to more Sunday lunches at her parents' place. He was really quite sweet when you got right down to it. Like a lost, misguided, motherless child.

'OK, OK,' said Tom. 'Just don't let it get out that I have feminist tendencies.'

'I don't know, that mightn't be a bad idea...' Kate trailed off, wondering what Medea Media had made of her fax. She hadn't heard a peep out of them since she sent it off.

'You carve, Paris – everyone else help yourself to veg and gravy,' Blue issued the same instructions as always and Kate sat back, her hands crossed against her bare tummy (she was wearing another crop top today – this time a red mock football shirt with white piping, short sleeves and a v-neck, which plunged lower than a *Sun* reader's IQ), surveying the scene.

She couldn't help but feel smug, somehow. *This* is what she'd been hankering after all these years – *this* was exactly the feeling she was trying to create with George, Decko, Jane and Seamus at home. Yes, she inwardly grinned, this was the family portrait snapshot that would hang forever in her mind's gallery.

At this thought, she shifted a little in her seat and sat up straight, her lips pursed in deep concentration.

Because it wasn't the perfect picture, was it? For a start it should have been Seamus sitting there, not Tom – the man who habitually humiliated Kate, unable to keep his hands to himself where women were concerned.

Kate wondered whether Tom used his serial shagging as a form of revenge – perhaps as a way to get back at his mother for leaving him. He never allowed himself to get really close, truly intimate with Kate and yet was capable – albeit fleetingly – of letting his defences down, and the facade drop for Blue.

And what was with Paris being so distracted all the time? What was he so pre-occupied with? Maybe Blue was up to something. She *had* acted a tad strange that day they'd met for lunch in Covent Garden, hadn't she? And what – or who - was she preening herself for when she walked back into Carluccio's?

And as for Steve – well! Mardy, miserable and maudlin one minute – creasing up with laughter the next. He did seem to chat to Tom a fair bit yesterday at the football, come to think of it...But who knew he and Tom would get along so well, bonding over boobs and beer?

Kate thought something time-travelly might happen any moment when all sounds around her disappeared, like someone had turned the volume right down or pressed the mute button on a remote.

She watched in silence as Tom, Steve and Blue tucked heartily into their meals, talking with mouths full and gesticulating wildly as another hilarious story was told. Paris, though, remained quite slow, almost completely still, as he chewed his carrots and peas and stared at the silver gravy boat.

They were all obviously so much more messed up than Kate had ever realised – a clutch of Pandora's

Boxes, wriggling and squirming with secrets a-plenty on the inside: secrets too terrible to unleash.

She never would have noticed any of this the first time round, when she was so much younger and always took everything at face value. And anyway, she was too busy living her hedonistic whirl of a life to stop and consider what might or might not be going on in other people's worlds.

She zoomed in on Steve. He was a viper's nest of complex emotions, that was quite clear. But would his demeanour and outlook be changed, simply because he was going to be forced to fend for himself without the financial help of his family?

And what about Tom?

Oh, bloody men – they were always so confusing! No change there, then, she thought to herself. Though something big *had* changed – Kate's estimation of Tom. She had really seen a more rounded, 3-D version of him today – but so what? That didn't mean she had to move in with him, did it? And how could she even *entertain* the thought of sleeping with him? She did remember thinking he was quite the master swordsman when it came to their shenanigans between the sheets the first time round... And she *had* dreamt about this moment for such a long time...how could she back out now, when her chance to right the wrongs of her past had finally come? How could she *not* see her fantasy through to fruition?

But she was a happily (ish) married woman! Wouldn't that make her no better than Tom – a philanderer with a heart like a fridge?

But wait – what had Georgia said yesterday? Something about Kate taking her life and herself too seriously? And wanting to control everything and everyone around her so much, she'd lost all sense of fun and had become a crashing bore? Or words to that effect?

She felt dizzy. But what about Seamus? And what about the kids? It would be like being unfaithful, wouldn't it? Well, no, not technically... because it was, quite literally, all in the past! She could *easily* get away with it – she'd slept with Tom loads of times in the past, way before she'd ever met Seamus, so she wasn't sailing through uncharted waters exactly or doing anything *illegal* in a relationship sense. And now she had the chance to do it all over again, but better – no one need ever know!

Besides, she knew only too well that at her birthday party, Tom was going to run off with Tasmin – exactly as he did the first time round – so where was the harm in making hay while the sun shone? And who knows? She might be propelled back to 2014 at any moment – especially considering the sound had completely vanished in a scary, vortex/continuum/quantum thingamajig kind of way – how would she feel if she woke up back at home amongst her full-on family, knowing she'd blown the only chance she was *ever* going to get?

I'm going to go for it. I don't have any other choice!

But despite her inner sex goddess winning this internal debate, something still niggled at her. It was like the spirit was weak, even though the flesh was very willing indeed.

All at once, someone pressed the mute button and noises were well and truly on again.

'Honestly, we was robbed!' Tom was saying.

'No we weren't,' Steve countered. 'The score reflected the level of play between the two teams. England was totally on a par with Switzerland. We deserved to draw.'

Paris jumped and spluttered, like an old jalopy trying to re-start its engine.

'Did someone say par?' he winked at Kate as though she was six years old.

Kate smiled weakly back. Something was troubling her dad and it made her sad to think of him in turmoil.

'I'm just saying,' Tom went on, totally ignoring Paris 'that we really stand a great chance of winning this tournament if we *get the goals*. It's no use playing brilliantly but not scoring – or worse, playing just as well as everyone else, but not asserting our authority over them, dominating them as they deserve to be dominated. Because mark my words, the Empire shall rise again and come the end of June, that trophy will be ours!'

'All right, all right,' said Steve, leaning back in his chair as though the blast from Tom's mock-jingoistic rant was so strong, it was nearly pushing him off his chair.

‘Shall we leave football for a minute or two?’ Blue suggested. ‘There must be some other news we’d all be interested in hearing, mustn’t there?’

Four faces stared blankly back at her, the three men looking decidedly dumb and even a little bit bovine as they chewed their food and let their eyes droop.

‘Kate?’ Blue prodded her daughter. ‘Anything you want to tell us? Anything at all?’

As she walked behind Steve, carrying bowls of vegetables back into the kitchen, Blue nodded at him and widened her eyes at Kate, wondering when on earth she was going to take the hint.

‘Oh, uh, yeah,’ Kate coughed. ‘Yeah – everyone? Tom and I are moving in together. I figured he’s been asking me for so long, I had to agree to it just to get him to shut up!’

Paris looked a smidge more perturbed than he had just seconds before, but no one except Kate seemed to clock this. Blue, at the other end of the spectrum, came running back into the dining room and clapped her hands together, like an excited schoolgirl.

‘Ooh!’ she squeaked. ‘How simply *wonderful,* Katie!’

‘Calm down, *Blue*,’ sneered Steve. ‘It’s not as if she’s marrying royalty or anything!’

‘Really?’ Tom nearly choked on his mint sauce. ‘Are you sure? I mean, are you really sure you want to?’

Tom sounded quite uncharacteristically humble and unsure of himself. It was as though he he'd just won the lottery and couldn't quite believe it.

'Of course I'm sure,' said Kate, her voice wavering with obvious uncertainty. She was flattered by Tom's reaction and feeling strengthened by it, decided to issue a warning from her unprecedented position of power. 'But you hurt me – just once – and you won't know what's hit you.'

'But I will,' said Paris who was abruptly coming to life again at the mention of his little girl in pain. 'And it'll be *me*. I'll hunt you down and kill you like the dirty dog you are if you hurt one little hair on that girl's pretty little head.'

Taken aback by the brutality and ferocity of Paris' little promise, everyone fell silent, save for a very loud GULP reverberating from Tom's throat.

This barely contained aggression was so unlike her dad, thought Kate. And that threat! It must have come from an old Western or something – maybe he'd simply forgotten the bit about 'yer yellow-bellied varmint'. But wherever it came from, it was definitely heart-felt, of that there was no doubt.

'I hate to be a wet blanket,' Steve began.

'Do you?' Kate put it to him. 'Do you *really*, Steve?'

'You know I do! I just want to be sure that you've really thought this through, considered all your options and..and taken everyone into account.'

'Georgia doesn't know yet,' Kate admitted. 'But

she'll be fine with it, I know she will. She'll just have to get another tenant in – there's no way she'd ever move out of that fantastic flat.'

'But what about me?' Steve sounded like the small child now.

'What about you?' Blue said sternly, but turned away to face the kitchen as soon as she'd said it, lest her family see her chin quivering with emotion.

'You'll have to get a job and support yourself,' Paris came to the party, looking Steve straight in the eye and telling it like it was.

'How?' Steve pouted and folded his arms over his chest, slumping down into the back of his chair.

'You'll think of something,' Kate said, trying to sound encouraging. 'And I'll help you – we all will. I'm sorry, Stevie – but there's no way I'll be able to pay your way as well as the rent on our new flat – especially if we're moving to Notting Hill like Tom wants to.'

Steve's bottom lip jutted out so far from his face, he started to look like one of those Yanomamo Indians of the Amazon complete with lip plates. Or like Decko when he didn't get his way. Kate had never noticed the striking resemblance between Steve and Declan before – probably because Steve had never been to visit, and hadn't even met the kids since they'd been born.

Instantly, Kate realised the severity of the situation – her relationship with her brother was on the line, here, the stakes so high that if she wasn't careful, she knew she might never see him again.

Everyone except for Steve stood up and started bustling about the table, clearing plates and picking up glasses. Talk turned to football again, then the weather and eventually to how delicious that roast was and whether it was Welsh or New Zealand lamb because it was so melt-in-the-mouth tender, it was incredible...

BANG!

The front door slammed, knocking a row of kitsch but relatively inoffensive figurines off the sideboard. The foursome making themselves busy in the kitchen looked up from what they were doing and swapped wide-eyed, worried glances.

'Steve?' Blue called.

'STEVE!' shouted Kate, dropping the china cup she was drying and running for the door.

15

‘So where’s he gone, then?’ Georgia had called Kate at the office first thing on Monday morning.

‘I don’t know,’ sniffed Kate. ‘But it’s all my fault! Just because I wanted to see what it was like to have sex with Tom again! I’ve been so selfish, blaming Steve for Tom running off with Tamsin –’

At that moment, as if on cue, Tamsin appeared out of the blue, right beside Kate’s desk, gurning like the cat who’d got the cream.

‘What *are* you banging on about, Kate? You’re not making any sense!’ Georgia said.

‘I’ve, um, got to go – call you later,’ she said and swiftly hung up.

‘Morning, Kate,’ Tamsin said sweetly. ‘I was just wondering how things were going with *LASHED* and Medea. Do you need any help handling it? I could really use the experience and to work with you on this one would be a once in a lifetime opportunity.’

Smarmy little -

‘Kate!’ boomed Archie.

Kate excused herself and nearly broke into run, she couldn’t get away from Tamsin’s personal space fast enough.

‘So, good weekend?’ Archie plumped for his usual opening gambit.

‘Yeah, not bad,’ came Kate’s by now stock reply.

'What about the match, eh? Good start or what?'

'Yeah, great! And how exciting was the atmosphere?! Honestly, it was exactly how I remembered it – like one big love-in, all of us united against a common enemy – every other team! Brilliant.'

Kate perched her bum on the corner of Archie's desk and shook her head slowly, narrowing her eyes and looking out the wall of window, as if she was a General reminiscing about long-lost military glory.

'Yeah, right,' Archie pulled his chin to his chest and gave her a funny look. 'So anyway. I just got a message from Medea Horton, the boss of Medea Media. Apparently she's sent us loads of emails respectively, but our system's been shut down for God knows how long. And the upshot of it all is...' Archie drummed his fingers on the edge of the desk, '...she wants to have a meeting with us. You, me and Tom. To nut out the terms of our apology, she said.'

Kate's heart jumped. She wasn't much of a one for confrontation at the best of times – but with Steve AWOL and her move to Notting Hill imminent, she felt like she had enough to contend with.

'Kate? Are you OK?' Archie asked.

'Fine, fine,' she lied. 'I've just got so much to do and-'

'Any ideas re: *Mad Fer It!*?' he cut her off, tapping his fingers impatiently on his lifeless computer keyboard.

'No, not really,' she said, unable to get Steve off

her mind.

'Nothing? Not even the germ of an idea? I must say, Kate, I'm a little disappointed in you. You're usually so quick off the mark, so sparky. What's up?'

'Oh, nothing...'

'Kate? This is me you're talking to, go on, tell me all about it.'

Kate looked at him and seriously considered it. He was, apart from Tom and Seamus, her closest work friend after all.

But if she told Archie that she'd been transported from her steamy, chaotic suburban kitchen in 2014 to her old body, job, boyfriend and free, well-sleeping, childless state in 1996 – exactly how, she had no idea – what would he say?

If she explained to him, as best she could, that this was the second time she'd lived through Euro 96 and she could place a bet with Ladbrokes that would mean she would never have to worry about money ever again in her life – and nor would her kids and her kids' kids ad infinitum – how would he react?

Imagine she *did* fill Archie in on what had happened in the past week – would he laugh at her? Call her crazy? Slap her cheek and tell her to snap out of it?

Kate decided she couldn't take the risk of telling him about the time travel, but she could let him in on the Steve situation. She took a deep breath and looked him straight in the eye.

'It's just my brother. You know, Steve?' she

couldn't remember whether Archie and Steve had ever met. 'I don't understand it entirely, but he's got the right hump with me because I can't afford to pay for his life anymore.'

'Right,' Archie nodded sagely. 'And why not?'

'Because I'm moving out of the West Hampstead flat we share with Georgia –'

'Ah, the lovely and fragrant Georgia,' Archie said, his eyes twinkling.

'...and I'm moving into a flat in Notting Hill. With Tom.'

'You never!'

'Am so,' she smiled, for the first time this morning.

'But Kate – now don't take this the wrong way or anything – and I love Tom, man, you know I do – great bloke to have at a party – but, well, I...you can do so much better than him, that's all.'

'Oh, I agree,' she said, surprising the hell out of Archie and making him sit up that little bit straighter. 'And I will, believe me. Just not yet. Just let me have my last hurrah the way I've dreamt about it for the past 18 years.'

'You've wanted to move in with Tom for the past 18 years?' Archie looked confused. 'But you only met him when you started to work here...I don't underst-'

'Knock, knock!' Seamus said with a lopsided grin as he rapped his knuckles on Archie's door.

If only Archie knew, thought Kate.

'Ah, Shane,' said Archie, standing up to make way

for Seamus to get in front of his computer.

'Seamus,' Kate said, correcting him.

'Sorry, *Seamus*,' Archie said.

'That's quite all right,' said Seamus, who seemed to have gone from 0 to 60 in terms of confidence in the last week. 'Now are you sure you've got everything turned on?'

Seamus disappeared under Archie's desk and in a muffled voice said:

'Ah, there's your problem right there. Modem wasn't plugged in.'

'Ah,' Kate and Archie echoed, as if they knew what a modem was.

Seamus reappeared in front of Archie's desk and drew himself up to his full height. And quite impressive he looked, too, Kate couldn't help but note.

'How'd you enjoy the match, Archie?' Seamus asked.

'Fantastic,' Archie replied. 'Aren't you going to ask Kate? She watched it, too...'

'Oh, I know what Kate thought – I was right there, watching it with her,' Seamus said with – what was it - *pride*? 'How did you go with your idea to save your favourite teen mag, Kate? What did Archie think?'

There was something quite different about Seamus today. And Kate was taken aback by how attractive she found him.

'Kate?' Archie turned to her. 'You said you didn't have anything!'

'Oh!' Kate dragged her eyes away from Seamus.

'It was actually Seamus' idea, really. Um, how about in a bessie mates special or something, we get the Oasis lads in a boxing ring with the Blur boys and get them to fight out their friendship problems – ie interview them about what annoys them most about each other – and then, in a world first, get them to kiss and make up. Lots of pix of them hugging and messing about in their satin shorts and stuff and –'

'My God, Kate – that is woeful!' Archie laughed.

Seamus looked crushed. So did Kate.

'They'd never do that! Never in a million years! Far too uncool!'

'But...but what if –'

'I must say I expected better from you, Kate,' Archie said as he wiped a tear of mirth from his eye. 'Keep thinking, though – maybe without the aid of alcohol this time.'

'Well, also,' Seamus diplomatically began, changing the subject, 'I wanted to let you know that the IT department is quickly expanding – yay – and I have employed a new member of the team. His name is Kevin -'

'Of course it is!' Archie started laughing again.

'...and he will be starting any day now, so...'

'So it'll be nerd-a-rama soon!' Archie had to hold onto his stomach, he found himself so hilarious.

Kate had never seen Archie like this before – he was being cruel and unkind and unnecessarily mean.

What was it with everybody lately? Everyone acting out of character, not being the constantly lovely, predictably *nice* people she used to know? Why were they all so different from the way she remembered them?

'Come on, Seamus,' Kate said, steering him out of Archie's office by his elbow. 'Will you tell me if my modem's turned on now, too?'

*

Kate had hooked her arm in Seamus' as they left Archie's office and the Mike Flowers Pops version of *Wonderwall* was playing on the radio outside, amongst the cubicles and her laughing colleagues, thwacking each other with rulers.

'What would you say to side burns?' Kate asked Seamus as she watched some young scamp proudly combing his in a mirror atop a tall, grey steel filing cabinet.

'Um – run them under a cold tap? Call 999? Same as I'd say to front or back burns, I suppose...' Seamus chuckled.

Kate shot him the look she usually reserved for George when he was experimenting with jokes and word play – a fond look that said 'not bad, but needs a little work'.

'Side *boards* then,' she giggled, despite herself. 'Like that boy has, over there?'

'Boy? *Man*, more like!' said Seamus with a slight hint of admiration in his voice. 'I've already started thinning out, I doubt whether I'd be *able* to grow anything as impressive as that. But they do look rather good, in a very mod way...'

The pair had reached Kate's desk and she sat down in her swivel chair while Seamus looked around, leaning on her desk one minute, folding his arms across his chest the next and finally running both hands through his hair (ever-so-gently, of course, so as not to cause any unnecessary fall out) before he curled them into fists and stuck them on his hips.

'So what was it you wanted me to do?' he asked.

'Could you get my modem working again, please? And then can you help me find some search engines? I can't for the life of me remember what they're called and I really want to find out –'

Seamus momentarily put one hand on Kate's thigh as he got down onto his knees and peered into the small dark recess under her desk.

'Oops, sorry about that...just needed something to hold onto...'

'That's OK,' she said softly, realising in that instant that she didn't mind. Didn't mind at all. She watched the top of his head that, she noted, seemed to be thickly thatched and not thinning in the slightest. She remembered that Seamus had always done that – thought he was much balder than he was. It was like her with her weight – she always thought she was about one to two stone heavier than she was. It was exactly the same thing, come to think of it. Why do we always do that, she asked herself. Why do we exaggerate and make much worse the thing we're most concerned about?

She made a mental note to stop that once she got

back to 2014. She vowed to be healthy and happy and not obsess about how she looked and how everything was going south – or had already gone south, left ages ago – no! Stop it! There will be no more room left in her fabulously fulfilled, busy, happy life for such negative self-talk, as Georgia called it, when she got back.

If she ever got back.

'I've got to know how long I've got left here, Seamus. I simply have to know!'

Seamus, holding onto five thin black wires, backed out from under her desk and sat on his haunches, looking quite pleased with himself.

'The information superhighway is an amazing thing – but no one knows that sort of stuff – that's between you and, er...' Seamus pointed up towards the ceiling.

'Who? Management?' she said, knitting her brow. 'Someone on the fifth floor?

Seamus leant towards Kate, saying in a whisper, 'No, no - *your maker*.'

'What *are* you talking about?' Kate was beginning to get a little irritated.

'I could ask you the same thing,' Seamus got up, holding the wires to his chest. He tossed his hair a bit and thrust his chin in the air, looking like he'd just said he didn't want to play anymore and he was going home with his ball.

'Urgh,' Kate grunted. 'Just give me the names of some search engines and I'll look it up myself.'

Seamus wrote three names down on the A4 pad sitting at the side of Kate's desk.

'There you go,' said Seamus, dropping the pen on top of the pad and readjusting the wires under his arm, as though they were a clutch bag. 'Now when are you going to take me shopping?'

But Kate was already getting busy with her keyboard, typing in 'time travel' and watching her screen, wide-eyed and expectant.

'Argh!' she harrumphed. 'Why does it take so bloody long?'

'Well, technically- speaking –'

'And where the hell is Wikipedia?'

'Wiki-*what*?'

'Oh, never mind!' she cut Seamus off. 'I'm going to have to go to the library. Ha! Imagine! I've only been in the kids' sections of libraries, lately – sitting on brightly-coloured cushions for story time with Baby Jane. That is, if there are any libraries left – God knows they're shutting them down with such gay abandon these days, is it any wonder we're... all so...computer...obsessed ...?'

She glanced up at Seamus who was looking down at her, an expression of vague concern on his face.

The air between them hung heavily for a few portentous seconds before the rest of the office appeared to melt away and whirl around them at supersonic speed, turning everyone and everything into merely spinning atoms, while the two of them stayed stock still, gazing into each other's eyes.

The moment was loaded - fairly *dripping* with meaning.

'You know, you seem so familiar to me,' Seamus furrowed his brow, his forehead creasing in its usual spot. 'I just can't work out where from.'

Kate nodded encouragingly and stayed silent, wanting to squeeze all possible droplets of romance out of it, like it was a sponge, soaked in the wonderful memories of their relationship.

She took a deep breath as he opened his mouth to speak.

'Maybe I've seen you on the bus... um...do you ever catch the number 19 to Clapton Pond?'

Kate shook her head and felt her face forming into that look again, the one she reserved for George and his jokes. Because really, was this as good as it was ever going to get with Seamus? Was this the best he could do to sweep her off her feet? Swivel chair, whatever.

Kate willed him on, moving her head back and forth, inching herself ever forward, as though her chair were a rocking horse and she was coming down the straight, winning by a nose in her imaginary race.

Come on, Seamus! You can do it!

'All I know is that I feel somehow safe with you. And that every morning when I wake up, ever since we met, I just can't wait to see you.'

Kate's breath caught in her chest.

That's better...keep going, keep going!

'Weird, eh?' he raised his eyebrows.

The office careening around them slowed down and within a couple of seconds, came to a standstill.

The air thinned out, *Return of the Mack* started up on the radio and people carried on exactly as they had before, no one commenting on or in any way acknowledging what had just happened. As though it hadn't.

Seamus said he'd better be going and looking confused, sloped off down the corridor to The Lift.

Tamsin's tinny voice got louder in Kate's ear – she was walking towards the reception desk with Lucy, barking orders about some fax or other that Lucy was to send.

And then, when she saw Tom swagger in, singing along with the song, as though he himself *was* the Mack and this was his triumphant return, she sighed.

'All right, Babes?' he upped the Cockney as he perched on the corner of Kate's desk, chewing gum rapidly and whipping off his Aviators.

Kate smiled the way she would at a puppy's vain attempts at climbing up a couch too tall for him, where no purchase could be found. Because Tom was quite sweet, really – trying so hard to impress and be cool all the time.

'Right. Coupla places to see up West tomorra, which I have 'igh 'opes for. And what's this about a meeting with Medea?'

'Ah – I dunno,' Kate said. 'As far as I know we haven't set a time or place or anything yet-'

'I hope you don't mind,' Tamsin butted in, 'but I

took the liberty of organising this meeting for you. Medea Horton – she's the, ah,she's the boss of Medea Media, right?'

Tom and Kate nodded.

'Well, the only time she could make it was this Friday, but I know you're off to Guernsey then, Kate, so I scheduled it in for, um this afternoon.'

Kate gasped.

'I know it's short notice,' Tamsin said apologetically, 'but that's the only other free slot she had and –'

'Hey, hey,' said Tom, standing up and putting his hands on Tamsin's shoulders. She, in turn, looked up at him with such reverence, it was as though the very hands of God were upon her.

Kate rolled her eyes skywards and mumbled 'Oh, *please*.'

'It's all OK,' Tom continued in soothing tones. 'You did the right thing, as it goes. This whole Medea thing's a storm in a tea-cup. Or a D-cup, more to the point!'

Tamsin tittered and Tom looked appreciative. Kate couldn't believe the cheesiness of what she was witnessing.

'Anyway, the sooner we get it over with, the sooner we can get back to doing what we do best!'

The radio went off, the shuffling of papers stopped and rulers ceased their incessant thwacking – the atmosphere was so heavy with anticipation, all eyes on Tom, and so quiet, you could hear a spitball drop.

Tom flashed a nervous look at Kate. He desperately needed help, here – a prompt.

'Profit, good ti-' she began in a whisper out the side of her mouth.

'Fuck profit! PARTIES, good times and banter!' shouted Tom to rapturous applause from the rest of the office – and a squeak of pure delight from Tamsin.

16

Kate, having reduced Medea to her own prejudiced cultural stereotype in her head, imagined she would be heavy-set with purple DMs, black leggings, floaty purple shirt, a black velvet waistcoat (XL) or shapeless, manly, oversized denim jacket and a buzz cut.

But when Medea Horton walked into the PGT&B offices that afternoon, it was as if she was doing it in slow motion. Her long, wavy, blonde tresses bounced on her slim shoulders as though she were wading through waist-height wheat sheaves on a bright blue-skied, sunny, spring day.

Her cream silk shirt's top button was undone, to a very business-like but un-dorky level, her dark blue suit jacket slung casually over her arm. Her heels sank in to the plush pile carpet of the meeting room, but this was nothing Medea couldn't handle.

She smiled a dazzling, straight-toothed, positively *radiant* smile and extended her beautifully-manicured, soft hand to Kate.

Medea's gold watch dangled elegantly on her delicate wrist and when she looked as if she was about to say something, Kate expected a symphony to start up.

'Hello there! I'm Medea. And you must be...?' she said in a heavy Scottish accent.

'Kate,' said Kate, standing up too fast and bashing her knees on the table. 'Um, I'm Kate and this is Tom,

Editor of *LASHED* and Archie, head of PR at PGT&B.'

Kate swept her hand in the men's direction, but could detect no movement nor hear any sound from them.

She tore her eyes away from Medea and instantly saw why: both Tom and Archie were slack-jawed and speechless, struck dumb, quite literally, by Medea's stunning beauty. Their eyes were out on stalks. And despite the fact that Tom saw thousands of gorgeous (albeit scantily-clad) women every day as part of his job and Archie was a professional who always remained calm in a crisis, these two were hopelessly, helplessly mesmerised.

'Guys? GUYS!' Kate tried to get their attention with a little light shouting and a knock on the table.

'Yes, yes, of course,' said Archie distractedly, glancing at Kate and spluttering a bit as though he'd just been woken up. 'Ah, yes. Do...ah... take a seat.'

In a rare display of competitive chivalry, Archie and Tom swapped goading glances for a millisecond and then simultaneously shot out of their seats, racing for the chair nearest the door, both fumbling with the back of it and elbowing each other out of the way.

'Pathetic,' said Kate quietly, raising her eyes to the buzzing, on/off strip lighting hanging from the ceiling.

Medea laughed.

'It's quite all right, fellas, I can manage to pull my own chair out, thankyou.'

Summarily dismissed, the two men backed away, never taking their eyes off her, mumbling apologies and returning to their own chairs.

Bet it happens all the time, thought Kate.

'It happens all the time,' said Medea and smiled at Kate. 'No big deal. So. Shall we get down to business?'

'Yes,' said Kate, surprised how there was no football talk, taking up the whole meeting time, resulting in another meeting having to be planned for the following week – for that's how meetings at PGT&B were notorious for panning out. 'Would you like some water? Coffee? Tea?'

'Beer? Wine? Me?' grinned Tom, suspecting he was getting his mojo back.

'No, no thanks. I'd rather just crack on if we could – I've got back to back appointments this afternoon.'

'How about a front to front appointment –' Archie whispered to Tom.

'Ah, I think Medea's right,' Kate cut Archie off. 'Let's get on with it.'

'Right,' said Medea ignoring the leering lads and looking straight at Kate. 'Now, as both magazine publishers and women, we strongly object to the imagery, tone and blatant male sexual aggression that magazines like *LASHED* perpetrate and purport is normal – and even worse, agreeable - in our society.'

Kate nodded.

'Now hang on a second,' said Tom, 'what does purport mean?'

Archie and Tom exchanged schoolboy sniggers and Kate registered a distinct sinking feeling.

'And while we're perfectly open to the ideas you expressed in your fax, Kate, we don't actually believe it, in the case of *LASHED* for one cold, hard minute. I mean, how stupid do you think we are?'

'But...I –' Kate stammered.

'However. We are *very* interested in doing business with you. Not getting into bed with you, as such...'

Archie and Tom couldn't help themselves when they heard this phrase and, clutching their stomachs, howled with laughter.

'Oh, here we go,' Medea went on.

In an instant, the room fell silent. Tom and Archie coughed and sat up straight, recovering remarkably fast from their little bout of schoolboy hysterics and all three PGT&Bers were in Medea's thrall.

'Are you quite finished? Now. We definitely want to take you up on your offer of free advertising on prominent *LASHED* pages for a year.'

'You are?' Kate was surprised. 'I thought if you wanted to see us in person, you probably weren't going to go for it at all.'

'Well,' said Medea softening, 'we're only a small business and we are starting to struggle a bit, what with the rise of the lad and so-called irreverent, binge-drinking "ladettes" eclipsing us and our comparatively sober views...'

Kate, Archie and Tom all nodded, willing her on.

'It's a long story,' sighed Medea. 'But suffice it to say I want us to be a success on our own merits. I set the company up myself and I want to prove that our values and ideals are still relevant today – and are, indeed, crucial to building a decent, fair, nurturing society for all. I know it sounds a bit high-minded and out of step with today's individualistic, hedonistic, party, party, party attitudes, but, well, there we are.'

'Good on you,' Kate said, admiring Medea more and more with every passing moment.

'But the advertising is not all I'm after,' Medea said quickly, sensing her audience was not only captive but even in a bit of a trance and, therefore, totally receptive to anything she had to say. 'I also want a regular, monthly spot – a column or something – in not just *LASHED,* but another of your publications. Any ideas?'

Kate snapped out of her semi-hypnotised state and jumped out of her chair a little bit when she shrieked, 'Yes!'

Everyone looked at her expectantly.

'I think *Mad Fer It!* could really do with something like this – as long as you could dress it up, make it funny and relevant to 12-year-old girls – you know, focus on pop stars and movie stars and not take yourself too seriously and lean more towards girl power than radical feminism... Don't you think, Archie?'

Archie stroked his chin.

'Oh, come on, Archie!' Kate pleaded. 'Medea'd

be a great role model for young girls – she's beautiful and ballsy and cool – and with some help from the *Mad Fer It!* editorial team, we could really produce a ground-breaking, history-changing – I mean, history-*making* – feat, here!'

'I love it!' beamed Medea.

'What about me?' Tom pouted.

'What about you?' Archie countered.

'Well, don't I get a say in any of this? I'm only the Editor of *LASHED* with 100% editorial control, you know. It says so in my contract,' said Tom coming over all Elizabeth Taylor in a strop.

'Well, go on, then,' Archie said. 'Enlighten us with your views.'

'I think we should all go to O'Flaherty's to celebrate – and, ah, plan your first column, Medea. Who's with me?'

'Love to – but I've got to run,' said Medea, standing up and pushing her chair out with the backs of her knees. 'Another time, maybe?'

Tom was transfixed again.

'Yeah, sure,' he drooled. 'Any time at all.'

17

'It was as though I was invisible!' Kate moaned to Georgia as they waited in the queue to board the plane to Guernsey.

'Well, I hate to say it, Kate, but that's what Tom's like. It's what he's *always* been like. What he always *will be* like.'

'I know, I know,' Kate sighed at the hideous, three shades of blue, swirly airport lounge carpet. 'I just thought...I'd seen a different side to him, lately, that's all.'

'Well, he's a bastard,' said Georgia matter-of-factly. 'He'll never change. And to salivate all over that girl in front of you, well, bah! Don't waste any more of your time, Kate. You know he's beneath you, don't you?'

'Chance'd be a fine thing,' said Kate, a wicked smile creeping onto her face.

'Honestly – what would Medea say?' Georgia sniggered.

The pair withdrew back into their own respective head spaces in quiet contemplation of things to come.

Georgia had packed several tiny bikinis, and so, in anticipation, had also had everything even remotely resembling hair waxed, plucked or shorn off her body. Despite the fact that the pregnancy hormones racing around her system made her skin so much more sensitive, she was determined to ignore the whole baby thing and carry on as normal. Which is why she even went so far as to have a Brazilian.

'I plumped for a small, but oh-so-sexy landing strip,' she proudly showed Kate the night before. 'Get a load of *this*!'

'Yowch!' Kate recoiled in horror. 'You look like a plucked chicken! With a black go-faster stripe on your...on your...you know, *there*.'

'It'll calm down,' said Georgia, pulling her pants up and plonking herself down in front of the telly. 'And when it does, I'm going to look fabulous.'

'To who? Or should that be "whom"?' Kate wondered out loud.

'I don't know, do I?' Georgia said tetchily. 'Whosoever gets lucky enough to see me in all my glory, I suppose.'

'Yeah, right,' Kate scoffed. 'Because you're going to be getting so much action in Guernsey in the two days we're there...'.

'Well, a girl's got to be prepared,' Georgia said. 'And nothing quite says "preparation" than a Brazilian.'

Or tarty desperation, Kate thought and breathed out through her nose. It whistled.

'Well, I wouldn't expect a Granny like you to get it,' Georgia shook her head at Kate, 'I mean, you're so po-faced and...I dunno...*mumsy*, lately, it's as though you've aged 40 years and forgotten how to have fun.'

'Hang on!' said Kate, looking up from her suitcase at Georgia. 'I haven't forgotten how to have fun! I love fun! I'm taking off for a quick holiday – that's fun!'

Georgia widened her eyes at Kate as if to say, 'got any more examples of extreme good-time seeking?'

'Um,' Kate stalled for time 'and I had drinks with you at the football the other day – that was fun!'

'You don't fool me, Kate,' said Georgia, getting up off the sofa and looking under cushions for the remote. 'I may have been on one, but that didn't stop me noticing your return to limes and sodas after the match. Honestly – the way you've been behaving lately, anyone'd think *you* were up the duff!'

'Oh, as if!' scoffed Kate, whose hand instinctively sought out her flat tummy as if to double check there was no visible bump there as well as marvel at its tight, smooth, youthful feel. 'I haven't even had sex yet, since I got back–'

'Back? Back from where?' Georgia pulled her chin into her neck in disbelief. 'Work this afternoon?'

'No, I mean,' Kate blushed, searching frantically for a way to back pedal her way out of this one. 'Um, that is to say, we, ah, we never seem to get the chance what with all the big nights Tom has and stress at work...'

'There you go again, sounding old before your time,' Georgia sighed. 'You're only turning 27 in two weeks, Kate – not 87! Now where's the bloody remote?'

Kate shrugged her shoulders and studied the contents of her suitcase in an effort to look unfussed.

But she was fussed – really fussed.

What *was* wrong with her, she asked herself. If she

was so keen to get at it with Tom, which she thought she was, why hadn't she? She'd been through it a million, trillion times in her head – Seamus and the kids would never know and she'd been dreaming about this opportunity for *years*. She had no doubt a big clock was ticking loudly somewhere, counting down the minutes and seconds until her time back in the past was up. And she couldn't bear it if her second chance in 1996 came to an abrupt end and she still hadn't managed to sleep with Tom.

'Not even that lazy sex, when you're still half-asleep and groggy and-ah! Here it is! It's always the last... place... you look,' Georgia said as she lay flat on the floor, coaxing the remote out from under the couch with a squash racket that had been lying around on the designer-distressed coffee table.

'What are you so keen to watch, anyway?' Kate gave a light laugh, relieved the subject was exiting her sexless waters and entering that great leveller, the wonderful world of TV.

'Top of the Pops, 'course,' Georgia said, sitting herself down and plumping up the cushions behind her back nicely.

'Oh, yay!' Kate couldn't help herself exclaiming. 'Who's going to be on?'

'Dunno,' said Georgia through a mouthful of Cheesy Wotsits. 'I'll just see, then I'll get straight on with packing.'

Kate grabbed the pack of E-numbered madness off Georgia and flumped down next to her.

Ooh, this was going to be good, she thought, enthusiastically stuffing her face with God-knows-what chemicals and toxins. She'd missed decent music so much in the noughties – not that she managed to keep up with the latest sounds or anything – she was far too busy trying to carry Baby Jane around to worry about carrying a tune anymore. And as for lyrics, as long as she could recite *Fireman Sam* and *Fifi and the Flowertots* in times of duress as a way of calming her tantrumming kids down, she didn't really care that much whether she knew the words to Rihanna's latest hit – let alone remember how *Rapper's Delight* went.

Still, she noted sadly, it seemed that with every passing year, another part of her once quite good voice and diverse musical repertoire disappeared and she sounded more and more like her own mother who was tone deaf – an utterly *atrocious* singer, made fun of by Kate and Steve incessantly.

Kate's timing was slightly off these days, too - she couldn't quite hit the right notes and – worst of all – she'd mumble the words in the trickier bits of songs she once knew so well and loved so much – usually seconds after turning up the car radio and proclaiming to the kids: 'I love this song! Played it a gazillion times! I must know it better than I know myself!'

She would often count herself lucky that she was in the car at these moments and not facing the kids, so they could interpret her mumbling and sudden dips in volume as concentrating hard on driving as opposed to simply being rubbish at singing.

But, of course, the kids didn't notice either way. As they got older, it seemed to Kate that they just ignored her most of the time, as though she was an unseen fairy at the bottom of the garden who looked after everyone tirelessly and never expected any acknowledgement or – God forbid! – thanks.

Kate wanted to spit the Wotsits out, they tasted so ridiculously plastic and manufactured. But she didn't want to draw any more attention to herself, so she handed the packet back to Georgia and wiped her bright-orange-stained fingers on that week's *Radio Times*, a small stack of them sitting underneath the squash racket on the table where she and Georgia were both resting their feet.

'Oh no!' she shrieked. 'It's not on tonight – they've switched it to Friday!'

Georgia wheeled her torso around in shock.

'They can't do that – Thursday night's *Top Of* is an institution!'

'I seem to remember reading something about it in *Mad Fer It!*,' Kate said. 'It's apparently a bid to catch the going out crowd before they go out, or there's less competition on Friday nights or something...'

Kate picked up the pile of RTs and began leafing through them, but Georgia was speechless, still staring at Kate in shock.

'It's all right, though, George, don't be too upset,' said Kate, sounding, just for a split-second, as though she was soothing her eldest son after he'd scraped his knee or had a run-in with the school bully. 'It's not like they've cancelled it altogether. It'll just take some getting used to, that's all.'

'It's all right for you, Gran – you probably *want* to stay in and watch telly on Friday nights, rest your weary bones after the week from Hell. It's one thing to love good telly – as we all do – but quite another to be so dull that you'd actually *prefer* to stay in and watch it rather than go out and experience life. Isn't it? Kate? Kate!'

Now it was Kate's turn to be shocked. As she thumbed through the older copies of *The Radio Times*, she saw that the night she'd been transported back in time, the last episode of Series One of *This Life* had been on. So while she was out disgracing herself all over town, she could have been at home drooling over the lovely Jack Davenport.

'Oh, bollocks!' she mumbled.

'Is so! God, you're such an old biddy – '

'No, no,' said Kate, 'although yes, you're right, I probably am old before my time – in so many ways – but we missed the last episode of *This Life* last week. *That's* what I'm saying is bollocks.'

'Oh,' Georgia calmed down. 'Don't know what I'm getting so het up about, Kate, sorry.'

'Maybe those pregnancy hormones are –'

'No, no, NO!' Georgia covered her face with her hands in frustration. 'Leave it alone, will you?'

Kate bit her lip and extended her hand to Georgia's shoulder. She didn't have to say anything, Georgia knew this gesture said, *I'm sorry, I'll shut up now, promise.*

'That show's crap, anyway,' Georgia eventually said through her fingers.

'But you used to love it!'

'What do you mean, "used to"?'

'We get right into watching the trials and tribulations of a share house full of hard-living young lawyers...' Kate read out the Radio Times' description. 'And the guy who plays Miles is a bit on the tasty side, isn't he?'

'Not bad,' Georgia slowly nodded her head in contemplation. 'I actually don't mind the guy who plays Egg, either, if we're being honest.'

'Which we are,' Kate pulled Georgia in to her for a hug.

'Yes, we are. But I still prefer to actually leave the house once in a while and try to *live* this life - instead of watching other people's fictional versions of it...'

Kate thought back to her first night in 1996 the second time around and shuddered.

'Oh, do shut up,' was all Kate could think of to say. 'You've got the waxing done, now get those bikinis packed - you never know who you might meet in Guernsey, do you?'

At this, Georgia beamed and fairly leapt off the couch to finish packing.

And now, here they were lining up to board the plane that would take them away from all this, give them time to talk and think and take long, soulful walks along warm, windswept beaches. And, Kate hoped, give her the chance to talk Georgia out of what she knew would be the most disastrous decision of her life.

*

'I'll freeze my tits off out there – no way am I taking my jumper off, let alone actually getting in the water!' laughed Georgia as she shivered, trying to flick her towel out and get it lying straight and in an orderly fashion on the wind-whipped sand.

Kate threw her head back and guffawed at the sight and sat down on the sand, her only concession to beach wear being that she'd rolled her combats up a bit. She'd taken great delight in seeing how her large, loose-knit boat neck cornflower blue jumper hung casually yet sexily on her almost angular frame and when she hugged her knees to her chest, she nearly yelped at how easy it was, how there were no rolls of flesh getting in the way.

'This'll brush the cobwebs away,' she said, squinting as some dried seaweed blew into her face and got tangled up in her hair. 'There's something so much more romantic about a beach in the cold, don't you think?'

'You'll have to speak up!' Georgia yelled back. 'I can't hear you over the roar of the Force 10 hurricane!'

It *was* blowing a gale, Kate had to agree.

'I said, DON'T YOU THINK A BEACH IS MORE ROMANTIC IN WINTRY WEATHER? SO MUCH MORE DRAMATIC AND BROODING –'

'For GOD'S SAKE, Kate – for the last time, I AM

NOT BROODY!'

'What?'

'Eh?'

As Kate felt the first few drops of rain on her face, she cupped her hand around Georgia's ear and shouted:

'Shall we go back to the hotel and watch the football? Have a hot toddy or two?'

'NOW YOU'RE TALKING MY LANGUAGE!' screeched Georgia, stuffing her obstreperous towel into her beach bag and scowling as she threw her bottle of Reef Oil on top of it, as though it were her summer holiday accoutrements' fault the weather was so unsuitable for sunbathing.

The match had already started by the time they had got themselves organised at a warm table for two. It was a bit further away from the throng clustered around the bar and loudly watching Scotland v England, so the girls could talk unhampered by football and the inevitable disappointment from lack of goals.

'I'm not really that into all this Euro '96 palaver, anyway,' Georgia said, taking great gulps of her drink.

'Oh, yeah?' Kate widened her eyes in disbelief. 'You looked like it was a matter of life and death, like your life depended on it last weekend when we were watching it at O'Flaherty's...'

'Well, it did, in a way,' Georgia grinned. 'I mean, there was no way I was going to pull that football hooligan if I didn't pretend to be obsessed by the game.'

'Match,' Kate corrected her.

'Whatever. I just feel like ever since Simon dumped me and I've been lumbered with *this*,' she pointed to her tummy 'I need to sort myself out. And fast.'

'Well, you do,' Kate saw her chance and pounced. 'But you need to be sensible about this. Grown up.'

'Ha!' Georgia spluttered, spitting a wee dram of whisky out onto her chest. 'Like you, you mean? Miss Boring 1996? I'm surprised you didn't know the weather here was going to be so crap – I mean, I bet you listen to The Shipping Forecast all the time, for a little excitement, hmmm?'

'Give me a break, George,' Kate sipped her toddy, a tad wounded. 'All that guff about me being old is starting to get a little bit...um...old, now. And anyway, there's really no need to be so nasty. I'm only trying to help.'

The good time in Guernsey Kate had looked forward to so much, was turning out to be as much fun as a wet weekend in Whitstable. Without the glitz and glamour.

Kate knew that Georgia was capable of being a tad on the tetchy side at the best of times. But woe betide (*woe betide? She really was talking like an OAP!)* anyone who tried to talk to her rationally when she was pregnant – because then she was, apparently, a veritable tempest. Just like the storm brewing outside.

Silence descended upon their table. But at the bar,

the cheers and groans of near-miss goals and penalties being wrongly awarded carried on apace.

Kate and Georgia craned their necks to see what was going on for a few moments and then lapsed back into easy conversation.

'I'm sorry,' Kate offered her apologies first, figuring she might as well, considering she was older, wiser and, obviously a million times more boring.

'Ach,' said Georgia, downing her third or fourth whisky and sounding more and more Scottish as a result. 'Never ye mind, Lassie, never ye mind.'

Georgia's (pretty bad, actually) accent elicited some dirty looks from the men at the bar, but they were soon distracted by great whooping and hollering from the rest of the crowd.

The pair got up and joined the revellers at the bar and were duly and enthusiastically informed about what had just happened. One young gun breathlessly told Kate and Georgia – who were both genuinely interested and excited - that McManaman had passed the ball to Neville who then made an excellent cross to Shearer who, in turn, headed the ball into the net – and England into the lead.

'I knew that McManaman-amanaman was a man... amanaman...one to watch,' Georgia swayed and slurred ever-so-slightly.

It was 52 minutes into the match. Soon after, Scotland nearly equalised, but the England goalie with the unfortunate surname Kate couldn't help commenting on (because, really, who could resist not taking the mickey out of someone called Seaman?) deflected the ball.

The tension was mounting, the taste of victory palpable - and being a part of it, as the curtain rain lashed the hotel's floor-to-ceiling windows, was the best fun Kate had had since...well, since she'd watched any Euro '96 matches the first time round, really.

'Ooh, don't think much of the colour,' Georgia whispered loudly to Kate when Paul Gascoigne's shock of lurid blond hair filled the TV screen.

'Nah,' Kate nodded. 'And with that super-short cut, he looks like a fat, ugly Yazz. Remember her? From the 80s? She sang *The Only Way Is Up*?'

Kate, who had, by this stage, also managed to knock back a few whiskies, attempted to jog her friend's memory with the wrong words accompanying her out of time, out of tune version of the old hit.

'I thought I was a (mumble, mumble), ooh for somethin' you today...but bein' on the...and now the only way is up! Bay-beh! For you come on now!'

'Can't say it sounds familiar,' Georgia laughed. 'You sure it was the 1980s and not the 1880s? You are a little on the ancient side, remember.'

'Cheeky moo,' Kate muttered and drained her drink, muscling through the scrum of punters standing broad-shoulder-to-broad-shoulder at the bar.

'Are you blind, Ref?' the crowd chorused as a penalty was awarded to the Scots.

Seaman turned the near-goal into a near miss and then, with eleven minutes to go, Gazza (he of the comedy barnet), kicked the ball, in a rather astonishing, brilliantly-executed volley, into the net.

The 'dentist's chair' celebrations that followed, whereby his teammates sprayed water into a prone Gazza's open mouth, mirrored a boozy drinking game the England team had been busted playing a few weeks before. Or so the young football fan hugging Georgia and squeezing her tight in his delight informed them.

'Woo-HOO!' Kate joined in as she weaved her way back to Georgia, remarkably not spilling a drop from the four short glasses. 'It's looking good for us now –'

'Don't say that!' Georgia and her man said in unison. 'You'll jinx it!'

But she didn't – England virtually *romped* home, winning convincingly, 2-nil.

The roar when the whistle blew at full-time was so loud, Kate covered her ears as she jumped up and down with the rest of the gang.

'Too loud for me,' Georgia bent away from the football fan's embrace and shouted in Kate's ear.

'All right, all right!' Kate shouted back. 'No need to yell! Amazing as it sounds, I'm not deaf, yet, you know. And I do still have all my own teeth!'

'I'm not feeling so great, Kate, think I'll...just sit down over there for a minute.'

Georgia extricated herself from the over-zealous fan with the incredible wandering hands and staggered to the table they'd been sitting at before, near the window.

Kate followed and, in her merry state, thought now was the perfect time to talk Georgia out of that termination.

She plonked herself down in the wicker chair next to Georgia's and started the spiel she had so diligently prepared earlier, on the plane the day before.

'I know it doesn't fit into your life right now, but you might want kids later on...and, God, I might as well tell you the truth, George,' Kate took a deep breath, about to spill the beans.

Here goes, she thought to herself. The moment when her friend had no choice but to declare her insane and section her.

'You'll probably think I'm mad, but...Well, the fact is, George, that I'm here from the future – 2014 to be exact – and having lived through all of this before, I know that the abortion you're about to have will render you completely infertile and totally distraught.'

Georgia glanced at Kate, her face all screwed up, her complexion ghostly.

'I know it sounds crazy, but –'

In that very instant, Georgia let out a frighteningly shrill and sharp scream and, clutching her stomach, slumped off her chair onto the floor, curling up in the foetal position and crying her eyes out.

'George!' squealed Kate, darting down to the floor to tend to her best mate. 'George? Can you hear me?'

But all Georgia could do was stretch her legs out and then bring them back up to her chest quickly, writhing about in obvious excruciating pain.

‘Help me,’ Georgia sobbed weakly, reaching out a hand for Kate to hold.

‘AMBULANCE!’ Kate’s loud voice went all deep and gravelly and authoritative. ‘We need an ambulance here NOW!’

Kate placed Georgia’s head gently on her lap and stroked her hair, trying hard not to notice the bright red blood pooling on the carpet underneath Georgia’s backside.

18

'You don't half come out with some tosh, sometimes,' Georgia said to Kate as she propped herself up in her bed back at home in West Hampstead. 'What was all that "I come to you from the future" rubbish you were spouting in Guernsey? And do stop fussing, really. I'm fine.'

'Well, just to be sure, take it easy for a few days,' Kate replied, ignoring Georgia's remark and smoothing down the Persil-fresh, deep purple duvet cover she'd just put on – the all-white linen that had been there only minutes before seemed to Kate as though it was flirting with stain-related disaster.

'You're going to make someone a great wife someday,' said Georgia softly, 'and when you have kids, they'll be the luckiest little sods alive.'

As soon as the words escaped her lips, Georgia looked downcast.

'You reckon?' Kate scoffed, sitting on the edge of the bed like it was a horse and she was riding side-saddle. 'Try telling that to...Georgia? Are you OK? Do you want to talk about it?'

Kate hadn't seen Georgia's miscarriage coming – it wasn't what had happened the first time around, after all – and she felt strangely responsible, as if she should have known, been able to forewarn and protect her friend.

Georgia rolled her eyes as she studied the right

hand bottom corner of her duvet.

'Not really,' she mumbled.

'Oh, come on, Georgie, that's not like you – you always say there's no cure like the talking cure.'

'I do?' Georgia looked up in surprise.

'Yeah!' Kate's eyes scudded away from Georgia's, aware she'd wandered into inexplicable time travel waters again. 'I'm sure you do. All the time! Anyway, moving right along...'

Kate coughed and stood up.

'More tea?'

'No thanks, Mum,' Georgia smiled. 'I might just see if I can have a little snooze-ette, if you don't mind – a well-deserved power nap for the infirm. And you go to work, go on! I'll still be here when you get home. I'm going nowhere...*fast*!'

But Kate couldn't drag herself away. She remembered how knocked about she'd been by the miscarriage she'd suffered six months before she fell pregnant with George and how alone and unbearably sad it had made her feel. And even though Georgia was a totally different animal to her, she was convinced that there, somewhere, buried deep beneath that tough, unfazed exterior, Georgia felt exactly the same way.

'So, how are you, Georgie? I mean, really. In yourself,' Kate said in what she hoped was the tone of voice a calm, professional psychologist might use.

'Knackered,' came Georgia's reply, as she made a point of closing her eyes and rolling onto her side, away from Kate.

Kate was, however, undeterred by Georgia's obvious shut down signals.

'I know when I had my –' she cut herself off and scanned the bedroom for inspiration, something to help her rephrase what she was trying to say. 'In the stuff I've read about miscarriage – women's mag stuff and the odd newspaper article, it seems that no one really wants to talk about it much and, as a result, the emotional trauma continues and escalates, untreated, only to come out in other self-damaging ways.'

An exaggerated, obviously fake snore rattled the walls and rippled the sheets where Georgia lay.

'Oh, come on!' Kate playfully slapped Georgia's rump.

Georgia laughed and rolled onto her back, pushing herself up with her hands, making Kate jump to attention and rearrange the pillows behind her against the wall.

'I'm fine, really,' Georgia insisted.

'Really?' Kate didn't buy it.

'I'm more upset about Simon dumping me than losing the baby, if you really want to know.'

Kate did really want to know, she wanted the truth – desperately. But this wasn't anywhere near what she wanted to hear and she couldn't quite believe her ears. It was as though Georgia's brutal honesty sharply and swiftly offended Kate's moral code, made a mockery of all she held dear. And she couldn't let it lie.

'I'm not sure I –' Kate began.

'It's quite simple, really, Kate,' said Georgia,

fixing her dark, brooding (though not, obviously, *broody*) eyes on her best friend 'I'm too young for kids – I don't want them. Not yet. Maybe never. I don't know. Same as you, really – or the same as you *used* to be, at any rate. I don't know why you're having such a hard time with this all of a sudden. Anyone would think you were married and middle aged and *you'd* had the miscarriage or something.'

Georgia inspected her fingernails and decided that chewing the side of her thumb was a pretty good option at this point.

'I just know you,' Kate said softly, tilting her head to the side for added effect 'and you're not that shallow – not as unaffected by life as you try to make out sometimes.'

'Oh yes I am!' Georgia slapped her palms down on the duvet cover. 'I'm deeply shallow, actually, I'll have you know. And I resent any implication to the contrary!'

Kate grinned. Somehow in the melee of the past few days, she'd seemed to have forgotten that, at 27, the pair of them were really only interested in men, sex, going out, having fun and trying to hold down a decent-enough job that would pay for all of the above (except the sex, neither of them had ever had to pay for that). It was day-to-day living, lurching from one ill-fated affair to the next, recovering unfairly fast from hangovers and giving scant thought to the future, because the present, not the past, was, quite frankly, such a blast.

How could she have, Kate mused to herself? She'd only been dreaming about these comparatively carefree days for most of her life as a mother – how could she so quickly have dismissed her and Georgia's favourite pastimes as the folly of youth and somehow invalid? Not real? Unimportant and silly? How had she become so smug and patronising and judgemental? So *old.*

'Kids,' she muttered, answering her own question.

'Oh, God - what now?' Georgia groaned.

'Ha! I mean, kids, eh? Who needs 'em, right? We are far too young and clever!'

As Kate quoted the pair's favourite line from *Come On, Eileen*, a glint of recognition sparkled in Georgia's eyes.

'Thank God you're back,' Georgia wiped imaginary sweat off her brow. 'That motherly stuff you were doing was really starting to freak me out!'

'Yeah, me too,' Kate chortled. 'Right. So. You stay there, get better, whatever, and I'll, um, leave you to it.'

As if they'd done it a thousand times before and their moves had been honed, carefully choreographed over the years, Kate got off the bed and Georgia picked up a dog-eared copy of Men Are From Mars, Women Are From Venus from her bedside table.

*

Kate busied herself about their flat, doing things she knew she was good at – taking clothes off the radiators and clothes horses, folding them, putting them away neatly in their own little drawers dedicated to tops or knickers or trousers.

She heard her grandmother's voice in her head saying: 'A place for everything and everything in its place,' and felt a sudden rush of love for her family and an almost overwhelming desire to get back to them.

What were they doing without her, she wondered. The house must be a right tip by now – beds unmade, toys strewn all over the place, dirty nappies stinking out the bin, greasy washing up left lying in a sink full of cold, sud-less, grey water...Were they wondering where she'd got to? Or maybe they were frozen in time and their lives were all on hold, in suspended animation until she get her little adventure out of the way and came home.

'Home,' Kate said out loud and sighed.

When she did get back, she continued asking herself, would she simply land in the fuggy kitchen and pick up where she'd left off? Would everyone just carry on as if nothing had happened? Would the kids be fighting, the porridge burning, Seamus getting more emotionally distant, she, herself, getting more and more frustrated when she thought of ambitions unfulfilled, and all the while her Marigolds perishing alongside her spirit?

She shook the thought out of her head and instead focussed on her (sometime) ability to make a mess tidy, her way with turning chaos into order. Or, if not exactly *order*, as such, then a weeny bit *less* mad.

She thought of how she secretly quite liked it

when the kids were sick back in the noughties – she loved giving her soothing, comforting bedside manner a good workout. She never thought she would, being a driven career girl and all, but she really enjoyed helping to make other people feel better, too.

In fact, having given up the idea of ever returning to full-time paid work (at least until the kids had left home), she might say she even *preferred* looking after the kids to working for The Man, dancing to the beat of someone else's drum for a wage. Because as far as job satisfaction goes, she thought, being a full-time mum sure took some beating.

Or, she smiled to herself, being a full-time mum, you sure took a beating.

Kate sighed again as she emptied the dishwasher. Whichever way she looked at it now, she couldn't help but come to the conclusion that her life as a wife and mother was as good as it was ever likely to get. And that wasn't such a bad thing.

In fact, in cold, hard, actual fact, she was beginning to think it was rather a great thing.

I take it all back! I love things just the way they are at home –Shay exactly as he is, the kids the same - don't go changing anything, please!

'Oops,' she said out loud, holding a spotless wine glass up to the light. 'Here I go, donning my rose-coloured glasses again.'

She reined herself in, trying to be careful not to go overboard as per usual and make absolutes of everything, look at a situation or a film or a haircut, even, as 100% fantastic – or 100% terrible, with no in betweens. Because unfortunately, coupled with her penchant for nostalgia, Kate also had a tendency to turn the grey and murky into black and white. And in her heart of hearts, after much trial and error and having been around the block several hundred times, she knew there really was no such thing.

Of course little improvements could be made to her life in 2014. *Of course* certain, insignificant things that didn't really matter could be altered just a smidge and life as a whole would be more fluid, more relaxed, more enjoyable.

Of course nothing was perfect.

Like Seamus, for example. If only he could be more confident in himself, see how smart and good-looking he really was, maybe then he would realise his dreams and their lives together would be so much more...passionate and exciting and fulfilling.

And the kids. Don't get me wrong, she thought, they are three gorgeous, adorable little bundles in every way. But it would be nice, sometimes, every now and again, if they didn't fight and did their homework and cleaned their rooms without being nagged to death about it. And if Baby Jane would sleep for 12...eight – hell, if Baby Jane could sleep for more than *three* hours straight, that would really be something to write home about.

And if they could all just give her a little bit of *respect...*

'What you want!' she declared, off-key. 'Baby I

got it!'

'What?' came Georgia's groggy voice from her bedroom.

'Nothing, nothing,' Kate called back. 'Just thinking out loud, that's all.'

'Haven't you got your appraisal today?' Georgia asked. 'Shouldn't you be shuffling off to work?'

Oh God. Kate had forgotten all about that!

Her appraisal. Where she would be hauled over the coals for a) the enormous amount of days she'd called in sick (hungover) so far this year and b) never quite reaching the impossibly high goals and targets Archie would always set for her.

The Appraisal. Where she would be told she had to go on various grandmother-sucking-eggs training courses to 'up her capacity' as a PR guru.

Or, her chance to have *her* say and suggest ways of improving the company's performance for *her* benefit, as the bosses were always so keen to put it.

They were so into spin at every possible turn, PGT&B, that even a sacking was called a 'voluntarily exit, swift-stylee' (if, indeed, it was ever mentioned at all after the fact) and when someone didn't get a promotion or a pay-rise, it was referred to as 'consolidation and stabilisation of the status quo' – which, of course, was crucial to the smooth running of the operation. And crucial for ensuring that management always got *their* pay-rises and bonuses, too.

Kate, like every other right-thinking minion –

senior minion, maybe, but minion nonetheless – in the world, *dreaded* their appraisal.

Or, at least, she *used* to.

Today, though, she couldn't wait to get her hands on Archie's Fred Perry lapels and tell him exactly what she thought about how the company – and, in particular, her department - was run.

Today, she fairly tripped over herself when she broke out into a skip in order to get to the bathroom and her make up bag fast.

'To-day is gonna be the day...' Kate sang slightly out of time in her best nasal, Manchester drawl, as she gussied herself up (which, on the cusp of 27 years old, merely meant a few dabs of some wet/dry foundation, a couple of brushes of mascara and a quick slick of lippie as opposed to being on the cusp of 45, which meant serious consideration of botox, fillers and lipo).

The phone rang just as she was on her way out, and once she'd squeezed her arms into her short, tight, faded denim jacket, she picked up the receiver.

'Hey Baby,' came Tom's undeniably sexy voice, 'it's your dream man, here...'

'Hi, hi, hi, Tom,' she said, panting a bit, 'I'm just going out the door –'

'Relax, Babe – chill,' he said, 'I know I make you breathless...and...and that's why I'm calling, actually.'

'It is?'

'Yeah. Call off the dogs, the search is over – I've found us the perfect love nest. In Notting Hill. And as soon as you think G can cope without you and your

Florence Nightingale act, you can move on in!'

'Oh, Tom!' Kate said, hoping that Tom didn't pick up on the slightly scared quaver, the almost inaudible, trepidatious tone of her voice. 'That's brilliant news! But I'll see you at work – I've got to run, now – my appraisal's in an hour!'

19

'I'll pour,' Kate said, taking charge of the sturdy silver tea pot and two china cups on saucers that were sitting in the middle of Archie's desk. 'Milk in first or last?'

'Last,' Archie said slowly. 'Exactly the same as all right-thinking Englishmen have it.'

Archie watched her suspiciously as she carefully dropped two sugar cubes into his cup from the mini silver tongs, gave it a quick stir and in one fluid movement, tapped the teaspoon lightly on the rim of the cup, placed said spoon on the saucer and leant over Archie's desk to place the whole lot in front of him.

'Thankyou,' he said, bringing his huge swivel chair closer to the desk. 'I did ask for some Hob Nobs, but they don't seem to have materialised...'

'Oh, that's OK,' Kate said, pretending she wasn't bitterly disappointed by this outrage of an oversight. She swallowed as quietly as she could, hoping to hide the fact that her mouth had been watering and her eyes had lit up ever since she'd spied the biscuit tin.

'I...ah...' Archie faltered.

'That's easy for you to say,' Kate grinned.

'Um, well, actually,' Archie did his best to look deadly serious and carry on. 'I'm not sure how to go about this, Kate. We've been close friends as well as colleagues for quite some time, now...'

Oh, God. Like a bolt out of the blue. This is it. He's firing me! Gird your loins, girl, here it comes...

'...but I still haven't got the faintest idea why

you're behaving like such...such an old lady, lately.'

'What?' Kate nearly spat out her tea. 'What do you mean, "old lady"?'

'Well, no offence, obviously, but playing mum, pouring the tea, taking time off to tend to your flatmate, seemingly at odds with all of us here – I mean, your ideas are a bit, to put it bluntly, *crap*, lately. And you seem to have forgotten that you're in PR – it's your *job* to party with the best of them – not come over all sensible and opt for Radio 4 and an early night.'

Kate was gobsmacked. Her mouth had fallen open at the start of Archie's little rant and had remained quite plainly agog until its end.

'I...uh...' now it was Kate's turn to stumble over her words.

'I don't mean to be rude and I'm sure we can talk openly with each other, but I believe it's professionally – and probably morally, too – incumbent on me to bring to your attention exactly how...how...'

Kate arched her eyebrows, widened her eyes and willed him on.

'...how unutterably *boring* you've become.'

'Well!' Kate managed, after fighting for a few seconds to get her lips out of the 'agape' position in an effort to form some words. 'I never!'

Archie rolled his eyes to the ceiling.

'See what I mean?' he sounded exasperated. 'You talk like my Granny!'

At this, Kate took a little bit of umbrage. And a

speedy good look at herself.

She had been holding her saucer in her lap with one hand, and was hovering her cup over the saucer in her other hand. Her legs were crossed neatly at the ankle and tucked under her chair, to the right. Her back was straight and at that very moment, she imagined herself looking like her own granny, striking a pose favoured by those well-over 50. In 1950. In fact, she thought, the only things missing were a small hat and kid gloves.

She put her tea on Archie's desk, making sure to slosh some into the saucer and slouched down into the back of the chair. She shook her Jennifer Aniston hairdo and gave a small cough.

'Is this my appraisal or are you just having a pop at me as some kind of a warm-up?' she said, her chin jutting out, helping her assume an air of indignation. 'Is this your major criticism of me?'

Archie nodded and smiled with relief.

'Yes it's your appraisal, yes it's my main criticism and –'

'Life can't always be one big, long episode of *Men Behaving Badly*, you know, Archie,' Kate said, crossing one ankle over her opposite knee and sitting in a decidedly male manner.

Regardless of her newly-adopted relaxed way of sitting, though, she still sounded a bit school marmy. A fact that hadn't escaped Archie's ears.

'Just listen to yourself, Kate!' he yelped. 'Since when did you get to be so bloody sensible? Honestly, you're like Julie Sodding Andrews in khaki combats!'

Kate glanced at her thin thighs and ludicrous white plastic high-heeled Spice Girls sneakers and tutted.

She allowed her thoughts to go off on a tangent at this point, wishing she had just one ounce of the poise, the warmth and the great fun ideas that Julie seemed to have for all those kids in *The Sound of Music* – and there were seven of them!

Kate felt herself frown when this happy, serene, contented snapshot of caring womanhood and doting children on lush, green hills was replaced by her shouting at her three frightened kids, all looking up at her, terrified in a damp, dull, peeling-lino-floored kitchen. She flinched as she pictured serpents snaking their way through her wild hair and when she felt the crushing weight of that all-too familiar clenched-teeth tension hanging heavily over their home like a big, black cloud, she shook her head and swore to herself that when she got back to 2014 – *if* she ever got back to 2014 – she would channel her inner Julie daily and banish her outer Medusa forever.

Kate confidently placed both feet flat on the floor, sat up and, like every granny who'd ever gone before her, said:

'Good manners cost nothing, Archie. And if being sensible and boring means I'm nice to everyone and take the time to get to know everyone from the receptionist to the new IT guy –'

'Urgh,' Archie looked away, disgusted. 'I was wondering when we'd get to him. Honestly, Katie, I don't know what you see in him.'

Kate stopped short and bent her head so far to the right, her ear almost touched her shoulder.

'What are you talking about?'

'I've seen the way you look at him, Kate. That dweeby guy from the basement who can't put one foot in front of the other without tripping over filing cabinets and leaving carnage in his wake, demolishing everything in his path.'

'You mean Shay...I mean, Seamus? I suppose he can be a bit clumsy...' Kate said surprisingly fondly. 'But his heart's in the right place. And if you weren't so quick to judge, you'd find out he's a pretty nice guy, too.'

'I don't care about him, whatever-his-name-is – '

'Seamus,' Kate helped him out.

'I said I don't care!' Archie's bottom lifted a centimetre or two out of his chair, such was the force of his declaration.

'All right, all right,' said Kate, patting the air in front of her with her palms, trying to calm him down a bit.

God, she thought. What's with everyone at the moment? Why is everybody acting so strangely? Paris, Blue and Steve (who was still MIA) had all been weird, Georgia not wanting to bang on about her feelings ad infinitum, the hapless Seamus, Tom actually seeming quite sweet and homemaker-y – or at least not being a *complete* and utter heartbreaker (say, 80-85%, so far) – and even Archie was acting out of character. What on earth was going on?

It was all so odd. Could it possibly be that her little nostalgia problem – if she could call it a *problem*, as such – was to blame? Could it be the fault of those rose-coloured glasses she was so keen on wearing?

Because no one was exactly how she remembered them, let's face it – not even her own good self. And now it was making her feel uneasy. At least in her mind's eye, she knew where she stood – the cast of thousands in her past life were one-dimensional and their character traits set in stone.

But here, in reality – if, indeed, that's where she was – things were quite different.

Perhaps her ageing, wearying memory had let her down. She seemed to have forgotten long ago that most people have several sides to them and aren't always kind or funny or selfish, but more likely a mish-mash of good, bad *and* ugly.

'Earth to Kate? Come in Kate!' Archie was looking a little worried now.

'Oh, sorry, Archie, I –'

'I don't get it,' he said, slumping back on his chair. 'You have all these early nights, never get caught up in the fun of a big session, never let the partying get the better of you – and yet you look shattered. Is something bothering you? Are you losing sleep or something?'

'Oh, no – it's wonderful,' Kate stretched out dreamily, temporarily forgetting herself. 'You have no idea – I've got the double bed to myself, the kids aren't waking me up several times a night, I'm not getting up to wee every two hours – I don't think I've slept this well for, God, at least ten years!'

'The *kids*? You mean Georgia and Steve wake you up all the time?'

'Er, no... yes, yes!' She backtracked over her own foot and yanked it out of her mouth. 'Always playing loud music and playing drinking games into the wee hours in the front room –'

'Which is exactly what you should be doing, too, Kate! Be honest with me - why aren't you out, making merry with clients more often?'

Kate considered being truthful with Archie for a nano-second. And then dismissed the idea as preposterous just as quickly. If he only knew what secret she was harbouring, he'd have her carted away by the men in white coats in a flash, for sure.

How could she tell him that she'd travelled back in time and even though she looked like the vivacious, bubbly 26-year-old fun-loving girl he knew so well, she was actually a knackered, exhausted 44-year-old mother of three who even *she* didn't want to know most of the time?

How could she say to him that sure, her work may be a little on the lack-lustre side at the moment, but on the bright side, at least she was getting all that delicious, much-needed, unbroken sleep?

She couldn't, that's how. She was just going to have to come up with something good. Something believable. Something that Archie would think a 26-

year-old girl like her would be rocked to her very foundations by. A family problem? 'That time of the month' troubles? A hangnail?

As soon as she began racking her brains, searching for a plausible answer to his question, Archie's office door burst open.

'Roll up, roll up!' said Tom in his best circus ringmaster's voice, 'Step right this way!'

There he stood, looking rather cute, with his legs astride, his tight, white canvas jeans hugging his muscular thighs nicely and his white cheese cloth billowy shirt bestowing upon him a decidedly Mr Darcy disposition.

Archie looked at Kate and nodded slowly, a smile of sudden realisation and simultaneously satisfaction spreading across his face. Kate returned his look as if to say: 'Yes, Archie, you're right – it's Tom. *He's* the problem. Relationship in a bit of turmoil at the mo'. It's not easy going out with the Leader of the Lads, you know.'

'Hoo! Is it hot in here?' Kate said, fanning herself with her right hand.

'No,' sneered Archie, 'you're probably just having a hot flush.'

Archie looked admiringly back to Tom and said: 'So go on, Tom – what's your latest caper all about, then?'

'We're throwing a party to welcome Medea, our hottest, coolest new columnist to *LASHED*. Damien Hirst'll be there – it's in honour of all *enfants terrible* at Quo Vadis – you know, that great restaurant in Soho? Thought it'd get us some good publicity. And bring a bit of culture to the masses, a bit of testosterone-fuelled art the way it should be done...'

Now it was Kate's turn to sneer.

'Ooh, no. All those poor cows suspended in formaldehyde –'

'Sounds like some of my ex-girlfriends,' Tom guffawed. 'Sorry, sorry. Kate, I will not take no for an answer – you are coming to this gig. With me. NOW.'

'She likes her men to be forceful,' said Archie, in a strangely sullen manner, Kate thought.

Yes, it was definitely sullen. And sarky. Archie was acting like a sulky teenager and it didn't suit him.

An almighty crash broke Kate's reverie and all three heads turned to Tamsin's desk in the open-plan office.

'I said re-boot it, not put the boot in!' cried Seamus from somewhere under the debris of fallen papers and computer equipment.

Tamsin stood there, her eyes huge, her hands up to her mouth, static with shock that she could have killed half of PGT&B's IT Department with just one swift kick from her stilettoe-shod foot.

Kate looked at Archie who shook his head and said: 'Typical.'

Her attention was diverted, then, to a soaking wet cagoule flying past the windows of Archie's office, spraying the glass with water as it went.

'Hang on, mate, I'll get you out. Just don't move,

OK?' said the racing cagoule.

'Who's that?' Tom asked no one in particular.

'I'm not sure, but I think it's Kevin. The IT department's newest - and nerdiest – recruit,' said Archie, his top lip curling so hard, with such contempt, that it was quivering with the effort.

'Ah, they're always called Kevin, aren't they?' chortled Tom. 'I mean, there's always one nerk in every group of guys who's called Kevin, isn't there? Drummers in bands, usually. It's the classic dork's name.'

'Well, I'm in – well up for a night out,' said Archie. 'What's it gonna be, Kate?'

Kate bit her lip.

There was that mum-in-charge side to her which made her straighten up, push her shoulders back and want to say, 'oh, grow up, Archie – I've got a stack of washing to get through and there's no way I'll cope tomorrow with all you demanding kids on three hours sleep!'

Equally, however, there was the other side to her, that live for today, youthfully exuberant, slim, vital part that wanted to say 'Way-hey - let's go!'

But what about that deep, satisfying sleep and those fabulous feature-length dreams? Could she sacrifice 8-10 solid hours in picturesque Noddington for a potentially 'fun' night out? When her idea of the best, most fantastic fun night possible was one of end-on, hard-core, full-on uninterrupted snoozing?

'But it's so nice just to sleep,' she said, her voice

taking on a peculiar timbre, a deep growl almost, as she said the word 'sleep'.

She struggled with her schizophrenia, grappled with her notions of a good time and wrestled with her hopelessly conflicted split personality for, ooh, about four seconds, before Archie made her mind up for her.

'Come on!' he grabbed her elbow. 'You can sleep when you're dead.'

'All right,' she acquiesced, thinking she might as well make the most of looking young, if not feeling it – and prove to Archie, in the process, that she still had what it took to be tops in the PR world.

'That's my girl,' Tom put his arm protectively around her shoulder and the three of them wandered off, doing the Monkees' overlapping knees walk in the direction of The Lift.

So here she was, on the verge of something beyond exciting: a night on the tiles in a premier restaurant, the chance to quaff wine (in moderation in Kate's case) and the once (or twice, in Kate's case) in a lifetime opportunity to chat to some potentially really interesting celebrities. She should have been thrilled. Tamsin would have been. *She* wouldn't have been able to wipe the loopy grin off her face. But instead, as they waited for The Lift in silence, Kate's smile quickly faded to be replaced by a grimace.

She felt that gnawing, empty feeling in her stomach again and stroked her flat belly as if trying to rub it out.

'We'll get something to eat there, Babes,' said

Tom, noticing her slightly pained expression and stomach-touching.

'No, I'm not hungry,' said Kate, furrowing her brow. 'Hang on a sec – I'll be right back.'

Tom and Archie watched as Kate disappeared down the hallway, past reception and ran up to Kevin and a dishevelled Seamus.

Panting – because even though she looked trim, she was still a total stranger to exercise and fitness was, to her, a dirty word – she said:

'Seamus! Help!'

Seamus, who was trying his best to disentangle himself from a bird's nest of wires and cables that had virtually wrapped him up like a mummy, glanced up. He did a classic double-take when he saw the look of consternation on Kate's face and tried to wriggle free of his cable cocoon. But it was useless – resistance was futile.

'Stop jiggling about,' laughed Kevin , 'you're only making it tighter!'

Tamsin giggled and even Kate wanted to chuckle – he did look ridiculous like that – how did he get himself into such ludicrous scrapes?

'Um,' mumbled Seamus when he noticed everyone in the office laughing at him. 'I'm a bit tied up at the moment. Would you like to make an appointment and I can speak with you later?'

Kate gently pushed Kevin out of the way and wrapped her arm around Seamus' back. She urged him to move forward, as she slowly shuffled him away from their colleagues' pricked up ears.

'You have GOT to help me get back home...I mean, get me some info for my new mag,' Kate whispered to Seamus out of the side of her mouth.

Seamus jumped like a kangaroo (though not quite as effectively or gracefully) by her side, trying to keep up with her.

'Are you bibbling about time travel again?' he managed to say, even though the wires were getting quite tight around his chest and he was hopping about like a giant mouse stuck in a lasso.

'Yes,' Kate looked over her shoulder and beamed at Tamsin and Kevin who were standing there gormlessly watching Hop-A-Long Seamus make a total tit out of himself. Again.

'I've done some research for you already,' said Seamus, getting breathless. 'And I think I know how it works. It definitely is possible –'

'I know!' squeaked Kate. 'So...shall we meet somewhere? So you can tell me all about it and I can get my pitch straight, promise the great gift of time travel for one lucky reader on our cover every month?'

'Yeah, OK,' said Seamus, a tad wheezily. 'But what about your side of the bargain? When are you going to help me out with clothes? And tell me how to talk to women?'

Kate had forgotten all about that.

'Let's combine the two. We'll go shopping next Saturday. How about that?'

'Next Saturday?' he said, scanning the inside of

his eyelids as if that's where he'd stuck his daily planner. 'The twenty-second?'

'Yep,' said Kate, glancing at Tom and Archie who were standing at The Lift craning their necks to see what she was up to.

'It's a date!' said Seamus, brightening up. 'Of sorts...um...we'll need to get an early start, though – it's Spain v England in the afternoon. Kick off's at three.'

'It's a deal,' said Kate, grabbing some scissors off a nearby desk and snipping Seamus out of his flexy prison and on towards freedom. She darted away from his side and cantered, triumphant, back to The Lift.

'Super Gran,' grinned Archie as suddenly The Lift pinged, the doors opened and all three of them nearly snapped their necks in their haste to get into it.

20

Looking around the restaurant, Kate couldn't help but feel completely out of place.

All the other women there, as far as she could see, were outrageously beautiful, statuesque models and/or painfully, achingly cool, fascinating artists.

And all the men completely ignored her. Now this, as a dishevelled, harried mother-of-three, she was used to. But surely it hadn't been like this when she was 26 the first time around...

It was the kind of do she'd been dreaming about being invited to ever since she left the media whirl way back when – the kind of thing she was used to and thought nothing of once upon a time. But now, in a cruel twist of irony, she found herself wishing she was at home.

I mean, she said to herself, it's all well and good looking fabulous and having sparkling, witty conversations with your intellectual equals, but what's wrong with teaching a toddler to talk? Sure, you babble on endlessly about fire engines and *Dora the Explorer*, granted – but is there anything inherently *bad* about that? *Au contraire*, she said to herself in her best French accent, it's a far, far better thing to do than ponce about getting pissed on expensive bubbly and braying to anyone who'll listen about how wonderful you are, that's for sure.

Yep, youth is definitely wasted on the young, she snorted into her mini bottle of Moet, blowing extra bubbles with the straw.

She never thought she'd hear herself say it, but as she felt her tummy, she told herself that not only was she missing the kids and home, she was actually missing the flabby, wobbly bits of her old body. Because at least you knew where you were with a stomach you had to tuck into your knickers and cellulite that no longer surprised you.

And the pressure on these youngsters! Not only did they have to *look* great all the time, flaunting their flawless skin and tight flesh, but they had to constantly *act* perky, too. What, in all honesty, could possibly be *wrong* with slobbing out in front of the telly in hideously unflattering, threadbare-at-the-thighs leggings?

Kate smiled at the thought and felt a deep yearning, a longing for the sense of freedom, comfort and joy that only an oversized fleece can give.

But it was more than that – more than simply the sartorial expression of contentment that she missed – it was the easy relaxing of tension: the tension to perform like a monkey, to be cute and smart and popular, all the while keeping your tum in trim and being a contender for Rear of the Year contests.

That was it, Kate thought – that was what she'd been searching for back in 1996 - that elusive feeling you get when you know you're happy and you don't have to try so hard anymore. The feeling you get when you're *home*.

No wonder she hadn't felt it yet – she was as far

away from home as it was possible to be, at Quo Vadis with all the bright young things of the day. And to top it all off, all she could think about was ironing and burnt porridge and an oven that was a million light years away from cleaning itself.

She felt like a mousey housewife at her ebullient husband's work do; a perplexed, childless adult at a kid's party - a veritable fish out of water.

She scanned the room and saw Tom, who'd pretty much deserted her the minute they'd arrived. She watched him (in between toilet trips so frequent, Kate almost started to worry for his prostate), as he busied himself schmoozing his way around the room, eventually settling on a slightly less-than-delighted looking Damien Hirst.

Tom was talking ten to the dozen and laughing uproariously at yet another of his own jokes. Damien held his glass aloft in the direction of the waiters as if to say: 'More here, please. QUICK!'

Kate felt dreadfully alone.

She marched purposely, pretending she was confident, to the bar and tried to look unfazed, as though she came to these sorts of shindigs all the time and found them, quite frankly, to be a bit of a *bore*.

Her heart leapt when she spotted Archie near the windows. She was almost about to join him when she clocked that he was flanked by an Amazonian model on one side and Vic Reeves rubbing his thighs at said model on the other.

Kate thought better of it and turned round to face

the barman.

'Another one of these, please,' she said to him who, in turn, nodded to a tray further down the end of the bar.

Of course, you silly moo! You don't have to order or pay for drinks at events like this!

Embarrassed by her gaffe – even though no one had noticed – she sheepishly wandered towards the tray.

She picked up a mini bottle of Moet, adjusted the straw, took a sip and furtively earwigged on the conversation going on next to her.

A tall woman, with slitty eyes and a wonky mouth when she laughed was holding forth about her latest triumph.

Kate looked closer and realised it was Tracey Emin, the notorious artist who was once lauded as the spokesperson for a generation of disenfranchised women.

Kate forgot herself and muscled her way in to the cosy chat.

'Yeah,' said Tracey, who couldn't have sounded more bored. 'Fourteen days, holed up in a studio in Stockholm, alone except for paint and canvases, naked and being filmed.'

'Wow,' muttered Kate, as the other two women left, leaving just Tracey and Kate to talk.

'I wanted to feel real,' Tracey said. 'And break the painter's block that had hounded me for six years.'

'That's really interesting,' said Kate.

'I know,' said Tracey flatly, looking over Kate's head and stepping up on tippy-toes in an effort to search the room for someone better to talk to. 'It worked, of course, and I made some great art. But now I need something fantastic again. Inspiration can be so hard to come by.'

'Don't I know it,' laughed Kate. 'You should try finding the inspiration to keep a house clean and tidy when you get no help, no thanks, no appreciation, not even any acknowledgement for it – and not even a sniff of any money for it! Now *that's* an art...'

Tracey glanced down at Kate and looked away quickly, as though Kate was making some annoying sound, like a mosquito, and was best ignored.

'Well,' said Kate nervously. 'Speaking of, I'd better make a move, get home soon. Flats don't clean themselves, do they? And as for my bedroom, the bed's unmade, there's dirty knickers everywhere –'

'What did you say?' Tracey's eyes bored into Kate's fiercely.

'Um, nothing, I -,' Kate backed away from the artist's intense gaze. 'I'm just saying my room's a mess and I haven't made my bed in, God, *years* and –'

Tracey dropped her cigarette into her glass and grabbed Kate by the shoulders.

'Go on,' Tracey rasped, blowing smoke in Kate's face.

'About what?' Kate said, getting a little frightened now.

'Your bed.'

‘I dunno,’ Kate shook off Tracey’s bony hands as the penny dropped. ‘It’s just a total mess – the physical reflection of me and where my mind’s mostly at, I suppose. I mean, the sheets are dirty, the duvet’s a disgrace, and the floor next to it, with all the used tissues, empty bottles of booze, the diaries telling a thousand tales of woe and heartbreak...’

‘Yes, yes, YES!’ screamed Tracey, putting her arm around Kate and steering her towards the Ladies. ‘Tell me more, tell me more!’

Kate proceeded to describe her bedroom in West Hampstead, giving Tracey Emin the idea that was to send her skyrocketing into the stratosphere of the world’s truly great artists.

Which gave Kate a massive injection of confidence. After all, she was old enough to be the mother – or, at least, the older auntie or big sister - to most of the people at this party – why should she feel so self-conscious and shy?

Talking to Tracey had given Kate a spectacular buzz. Much better than the one that made Tom disappear into the Gents time and time again, only to come out with his arms draped all over Liam Gallagher, football lout/best-male-mates style.

‘Hey, hey hey!’ Tom made a bee-line for Kate and Tracey when his bleary, but furiously flickering eyes finally landed on them. ‘I see you’ve met my girlfriend –’

Girlfriend? *Girlfriend?* Who was Tom talking about? The word sounded so weird to Kate, she was momentarily disorientated.

It was such a young and flirty and carefree word – like the kind of word you'd use for someone you went camping with in France for the summer. The kind of word you'd use for someone who had super-long legs and wore cut-off jeans - Daisy Dukes if you will – who rode a big, old fashioned unwieldy bike and laughed a lot and had straight, long, fringe-less hair, highlighted by the sun and their light disposition.

But Tom was referring to Kate. This she knew because he planted a big, wet, stumbly kiss on her mouth.

'Yeah, yeah,' said Tracey, sparking up and drawing deeply back on a filterless cigarette. 'But I gotta run, Hon. Thanks for the, um, chat, um...'

'Kate,' Kate reminded Tracey of her name. Not that she'd ever asked her, mind.

'Kay, right! Laters, then!' Tracey kissed Kate on both cheeks, smiled at Tom and Liam and positively lurched into the arms of Medea who was approaching their little circle.

'Meds, I'd love to talk, but I've got to go – when the muse strikes and all...!'

And off she went, scurrying down the stairs in a bid to make it back to her studio before the idea of showing Tracey's personal history and womanhood's universal pain and slovenliness in the shape of her unmade bed deserted her.

'Ah!' said Tom, reeling around to welcome Medea into the fold with outstretched arms. 'Medea, *my de-*

ah!'

Medea smiled and kissed an effusive Tom on both cheeks, then did the same to Kate.

'Oi, oi!' piped up Liam. 'Forgetting someone?'

Medea smiled beatifically and turned to face Tom.

'I don't believe you've met Liam?' Tom said. 'Liam Gallagher, lead singer of phenomenally successful popular modern rock band Oasis. Have you heard of them?'

'Yes,' said Medea. 'Of course I have. I didn't know you were an art fan, Liam. What do you think of the artists here today?'

'Fookin' puffs, the lot of 'em,' said Liam, slowly half-running on the spot, like he was limbering up and about to go on the pitch. ''Cept that Hirst bloke, he's all right. I'm mad for 'im, me.'

'Ooh!' said Kate. 'Which reminds me. Now, Liam, remember the last time we met, you said you were mad for *me*? Remember saying I was gorgeous and you'd do anything for me?'

Which prompted Tom and Liam to grab hold of each other by the shoulders and sing along with *You're Gorgeous*, the Babybird song which was playing quietly in the background.

Kate was on a roll. She tried to reach up to Liam's shoulder to grab a hold of him, so he couldn't get away from her and her cunning plan. But she needn't have bothered - Liam ably assisted her by sitting down on a chair at a nearby table and pulling her onto his lap.

'Woah, I say!' said a shocked and inexplicably

aristocratic-sounding Tom.

'It's OK,' said Kate, relishing the fact that for once she could sit on a man's knee and not worry that she was going to make his legs buckle under her weight. 'It's work, remember?'

Tom shuffled about a bit until Medea slid her arm through his and walked him over to another table, suggesting they discuss in detail her first column for *LASHED*.

'So here it is,' Kate said soberly, her knees together, ankles crossed and hands in her lap as she looked down on Liam. 'I will go out with you – wherever you want – if you do me this one small, teensy little favour.'

'I said I'd do anything,' he stared up at her.

Kate had to fight the urge to tickle him behind the ear like one might do to a Labrador puppy and let her gaze linger on his striking bluey-green eyes a little too long.

Misreading the signs of affection for lust, Liam stretched his neck up and moved in for the kill, his right hand gently pushing the back of her head down so that their lips could meet.

Kate jumped up.

'Uh-ah-ah,' she said, wagging her finger at him and keeping her cool admirably. 'Favour first.'

Liam, who looked for a micro-second like he was going to lose his famous temper, let a grin wrap itself around his lips and pulled Kate back down onto his lap.

'I only wanted to kiss your cheek,' he said.

So it was Kate who'd misread the signs! She didn't know whether to feel insulted or relieved, so she decided to ignore it and continue on her quest.

'See your friends, Damon and Alex from Blur over there?' Kate pointed at Liam's main rivals who were arguing about something, gesticulating wildly in front of a glass case containing a dead cow.

'Chelsea-loving, mockney art school ponces –'

'That's right,' Kate cut him off before he got too het up. 'I want you and your brother, Noel, to dress up in boxers' satin shorts and tops and get into the ring with them –'

'The only fookin' rings I'm gonna get into–'

'Here's the deal,' Kate sighed, wanting to wrap this up fast. All the smoke was making her dizzy and although he was undeniably good looking, Liam was so young, he simply wasn't her type anymore. 'You and Noel make friends with Damon and Alex in a mock boxing match. *Mad Fer It!*, everybody's favourite teen mag, will be there to interview you all about your rules of friendship and how sometimes falling out can be the best thing to bring mates back together.'

Liam sniffed loudly and coughed. He stared at Damon and Alex through his mauve-coloured John Lennon glasses and stroked his stubble.

Kate got up, imagining this was his lesser-spotted pensive look. And even though the thick, swirling smoke of a million cigarettes was making it hard for her to breathe, let alone see, she could tell that he was considering her proposition seriously.

'You do that for me and I'll do whatever you want – within reason, of course – for you.'

Kate couldn't quite believe that Liam seemed to have fixated on her – short, average, girl-next-door her, when he could have all the ridiculously stunning women in the world he wanted. It didn't make sense to her. Nor did it appear to make any sense to a rather miffed-looking Patsy Kensit who was striding over towards them.

Sensing she might never get the chance again, Kate dared to derail his train of thought slightly and ask him another question.

'Liam, why are you so interested in me?' she said quickly, looking fearfully over her shoulder at a fast-approaching Patsy.

'I like you, that's all,' he smiled softly.

Kate tilted her head to one side and was thinking how adorable he was, really, like George and Decko when they were five – all rambunctious and lively – but sweet and loving and ready to smother their mother in kisses at a moment's notice, when Liam spoke again.

'You're different. Wise. You remind me of my mother, I suppose – strong and smart. Not in a sick way or nothing – I love my mum. And there's something of her in you, I think. Is that an awful thing to say?' he said looking more vulnerable than Kate could ever have imagined.

‘No!’ she squealed. ‘It’s the finest compliment you could ever give a woman, actually. Because, well, you think your mum’s amazing and wonderful, right?’

‘I’ll kill anyone who says different,’ he said, squaring his shoulders back and jutting his chin out.

‘Your mum must be so proud,’ Kate said, just in time to see a woman’s hand swoop down and softly slap Liam’s cheek.

‘You flirt!’ Patsy shrieked with a half-laugh, as though she was trying to show everyone that she didn’t really mind. ‘You’re *terrible*!’

Kate leapt up and stood, suddenly dwarfed, next to Patsy. Liam looked up at Patsy, then down at Kate. Up to Patsy, down to Kate. Patsy, Kate, Patsy, Kate.

Patsy folded her arms across her chest and pursed her lips. Kate put her hands on her hips, to a) prove to herself that they were still virtually non-existent, despite how old she was feeling and b) to adopt a particularly motherly pose as part of her persuasion tactics.

‘I’m a dab hand with a roast,’ cooed Kate. ‘And my Yorkshire puds are second to none...’

‘I’ll do it!’ Liam said, slamming his hands down on the chair’s arms and hauling himself up out of his sitting position. ‘If Our Kid’s still talking to me, I’ll sort it. Now, let’s fookin’ celebrate!’

Patsy unfolded her arms and dragged his head down to her breast, laughing.

‘He’s like a big kid, isn’t he?’ she addressed Kate.

‘Yeah,’ Kate laughed, relieved things hadn’t

descended into an unseemly cat fight and Liam had actually agreed to do her bidding.

It took a while to sink in, because she couldn't quite believe that the infamous Battle of Britpop would be fought and won in the pages of *Mad Fer It!* and everyone would be friends again, not fierce rivals wishing AIDS and death upon each other.

Archie was going to fall off his chair when he heard about this! And all because Kate reminded Liam of his mum. HA!

Now all she needed to do was get Damon and Alex in on the story and she could go home, a good night's work done and dusted.

Leaving Liam and Patsy to it, Kate headed for Tom and Medea who were engaged in a deep and no doubt meaningful conversation with Damon and Alex in front of a badger and a hedgehog suspended in a vitrine case full of formaldehyde.

'...more for the nursery, I think – you know, cute, cuddly little animals to keep the baby company at night,' Alex was saying.

'Or to scare the life out of the poor little blighter,' Damon replied.

'In my experience,' Kate joined in, 'babies don't ever sleep, no matter what you do. So whether you opt for stuffed animals, musical mobiles or even a dead, dissected hamster in a glass cage, you can forget about sleep for approximately five years, give or take a day or two for when your little one's sick and you resort to MediSed in a last ditch attempt to save your sanity!'

She reached into their little circle and grabbed a mini vegetarian pizza off a tray, popped it into her mouth and grinned at the taken aback foursome.

'What do you mean, "in your experience"?' asked Tom.

'Do you have younger brothers or sisters?' piped up Medea. 'Did your mother have a menopause baby or something?'

Suddenly, Kate felt the confidence drain out of her and she wondered why on earth she had opened up her big mouth.

Still, she reasoned with herself, she had to break into their convo somehow – and this was as good a way as any, considering she now had their full and undivided attention.

'Ah, no, my,' this thinking on her feet, endlessly trying to cover her tracks was really starting to get on her nerves. She couldn't take much more, desperately trying to remember every little lie she came out with. 'My, um, auntie is a midwife and she always says it's futile to think that anything you do has an effect on whether a baby sleeps or not. She says they have minds of their own and will sleep when they want to and not a moment before.'

Damon and Alex turned back to look at the badger/hedgehog ensemble, as did Medea and Tom.

Kate's innate good sense told her she'd lost her audience. How was she going to ask the Blur boys to do the boxing ring thing? And how on earth was she going to convince them to say yes?

'Babes, can I have a quick word?' she jerked her head towards a corner of the room as she tapped Tom on his shoulder.

'All right, love,' said Tom with a wink. 'If it can't wait. And I'm pretty sure it can't...'

They moved over to a quieter corner and Tom put his arms around Kate's neck, puckering up in preparation for a super-smooch.

'Hang on, hang on,' said Kate, turning her cheek to him and pushing his chest away with her palms. 'I've got a huge favour to ask first.'

'OK – but make it quick,' gasped Tom.

'OK, well,' Kate took a deep breath. 'I want you to ask Damon and Alex Blur –'

'That's not their last names, you know,' Tom scoffed.

'I know – but that's what *Mad Fer It!* calls them – and I want – no, I *need* you to ask them to agree to be in a photo shoot with Liam and Noel –'

'Oasis?' he smirked.

'No, Liam and Noel *Gallagher*, in a boxing ring in satin shorts and tops, burying the hatchet and talking to the features team about mates and falling out and making up again.'

Kate took a noisy, wheezy breath in, her lungs desperate for air.

Tom, however, just stared at her.

After a few seconds – which must have seemed like hours to Tom and his addled brain – he started to laugh.

'That's the stupidest thing I've ever heard!' He slapped his knee, cowboy-style for added emphasis. 'Why didn't I think of it?'

Tom suddenly went all serious and pulled Kate in close to whisper in her ear.

'I will ask them for you, if the *LASHED* team are allowed to be at the shoot, too, and get their own adult, blokey take on the proceedings.'

'Can't see why not,' said Kate. 'Two birds, one stone – it's a yes from me!'

'*And...*' Tom got a glint in his eye. 'you promise to come home with me soon and let me have my wicked way with you. Let's christen our new pad in fine style.'

Kate giggled and nodded a rather effusive 'yes' that took her a bit by surprise.

God, she thought. All this promising favours of a gastronomic or sexual kind just to get a magazine out of trouble? Talk about dedication to the cause – it gave a whole new meaning to the phrase *job satisfaction.*

Still, she figured she might as well do what she'd set out to do – feel young, free and easy again – and sleep with her old boyfriend who had been, quite literally, the man of her dreams.

Medea and Kate made small talk while Tom, Damon and Alex went off somewhere 'for a private, little chat' Tom called it, as he tapped his nose in a nudge, nudge, wink, wink kind of a way.

When they returned, all three of them had contracted a nasty case of the sniffles.

'It's that bloody cold room where Damien stores

his carcasses,' smiled Alex. 'You just go to see an installation and pow! You're struck down with the lurgy!'

'Yes, but is it art?' Damon asked as he stroked his chin.

*

'So?' Kate linked arms with Tom as they weaved their way through Soho to get to Tottenham Court Road tube station.

'So...' Tom teased her, withholding the vital information. 'They're in!'

'They are?'

'Yup!'

'Did they take much convincing?' she asked.

'Nothing I couldn't handle,' Tom answered, proudly straightening up his Ben Sherman button-down collar. 'Actually, they were like putty in my hands. Said they were really looking forward to it.'

'That's amazing!' said Kate, truly astounded. 'I'd better organise it as soon as possible – best not give any of them the time to change their minds and pull out.'

'Bet that's never happened to you before,' Tom said, a tad creepily.

Kate bit her lip. She couldn't bring herself to even laugh nervously at his comment - she was too busy being wracked with guilt over wilfully being unfaithful to 2014 Seamus who, for all she knew, had been electrocuted on the golf course in that torrential storm.

Oh God, oh God, oh. My. GOD!

This was it, she thought to herself as they snuggled up close together on the packed train home. She was finally going to get the chance to relive the best sex of her life. With the best lover she'd ever had. The best *boyfriend* she'd ever had. The one she probably should have married. Or, at least, the one she wished she'd had the opportunity to turn down before he ran off with that Tamsin at her birthday party.

Not that she felt as strongly about that as she used to. Now, having seen both him and Seamus as their younger selves, she could see why she ended up with Seamus after all. Because now, with her 44-year-old eyes, she was no longer seduced by the trappings of wealth and power and proximity to celebrity – this time in 1996, she could see what really mattered, what foundation a solid relationship should really be built on: shared, common interests, a good sense of humour and a top drawer full of mobile phone chargers and allen keys.

Tom was stroking Kate's back as she leant into him, his back against the glass, partitioning the seats from the standing area. Kate closed her eyes and tried to take it all in: she knew Georgia would be asking for all the gory details later – and she also wanted to make sure she remembered everything for posterity – correctly and exactly as it was, this time – completely without any rose-coloured glasses.

His shirt smelled of beer and cigarettes, but underneath that, was his signature scent – some expensive eau de cologne Kate could never remember the name of – and it was making her giddy.

'Mmm,' she hummed, unable to help herself or wipe the smile off her face.

He didn't hear her over the din of the train rumbling along the rails, but he did feel the vibrations in her chest and moved his hand to the back of her head. He stroked her hair like it was the ear of a thoroughbred Afghan hound and she wondered whether her Jennifer Aniston cut would weather the storm of rampant, wanton, most probably *really dirty* sex with Tom.

When they hit the chilly night air, coming up out of Notting Hill Gate Underground station, Kate felt light-headed, as though *she* was the one who'd been making surreptitious trips to the loos all evening.

'You don't know how long I've waited for this, Tom,' she said, rubbing her cheek against the scratchy, woollen sleeve of his coat as they walked.

'Oh, I know, Babes,' he said. 'The things I'm going to do to you when I get you home...A-ha! And here we are!'

Tom unlocked the front door to the narrowest, most low-ceilinged hallway Kate had ever seen. It was like something out of *Alice In Wonderland.*

'Bit poky, this front bit, sorry,' Tom yawned as he apologised.

'No, no – it's great!' Kate lied. 'It's chic, *bijou* even.'

That's exactly what I said when I first saw it,' Tom said, looking at Kate with a gleam in his eye she'd long forgotten.

'Come 'ere,' he growled, pushing her up against the wall and kissing her. She felt little sparklers begin to fizz and pop somewhere deep down at her very core and she closed her eyes again, letting the moment take her over.

'Mmmm,' Tom was the first to break away from their hot and hasty embrace. 'But wait, there's more! Wanna see the rest?'

He grabbed her hand and led her up the stairwell so slim, she was glad she wasn't carrying any excess poundage. When they walked round the bend and got to the top of the stairs, he pushed open the front door to their flat.

'Et voila!' he said.

'Wow,' she replied. 'When have you found the time to do all this?'

The walls were covered in not paint, not wallpaper, but Elmo-from-*Sesame-Street* red fur.

Kate's mouth couldn't help but turn down at the corners as her eyes drank in the ambience of the room. After careful consideration lasting at least three seconds, she concluded it was a tribute to Playboy mansion, Hugh Hefner-style, 70s sex. And she didn't mean sex in your 70s.

'One of the girls at work – Tamsin or something – she helped me,' he said, kicking off his desert boots and guiding her into the bedroom.

'And now, for the *piece de resistance*,' he said, making Kate bristle and wonder why he was saying so much in French in his corny accent.

A big, round, purple crushed velvet waterbed took pride of place in the centre of the room. Tom flopped onto it and lay on his back, his body undulating and bobbing about like a sailboat in slightly choppy waves.

'What do you think?' he said, staring at the ceiling.

Kate's eyes followed his and she gasped when she saw what was blu-tacked up there – poster overlapping poster of England players. It was like walking into George's room, a little boy's safe haven, the walls covered with portraits of his footballing heroes.

Kate kicked off her shoes and tried to stay in the mood, even though seeing those pictures alerted her to the fact that this coupling was fifty shades of wrong.

She slid on the velvet towards Tom and told him she loved what he'd done with the place.

'Yeah, it's great, isn't it? Especially now that Euro '96 is on. I can easily change my Fantasy Football team line-up with a new pic and a quick flick of the old sticky tape, cos the lads at *Back of The Net!* magazine always slip me a complimentary copy of their latest poster mags and...'

Tom was now even *sounding* like a ten-year-old boy, all gushy and over-excited about... *football*.

The more Tom burbled on, the more Kate realised she couldn't go through with it. She just couldn't sleep with this man-child, this immature boy who'd rather talk about the beautiful game than his beautiful girlfriend.

As he wittered their valuable foreplay time away, Kate grappled with her memory as she tried to locate, in the songwords part of her brain, the lyrics to *Greetings To The New Brunette*, a particularly apt Billy Bragg song that came to her mind. She furrowed her brow as she tried to remember the lines about lying back and thinking of England, but not having a clue who was in the team. Or something like that, anyway. The tune was lost to her years ago, she realised, the second she tried to hum it.

But back to Tom, she shook her head in irritation. Should she or shouldn't she?

Kate thought hard, looking up to the football-covered ceiling for inspiration and biting the inside of her right cheek.

But as soon as she'd made up her mind to abort her mission, she became aware of a small grunting noise that was getting louder and louder.

'Tom?' she said, looking around the room wide-eyed, expecting to see a snuffling mouse or family of rats any minute. 'Tom?'

When she turned to look at him, to nudge him into action, she noticed he wasn't moving.

'Tom?' she said again, grabbing a hold of the arm nearest her and shaking it. 'Tom? *TOM!*'

Kate sat bolt upright. What was she going to do? Was he dead? Bloody hell! How could he...well, God knows he'd probably snorted the GDP of a small South American country up his nose in the past couple of hours, so...

This was no time for moral judgements or amateur forensic science, she scolded herself. But what was it time for then?

She knelt beside him and fumbled around trying to hold up his arm, feeling for a pulse on his limp wrist.

'Come on, Tom,' she said through clenched teeth. 'Come ON! Breathe will you?'

She bent down and put her ear to his mouth, not caring that her Rachel hairdo was falling all over the place and getting badly out of shape.

Nothing. She heard not a sound.

Until, suddenly, like someone coming to the surface of water after diving in too deep and running out of breath, a gasping, rasping 'Nyeurrrrgh!' came from the corpse.

Kate was catapulted back by fear, falling off the bed and bumping her head against the mirrored built-in wardrobe. Definitely *not* the spot she'd imagined her head to be banging against in the bedroom tonight, she thought, as she rubbed her sore head and winced.

'What's wrong with you, Gazza?' squeaked a frightened-sounding Tom. 'Hoof it down the pitch! Go on, my son!'

Tom was alive! He'd come back to life!

'Alan? Is that you, Mr Shearer?' Tom said, even more bewildered this time.

'No, it most certainly is not,' said Kate, standing up and walking towards him. 'And what the hell do you think you're doing, passing out on me like that? You gave me the fright of my life!'

But Tom simply shut his eyes, fell back on the bed, turned to the side away from Kate, curled his knees up to his chest, stuck his thumb in his mouth and proceeded to sleep like a baby.

Or, more accurately, sleep like a heavily-intoxicated man, if what Kate's midwife auntie said was true.

21

Kate woke with a start at 5:30 the next morning. She felt extreme discombobulation as she looked around her and saw absolutely nothing even remotely familiar.

Had she looked up to the ceiling, of course, she would have been instantly reminded of George and Decko's walls at home, but you never think to look up, really, do you?

Tom was snoring his head off next to her and she cursed her body clock that was still sometimes running on Baby Jane time.

She smiled as an image of a giggling Baby Jane spread over the screen in her mind, and she wondered, for the umpteenth time, who she'd inherited her soft but crazily static, spiky baby hair from. Seamus and Kate often laughed about that shock of hair and how it made their girl look like a white, one-year-old, blonde Don King.

Speaking (to herself) of mega-rich boxing promoters, she congratulated herself on the coup of the century – if it all came off and Liam et al could all make up and be friends, then she really would have changed history – saved a magazine, proved to Archie that she still had what it took, helped the silly little boys grow up...

Tom grunted and spluttered like he was choking and then, as quickly as it had begun, his breathing settled down again into the deep, guttural snore that meant he was, to carry on a theme, out for the count.

Totally KO'd.

So much for the amazing sex with Tom she was sure she was going to have last might. Still, she consoled herself, maybe it just wasn't meant to be. Obviously, Fate had a different idea about what her trip back in time was all about.

Which was...*what*, exactly?

Clearly it wasn't about hooking up with her old flame and igniting the bed again, so hot were their sex sessions, so legendary in her memory.

But was it really about being any good at her old job? Saving Georgia from certain disaster? Having a flat belly?

Had she been sent back to 1996 to ruin Steve's life? She hadn't heard from him for nearly a week now – where *had* he gone?

The old Travis song sprang into her mind and she sang the wrong words, slightly out of time and tune, to herself for a few seconds.

'Driftwood,' she said out loud, shaking her head sadly. Tom didn't stir.

Kate threw back the light duvet and sat up. She was still wearing her khaki combats (they were clean on yesterday) and her red and white crop top faux football shirt. She adjusted the strap of her M&S bra and tried to make the most of that moment, knowing that once she'd had all the kids, she'd never be able to be an off the peg bra girl again. She looked down and admired her medium-sized chest, proud of its perkiness.

And then she sighed. She hadn't thought she'd ever get sick of seeing herself slim and youthful, but to be honest, it wasn't all it was cracked up to be.

She rubbed her belly, which, in her sitting position only had about three half-centimetre thick folds on it and realised, for the very first time in her life, that she was a bit of a walking cliché.

For she'd often read about women who said they loved their caesarean scars and their flabby, stretch-marked stomachs, because they were a constant reminder of their beautiful babies, their wonderful kids, their fantastic families.

And this was how Kate felt right at this moment – her flat, taut tummy meant she didn't have George or Decko or the adorable Baby Jane. And her faithful, loving (if not a tad badly-dressed and golf-obsessed) husband, who could always make her feel better by making her laugh was nowhere to be seen, either.

With not so much as a by your leave, she jumped out of bed, hopped around the disgusting fur-covered bedroom as she pulled on her high heeled trainers, threw her mini leather backpack on and bolted for the front door.

She couldn't wait for Seamus to pfaff about, getting tangled in wires and dropping modems on his feet in his attempts to help her find a way back – as a mother and a wife in real time, she knew that if you wanted to get something done – and get it done properly – you had to do it yourself.

Surely, she reasoned with herself, there'd be some

reference books at work – or maybe in the archives of the TV listings mag, *Your Viewing Pleasure,* they'd have some info on Dr Who telling us how he got about in different time/space continuums. Or Catweazle! Now, just how did *he* get transported through time from the middle ages to the early 1970s?

And there must be *something* about time travel on the internet by now – it wasn't *that* fledgling a thing.

As she skipped down the stairs, two-at-a-time, she did her best to ignore the intense gnawing emptiness that was threatening to eat her up from the inside. It was like full-on period pains – or worse, *contractions* – and she felt instinctively that something was changing, the sands were shifting.

Then again, maybe it was just her sciatica rearing its ugly head.

She was starting to feel a little confused. She couldn't quite believe it herself, but could it be that she, the nostalgia nut, the has-been queen had perhaps had enough of the past now? She couldn't help but think that in comparison to what she had back in 2014, with all its problems, dysfunctionality and hectic mess, being nearly 27 years old in 1996, being free, single and unencumbered by anyone or anything, going out and drinking all the time was, quite frankly, a lot more dull than she'd remembered.

At the bottom of the stairs, she tried to force her arms into the sleeves of her tight denim jacket, but they just wouldn't go all the way, only up to her elbow. Kate quickly tore the jacket off and inspected her arms.

Were they a tad...*fleshier* than they were yesterday?

She told herself there was no time to worry about that now and in that instant she was overwhelmed by a profound sense of urgency. She took off out of the flat, ran into the street and fled towards Notting Hill Gate tube.

But in her speed to catch the train out of there, to anywhere, somehow the heel of her right trainer got caught between two paving stones and she tumbled down to the ground, landing on her bony bum.

Bayswater Road was reasonably packed now, with workers off to start their days early and rich trustafarians returning home from their nights out, but not one person stopped to help her. In fact, one or two men in Burberry trench coats actually trod purposefully on the straps of her backpack as they stomped past.

'Typical,' she said out loud. London was not famous for its friendly, helpful citizens, so she pulled herself up and, rubbing her hip and the small of her back, just like she did after carrying Baby Jane for too long, and hobbled down into the underground.

Sitting on the train to Tottenham Court Road, she thought of her *family of origin*, as Georgia would call it – Steve, Paris and Blue - and wondered what the hell was happening to them. She wished she had her mobile on her now, so she could call them, rally the troops and get them all together. Because then, surely, they'd all be happy again, wouldn't they?

Lost in her own inner world, she beamed at the

mental picture of everyone clustered around the Christmas tree when she was a kid. Like a human ViewMaster, she flicked over to the next Clinton's card, chocolate box image of Blue, Paris, Steve and Kate all sitting at the dinner table, mugging for and raising their glasses to the camera, their fabulous Sunday lunch spread out as though Nigella Lawson herself had set it up.

She felt all warm and gooey inside, like the liquid centre of a Lindt Lindor ball.

'I mean,' she mumbled, 'what can make you happier than family?'

'Chocolate,' said the woman sitting opposite her with a smile.

'Cider,' piped up a Worzel Gummidge, trampy-looking guy, propping up the glass partition.

'Football,' chorused a boy and a girl sitting down in their posh school uniforms, while their daddy hung on the strap above them.

Now that's more like it, Kate thought – that's the sort of community, spirit of the blitz Londoners were supposed to pull out of the bag in times of trouble. She couldn't get the surprised look off her face and felt compelled to join in.

'Actually, sleep – *lots of sleep* - would be my number one essential item for guaranteed happiness,' she smiled.

'Health,' a hoarse old man said. 'You've got nothing if you haven't got your health.'

Everyone nodded.

'What about love?' a middle-aged Caribbean woman asked.

'Nah - money,' a bespectacled, 30-something City-type said matter-of-factly.

'Time,' the old lady sitting next to Kate said in a husky, barely audible voice as she touched her arm. 'More time.'

And everyone fell silent.

*

It was weird getting to PGT&B so early. For a start, she didn't have to wait long for The Lift at all – within five seconds, she heard the PING! and stepped in to the mirrored box.

As per usual, she studied her face in the mirrors as she was carried up to the third floor.

It all looked pretty much the same as it did the day before and the day before and the day before *that* – but Kate was sure she could see an ever-so-slight sag around her jawline. No one else would be able to notice – except maybe Georgia – but there was definitely some fall going on there.

'Nah, couldn't be,' she said chirpily and turned away.

As she limped into the empty office, rubbing her still-sore bum, and wondering whether she would have to have a hip replacement operation when she got back to 2014, it suddenly struck her that it was a week and a half until her birthday.

In just over a week, she would be turning 27. Or, if she made it out of 1996 before then, 45. She wanted it to be the latter. *Desperately*.

She picked up her speed and lop-sidedly trotted up to her desk. When she pulled her chair out, plonked herself in it and wheeled herself up to the edge of her desk, she let out an eardrum-bursting shriek.

She leapt out of her seat and stumbled backwards towards Lucy's reception desk, saying: 'Don't hurt me, you stay, I'll go. Please don't hurt me!'

As the vaguely familiar figure emerged from under her desk, drawing itself up to its full, dishevelled height, she brought her forearm up to her eyes, like a 1950s schlock film actress, shielding her beautiful face and delicate, porcelain skin from some gruesome monster.

She held her breath for what seemed like ages until it spoke, this creature from the black lagoon (the mysterious space, home to all manner of crumbs, unidentifiable food stuffs, spilled fizzy drinks and God knows what else under her desk).

'Calm down, calm down,' it croaked and then cleared its throat. 'It's only me!'

'Steve!' Kate yowled, bringing her arm down as soon as she heard his voice. 'What? How? Why?'

'You forgot where and when,' he yawned, stretching his balled fists towards the ceiling and exposing his hairy tummy. 'Us journalists must always remember those five crucial questions.'

'What do you mean, "*us journalists*"? And what the *hell* are you doing here?' Kate sounded like her old self more and more – and when she said this last part, she placed her hands on her hips, tapping the toes of her right extended foot as if she were wearing a pinny and telling her boys off for traipsing mud through the house or something.

'I've been working as a journo - doing some work for your boyfriend, as it happens,' said Steve. 'He said he saw something in me, some potential that Sunday lunch at Mum and Dad's and told me to come and see him the next day. I've been working here ever since.'

'Really? He never said anything to me...' Kate furrowed her brow and shook her head. 'God, he really is *sooo* much a nicer guy than my memory gives him credit for.'

'Yeah, he is,' Steve agreed, scratching his stubbly cheek. 'But I had nowhere to kip, so I thought I'd doss down here.'

'But why under my desk? Why not under your own at *LASHED*? And why didn't you call or leave a message – or just leave me a note on my desk or something?'

'I was embarrassed, wanted to show everyone I could do things on my own first, before I got in contact. But I missed you – hence the sleeping under your desk, worshipping at the space where your feet had once been. And...well, I don't exactly have my own desk yet,' Steve looked sheepish, 'and I haven't been paid yet, either.'

Kate stood there speechless and let her heart rate get back to normal. Which gave her time to take it all in, figure out a plan and carefully consider her response.

But before she had a chance to completely calm down, her chin wobbled and crinkled up for a moment before she burst into tears, flinging herself at her long lost brother.

Her sobs came thick and fast, as though she was making up for lost time. Steve held his sister close and they stayed like this for ages, until eventually Kate pulled back, wiping her eyes.

'Come back and live with me and Georgia – how could I have let you go in the first place?!'

'I dunno,' grinned Steve. 'You weren't always so heartless and selfish...'

'And as for the money, well, we'll sort that out as soon as Tom comes in this morning. If he makes it in at all, that is,' smirked Kate. 'Tea?'

The pair meandered over to the small office kitchen and Kate popped the kettle on.

Steve crouched down and bobbed on his haunches while he sniffed the eight open milk cartons languishing in the bar fridge door.

'Cottage cheese,' he grimaced and poured the contents of seven down the sink.

'So what's the story, Stevie?' Kate said bluntly to her brother. 'Why did you run off like that at Blue and Paris' place?'

'Mum and Dad's place, you mean?'

'Yes, you know I do.'

'I don't know,' he said, putting the last carton on the kitchen bench. 'It all got too much for me, I suppose.'

'What did?'

'The pathetic games people play.'

'Who?'

You don't know?' Steve asked.

'No – tell me,' Kate said.

'You really don't know, do you?'

'Steve! Tell me!'

Kate's worry line, the little crevice between her eyebrows, was deepening into more of a crevasse now.

'Here goes,' Steve said slowly. 'Mum's been having an affair. With the guy next door. She met him at a swinger's party.'

Kate didn't move, not even her mouth flopped open in shock or horror or sheer disbelief.

'Yep,' Steve carried on. 'Dad knows and has been trying to come to terms with it for months now.'

'But –'

'I know, I know. Swinging! It's so...so...so 70s!' Steve sneered. 'And so awfully *suburban*!'

Kate couldn't really compute all this and felt as though her confusion was really settling in now, threatening to completely overwhelm her. Not, she thought, totally dissimilar to the way she felt when Declan was first born and she struggled without her parents to cope with two under two.

She felt almost exactly the same, come to think of it, her heart rate quickly increasing, her breath getting shallow, the world spinning around her as her eyes darted this way and that, trying in vain to find a focus, a point of stillness and stability, an anchor.

'Are you OK, Kate?' Steve put his arm around her.

'I...I think I need to sit down,' she managed to stutter, as he helped her to a chair in Archie's office.

'It's bizarre, I know,' said Steve over his shoulder as he went back into the kitchen to make the tea.

Kate could hear cupboards opening and closing and then Steve saying, in disgust: 'What? No Hob Nobs? Call yourselves a media company? It's a bloody disgrace!'

Kate half-smiled and rubbed her forehead, waiting for the migraine to hit.

Steve came back into Archie's office with their tea and perched on the edge of the desk in front of Kate.

'You don't look so good, Kate,' he said, genuine concern in his voice.

'And you don't smell so fragrant yourself,' she said a tad shakily. 'When was the last time you had a bath?'

Steve just snorted as he brought his mug of tea up to his lips, making little ripples on the surface of the milky, beige beverage.

'Right. One thing at a time,' Kate said, trying to compartmentalise and sort her head out. 'We'll get to Paris and Blue later. But first, tell me something.'

'Anything, Sis,' said Steve.

'Why was me leaving our flat such a horrendous thing for you? And why are you so *angry* all the time?'

'I don't know,' he said quietly. 'Actually, that's a

lie. I've had some time to think about it and I think I do know why...'

Kate noticed Steve's eyes getting watery and wanted to suffocate him with hugs and smother him with kisses. God, she thought, this is *just* like having a baby – the sudden rush of love, the confusion, the pandemonium in your heart, the dizzy, elated way you feel – even long after the morphine's worn off.

'No, no, no,' Steve repelled her advancing arms. 'Just let me get it all out, will you? I've been bottling it up for years, I might as well let it all out now.'

Kate shifted in her seat.

'Are you sitting comfortably?' Steve asked. 'Then let's begin. As you know, I was born a couple of years after you and that, unfortunately, was my first mistake.'

'What do you mean?'

'I mean that I've always felt like second best, always in your shadow – and not in a wind beneath your wings kind of way.'

They both smiled at this point, sharing the memory of watching *Beaches*, one of Blue's favourite movies on video over and over again, until they knew all the lines off by heart.

'It's only recently that I've been able to put it into words, but I think I've always had this overriding feeling that somehow, because I wasn't *you*, I was always a great disappointment to Mum and Dad.'

Kate shook her head as if to say 'no, that's not true', but Steve ignored her and continued.

'It's nothing that you did, you were just a kid and the apple of your parents' eye – no, it was what Mum and Dad did – all that bullshit about calling them by their ridiculous, made-up names, all that finding themselves and asserting their own individuality upon the family unit – that's what made me feel surplus to requirements. That's what made me feel insignificant and insecure and...unwanted and unloved, basically.'

'But there's no way they –'

'They may not have *intended* for that to happen,' Steve cut Kate short, 'but that's what *did* happen. That's how I interpreted Blue's constant bid for independence and freedom – a rejection of *me*.'

Kate wanted to tell him to stop it – stop being so ridiculous and selfish and pathetically childish and me, me, ME! She'd always suspected this was part of Steve's problem – the sibling rivalry, the vying for their parents' attention and approval. And then there was the inevitable coming second, always feeling second best - effectively, to his mind, always coming *last*.

She wanted to tell him to grow up and consider someone else for a change. Why, for God's sake, was it so traumatic for him that his mother was a fully-formed, well-rounded individual? Wasn't it enough for him to know that she'd sacrificed her career for her children? That she never reached the lofty heights Paris had, because she took six years off her paid working life to look after her small family, before they went to school? Didn't it ever occur to him that, yes, she was their mummy – but she was also a grown-up *person*, one with normal adult needs and desires?

So their mother had sought a life beyond the four confining walls of home – was that so wrong? So she was interested in millions of things other than her kids – wasn't that a good thing? Why did it have to have such an adverse affect on *him*?

Poor old Blue – she was hardly *Mommie Dearest*, a schizophrenic, neglectful, nasty, nutty mother. But here was Steve, blaming her for all *his* issues.

On the flip side, though, Kate completely understood how Steve felt. Because even though she didn't like to admit it – even to herself – she, too, had sometimes felt abandoned and nowhere near as important to her mum as her work or friends or, clearly, her romantic, emotional and sexual needs.

In the quiet surrounding them, Kate felt the creeping realisation that everything she was saying in her head about Blue sounded spookily familiar to her. Suddenly, like the bolt of lightning that brought her here, she was struck by clarity.

She was, as a mum, exactly like Blue. She had become just like her own mother!

Kate felt the irresistible urge to defend her mother. And herself.

'But just because she's our mum doesn't mean she can't be a whole load of other things too. Does it? I mean, why can't she seek out fulfilment in life in all sorts of different areas?'

'I dunno. Maybe women can't have it all,' Steve

stared out the window at the city skyline. 'Or maybe she just could have made a bit more of a fuss over me – and Dad. Maybe she could have been a better role model for me, showed me what loving relationships looked like. If she hadn't been so busy being frustrated with her lot and yelling at us all the time and going on about what she could be doing if she didn't have us and how she made a huge mistake getting married and having kids –'

The hairs on the back of Kate's neck stood up. This was getting too close for comfort.

'She never said that!'

'Oh yeah? You didn't hear her,' Steve opened his eyes wide and glared at Kate. 'I wasn't supposed to, either, but she said it all right. Several times, whenever she and Dad were rowing in their bedroom.'

'You sneaky little...what else did she say?'

'Nothing much,' Steve said, looking out the window. 'Except that she married the wrong guy and her life would have been so different and so much better if she'd only stayed with the love of her life, the one she had electrifying sex with before she even met Dad.'

Kate's mouth fell open at this point.

Eventually, after several dry-mouthed swallows, she regained the power of speech.

'When did you hear all this?' she croaked. 'And why didn't you tell me immediately?'

'It was *ages* ago - about seven years,' Steve shrugged. 'You'd gone off to University and were too busy and bohemian to talk to your little brother about family matters, stuff about home anymore.'

Kate nodded – Steve was right - that was *precisely* how she'd felt at the time.

She pictured herself and Georgia in their trademark jet black tights and turtle necks, smoking anything they could get their hands on, listening to The Smiths and downing bottles of red as though they were starving beatnik artists in a Stella Artois ad. Now *there* was a simpler time – why oh why couldn't she have been taken back to 1987?

'Mother's guilt,' Kate suddenly said authoritatively. 'It's not easy juggling a house and kids and a husband who'd rather play golf than take you out for dinner, you know. I bet she felt so guilty about harbouring those thoughts, those fantasies about her ex – and she couldn't bear it. That's why she lashed out and that's why she eventually had some tawdry, grotty, ghastly affair with some hideous old man.'

'Sounds like you've thought about it more than I have,' said Steve, picking up their empty tea mugs. 'I've kind of forgiven her – and Paris, now, anyway. They were only doing their best, trying to live their lives at the same time as making decent ones for us. How's that Philip Larkin poem go? Something about how your mum and dad don't mean to, but they really fuck you up?'

'Yeah,' smiled Kate. 'Something like that. Have you thought about therapy? Prozac?'

She thought about Georgia and how she swore by

a combination of the two.

'Why is a chemical the answer?' Steve stared her down. 'No one knows what long-term effects these drugs have and I've taken my fair share of Es – which, let's face it, is exactly what anti-depressants are – and nothing's changed in my head. Except that I've had some wicked , completely brilliant nights.'

Kate nodded.

'And some horrific comedowns,' Steve went on softly. 'I just can't help but think if only Mum had been happier, though, then she wouldn't have wanted another life and I wouldn't have turned out –'

'GAY!' Kate propelled herself out of her chair. 'I knew it! You're gay, right? Ah! *Sooo* obvious.'

Steve threw his head back and laughed.

'Miserable! I was going to say *miserable*,' he shook his head, smiling. 'You're a real piece of work, you are. No. I am definitely not gay. Not that there's anything wrong with that...'

'Allo, allo, allo!' Archie interrupted them from the doorway. 'What have we here, then? Taken over my office already, have you, Kate?'

Archie sauntered in and, in a decidedly proprietorial move, threw his bomber jacket over the back of his oversized chair. It was the sartorial equivalent of peeing on it, Kate thought to herself.

'Sorry, Archie,' Kate began, 'I just wasn't feeling too well and –'

'Yes, yes – I imagine your celebrations with Tom last night did get rather, shall we say, exuberant?'

'Eh?' Kate and Steve grunted in unison.

'I heard about your success with the Britpoppers,' Archie went on. 'But it hasn't happened yet. If – and it's a big if – IF you pull it off, then maybe we'll talk about you having your own office.'

Well whoop-de-doo, Kate said to herself.

'But you've got a long way to go, baby, before you can handle things at my level,' Archie said. 'And Steve! What are you doing here? Is it a family takeover or something?!'

'I was just leaving,' said Steve, practically running for the door. 'See you soon!'

Archie raised his eyebrows at Kate expectantly as he sat down and rested his Chelsea-booted feet on his desk.

'Um, right,' said Kate. 'I'd better be going, too, I suppose. Really start getting to grips with the shoot, set it up for sometime this week.'

'Good girl,' Archie said, in patronising tones. 'I'm sure you have a lot of work to get on with. Close the door on your way out, would you?'

Kate stood up and turned to leave. But as she reached the door, she stopped and said:

'Archie? Have I done something to upset you?'

'No,' Archie scoffed. 'What makes you say that?'

'Because lately you're being a bit, I dunno, *mean* to me.'

Archie looked perplexed and shook his head.

'You seem annoyed with me, short with me most of the time.'

'I've always been short,' he grinned.

'Are you sure?' she pressed on. 'I mean, you're sure I haven't said or done something to –'

'Yes! I'm sure! Now go on, get out of here – I want you to have set up the shoot of the century before lunchtime!'

'Yes, Sir!' She saluted, turned tail and marched out of there.

But before she got down to work, there was a rather more pressing phone call she had to make.

22

‘G?’ said Kate.

‘’Yeah, it’s me,’ yawned Georgia. ‘Where are you, you dirty stop out?’

‘At work. Stayed at Tom’s new place last night and, I, I just don’t think it’s going to work, you know? I want to come home.’

‘You’re in luck, Lady – I haven’t had a chance to rent your room out yet – even though they’ve been *queueing* down the street...’

‘Great, brilliant. And how about you? How are you feeling?’

‘Fantastic. Top of the world. Never felt better in my life.’

‘Still crap, eh?’

‘No, I’m serious. I’m going to go back into work this afternoon. I’ve completely recovered from my trauma physically, now it’s simply a matter of sifting through the emotional detritus.’

‘Wow,’ said Kate. ‘How are you going to do that, then?’

There was a brief pause, and Kate expected Georgia to say ‘see a psychiatrist for 15 years get a permanent prescription for Zoloft’, but she didn’t.

‘Get right back on that horse, get out there again and settle down with a *decent* man.’

‘But where are you going to find one of those? Pubs and clubs are full of morons and – ’

'I think I may have already found him,' said Georgia with a giggle.

'Who?'

'That guy who helped us home that night – the guy who works in your company – the gentlemanly one, you remember!'

Kate tried to picture any decent, gentlemanly men she knew at PGT&B. She drew a blank.

'You know! The speccy, dweeby one! With the Irish name...'

'Seamus?'

'That's the fella!'

'But you can't! I mean –'

'Why not?' Georgia sounded offended. 'He did seem interested, a bit, that night...'

'Oh, God, G! He's only human! But you can't have him, he's taken.'

'He is not!'

'Not yet, maybe – but he will be. Any day now, if my predictions are correct...'

'Yeah! By me!'

'No! That's not fair!'

Kate had lost many a man to the charms of her best friend over the years – but she wasn't prepared to sacrifice this one.

'You have such a massive head start, such a huge advantage, you with your Beatrice Dalle-ness and everything!'

'OK, OK, calm down,' Georgia said, audibly taking a drag on a Malboro Light. 'Hey...you haven't got your eye on him, have you?'

Kate looked furtively over the top of her carrel and checked to see who was around and wished she had her own office right now, with the door shut, so she could speak freely without all her colleagues hearing her and thinking she was a) mad and b) had terrible taste in men.

Her eyes met Tamsin's, who was wriggling her way over to Kate's desk in an impossibly tight, mid-calf length boucle pencil skirt. That, coupled with her black patent platform pumps gave her a Minnie Mouse-ish appearance and instead of looking sexy, Kate thought she looked comical, bordering on the ridiculous.

Then again, she told herself, she would think that, wouldn't she?

Tamsin hovered over her, waving the monthly targets and bonuses for the marketing department in Kate's face and mouthed: 'I'll take them in to Archie first, yeah?'

Kate always wanted to have a look at how she and the rest of the team were doing before Archie – so she could be prepared for either a pat on the back or a bollocking. But right now she didn't care about those meaningless facts and figures – it was more important to save Seamus from the Georgia's scarlet-talonned clutches!

'Whatever,' Kate whispered, waving Tamsin away.

'Excuse me?' Georgia said. Kate could hear her

best friend's eyebrows rising.

'No, not you,' said Kate. 'Just some annoying little...now you listen here, Jolene. Keep your hands off Seamus – don't take him from me just because you can!'

Georgia didn't say a word. Kate imagined the quiet on the end of the line was what was known as a stunned silence.

'But he's so clearly not your type,' said Georgia, sounding confused.

'Is too!' was all Kate could think of to say.

'Is not!'

'Is too!'

The pair of them continued sounding like George and Declan bickering over their Matchbox cars for a while before they broke into a fit of the giggles.

'Anyway,' Kate said, wiping a tear from her eye, 'I didn't ring you so we could fight over boys, I wanted to tell you about Blue and Paris, get some advice.'

'Do spill,' said Georgia.

'Well,' Kate hunched over her keyboard and cupped her hand around the phone receiver in an attempt at privacy. 'They tried swinging and now Blue's taken up with one of the swinging old guys they met. She's having an affair!'

'What?!' Georgia coughed and spluttered.

'I know! But what do I do now? I'm meeting Blue for lunch – should I confront her? Ignore it? Console and comfort Paris? What's a daughter to do in this sort of a situation?'

'Keep her snout out!' Georgia's pitch escalated. 'I dunno – how the hell should I know?'

'You're the one reading *Men Are From Mars* –'

'What's *that* got to do with it?'

'Well, is Dad disappearing into his cave the more Mum comes out of hers? How can I fix them up? What's the solution?'

'You can't,' Georgia said deadpan 'and there *is* no solution. Can't you just let them live their lives the way they want? Why do you have to interfere all the time? You can't *fix* them. Relationships are complex things. Men and women are complex things. Well, *women* are complex things...'

Kate was stopped short by Georgia's precise assessment of the situation.

'So tell me,' Georgia went on. 'Why exactly can't I go for Seamus?'

'You just can't! Um, for the sake of your own happiness, Georgie! He'd really get on your nerves after a while, once the novelty of going out with a geek wore off. It would be so boring, so predictable, you'd grow to hate his safeness and predictability – it'll drive you mad. Sorry, it *would* drive you mad. Madd-*er*. Trust me on this one.'

'Why should I?'

'Because you just have to! Honestly, G, you've got to believe me! You don't want him. I just *know* that he can never meet your emotional needs...'

At that moment, Kevin popped his head up over

the back of Kate's carrel and waved a tangle of cables at her like he was a deranged octopus.

'I'll just plug one of these in – if I can find the right one – and we'll see if we can get you online without a modem,' he whispered, as though it was some great state secret.

'...but I think I might just know a man who can...,' Kate said slowly, putting the phone down on Georgia without even waiting for a reply.

*

Kate was in an organisational frenzy. It was either feast or famine with her (usually feast, let's face it, especially where Terry's Chocolate Oranges were concerned), but when she got going on something (except, unfortunately, ironing, which she could never really get excited about), she was often an unstoppable tour de force.

She called Liam and checked that Noel had agreed to the shoot – which, quite surprisingly, he had. She got their sizes ('Massively enormous' and 'tiddly' respectively, according to Liam), confirmed with the eager Blur boys' people and called the All Stars Boxing Gym on Harrow Road to set up a time.

She went down a level to the teen floor of PGT&B and chatted to the *Mad Fer It!* team who were, understandably, beside themselves with excitement.

Kate was thrilled, too.

And when she found herself squealing and jumping up and down while spinning around in a ring-a-ring-a-roses kind of a way, with everyone who worked on the magazine, she felt young and fresh and vital and truly lost in the moment.

Until her back gave out, that is, and she had to be helped to a swivel chair so she could sit down under the poster-covered Take That RIP memorial wall.

*

'Even now it's a mug's game,' Kate muttered to herself as she checked out her body's profile in The Lift mirror. 'I should've known better than to look.'

Mere days before, where there had been nothing but tight, smooth flesh, she could now detect the beginnings of a bit of a paunch poking out from the bottom of her crop top.

Must be all those carb-heavy beers I've been necking, she thought. Even though she had actually been quite abstemious lately – unlike how she obviously was in 1996 the first time round. Honestly, she shook her head, studying the grubby carpet, was that really how most young women behaved back then? Badly? Like little boys?

She thought of Baby Jane and her wide-eyed innocence. She thought of the big, bad world out there, lying in wait to corrupt her little girl and steal away her sweetness. She started to well up picturing Jane as a poor, defenceless, motherless child, sitting in a pooey nappy on the kitchen floor, arms stretched up as if to say: 'Mummy! I need you!' in international body language.

Kate winced as she imagined the contents of Jane's nappy – and then gasped as she felt her panic rise. What if she never got back to 2014? What if she was stuck in 1996 forever?

'I have GOT to get back!' She declared, just as The Lift pinged and landed with a jolt on the ground floor.

'Calm down, Gorgeous,' said Tom, who was standing there with Tamsin. 'Where's the fire?'

Kate looked at the both of them and, expecting to be nearly knocked down with righteous indignation and rabid jealousy, surprised herself no end when she felt nothing. Nothing at all. Except a slight rumbling in her tummy. Well, Tamsin *was* clutching a bag full of unbelievably delicious-smelling cakes and assorted goodies from Patisserie Valerie and the buttery, sugary whiff surrounding her was almost intoxicating.

'Oh, ah – I've got to meet Mum – I'm late as usual!' said Kate.

'Hey! Wait!', Tom wheeled around, trying to grab Kate's elbow as she whizzed past. 'What time did you leave this morning?'

'I dunno,' Kate pulled her elbow into her ribs and picked up her pace, shouting over her shoulder. 'Early. I'll see you later, yeah?'

'I really think we need to...,' Tom didn't finish his sentence, he just sighed and turned away, stepping into The Lift.

And just as the shiny silvery mirrored doors began to close, Kate saw Tamsin batting her eyelashes like mad.

'Talk?' Tamsin purred. 'Were you going to say

"talk"? Because if you ever need a sounding board, Tom, I'll always be there for you.'

That'd be right, Kate snorted to herself as she battled with the early lunchtime crowds in Oxford Street, Tamsin just couldn't *wait* to get her hands on Tom, could she?

Passing through Soho, making her way to Covent Garden, Kate realised she could *understand* why she used to be so crazy about him and how her heart could have been so smashed when he took up with Tamsin all those years ago. But it just wasn't there for her anymore, she simply didn't feel it the way she had.

Thank God he *had* passed out last night and been totally incapacitated, unable to perform – imagine the guilt she'd be drowning in today if they *had* actually shagged!

Kate smiled thinking of how close she'd come, how narrowly she'd avoided unbearable remorse. And just as she was thinking about how she never thought she'd *ever* be so cool and calm – almost detached – about Tom, Blue came trotting up to her.

'Darling!' she panted. 'Change of plans – I can't meet you for lunch today.'

'What?' Kate scrunched up her face. She was starting to get really quite annoyed with her mother. 'But you said –'

'I know, I know,' Blue looked over Kate's shoulder and then behind her own, as if she were a fugitive on the run from the law, a hunted woman. 'But something came up and I just couldn't get out of it.'

Kate scrutinised her mother. She was wearing a cream, layered ensemble of indiscernible lines – like something Dame Judi Dench would wear – sophisticated and flowing, covering a multitude of sins, as Blue would say, but still looking stylish and expensive.

Her make-up was expertly applied – the perfect shade of foundation with not-too powdery a finish, a few subtle yet effective brush strokes of blush to highlight her sharp cheekbones, several coats of strong yet decidedly un-clumpy mascara to bring out and frame her beautiful bluey/green eyes and a glossy lip tint that complemented her colouring perfectly, no doubt with an SPF of 60 in it (Blue was nothing if not practical, underneath all that glitz and glamour).

She looked comfortable, well-put together, well-preserved and, Kate's breath caught in her throat, *very attractive*.

Kate thought of herself back home when she was happy and comfy and relaxed – and vowed to burn every cheap, nasty and hopelessly uglifying fleece and pair of jogging bottoms she owned when she got back to 2014. Better alert the council, then, she thought – don't want her no doubt massive funeral pyre to piss the neighbours off. Or maybe she should wait till bonfire night, donating her gargantuan 'joggers' to any Guys needing bottoms. If anyone would accept them.

A jaunty scarf, one Kate had never seen before, was casually draped around Blue's neck, discreetly concealing the wrinkling skin wrapping itself around

Blue's throat. Kate's eyes lingered on it, as she searched for the words to express her disappointment and growing irritation.

'Liberty,' said Blue, by way of explanation. 'It was a gift.'

Kate's eyes shot up to Blue's.

'From a...a friend,' she smiled, turning her body half around, nervously and then holding onto her daughter's forearms with an urgency Kate found unsettling.

'Look, I've got to go, now, Darling. But Sunday lunch? At ours? Bring whoever you like and – have you heard from Steve yet?'

Kate's eyes were inadvertently turning into slits as she looked her mother up and down.

'Yes,' she said curtly, as though she was unsure as to whether it was any of Blue's business.

'Oh!' Blue's hands shot up to her mouth, without actually touching her face, lest she muck up her make-up. 'How is he? Where is he? Is he all right?'

Blue suddenly looked frightened – and it aged her at least ten years.

'Yes, he's fine,' Kate softened a little bit at this display of motherly concern. 'Don't worry, he's fine.'

Kate decided against adding 'no thanks to you', and instead, smiled.

After all, she thought, she was starting to really understand how her mother must have felt all these years, bringing up two kids with a distant husband and nothing to fall back on when the nest inevitably emptied.

She put her hand on Blue's shoulder and said:

'You go, Mum, it's OK – I've got plenty of work to do and I'll see you on Sunday. Go on, go!'

She shooed Blue away, watching as her mother skipped happily into the crowd. But where was she going? And why was she dressed so smartly? Who on earth could she be seeing? Who could *possibly* be more important than her daughter, back from the future, with only limited time to sit and talk and make the most of each other?

Kate instinctively felt it, then – the second best-ness Steve had talked about. Now she really knew how he felt, how awful it was to suspect you were languishing low, lingering somewhere at the bottom of a long list of your parents' priorities.

She felt the irresistible urge to follow her, and quickly took off after her, like Usain Bolt out of the starting blocks - albeit with a dodgy hip, an aching back and a really sore ankle.

She managed to catch sight of Blue's scarf, so exquisite was it, flying behind her mother's head as she weaved her way through the throng, and did her level best to hobble faster, the pain visible on her knitted brow, her lips forming the shape of a cat's bum as if she was continually saying 'ooh, me aching bones!'

In her haste, she bumped into people and nearly skittled a toddler hanging onto his mother's hand. She bashed other short people's shoulders as she rushed and didn't even turn back to say sorry or help with a bag of groceries she'd knocked out of a trendy, young woman's hand.

A path cleared before her and there in front of her, stood stock still on the Covent Garden cobbled street, was a tall, incredibly skinny, lanky man with a dark, shaggy hairdo, full-fat, Rubens-esque lips, black cords, black desert boots and a plain black leather jacket.

He watched her in disbelief, his mouth hanging open as Kate hurried on, aware but seemingly uncaring about the carnage she was leaving in her wake.

Kate, herself, did a classic double-take when she got closer to the guy, realising it was the strikingly beautiful Richard Ashcroft from The Verve, and wondered whether they'd released the brilliant Bittersweet Symphony yet. She made a swift mental note to Google that when – *if* – she ever got home, and hurried after her mother, who was taking a right turn and dashing into Carluccio's.

When she got there, Kate stared through the plate glass window at the front of the restaurant and gasped when she saw Blue smoothing down her hair, passing a hand self-consciously over her linen-trousered bum and proceeding to snog the tanned, weathered face off the grey-haired gent who stood up to greet her.

'Get a room,' Kate tutted.

She'd always been a little uncomfortable with full-on PDAs, but now she was positively squirming with the unease of it all.

Maybe it was because she was the public and her

mother was the displayer...and the object of her mother's unseemly display of affection was most definitely not her father.

23

Even though it had been cleared of its usual punters and had been closed to the public for the day, All Stars Boxing Gym was a hive of activity.

The air fairly fizzed and popped with excitement as the *Mad Fer It!* team fussed over their favourite pop stars and the *LASHED* lot tried to make out that they couldn't care less.

Medea – who probably really didn't give a toss – had been sent to cover the shoot for her first column. She chatted idly to Damon and Noel, respectively, looking more bored than all the rest of them put together, until Tom arrived, when she lit up like a Christmas tree.

'I've brought everything we'll ever need for the best shoot ever,' he announced, wiping his nose with his index finger.

'Did you bring batteries?' Medea asked him. 'Only I think mine are running out and I'll need my dictaphone to work without a hitch today - I really want to catch the fun mood, the friendly ambience for my first piece.'

Tom replied in the affirmative, desperately trying to keep the enthusiasm out of his voice. Kate couldn't tell whether he was suppressing the whelps of an excited puppy because of Medea's presence and undeniable beauty – or whether he was simply over the moon to be in the same room as his style and musical heroes.

Either way, she thought, he looked happier than she'd seen him for ages. Now if only she could keep him at arm's length, keep on avoiding having the awful break-up chat that they obviously had to have, everything would be perfect.

Steve wandered over to the tea and biscuits table, where Kate was making short work of a packet of Penguins.

'You'd better take it easy with those,' he teased gently. 'You've been looking a little podgy, lately, Sis.'

'How *dare* you?' replied Kate, through a mouthful of chocalatey crumbs.

'I can always go and get some more,' squeaked Tamsin, who seemed to have appeared out of nowhere.

'What are you doing here?' Kate couldn't help but ask.

'Archie sent me,' said Tamsin, smugly. 'He said he wanted me to make sure everything went smoothly until he could get here.'

'Did he now?' Kate raised her right eyebrow.

Tamsin nodded superciliously and inched her way in between Steve and Kate, pouring herself a brew.

'Is Lucy coming down, too?' Steve asked.

'Who?' Tamsin asked.

'The third floor receptionist? Lucy? With the long, dark hair that looks perfect and smells –'

'A hundred times better than you, Steve,' Kate coughed, exaggerating the effect of the overpowering

BO emanating from her brother, by holding her screwed-up nose. 'Have you showered yet?'

'Showering's for puffs,' said Liam, bounding over to the group and grinning as he bent down to give Kate a hug.

Tamsin giggled nervously and Steve stared at the Oasis frontman in awe.

In the absence of any idea about what to do herself, Kate patted the top of Liam's head. She couldn't have been more patronising if she'd tried and scolded herself for her inappropriate gesture.

'Make-up lady's here, Liam,' shouted the picture editor from *Mad Fer It!* from the dressing rooms, freeing both Kate and the pop star from this uncomfortable, awkward moment.

'Make-up's for –'

'Puffs,' Kate, Steve and Tamsin all said in unison, laughing and hoping that Liam wouldn't take offence and knock their collective blocks off.

'You're learning,' laughed Liam, pointing his finger at the threesome and backing away, his long arms swaying and his bandy legs bending at the knee, making him look positively simian. 'You're learning.'

Sitting down on the cream-coloured plastic chairs, Kate noticed Tamsin was carrying what appeared to be a small shoebox. She placed it on the tiny strip of material masquerading as a mini skirt (which barely covered her knickers) when she sat down and stared at it lovingly.

'What *is* that?' asked Kate.

‘Oh this little old thing?’ Tamsin’s voice went all high and squeaky, like she was an impressionable young country singer being asked what her guitar was by some grizzled, old Nashville record company CEO.

Kate nodded.

‘It’s the office mobile phone,’ Tamsin answered, proudly. ‘Archie wanted me to be contactable at all times.’

The shoebox rang.

‘Oh!’ Tamsin shrieked, jumping up and sending the phone tumbling to the floor. ‘Cheeky thing vibrates!’

Steve did the chivalrous thing and picked up the vibrating brick, handing it to Tamsin as he body-popped, pretending he had been given an electric shock by the new-fangled, alien-looking mobile telecommunications device, as Seamus would say.

‘Hello? HELLO!’ Tamsin yelled into the receiver, once she’d fumbled about with it a bit, got the wrist strap and antenna untangled from her hair and flipped open its retractable mouthpiece.

Archie’s voice crackled through the line.

‘YES, YES – THEY’RE ALL HERE – YES, EVEN NOEL – YES, SHE’S HERE...HANG ON...HE WANTS TO SPEAK TO YOU, KATE!’

‘All right, all right - no need to shout,’ Kate said extra-softly, to highlight Tamsin’s unnecessary decibels and took the phone from her colleague. With both hands.

‘Hiya Arch,’ she said into the phone, nearly

toppling over ear-first with the weight of the thing.

Much to Tamsin's visible annoyance (she folded her arms across her tight cashmere sweater, looked very cross and actually uttered the famous phrase: 'harumph!' as she stamped her high-heeled foot), Kate wandered off towards Tom and Medea sitting outside the dressing room, studying the scuffed lino while she walked.

'No, no, it all seems to be going well, so far, touch wood,' she playfully, lightly knocked on Tom's head as she passed him and Medea, deep in editorial conference. 'No bust-ups whatsoever. All rivalries appear to be in check, so far –'

'But that's exactly what we DON'T want!' Archie barked at her. 'We need drama! We need conflict! Come on, Kate – you've got two of the most volatile, unpredictable personalities in there – make some waves! Wind 'em up! We've got to milk the publicity on this for all it's worth – and then some!'

'But –'

'And if it doesn't kick off, front page of the red tops-stylee, don't bother coming back to work – I'll get Tamsin to clear your desk for you. In fact, consider yourself sacked as of immediately. HR will forward you your P45!'

Kate was stunned. Her mouth was moving, but no words came out. She must have looked like a fish out of water, an old trout, landed in a boxing gym, taking great gulps of air in vain.

What *was* wrong with Archie? What had she done

to provoke his ire so?

'Archie, I hardly think that's fair –'

Click.

Bloody hell, Kate thought, as she walked back to Tamsin, smiling weakly at Tom and Medea and the outrageously famous pop stars lounging about in the ring, looning about on their guitars with boxing gloves on, waiting for their turn with the make-up and hair lady.

Tamsin looked more smug than usual when she clocked Kate's confused, hurt countenance and snatched the phone off her.

'Cracking the whip a bit too much for you today?' said Tamsin, oozing smarm everywhere.

Kate glared at her and was almost relieved that she was still bereft of the power of speech – she felt as though the red mist might descend upon her any minute now, and she wouldn't be responsible for what great vengeance her tongue might unleash on silly little Tamsin. Who was about two feet taller than Kate.

'I don't have to put up with this,' muttered Kate narkily as she swiped her khaki anorak off a chair, folded it over her left forearm, turned tail with her nose and chin in the air and stormed out of the smelly old gym. 'I'm going to give that Archie a piece of my mind.'

But by the time she got back to the office, Archie was nowhere to be found.

'Lucy?' Kate approached the reception desk. 'Have you seen Archie?'

'Hmm?' said Lucy, looking over the top of her magazine. 'Who?'

'Archie! The boss! The Big Cheese! The Big Kahuna!'

'Oh, ah, have you checked in the –'

'He's not at his desk, not in the tea room, not upstairs in the *LASHED* office – nowhere! Oh, Archie – where are you?'

'Well, he's not in there,' said Seamus as he walked out of the Gents doing up his fly. 'What's the panic?'

'Oh, nothing,' Kate breathed hard, steam still coming out of her ears. 'Just a work problem.'

'Maybe he's gone down to the shoot,' offered Lucy.

'But I was just there,' Kate said, trying to calm herself down.

'Lucky you,' Lucy said under her breath. 'How is it all going down there, then?'

'Good, good,' said Kate. 'Too good for Archie, though – not enough bad feeling, no real fisticuffs.'

'So everyone really has kissed and made up?' asked Lucy. 'They are all friends again?'

'So far so good,' Kate smiled at the young girl and remembered what it felt like when your pop star heroes were your whole world, when they mattered to you more than your family, when your whole identity was wrapped up in their personas.

'And who else is there? I mean, who's covering it for, um, *LASHED*?'

'Medea and Steve, I think,' said Kate, who couldn't wait to read their different takes on the same event. 'Tell you what - why don't you go and see for yourself? Go down to the shoot, check it all out first-hand? And if Archie's there, tell him I'm looking for him.'

Lucy didn't need to be asked twice and leapt up, vaulting over the reception desk, bolting past The Lift and taking the fire stairs, two-by-two. She didn't even remember to take her handbag, she was in such a rush.

For some unknown reason – maybe it was a force of habit – when Kate turned around, her eyes were drawn towards Seamus' crotch area, where a big wet patch had taken on an oblong shape. She'd seen it now nigh on a trillion times and knew exactly what it was, despite Seamus' lame excuses.

Seamus looked down to see what Kate was gawping at and blushed.

'Oh, uh, th-that,' he stammered. 'It's the cold tap in those toilets – comes out with such force, it nearly hits you in the eye as it splashes off the basin.'

He laughed nervously and added: 'The *eyes*, I mean, the eyes in your head.'

Kate felt a wave of disappointment wash over her. Twenty years, she thought to herself. Do I have to suffer through *at least* the next twenty years of my life with a man who blames his poor willy-shaking technique on faulty tapware?

At first she thought it vaguely amusing, way back when, but after three kids and being relegated to a tedious existence in the suburbs, Kate had begun to see such sloppy behaviour as merely pathetic.

'You just didn't dry yourself properly,' she said deadpan and turned away in disgust.

'Yes I did! Honestly,' protested Seamus, 'it's cold water! From the outside. From when I was washing my hands! Aren't you pleased I was *washing my hands*? How many blokes do that?'

But Kate dismissed him with a click of her tongue and a mumbled 'whatever' as she tried to make out what kind of alien life force had landed on her desk.

'At least I was washing my hands,' Seamus murmured again, feeling quite sorry for himself at this, as far as he could see, unsolicited attack.

'What's all this?' Kate asked, holding up a black box and a nest of wires.

'Oh, I'm just trialling some new equipment on your computer,' Seamus' eyes lit up and he almost skipped to her side. 'That's the old modem which, as you can plainly see, is quite clunky and cumbersome.'

Kate could, indeed, see that. But what took her by surprise, what she hadn't necessarily seen so clearly before, was Seamus' obvious passion for all things techie. She softened to him at this point, forgetting all about the wet patch.

'You love it, don't you?' she stated rather than asked.

'Pardon?' he replied, wide-eyed.

'All this new-fangled technological stuff,' she air-typed and jerked her head towards her computer monitor and keyboard.

'Oh! Yes, yes,' he nodded emphatically. 'It's fascinating, really, how...'

Kate didn't hear the rest of Seamus' sentence – she was too busy trying to hold onto the edge of her desk as the world, with Seamus at its centre, seemed to spin around her.

Bugger, she thought. I bet this is it – I'm going to be shunted back to 2014 right now and I didn't even manage to sleep with my one true -

The spinning slowed down a little bit, while Seamus continued to burble on, but suddenly, all Kate could hear were soaring violins. She felt more than heard the vibrations, the hum of his voice in the background and could see him getting more and more animated as he took the top off the computer and showed her the delights it contained.

A creeping sense of sickness started working its way up Kate's body from the tips of her toes to under her arms, making her armpits bristle.

She must be being sent back to the future – unless she was simply having another hot flush. She felt dizzy and discombobulated, so she closed her eyes and held her breath.

Slowly, like she was coming to after being knocked out, Seamus' voice grew louder and she felt the spinning stop.

'...and so, yeah, I suppose it's my dream, now – to start up my own company, make several million, make the most of the internet while I can and use my millions for good, helping other people less fortunate than myself. My philanthropy could really be financed by what I like to call *the full-stop, 'c' 'o' full-stop 'u' 'k' explosion –'*

Kate saw Seamus wriggle his fingers like fuzzy bunny ears at her as he said the last bit and noticed that, for the first time since she'd been back in 1996, Seamus looked all pleased with himself, like he was the cat who got the cream, as though there might be some confidence buried deep down in there somewhere. Very deep.

'Could catch on,' came Kevin's voice, his face slowly coming into focus for a bleary-eyed Kate.

'Are you all right, Kate?' asked Seamus.

In an unprecedented act of chivalry, Kevin whipped off his damp cagoule that smelled like a wet dog and put it over Kate's shoulders while simultaneously guiding her down into her swivel chair.

'I've got it, I've got it,' said a slightly annoyed Seamus, elbowing Kevin out of the picture and trying to pick Kate up. 'Would you like an Irn Bru? Red Bull? Beer?'

He really was as clueless as he looked.

'No, no thanks - I'm fine,' Kate said, rubbing her forehead. 'Just got a bit dizzy, that's all.'

The genuinely concerned Seamus held her as if he were carrying her over the threshold and Kate looked up at him with what felt like new eyes. They felt wider, bigger, brighter. Or maybe that was just her future.

'Have you...erm...I don't really know how to put

this, but have you been...ah...scoffing a lot of chocolate lately?' Seamus stuttered.

Kate looked at him and smiled beatifically as she felt warmth flood her veins, making her imagine them with caramel flowing through them, instead of blood.

'Hmmm, caramel, toffee...' she smiled blissfully.

'A-HA! I thought you looked a little bit...I dunno...*chunkier* than when we first met!' declared Seamus, dropping her roughly into her chair. 'So you *have* been getting my little gifts, eh? I hope you realise that not just anyone gets my last Rolo, you know.'

'You really have no idea, do you?' Kate sat up, her interior caramel cooling and hardening rapidly. 'You just don't say *anything* to a woman about how she looks or what she's been eating. Unless it's "wow, have you lost weight?" or "have my chips, I don't mind – honestly, there's nothing of you"'

'But I –'

'Ah, forget it,' Kate heaved a sigh. 'Just the one Rolo, then, was it?'

'Well, no,' said Seamus looking hurt. 'The last Rolo in my daily packet. So, I dunno, 10 Rolos altogether?'

Kate's chin crumpled as she chewed her bottom lip. Maybe he wasn't so hopeless with women after all.

24

'Oh, come ON!' Kate huffed when she woke up on Saturday morning. 'How can I *still* be here?'

Somehow, with her tummy swelling and her arms puffing up (not to mention her jowls making an unwelcome appearance and her eyelids looking heavier), she thought she might have woken up in 2014.

But here she was, still in her bedroom of the West Hampstead flat, a clueless Seamus to take shopping in an hour, followed by a football match at smoky, rowdy O'Flaherty's.

To think she would have given her left (pudgy) arm for such an experience a few weeks ago – to be right in the thick of it again, footloose and fancyfree, with no familial responsibility, no ties that bind to hold her down – who wouldn't be over the moon to have that chance again? But now, instead of throwing off the shackles of her life as a wife and mother and leaping into the past with gusto, she felt sad to be without her adorable little handbrakes - now she was starting to feel quite uncomfortably *stuck*.

Chains by Tina Arena bellowed out of the radio.

'You said it, Teen,' Kate muttered to herself as she slid out from between the sheets.

'Oooh!' she drew a sharp inward breath.

The sciatica at the top of her left buttock was really pinching now – only to be outdone by the sudden, searing pain in her right hip. She lay back down, musing about how she supposed the flesh could go back in time, ironing out the wrinkles and disintegrating some unsightly flubber in the process – but the bones, dem bones, dem bones, dem dry bones – there was no way they could ever be 26 again.

Carefully and in slo-mo, Kate raised herself up to a sitting position and from there, managed to push herself up with her arms to a Neanderthal Man, hunched over, knuckle-dragging standing stance.

She swore she could hear herself creak as she straightened herself out and drew herself up to her full height. She placed her open palms on the curve of her waist and was instantly gratified to find it was still slim. Not as slight as it had been 10 days ago, granted, but at least it was still *there*, unlike her waist in 2014, which had vanished, missing in action, sometime around 2004.

And so were her smooth, barely-there hips - a million miles away from the rest-a-pint-on-them shelves they would one day become.

She wondered whether it was glucosamine or cod liver oil that the oldies took for their joints and made a mental note to herself to buy a couple of vats of each when she was in town, next, picking up her pensioner's bus pass.

She thought how great it would be to have free off-peak bus travel, actually – just think of all the places she could go! Other towns not within walking distance, London...um...But then her eyes fell to the floor and she sighed, imagining that the brilliance of the bus pass would be rather cancelled out by the inevitability of having to get up the bus's steps on a zimmer frame – if you managed to remember it as you left the nursing home.

Kate looked at herself in the long mirror attached to the inside door of her flimsy, pine wardrobe.

'And what's so amazing about London, anyway?' she asked her reflection.

It didn't answer her, but she stared at it for ages, just in case.

Her body was still a marked, major improvement on the latter day version, but she could definitely see the signs pointing to where her body was heading: due south, no stopping on the hard (sloping) shoulder.

She stepped closer and scrutinised her face. And for the first time ever, she didn't grimace as she felt the beginnings of her jowls – and she barely flinched as she felt her brow line sagging down, nearly meeting her eyelashes.

In fact, she broke into a grin that wouldn't look out of place on a horror movie deranged clown's face.

Her chin dropped to her chest (which, she noted, didn't cause her any pain, as it used to, due to her sharp, some would say *pointy* chin) and she saw that Seamus and Steve were right – her belly was rounding out rather nicely, thankyou very much.

She was convinced all this body expansion and face droop meant she was being prepped for being flung back to the future. And this put a spring in her step and a song in her heart as she threw on a way too short, flowery baby doll dress and her Doc Martens boots that came up past her thin, bony, but still a little bit sore ankle.

Stylish *and* supportive, she congratulated herself on her wise choice of footwear as she did up the laces. You can't be too careful with dodgy old bones and ankles and metatarsals these days, her inner OAP said prudently.

She'd always longed to have the kind of tall, thin body that could carry off floaty dresses teamed with clunky boots and even make that particular ensemble look *sexy*. She wanted to look like Diane Keaton in *Annie Hall* – Diane Keaton in anything, really – all lithe and coltishly limby.

But she was always far too short and chubby for that sort of caper – or, at least she always *thought* she was.

Today, however, she felt like she could give even Audrey Hepburn a run for her money, because stop press, she actually looked...quite good!

Go on, say it out loud, like you're talking to your best friend - make yourself really believe it!

'You look great!' she obeyed herself.

Perplexed by this uncharacteristically positive self-talk, she narrowed her eyes, bit the inside of her cheek and wondered fleetingly whether it was her body dysmorphia that was in full swing or whether her eyesight was now officially up the spout.

She had been feeling a little out of focus, a bit blurry, slightly off-kilter ever since she...Kate couldn't remember when, she surprised herself to acknowledge.

She peered at herself and assumed an air of fragile confidence.

'Yep, you look great!' she said again. 'Even though you're porking out, it's now or never to start loving your body. No matter how much it makes the ground beneath you shake.'

Kate wandered cautiously into the kitchen.

'Brave, Our Kid,' said Steve in a shockingly bad Mancunian accent. 'Do you really think you should wear that?'

'Don't listen to him,' said Georgia through a mouthful of toast. 'You look fab. All you need is a hat with a massive flower on it, like Blossom, and you're away!'

Kate wasn't sure whether Georgia was taking the mickey or not, so she simply worked her lips into what she hoped was an enigmatic smile (although she had no idea how to do this, so ended up looking rather more Irritable Bowel Syndrome than intriguing) and sat down on the kitchen bench.

She self-consciously tugged at the hem on her dress, trying to pull it over her plump knees, even though they were out of sight, hidden underneath the heavy oak table.

'Where you off to, anyway?' asked Steve.

'Shopping first, football after,' Kate replied, helping herself to an unfeasibly large bowl of Crunchy Nut Corn Flakes.

'That's not like you,' said Georgia gathering up

her thick, dark hair into a ponytail and securing it with a fluoro orange scrunchie.

'Oh!' cried Kate. 'I haven't seen one of those for...'

'Yeah, sorry,' said Georgia. 'I raided your supply ages ago – haven't had the time to get any more.'

Kate screwed up her face and stared at Georgia. How she could wear neon-coloured hair bands and still look beautiful, was beyond her. The bright colours always clashed with Kate's skin tone whenever she tried for a casual up-do, and made her look like some saddo who never got over the 80s.

'Ahem,' Kate coughed. 'Forget about it – with all these layers, I can't do anything with my hair, except the Rachel.'

'And even that's not going too well, lately, is it?' said Steve sarkily as he got up to put his cereal bowl in the sink.

Little wonder, she thought, that she was so insecure about her looks, when those closest to her took potshots at her appearance as a matter of course.

'What's with you this morning?' Kate said, starting to get a little tired of Steve's verbal assault.

'Oh, nothing, nothing,' he said, frowning. 'I'm sorry, Sis, I don't know what's wrong with me – you look fine. Honestly.'

Fine? *Fine?*

'Gorgeous, you mean,' Georgia corrected him. 'Fine is for weather, not women.'

Good line, G, thought Kate. She repeated it in her

head three times in an effort to remember it for when Seamus said the exact same, infuriating thing back in 2014.

'You're right, you're right,' said Steve, putting his hands on Kate's shoulders from behind and bending down to kiss her cheek. 'You look gorgeous. I'm just a little tetchy this morning because I've got...a date!'

'A *date*?' the girls chorused.

'Who is he?' Georgia teased him.

'*She* is someone you don't know,' Steve said. 'Or don't know very well. Yet.'

He turned his back and hightailed it out of there before his flatmates could grill him any further about his fledgling love life.

'I'll see you at O'Flaherty's!' he yelled as the front door slammed heavily behind him.

*

Despite the warm air, Kate shivered a little as she stood out the front of Selfridge's, waiting for Seamus.

Her knees hadn't been this exposed for centuries and the body-loving, confident attitude she had assumed only an hour ago, had all but deserted her as she hugged herself, glad of the last-minute Hennes pin-striped blazer she'd grabbed on her way out of the flat.

Not that she was into or even normally *aware* of labels – unless they were of the Primark or TK Maxx bargainous variety. In fact, she didn't care for shopping much, either, if truth be told.

Well that wasn't entirely true. She loved baby shops and getting cute outfits for Baby Jane. She'd even got a kick out of kitting the boys out in what she thought were trendy clothes. Seamus, of course, was a lost cause, his already woeful dress sense sacrificed on the altar of golf (argyle jumpers and nylon slacks) years ago, so she didn't have to bother there.

But when it came to clothes shopping for *herself*, Kate just couldn't get into it.

Just like her old size 12 jeans.

Perhaps it was the fact that she was entering (or had already entered) that phase of life where comfort was more important to her than being on-trend; for at 44, she wore Fit Flops rather than Havaianas, Hush Puppies as opposed to killer heels and she looked in M&S for whole, shapeless outfits (usually in Menopause Blue) – not just bras and knickers anymore.

Maybe it was because she found the whole depressing experience a colossal waste of time, when nothing ever fit or looked good on her, she had no idea what was age appropriate and she was constantly shocked by the old woman she saw staring back at her from changing room mirrors.

She much preferred shopping for food at Waitrose or Sainsbury's, lulling herself into a false sense of domestic goddessery, where her fantasies of preparing perfect three-course meals for her wonderfully erudite, Wildean, very-possibly-on-the telly friends could come crashing to the fore. She often imagined their faces as they took their first bite of her tiramisu, their eyes closing in ecstasy as they lustily declared her dessert

'Heavenly'.

She loved food (clearly) and she loved *shopping* for food. Nothing cheered her up more than a recently-stocked, full fridge. But clothes shopping? Meh.

But anyway, she reminded herself, this little expedition was all about Seamus. Because not only did she have to secure Seamus' help if she was ever to get back to 2014, it was also the perfect excuse to just spend some time with him, alone together.

She wanted to get to know him again, find out what it was about him that made her fall in love with him in the first place.

Given her attitude to clothes shopping, though, how on earth was she going to save Seamus from a life of leisure suits and other trainspottery garb? Particularly when she herself had known some tragic outfits of her own? Still, she reasoned with herself, she *had* to have more dress sense than he did. God knows, Timmy Mallet had more taste in his *hat* than Seamus had in his entire wardrobe.

When he ran up to her (Seamus, that is, not Timmy), out of breath and panting, his spray jacket flapping about behind him, Kate greeted him with a tentative kiss on the cheek and a quiz.

'First up, let's test your fashion IQ,' she said, wondering for a second whether she had been working with magazines for far too long. 'For instance, what do you think of what I'm wearing?'

'Yeah,' he answered distractedly, panting like a dog. 'Yeah, it's fine.'

'Fine?' she shook her head, as though she couldn't quite believe what she was hearing (even though, of course, she'd heard it a million times before from Seamus and had even come to expect it as his stock response to just about any question she threw at him). 'Fine is for weather, not women.'

So proud of herself and her short-term memory, she nodded as if to say: 'Oh yeah, Baby, that's what we're dealing with here, wit *and* repartee!'

'Oh, I didn't mean to sound – '

'Like a typical bloke?' she finished his sentence for him, feeling as sharp as a tack.

'No, I – I actually think it looks fantastic!' Seamus' voice cracked when he said 'fantastic'.

'Oh,' Kate looked down at her spongy knees and put her hands on her hips. 'This old thing?'

'No, not you – your dress!' Seamus tried to elbow her in the ribs, but only made it to her upper arm, such was their height difference.

Kate's arms dropped to her sides and she pulled a pretend offended face.

'Let's head to Topman, see what they can do for you,' she said, steering him towards Oxford Circus.

Not twenty minutes later, Seamus pulled back the changing room curtain for his big reveal. There he was, this six foot two gentle giant in skinny jeans, a white t-shirt with a red checked lumberjack shirt tied around his waist, Reebok pump high-top sneakers and a baseball cap dangling from his fingers.

'It's just not really...me,' he said quietly. 'All feels

a little bit too East 17 to me. But if you like it...'

And she did. Sort of. She was so used to seeing Seamus as the trainspotter that style forgot, she was desperate to get him into something young and cool while she had the chance.

But even she found Seamus tarted up like he was the sixth member of *One Direction* a bit mutton dressed as lamb... if you could say 'mutton' for men.

Kate didn't think you could. And anyway, I sound like an ad for aftershave, she giggled to herself – Try new Mutton For Men – and have the ladies baa-ing for more/and send the ladies baa-ing mad/and you'll never baa up the wrong tree again/the hottest aftershave known to man – baa none...

Focus, Katie, focus.

Maybe she meant *rammy* – more rammy than lamby? No, that didn't sound right. Ram dressed as lamb. Yes! That was it.

'Hmmm,' she said, rubbing her slightly-less defined chin. 'Bit rammy, you're right. How old are you again?'

'Twenty six,' he answered. 'Why?'

Kate shook her head quickly, as though his very question was a massive irritation.

'It's just...why do you insist on looking so, so old? So old way before your time?'

'I didn't think I did,' he replied, sounding a smidge hurt. 'But even if I do, what's wrong with looking old? What's so *bad* about old?'

That shut her up. Kate couldn't find the words to

express how she felt about age – especially as she'd done somewhat of a 360 in the past few days, where her attitude towards her ageing body was concerned.

'Nothing,' she eventually managed as Seamus drew the changing room curtain and got back into his own clothes. 'There's nothing bad about it at all. I just think that while you're young, you might as well make the most of it – all that tight skin, all that wrinkle-free flesh –'

At that moment, Seamus emerged, rubbing his just-about-to-start-balding-any-minute pate.

'Ah, it's not all it's cracked up to be,' he grinned, the twinkle in his eye burning bright.

'You see?' said Kate, holding out her hands in exasperation. 'You've got a full head of hair and you're acting as though you're flaming Kojak!'

'All right, all right,' said Seamus, his smile fading and the twinkle dulling. 'Keep *your* hair on!'

'You'll be growing hair out of your ears and nostrils before you know it, your nose getting bigger and more bulbous...'

'And on that bombshell...' Seamus smiled, handing the rammy clothes back to the bored salesgirl at the counter.

As the pair walked out of the youth-crazed shop and meandered up Oxford Street, Kate began her sermon.

'I just think you're really quite good looking, you know, and you don't do yourself justice wearing all that boring old non-descript gear,' she explained. 'I mean, as a girl, sorry, a woman, rather, I know that when you think you look good you feel good. Or is it vice versa? Bugger! I can never remember which way round they go... Anyway, the point is, your confidence soars when your outer self is as interesting or as charming or as amusing or as good-looking as your inner self and-'

'What a load of old –'

'It's true!'

'So do you think I'm charming and funny, too?'

'Only if you're wearing that football shirt as some sort of a joke,' she smiled up at him.

Seamus stopped mid-lope and held onto Kate's elbows gently, turning her around to face him.

'I've never said this to a girl – *a woman* – before, Kate, but I want you to know that you can count on me –'

'Yes?' Kate looked past Seamus' daggy NHS specs, deep into the dark brown pools that were his eyes.

Here it comes, she thought, his declaration of hero-like manliness, how he's hot but dependable; fun and feisty, desperate to dedicate his life to making his family happy.

Kate drew in a deep breath, nearly paralysed by the potential poignancy of the moment.

His gaze bore into hers, their eyes moist with meaning.

And then he said:

'You can count on me to never, *ever* joke about

Liverpool.'

*

Kate let Seamus keep his almost-cool spray jacket - only because they saw a couple of the guys from Ocean Colour Scene wearing them as they trawled about the shops in Carnaby Street and Seamus pleaded with her to let him hold onto it, saying there was proof that he was a trend-setter not a trainspotter. But as they passed a bin on their way to O'Flaherty's, she wrestled it off him (and the plastic bag containing his too-tight denim jeans, his kayak shoes and his seventies body shirt that was giving off so much static electricity, even the hairs on Seamus' arms were standing on end) and chucked them all away.

Before they walked into the pub, Kate admired her handiwork.

'You look great, Seamus,' she reassured him. 'Really good.'

'You sure it's not too try-hard?' his eyes searched hers, a thin layer of uncertainty coating his words.

'Don't be ridiculous,' Kate dismissed him. 'you're just not used to looking so hot. It'll take your brain a while to catch up. In the meantime, I suggest you get some new glasses. Or why not go for contacts?'

Seamus shook his head at this and she realised she was pushing him too far, too fast. He'd only just summoned up the courage to ditch his dodgy shoes – now the only familiar security blanket he had left were his outdated spectacles, why would he toss them, too?

'All in good time,' she smiled, silently

encouraging him to trust her, embrace change and make an appointment at SpecSavers. He had, after all, gone leaps and bounds in the style stakes today and if he carried on like this, Kate thought, she'd have to beat the competition off with a stick.

Speaking of competition, as they pushed the saloon doors open, Georgia bounded up to them.

'A-HA!' she slurred, unsteady on her feet already. 'I KNEW you were up to something, Kate! Knew you wanted him all to yourself!'

Kate directed her best friend away from her husband-to-be and manoeuvred her through the rowdy crowd towards the other end of the bar.

'God!' Kate exclaimed. 'Was it just us or was everyone drinking like fish in 1996?'

'What ARE you on about, Kate? Just get me another vodka Red Bull and show me the guy you want to set me up with. You said he worked at PGT&B?'

Kate scanned the pub, standing on the metal pole at the foot of the bar, like a springbok looking for safety in the wide open, dry, African plains - all rigid of back and jerky of head movement. But she couldn't see Kevin anywhere. Not that that meant anything – due to her restricted height and slightly blurry aspect, she couldn't see much at all. Kevin could well be there, it's just that Kate wouldn't know it.

What she did know, though, was that Archie, her arch enemy it felt like these days, was on her horizon. She could feel it.

Her eyes darted left and right and then BULLSEYE! Her gaze locked onto his and he called her name as he approached.

'Kate!' he yelled, standing on his tip toes as punters barged into him, their lager sloshing out of their pint glasses and splashing onto his shirt.

Pubs where you couldn't get a seat were no place for those shorter in stature, Kate thought to herself as she looked around for a vacant table. When she couldn't see one, and Archie began to close in on her, she fought the almost irresistible urge to flee.

'Kate!' he muscled his way through the burly blokes surrounding the girls and looked up at Georgia, as though he'd only just noticed how positively Amazonian she was, compared to his little tiddly self.

This'll be interesting, Kate thought.

'I'm so glad I found you,' he said, short of breath (as well as height, Kate noted, bitterly). 'I wanted to apologise for, um, sacking you over the phone the other day and explain why I've been behaving so badly towards you lately.'

Georgia raised her eyebrows, shoved her glass in her mouth and gulped thirstily.

'Could we talk somewhere a little more private?' he asked, looking decidedly awkward.

'Oh! Don't mind me,' said Georgia, her straw still in her mouth. 'I was leaving, anyway. I believe there's a man somewhere out there with my name on him.'

Kate felt her stomach lurch, hoping against all hope that Georgia didn't mean Seamus. Because no man stood a chance against her feminine wiles! Even if said wiles were a little slow due to their being drenched in vodka.

She took a deep breath through her nose and tried to calm herself, find her centre, as Georgia had told her to do so many times when the kids were driving her crazy and her OCD was threatening to make the whole family mad.

'So, young Archie,' she said, in only slight patronising tones. 'What have you got to say for yourself, then?'

'I want you to come back to work – I miss you! And we need you.'

Kate scoffed at this.

'HA! Why should I? You've been totally horrible to me lately and –'

'I know, I know,' Archie cut her off. 'But I can explain.'

A space cleared next to Kate and Archie leapt up onto the empty bar stool that was revealed, like a 10-year-old gymnast, straddling the horse.

'I'm listening,' Kate said, trying to fold her arms across her chest, but not being able to, due to her bust doubling in size right before her eyes.

Oh Lord, Kate said to herself. So they're getting bigger now, too! Back to my post three baby-size, I'll wager. What's the bet I'll be back in a 16DD and lounging about in 2014 before I've even finished this pint!

'Blimey,' said Archie, unable to tear his gaze

away from her bosoms.

'You were saying?' Kate said, taking another mouthful of beer and playing with the condensation on the glass with her fingertips.

'Right, yes, I, ah...I wanted to apologise for acting so weirdly around you lately – it's all my fault, of course.'

'Of course,' Kate echoed.

'I couldn't help it,' Archie carried on. 'I've had a crush on you ever since we met and even though I knew, deep down, that we would probably never get together, that didn't stop me getting insanely jealous whenever what's-his-face craned his scrawny neck into your orbit.'

'What?' Kate took a step back. 'Who?'

'You know,' said Archie, looking to the floor as if he was about to spit in disgust. 'That IT guy, Wayne or Shane or something.'

'*Seamus*, you mean?'

'Yeah, something like that,' Archie said quickly, as though he was annoyed for conjuring up the mental image of the very man he wanted Kate to ignore. 'I could see why you'd go for Tom – hell, even *I'd* go for Tom! But that dweeb? What's he got that I haven't got? Don't answer that. Anyway, he's not important. What *is* important is that I couldn't handle the impotent anger that descended upon me every time I thought of you with him and...and so -'

'And so you acted like a total bastard?' Kate helped him out.

‘Yes,’ said Archie sheepishly. ‘Can you ever find it in your heart to forgive me?’

Kate looked off into the middle distance as though she were seriously considering his question.

‘Kate?’ Archie said after a few minutes. ‘Kate, I’m so sorry. I’ll do anything to have you back! Just name your terms and -’

‘Quite frankly, Archie, I’m not sure I want to come back,’ she said slowly. ‘I mean, there’s the stress, the long hours, the crap pay...’

‘A four-day week, then, how would that be?’

‘Hmmm,’ hummed Kate, sure she could see some sweat forming on Archie’s brow. ‘I dunno. That open-plan office is getting me down a bit...’

‘You can have your own office! You can have mine! Would that help?’

‘And my salary – it’s so rubbish! Barely keeps me in rent and microwave meals for one...’

‘Now hang on a second, Kate, now you’re just taking the piss!’

But just then, out of the corner of her eye, she caught sight of something so striking, so compelling, so *gorgeous*, she simply had to ignore everything around her and stare at it.

The crowd noise died down to almost nothing and everybody else in the packed pub morphed into one slow-moving mass. And what came into sharp relief, where the spotlight was shining brightest, was on the profile of an impossibly handsome man. A man who was wearing an outfit that would make Paul Weller sigh with unbridled envy.

The dashing figure turned to look straight at Kate and when their eyes met, she felt her knees buckle.

25

'Come in, come in!' A pleased-looking Paris ushered Kate, Seamus, Steve and Georgia into the front hall of the family home in Ickenham.

And as the intoxicating aroma of Blue's roast lamb and perfect potatoes drifted into their nostrils, all four guests swooned simultaneously, with Seamus and Georgia saying in unison:

'Smells great!'

'Steven! I'm so glad you came!' Paris couldn't help himself and flung his arms around his son.

Steve looked a tad taken aback, but smiled cautiously and patted his father's back in return.

'We've missed you so much! Please don't ever, ever disappear like that again, you hear me?'

Paris in protective father mode was something rarely seen, what with Blue being the dominant one, having worn the trousers for so many years and all – but when he was in full swing like this, Kate felt her heart swell with pride.

That's the way a dad should be, she thought to herself – strong, forthright, quick with a manly hug whenever needed. Quick with a manly hug at any time, actually – because who could ever get enough of that safe, secure, snug feeling a bear hug brought?

She looked at Seamus intently, loving the fact that he was trying to grow sideburns (at her suggestion), and tried to instill in him, by sheer force of will, Paris' brilliant dad qualities.

Paris reluctantly let go of a perplexed Steve and turned his attentions to Kate.

'Ah, my princess! Let me look at you!' He took hold of her hands and nodded approvingly. 'Nice to see you finally putting some meat on those bones, Gorgeous!'

Before she had time to get offended, she got a whiff of his sweet breath and realised that the return of his normal bubbly good humoured self had been ably assisted by alcohol. And when her dad's body engulfed her own, she closed her eyes, savouring the moment. His arms wrapped around her back, she imagined a big, avuncular gorilla was embracing her, grinning at the bliss of it all.

How she'd missed the physical contact with her dad – with both her parents, to tell the truth.

Because it was all well and good people saying your loved ones were always with you, even once they'd passed over to the other side. Kate had often found comfort in telling herself exactly that. It had got her through some tough times, and she still spoke to them both regularly, addressing the air around her as if they just might magically appear if she begged for long enough, cried hard enough. But a real hug took some beating.

'Come on through, everybody!' called Blue from the kitchen. 'I'm pouring some more champagne and we don't want it to go flat, now, do we?'

'Ooh! Champers!' trilled Georgia as she kissed

Paris on the cheek. 'What are we celebrating?'

'Life!'Paris chuckled as he looked deep into Seamus' eyes and extended a liver-spotted rough-hewn hand. 'Now, Kate? Aren't you going to introduce us?'

'Oh! Sorry, Paris,' said Kate. 'This is Seamus, my...my friend, Seamus.'

'Pleased to meet you, Mister –'

'Pah!' exclaimed Paris. 'No need for that, young man – we don't stand on stuffy ceremony here. Please call me Paris. And the little lady in there –'

'Oi!' boomed the little lady from the kitchen.

'...sorry, the woman of my dreams in there, goes by the beautifully apt name of Blue.'

'Right, right,' said Seamus, ducking his head in deference as Kate gently put her hand on the small of his back and guided him down the hallway.

In the warm open plan kitchen, French doors opened onto the garden in full bloom, Kate watched as Blue hugged her son for all she was worth.

'You're not getting away this time,' Blue said, her voice muffled as she squashed her face into his shirt. 'I refuse to ever let you go!'

'Well, can you just...loosen your grip... a little bit?' laughed Steve through short breaths. 'I can't breathe!'

'And where's my kiss hello?' beamed Georgia as she approached Blue, resting her hand on the matriarch's shoulder.

Georgia loved coming to Kate's parents' house. Blue and Paris had often acted like surrogate parents for her, always there for her when she rowed with her own mother (every Friday night for five years) and treating her as one of the family.

'Ah, my third child,' cooed Blue. 'Why haven't we seen you for such a long time? Especially when you needed us most, when you had your misc-'

'Oh, I'm fine, Bluey,' Georgia cut her off. 'Minor blip and now I'm back – better than ever and absolutely *starving*!'

'Well, sit down,' Blue tore herself away from Steve shortly after she pinched his cheeks puce. 'I thought we could start in the garden, it being such a lovely day – and then migrate inside for the main event.'

Kate drank in the wonderfully warm, family scene before her. She felt oddly detached, as though she were having an out of body experience and she was hovering above somebody else's perfect, functional family.

Seamus looked at Kate, feeling half like the invisible man, half like the jolly green giant, given that he was quite big and burly at 6' 2" and 13 stone. He stared at her who, in turn, was staring at the oven, her head cocked to the side, a slightly unsettling smile glued to her lips.

He badly needed her direction and so, to get her attention, coughed her name discreetly.

'Ka-hoh! Kay-hate! Kay-hoh hoh-hoff!'

'Hmmm?' Kate blinked repeatedly, as though she were waking from a dream.

‘Ooh, that sounds nasty,’ Blue addressed Seamus, her concern genuine and mumsy. ‘I’ve probably got some Tixylix here somewhere. I’m Blue by the way. Please excuse my daughter – manners of a woolly mammoth.’

‘That better not be another reference to my recent – and ever-so-slight weight gain...’ Kate said. ‘Blue? This is Seamus.’

‘Nice to meet you,’ said Blue, clasping her hands together and letting them rest on her chest. ‘Very nice indeed.’

Kate and Seamus both shifted about uneasily as Blue looked him up and down.

‘Although, I think you’ve got something stuck to your face.’

With the index finger of her right hand outstretched, like ET pointing to the sky, Blue skipped over to Seamus and tried to pull off the patchy bits of hair covering his cheekbones.

‘It’s just...a bit...of fluff...’

Seamus pulled away and rubbed his cheek.

‘Actually, they’re my sidies,’ he said sheepishly. ‘Or will be, eventually.’

Blue looked at him, puzzled.

‘Sidies? What on earth –’

‘Sideburns, Mum,’ Kate muttered, her tone slightly irritated. ‘You know, mutton chops! Anyway, leave him alone, will you? And can we eat? We’re all wasting away, here!’

Blue raised an eyebrow, pursing her lips as she

made a point of glancing southwards at Kate's bottom and Paris herded the group outside.

Once in the garden, the Pimm's and the champagne flowed – for everyone but Kate, that is.

'You know, you lot can really put it away,' she couldn't help but comment, a touch of the school marm to her tone.

'So can you,' Steve retorted. 'Usually you can, anway.'

'Yeah,' said Georgia, putting her glass down for a split second and sparking up a Marlboro Light. 'And she doesn't smoke anymore. Must be why she's stacking on the weight a bit.'

'I'll have you know,' said Kate, 'that I am not "stacking on the weight" as you so delicately put it, Georgia – I am simply becoming a proper, grown-up woman, getting my priorities straight, keeping a clear head and gaining some lumps and bumps along with my maturity.'

Kate took a sip of her lemonade (home-made – Blue was pulling out all the stops on the domestic front today) and winced as she heard what she'd just said and realised how boring, old and farty she sounded.

'I mean, I might be getting, um, a tad *curvier*,' she went on, trying to redeem herself, 'but that's what real women look like as they get older. And there's nothing wrong with that at all, is there, Blue?'

Kate looked at her mother accusingly.

'A bit of extra padding can be quite sexy, don't you think?'

Now it was Blue's turn to move herself about in her chair uneasily.

'I don't know whether I'd be qualified to answer that,' she said, coyly playing with a silver tendril of hair that had fallen out of her up-do as she glanced coquettishly at Paris.

'I am, though,' Paris chortled. 'And I can tell you right here and now that yes, everyone, a little cushioning in all the right places can –'

'...can really make a man hungry,' Steve butted in, pushing himself up by the arms of his chair and crossing his legs theatrically, like Kenny Everett on his video show. 'When's lunch, Ma?'

'Ooh! Yes,' Blue clutched the lapis lazuli beads that hung around her neck. 'I nearly forgot! Come on in, everybody. Paris, Darling? Would you get the joint out and wrap it up in tin foil, let it sit for 20 minutes? Get the veg out and start on the gravy, too, would you? I just want to have a little word with my devoted daughter, here.'

Kate looked at Seamus, almost apologetically, and motioned for him to follow Paris and Steve inside.

'I'll be in in a sec,' she whispered to him, reassuringly. 'Go on. Georgia'll look after you.'

'That's what I'm afraid of,' said Seamus at the same moment as Georgia linked her left arm into his right.

'Come on, you great hunk of man,' said Georgia, rubbing her right hand up and down what would have been his bulging bicep, if he'd had any muscle tone whatsoever.

Blue busied herself picking up the pitcher of Pimm's and a couple of empty glasses. She didn't even look Kate in the eye when she spoke to her, so terrified was she of the answer.

'So, Dear,' she began. 'You've gone off the booze and fags, there's a - shall we say - *thickening* around your middle...'

'I'd hardly say thickening,' Kate interrupted, her chin falling to her chest as she inspected her waist.

'Are you pregnant, Kate?'

'What?' Kate could hardly believe her ears.

'I beg your pardon, you mean,' her mother corrected her.

'No!' Kate slurped up the last bits of creamy potato and leek soup that Seamus and Georgia had left in their respective bowls. 'Of course I'm not!'

Blue either didn't hear her daughter's response – or flatly didn't believe her, because she carried on regardless.

'And is that nice young man, the one with the hairy face – is he the father? What the hell happened to Tom? And why don't you tell me anything anymore?'

'No!' Kate cried. 'No, I am not pregnant. And no, Seamus isn't the father, either.'

She stopped herself when she heard these words and shuddered to think how close she came to going off with Tom and effectively erasing Seamus from her life. She screwed up her nose, thinking that if she'd ignored Seamus and rid herself of him, then, as a result, so George, Declan and baby Jane would disappear, too.

'And Tom?' Blue pressed. 'Last I heard you were moving in together - what happened there?'

'Nothing, really,' Kate said, trying hard to remember what had actually happened. 'I did move in with him. For one night. But I think we both realised it wasn't going to work. I love him, in a way, and think he's a nice guy and everything –'

'Well, he did save our Steve from rack and ruin,' Blue looked at Kate with wide eyes. 'Or worse...'

'I know, it's just,' Kate squirmed and looked over the garden fence, 'he just didn't do it for me in the end.'

Kate dared to look at Blue. Blue softened and nodded as she picked up the soup tureen and began to head inside.

'Hmm,' she hummed, dreamily. 'I know exactly what you mean.'

'You do?'

'Yes, Darling, I do. Even women of *un certain age* need to get their rocks off from time to time, you know.'

'So that's what put this rather unseemly spring in your step, is it? You've been *at it*, like a dog in heat, have you?'

'Hardly, Sweetheart,' Blue laughed. 'A little less of *the dog*, if you don't mind.'

Kate thought of the suave man she'd seen Blue throwing herself at in Carluccio's and felt her face redden.

'But we did *do it*,' Blue's eyes sparkled. 'Yes, after a drought lasting more years than I care to remember, we finally had sex last night.'

This was it, Kate thought as she girded her loins – the moment she'd been waiting for. Her chance to really let rip, tear into her mum for being unfaithful to her dad, really let her know what she thought of such scarlet behaviour.

'Mum! How could you?'

Blue's starry eyes looked over her shoulder at her daughter as if to say: 'Darling! It really has been too long between shags for you, hasn't it?'

'Well...we did! And it was fantastic!' Blue squealed, suddenly looking ten years younger.

'Well I think it's disgusting,' Kate couldn't hide her displeasure. 'At your age! And what about poor Dad?'

'What do you mean, "at my age"? And "poor Dad" is just fine about it, thankyou very much. More than fine, actually – he's over the moon! Just look at him!'

Kate knitted her eyebrows. Was she missing something here, or was her mother saying that her father approved of her having an affair? With the old swinging guy from next door?

'Wait a minute,' she tugged at Blue's elbow and stopped her in her tracks. 'Are you telling me that Dad's OK with it? Happy about it, even?'

'Of course he is!' Blue pulled her elbow away

from Kate's grasp. 'He's bloody *delirious*, Darling!'

'This isn't right,' Kate shook her head, studying the ground at her feet. 'No, no – this is wrong on just about every level going!'

'What *are* you on about, Kate?' Blue said in hushed voice, as though Kate might be seriously mentally ill – or need a good lie down, at the very least.

'You can't make Dad try swinging and then run off with the first old guy who takes your fancy! Not when you've got a husband who loves you like crazy and kids who look up to you and depend on you for...for their moral guidance and everything!'

Blue took a step back, as though the strength of Kate's words was knocking her off her feet.

'Sit down, Love,' she said after a few seconds. 'I think you've got the wrong end of the stick.'

Kate and Blue put the crockery down on the grass and headed back to the shade of the John Lewis outdoor furniture set, complete with umbrella, that Blue and Paris had agonised over buying for years.

Sitting down, visibly shaken, Kate listened to Blue's side of the story.

'Sweetie Pie, I know how hard this must be for you to hear this, but I think it's important you do, so please, bear with me.'

Kate agreed to let her mother speak without interruption.

'While being a wife and mother is wonderful, it's not without its hardships and tough times. As a young mum – which you will find out soon, if you get a wriggle on – you devote all your time and energy to your kids. And it's a privilege to do so. But after a while, you start to realise that a big part of your old self and your old relationship with your man has gone AWOL – and try as you might, you just can't get it back.'

Blue looked anxiously off over the garden fence while she spoke, making Kate look behind her and wonder whether Sir Swing-a-lot was waving at her mum.

'Your profession has changed and moved on, so have your old friends and you're older, with responsibilities. You can never go back to how it was and thank God, really – I mean, when I think about what I used to find fun or important or necessary for a good life, I almost have to laugh. I mean, what a waste of time!'

Kate smiled at this and knew exactly what Blue meant. Even though she didn't agree with her 100% (Kate *had* managed to go back, after all – even though the past wasn't strictly as she remembered it), Kate could finally see that all the drinking and smoking and so-called 'partying' she used to do was now boring to her.

'One day you'll realise that things have changed – and you, yourself have changed - for a pretty good reason. And that good reason is family. It's the most important thing in life, without a doubt.'

'So why –'

'Ah-ah-ah,' Blue sing-songed, wagging her finger at Kate. 'Let me finish. Now where was I? Um, jeepers, my memory is definitely not what it used to be, that's for – ah! Family, that's right! *Family.* So while family is the most important part of a woman's life, it's not the *only* part. Some women are satisfied with taking care of their family – whether that involves working at a job to bring in money or working tirelessly at domestic duties for no pay at all. But some women – and I am, rightly or wrongly, one of these, Love – need more excitement, more drama, more *danger* in their lives than living vicariously through their husband and kids can bring.'

Kate felt just like she used to as a six-year-old kid when she'd ask her mother what a particular word meant, only to receive a lecture on the word's etymology and modern usage by way of a thousand examples.

Kate wanted to get to the nub of the matter quickly, just as she had way back then – and nodded impatiently, as if the increasing speed of her head movement was going to give Blue a subliminal message, and her mini seminar would be wrapped up fast as a result.

'Which is why I thought swinging – despite it sounding silly and suburban – might be a good idea for your father and me. I thought it might help us rekindle the spark, relight the fire, as Lulu sang with that all-boy pop group...what were they called again?'

'Take –'

‘Take That!’ Blue jumped up a little bit out of her chair, she was so excited to have remembered something from the recent past with only a teensy bit of prompting. ‘Yes, Take That, that’s right.’

‘YOO-HOO, YOU TWO! COME ON!’ Paris called out from the French doors.

‘Won’t be a minute,’ Blue yelled back.

Kate hoped she was telling the truth – she was keen to get at one of her mum’s roasts while she still had the chance and her mouth started watering at the thought of it.

‘Now I’ve totally lost my train of thought. Where was I?’

‘You were relighting your fire with Dad.’

‘Yes, yes. Well, anyway, to cut a long story short, it wasn’t for us. We both felt too self-conscious and embarrassed and no one did it for me quite like your father. Apart from this one man, a really nice man called Terry.’

Kate stiffened as she pictured this Terry groping her mother in Carluccio’s again.

‘Turns out,’ Blue continued, ‘when we went into Julia, the woman hosting the party, when we went into Julia’s bedroom, Terry didn’t want to go through with anything physical, either. So while Paris was in the living room, talking to Marjorie Bentham and Terry’s wife, Sadie, I was in the bedroom, getting on like a house on fire with Terry, with him chewing my ear off – not literally, you understand, nothing physical went on – about the adventure holiday business for the over

60s he wanted to start up.'

Kate looked vexed and tired at the same time as she stifled a yawn with one hand and rubbed the back of her neck with the other – it was getting quite sore with all the rapid nodding she'd been doing.

'And so there we are,' said Blue, slapping her hands down on her knees, which Kate mis-read as a gesture of chuffed conclusion. But Blue was far from finished.

'So I'm going to go into business with Terry, which has given me a new lease of life, a whole new start, professionally. And now with all that creativity coursing through my veins, it's really got my juices flowing again – pun well-intended – and, consequently, as your father was saying only this morning, it's given me a sort of glow, a new vibe, that's not only wildly attractive and irresistible to him, but something that's taken years off me.'

Blue paused momentarily.

'It's like we've rediscovered why we fell in love with each other in the first place, all those hundreds of years ago. Me with my energy, him with his protective manly vigour – we feel like teenagers again!'

Blue sighed and looked wistfully at the daisies and dandelions not far from her feet. Kate wondered whether this was her chance to jump into the conversation.

It wasn't.

'But anyway, Snuggle Pot, you don't want to hear about our sex life!'

'No!' said Kate, relieved, starting to get up. 'I don't!'

'The point I'm trying to make is that I was running to stand still - happy, but unfulfilled by being a wife and a mother. So I rose to the challenge and reinvented myself, found something new that I was passionate about and dredged up from somewhere the courage and confidence to go for it!'

Kate's tummy rumbled loudly and when she put her hand to it, she felt its fleshy softness, reassuring her in its familiarity. This was how she was used to her stomach feeling to her touch, and she was convinced that every inch she gained on her body now meant she was getting closer to getting home.

'Thing is, Darling, you can never go back – not to how *you* were, not to how *things* were. You've got to move, evolve and change with the times. Which is great! It's so exciting! And that's what life's all about, what living is all about – the here and now. Lord knows life's too short and no one knows what the future will bring -'

Kate got a little teary at this juncture and her chin dimpled with the effort of staving off a good old cry.

'What's the matter, Kate, hmmm?' Blue asked, getting up and walking around to Kate, putting her arm around her daughter's shoulders and pulling her head to her pinny.

Blue – or, rather, Blue's pinny - smelled of Comfort fabric conditioner, roast dinners, chocolate chip cookies and bread and butter pudding.

Somewhere in that heady mix was the smell of cigarettes and red wine, left over from the days when the whole family indulged their vices a little too enthusiastically. It seemed to Kate, in her upset-but-happy, relieved-yet-anxious state, that the top notes were all about the safety and security of the home, just about managing to contain the unruly, rebellious middle and bottom notes.

Kate lost herself in these aromas for a short while, letting her mind swim in the great memories they evoked. Like the kids' birthday parties full of tears and tantrums and bikes and scraped knees; the adults' dinner parties, where Kate and Steve would sneak wine and whisky all night, listening to the grown-ups get sillier and more slurry with each passing course; the camping holidays that went horribly, hopelessly, hilariously wrong which were the stuff of family legend, now – folklore to be passed down through all subsequent generations.

Kate's thoughts quickly jumped over the family fence and fairly raced back to her own kids. Oh, how she wished she had her iPhone on her now and she could quickly trawl through the million photos of her three beautiful bundles. What she wouldn't give to proudly show Blue the fruits of her and Seamus' loins.

Slowly she became aware of something buzzing around her head. As it got a little louder, it became clear that it was the sound of someone talking. Blue was still banging on!

'...because the greatest gift of all we can give to

our children is the confidence to get out there, keep on moving and always be themselves. If I had to give you one bit of advice that I thought would see you right through life it would be this, Darling: happy wife, happy life. Constantly jabbering on about what's wrong or what used to be is a sure-fire way to guarantee a miserable life. For all the family. Find who you love, someone who makes your knees go weak - you'll know in your heart of hearts when you find him - settle down, have a family, build a bank of wonderful memories together and don't forget to find a little something for yourself, discover something you love doing. Love what you do and you'll never work a day in your life, as they say! And don't ever hold onto the past and the way things were – embrace the future and its amazing possibilities. It's the best recipe I have for a fulfilling life.'

There was a lull as Blue stopped for breath, and Kate pondered the wisdom of her mother's words. Despite the fact that they'd come a little bit too late. Then the sound of snoring filled the air.

'Kate? Kate! Are you asleep?'

Kate looked up at Blue and beamed.

'You little... rascal!'

'Just teasing, Ma,' Kate laughed, as the whole family used to after winding poor old Blue up about something or other.

'Yeah, well,' Blue grinned. 'I'd better get back inside before your baby brother gets too jealous and thinks you get all the attention.'

The pair got up, and as they got closer to the French doors, caught sight of Georgia tracing a decidedly uncomfortable Seamus' sideburns with her index finger while Steve and Paris looked on.

'And speaking of teasing,' Kate squinted to get a better look. 'Think I'd better save Seamus from Georgia. And himself.'

26

'You loved it!' Kate elbowed him in the ribs.

'I did *not*!' grinned Seamus. 'You know me – I *hated* it!'

Kate bit her tongue and realised that, yes, she did know him. Pretty well, come to think of it. And he really would have felt intensely uncomfortable when Georgia was making her moves, her unwanted advances towards him at lunch on Sunday.

But today was Wednesday – Wednesday, June 26 1996 – the day the advance copies of the latest issues of both *Mad Fer It!* and *LASHED* came into the office, with the Germany/England semi-final to look forward to later on.

It was a big day, and even though Kate hadn't officially gone back to work yet, she had come in early, so as not to miss the initial reactions from everybody and was killing time down in the basement of the PGT&B building, with the whole IT department – both Seamus *and* Kevin.

'So you couldn't help yourself, couldn't keep away any longer, could you? You just had to come and see where the magic happens,' Seamus had said when she'd strolled in. 'The heart of PGT&B's publishing operations, the very *nerve centre*, if you will.'

Or 'nerd centre', as Archie called it.

'The mags will be coming in upstairs any minute – why don't you two come up and see them with me?'

Kate said as she flicked through a dog-eared copy of *Back of the Net!* sitting on Seamus' desk. 'And also, I wanted to invite you two to my birthday party this Saturday.'

'The night before the final on Sunday,' Seamus said.

Kate resisted telling him that England were going to be knocked out of the competition tonight and he might not be as interested in watching the match the next day, if his team weren't playing in it. Then, quick as a flash, she wondered whether she should get down to Ladbroke's and put a bet on tonight's game going to penalties and Gareth Southgate subsequently missing his, effectively costing the country the game and, in turn, the chance to win Euro 96.

As she grappled with the ethics of the monumental cheat she was considering, Seamus spoke.

'I'm in!' he chirrupped. 'How old are you turning?'

'Forty-fi-' Kate stopped herself and, with the aid of her fingers and a chewed Bic biro sitting on top of a scrap of paper (mental arithmetic not being her strongest suit), counted backwards from 2014 to 1996, and then subtracted 18 from 45.

'Twenty seven,' she said finally, triumphant. 'God! Twenty seven! Who'd a thought...'

'Getting old there, Dear,' said Seamus softly. 'I said YOU'RE GETTING OLD, THERE, DEAR! Any minute now, you'll be 30 and then that's it. It's all over.'

'Doesn't have to be,' said Kate. 'It's all in how you look at it. Perspective is everything.'

Seamus pushed his glasses up with the tip of his middle finger and groaned.

'Next you'll be saying rubbish like "age is just a number" and "life begins at forty" and "you're only as old as the man you feel"'

'Yeah, I know!' Kate laughed at the ridiculousness of it all, wondering whether she had ever, in all sincerity, uttered those sorts of phrases. 'Or "ninety-eight years young" or whatever...'

'Speaking of, are Blue and Paris coming to your birthday bash?' Seamus asked. 'I've got a few questions about my swing I'd like to put to Paris.'

'No, actually,' Kate sighed. 'No, they won't and I'm a bit disappointed about that, to tell the truth. I thought they might be able to at least drop in and say hi.'

'Why aren't they coming? Got a better offer, did they?'

'Well, yes they did. They're going to be jumping out of a plane somewhere in Devon, I think. Skydiving. It's all a part of them trying out adventure holidays for the over-60s. They're setting up a business with a...a friend of theirs.'

'I think that's a cracking idea,' said Seamus, scratching his cheek in a deep-in-thought kind of way (although it's entirely possible that it was more a why-am-I-trying-to-grow-these-ridiculous-sideburns-when-they-make-my-face-so-unbearably-itchy? kind of way). 'They'll need a strong presence on the internet, definitely – especially when the OAPs of tomorrow are going to be more web-savvy than even I can imagine...'

Kate smiled. That was her Seamus, that was her man – always looking to the future, never dwelling in the past.

'You're right,' Kevin piped up. 'You know, there's something in that, what you just said.'

Kate's eyes were drawn to the place Kevin's voice had come from, and could see that he still had his cagoule on, even though he was sitting down in front of his monitor, barely visible amidst the towers of manuals and newspapers.

'Yes, I know,' Seamus spoke slowly and confidently. 'OAPs are going to need to be totally *au fait* with the internet and Kate's parents' new business will need a strong presence on the web...'

'And if,' Kevin went on, standing up and shedding his geeky coat. 'If, as you predict, the interweb is going to take off in amazing ways, older people and techno-doofuses alike are going to need some help getting to grips with all it has to offer.'

Seamus stuck out his lower jaw and continued clawing at his cheeks.

'And they'll need someone in the know, someone who can speak to them in their language, on their level to explain it all,' he said, his eyes bulging and blinking the more he saw into the bright future. 'Which is exactly where we come in! We'll talk to businesses, individuals – anyone who needs our help – and can pay us handsomely for it...That's it!'

'What?' Kate blinked.

'Don't you see?' Seamus wheeled around, spinning in a semi-circle, his khaki parka flying out behind him as though it was a superhero's cape.

'We'll start up our own web consultancy, bring IT to the masses, debunk the mysteries of the information superhighway!'

'Well, not too much, I hope – don't want to do ourselves out of any business –'

'Oh!' Seamus clapped his big, dry hands together and brought them in to his chest. 'There's no end to what we can do with this! Course, we'll need some good marketing behind us, so people will know we're out there...'

Seamus and Kevin stared at Kate.

'Who? Me?' said Kate. 'Oh, no – you don't want me, I'm too much of a flibberty-jibbet –'

'Flibberty – *what*? You sound like my grandmother! Next thing you know, you'll be knitting me a scratchy jumper and giving me 50p for Christmas!' Seamus laughed.

'I'm way too unpredictable, much too unreliable – you never know where you are with a girl like me – I'm here one day, gone the next!'

Kate crossed her fingers behind her back hoping against all hope that this really was the case and any minute now, some invisible force would fling her straight back into the future.

'Well, it's either you and you come into business with us – or some other company benefits from our talent and expertise.'

'Not to mention modesty,' Kate muttered, surprised at Seamus' sounding so self-assured all of a sudden.

'But how are we going to get the money together to set ourselves up in business?' Kevin wondered out loud, emerging from the manual and magazine mountain. 'I mean, start-up costs will be through the roof – we'll need equipment, advertising, a premises to rent...'

A silence descended upon the threesome as they thought about this.

'That's assuming we're partners, right Shay? I mean, we're in this together, right? It'll be half my business, too, yeah?'

'Of course!' said Seamus. 'Fifty-fifty, equals, straight down the middle. Unless Kate wants in, too, then all the colossal profits will be split into thirds. Now, we'll need a name – something catchy that says what we're all about...'

More chin rubbing, cheek scratching and jowl stroking (this was mainly Kate) ensued.

'What about...the it boys?' Kate offered to a sea of blank faces before her. 'You know, like Tara Palmer Thingy and Tamara Beckwith – they're it girls, right?'

Kevin and Seamus swapped glances, not getting where she was going at all.

'But instead of *it*, we cap it up, so it's IT! Geddit?'

‘Um,’ Seamus and Kevin ummed in unison.

‘The IT Boys! Like *it boys*, right, but IT!’ Kate carried on, losing them completely.

‘Let’s think on,’ said Seamus, flashing Kate a sympathetic smile. ‘But in the meantime, how are we going to raise the finance for our fantastic venture? Any ideas? Anyone?’

‘No,’ said Kate forlornly. ‘And anyway, the mags will be arriving right about now upstairs – wanna come with?’

‘I think we should stay down here and plot our escape from the corporate jungle,’ said Seamus, clearing his desk of all its debris with one sweep of his right arm.

‘OK,’ said Kate, turning to leave. ‘But you are going to come on Saturday, aren’t you? At The Prince Bonaparte pub on Chepstow Road. About one o’clock? That means you too, Kevin.’

‘Really? Well, yeah! That’d be great!’ squeaked Kevin who sounded like he didn’t get out all that much.

*

As soon as Kate stepped out of The Lift and into the third floor, she knew the magazines had turned up and that, as a result, some seismic shift had taken place.

The squeals and peals of laughter coming from the marketing department – particularly Tamsin – brought to mind George and Declan when they were three and two years old, respectively, and they went on the tea cup ride at Longleat.

Kate felt the knot of excitement in her tummy and couldn't wait to get her hands on the magazines. As she strode over to her desk, Tom jumped out at her.

'I've been looking for you everywhere, but you've been so hard to find,' he said, very possibly quoting lines from an old song, although Kate couldn't be sure. 'Where have you been?'

'At home,' she replied breezily. 'West Hampstead home, I mean.'

'We really need to talk – I've been going out of my mi-'

Never one for confrontation of any sort – particularly the public kind – Kate cut Tom off before he had a chance to finish.

'Ooh, look! There's the latest copy of *LASHED*! It's my favourite magazine, don't you know. Course, I only read it for the articles and comment on current affairs – I find it's brilliant at raising consciousness. And it has some *excellent* columnists writing for it...'

She winked at Steve and picked up the heavy glossy with the boxing ring and all four Britpop boys adorning the cover, Liam's face the biggest, naturally, looking like it was almost about to burst through the expensive paper stock .

Flicking through endless pairs of boobs and oiled-up flat bellies, Kate eventually found Steve's piece, about the shoot at the gym and read the intro out loud:

When we asked the two biggest bands on the planet to stop their sniping and play nice, we didn't even think they'd answer our calls, let alone show up to the shoot. But they did. And so we got bold in this, the coup of the century, and told them to kiss, make up and walk away the best of friends – or else. So did they? Or did they look back in anger? Steve O'Toole finds out...

'Great stuff, Steve!' Kate looked at her brother, blushing in front of her. 'Like your pen name, too – O'Toole!'

'They do it to all the new recruits,' Steve said. 'Make up a surname alluding to your manhood.'

'How grown-up of them,' Kate mumbled, holding the magazine in and out in front of her face as the words on the page wobbled about in a fuzzy mess.

'Ah! It's all gone blurry,' Kate said, bringing her fist up to her face to rub her eye, just like Baby Jane did when she was dog-tired. 'I'll have to read the rest later, when –'

'Here,' came Medea's velvety voice out of nowhere. 'Try my reading glasses – they're not prescription as such, just magnifying glasses, really, from Boots.'

Kate reached out and put the old lady link chain over her head and the frames on her face. They fitted rather nicely, she thought to herself, and reasoned that if the stunning Medea had to wear granny glasses, complete with an ugly plastic chain attached with little black rubber bands to the glasses' arms, then the thought of getting her own pair back in 2014 wasn't so dreadful.

While Kate fiddled with her face furniture, Medea

grabbed the magazine off her, turned to her column in the book and thrust it back at Kate, placing it right under her nose.

Kate looked down and began to read, the words fairly jumping off the page at her. Honestly, she thought, these glasses are incredible - it's like the letters are in HD, they're so crisp and clear!

'Let's see,' she said out loud. 'Our woman with more front than Blackpool –'

'Way-HEY!' came the chorus of 12-year-old marketing boys in the background.

'...Medea Hor'nbag...'

Kate looked over the top of the magazine and turned her mouth down at Medea who, in turn, winced at the discomfort of her name being bastardised in such a sleazy way.

'...blah-de-blah-de-blah,' Kate continued quickly. '...what really happened when Britpop boys Liam, Damon, Noel and Alex got together ... boxing clever...yermmurmer...rarely if ever has such a revolting display ...hang on! Such a revolting display of stags swaggering, rutting and burping as though part of an erotic mating ritual – with each other! Ah ... homoerotic ...um ...fragile male ego ... pathetic posturing, zero intelligence, more artistic integrity in my arse ...talentless twerps ...chauvinist pigs ...

Kate dropped the magazine down from her face and stared at Medea who was, she noted, in fantastically sharp focus.

She carried on reading.

‘Just like the pages of the disgusting rag you’re holding ...worthless, sexist, about as funny as a fart in an elevator ... boorish and boring ... ’

Kate’s mouth hung open and she searched Tom’s eyes for some sort of ocular explanation.

None was forthcoming – in fact, Tom looked more frightened than in the mood to discuss his editorial decision.

‘Have you taken leave of your senses printing that?’ Kate quizzed him.

‘But she’s right!’ Tom whimpered. ‘I just couldn’t go on living a lie, so I decided to go out with a bang and tell the world what I really think.’

‘Using Medea Hor’nbag as your mouthpiece,’ Archie joined in, reaching up a little to pat Tom on the back. ‘Genius, Tom, genius. It’s hilarious! The readers will get it – they’re a smart bunch who love nothing more than having a laugh at their own expense! It’s brilliant – well done.’

‘Have you seen my Ed’s Letter?’ Tom asked Archie.

‘No – what does it say?’

Kate flipped back to the front of the magazine and saw, under a picture of Tom beaming and waving, in bold capital letters:

I QUIT!

‘But why?’Archie whined. ‘This is going to fly off the shelves – you’re going to be massive!’

Tom shifted about from foot to foot and coughed, clearing his throat in preparation for his speech.

'I figured that, in the end, domination of the media world isn't going to make me happy. In fact, it's turning me into a bit of an alcoholic, drug-addled twat, to be completely honest,' Tom looked sheepishly at Kate at this revelation. 'I want to have a family one day – one day soon – and I thought if I ended up having a daughter, how could I possibly explain all this to her? I'd be so deeply ashamed, as though I'd betrayed her and her sex before she'd even been given a chance to make her mark in the world.'

He took a breath and turned his gaze from Kate to Medea.

'I want my daughters – my kids, whichever gender they belong to – to know that I'm behind them one hundred per cent – and that being a girl isn't a handicap – or shouldn't be – and that she can do anything she wants to do, regardless of the misogynistic world she lives in. I want her to know that she'll have more than just her looks – which are bound to be gorgeous, may I add – to offer the world. And I want them to be proud of me – not embarrassed.'

Kate watched Medea nod at Tom, silently encouraging him.

'I suppose,' he went on, 'something – or someone – has finally made me realise that none of this is me at all – not the real me, anyway. Not the me I actually like. And it's not what I want my life's work to be, not how I want to be remembered, either. So that's it, folks. So long and thanks for the mammaries.'

Tamsin tittered.

'Sorry,' Tom guffawed. 'Couldn't help myself.'

27

The big cheeses at PGT&B gave everyone the rest of the day off, so they could celebrate their magazines' reversals of fortune and prepare for the Euro 96 semi-final between England and Germany, starting at 7 p.m.

Of course, for just about every employee of PGT&B, that meant a quick trip to the offie to stock up on fags and then straight down to O'Flaherty's to get a good seat in front of the big screen. And, obviously, get a few bevvies in before kick off.

The banter and the pints flowed – even Kate managed to gulp down one or two as the excitement and anticipation grew.

Or maybe it was more like three or four pints, Kate couldn't quite remember.

Whatever she'd drunk, though, she placed the blame squarely at the feet of alcohol for what transpired a few hours later.

'It's the best mag in the world - ever!' *The Mad Fer It!* team chanted over and over as they clinked glasses, spilling sticky lager on the pages of the Friendship issue.

'I love the photos of them, looking so scrawny in their satin shorts – but acting like they're the Jets and the Sharks!' Kate said.

She carried on leafing through her favourite fortnightly and giggled at the captions accompanying every photo. Not a single opportunity to take the mickey out of pop stars was missed and she was surprised at how near the knuckle some of their comments were. She was also puzzled as to why she hadn't remembered that this funny, ballsy team managed to get away with magazine murder week after week. Or, more accurately, every two weeks.

Suddenly the Editor came running into O'Flaherty's, her cool junior Debbie Harry exterior completely ruffled.

'You're not going to believe this, troops,' she panted, slinging her army surplus bag down on the floor and shakily sparking up the first of approximately fifty fags. 'But I've just got off the phone to Robbie –'

'Fowler?' some young wag piped up, the football theme seeping into every conversation.

'No!' said the Ed. 'Robbie, you know!'

'Off *EastEnders*?' offered another scamp. 'Did you get to speak to Well'ard, too?'

'No!' Williams, you pratts, *Williams*! He got an advance copy of this issue and he loved it so much, he says it's given him a fantastic idea...and guess what!'

'He proposed?' another cheeky monkey suggested.

'He wants to do a duet with you?' guffawed the picture editor.

These kids – although they were mostly only five or six years younger than Kate - knew no respect, clearly. It was no wonder they managed to produce such a witty magazine with such alarming regularity. Kate was full of admiration for their flagrant disregard for authority – so much so, she forgot herself for a second or two.

'He wants to kiss and make up with Gary Barlow? Get Take That back together?' Kate beamed.

'Ha! Yeah. Like that'll ever happen,' the Features Editor said sarkily and joined in with the rest of them, sneering at the very suggestion.

For a bunch of bright young things, they weren't half a surly lot, thought Kate. They think they know everything, don't they? Well on this occasion, Kate's chest almost swelling with pride (or was that her bosoms growing again?), she knew, beyond a shadow of a doubt that they were wrong.

'You're all way off,' said the Editor, regaining a little of her usual composure. 'No, he said that he's going to fabricate a row with his new best friends, Liam and Noel, and he wants us to cover it every step of the way. Reckons he's going to create a feud that will culminate in him challenging Liam to a boxing match at some awards do or something and we get to have exclusive rights to everything – he won't make a move without us!'

'You mean like how Liam and Noel sang "shite life" instead of Parklife at this year's Brits – just to hack Blur off?' the picture editor asked.

'And how Jarvis Cocker wiggled his hands and his bum on stage to really cheese Michael Jackson off?' the sour-faced intern asked.

'Yes!' enthused the Editor. 'Seems awards ceremonies are where it's at these days, if you want to draw attention to yourself!'

Impressed noises and excited murmurs spread around the table like Marmite.

'And the best bit?' the Editor went on.

'But wait! There's more!' The chief sub screeched.

'This means there's no way they'll fold us! We've won ourselves an enormous stay of execution! We will survive!'

The hard-drinking Editor ordered a bottle of Jack Daniels to celebrate.

As the whooping and cheering escalated and there was still just over an hour to go before the match began, Kate decided it was time to use her insider knowledge for good and so took her leave, mumbling something about going to see a man about a dog.

*

When she got back to O'Flaherty's (or O' Farty's as Seamus pronounced it), the tension was palpable. A large table with an excellent view of the screen saw Georgia, Steve, Archie, Tom, Tamsin, Lucy, Medea, Seamus and Kevin sat round it. Kate spotted the spare chair in between Georgia and Seamus loaded up with bags, light jackets and cardis for if it got a bit chilly later.

'It's such an amazing feeling out there,' she said, scooping the clothes off the chair and carefully placing them by her feet, only for them to be kicked mercilessly under the table during the match that was about to start.

'It's not too bad in here, either,' said Georgia

casting a lusty glance at all the men present.

'Actually,' said Kate. 'Have you met everyone here?'

'Yep – the lovely Seamus introduced me while you were – where were you just now, anyway?'

'Um,' Kate racked her brains for a plausible excuse for not being in the thick of it for the whole afternoon. 'Just ducked down to the, ah, National Portrait Gallery.'

She didn't know where that came from – somewhere deep down inside her belly full of regrets, she supposed – visiting the NPG more often was always on her long list of things she wished she'd done more of.

'Ah! A woman after my own heart,' shouted Tom. 'What are they showing there at the moment, Kate? Any special exhibitions?'

'Just...lots...of...portraits, really. You know, the usual stuff.'

Tamsin batted her eyelashes at Tom and said:

'Speaking of portraits, we never did get to do that glamour shoot starring, er, *me* – did we? Perhaps we could do some private photos later – I'm sure I have a Polaroid camera at my place...'

Tom shuffled about in his seat and didn't know where to look. Neither did anyone else.

'All right, then, everyone,' said Archie, popping the big balloon of unease that hung heavily over the table and turning to face the screen. It's about to start.'

'Well, someone's going to have to tell me what's

going on,' purred Medea. 'I'm not terribly *au fait* with soccer, you see.'

'Football!' the table said as one.

'I'll keep you up to speed,' said Tom. 'I like nothing more than explaining the beautiful game.'

'And hearing the sound of his own voice,' Georgia whispered to Kate.

Kate snorted and looked at Tom fondly. It had surprised her that he'd revealed such well-hidden depths lately - and she couldn't believe how wrong she'd got him in her memory. To her mind in 2014, Tom was a bit of a one-dimensional figure with an eye for the ladies, a masterful, wildly satisfying sexual technique and a pornographer's attitude towards love and commitment. But now she realised he was just as confused and scared as everybody else out there in the melee, desperate to find themselves and, with any luck, true love.

He could still be in possession of fantastic skill when it came to making love, Kate wouldn't know – but this made her think that perhaps it wasn't one person who controlled the greatness of a love-making session – but rather the way the two people worked together, cared about each other and couldn't help themselves fancying the pants off each other.

She looked at Seamus crossing his long legs in the chair next to her. This made the cuffs of his well-cut, light tobacco-coloured cord trousers rise, revealing a black sock positively festooned with mini Bart Simpsons, grinning his little yellow head off poking out over the top of his desert boots.

Yep, Kate told herself, there is definitely no rhyme or reason to this love game.

'GOAL!' the pub suddenly erupted.

'I say,' said Medea. 'That was quick!'

'Shea-rer, Shea-rer!' chanted Tom, jumping up and down like Declan on the pogo stick Kate had bought him from her favourite online shop, Retro Toys Were Us.

The already-super charged atmosphere ratcheted up several notches at this early suggestion that England might actually beat Germany and Kate basked in the ambience, remembering how ecstatic everyone had been at this point all those years ago.

She almost couldn't bear to think how devastated everybody in the pub – in the country – would soon be.

She got up to order a lemon, lime and bitters at the bar, figuring there'd be no queue, considering everyone else would be far too busy hugging and crying and generally being jubilant.

But she couldn't battle her way through the crowd. The pub was completely rammed. Getting bumped and jostled about like a pinball, she managed to make her way to the perimeter of the pub and, with her back against the wall, manoeuvred herself to the bar.

By the time she got the Australian barmaid's attention (which took a while), Germany had equalised.

She knew this for sure, because once the unsportsman-like groans of the England fans died down, she heard Tom, in his Cockney accent say:

'Ah, now Medea, *me de-ah*,' Kate could hear him smile a little at his pupil and the way he played with her name, 'now we need to get another goal and not let the Germans get any more goals.'

Apples and pears, whistle and flute – why did Tom lapse into Cockney when excited or upset or being candid? Was it his involuntary way of exposing the real him? The vocal equivalent of shedding his artificial skin and letting us all see his real self via his glottal stop?

'Well, *der* - any fool knows *that*,' said Medea. 'I meant I don't get things like the offside rule and penalties and stuff.'

You won't have to wait long for a heated discussion on the merits and disastrous drawbacks of the penalty shoot-out, thought Kate.

But in reality, they did. And after seventy-four more minutes of play and continuous standing at the bar, Kate's feet, adorned by her stiff, new, all-white Adidas trainers, were killing her.

Then, three minutes into extra time, Kate heard Georgia yell:

'Oh, McMan-aman-aman-aman-aman! How *could* you?!'

'If 'e'd'a go' tha' in, we'd a' won,' Tom said, now sounding like a Welshman with several missing teeth and a swollen tongue. He must be really nervous, thought Kate. But what could be making him like that? Or, more to the point, *who*? Or should that be *whom*?

As Kate grappled with her internal grammatical mistakes, Germany must have scored, judging by the boos and bitter mutterings from all those of normal height around her.

‘’Ang on, ’ang on - ah, right – so the ref’s not allowing that goal,’ explained Tom. ‘Foul, apparently.’

‘What did he do that was so foul?’ Medea, Tamsin, Lucy and even Georgia all asked at the same time.

‘Um,’ Tom stalled for time, ‘Now if Gazza can just get...it...DOW!’

The punters roared with disappointment, signalling to Kate that Gazza had, indeed, missed.

‘Righ’,’ said Tom, smacking his lips. ‘Now it’s a pen-al-ee ’uck-in’ shoo ow –’

‘I can’t understand a word he’s saying!’ laughed Medea.

‘He said it’s a penalty shoot out,’ Kate heard Kevin say. ‘It’s a bit like tennis when it goes to deuce, you know, 40-all.’

‘Oh! Why thankyou, kind sir, for explaining it to dumb little old –’ said Georgia in a Southern belle accent, cutting her own sarcastic self off. ‘Well ’allo,’allo, ’allo! What have we here, then?’

Georgia must have turned to face Kevin, because Kate couldn’t quite make out what she said next, although it sounded a bit like ‘Ding dong! Now where did you come from? I don’t believe we’ve been properly introduced.’

Kate was convinced she could hear Kevin blush,

though, and smiled, picturing him pushing up his glasses, starting to sweat.

Five times the crowd cheered and brayed and five times they ignored the German goals, talking over them, as if they didn't matter and were simply a dull, but necessary formality.

Then it was Gareth Southgate's turn. Kate hid her face with her hands, turning round to the bar.

She desperately wanted to make it back to her table for this bit, be there with her shoulder for Seamus to cry on when it all went so horribly wrong, but she couldn't for the life of her break through the wall of bodies, several layers deep, blocking her way between her and her table of friends.

So she gave up trying, just as a hush fell on the crowd, breezing through the pub, like an invisible, silent cumulonimbus, a hazy, cloudy portent of doom. All you could hear were the nervous gulps of a group of people gripped by impending, crushing defeat.

You could have heard a pin drop – and Tom's aitches, as he continued with his running commentary in Medea's ear.

'So this German fella, *Moller*,' he sneered. 'Just 'as to 'oof it in and crash, bang, wollop! We're out of the competition.'

The faint sound of boot on ball felt like a kick to the nation's collective stomach. And the nation howled in response.

'NO-O-O-O-O-O-O-O!'

The air filled with grief and despair and, just like

the first time round, Kate felt like crying.

And as the final whistle blew, the tears, the wailing and the gnashing of teeth reaching fever pitch, Kate slipped out of the pub and headed back into Soho.

28

'So when I got into work on Friday morning,' Seamus said, 'seven a.m., as usual –'

'As you do,' Kate butted in.

'Yes, as I do, every day. Well, every *week* day, of course – I'm not that keen!' Seamus snorted.

They were walking along Bayswater Road, past Hyde Park, on their way to the Prince Bonaparte pub, right down the bottom of the dodgier end of Chepstow Road. If there *was* such a thing as the dodgy end of the street, of course, flanked as it was on either side with outrageously expensive-looking white-stucco Victorian terraces.

'So you got into work at seven,' Kate prompted him, looking behind her for a second, to make sure Georgia and Steve and Kevin were still there.

'Yeah – and sitting on my keyboard is a plain A5 envelope.'

'Really? How fascinating!'

'No, listen,' smiled Seamus.

'Is A5 bigger or smaller than A4?' Kate crinkled her nose. 'I can never remember.'

'Smaller,' he said authoritatively. 'The larger the number, the smaller the size. So A1 is bigger than A2. A3 is bigger than A4 and so on and so forth.'

'Yeah, yeah,' said Kate, rolling her eyes and pretending to yawn at Georgia who had linked arms with both Steve and Kevin, walking ten or so paces behind her and Seamus.

'Well anyway, I opened it and I nearly fell backwards in a crumpled heap –'

'Ooh, make sure you don't – not in that gorgeous brushed cotton parka, anyway – cost a bomb, that did.'

'...because there was a MILLION POUNDS in there!'

'Shhh,' Kate put her index finger to her badly, heavily-lined lips which, unfortunately made her look far more Robert Smith than Julia Roberts.

'What's that about a million pounds, Shay?' called Kevin.

'Nothing, nothing,' said Kate.

'Your shout, then Seamus – if you're talking about that kind of money!' Steve joined in.

'Yeah, so,' Seamus carried on. 'I thought I'd take it to the police, see if anyone's lost it.'

'You *what*?' Kate stopped dead in her tracks.

'Well, it's not mine and it's an awful lot of money – someone's bound to be missing it...'

Kate felt her frustration levels rise sharply, exactly as she did when George or Declan ran rings around her, answering back and refusing to do what she asked of them, making her realise, always too late, that she was fighting a losing battle, simple and irrefutable logic being her kids' usual weapon of choice.

She frowned.

Take the money and run, you fool! This could set you – set us all up - for life!

As they walked, Kate steered Seamus away from

every newsagent's sandwich board they passed, so as to avoid the day's headlines screaming at him:

BOOKIES BANKRUPT! said one side.
BIZARRE BET PUTS BOOKIES OUT OF BUSINESS shouted its other side.

Kate pointed out how pretty the trees were at this time of year and when the pleasant breeze carried the vaguely familiar half-singing/half-yodelling voice to their ears, she knew she'd stumbled upon a big enough distraction.

'Good old Alanis,' she giggled. 'What's she warbling on about now?'

'Irony, most probably,' said Seamus. 'I was actually going to ask you if you wanted to go to the Prince's Trust concert in Hyde Park with me today – as a birthday present – but you got in first with your pub party and...and anyway, I couldn't get tickets.'

'Oh, that's sweet Seamus,' she said, looking up at him as they walked. 'Well, now we can hear it for free – and not have to use a port-a-loo when we need to spend a penny.'

Spend a penny? Now where the hell did a twee, old-fashioned phrase like that come from? Kate felt she was getting older by the second.

She pictured her personal portrait in the attic, a la Dorian Gray, and wondered whether hers was faulty. So instead of halting the ageing process while she enjoyed her youth, her painting was speeding it up.

'There you go, sounding like my grandmother again,' Seamus grinned, cautiously putting an arm around Kate's shoulders. 'Which is fine by me - I loved my Gran. Gutted when she died.'

Kate shook her perfect Rachel 'do and looked up.

'Was that rain?' she asked, holding her hand, palm-side up to the greying sky.

'Nah, it can't be,' said Seamus. 'I was surfing the net this morning and found a weather site. Pretty amateur it was, but it said London would be dry today – if not bright and sunny.'

Kate could have sworn she'd felt a raindrop and so, keen to avoid frizz and follicular mayhem on her birthday, she pulled Seamus underneath a newsagent's awning.

WAS MATCH FIXED? asked the sandwich board next to them, with
WE WAS ALL ROBBED! emblazoned all over its other side.

'Oh yeah,' said Seamus – did you read about that? How someone won an absolute fortune placing a spookily accurate bet on Wednesday night's match? It was as if the person who did it knew exactly what was going to happen, like, down to how many blades of grass the players would crush or something.'

'No, no, I hadn't heard,' Kate said quickly. 'Oops,

looks like it was a false alarm, no rain here – let's get to the pub. Pronto!'

They picked up the pace and Kate directed the conversation back to Seamus' windfall.

'So what did the envelope say? You know, the envelope with the money in it?'

'Nothing,' he said. 'I told you it was plain.'

'It didn't have your name on it? In blue pen? With a little love heart next to it?'

Kate was sure she'd addressed said envelope to him. She distinctly remembered toying with the idea of writing 'For The IT Boys' on the front, but thought it might be too obvious who it was from, then, might really give the game away. Even though she knew that Seamus didn't like the play on words. Or give a damn about It Girls, let alone IT boys.

She can't have been that drunk, can she?

'Don't think so,' Seamus answered. 'Hang on, I'll check.'

Kate gasped as Seamus pulled the envelope out of his deep parka pocket.

'Put it away,' she hissed at him. 'Put it away!'

He did as he was told and as soon as the envelope was safe, Kate grabbed him by the elbow, looking nervously over both her shoulders.

'What? What's going on?' Seamus' voice cracked.

'Nothing! But, you know – you don't want to be flashing that amount of cash about in the street. You never know who might snatch it off you.'

'Kate, do you know something about this money?'

Seamus held her still and locked his eyes onto hers.

This was getting too tricky, she thought. Seamus with his do-goody ideas and lofty morals would never understand her reasons for betting. He *might* get that she'd come to the past as a visitor from the future, but gambling? And then using her ill-gotten gains to feather their own nests? When every night on the news tales of war, poverty, hunger and misery bombarded them?

'Because if no one claims it from the police station, I think I might do something really worthwhile with it – like give it Great Ormond Street or some needy charity. Hey! Maybe I'll even use the money to start a charity of my own...'

Seamus had a bit of a Mother Theresa thing going sometimes, Kate remembered. Which was another reason she'd fallen for him the first time round.

He'd always been a boy scout in long pants, forever wanting to do the right thing, never letting a chance for the caring, compassionate, philanthropic side of his nature to pass him by.

As if to illustrate her point, a beggar on the corner of Westbourne Grove and Chepstow Road mumbled something about food and shelter, holding out his hand to them. The pair suddenly felt painfully bourgeois and middle class as they stood there, about to enjoy an afternoon of drinking alcohol out of a glass, with a greasy, delicious kebab to look forward to on the way home to their safe, warm beds.

Seamus glanced down at the beggar and put his

hand in his pocket. Right at that moment, Kate was adamant that from somewhere in the distance, she could hear Alanis singing about putting her one hand in *her* pocket...

Don't do it, Shay! Don't do it! Think of the kids! Please don't do it!

'There you go, mate,' said Seamus cheerfully, as he pushed a couple of fifty-pound notes into the beggar's hand. 'Get yourself a nice cup of tea.'

Kate laughed with relief and brought her hand up to her chest.

'I may be kind-hearted,' he gazed at her, bending his head down close to hers. 'But I'm not stupid.'

'My hero,' she whispered, standing on tippy-toes to kiss him full on his plump, juicy lips.

*

Kate was truly touched to see so many familiar, smiling friendly faces as she walked through the front door of the Bonaparte, holding Seamus' hand.

'Happy Birthday!' Archie, propping up the bar, was looking extremely pleased with himself as he raised his pint to Kate.

She figured he must have finally recovered from his bout of jealousy and come to terms with the very real possibility that faint heart may well have won fair lady this time. If she was to be so bold so as to refer to herself as 'fair' - or, indeed, a 'lady'.

Not that Seamus would be so pleased if he knew she thought of him as having a faint heart, but still. She wasn't thinking out loud for once – and Lord knows he was no mind reader – because, really, just look at those shoes! If he'd had the merest smidge of ESP, he'd have been able to hear her shout: 'NO! NEVER WEAR POLISHED BLACK BUSINESS SHOES WITH SUIT PANTS! YOU LOOK LIKE ONE OF THOSE SLEAZY GUYS IN LOS DEL RIO...HEY, MACARENA!'

As she approached Archie, lips puckered, reaching out for the flesh on his right cheek, Tamsin coughed her exaggerated dumb blonde helium cough (which made her sound like Daisy Duck while simultaneously looking like Minnie Mouse – a rare and true talent, to be sure) and made her presence known. But not before Kate's lips coincided with Tamsin's cheek, much to the amusement of the onlookers.

'Steady on, girls,' laughed Archie. 'There's more than enough of me to go around!'

'Now that's something you don't see every day,' sniggered Seamus. 'Although it might be nice if you did...'

'Urgh!' grunted Kate, resisting the overwhelming temptation to wipe the back of her hand across her mouth, as if to rid herself of Tamsin germs. But she wasn't that childish. And anyway, she'd spent ages applying her brown lipstick that morning - carefully colouring in a millimetre outside her natural lip line, so that everyone would think her pout was actually quite full (as opposed to being really rather thin) – and she couldn't bear to smear it off now.

'Woo-hoo!' Georgia, Steve and Kevin cheered in

chorus as they bounded up from behind.

'So who's getting some birthday action, eh?' Georgia elbowed Kate in the ribs. 'I knew it! I knew you were saving him for yourself!'

'You don't want him, G – really, you don't,' Kate whispered in her ear.

'No, I know,' Georgia agreed cheerfully. 'I've got my eye on another prize, as a matter of fact.'

Georgia looked wantonly at Kevin. Kate followed her best friend's gaze and felt a twinge of pity for poor Kevin. Georgia would, no doubt, eat him alive. He would never know what had hit him.

'Happy Birthday, Kate,' came a rather timid female voice behind her.

She turned around and saw Lucy, the receptionist, offering Kate a little ESPA bag.

'Oh, Lucy!' squealed Kate. 'For me? You really shouldn't have – that stuff's way too expensive for someone on your salary!'

'Well,' her big, blue eyes blinked with shyness, her lashes enviably thick and long, 'it's from both of us, actually. Just to say thanks.'

'Thanks?' Kate looked over shoulder to see who Lucy was batting her eyelashes at. 'What for?'

'For bringing us together,' said Steve, stepping into Kate's view and sliding his arm across Lucy's shoulders. 'If it weren't for you, I'd never have met Tom or slept under your desk or had early morning coffee sessions with this lovely young lady here...'

Lucy gazed up at Steve and he grinned.

‘Awww,’ Kate cooed, wondering if it was true what they said about boys never quite getting over their love for their mothers – because Lucy’s eyes were exact replicas of Blue’s. And her own, come to think of it.

Images of George and Declan flooded her head; George’s fourth birthday party, where he hugged her so hard, she had bruised ribs for weeks after. And Declan’s first day at Reception where he wept, miserable and inconsoleable for so long, she had to take him home again. It took him a good six months before he could leave her in the morning without sobbing and holding onto her leg like it was his life support machine.

Even now, she reminded herself, he wasn’t exactly enamoured with the idea of not being with his mummy 24/7. He still slept in between her and Seamus quite often, which, she only ever admitted to herself, she actually *loved*, despite the interrupted, rubbish night’s sleep she would have as a result. Especially when she had to get up at 5 a.m. for Baby Jane.

She thought of the three of them from an aerial viewpoint, all snuggled up together, limbs entwined, their breathing in sync with each other...or at least, Kate and Declan’s were – in her mind’s eye, Seamus looked like he was about to fall off the bed, his back turned to the cosy wife/son twosome.

Kate frowned. The fact that she and her husband weren’t ever in the same room together *alone* anymore – let alone the same time zone - might really have something to do with the fact that they hadn't made love for...ooh, let's see...how long was it again?

'Absolutely yonks,' she said out loud, starting to panic. 'Argh! I'm never going to get back, am I?"

Suddenly, Tom's beaming face came sharply into focus.

'Ah, well,' he said, scuffing his Cuban heels nervously on the original Edwardian floor boards. 'That's what I've been meaning to talk to you about, Kate. I'm not sure how to say this, but...I don't think we should get back together.'

'And happy birthday to you, too!' Kate grinned, unfazed.

'Yes, yes, sorry,' he muttered, kissing her cheek. 'Happy birthday. I just don't think it's going to work between us. I think you're a great girl and so much fun and –'

'Just not *that* great or *that* much fun,' she finished his sentence for him.

'No! Don't be silly!'

He looked distracted, though, Kate thought. And seconds later, she found out why. When a pint of Caffrey's appeared out of nowhere over her shoulder, she followed the graceful, elegant hand holding it in slo-mo, her eyes finally coming to rest on the stunning face of none other than Medea.

'To be perfectly honest,' Tom went on, slipping his arm around Medea's tiny waist and pulling her into their conversation, 'In this case, it really *is* actually me, not you. I'm so sorry, Kate, but...well, I've met someone else.'

As he said the last bit, he looked longingly into Medea's eyes. Kate could hear both their breath getting shorter and more urgent. Their heads moved closer and closer...until they could resist no more, and proceeded to snog the very face off each other.

'Blimey,' muttered Kate as she left them to it and made her way over to two leather sofas facing each other, a low coffee table in the middle, separating them.

The couch backed up against the wall was packed to capacity with Archie sitting next to Tamsin. Tamsin was fixated on Archie, hanging on his every word, her bum pointed pertly at Steve who was sitting up straight next to her. He looked the happiest she'd seen him in years, talking animatedly with Lucy on his lap, his hand proprietorially resting on her knee.

Kate wriggled her bum down into the small space between Georgia and Seamus on the opposite couch, buoyed by how completely painless and hurt-free her break up with Tom had just been.

'Oops, sorry!' Georgia growled as her thigh slammed up next to Kevin's, sitting there quite innocently and unsuspecting at the end of the sofa.

She looked at Kate and said:

'You might want to go easy on the pies, my friend. But in the meantime, what say you and me and Beavis and Butthead here get totally and utterly wasted?'

Kate drew in a sharp breath and held it. She'd love to really let loose and have a taste of some of the pure, unadulterated fun she used to. But what about her hangovers? That lasted three-four days, depending on whether she smoked or not? And what about her waistline – Lord knows how many Weight Watchers points are in vodka Red Bulls...

She chewed the inside of her right cheek, looked out of the Georgian windows and saw the dark grey clouds rapidly rolling across what had, minutes before, been bright blue sky. The lights inside the pub flickered on and off, making a hissing sound as the first dollops of hard rain forced the punters sitting outside to run for cover inside.

Lightning streaked across and lit up the sky like spindly, sharp, blindingly white branches of light, threatening to electrocute and disintegrate the chimney pots of Notting Hill.

And then the thunder hit – as loud and as terrifying as though Thor himself had brought his hammer down with truly great vengeance right on the rickety old roof of the Bonaparte.

'Ooh!' Tamsin squealed and leapt into Archie's delighted arms.

The rain pelted down on the pavements, bouncing off the stone slabs like they were mini cement trampolines, the wind howled and raged - and Kate watched it all, transfixed.

But the heavier and more oppressive it became outside, the more levity she felt. It was as though a great weight had been lifted off her shoulders for the first time in a hundred years and she felt...not tied, not bound...but deliriously, deliciously *free*.

She quickly reasoned with herself. She was clearly never going to make it back to 2014, she didn't have any kids or job responsibilities to consider and, quite frankly, at this stage in the game, she'd had quite enough of being so prim and proper and old before her time.

'Oh, sod it,' she yelped. 'I'm in. Let's get trolleyed!'

As the rain storm turned torrential downpour and the barmaid had to turn *Champagne Supernova* up to drown out the dreadful roar of the rotten weather, Kate put one arm around Seamus' broad shoulders, the other around Georgia's bony back and began to sing her little heart out.

'Someday blah-blah-blah me,' she caterwauled, slowly becoming aware that hers was a solitary (out-of-tune) voice echoing and bouncing off the grey concrete walls of what looked like the inside of the Blackwall Tunnel whooshing past her.

'Cor between the...'

Suddenly she felt herself falling fast, her Rachel 'do hanging hopelessly in her eyes, getting itself completely out of place, despite spraying nearly a whole can of Elnett Extra Hold on it earlier that morning.

And as an almighty crack of thunder frightened the life out of her, making her shut her eyes tight, she clapped her hands over her ears.

'...land-SLL-I-I-I-I-I-I-I-I-I-I-I-I-I-I-DE!' she

screamed in muffled triumph, a tiny bit chuffed with herself for finally getting one word right.

29

'Oh, there you are! Darling where've you been?' someone who looked a lot like Seamus cocked his head to one said and smiled as he set out cutlery on the huge, long oak dining table. 'I've been looking all over for you. They want you to accept the award for me, considering I'll be in India when they're holding the ceremony.'

Kate brushed a few fine strands of hair from her face and looked around her feverishly, like she'd just been teleported back to another time and another place. Which, in actual fact, she had.

Her head darted behind her, to her left, to her right and she gripped the edge of the luxuriously soft, rich milk chocolate-coloured nubuck leather sofa with her fingers.

An enormous mirror, framed in oak, hung on the wall to her right and seconds later, she shot up out of her seat and racing up to it, desperate to get a look at herself.

Gone was the Rachel 'do (which, let's face it, never really worked all that well on her hair with her and was always far too much trouble to maintain) and in its place, a short-ish, sophisticated layered dark brown bob. Several grey hairs around her temples acted like visual klaxons to her fascinated gaze, but actually, she quickly thought, they made her look... rather *distinguished*.

She pointed her chin to the ceiling and studied her

neck – yes, it was a teensy bit crepe-y and yes, those jowls she so fretted about had definitely taken up permanent residence along her jawline. But instead of shock and panic, Kate felt calm and cool.

No matter how tightly she stretched the loose skin up and pulled it behind her ear lobes, when she took her hands away, the sag was swift and inevitable. She did this several times, just to be sure, and felt a strange sense of relief every time, as though this was what she wanted to see, this was how things *should* be.

Her skin felt soft and dry – as opposed to slightly greasy and prone to break outs – and she noticed that her face powder stuck well as a result and didn't look too caked on.

And even though her upper eyelids drooped a tiny bit lazily over her blue eyes, they still shone brightly back at her, twinkling excitedly, as she saw the reflection of their family planner on the kitchen wall screaming the date at her.

29 JUNE, 2014

And underneath that, with lovehearts and balloons obviously drawn by kids, the words that made her heart sing:

MUMMY'S BIRTHDAY!!!!

A satisfied smile curled itself around her lips.

'Oh, here we go – earth to Kate, come in, Kate...' Seamus sighed wearily.

'Hmmm?' she turned around and faced him. And

was struck by how handsome he looked.

He was wearing a lightweight black sweater, the sleeves pushed up to reveal tanned, manly, hairy forearms. His trousers were tobacco-coloured and tapered at the ankle – were they skinny jeans? Her fashion-retarded Seamus? Her eyes dropped to his feet and she brought her hand to her chest, taking in a sharp breath, when she saw they were shod in a moccasin-y-type French-looking loafer - without socks!

'The award? For services to the IT industry?' Seamus sounded a bit bored as he carried on setting the table. 'They want to give me a lifetime achievement for setting up the Institute for the Technologically Challenged. No biggie. But I'll be helping out at our orphanage in Kerala, so I won't be able to pick it up. I know it's a pain – but would you mind accepting it for me? It's your marketing genius that put us on the map, anyway...'

Kate stared. Her mouth dropped open and she felt the flesh between her chin and the base of her throat wobble a bit. Who was he? Who *was* this amazing man?

'Course,' Seamus carried on, 'we never would have been able to do any of it if we hadn't ever had the cash and the *cojones* to set up our own consultancy, all those years ago. It's hard to believe that once upon a time we were trapped in the basement of PGT&B, putting up with abuse from the suits and feeling like second-class citizens.'

He stopped and looked out the wall of glass doors,

opening out onto the garden, manicured and lush, complete with trampoline and covered sundeck.

'I'm always a wee bit embarrassed that we profited so hugely from the internet and people's fear of it, to be totally honest,' he went back to laying out the cutlery that looked suspiciously like real silver. 'But, you know, what else could we do?'

Kate couldn't believe her ears. For a start, Seamus was talking like someone who was at home in their own skin – someone who knew his own mind and wasn't backward in coming forward. He sounded so confident, so comfortable. And it fair blew Kate away.

She coughed and steadied herself on her pins, wandering back through the unnecessarily large downstairs open plan, Swedish blonde-wood-floorboarded room to the couch and sat down.

'What's this?' she addressed no one in particular.

A massive magazine sat on the coffee table, with a pair of pinky-purpley-framed glasses on top of it. She carefully picked up the glasses and placed them gingerly on her face. They were a perfect fit! And all of a sudden, it was like the world around her had gone 3-D, not the slightly fuzzy, blurry aspect she was used to.

She dragged the magazine off the table – for it weighed a ton – and dropped it on her lap. Detail from *Dejeuner Sur L'herbe* (the naked lady in the foreground) was on the cover and Kate said the mag's title out loud when she read it, all big and bold in confident capital letters.

'FRAME.'

'Yeah – the latest issue from Tom and Medea,' said Seamus. 'Came in the post this morning. Special birthday issue, apparently.'

'Is it art?' she said absent-mindedly, flicking through the weighty tome.

Seamus scoffed.

'The eternal question, my Dove. They said to give you their love, of course, and apologies that they couldn't make it today – art fair in Bologna or some such.'

She looked up from the magazine and scratched her head.

'I'm off to St Andrews on Wednesday, too, Hon, remember? It's our annual trip. Ooh, which reminds me – Paris wanted me to ask you whether you'd mind if Blue stayed here with you and the kids while we're away. Her leg's healing up nicely, apparently.'

'She's here? *They're alive*?'Kate heard her voice crack and felt her eyes water.

'She only broke her leg, Darling – Paris managed to abseil down Big Ben with no trouble at all, so he's been able to run around after her at their place. But even convalescing and bed-ridden, she's getting a little under his feet, so, as you can imagine, he's rather champing at the bit to get away.'

'I...I...' Kate stuttered.

'Honestly, Katie,' Seamus looked at her as though she was mad. Or a bit thick. 'Were you on one of your nostalgia road trips when you spoke to them last night?

You seem ever so spacey. And I thought you'd sworn off living in the past, anyway... '

At that moment, she became aware of a familiar sound, music not unlike what she'd been hearing in the Bonaparte mere moments before.

'Who's this?' she pointed at the ether.

'What? The music?'

'Yeah,' she tilted her head back, as though the answer might be painted on the ceiling.

'Blurasis, of course,' he went to the fridge and took out several bottles of Veuve Clicquot. 'The finest supergroup since, oh, God, I don't know.'

'Blur-*asis*?' she brought her head back down and squinted at him as though she couldn't be sure that she'd heard him correctly.

'Yeah,' he let out a little laugh, as though he was talking fondly about good friends of his. 'Although Noel really should have let the fat dancer from that boyband have a bit more say in their name. Still, That Blur Asis? I don't think so - doesn't have quite the same ring to it, does it?'

Kate looked at him, confused.

'Muum!' George shouted from somewhere upstairs. 'Where's my iPad?'

Kate's mouth rounded itself into an 'O' when she heard this. Her boy! Her baby boy!

'Don't shout from up there,' Seamus yelled. 'Come down here and talk to your mother like a proper person!'

'Just tell me where it is!' George sounded

exasperated.

'It'll *be* where you *left* it!' Kate and Seamus said in unison, grinning at each other.

'I'll go,' Kate beamed, the urge to see her offspring – even in its groaning, surly state – overpowering her.

But when she got to the top of the stairs on the first floor landing (there was at least one other storey on top of this one, she was delighted to see), she gasped.

The toys, the clothes, the books, the unidentifiable chaos and clutter greeting her was reminiscent of their old place, the place that could never be clean or tidy for more than five minutes every month – the place she thought she'd left behind.

'Mummy!' a jubilant Declan came crashing into view, clutching his teddy and crunching over the debris separating them.

Kate stretched her arms out and felt her face crumple, crying as she dragged him to her.

She inhaled the delicious scent of her youngest boy; the hair that had yet to be infused with sweat and Eau d'Adolescent and instead still smelled strongly of Johnson's Baby Shampoo, the summer pyjamas with the merest, lingering whiff of Tesco own brand fabric conditioner still in its weave – and the smooth, baby soft skin of his neck, that was a heady mix of soap and sleep and warmth.

'I have missed you SO much, young man,' she sniffed into his shoulder, her embrace tightening.

‘Mum,’ he tried to escape, ‘you’re hurting me! I...can’t...*breathe*!’

Reluctantly, she relinquished her grip on Declan and beamed at him, wiping her tears away.

‘Why are you crying, Mummy?’ he said, looking almost unbearably cute and impossibly doe-eyed. ‘It’s your birthday – you should be happy!’

‘Oh, I am, Sweetheart,’ she laughed. ‘I *am* happy. Delirious, even!’

Declan looked perplexed – strikingly similar to the way Seamus had regarded her only minutes before – and so, not wanting to scare him, pulled herself up to her full height (about two - three inches, tops - taller than Decko himself), took his tiny hand in hers and trampled over the mess, following the sound of some ridiculous computer game to George’s bedroom.

‘George!’ she trilled when she saw him lying on his stomach across his unmade bed.

Nothing. He didn’t even look up.

Kate wasn’t about to take him ignoring her for an answer, so trotted up to him, tickling his ribs and getting ready to hear that gorgeous, contagious giggle he used to do whenever they played and joked around together.

‘Get *OFF*!’ he bellowed, his annoyance casting a pall over the sunny reunification proceedings. ‘Ah, you made me lose my concentration, Mum – why do you always have to do that?’

He tutted and moved himself to the end of the bed, legs dangling over the edge and still didn’t even look at her.

'Charming,' she said, dejected. 'It *is* my birthday, you know. Maybe just one day a year you could be –'

But suddenly she got that sinking feeling and instinctively knew that trying to talk George round to being affectionate and demonstrative towards her was a losing battle.

'Isn't it marvellous?' she said, looking down at Declan who was looking lovingly up at her.

'Yeah!' he said, effusively, turning his attentions to George. 'I want the iPad! Gimme it, George, my turn!'

Declan pounced on George and the fists flew. The pair tumbled off the bed, grappling with each other and Kate took a step back, not having a clue what to do, conflict resolution being yet another of her weak points.

'Shay –?' she shouted.

Kate didn't finish his full name in her distress call, for as she turned around, there he was, walking casually, broad-shouldered and capable, into the boy's bedroom.

'All right, all right,' he said, his voice dripping with gravitas, all authoritative and, actually, Kate thought, extremely sexy. 'That's enough, now – break it up you two.'

He expertly pulled the brawling brothers apart, sitting them on the bed, either side of him and started to soothe the savage beasts.

'Now what's all this about, then, eh? If you're

fighting over iPads again, I'm just going to have to confiscate them, understand?'

The two boys pouted and bickered about who started it and whose iPad it really was.

Just then, the doorbell rang. But Kate was frozen to the spot.

With one son under each arm, Seamus looked the very picture of the masterful family man and Kate could have sworn she felt something stir in her stomach at the sight.

'You go, Katie – I'll sort these two out.'

She turned to go downstairs, looking over her shoulder to get a last glimpse of the boys collapsing into fits of hysteria, their father tickling them and playfully diving onto the carpet as he let them attack him.

And as she trudged downstairs, her Hush Puppies with a cork wedge heel denting the luxurious wool Berber ever-so-slightly, she wondered where it had all gone so ridiculously *right*.

Opening the heavy door, stained glass panels letting in shards of coloured light, a small pair of pudgy arms nearly punched her in the face.

'Happy birthday, Mummy!' said Georgia in her baby voice as she waved Baby Jane's arms about.

'Oh!' Kate squealed. 'Come here, Baby!'

She virtually snatched Jane away from Georgia in her haste to hold her to her breast, but no one seemed to notice.

'Happy birthday, Darling girl,' Georgia said,

bending down to kiss her best friend a nano-second before she moved swiftly on, wondering loudly who was playing such rubbish music. 'Can't you put some Kajagoogoo on?'

'Happy birthday, Katie,' said Kevin standing in the doorway, his designer stubble scratching her skin a bit as he kissed her continentally. 'And this little person wants a kiss, too. Go on, Dylan, give Auntie Katie a kiss!'

With Baby Jane on her hip, Kate looked down to see an astonishingly beautiful little boy pouting like someone she knew so well and holding his arms out to Kevin so that he'd get picked up.

'And who's this?' Kate asked.

'Our son? Your God son, remember?' Georgia called back to her. 'Any recollection of the years of heartbreak and misery we spent on IVF? Hmm? Until we gave up and got lucky totally by accident in the Algarve that summer? Really, Kate, you can be so ditzy sometimes.'

Kate was stunned. That Kevin and Georgia were clearly a couple was enough to render her speechless. But to see the remarkable result of their union of beauty and the geek in front of her like this, in living, breathing colour? It was all nearly too much for her.

'Move along, move along,' came Steve's voice from somewhere behind a dazzling pair of sapphire eyes.

'Come on, Luce,' Steve continued. 'Give the old girl a peck and let's get this party started!'

Kate, a little shell-shocked, nearly shut the door when Steve had finished placing presents at her feet and left, conga dancing down the hallway, his hands holding onto the lovely Lucy's still-slim hips.

But at the precise point that she was betting herself that Lucy hadn't had kids, hence the narrow hips, and she expected to hear the clunk of the front door closing, instead, Kate heard a gravelly voice growl:

'Hey! Hang on! Lady with a baby coming through!'

She yanked the door open and there stood a hugely pregnant woman, nearly dwarfing the already-small man standing next to her, such was her mammoth girth.

'Oh!' was all Kate could manage as she thought back to the last time she'd seen these two – and pictured them cosying up together on one of the couches at the Bonaparte.

'Don't just stand there gawping,' Tamsin said, barging in and touching Kate's cheek briefly with her own. 'Now what does a girl have to do to get a drink around here – break her own waters?'

A totally bald Archie looked at Kate apologetically and kissed her, grabbing and holding her hand for a split-second.

'Happy birthday, Kate,' he said softly.

Kate, who was just that little bit taller than Archie, thanks to those wedge heels, looked down on him and held his gaze.

'Thanks, Arch,' she said. 'It's good to see you

again.'

'It's only been a couple of weeks,' Archie replied gruffly, spoiling what Kate had thought was a rather poignant moment and let go of her hand. 'No need to get all sentimental.'

*

At one end of the table, way down the other end of the room, Seamus sat feeding Baby Jane in her Stokke chair next to him. Right up the other end of the table sat Kate, surveying the celebratory scene before her.

She watched with near-to-bursting pride as her family chattered and joked with her friends. She even included Tamsin in this group and watched her bat Archie's hand away from the small of her back.

'Try any crap like that in the delivery suite and I won't be responsible for my actions,' she said curtly.

Kate laughed – an easy, relaxed laugh – and pinched herself on both bingo wings, to check that a) her arms were back to being reassuringly flabby and b) she wasn't dreaming.

She closed her eyes and breathed in the sweet perfume of her favourite flowers. White and pink lilies were everywhere – on the table, in the kitchen, on the hallstand - and as she let their smell overtake her, she felt an arm slip around her waist.

She immediately stiffened and sat up straight, trying desperately hard to hold in her stomach.

'Ah, it's no use,' she said, exhaling loudly. 'After three babies and countless cupcakes, there haven't been any muscles down there since –'

'Who cares, Kate?' Seamus said, bouncing on his haunches next to her, his shaved head, stylish sideburns and barely-there beard making him look rather dashing. 'Your body has given us our beautiful kids - why would you want it to look different?'

Kate felt her eyes slide rapidly from Seamus' right to his left, his right to his left, searching for signs that this was an elaborate ruse and he was about to present her with liposuction or a face lift for her birthday.

'Are you serious?' she asked him.

'Never been more so,' he said, his voice deep and steady.

Kate felt a vague dizziness descend upon her and she fanned her face with her right hand.

'Is it getting hot in here?' she asked no one in particular, giggling like a schoolgirl.

'Open your presents! Open your presents!' George chanted, making minuscule dents in the table as he banged his knife and fork onto it.

Decko copied his big brother to the letter and soon the whole table had joined in.

Kate, although obviously keen to find out what she'd been given for reaching the ripe old age of 45, didn't want to break the spell she was under. And she was rather pleased with herself that she could string a sentence together at all, when she stared into Seamus' eyes and said:

'No matter what's happened in the past and no matter what the future holds, I just want you all to know,' she paused and looked meaningfully into everyone's eyes at this point as her chin dimpled, holding back a veritable flood of tears, 'that this – this here, this now – *this* is the best present ever.'

Both guests and family groaned in response to Kate's uncharacteristically mushy declaration, but Seamus simply cupped her cheek (and jowl) in his hand and let his gaze fall softly, intensely upon her own.

She felt sweat bead on her upper lip and something flip in her stomach again, as if trapped butterflies were flitting about in her belly. And at that moment, everything except Seamus disappeared from focus, becoming one big, shapeless, amorphous mass rolling around her head like fog.

But she didn't wonder what on earth was going on. She didn't leap to the conclusion that menopause was well and truly under way and she was experiencing a hot flush. She didn't ask herself whether she was coming over all unnecessary and lusty - nor did she entertain the possibility that she was even the slightest bit inebriated.

This time there was no doubt in her mind as to what this feeling was. She closed her eyes and let it wash warmly and deliciously over her, as though she was lying under a chocolate fountain with her mouth wide open on a guilt-free designated diet-break day.

It felt good. It tasted sweet.

And this time, she knew it was love.

THE END

6186024R00232

Printed in Great Britain
by Amazon.co.uk, Ltd.,
Marston Gate.